INTRODUCTORY

DOS 5.0/6.0/6.2

WITH WINDOWS™ 3.1

INTRODUCTORY

DOS 5.0/6.0/6.2

WITH WINDOWS™ 3.1

HARRY L. PHILLIPS
Santa Rosa Junior College

Course TECHNOLOGY

Course Technology, Inc. *One Main Street, Cambridge, MA 02142*

Introductory DOS 5.0/6.0/6.2 with Windows 3.1 is published by Course Technology, Inc.

Vice President, Publisher	Joseph B. Dougherty
Product Manager	Darlene Bordwell
Director of Production	Myrna D'Addario
Senior Production Editor	Kathryn Dinovo
Composition	Gex, Inc.
Production Assistant	Christine Spillett
Copyeditor	Joan Wilcox
Proofreader	Joyce Churchill
Indexer	Sherri Dietrich
Product Testing and Support Supervisor	Jeff Goding
Student Testers	Chris Greacen
	Rich Gorham
	Kevan Schultz
Photo Researcher	Elyse Rieder
Prepress Production	Gex, Inc.
Manufacturing Manager	Elizabeth Martinez
Senior Design Specialist	Kim Munsell
Cover Designer	John Gamache

ISBN 1-56527-151-3

Printed in the United States of America

10 9 8 7 6 5 4 3 2

From the Publisher

At Course Technology, Inc., we believe that technology will transform the way that people teach and learn. We are excited about bringing you, college professors and students, the most practical and affordable technology-related products available.

The Course Technology Development Process

Our development process is unparalleled in the higher education publishing industry. Every product we create goes through an exacting process of design, development, review, and testing.

Reviewers give us direction and insight that shape our manuscripts and bring them up to the latest standards. Every manuscript is quality tested. Students whose backgrounds match the intended audience work through every keystroke, carefully checking for clarity and pointing out errors in logic and sequence. Together with our own technical reviewers, these testers help us ensure that everything that carries our name is error-free and easy to use.

Course Technology Products

We show both *how* and *why* technology is critical to solving problems in college and in whatever field you choose to teach or pursue. Our time-tested, step-by-step instructions provide unparalleled clarity. Examples and applications are chosen and crafted to motivate students.

The Course Technology Team

This book will suit your needs because it was delivered quickly, efficiently, and affordably. Every employee contributes to this process. The names of all our employees are listed below:

Tim Ashe, David Backer, Stephen M. Bayle, Josh Bernoff, Erin Bridgeford, Ann Marie Buconjic, Jody Buttafoco, Kerry Cannell, Jim Chrysikos, Susan Collins, John M. Connolly, David Crocco, Myrna D'Addario, Lisa D'Alessandro, Howard S. Diamond, Kathryn Dinovo, Katie Donovan, Joseph B. Dougherty, MaryJane Dwyer, Chris Elkhill, Don Fabricant, Kate Gallagher, Laura Ganson, Jeff Goding, Laurie Gomes, Eileen Gorham, Andrea Greitzer, Cathie Griffin, Tim Hale, Roslyn Hooley, Tom Howes, Nicole Jones, Matt Kenslea, Kim Mai, Susannah Lean, Suzanne Licht, Laurie Lindgren, Elizabeth Martinez, Debbie Masi, Dan Mayo, Kathleen McCann, Jay McNamara, Mac Mendelsohn, Laurie Michelangelo, Kim Munsell, Amy Oliver, Kristine Otto, Debbie Parlee, Kristin Patrick, Charlie Patsios, Jodi Paulus, Darren Perl, Kevin Phaneuf, George J. Pilla, Cathy Prindle, Nancy Ray, Marjorie Schlaikjer, Christine Spillett, Susan Stroud, Michelle Tucker, David Upton, Mark Valentine, Renee Walkup, Lisa Yameen.

Preface

Course Technology, Inc. is proud to present *Introductory DOS 5.0/6.0/6.2 with Windows 3.1*, designed for a first course on today's most popular operating system, DOS. This text, targeted at beginning students, clearly describes concepts related to DOS, the DOS Shell, and Windows operating environments. It is designed for use in a first half-semester or short (eight- to nine-week) course in DOS. It is also ideal for a self-paced DOS course that relies on independent study, with minimal direction from the instructor. The text assumes the student has no knowledge of DOS.

Organization and Coverage

Introductory DOS 5.0/6.0/6.2 with Windows 3.1 contains an "Essential Computer Concepts" chapter, six DOS tutorials, and two Windows tutorials. "Essential Computer Concepts" presents an up-to-date overview of computers and covers basic hardware and software concepts. The six DOS tutorials provide hands-on instruction. In these tutorials students learn how to use DOS and the DOS Shell for disk, directory, and file management on computer systems with hard drives and one or more diskette drives. Students perform operations from both the DOS prompt and the DOS Shell so that they know how to complete tasks in both environments. Special icons in the margin of the text call students' and instructors' attention to differences among DOS 5.0, 6.0, and 6.2, the three DOS versions covered in the book. Mouse icons also call out special steps for mouse users, where appropriate. The two Windows tutorials, again with hands-on instruction, introduce students to basic Windows features, emphasize the use of the mouse, and describe how to use File Manager for disk, directory, and file management operations.

Approach

All of the components of this text—"Essentials Computer Concepts," the DOS tutorials, and the Windows tutorials—are unique in their approach. They motivate students by demonstrating why they need to learn the concepts and skills described in the tutorials. This text teaches DOS using a task-driven rather than a feature-driven approach. By working through the tutorials—each motivated by a realistic case scenario—students learn how to use DOS in situations they are likely to encounter in the workplace, rather than learn a list of commands one by one, out of context. Each discussion motivates students by explaining *why* they will perform a given task.

Features

Introductory DOS 5.0/6.0/6.2 with Windows 3.1 includes the following features:

- **"Read This Before You Begin" Page** This page is consistent with Course Technology's unequaled commitment to helping instructors introduce technology into the classroom. Technical considerations and assumptions about hardware, software, and default settings are listed in one place at the front of the book to help instructors save time and eliminate unnecessary aggravation.
- **Objectives** A list of objectives at the beginning of each tutorial orients students to the goals of that tutorial.
- **Tutorial Scenario** Each tutorial begins with a short problem that students could reasonably encounter in business so that the process of solving the problem will be meaningful to students.

- **Step-by-Step Methodology** The unique Course Technology, Inc. methodology keeps students on track. They click or press keys, always within the context of solving the problem posed in the case. The text constantly guides students, letting them know *why* they are pressing the keys and describing the results. The numerous screen shots include labels that direct students' attention to what they should look at on the screen.
- **Page Design** Each page is designed to help students easily differentiate between what they are expected to *do* and what they are expected to *read*. The steps are easily identified by the typeface and numbered bullets.
- **Chapter Summary** Each tutorial concludes with a concise overview of the features and topics covered in the tutorial.
- **Command Summary/Features Summary** The Command Summary at the end of each DOS tutorial and the Features Summary at the end of each Windows tutorial provide important reference tools for students prior to examinations.
- **Questions** Each tutorial contains meaningful, conceptual questions that test students' understanding of what they learned in the tutorial.
- **Tutorial Assignments** These assignments provide students with additional practice on the skills they learned in the tutorial. Students practice by modifying the problems they solved in the tutorial and by applying what they learned to solve new problems.
- **DOS and Windows Reference Cards** Removable command and features summaries at the end of the text provide a handy, quick reference for all DOS commands and Windows features covered in the book.

Supplements

- **Instructor's Manual** The Instructor's Manual is written by the author and is quality-assurance tested. It includes:
  - Answers and solutions to all the Questions and Tutorial Assignments
  - A disk containing solutions to all the Tutorial Assignments
  - Tutorial Notes, which contain background information from the author about the tutorial scenario and the instructional progression of each tutorial
  - Technical Notes, which include troubleshooting tips as well as information on how to customize the student's screens to closely emulate the screen shots in the book
  - Transparency Masters of key concepts, selected by the author
  - Sample course syllabi
- **Test Bank** The Test Bank contains more than 50 questions per tutorial in true/false, matching, and short-answer formats. Each question has been quality-assurance tested by students to achieve clarity and accuracy.

Acknowledgments

I want to thank John Connolly, President of Course Technology, Inc., for his initial and ongoing commitment to the production of high-quality textbooks. I also want to thank the dedicated staff members of Course Technology for their invaluable professional contributions to this textbook. In particular, I thank Joe Dougherty, Publisher, for initiating this project and for his ideas, interest, and ongoing support. I especially thank Darlene Bordwell, Product Manager, for her insight, support, cooperation, and successful management of this project. As my primary contact on a day-by-day basis, Darlene facilitated and guided this project with grace and ease.

In addition, I thank Jeff Goding, Product Testing and Support Supervisor, for his supervision of the quality assurance process. The student testers, Richard Gorham, Kevan Schultz, and Chris Greacen, thoroughly tested the text and offered valuable suggestions for improving the quality of the presentation. I thank Kathryn Dinovo, Senior Production Editor, for carefully supervising the final assembly of the book; Kim Munsell, Senior Design Specialist, for her contributions to the book's design; Joan Wilcox, Copyeditor, for her editing and for her suggestions, which improved the flow and comprehension of the text; and Joyce Churchill, Proofreader, for verifying the accuracy of the final text.

The reviewers of this textbook—Susan Isermann, Illinois Valley Community College; Charles Fromme, Queensborough Community College; Lloyd E. Stallkamp, Northern Montana College; Kathy Medved, Pierce College; Stephanie J. Snyder, Lake Tahoe Community College; and Patrick Chan, Porterville College—all offered constructive comments on the direction and coverage, as well as the presentation of concepts and features, and deserve special thanks for their efforts.

Finally, I thank my many friends, coworkers, colleagues, family, and parents for their unqualified support while I worked on this project.

Harry L. Phillips

Brief Contents

Essential Computer Concepts **EC 3**

Introductory DOS 5.0/6.0/6.2 Tutorials **1**

Tutorial 1 Understanding DOS 3

Tutorial 2 Displaying Directories 41

Tutorial 3 Working with Files 77

Tutorial 4 Using Subdirectories 113

Tutorial 5 Managing a Hard Disk 165

Tutorial 6 Backing Up a Hard Disk 207

Windows 3.1 Tutorials **257**

Tutorial 7 Exploring Windows 3.1 257

Tutorial 8 Using File Manager 287

Glossary **321**

Index **328**

Table of Contents

Essential Computer Concepts *EC 3*
- **Objectives** *EC 3*
- **What Is a Computer?** *EC 4*
- **Types of Computers** *EC 4*
- **Types of Microcomputers** *EC 7*
- **Major Functions of a Computer** *EC 8*
- **Computer Hardware** *EC 8*
  - Input Devices *EC 8*
  - Memory *EC 12*
  - Processing Hardware *EC 13*
  - The System Unit *EC 15*
  - Output Devices *EC 17*
    - Monitors *EC 17*
    - Printers *EC 18*
  - Disk Drives and Storage Media *EC 19*
  - CD-ROMs and Optical Disks *EC 23*
  - Modems *EC 23*
- **Computer Software** *EC 23*
  - Systems Software *EC 24*
  - The Development of DOS *EC 25*
  - Applications Software EC 27
- **Networks** *EC 31*
- **Summary** *EC 32*
- **Questions** *EC 33*
- **Essential Computer Concepts Index** *EC 37*

1 Understanding DOS *3*
- **Objectives** *3*
- **What Is the Role of Operating System Software?** *4*
- **Using MS-DOS and PC-DOS** *4*
- **Using Files and Filenames** *5*
  - Using File Extensions *6*
- **Using Drive, Directory, and Path Names** *9*
- **How to Follow the Numbered Steps in the DOS Tutorials** *10*
- **Starting a Computer System** *10*
- **Working at the DOS Prompt** *12*
- **Identifying the Version of DOS** *13*
- **Changing the Date** *14*
  - Using the Repeat Key *15*
- **Using DOSKEY** *16*
- **Setting the Time** *17*
- **Clearing the Screen** *18*
- **Formatting Diskettes** *19*
  - Diskette Storage Capacities *20*
  - Using the FORMAT Command *20*
  - The Importance of the Format Capacity Switch *20*
  - Preparing Your Diskettes *21*
  - Identifying Storage Capacities of Diskettes and Drives *21*
  - Formatting a Diskette *22*
  - Assigning a Volume Label *24*
  - Evaluating the Disk Storage Space Report *25*
  - Caring for Diskettes *26*
- **Changing the Default Drive** *27*
- **Using the Help Switch** *27*
  - Printing the Help Screen *28*

Making a Copy of a Diskette *29*
Understanding the Syntax of the DISKCOPY Command *30*
Using the DISKCOPY Command *31*
Finishing Your Work Session *34*
Summary *35*
Command Reference *36*
Questions *37*
Tutorial Assignments *38*

2 Displaying Directories *41*
Objectives *41*
Displaying a Directory *42*
Pausing a Directory Listing *44*
Viewing a Wide Directory Listing *45*
Viewing a Directory of the Default Drive *46*
Specifying a Sort Order for Directory Listings *46*
Using Sort Order Parameters *47*
Displaying Directory Listings in Lowercase *50*
Using Wildcards *51*
Using the Question Mark Wildcard *51*
Using the Asterisk Wildcard *53*
Specifying Default Switches *55*
Using Command Line and Graphical User Interfaces *58*
Using the DOS Shell *59*
Using the Mouse *62*
Customizing the DOS Shell *62*
Displaying Directories in the DOS Shell *65*
Using Wildcards in the DOS Shell *67*
Exiting the DOS Shell *69*
Summary *70*
Command Reference *71*
Questions *72*
Tutorial Assignments *74*

3 Working with Files *77*
Objectives *77*
Getting Started *78*
The Importance of ASCII Files *80*
Viewing the Contents of an ASCII File *81*
Piping Output to the MORE Filter *83*
Viewing ASCII Files in the DOS Shell *85*
Printing an ASCII File from the DOS Prompt *89*
Printing an ASCII File from the DOS Shell *90*
Copying Files *91*
Copying a File Using One Disk Drive *93*
Copying a File Using Two Disk Drives *94*
Copying a File or Files from a Diskette to a Hard Disk, and from a Hard Disk to a Diskette *96*
Copying a File in the DOS Shell *99*

Renaming Files *101*

Renaming Files in the DOS Shell *103*

Deleting Files *104*

Deleting a File from Another Drive *105*

Deleting Files in the DOS Shell *106*

Finishing Up *107*

Summary *108*

Command Reference *109*

Questions *110*

Tutorial Assignments *111*

4 Using Subdirectories *113*

Objectives *113*

Managing Files *114*

Getting Started *116*

Printing a Directory *116*

Creating Subdirectories *117*

Changing Directories *120*

Moving Files to a Subdirectory *122*

Moving Files with the Yearly Income Projections *126*

Moving the Monthly Income Report Files *128*

Moving the Invoice Files *129*

Copying Files within a Subdirectory *131*

Expanding a Directory Structure *132*

Creating a Directory for Reports *134*

Viewing the Directory Structure *137*

Creating a Subdirectory in the DOS Shell *138*

Moving Files in the DOS Shell *140*

Refreshing the DOS Shell *143*

Completing a Directory Structure with the DOS Shell *144*

Expanding the Subdirectory Structure *145*

Extending a File Selection *147*

Expanding the Directory Tree *149*

Creating a Directory for Invoice Files *150*

Creating a Directory for Summary Files *153*

Navigating the Directory Tree at the DOS Prompt *154*

Stepping Down the Directory Tree *155*

Stepping Up the Directory *155*

Printing a Directory Tree from the DOS Prompt *157*

Summary *159*

Command Reference *160*

Questions *161*

Tutorial Assignments *163*

5 Managing a Hard Disk *165*

Objectives *165*

Getting Started *166*

Viewing the Directory Structure of a Hard Disk Drive *166*

Printing the Directory Structure of a Hard Disk *167*

Evaluating the Organization of Directories on a Hard Disk *168*

Recommending a New Directory Structure *169*

Developing a Strategy for Reorganizing a Directory Structure *170*

Modifying the Directory Structure *171*

Moving Files from Directory to Directory *172*

Verifying a Move or Copy Operation *172*

Removing an Empty Directory *173*

Reorganizing a Directory Structure with the DOS Shell *173*

Moving Files from Directory to Directory *175*

Removing an Empty Directory *176*

Completing the Reorganization of the Directory Structure *177*

Renaming Directories *178*

Locating Files in Directories *180*

Searching for Files in the DOS Shell *181*

Defragmenting Hard Disks and Diskettes *183*

How Does File Fragmentation Occur? *183*

Using the DOS Defragmenting Utility *186*

Checking the Directory Structure *186*

Loading the Defragmenter *187*

Understanding the Map of Disk Space Usage *189*

Selecting an Optimization Method *190*

Checking for Computer Viruses *194*

Sites of Infection *195*

Computer Virus Activity *195*

Anti-Viral Software *196*

Starting Microsoft Anti-Virus *196*

Displaying Information on Computer Viruses *197*

Scanning a Disk *199*

Summary *202*

Command Reference *203*

Questions *203*

Tutorial Assignments *205*

6 Backing Up a Hard Disk *207*

Objectives *207*

Backing Up Files, Diskettes, and Hard Disks *208*

Getting Started *209*

Formatting Diskettes for a Backup *210*

Using the BACKUP Utility *211*

Viewing the Contents of the AceForms Directory *212*

Backing Up the Aceforms Directory *214*

Checking the Backup Process *215*

Removing a Directory *217*

Restoring Files from a Backup Set *217*

Performing a Backup and Restore from the DOS Shell *219*

Using MSBACKUP *220*

Running a Compatibility Test *222*

Performing the Test Backup *226*

Verifying the Backup Process *227*

Backing Up a Directory *231*
Creating a Setup File *232*
Changing the Settings in a Setup File *234*
Starting the Backup *236*
Verifying the Backup *238*
Removing Part of the Directory Tree *239*
Restoring Directories and Files *240*
Verifying the Restore *243*

Using XCOPY for Backups *245*

Finishing Up *247*

Developing a Backup Strategy *248*

Summary *250*

Command Reference *250*

Questions *252*

Tutorial Assignments *254*

7 Exploring Windows 3.1 *257*

Objectives *257*

The Windows 3.1 Graphical User Interface *258*

Starting Windows *258*

The Windows Desktop *259*

Identifying the Elements of a Window *259*
Using the Control Menu *263*

Examining the Program Manager Menus *264*

The Options Menu *264*
The Window Menu *265*

Using Help *266*

Opening the Main Group *270*

The Control Panel *271*
Using the MS-DOS Prompt *272*

Moving a Window *273*

Changing the Size of a Window *274*

Cascading and Tiling Windows *277*

Selecting a Window *279*

Exiting Windows *281*

Summary *281*

Features Reference *282*

Questions *283*

Tutorial Assignments *284*

8 Using File Manager *287*

Objectives *287*

Using File Manager *288*

Formatting a Diskette with File Manager *290*

Copying the Contents of a Diskette with File Manager *293*

Selecting a Drive with File Manager *295*

Expanding the Directory Tree *296*

Selecting a Directory *297*

Organizing the Display of Filenames *297*

Renaming and Copying Files *303*

Modifying the Directory Structure *307*

Removing a Directory *309*

Reorganizing the Directory Structure *311*

Renaming a Directory ***311***
Creating a Directory ***313***
Moving Files ***314***
Exiting Windows ***316***
Summary ***316***
Command Reference ***317***
Questions ***317***
Tutorial Assignments ***319***

Essential Computer Concepts

Essential Computer Concepts

OBJECTIVES

In this chapter you will learn to:

- Define and describe a computer and its major functions
- Distinguish among a microcomputer, a minicomputer, a mainframe, and a supercomputer
- Describe the major hardware components of a computer
- Describe the functions of common input and output devices
- Understand the function of processing hardware
- Measure storage capacities of memory and disks
- List the sizes and capacities of common storage media
- Describe the major types of computer software, including systems software and applications software
- Understand the importance and use of computer networks

WHAT IS A COMPUTER?

A **computer** is an electronic tool that automates tasks by performing operations at remarkably fast speeds. These operations include mathematical calculations, comparisons of numbers and characters, restructuring of text, and the display of graphic images. Computers therefore organize and process **data**—facts, figures, and images—to produce useful information.

To accomplish these operations, computer systems must include specific types of hardware that operate under the control of software. The **hardware** includes the physical components that enable the computer system to access, process, display, and print data. The **software** consists of **programs**, or sets of instructions, for accomplishing a task. One important and indispensable software component is the **operating system**, which manages the operation of the computer system and the use of other software.

Businesses use computers to manage financial information, produce business projections, develop business strategies, enhance the preparation and presentation of important business documents, design graphics, transmit information nearly instantaneously from one business office to another around the world, handle business transactions, and perform many other essential business tasks. Computers improve the productivity and efficiency of employees, and enable businesses to meet timelines critical to their success in the marketplace. Computers also play an important role in agriculture, industry, engineering, aeronautics, astronomy, space exploration, oceanography, the biological sciences, physics, mathematics, medicine, the judicial system, politics, environmental studies, music, and the arts.

TYPES OF COMPUTERS

Computers often are classified by their size, speed, and cost. **Microcomputers**, or **personal computers (PCs)**, are priced from $500 to $15,000 for individual and business use. Microcomputers are designed for use by a single person and easily fit on a desktop (Figure 1). **Laptop computers** are smaller microcomputers that fit comfortably on your lap (Figure 2). **Notebook computers** are even smaller microcomputers that can easily fit into a briefcase (Figure 3). Laptop

Figure 1
Microcomputers in an office environment

and notebook computers are compatible with other, larger microcomputers. They use the same operating system and can share software and data. Microcomputers of all sizes are used extensively in businesses of all sizes as well as for personal use.

Figure 2
A laptop computer

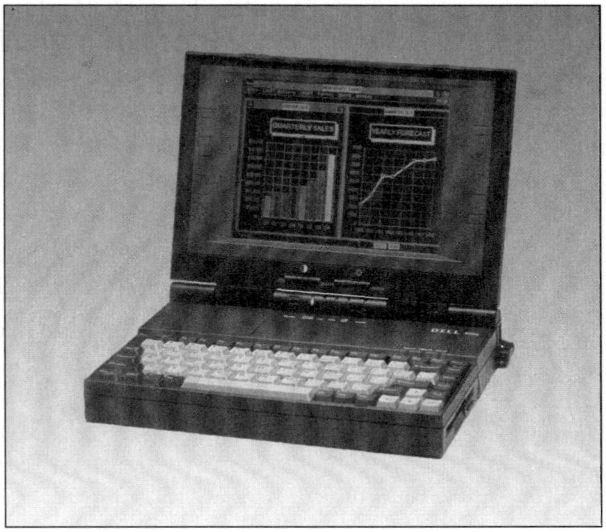

Figure 3
A notebook computer

Large businesses, government agencies, colleges and universities, and other institutions also use larger and faster types of computers called **minicomputers** (Figure 4). Minicomputers require more office space than microcomputers, operate 3 to 25 times faster than microcomputers, store and

Figure 4
A minicomputer

process much larger quantities of data, and are priced from $15,000 to $500,000. Minicomputers can support multiple users working on **workstations**, or computer **terminals**, in remote offices.

A still larger and more powerful type of computer is the **mainframe computer** (Figure 5). Mainframes have even larger capacities for storing and processing data, run 10 to 100 times faster than microcomputers, require a specially controlled environment, and are priced from $100,000 to $2,000,000. Mainframes also support a much larger number of multiple users than minicomputers.

Figure 5
A mainframe computer

Supercomputers, the largest and fastest computers, expend so much energy that they require their own internal cooling systems to dissipate the heat generated during their operation (Figure 6). Supercomputers are expensive, often costing hundreds of millions of dollars. Only the largest corporations, government agencies, and universities can afford supercomputers. Typically, supercomputers run 50 to 10,000 times faster than microcomputers and handle such complex problems as weather forecasting, earthquake prediction, and petroleum surveying.

Figure 6
A Cray supercomputer

As a result of the rapid changes in technology, the criteria used to distinguish these types of computers is also changing. For example, newer and more sophisticated types of microcomputers outperform some minicomputers.

TYPES OF MICRO-COMPUTERS

Most microcomputers use one of two similar operating systems to manage the internal operation of the computer system: PC-DOS (Personal Computer Disk Operating System) or MS-DOS (Microsoft Disk Operating System). IBM Corporation assembles IBM PCs that use PC-DOS. Other manufacturers, such as Compaq and Dell, assemble IBM-compatible microcomputers that use MS-DOS. Both IBM PCs and most compatibles contain Intel microprocessors. The **microprocessor** is a special computer chip that processes data using program instructions. Over the years, Intel Corporation has produced new and more powerful microprocessors for use in IBM PCs and compatibles.

In contrast, microcomputers produced by Apple Computer, such as the Macintosh, use microprocessors produced by Motorola and use a different operating system. These microcomputers are noted for their high-quality display and graphics and ease of use as well as desktop publishing capabilities.

MAJOR FUNCTIONS OF A COMPUTER

Computers perform four basic functions: input, processing, output, and storage (Figure 7). **Input** refers to the process of providing data and instructions to a computer system so that it can accomplish some type of useful task with that data. **Processing** refers to the ways in which the computer uses input to produce meaningful information. Processing includes operations such as arithmetic computations, logical comparisons, rearrangement of data, and the production of images or pictures. **Output** refers to the transmission of the results of computer processing to you, the user. For example, the computer might display or print the results of processing, thus producing output. **Storage** refers to the process of recording data and information to some type of permanent storage medium, such as a disk or magnetic tape, for later use. To perform these basic operations, a computer system must include both hardware and software.

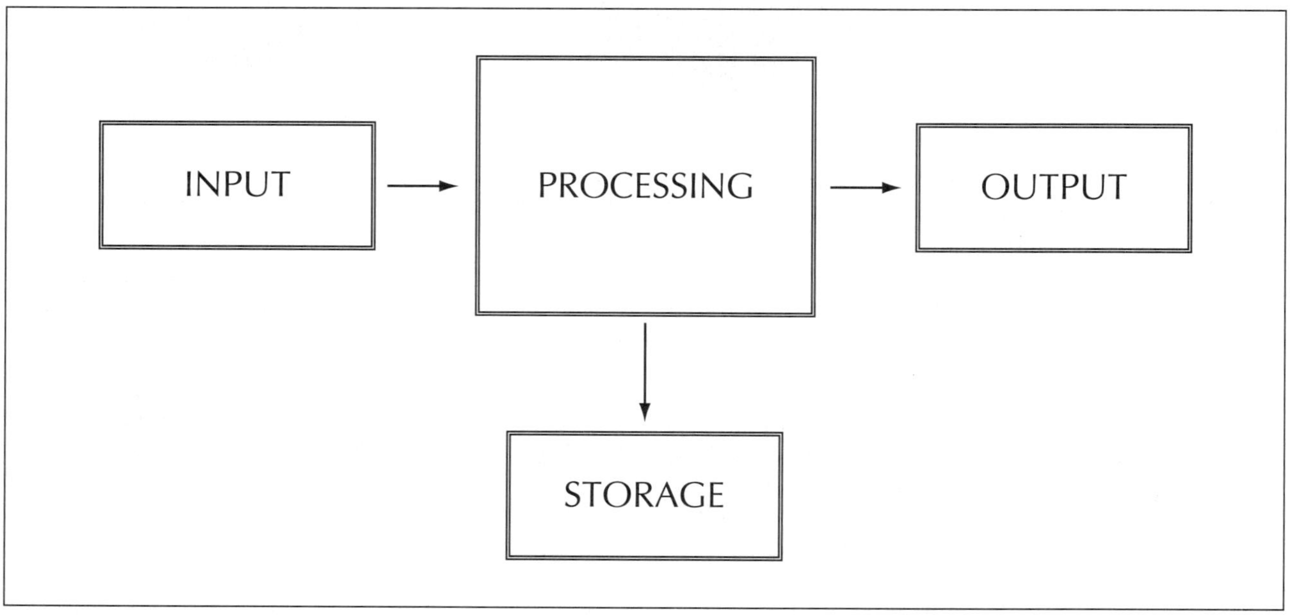

Figure 7
Major functions of a computer

COMPUTER HARDWARE

Computer hardware is typically divided into four categories to reflect the types of activities that the hardware performs: input devices, processing hardware, output devices, and storage media (Figure 8). The term **device** refers to a component within a computer system. The standard hardware components in a microcomputer system include a keyboard, a system unit, a monitor (or video display unit), disk drives, and a printer.

Input Devices

You use **input devices** to provide data and **commands** (instructions) to the computer. The two primary microcomputer input devices are the keyboard and the mouse.

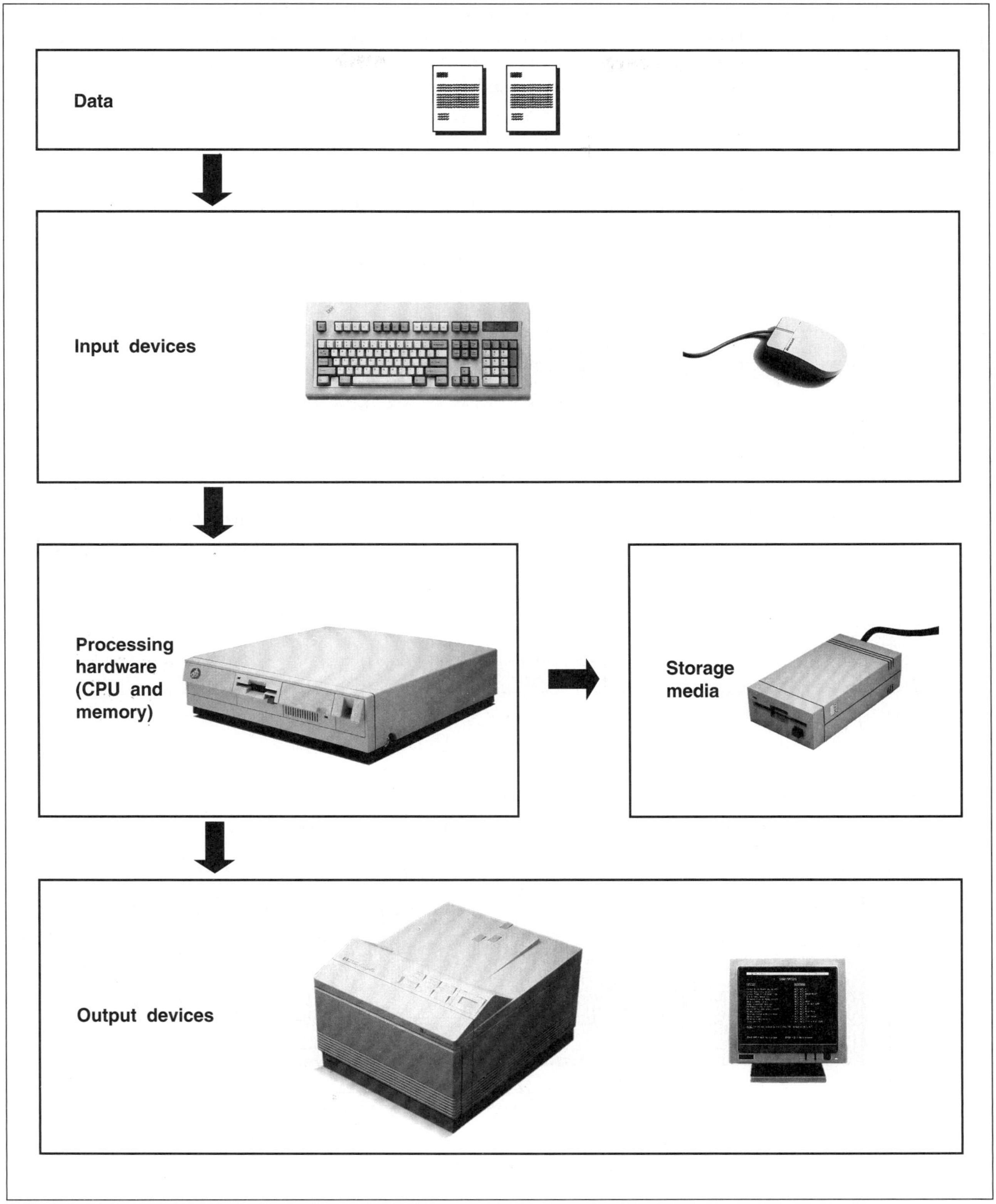

Figure 8
The relationship among input devices, processing hardware, output devices, and storage media

Most of the keys on your computer keyboard work just like the keys on a typewriter. Some features of a computer keyboard, however, are unique to computers. Figure 9 shows the standard 83-key keyboard, and Figure 10 shows the more common enhanced 101-key keyboard.

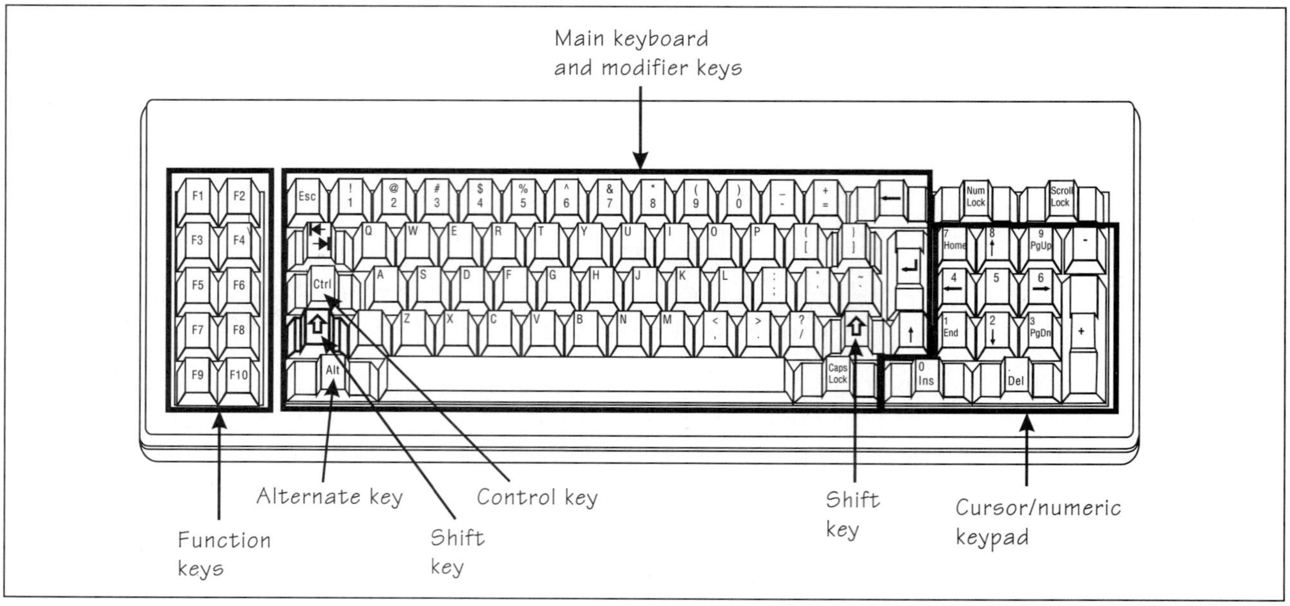

Figure 9
The standard 83-key keyboard

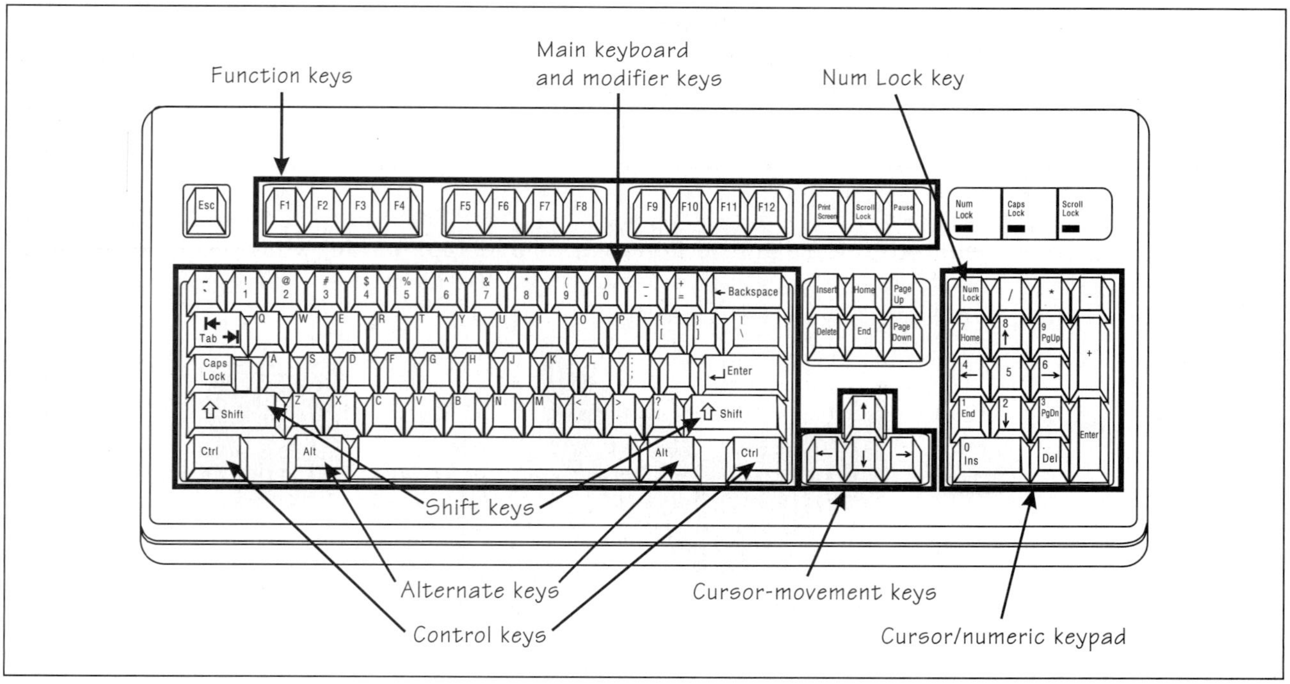

Figure 10
The enhanced 101-key keyboard

These computer keyboards include groups of keys that form the main keyboard, numeric keypad, cursor movement keys, editing keys, and function keys. The keys on the main keyboard work like the keys on a typewriter. To type text, you just press the keys. Sometimes you press more than one key. A **modifier key** is a key that is pressed in conjunction with another key to change the keyboard output. For instance, to type uppercase letters or symbols, such as the colon (:), you press the Shift key (a modifier key) and, while holding it down, press the desired keyboard letter or symbol key, and then release both keys. In addition, you can combine modifier keys, such as the Shift key, the Alt (alternate) key, and the Ctrl (control) key, with other keystrokes to accomplish special tasks, such as saving or printing data, within particular programs. It is important to remember that these key combinations vary with the type of program you use.

The **numeric keypad** on both the standard and the enhanced keyboards is located to the right of the main keyboard. You can use the keys on the numeric keypad in two ways: to enter numbers or to move the cursor. The **cursor** is either a blinking underscore character (_) or a small solid rectangle that marks where the next character that you type will appear on the screen. The Num Lock key permits you to alternate between entering numbers and moving the cursor with the numeric keypad. When you turn [Num Lock] on, you can use keys in the numeric keypad to type numbers and other special symbols, such as the decimal point, the plus sign, and the minus sign. When you turn [Num Lock] off, you can use keys in the keypad to move the cursor. This key is an example of a **toggle key**, a kind of on/off key that alternates between two uses each time you press the key.

Enhanced keyboards contain a separate set of cursor-movement keys between the main keyboard and the numeric keypad. Thus, you can leave [Num Lock] on, use the numeric keypad to enter numbers, and use the separate set of cursor-movement keys to move the cursor.

The **editing keys** allow you to change, or modify, what you type. The editing keys include [←] (Backspace), [Del] or [Delete], [Ins] (Insert), and [Esc] (Escape). The Backspace key deletes the character to the left of the cursor, and the Del and Delete keys delete the character at the cursor position. The Ins key is a toggle key that alternates between insert mode and typeover or overtype modes. In **insert mode**, what you type is inserted at the position of the cursor and characters to the right of the cursor are shifted to the right. In **typeover** or **overtype mode**, what you type replaces existing text on a character-by-character basis. Depending on the program you use, the Esc key clears or cancels editing changes.

The **function keys** are the keys labeled **F1** through **F10** or **F1** through **F12**. The function keys are located to the left of the main keyboard on a standard keyboard and above the main keyboard on an enhanced keyboard. You use the function keys alone or with the modifier keys [Shift], [Alt], and [Ctrl] to perform specific tasks, such as saving or printing. Programs that you use will assign specific operations to these keys, and these operations might differ among programs. For example, if you press the F1 function key, many programs, but not all, will display **help information**, which assists you with the task you are performing in the program.

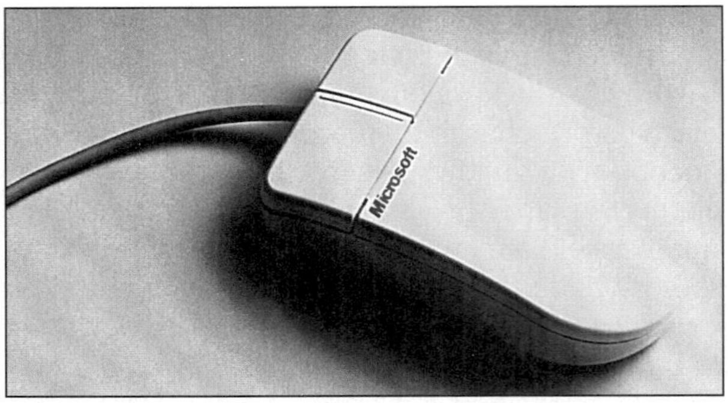

Figure 11
A mouse

Your computer system might also be equipped with a mouse (Figure 11). A **mouse** allows you to position a mouse pointer anywhere on the screen so that you can select options and perform specific operations. As you move the mouse over your desk with your hand, you also move the mouse pointer on the screen in the same relative direction. The **mouse pointer** usually appears in the shape of an arrow or a rectangle; however, its shape may change to reflect the type of activity you are performing in a program. Sometimes you can accomplish tasks more efficiently by using a mouse than by using a keyboard.

Another increasingly important input device is a scanner (Figure 12). A **scanner** is a device that you move over an image on paper to copy that image into the computer system and store it so that you can later enhance and print it. Although some graphics scanners are similar to copier machines, small hand-held scanners are a popular and less expensive alternative.

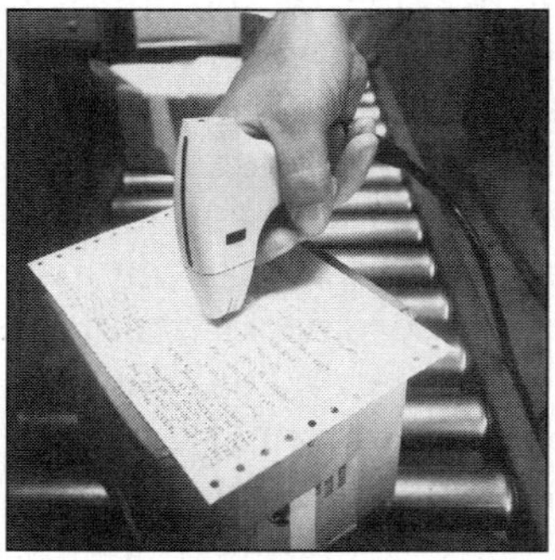

Figure 12
A hand-held scanner

Memory

One important hardware component used for processing is memory. The computer's **memory** consists of a set of storage locations where instructions and data are stored while you use a microcomputer. Computers store these program instructions and data with the use of electronic switches, which can be either *on* or *off*. By associating an *on* switch with the number 1 and an *off* switch with the number 0, we can represent computer data in the binary numbering system with the value 0 or 1. The values 0 and 1 are referred to as **bits**, or **b**inary dig**its**. Computers generally store data in groups of eight bits, called a **byte**. A byte with all eight bits set to 0 (i.e., 00000000) represents the whole number, or **integer**, 0. The integer 1 is represented by 00000001. The integer 2 is represented by 00000010. Figure 13 shows the binary representation of some of the integers from 0 through 255. Each byte can also represent a character, such as the letter A or the @ symbol. For example, in IBM compatibles, the letter A is represented by 01000001, B by 01000010, and C by 01000011. The exclamation point (!) is represented by 00100001, a period (.) by 00101110, and a plus sign (+) by 00101011. All instructions and data used by a computer must be encoded as bytes. As a computer user, you do not have to know the binary representation of numbers, characters, and instructions to use a computer, because the computer handles all the necessary conversions internally.

Number	Binary representation
0	00000000
1	00000001
2	00000010
3	00000011
4	00000100
5	00000101
6	00000110
7	00000111
8	00001000
⋮	⋮
14	00001110
15	00001111
16	00010000
17	00010001
⋮	⋮
253	11111101
254	11111110
255	11111111

Figure 13
Binary representation of some numbers between 0 and 255

In addition to bits and bytes, storage capacities are also measured and expressed as kilobytes, megabytes, and gigabytes. A **kilobyte** is 1,024 bytes, or approximately 1,000 bytes. The abbreviations K and KB are also used to indicate kilobytes. A **megabyte** is 1,024 kilobytes, or approximately one million bytes. The abbreviations M, MB, and meg are also used to indicate megabytes. A **gigabyte** is 1,024 megabytes, or approximately one billion bytes. The abbreviations G and GB are also used to indicate gigabytes.

A microcomputer contains two basic types of memory: Read-Only Memory and Random-Access Memory. **Read-Only Memory**, or **ROM**, is that part of memory reserved for special instructions and data that are required for the internal operation of the computer. The manufacturer places these instructions and data in ROM at the time it produces the computer. ROM includes instructions for starting the computer system, for testing the system components at start-up (the POST, or Power-On Self-Test), for locating drive A and C, and for transferring the operating system software from the disk in drive A or C to Random-Access Memory. The microprocessor can retrieve, or **read**, the instructions and data stored in ROM, but it cannot erase or change the data. When you turn off your computer, the instructions and data in ROM remain intact, ready for use when you turn the computer back on.

Random-Access Memory, or **RAM**, also stores program instructions as well as input you provide the computer and the data it processes. RAM is your workspace, or working memory. A computer's microprocessor can retrieve, or **read**, data from and store, or **write**, data to any location in RAM at any time. For example, when you create or modify a document, such as a letter, memo, or report, the document is stored in RAM as you work on it. Because this memory is **volatile**, that is, it is temporary and dependent on the availability of power, you must save your work on some type of permanent storage medium. If you turn the power off, or if the power fails, then any instructions or data stored in RAM will be lost.

The amount of RAM in a computer system can vary. When you purchase a computer system, you can specify how much RAM you want. Most computers today have 2, 4, 8, or 16 megabytes of RAM to meet the demands of software.

Processing Hardware

Another important and essential processing hardware component is the **microprocessor**, a specialized computer chip. The microprocessor constitutes the **central processing unit** (or CPU) of a computer system and is responsible for processing input to produce output. Figure 14 lists microprocessors used in IBM and IBM-compatible microcomputers from 1981 to 1993. Intel Corporation produced these microprocessors and assigned a number as the name for each one. Although these microprocessors differ in a variety of ways, including the design of the chip itself, the capabilities of microprocessors are generally described in terms of the amount of data they can process, the amount of data they can transmit or receive, their operating speeds, and the amount of memory they can access.

Microprocessor	8088	8086	80286	80386DX	80386SX	80486DX	80486SX	80486DX2	Pentium
Used in	IBM PC & IBM PC/XT	XT Compatibles	ATs (IBM PC/ AT & 286s)	386DX	386SX	486DX	486SX	486DX2	Pentium PC
Introduced	1981	1983–84	1984	1985	1988	1989	1991	1992	1993
Amount of data processed	16 Bits	16 Bits	16 Bits	32 Bits	32 Bits	32 Bits	32 Bits	32 Bits	32 Bits
Number of data lines	8	16	16	32	16	32	32	32	64
Amount of data transmitted	8 Bits	16 Bits	16 Bits	32 Bits	16 Bits	32 Bits	32 Bits	32 Bits	64 Bits
Number of address lines	20	20	24	32	24	32	32	32	128
Type of address bus	20-Bit	20-Bit	24-Bit	32-Bit	24-Bit	32-Bit	32-Bit	32-Bit	128-Bit
Maximum amount of memory addressed	1MB	1MB	16MB	4GB	16MB	4GB	4GB	4GB	Almost unlimited
Operating speed (clock rate)	5–8MHz	5–10MHz	8–12MHz	16–33MHz	16–20MHz	25–50MHz	16–25MHz	50–66MHz	60–100MHz
Math coprocessor	Not included	Not included	Not included	Not included	Not included	Included	Disabled	Included	Included

Figure 14
Microprocessors used in IBMs and IBM compatibles

A microprocessor uses **data lines** to transmit and receive data from other hardware components. The microprocessor can transmit one bit on each data line. The data lines as a group are called a **data bus**, which consists of the electronic circuitry that connects the CPU with internal and external hardware components. A microprocessor also uses **address lines**, which together constitute an **address bus**, to access memory. The number of address lines determine the maximum amount of memory that the microprocessor can access and use.

The speed of a microprocessor is determined by its **clock rate**, or **clock speed**. The computer clock is part of a group of electronic circuits associated with the microprocessor. You can think of the clock rate as the "heartbeat" or "pulse" of the computer; it controls the timing of operations within the computer. The higher the clock rate, the faster the computer. The clock rate is measured in millions of cycles per second, or **megahertz (MHz)**.

The history of microprocessor development is one of rapid technological improvements. In 1981 Intel developed the 8088 microprocessor for the IBM PC and PC/XT (XT stands for Extended Technology). This microprocessor processed 16 bits (two bytes) of data at a time, received and transmitted 8 bits (one byte), accessed 1MB of RAM, and operated at 5 to 8 MHz. This microprocessor, however, was soon updated by the 8086, which was developed for XT compatibles. It had 16 data lines, so it could transmit and receive twice as much information as the 8088. Next came the 80286 microprocessor in the AT (Advanced Technology), which accessed up to 16MB and doubled the operating speed of the 8088. Although some 286s are still in use today, the 8088 and 8086 are both outdated and are rarely used.

The next generation of microprocessors was the 80386DX. Introduced in 1985, this chip doubled the speed of the 286 in terms of data processing and transmittal, and has a clock speed two to four times faster. It can address up to 4096MB—or 4GB—of memory. The 80386DX was a popular but fairly expensive microprocessor; Intel introduced a slightly less powerful but cheaper version, called the 80386SX. Both microprocessors are in wide use today, although they are rapidly being replaced by the newer 80486 chip.

The first 80486 microprocessor, the 80486DX, was marketed in 1989, and has a clock rate of 25 to 50 MHz. It operates 50 times faster than the original 8088. The 486DX system includes a **math coprocessor**, which works in conjunction with the microprocessor to dramatically increase the speed of mathematical calculations and graphics processing. The math coprocessor enhances the overall performance of the computer. An even faster 486 microprocessor, the 80486DX2, operates at twice the speed of the 486DX. Again, because of the 486's popularity, Intel also offers a slightly less powerful system, the 80486SX, at a price that individuals can more easily afford. The 80486 series of microprocessors are in widespread use in homes and offices.

In 1993, Intel introduced its newest and most powerful microprocessor—the Pentium. This microprocessor operates twice as fast as the 80386DX2 and 200 times faster than the 8088. It has a clock rate of 60 to 100 MHz and can access a nearly unlimited amount of memory. The microprocessor has some unique features—such as the ability to process two instructions per clock cycle instead of one—that open up new possibilities for designing and using the newest types of software.

Understanding the features and capabilities of microprocessors is important when you purchase a computer system, evaluate new hardware and software for your computer, configure your system, and optimize its memory.

The System Unit

The microprocessor and the memory chips used for RAM and ROM are housed in the computer case, or **system unit**, on a system board. This **system board**, or **motherboard**, is a fiberglass board with electronic circuits etched, or printed, onto it. The **system bus** consists of the network of electronic circuitry that is responsible for transmitting data and signals between the microprocessor and various components as well as for storing information on the location of instructions and data in memory. The data and address lines, along with **control lines** for synchronizing operations, constitute the system bus.

The system unit also contains other circuit boards, called **adapter cards** or **add-in cards**, that enable the computer system to work with various types of hardware components included in the computer system (Figure 15 on the following page). These adapter cards are added into available **expansion slots** and attach to the main system board. For example, an adapter card might be added to a computer system so that you can use a mouse. The system unit also contains a power supply that provides power to all of the components in the computer system.

Figure 15
Slots in a vertically-configured microcomputer

The system unit uses **ports** as electronic pathways to pass data between the computer's microprocessor and its **peripherals**, the hardware components, such as printers and monitors, that are connected to the system unit. Microcomputers have two types of ports and use one of two types of techniques for transmitting data: serial and parallel (Figure 16). **Serial ports** send information between the microprocessor and other components one bit at a time. In contrast, **parallel ports** usually transmit eight bits, or one byte, at a time. For example, computer printers are often designated as serial or parallel to indicate the type of port to which they connect. Serial printers are usually connected to the port called COM1 or COM2 (for COMmunications port 1 or 2), and parallel printers are usually connected to the port called LPT1 or LPT2 (for Line PrinTer port 1 or 2). The port for the first system printer is designated PRN (for PRiNter) and usually corresponds to LPT1.

When you buy a printer or any other peripheral, be sure your computer has a port that matches the peripheral. For example, if a new laser printer requires a serial port, be sure your computer has an available serial port to which you can connect the printer. If not, you can buy and install a board, or add-in card, that contains one or more additional ports.

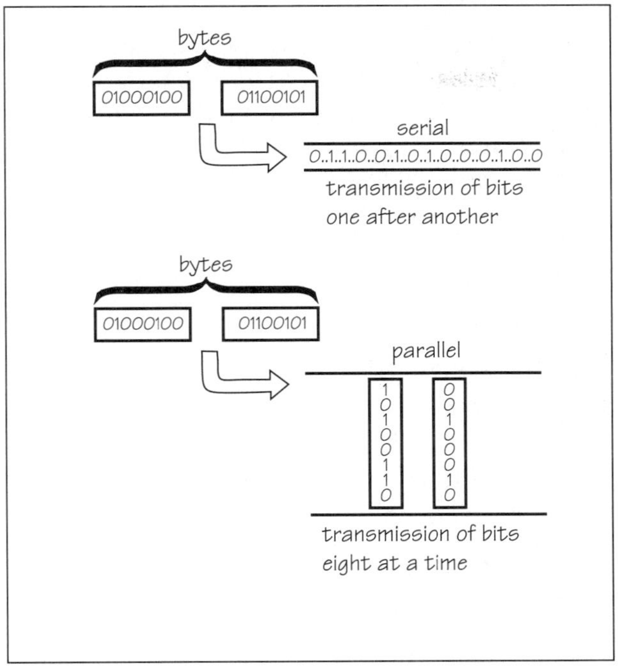

Figure 16
A comparison of data transmission using serial and parallel ports

Figure 17
A color monitor

Output Devices

The microprocessor uses **output devices** to display, print, or store information that results from processing data. The most commonly used output devices are monitors, printers, and disk drives.

Monitors

A **monitor** is a TV-like video screen that displays text and graphics (Figure 17). Most microcomputers use a **cathode ray tube**, or **CRT**, for displaying an image. Most laptop computers use a flat-panel display, such as a **liquid crystal display**, or **LCD**.

The text and graphics displayed on computer monitors are created with little dots of light called **pixels**—short for "picture elements" (Figure 18). Each pixel on a monochrome monitor has only one color—green, amber, or white—when the pixel is illuminated and no color (black) when the pixel is not illuminated. Each pixel on a color monitor, on the other hand, can appear in any of several colors.

The entire monitor screen is a grid of pixels that combine to create the illusion of a continuous image. For example, a **video graphics array**, or **VGA**, monitor has a 640 × 480 grid. There are 640 pixels across the width of the screen and 480 pixels down the length of the screen. If you multiply 640 × 480, you have a total of 307,200 pixels available for creating and displaying an image on a VGA monitor. **SuperVGA (SVGA)** monitors, with a resolution of 1024 × 768 pixels, have a total of 786,432 pixels and can display even more impressive graphics. The higher the number of pixels on a monitor, the greater the **resolution** and the clearer and sharper the graphics images it can display.

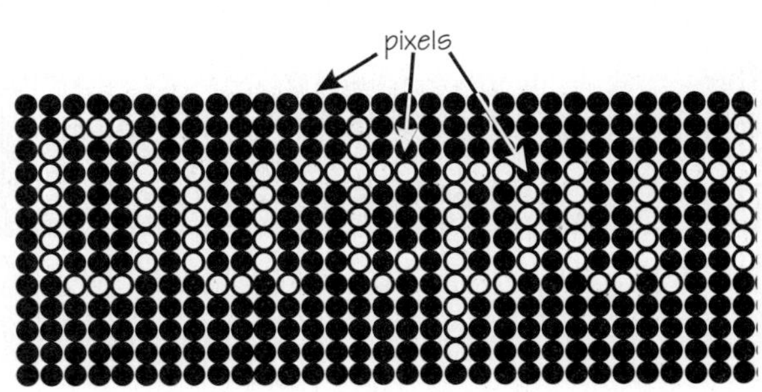

Figure 18
Illumination of pixels to produce a text image

Monitors have two display modes: text and graphics. In **text mode**, the monitor can display only text—letters, numbers, symbols, and special characters. In **graphics mode**, the monitor can display graphic images as well as text. All monitors have a text mode, but not all monitors have a graphics mode. A **video card**, or **graphics adapter**, mounted in an expansion slot on the motherboard in the system unit controls the display of text and graphics on the monitor.

Most monitors display 80 characters across the width of the screen and 25 lines down the screen, or approximately one-half page of information at a time.

Printers

A **printer** produces a paper copy of text or graphics processed by the computer. The paper copy of computer output is often called **hard copy**. Printers are classified as impact and non-impact printers. **Impact printers** produce a character on paper by striking a metallic element against an inked ribbon. **Non-impact printers** spray ink or use heat to fuse ink onto paper and thereby produce an image of a character.

The most popular impact printer is the dot-matrix printer (Figure 19). A **dot-matrix printer** uses small pins in the print head to produce a character composed of an array, or matrix, of dots. The dots are formed when the pins strike an inked ribbon. Less expensive dot-matrix printers have nine pins, whereas more expensive models have 24 pins and produce higher-quality output. These printers can operate in draft mode or near-letter-quality mode. In **draft mode**, the printer prints faster but produces lower-quality output. In **near-letter-quality (NLQ) mode**, the printer prints more slowly but produces higher-quality output. Figure 20 shows the text output from a 24-pin dot-matrix printer in draft mode and also in NLQ mode. Dot-matrix printers can also print graphics as well as text.

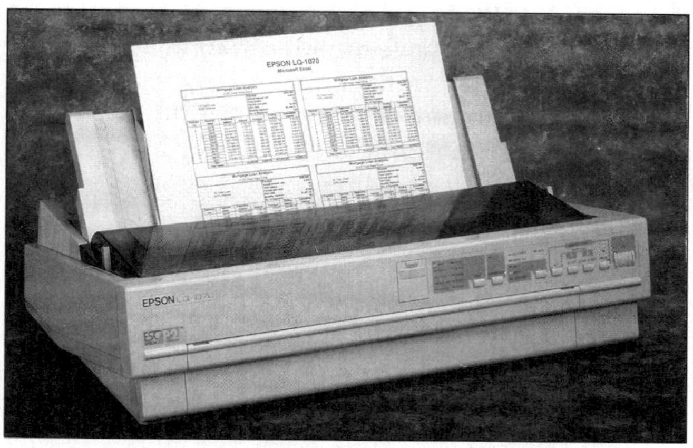

Figure 19
A dot-matrix printer

```
This is sample output from a
 24-pin dot-matrix printer
       in DRAFT mode

This is sample output from a
 24-pin dot-matrix printer
        in NLQ mode
```

Figure 20
Samples of draft-quality and near-letter-quality output from a dot-matrix printer

Figure 21
An ink-jet printer

The most popular types of non-impact printers are ink-jet printers and laser printers. **Ink-jet printers** spray tiny dots of ink onto the paper to form text or graphics (Figure 21). Most ink-jet printers are faster than dot-matrix printers. They produce graphics of reasonable quality and text of high quality.

Laser printers use a laser beam to form an electrostatic, or electrically-charged, image on a rotating photosensitive drum. These electrostatic areas on the drum then attract a black, powdery substance called a **toner**. Subsequent heating bonds the toner to the paper—similar to the process in a photocopying machine. The laser printer produces the highest-quality text and graphics of any type of printer (Figures 22 and 23). Moreover, laser printers are faster and quieter than dot-matrix and ink-jet printers. As a result of these features, laser printers are becoming the standard printer in the business world.

Figure 22
A laser printer

Figure 23
Sample output from a laser printer showing four fonts (different typefaces in different sizes)

Disk Drives and Storage Media

A **disk drive** is actually classified as both an input and an output device because the microprocessor can record data onto, or retrieve data from, secondary storage media in the disk drive (Figure 24 on the following page). A disk drive stores data in much the same way that a VCR stores images and sound, except that instead of advancing a tape, the disk drive spins a disk or diskette.

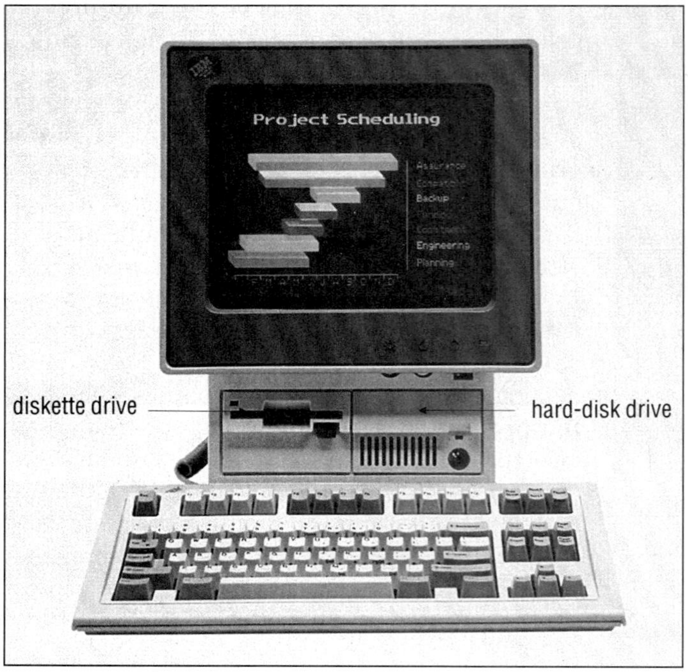

Figure 24
Disk drives in a computer

The most common storage media for microcomputers are diskettes and hard disks. Sometimes called a **floppy disk**, a **diskette** is a flat, circular plastic disk with a magnetic coating enclosed in a square case called a **disk jacket**. The most common sizes of diskettes for microcomputers are 3½ inches and 5¼ inches (Figure 25). The 5¼-inch diskettes have soft, flexible disk jackets and are usually stored in paper sleeves for protection. The 3½-inch diskettes have hard plastic cases and do not require sleeves. The most common types of diskettes are double-sided, double-density (DS/DD) and double-sided, high-density (DS/HD). On **double-sided** disks, information is recorded on both sides of the diskette. The terms **double-density** and **high-density** refer to the amount of information that is stored within a unit area on the diskette. High-density diskettes can store two to four times as much data as double-density diskettes.

The 5¼-inch double-density diskettes have a capacity of 360 kilobytes (abbreviated K), and the 3½-inch double-density diskettes have a capacity of 720K. The 5¼-inch high-density diskettes have a capacity of 1.2MB. The 3½-inch high-density diskettes have a capacity of 1.44MB.

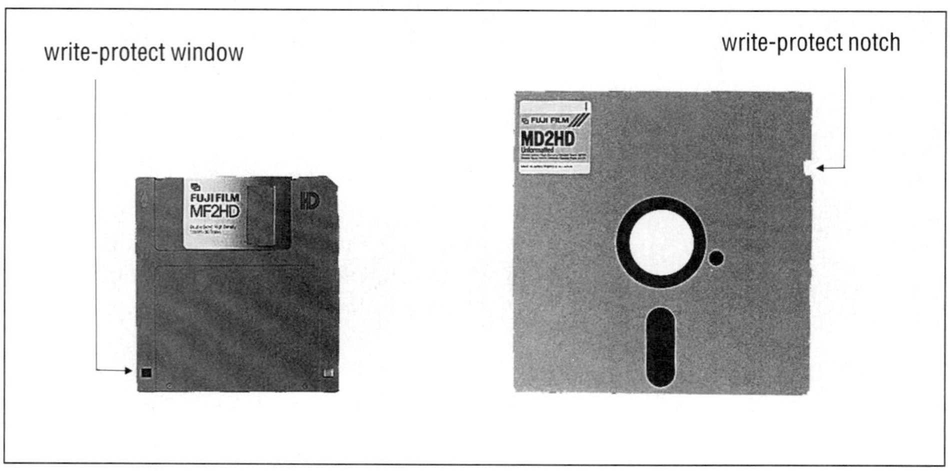

Figure 25
A 3½-inch diskette *(left)* and a 5¼-inch diskette *(right)*

Diskette drives are also available in double-density and high-density types. A high-density diskette drive can read from and record on both high-density and double-density diskettes. A double-density diskette drive, on the other hand, can read from and record on only double-density diskettes. Before you purchase diskettes, be sure they match your type of diskette drive. For example, if you have a 3½-inch high-density diskette drive, you should buy and use

3½-inch DS/HD diskettes. To distinguish between the two types of disks, note that the 3½-inch high-density diskettes have a hole in the lower-right corner, directly opposite the square hole with the write-protect tab (described below), whereas the 3½-inch double-density diskettes have only the square hole with the write-protect tab. In addition, high-density diskettes sometimes have "HD" written on their cases. Usually, however, you have to rely on the information printed on the packaging.

After you store information on a diskette, you might want to be sure that no one records more information on the diskette or erases the information from the diskette. For this purpose, diskettes provide **write protection**, which serves as a safeguard against losing valuable information. To write-protect a 5¼-inch diskette, you place a write-protect tab over the write-protect notch; to write-protect a 3½-inch diskette, you open the write-protect window by pressing a small square tab down so that you can see through a square hole in the diskette (Figure 26).

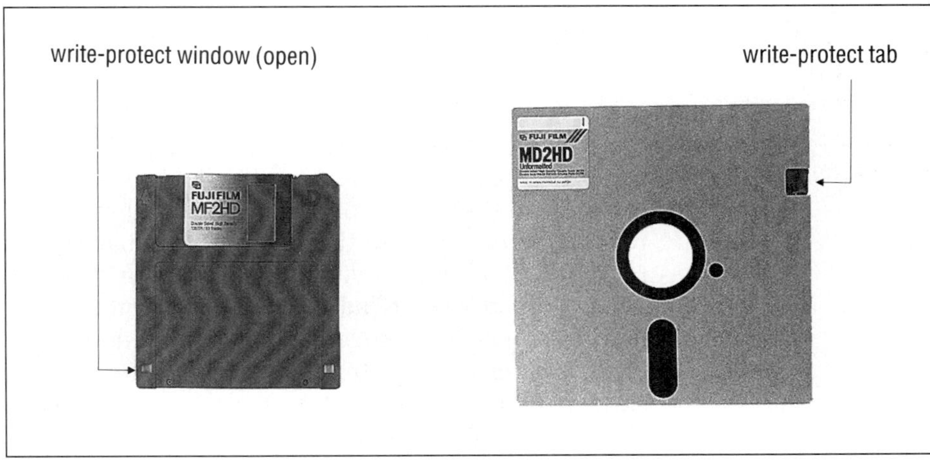

Figure 26
A write-protected 3½-inch diskette *(left)* and a 5¼-inch diskette *(right)*

Hard disks, also called **fixed disks**, consist of two or more unremovable metallic disks, or **platters**, with a magnetic coating on both sides of each platter (Figure 27 on the following page). The hard disk is mounted permanently within the system unit. Hard disks have two advantages over diskettes: speed and capacity. The speed of a hard disk is measured by its **access time**, that is, the time required to read or write a byte of data. A typical hard disk has access times one-third to one-tenth those of a diskette; therefore, a hard disk is 3 to 10 times faster at accessing data.

The capacity of hard disks is commonly measured in megabytes (MB). A hard disk with a capacity of 200MB can store the equivalent of about 80,000 pages of text, compared to only about 600 pages of text on a 1.2MB 5¼-inch diskette. Most microcomputer hard disks have capacities in the range of 20MB to 600MB. These high capacities are more than just a convenience; much of the work currently performed by businesses using microcomputers requires these higher-capacity hard disks.

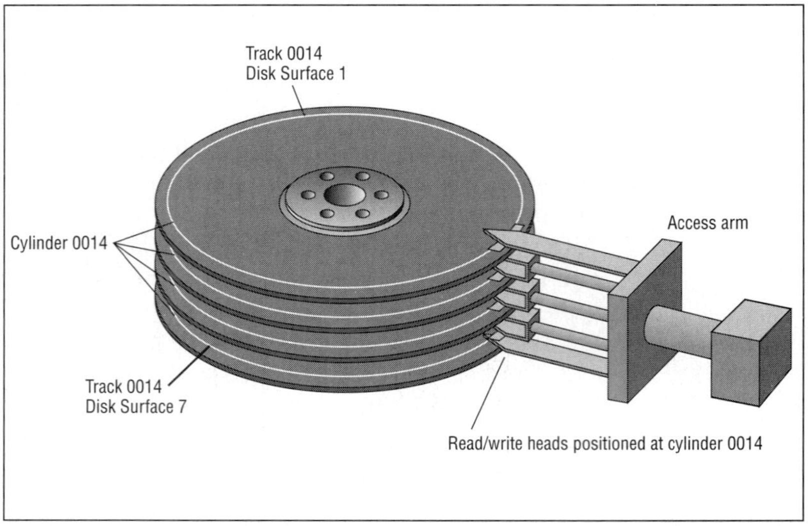

Figure 27
Read/write heads and platters in a hard disk drive

Diskettes spin in a diskette drive at 300 or 360 revolutions per minute, or rpm, whereas platters in a hard disk drive spin at 3,600 rpm—10 to 12 times faster. Hard disks spin continuously, but diskettes spin only when the computer reads from or writes to the diskette. As a hard disk or diskette spins, the computer reads or writes data onto a platter or diskette with the use of read/write heads. A **read/write head** consists of an arm that moves across the surface of a hard disk or diskette to locate and read data or to record data onto the surface of the platter or diskette. The read/write heads in a diskette drive rest on the surface of the spinning disk and access data through the **head slot** (or the oval-shaped recording window) on a 5¼-inch diskette or through the **access hole** on a 3½-inch diskette. A metal **shutter** covers the access hole when the 3½-inch diskette is not in the drive. Once inserted in the drive, the shutter opens to expose the access hole for the read/write heads.

In the case of a hard disk, the read/write heads fly on a cushion of air a few millionths of an inch above the surface of each disk platter (Figure 27). As a result, hard disks must be sealed within a unit that protects the hard disk from contaminants, such as dust, hair, and other minute particles. If a contaminant comes between the read/write head and the hard disk platter, the hard disk will suffer a **head crash** and the read/write head might gouge the surface of the platter. The hard disk is then unusable, and all the data on the hard disk is lost. A head crash can also occur as the result of a jolt to the system unit.

To reduce the likelihood of damage to one or more of the platters in a hard disk drive, newer computer systems have an **auto-park feature** that automatically moves and **parks**, or rests, the read/write heads in a **landing zone** on the innermost surface of the hard disk when you turn off the computer's power. The read/write heads then rest on a surface of the disk where no data is stored.

CD-ROMs and Optical Disks

CD-ROMs (Compact Disc Read-Only Memory) and optical disks are also popular storage devices. The CD-ROM disk is similar to an audio compact disc and requires a CD-ROM disk drive that is similar to an audio compact disc player (Figure 28). You connect the CD-ROM drive to your computer system via an existing port or through the use of an expansion card inserted inside the system unit. In a CD-ROM drive, a laser beam reads data stored on the CD-ROM disk. A CD-ROM disk can store up to 700MB of data; however, you can only read data from the drive. You cannot record data onto the CD-ROM diskette. You also need special software to operate the CD-ROM drive. CD-ROMs are commonly used to store reference information, such as legal precedents, medical information, encyclopedias, and catalogs, as well as graphic images and font files, which require an enormous amount of disk storage space.

Figure 28
A CD-ROM disk and CD-ROM drive

The **optical disk** is similar to a CD-ROM, but the primary difference is that you can record information on the optical disk using a magneto-optical drive. You can also use optical disks that require a **WORM** (Write Once, Read Many) drive. You can write to this type of optical disk, but only once.

Modems

Another common input and output device is a modem. A **modem** is a hardware device that enables you to transmit and receive data between your computer system and a computer in another office or location. The term modem is an abbreviation for **mo**dulator/**dem**odulator. When transmitting data, the modem modulates, or converts, digital electronic *on* and *off* signals inside the computer to analog wave signals in a telephone line. **Digital** refers to data stored in discrete units, such as 0s and 1s, whereas **analog** refers to data that varies continuously over a range, such as the amplitude of a sound wave signal. When receiving data from another source over the telephone line, the modem demodulates, or reverts, the analog wave signals in the telephone line to digital electronic *on* and *off* signals for use in the computer.

An **internal modem** is mounted on a card that is inserted into one of the expansion slots inside the computer, while an **external modem** consists of a separate hardware unit that connects to one of the serial ports on the computer system. Both types of modems also connect to your telephone or directly to the telephone jack.

COMPUTER SOFTWARE

Just as a tape recorder or a compact disc player would be worthless without tapes or compact discs, computer hardware would be worthless without computer software. As you've learned, software, also referred to as computer programs, consists of detailed step-by-step instructions that tell the computer what to do. Figure 29 on the following page illustrates an example of a computer program that prompts the user for a number, then computes and prints the square and the square root of that number.

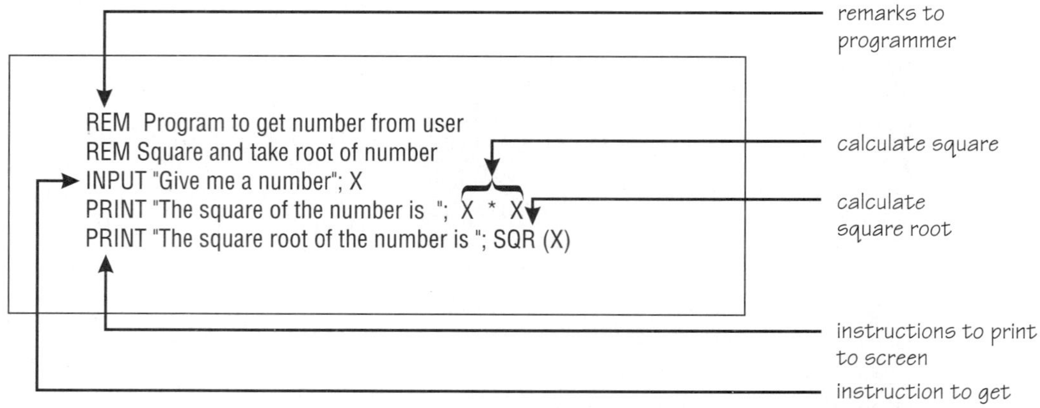

Figure 29
A computer program written in the BASIC programming language

The types of software that you use determine what you can do with your computer. For example, word processing software lets you use a computer to prepare documents, and graphics software lets you use a computer to create graphs and illustrations. Software can be divided into two general categories: systems software and applications software.

Systems Software

Systems software includes the programs that run the fundamental operations within your computer, such as starting the computer, **loading** or copying programs and data into memory, **executing** or carrying out the instructions in programs, saving data to a disk, displaying information on the monitor, and sending information through a port to a peripheral. Systems software includes three similar types of software: operating system software, system utility software, and programming language software.

Operating system software coordinates the activities within a computer, including all the input and output operations to and from the peripherals. The most popular operating system for IBM and IBM-compatible microcomputers is **DOS** (rhymes with "boss"), an abbreviation for **Disk Operating System**. There are two types of DOS: PC-DOS and MS-DOS. Microsoft Corporation developed both operating systems in conjunction with IBM and, as a result, PC-DOS and MS-DOS operate in a similar manner. (More about that in a moment.) This text focuses on the use of MS-DOS. Many operating system concepts and features that you will learn about in the following DOS tutorials apply equally well to PC-DOS and to larger, more powerful operating systems on minicomputers, mainframes, and supercomputers.

Another systems software program developed by Microsoft Corporation is **Windows**, a graphics-based operating environment designed to make your computer easier to use. An **operating environment** interfaces between the operating system (DOS) and an application or utility. The current version, Windows 3.1, offers an alternate approach to managing your computer system and its resources with a graphical user interface. A **graphical user interface** provides a more visual method for interacting with the operating system through the use of icons, menus, and multiple windows. **Icons** are images or pictures displayed on the screen that represent commonly used objects, such as a drive, disk, program, or file. **Menus** display a list of command choices. **Windows** consist of outlined areas of the screen, through which you use programs, view information, and display the contents of files.

Three other operating systems—OS/2, Unix, and Windows NT—require higher-performance computer systems with additional memory and disk space. Microsoft and IBM developed OS/2 (Operating System 2) for use on IBM microcomputers. OS/2 supports **multitasking**, the ability to use several different programs at the same time. Unix (Uniplexed Information and Computing System) not only supports multitasking but also **multiusers**; that is, several people, each with their own keyboard and monitor, can use the same computer at the same time. Microsoft Corporation's new Windows NT operating system supports multitasking and maintains compatibility with DOS and programs designed for use with DOS. Because OS/2 and Windows NT require a 32-bit internal data bus, these operating systems require computer systems with an 80386, an 80486, or a Pentium microprocessor.

All three of these operating systems also manage memory more efficiently than DOS. DOS has more widespread use because more programs operate under DOS, and DOS requires less memory and disk space.

System utility software includes special programs provided with operating system software to enhance the performance of your computer system, such as optimizing the use of memory, maximizing the use of storage space on a hard disk, correcting errors on a hard disk, obtaining technical or diagnostic information about your computer system, or preparing diskettes for use on a computer system.

Programming language software includes programs that enable you to design and write your own application software for use on a computer system. One popular programming language is BASIC (Beginners All-purpose Symbolic Instruction Code), an example of which you saw in Figure 29. On IBMs and compatibles, a version of BASIC is automatically provided with the operating system software. Microsoft supplies QBASIC (Quick BASIC) with MS-DOS 6.0. Other important and popular programming languages include C, COBOL (short for COmmon Business-Oriented Language), FORTRAN (FORmula TRANslator), and Pascal (named for mathematician Blaise Pascal).

The Development of DOS

Before the introduction of DOS, most microcomputers used another operating system called CP/M (Control Program/Microcomputers). When IBM decided to introduce its own microcomputer into the marketplace in 1981, one of its subcontractors, a small company named Microsoft, offered to provide the operating system software for the IBM PC. Microsoft then contracted with another company to complete work on an operating system named 86-DOS, which was similar to CP/M. DOS 1.0 resulted from this joint venture, and eventually Microsoft bought complete rights to the software. Since 1981, DOS has become the predominant operating system used on microcomputers around the world.

Microsoft and IBM have released different versions of DOS to meet the rapid changes in microcomputer technology. Many of the DOS versions extended support for new hardware components, added new features to extend the capabilities of DOS, provided new system utilities, and corrected problems in earlier releases. Figure 30 lists the DOS versions and some of their important features. You will examine many of these features in later tutorials.

Version	Date	Features
1.0	1981	The first version of DOS included basic functions required of an operating system: • Ability to use single-sided diskettes • Reading, writing, and managing files stored on disk • Loading and executing applications and utilities • Communicating with standard hardware components • Interpreting user commands • Programs for performing system-related operations
1.1	1982	Supported the use of double-sided diskettes
2.0	1983	Supported the use of hard disk drives and subdirectories
2.1	1983–84	Provided support for IBM's PCjr microcomputer
3.0	1984	Supported the use of larger hard disk drives and high-density 5¼-inch diskette drives
3.1	1984	Supported the use of computer networks
3.2	1985–86	Supported the use of 3½-inch double-density diskette drives
3.3	1987	Supported the use of 3½-inch high-density diskette drives, increased hard disk support, and improved support for languages outside the United States
4.0	1988	Supported the use of hard disk drives over 32MB, introduced the DOS Shell graphical user interface, and increased memory support
5.0	1991	Supported the use of extra-high-density diskette drives, introduced new disk and file management utilities, enhanced the DOS Shell graphical user interface, provided extensive on-line help, introduced the MS-DOS text editor, and improved memory management
6.0	1993	Supported compression of hard disk drives to increase storage space; multiple start-up configurations; increased Windows support as well as new utilities for optimizing memory, optimizing disk storage space, backing up and restoring data to a hard disk drive, checking for computer viruses, undeleting files, and unformatting disks
6.2	1993	Enhanced the disk compression (DoubleSpace) utility

Figure 30
Versions of DOS and their features

When DOS undergoes a major change, the number before the decimal point changes. For example, the change from DOS 5.0 to DOS 6.0 is a **major upgrade**. When DOS undergoes a minor change, the number after the period changes. For example, the change from DOS 6.0 to DOS 6.2 is a **minor upgrade**.

The PC-DOS and MS-DOS versions of 1.0 through 5.0 offer the same features. Starting with DOS 6.0, PC-DOS and MS-DOS differ in the types of utilities included with each software product.

Applications Software

A wide variety of software exists to help you accomplish specific tasks on your computer. This type of software is called **applications software**, because it allows you to apply your computer to accomplish a particular goal. The major types of applications software are word processing, electronic spreadsheets, database management, graphics, communications, and desktop publishing.

Word processing software allows you to create, edit, enhance, and print documents electronically (Figure 31). With a word processing system, you can produce many more types of documents and perform many more editing tasks than you can on a typewriter. For example, you can move text within and between documents, check spelling, create tables and columns, center titles, adjust margins, draw lines, change the appearance of text (to boldface or underlined, for example), and view how a document will appear before you print it. Word processing software simplifies the process of creating and printing headers, footers, page numbers, footnotes, and line numbers. Many word processing applications include advanced features for assembling and printing complex documents.

Electronic spreadsheets allow you to perform calculations on numbers arranged in a table of

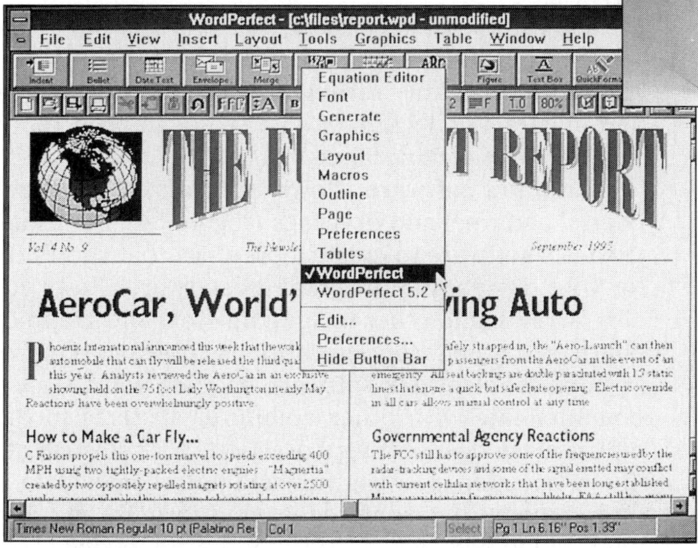

Figure 31
Example of a report produced with WordPerfect software and its pull-down menus

columns and rows on the computer screen (Figure 32). You can enter numbers, formulas, text, dates, and other kinds of data into the spreadsheet and automatically perform computations. By using the appropriate data and formulas, you can use an electronic spreadsheet to prepare financial reports and statements, analyze investment portfolios, calculate amortization tables, project income and expenses, and prepare a payroll.

Database software helps you manage information that is stored in the form of **records**; for example, information about employees, clients, schedules, supplies, equipment, inventories, or catalog entries (Figure 33). Database software

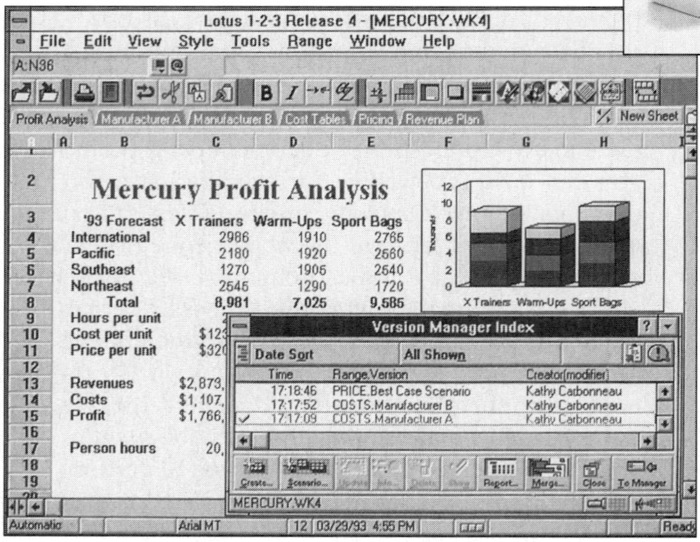

Figure 32
Example of a spreadsheet model created with Lotus 1-2-3 software

allows you to easily retrieve, search, sort, select, delete, organize, compare, and update a collection of data. You can print reports after selecting data, or you can print mailing labels.

Graphics software allows you to create illustrations, diagrams, graphics, charts, and freehand drawings (Figure 34). For example, you can use business graphics software to create a pie chart that shows the change in yearly income for your company. Most graphics software allows you to draw lines, boxes, circles, arrows, and other images; mix text and graphics; and enter data to create charts and graphs for your business presentations, reports, and newsletters.

Communications software enables you to use your computer system to communicate with other computer systems in the same office or in other offices around the country or world. With the use of a modem and a telephone line connection, you can transmit and receive data via electronic mail, participate in computer conferences and forums, and access on-line database and information systems. You can add a **fax board** to your computer so that you can send and receive facsimiles, or faxes. These faxes can include text as well as graphics.

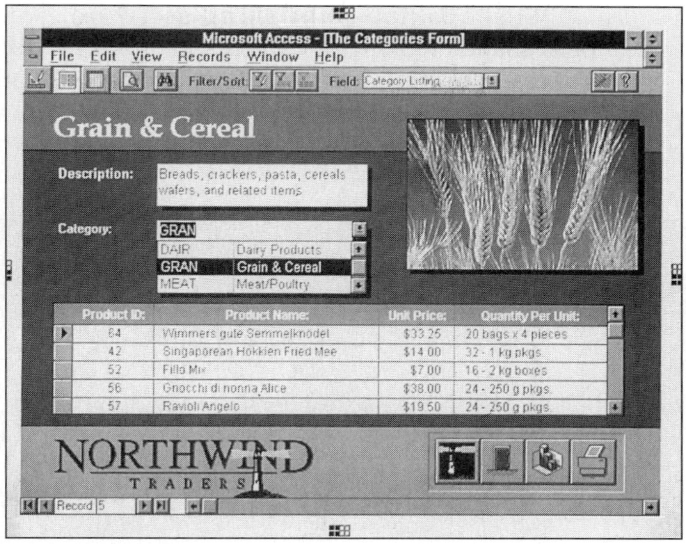

Figure 33
Example of a database created with Microsoft Access software

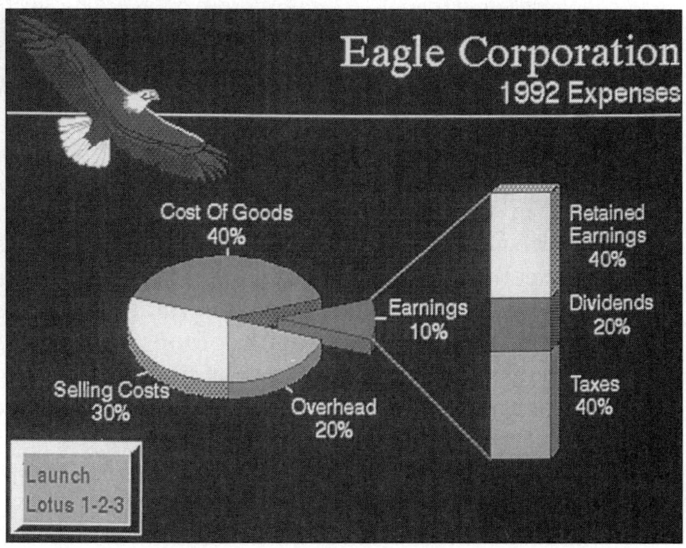

Figure 34
Example of a graphic design created with Harvard Graphics from Software Publishing Corporation

With **desktop publishing software**, you can produce high-quality, professional-looking documents for presentation or reproduction (Figure 35). You can combine text, graphics, and tables from other software applications into one final document. You can enhance the appearance of the final document so that it takes on a typeset appearance when printed.

Figure 35
Example of brochures produced with Pagemaker desktop publishing software

Yet another category of software, called **integrated software**, combines two or more applications into one product. Lotus 1-2-3, for example, combines an electronic spreadsheet application with a graphics application and a database application. Once you enter data into an electronic spreadsheet, you can use the same data to produce graphs and perform database operations. Lotus 1-2-3 also contains its own programming languages so that you can automate routine, repetitive operations with macros. A **macro** is a set of keystrokes or commands that executes an operation or set of operations.

Microsoft Works is another example of a popular integrated software package. Microsoft Works contains word processor, electronic spreadsheet, and database tools. You can produce charts or graphs using data in a spreadsheet. You can also place a spreadsheet or graph in a word-processed document or convert a spreadsheet to a database. You can even combine, or **merge**, a list of names and addresses stored in a database with a form letter created with the word processor to print personalized letters.

NETWORKS

In the business world you usually do not work alone but rather as part of a team. As a team member, you will probably use a computer **network**, a collection of interconnected computers and peripherals. A network allows you to share software, hardware, and data with other members of your team.

Typically, one of the computers on a network is equipped with a high-capacity hard drive and is designated as a **server**; that is, it "serves" the data to the other computers and peripherals on the network. The most common type of network involving microcomputers is a local-area network. In a **local-area network** (**LAN**), computers are joined by direct cable links and are located relatively close to each other, usually in the same building (Figure 36). Each computer in the LAN has a special **network board** inserted into one of its expansion slots, and each board is joined by an electrical cable to the server. Other computer equipment, such as laser printers and modems, may also be included in the LAN. Networks provide a standardized and predictable working environment for employees in a business and maximize the use of software and hardware resources.

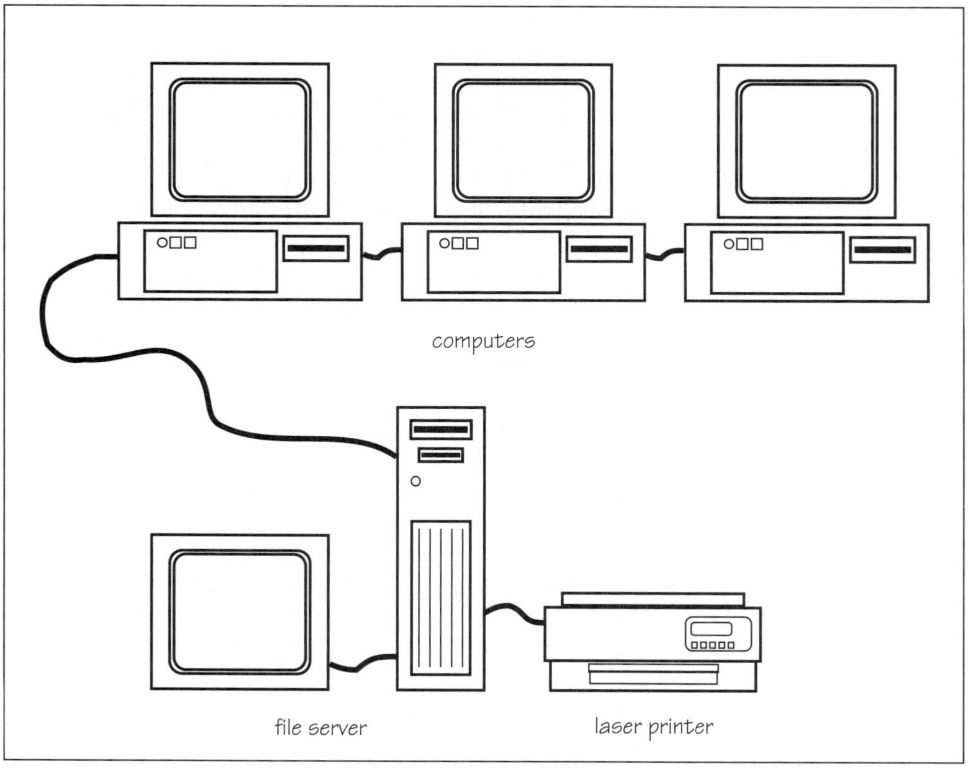

Figure 36
A local-area network, or LAN

SUMMARY

In this chapter, you learned that a computer is an electronic tool that uses software and hardware to perform many types of business tasks. Microcomputers, minicomputers, mainframe computers, and supercomputers differ in size, speed, processing capacity, and cost. You reviewed the four basic functions of a computer system: input, processing, output, and storage. You examined the major types of hardware devices: keyboard, mouse, and scanner. Processing hardware consists of the microprocessor, memory, and supporting electronic circuitry known as the system bus. You learned how Read-Only Memory (ROM) and Random-Access Memory (RAM) differ. You familiarized yourself with the units of measurement—bits, bytes, kilobytes, megabytes, and gigabytes—for describing the storage capacity of memory, diskettes, and hard disks. You examined the use of common types of output devices—monitors, printers, disk drives, CD-ROMs, and optical disks.

You examined the two major categories of software—systems software and applications software. You learned the importance of operating system software in managing the operation of a computer system. You examined the difference between PC-DOS and MS-DOS, as well as the versions of DOS. You learned about the use of system utilities and programming language software. You explored the uses of applications software—word processing, electronic spreadsheet, database, graphics, communications, and desktop publishing. You also examined the capabilities of integrated software.You learned that networks allow you to share software resources, hardware resources, and data with other individuals in your local workshop or located in a remote office.

QUESTIONS

1. Define or describe the following terms:
   a. Computer
   b. Hardware
   c. Software
   d. Memory
2. List and describe the four major functions of a computer system.
3. Describe each of the following hardware components:
   a. Keyboard
   b. Mouse
   c. System Unit
   d. Microprocessor
   e. Monitor
4. Identify the major groups of keys on a computer keyboard.
5. Describe the two types of memory used by microcomputers and how they differ.
6. Define or describe the following terms for measuring storage capacity on a microcomputer:
   a. Bit
   b. Byte
   c. Kilobyte
   d. Megabyte
   e. Gigabyte
7. Fill in the empty boxes in the following table with the storage capacities in kilobytes (K or KB) or megabytes (M or MB) of each type of diskette:

	3½-Inch Diskettes	5¼-Inch Diskettes
Double-sided, double-density		
Double-sided, high-density		

8. List the two major advantages of using a hard disk over a diskette.
9. What is a modem and how can you use it?
10. What is the difference between a serial and a parallel port?
11. What is the difference between text mode and graphics mode?
12. What is systems software, and why is it important?
13. List and briefly describe the six major types of applications software.
14. What is integrated software? What advantage does it offer over applications that focus on a single use?
15. What is a network? What is the advantage of using computer networks in business?

Photography Credits for *Essential Computer Concepts*

Figure		Credit	Page
1		Courtesy of International Business Machines	EC 4
2		Courtesy of Toshiba America Information Systems, Inc.	EC 5
3		Courtesy of Dell Computer Corporation	EC 5
4		Courtesy of International Business Machines	EC 5
5		Courtesy of International Business Machines	EC 6
6		Photo by Paul Shambroom, courtesy of Cray Research, Inc.	EC 7
8	keyboard	Courtesy of International Business Machines	EC 9
	mouse	Courtesy of Microsoft Corporation	EC 9
	CPU	Courtesy of International Business Machines	EC 9
	disk drive	Courtesy of International Business Machines	EC 9
	printer	Photo courtesy of Hewlett-Packard Company	EC 9
	monitor	Courtesy of I-O Corporation	EC 9
11		Courtesy of Microsoft Corporation	EC 12
12		Courtesy OptoWand, Inc.	EC 12
15		Courtesy of International Business Machines	EC 16
17		Courtesy of NEC Technologies, Inc.	EC 17
19		Courtesy of Epson America, Inc.	EC 18
21		Photo courtesy of Hewlett-Packard Company	EC 19
22		Photo courtesy of Hewlett-Packard Company	EC 19
24		Courtesy of International Business Machines	EC 20
25		Richard Morgenstein	EC 20
26		Richard Morgenstein	EC 21
28		Courtesy of Radio Shack/Tandy Corporation	EC 23
31		Courtesy of WordPerfect. WordPerfect is a registered trademark of WordPerfect Corporation.	EC 27
32		Courtesy of Lotus Development Corporation	EC 28
33		Courtesy of Microsoft Access	EC 29
34		The Harvard Graphics package photo is used with the permission of Software Publishing Corporation, which owns the copyright to such product. Harvard Graphics is a registered trademark of Software Publishing Corporation. Harvard Graphics is a product of Software Publishing Corporation and has no connection with Harvard University.	EC 29
35		Courtesy of Aldus Corporation	EC 30

Essential Computer Concepts Index

A

access hole, EC 22
access time, EC 21
adapter cards, EC 15
add-in cards, EC 15
address bus, EC 14
address lines, EC 14
analog, EC 23
Apple Computer, EC 7
application software, EC 27-30
    communications, EC 28
    database, EC 28
    desktop publishing, EC 30
    electronic spreadsheet, EC 27-28
    graphics, EC 28-29
    integrated, EC 30
    word processing, EC 27
auto-park feature, EC 22

B

binary digits. *See* bits
bits, EC 12
bytes, EC 12

C

cathode ray tube (CRT), EC 17
CD-ROM (Compact Disc Read-Only Memory), EC 23
central processing unit (CPU). *See* microprocessor
chips, EC 13
circuit boards, EC 15
clock rate, EC 14
clock speed. *See* clock rate
COM1-COM2, EC 16
commands, EC 8
communications software, EC 28
compact disc read-only memory (CD-ROM), EC 23
computers
    definition of, EC 4
    functions of, EC 8
    hardware for. *See* hardware
    software for. *See* software
    types of, EC 4-7
CPU (central processing unit). *See* microprocessor
CRT (cathode ray tube), EC 17
cursor, EC 11

D

data, EC 4, EC 14
    telecommunication, EC 23, EC 28
    transmission, EC 16-17
database software, EC 28
data bus, EC 14
data lines, EC 14
desktop publishing, EC 7
    software, EC 30
digital, EC 23
disk drive, EC 19
disk jacket, EC 20
diskettes, EC 20
    drives, EC 20-22
    sizes, EC 20
    types, EC 20
    write protecting, EC 21
disk operating system (DOS), EC 24-27
display modes, EC 18
DOS (disk operating system), EC 24-27
    development of, EC 25
    types of, EC 24
    versions of, EC 26-27
dot-matrix printers, EC 18
double-sided, double-density (DS/DD), EC 20
double-sided, high-density (DS/HD), EC 20
draft mode, EC 18
DS/DD (double-sided, double-density) diskettes, EC 20
DS/HD (double-sided, high-density) diskettes, EC 20

E

editing keys, EC 11
electronic spreadsheets, EC 27-28
enhanced keyboard, EC 10-11
executing, EC 24
expansion slots, EC 15

F

fax board, EC 28
fixed disks, EC 21-22
floppy disks, EC 20
function keys, EC 11

G

gigabyte, EC 13
graphical user interface, EC 25
graphics, EC 15
- adapter, EC 18
- mode, EC 18
- software, EC 24, EC 28-29

H

hard copy, EC 18
hard disks, EC 21-22
hardware, EC 4
- types of, EC 8

heads, EC 22
- crashes, EC 22
- parking, EC 22
- slots, EC 22

help information, EC 11

I

IBM Corporation, EC 7, EC 24-27
icons, EC 25
impact printers, EC 18
ink-jet printers, EC 19
input, EC 8
- devices, EC 8-12

insert mode, EC 11
integer, EC 12
integrated software, EC 30
Intel Corporation, EC 7, EC 14

K

keyboard, EC 8-11
kilobyte, EC 13

L

LAN (local-area network), EC 31
landing zone, EC 22
laptop computers, EC 4-5, EC 17
laser printers, EC 19
LCD (liquid crystal display), EC 17
liquid crystal display (LCD), EC 17
loading, EC 24
local-area network (LAN), EC 31
LPT1-LPT2, EC 16

M

macro, EC 30
mainframe computer, EC 6
major upgrade, EC 27
math coprocessor, EC 15
megabyte, EC 13, EC 21
megahertz (MHz), EC 14
memory, EC 12-13
- management, EC 25
- types of, EC 13

menus, EC 25
merge, EC 30
microcomputers, EC 4-5
- types of, EC 7

microprocessors, EC 7, EC 13-15
- history, EC 14-15
- speed, EC 14

minicomputers, EC 5-6
minor upgrade, EC 27
modems (modulator/demodulator), EC 23
modifier key, EC 11
modulator/demodulator. *See* modems
monitors, EC 17-18
motherboard, EC 15
mouse, EC 8, EC 12
- pointer, EC 12

multitasking, EC 25
multiusers, EC 25

N

near-letter-quality (NLQ) mode, EC 18
networks, EC 31
NLQ (near-letter-quality), EC 18
non-impact printers, EC 19
notebook computers, EC 4-5
numeric keypad, EC 11

O

operating environment, EC 24-25
operating system, EC 4
  types of, EC 7, EC 24-27
Operating System 2 (OS/2), EC 25
optical disks, EC 23
OS/2 (Operating System 2), EC 25
output, EC 8
  devices, EC 17-19
overtype mode, EC 11

P

parallel ports, EC 16
PCs (personal computers). *See* microcomputers
Pentium, EC 15, EC 25
peripherals, EC 16
personal computers (PCs). *See* microcomputers
pixels, EC 17
platters, EC 21
ports, EC 16
printers, EC 16
  types of, EC 18
processing, EC 8
  hardware, EC 13-15
programming language software, EC 25
programs, EC 4

R

RAM (random-access memory), EC 13
random-access memory (RAM), EC 13
read-only memory (ROM), EC 13
records, EC 28
resolution, EC 17
ROM (read-only memory), EC 13

S

scanner, EC 12
serial ports, EC 16
server, EC 31
shutter, EC 22
software, EC 4, EC 23-30
  application, EC 27-30
  systems, EC 24-27
  types of, EC 24. *See also* operating system
spreadsheets, EC 27-28
storage, EC 8, EC 12-13
supercomputers, EC 6-7
SuperVGA (SVGA), EC 17
SVGA (SuperVGA), EC 17
system board, EC 15
system bus, EC 15
systems software, EC 24-27
system unit, EC 15-16
system utility software, EC 25

T

terminals, EC 6
toggle key, EC 11
toner, EC 19
typeover mode, EC 11

U

UNIX (Uniplexed Information and Computing System), EC 25
upgrades, EC 27

V

VGA (video graphics array), EC 17
video card, EC 18
video graphics array (VGA), EC 17

W

windows, EC 25
Windows (program), EC 24-25
Windows NT (program), EC 25
word processing, EC 24
  software, EC 27
workstations, EC 6
WORM (Write Once, Read Many) drive, EC 23
write protection, EC 21

INTRODUCTORY DOS 5.0 / 6.0 / 6.2

Tutorials

Read This Before You Begin

To the Student

To use this book, you must have a Data Disk and a Windows Data Disk. Your instructor will provide you with a copy of the Data Disk and you will make your own copy of it by following the instructions in Tutorial 1. Later, your instructor will give you the Windows Data Disk, which you will copy for one of the Windows tutorials. See your instructor for further information. If you are going to work through this book using your own computer, you need a computer system running DOS 5.0, 6.0, or 6.2, Microsoft Windows 3.1, and a Data Disk. You will not be able to complete the tutorials and exercises in this book using your own computer until you have a Data Disk.

To the Instructor

Making the Data Disks To complete the first five tutorials in this book, your students must have a copy of a Data Disk. Later, you will need to provide your students with a copy of a Windows Data Disk for Tutorial 8. You can prepare these data disks from your Instructor Resource Disk. If some of your students will use their own computers to complete the tutorials and exercises in this book, they must first make a copy of the Data Disk for Tutorial 1 and the Windows Data Disk for Tutorial 8.

Installing the CTI Data Directories The Instructor Resource Disk contains a CTI Setup program that installs CTI data directories on drive C so that you can reproduce the Data Disk and the Windows Data Disk. The CTI Setup program also creates a subdirectory named AceForms for hard-disk backups performed by students in Tutorial 6. To use the CTI Setup program, follow the instructions provided in the Instructor's Manual that accompanies this text.

README File A README.TXT file located on the Instructor Resource Disk provides additional technical notes, troubleshooting advice, and tips for using the CTI Setup program in your school's computer lab. You can view the README.TXT file using any word processor you choose.

System Requirements

The minimum software and hardware requirements for your computer system are as follows:

- ◆ DOS 5.0, 6.0, OR 6.2 on a local hard drive or network drive.
- ◆ A 386 or higher processor with a minimum of 4MB of RAM (6MB or more is strongly recommended) for the Windows tutorials. The DOS tutorials can be completed on any computer system that supports DOS 5.0, 6.0, or 6.2 and that has the standard 640K of conventional memory.
- ◆ A mouse supported by Windows 3.1.
- ◆ A VGA 640 × 480 16-color display is recommended; an 800 × 600 or 1024 × 768 SVGA, VGA monochrome, or EGA display is also acceptable. The DOS tutorials can be completed with a monochrome monitor.
- ◆ 20 MB of free hard-disk space
- ◆ Student workstations with at least 1 high-density disk drive, preferably a 3½-inch disk drive. A 5¼-inch Data Disk can be prepared from the Instructors Resource Disk if you have a computer system with a 5¼-inch and a 3½-inch disk drive.
- ◆ If you want to install the CTI Data Directories with the CTI Setup Disk on a network drive, your network must support Microsoft Windows.

TUTORIAL 1

Understanding DOS

OBJECTIVES

In this tutorial you will learn to:

- Describe the basic functions of operating system software
- Select filenames
- Use drive and directory names
- Follow the numbered steps in the DOS tutorials
- Start a computer system
- Enter commands at the DOS prompt
- Identify the DOS version installed on a computer
- Clear the screen
- Set the date and time
- Use [F3] and DOSKEY to recall commands
- Use the Help switch
- Print a screen
- Format a diskette
- Make a copy of a diskette
- Turn off the computer system

Imagine you have just purchased your first computer system. From extensive research and careful evaluation of the capabilities of microcomputers, you discovered that you can use your new computer to prepare presentation-quality documents, develop a personal budget, keep business and personal records, and build valuable computer skills. You can streamline time-consuming tasks that you once did by hand so you can "work smarter."

The salesperson emphasized that you will need to invest some time up front to train yourself. You must understand the capabilities of the hardware and software included within your computer system. This initial investment in time will pay off in increased productivity in the future. Furthermore, with these skills, you will be able to troubleshoot many problems that might arise and install new software on your system.

After arriving home with your new computer system, you follow the instructions for getting started and set up your new computer system within half an hour. You examine the manual and other reference materials provided with the computer and learn that one of the most important types of software you will use is operating system software.

WHAT IS THE ROLE OF OPERATING SYSTEM SOFTWARE?

Operating system software manages the basic processes required of a computer system and, in the process, coordinates the interaction of hardware and software. For example, the operating system handles all input and output operations. As you type, the operating system interprets the keys that you press on the keyboard and then displays the corresponding characters on the monitor. The operating system also interprets instructions, or **commands**, that you enter from the keyboard. If you enter a command to use a software application or utility, the operating system locates the program instructions on disk. Then, it copies, or **loads**, those program instructions into the computer's memory so you can use that software. When you issue a command to save a document, the program you are using relays this request to the operating system, which then stores a permanent copy of the document on a hard disk or a diskette. If you want to print a copy of the document, the operating system handles the transfer of data from the software application to the printer. When you are ready to work with another document, the request is again relayed to the operating system from the program you are using. The operating system locates the document on disk, retrieves a copy of the document, and displays that copy on the monitor. If a hardware or software problem occurs while you are using the computer system, the operating system attempts to resolve the problem or notifies you so that you can solve the problem.

USING MS-DOS AND PC-DOS

As you learned in the "Essential Computer Concepts" chapter, the most popular operating system on IBM and IBM-compatible microcomputers is the Disk Operating System, known as DOS. *Disk* refers to one of the important hardware resources—hard disks and diskettes—managed by the operating system. DOS is actually a generic term for two related operating systems: PC-DOS and MS-DOS. PC-DOS is designed specifically for the hardware in IBM microcomputers, whereas MS-DOS is designed for the hardware in IBM compatibles. Although there are differences between PC-DOS and MS-DOS, both manage the hardware and software resources within computer systems in similar ways. If you are familiar with either PC-DOS or MS-DOS, then you will know enough about DOS to operate the other version.

This text covers the use of MS-DOS on IBM compatibles and focuses on three popular versions: MS-DOS 5.0, 6.0, and 6.2. Features of these versions of DOS are comparable to features included in PC-DOS used on IBMs. PC-DOS 5.0 is similar to MS-DOS 5.0, and PC-DOS 6.1 is similar to MS-DOS 6.0.

5.0

6.0

6.2

This text will use icons to identify features unique to a particular version of DOS. For example, if a feature is implemented differently in DOS 5.0, a DOS 5.0 icon will appear next to the text where the difference is discussed. Unless you see an icon denoting a specific version of DOS, you should assume that the concepts and steps under discussion apply to each of the three versions of DOS and that features operate the same way in each of these versions.

USING FILES AND FILENAMES

While you are working on a computer system, the computer's memory contains part of the operating system software. If you are using a word processing application to produce a document, the computer's memory also contains a copy of that software application and the document. If you turn off the power to the computer system, or if the power fails, you lose your working copy of DOS, the application software that you are using, and, more important, the document that you are creating or modifying. You can always retrieve another copy of DOS and the application software from your original disks. However, you must periodically save your work onto a diskette or hard disk to guarantee that you have a permanent copy of your document.

When you save your work, your document is stored in a file. A **file** consists of a certain amount of storage space on a diskette or hard disk that is set aside for the contents of a document. You must give each file a unique name to identify its location on a diskette or hard disk and also to identify its contents. A **filename** is one to eight characters in length. The characters can include letters of the alphabet and the numbers 0 through 9. For example, if you prepare a résumé, you might store the document in a file with the filename RESUME. If you produce two versions of your résumé, you might store the first version in a file named RESUME1 and the second in a file named RESUME2. You *cannot* use the same filename for two different files stored in the same location on disk, even if the files contain the same or similar information. If you attempt to use the same name as an existing file, you might replace the contents of the existing file with the contents of the new document.

You can also use certain types of symbols, such as a dash or underline, as part of a filename. For example, you might save a copy of your most recent tax records under the filename TAX-RECS or TAX_RECS. Since a filename *cannot* contain any blank spaces, the dash or underscore is commonly used to separate two parts of the same filename. You cannot use other symbols, such as a slash or asterisk, as part of a filename because these symbols are commonly used with DOS commands. To simplify the process of naming files, it is a good idea to limit the use of symbols in filenames.

You cannot use a filename that is the same as a reserved device name. A **device name** is a name DOS assigns to one of the devices, or hardware components, in a computer system. For example, DOS reserves PRN as the device name for the first printer port, so you cannot use it as a filename. Figure 1-1 lists the device names used by DOS. The NUL device is a special device used to store discarded bits of data.

Device Name	Meaning	Assigned To
LPT1	Line printer 1	First parallel port
LPT2	Line printer 2	Second parallel port
LPT3	Line printer 3	Third parallel port
PRN	Printer	First printer port
COM1	Communications port 1	First serial port
COM2	Communications port 2	Second serial port
COM3	Communications port 3	Third serial port
COM4	Communications port 4	Fourth serial port
AUX	Auxiliary device	First serial port
CON	Console unit	Monitor and keyboard
CLOCK$	System clock	System clock
A:	Drive A	First diskette drive
B:	Drive B	Second diskette drive
C:	Drive C	First hard disk drive
NUL	Null device	"Bit Bucket"

Figure 1-1
Reserved device names

Using File Extensions

If you need a filename that is longer than eight characters, you can include a **file extension** that contains an additional one to three characters. When you add a file extension, you use a period to separate the main, or **root**, part of the filename from the file extension. The file extension follows the same guidelines and rules as the main part of the filename. For example, you might use the filename RESUME.LTR for a file that contains a cover letter for your résumé. File extensions are usually optional, but some applications require a file extension.

File extensions usually identify the type of information stored in a file. For example, files with the file extension EXE (for executable) and COM (for command) are **program files** that contain program instructions for a software application or utility. Other types of files have file extensions that indicate they contain program code or settings used by programs. For example, files with the OVL extension are **overlay files**—files that contain a module of program code (such as a spelling checker) that is only loaded into memory when needed. Files with the INI extension are **initialization files** that contain settings used by programs. Figure 1-2 is a list of some of the important types of file extensions used for program files and auxiliary files included with a software product. These auxiliary files contain additional program code or data required by the application program you use.

File Extension	Abbreviation For	Example	Contents of Example
BAT	Batch file (User-Defined or User-Created Program File)	AUTOEXEC.BAT	DOS commands and other program commands that are executed when starting a computer
CNF	Configuration file	123.CNF	Configuration settings for Lotus 1-2-3 application software
COM	Command file	MOUSE.COM	Software for operating a mouse
EXE	Executable file	WP.EXE	WordPerfect application program
HLP	Application or utility Help file	WORKS.HLP	Help information for Microsoft Works application software
INI	Initialization file	WIN.INI	Initial settings used by Windows 3.1 operating environment software
OVL	Overlay file	SPELL.OVL	Spelling checker software used with Microsoft Works application software
SYS	System configuration file	CONFIG.SYS	Commands for configuring DOS when starting a computer

Figure 1-2
Important file extensions used for program and program-related files

Data files are files that contain documents or data. You usually produce these files with a software application or perhaps utility software. The software application or utility might assign a specific file extension to the file. For example, Microsoft Word, a word processing software package, assigns the file extension DOC to document files produced by that program. Figure 1-3 on the following page shows a list of file extensions assigned to data files by popular software applications packages.

File Extension	Meaning	Example	Example's Application Package
BAK	Backup file	5YRPLAN.BAK	Lotus 1-2-3
BK!	Backup file	RESUME.BK!	WordPerfect
DBF	Databasefile	CLIENT.DBF	dBASE
DOC	Document file	RESUME.DOC	Microsoft Word
PCX	Graphics file	FIGURE1.PCX	Collage Plus (screen capture software)
WK1	Worksheet file	5YRPLAN.WK1	Lotus 1-2-3

Figure 1-3
Some common file extensions assigned to document or data files by applications software

In many cases, you can choose your own file extensions to reflect the type of information a document contains. For example, you might use the file extension RPT for a document file that contains a report, such as CLIENT.RPT. Figure 1-4 shows a list of file extensions you might choose to use for data files. This figure also illustrates another valuable use of file extensions: If you have a set of documents that are related to each other (for example, budget documents), you can use the same word for the main part of the filename, but vary the file extension. All of the sample files in Figure 1-4 contain budget information for the 1994 fiscal year.

File Extension	Meaning	Example
DAT	Data	94BUDGET.DAT
DOC	Document	94BUDGET.DOC
FRM	Form	94BUDGET.FRM
LST	List	94BUDGET.LST
LTR	Letter	94BUDGET.LTR
MEM	Memo	94BUDGET.MEM
RPT	Report	94BUDGET.RPT
TBL	Table	94BUDGET.TBL

Figure 1-4
Some common file extensions for document files

Whenever you select a filename, use one that closely describes the contents of the file, so you will be able to find that file easily and distinguish it from other files.

USING DRIVE, DIRECTORY, AND PATH NAMES

In addition to providing a name for a file, you might also need to tell DOS which disk drive to use when it stores or retrieves a file. DOS uses **drive names** to distinguish the disk drives in your computer system. These drive names are device names for the disk drives. The drive names **A:** and **B:** are used for the first and second diskette drives. If you only have one diskette drive, you can refer to that drive as either drive A or drive B. The drive name **C:** is used for the first drive on your hard disk.

Your hard disk might be **partitioned**, or divided, into additional drives, with drive names such as D:, E:, and so on. On a computer network, you might work with network drives that have drive names such as F:, G:, or H:. Whenever you specify a drive name, you must always include the colon immediately after the letter of the alphabet that identifies the drive.

On a hard disk drive, program and document files are typically stored in separate storage compartments called **directories** or **subdirectories**. A good way to think of directories is to compare them to hanging files in a file cabinet. The hanging file is the directory. The individual file folders contained in the hanging file are subdirectories of that directory. In Tutorial 2, you will examine the concept and use of directories and subdirectories in more detail.

Directories have names similar to filenames. For example, you might have a directory named DOS that contains the program files that are included with MS-DOS 6.2, and another one named RESUMES that contains different versions of your résumé. When saving a file to a directory on the hard disk, you must specify the name of the directory. When you indicate the drive name, directory name, and filename for DOS to use when it stores or retrieves a file, you are identifying a **full path** for that file. For example, Figure 1-5 shows the full path for a program file named FORMAT.COM that is stored in a directory named DOS on drive C. Note that a Backslash (\) separates the drive name from the directory name, and the directory name from the filename. The full path identifies a specific location for your file. In Tutorial 2 you will examine more closely the importance and use of directories and paths.

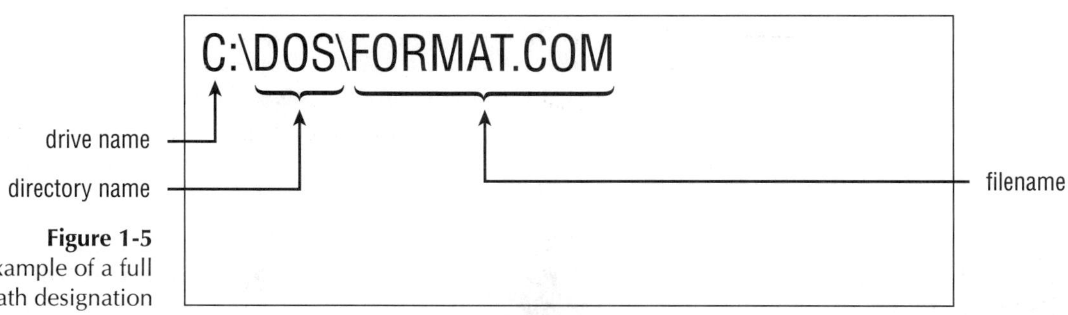

Figure 1-5
An example of a full path designation

As you work with DOS, you will find that there are some instances where you must specify the full path—drive name, directory name, and filename. In other instances, you may need to specify only part of the path because DOS makes an assumption about the remainder of the path. For example, if you do not specify a drive name, DOS assumes you want to use the **default**, or **current**, **drive**. The default drive is the current drive you are using. For example, the default drive might be drive A, B, or C. If you do not specify the proper path, then DOS might not be able to find the program or data file that you need to use.

HOW TO FOLLOW THE NUMBERED STEPS IN THE DOS TUTORIALS

Before you start your computer and learn more about DOS, you need to know how to follow the step-by-step instructions in this text. The steps are displayed as numbered items, as shown in Figure 1-6. *Do not attempt to follow these steps now.* They are only examples to demonstrate the way you use the tutorials in this book.

To access the DOS 6.0 and 6.2 Help system:

1. Type **HELP** and press **[Enter]**.
2. Press **[Tab]** and then **[↓]** (Down Arrow) until you highlight <Format>.
3. Press **[Enter]** to display a Help screen on formatting a disk.
4. Press **[PgDn]** to view subsequent Help screens.
5. Press **[PgUp]** to return to the first Help screen. On some computers, you can also use **[Ctrl][Home]**.

Figure 1-6
An example of step-by-step tutorial instructions

In Figure 1-6 notice that:

- The numbers, letters, and special characters that you will type are printed in a distinct bold typeface: Type **HELP**.
- The keys that you will press are printed in a distinct bold typeface: Press **[Enter]** means "Press the Enter key."
- Keys that you will press in *succession* are shown as follows: Press **[Tab]** and then **[↓]** (Down Arrow). This indicates that you press the first key and release it, then press the second key and release it.
- Keys that you will press *simultaneously* are shown as follows: On some computers, you can also use **[Ctrl][Home]**. While pressing and holding the first key, you press the second key, then you release both keys.

As you complete the steps, you will compare screen views on your monitor with those reproduced in the tutorials. Depending on the type of hardware you use, your screen views might be slightly different. Also, unless otherwise noted, the screen views illustrate operations performed with DOS 6.0. If you are using DOS 5.0 or DOS 6.2, you might see messages on the screen that differ slightly from those in DOS 6.0.

STARTING A COMPUTER SYSTEM

To discover how DOS and your computer system work, you will turn on your computer in a moment. The process of powering on a computer system and loading DOS into memory is called **booting** a computer system.

When you power on a computer system, you are performing a **cold boot**. During a cold boot, the microprocessor locates and executes program instructions for a Power-On Self Test (called a POST), which checks for hardware errors. The instructions for the POST are stored on a ROM chip. Then, the microprocessor uses additional program instructions stored on this same chip to check drive A for the operating system software. If the operating system software is not on the diskette in drive A or if drive A does not contain a diskette, it checks drive C for DOS. After it locates DOS on either drive A or drive C, it loads DOS into memory. Because DOS manages the computer, the system must be able to locate DOS and copy it into memory before you can use the computer. It is important to note that older PCs might require you to load the operating system from a disk in drive A; otherwise, you see an error message.

If you are using a computer and need to restart it for some reason, you can perform a **warm boot** by holding down [Ctrl] and [Alt] while you press [Del], then releasing all three keys. (You can also press the Reset button on your computer if your computer system has this button.) A warm boot clears memory of any programs and data. The microprocessor then loads DOS into memory, but skips the POST. This operation is also called a **system reset**.

Whether you perform a cold or a warm boot, the microprocessor loads the three DOS system files into RAM. The DOS **system files** contain the operating system software that manages the computer. On an IBM-compatible that uses MS-DOS, these files are named IO.SYS, MSDOS.SYS, and COMMAND.COM. On an IBM microcomputer that uses PC-DOS, the operating system files are named IBMBIO.COM, IBMDOS.COM, and COMMAND.COM. IO.SYS in MS-DOS and IBMBIO.COM in PC-DOS handle the basic input and output operations required of DOS. MSDOS.SYS in MS-DOS and IBMDOS.COM in PC-DOS manage the use of drives, directories, and files and constitute the majority of what you think of as DOS. COMMAND.COM in both MS-DOS and PC-DOS is the **command interpreter** or **command processor**. One of its primary functions is to interpret, or process, commands that you issue to DOS.

During the booting process, you will see additional information displayed on the monitor. This information may include technical specifications about your computer system and the amount of available memory, as well as information displayed by programs that are automatically executed when you boot. When you **execute** a program, DOS loads the program into memory and the microprocessor carries out, or processes, the program instructions.

You must know whether your computer system boots from the hard drive or from a diskette drive. This text assumes you have a hard drive. If this is not the case, your instructor will provide you with additional instructions for getting started and for completing the tutorials.

To perform a warm boot of your computer system:

1. If drive A contains a diskette, remove the diskette from drive A.
2. Turn the power switch on. You may also need to turn on the monitor. If the computer is already on, ask your instructor or technical support person for permission to turn it off and then on again. The computer system will perform a self-test and then load DOS into memory.
3. The easiest way to perform a warm boot is to simultaneously press and hold down **[Ctrl]** and **[Alt]** with your left hand, and then press **[Del]** with your right hand. Then release [Del], [Ctrl], and [Alt]. The screen will clear. During the booting process, you will see technical information about the computer displayed on your monitor. If you are using DOS 6.2, you might also see other information as it examines your system. DOS will eventually display the DOS prompt, which you'll learn more about in a moment. See Figure 1-7. In some cases, DOS might ask you for the current date and time before it displays the DOS prompt. If you do not see the DOS prompt on the screen, your computer system might be **customized**, or specifically configured, for your needs. For example, if a menu appears with a list of options for using your computer, ask your instructor or technical support person to show you how to exit to the DOS prompt.

6.2

6.2

If you are using DOS 6.2, you will see other information displayed on the screen. Just ignore these messages for the moment.

Figure 1-7
The DOS prompt after the system is booted

4. If DOS prompts you for the date, press **[Enter]** to accept the currently set date
5. If DOS prompts you for the time, press **[Enter]** again to accept the currently set time. DOS then displays the DOS prompt.

WORKING AT THE DOS PROMPT

The **DOS prompt** identifies the name of the drive from which the system booted or, in some cases, the drive that DOS automatically uses after the booting process is complete. If you prefer, you can change from this drive to another drive. The drive name shown in the DOS prompt identifies the default drive—the drive DOS uses at any given point in time to find files or execute commands. As you work, DOS keeps track of the current drive so that it can locate program and data files.

To the right of the DOS prompt, you will see a small blinking underscore called a **cursor**. The cursor identifies your current working position on the screen. If you type a character, that character is displayed on the screen where the cursor was positioned. The cursor then appears after the character you typed.

When you see the DOS prompt, you are working at the **operating system level**. You can enter internal and external commands to execute programs included with DOS. An **internal command** is a command for which the program instructions are stored in the computer's memory as part of DOS. In fact, the program code for internal commands is stored in the command interpreter, COMMAND.COM. DOS can quickly locate and execute program instructions for internal commands because they are stored in RAM and are easily accessed.

An **external command** is a command for which the program instructions are stored in a file on a hard disk or diskette. DOS must first locate the file with the program instructions. Then it must copy those program instructions into RAM so that you can use the program. It takes longer for DOS to locate and load an external command than an internal command because accessing disks is slower than accessing memory. External commands allow you to use the system utilities included with DOS.

IDENTIFYING THE VERSION OF DOS

After you boot the computer system, you may want to check which version of DOS is installed on your computer. Identifying your version of DOS is useful for several reasons. First, each version of DOS has slightly different capabilities. If you attempt to perform a certain operation with DOS and you experience difficulties, checking the version of DOS you are using will tell you if it is the one that contains this feature. The VER command—described below—is one of the first tools a computer specialist will use to troubleshoot a problem on a computer.

Second, if you are experiencing difficulties in using a software package on your computer system, you can contact the company that produces that software. One of the first questions a technical support representative is likely to ask you is what version of DOS you are using. The company representative uses that information as a starting point for finding the solution to the problem you are experiencing.

Finally, when you purchase a new software package, the instructions for that new software product may indicate that you need a specific version of DOS. Before you install the software, you should check the DOS version used on that computer system.

To identify the version of DOS on your computer, you can use the VER command, which is an internal command. Each command has its own **syntax**, which is the order in which you must enter a command. The syntax for the VER command is very simple:

VER

To use this command, you type VER at the DOS prompt and then press the Enter key.

Let's check your version of DOS.

To check the DOS version:

1. Be sure you see the DOS prompt. Then, type **VER**. It is important to enter DOS commands exactly as they are written, with the correct punctuation and spacing. However, case does not matter. You can use uppercase or lowercase. If you make a typing mistake, use the Backspace key to correct the error before you press the Enter key. If DOS displays the message "Bad command or file name," then you mistyped the command *or* DOS is unable to locate the program file for an external command. No harm is done. DOS returns you to the DOS prompt so that you can try again.

2. Press **[Enter]**. DOS displays your computer's DOS version number, and then redisplays the DOS prompt (Figure 1-8). When you press the Enter key after entering a command at the DOS prompt, DOS executes the instructions for the command. If you type a command and do not press the Enter key, nothing will happen.

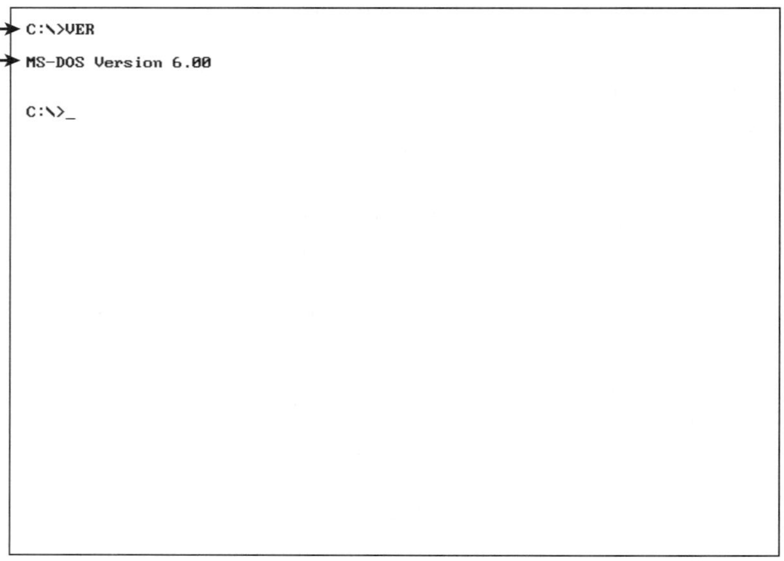

Figure 1-8
The VER command displays the version of DOS

CHANGING THE DATE

Next, you want to verify that the date and time are set correctly on your computer system. The correct date and time are important because DOS records the date and time with the filename when you save a file. Then, for example, if you have two versions of your résumé stored in two different files, you can check the date and time that each file was saved to determine which file contains the most recent version of your résumé.

You want your computer system to use the correct date and time, because you want to ensure that any files you create and save have the correct **date stamp** and **time stamp**. If you notice that the date is incorrect on your computer, you can use the DATE command to change it. The DATE command is another internal command, and its syntax is as follows:

DATE [*mm-dd-yy*]

To use this command, you can type DATE and press the Enter key, or you can type DATE followed by a specific date in the format shown and then press the Enter key. The information enclosed within square brackets is an optional **parameter**, or item of information. To indicate a specific date using the format shown in brackets, you type one or two digits for the month, a dash, one or two digits for the day, a dash, and the last two digits of the year.

Newer computer systems have a battery-powered "clock" that stores the date and time when you turn off the power to the computer. Earlier computer systems did not have this battery feature, and the date and time is not stored when you turn off the power to the computer. On these older systems, you have to enter and, in some cases, change the date.

To check the current date:

1. Type **DATE** and press **[Enter]**. On the next available line, DOS displays the current date, with the day of the week. On the line after the one with the current date, DOS displays a prompt for you to enter a new date (Figure 1-9). This type of *prompt* is an example of a request for information from a program. DOS also shows you the proper format for entering a date—mm-dd-yy.

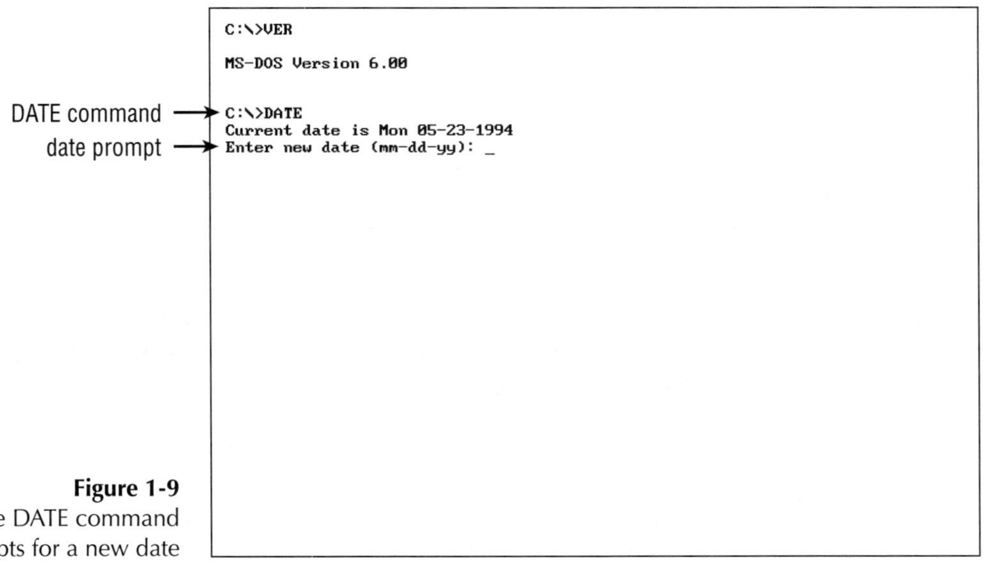

Figure 1-9
The DATE command prompts for a new date

2. Type the date of your next birthday. For example, if your next birthday is September 22, 1994, type **9-22-94**. Then press **[Enter]**. DOS displays the DOS prompt again. You do not type the day of the week. The operating system has a calendar that determines the day of the week from the date (e.g., that September 22, 1994 is a Thursday). If you enter the date in the incorrect format, DOS will prompt you for the date again.

Using the Repeat Key

To verify the new date, you can enter the DATE command again, or you can use the Repeat key, F3, to recall the last DOS command you entered.

To verify the date change:

1. Press **[F3]** (Repeat). DOS displays the previous DATE command that you entered (Figure 1-10). If [F3] (Repeat) does not work, you might have pressed [Enter] twice after the last command you entered. In that case, you will have to type the DATE command again.

```
C:\>VER

MS-DOS Version 6.00

C:\>DATE
Current date is Mon 05-23-1994
Enter new date (mm-dd-yy): 9-22-94

C:\>DATE_
```

newly entered date

DATE command repeated with [F3]

Figure 1-10
The DATE command repeated with the F3 function key

2. Press **[Enter]**. DOS displays the date that you previously entered and also automatically determines the day of the week for the new date—your next birthday. If you next used an application program to create and then save a file, DOS would record your birthday as the date the file was saved. That date would be incorrect. Let's change the date back to the current date.
3. Type the current date and press **[Enter]**. DOS displays the DOS prompt again.

If you know in advance what date you want to use, you can type the DATE command followed by the date. For example, if you want to change the date to July 9, 1994, you can enter DATE 7-9-94. DOS will not prompt you for the date and will not show you the date change.

USING DOSKEY

Although [F3] (Repeat) is useful, it allows you to recall only the last DOS command you entered. You can use a system utility called **DOSKEY** to keep track of the last 20 or so commands you enter at the DOS prompt, so that you can recall them rather than enter them again. To use this feature, you enter the command DOSKEY at the DOS prompt. Then you recall a command using the [↑] (Up Arrow) and [↓] (Down Arrow) keys.

DOSKEY is an external command with a complicated syntax and a variety of options. After you enter this command, DOS looks for a file on disk with a filename identical to the command that you type and with one of three file extensions—COM (for command file), EXE (for executable file), and BAT (for batch file). In this case, DOS will find a file named DOSKEY.COM and then load the program instructions stored in this file into RAM so that you can use the program.

DOSKEY is an example of a **Terminate-and-Stay-Resident (TSR) utility**. After DOS loads a utility such as DOSKEY, the TSR program remains in memory and active while you use other programs. In contrast, if you instruct DOS to load a software application and then exit that program, the program code for that application no longer remains in memory. That memory becomes available for other programs. If you use certain other utilities, the program code for that utility no longer remains in memory after the utility completes its operations.

To activate DOSKEY:

5.0 6.0 6.2

1. Type **DOSKEY** and press **[Enter]**. If you are using DOS 5.0 or 6.0, DOS will display the message "DOSKey installed" if DOSKEY is not already installed on your computer. If you do not see this message with DOS 5.0 or 6.0, DOSKEY is already installed. DOS 6.2 will not display a message.

DOSKEY keeps track of the commands you enter at the DOS prompt in a small area of memory known as the **command stack**. When the command stack fills up, DOSKEY eliminates the oldest commands so that it has room for new commands that you enter. After you enter a few commands, you will use DOSKEY to recall a specific command.

SETTING THE TIME

Next, you want to check the current time on your computer system to verify that it is correct. You use another internal command, TIME, with the following syntax:

TIME [*time*]

You can type TIME and press the Enter key, or you can type TIME followed by the time change you want to make and then press the Enter key.

To check the time:

1. Type **TIME** and press **[Enter]**. DOS displays the current time in hours, minutes, seconds, and either "a" for a.m. or "p" for p.m. For example, 1:54:31.12p means 1:54 p.m. and 31.12 seconds. On the next line, DOS prompts you to enter a new time. See Figure 1-11.

```
C:\>VER

MS-DOS Version 6.00


C:\>DATE
Current date is Mon 05-23-1994
Enter new date (mm-dd-yy): 9-22-94

C:\>DATE
Current date is Thu 09-22-1994
Enter new date (mm-dd-yy): 5-23-94

C:\>DOSKEY
DOSKey installed.

C:\>TIME
Current time is  1:54:31.12p
Enter new time: _
```

successful operation

time prompt

TIME command

Figure 1-11
The TIME command prompts for a new time

2. Type a new time that is one hour later than the current time and press **[Enter]**. For example, if the current time is 10:30 a.m., you type **11:30a** and press **[Enter]**. If the current time is 3:30 p.m., you type **4:30p** and press **[Enter]**. If you do not type "a" or "p" with the new time, DOS assumes that the time is an a.m. time. If you enter the time in the incorrect format, DOS will prompt you for the time again, or it might change the time to an incorrect time.
3. Press [↑] (Up Arrow). DOSKEY displays the previous TIME command. You can use this feature to recall previously entered commands at any time while you are working at the DOS prompt. Each time you press [↑], DOSKEY displays the last command you typed. To use a command you recall, you press the Enter key.
4. Press **[Enter]**. DOS displays the current time and prompts for a new time. If you now use an applications program to create and then save a file, DOS will record the incorrect time with the filename. Let's change the time to the current time.
5. Type the correct time in the proper format and press **[Enter]**.

Like the DATE command, if you know in advance the time you want reflected in your time stamp, you can enter the new time with the TIME command. For example, if you type "TIME 5:00p" and press [Enter], DOS will make the change and display the DOS prompt again, without asking you for any other information.

CLEARING THE SCREEN

Notice that the screen is cluttered with commands, messages, prompts, and your responses to the prompts, and you are now entering commands at the bottom of the screen. To clear the screen so that you can work more easily, you use another internal command, the CLS command, with the following syntax:

CLS

Clearing the screen before issuing commands is a good habit to develop because you can focus on one command operation at a time.

Let's clear the screen.

To clear the screen:

1. Type **CLS** and press **[Enter]**. DOS clears the screen and displays the DOS prompt and cursor in the upper left corner of the screen.

Now that you understand how to work with DOS commands, this is a good opportunity to stop for a few minutes and take a break.

FORMATTING DISKETTES

When you acquired your computer, it is likely that you also bought a word processing software package. Now you want to use this software package to design a new résumé. Until you learn more about how to use a hard disk, you decide to store the final copy of your résumé in a file on a diskette. One advantage of using a diskette is that it provides you with portability. You can carry the diskette with you and print copies of your files from any computer that has the same word processing software you have.

DOS requires that you use a formatted diskette in a disk drive. A **formatted diskette** is a diskette prepared by DOS so that DOS can store data on it. You can purchase **unformatted**, or blank, diskettes as well as **preformatted** diskettes. Some manufacturers of diskettes format the diskettes before selling them. These preformatted diskettes cost more, but you do not need to spend time formatting them before you can use them. You must format an unformatted diskette before DOS can record data on the diskette.

During the formatting process, DOS magnetically creates concentric recording bands, or **tracks**, on the diskette (Figure 1-12). DOS then subdivides the tracks into sectors. A **sector** is the basic unit of storage space on a diskette or hard drive. Each sector on a diskette can store 512 bytes of data. That means that you can store 512 characters, or approximately 10 lines of text, in a sector.

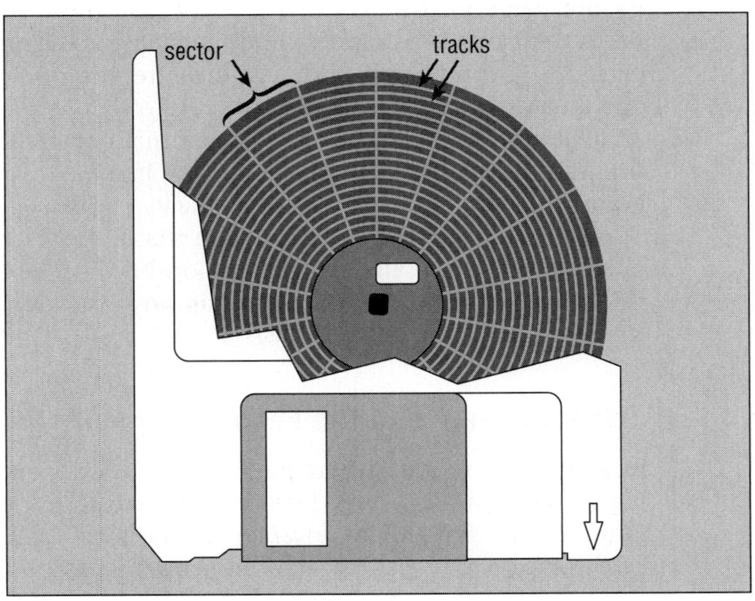

Figure 1-12
Tracks and sectors on a formatted 3½-inch diskette

Diskette Storage Capacities

Diskettes are sold in three common storage capacities: double-density, high-density, and extra-high-density. A high-density diskette stores two to four times as much data as a double-density diskette. An extra-high-density diskette stores twice as much data as a high-density diskette. Because diskettes are available in two sizes (5¼" and 3½") and three storage capacities, you want to be sure that you purchase the proper type for use in your computer (Figure 1-13). The difference in storage capacities depends on the number of tracks and sectors formatted on each side of a diskette. (For a review of the differences between 3½-inch and 5¼-inch diskettes, see the "Essential Computer Concepts" chapter at the beginning of this book.)

Figure 1-13
Characteristics of diskettes

Size	Density	Storage Capacity	Sides	Tracks	Sectors	Bytes per Sector	Sectors per Allocation Unit
5¼″	Double	360K	2	40	9	512	2
5¼″	High	1.2M	2	80	15	512	1
3½″	Double	720K	2	80	9	512	2
3½″	High	1.44M	2	80	18	512	1
3½″	Extra-high	2.88M	2	80	36	512	1

Using the FORMAT Command

To format a diskette to the maximum capacity of the disk drive, you use the FORMAT command, which has the following syntax:

FORMAT *drive name*:

The drive name is a required parameter or item of information. You must specify the name of the disk drive. If you use this syntax, you must also use a diskette that has the same storage capacity as the disk drive you are using. For example, if you want to format a diskette in a 3½-inch high-density disk drive, you must use a 3½-inch high-density diskette.

The FORMAT command is an external command, so DOS must locate the program instructions for this command in a file on disk and then load the program into memory so that you can use it.

You can also reformat a diskette that already contains information. If you do, you will erase all the information on the diskette. Before you format a diskette, be sure it does not contain any important information or software that you need.

The Importance of the Format Capacity Switch

In some cases, you might need to format a double-density diskette in a high-density or extra-high-density disk drive. If this is the case, you can use the **Format Capacity switch**, /F:<*size*>, with the FORMAT command to ensure that DOS formats the diskette to the proper storage capacity. (A **switch** is an optional parameter that modifies the way in which a command operates. A switch starts with a Slash (/) and is followed by one or more additional codes.)

When you use the Format Capacity switch, you type the FORMAT command and then type /F, followed by a colon and the size, or storage capacity, of the diskette. DOS uses the word *size* to indicate capacity. When you specify the size, you list the storage capacity in kilobytes or megabytes. For example, if you want to format a double-density diskette in a high-density drive A to a storage capacity of 720K, you use the following command:

FORMAT A: /F:720

When you type a switch with a DOS command, you do not need a space before the switch. However, a space before the switch makes the DOS command easier to read.

If you forget to use the Format Capacity switch and format a double-density diskette as a high-density diskette, DOS might report a large number of defective sectors.

Preparing Your Diskettes

Your instructor or technical support person will assist you in the preparation of data diskettes that contain the files you will use to complete the tutorials as well as the end-of-chapter Questions and Tutorial Assignments in this book. Because this text assumes you will use a computer system with a 3½-inch double-density or high-density disk drive, you will need two 3½-inch, double-density diskettes. You will use one diskette to work through the tutorial steps in each chapter; you will use the other diskette for the end-of-chapter Questions and Tutorial Assignments. Initially, both diskettes will contain the same data. However, as you complete the tutorials and the end-of-chapter Questions and Tutorial Assignments, the contents of the two diskettes will change. As you proceed with the tutorials and end-of-chapter Tutorial Assignments, you might need additional diskettes to practice DOS commands.

First, you should label each diskette to identify which diskette you will use for the tutorials and which diskette you will use for the end-of-chapter Tutorial Assignments. You can use the blank adhesive labels provided with the diskettes when you purchased them. Before you place labels on the newly formatted diskettes, you should write a short description on each label to identify the diskette's intended use and contents. If you have already placed the blank labels on the diskettes, you can use a felt-tip pen to gently write the description on the label. Do *not* use a ballpoint pen or pencil to write on the label. You might damage the surface of the diskette.

On one label, write "Tutorial Disk," and on the other label, write "Exercise Disk." Then place the labels on the diskettes. Figure 1-14 shows how to place a label on a 3½-inch diskette.

Identifying Storage Capacities of Diskettes and Drives

Before you can format a diskette, you must know the capacity of the diskette you want to format and find out whether your computer system has a double-density, high-density, or extra-high-density disk drive. You might need to use the Format Capacity switch to format the diskette to the proper capacity. Check the labeling on the diskettes and your disk drive unit for the storage capacities of the diskettes and drive.

Double-density diskettes might be labeled "DD" or "DS/DD" (for Double-Sided, Double-Density), high-density diskettes "HD" or "DS/HD" (for Double-Sided, High-Density), and extra-high-density diskettes "ED." Also, double-density diskettes have one square hole for the write0-protect tab; high-density diskettes have two square holes, one directly opposite the other on the sides of the diskette. Extra-high-density diskettes have two square holes, each at positions opposite each other on the two sides of the diskette. Double-density diskettes might be labeled "360K" or "720K," high-density diskettes "1.2 M" or "1.44M," and extra-high-density diskettes "2.88M." Double-density diskettes might also be labeled "1M," high-density diskettes "2M," and extra-high-density diskettes "4M"; however, these diskettes are not formatted to these capacities. You might also find that the disk drives or disk drive ejector buttons are labeled with the proper storage capacity of the disk drive. If you are unsure, ask your instructor or technical support person for assistance.

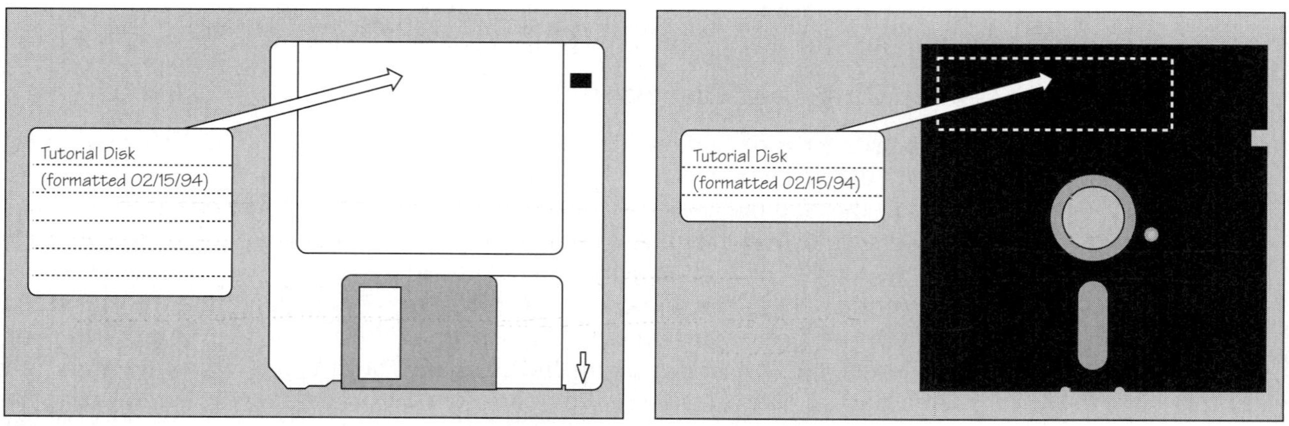

Figure 1-14
Applying an adhesive label to a 3½-inch and a 5¼-inch diskette

Formatting a Diskette

Now you are ready to format the diskettes that you will use for the tutorials and the end-of-chapter Tutorial Assignments.

To format a diskette:

1. Insert an unformatted 3½-inch double-density or high-density diskette into drive A or B and, if necessary, close the drive door. See Figure 1-15, which illustrates how to insert a 3½-inch diskette into a disk drive.

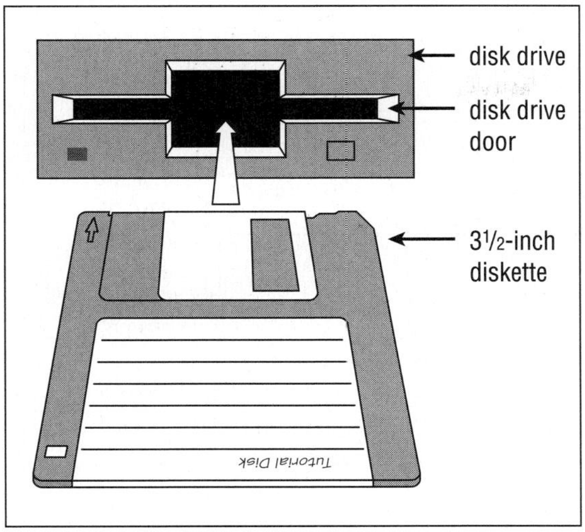

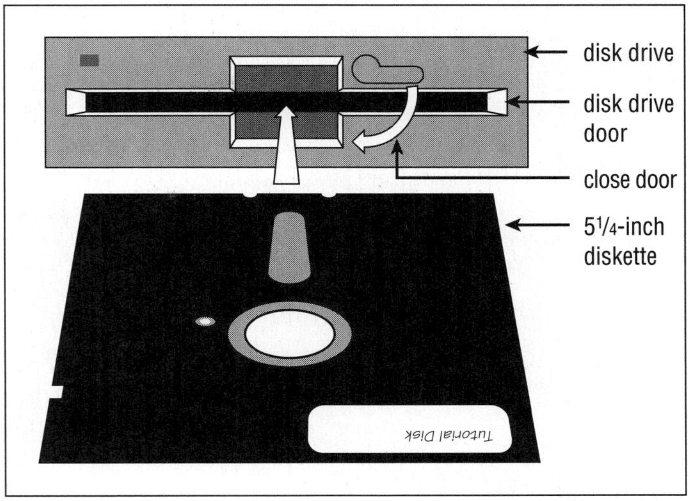

Figure 1-15
Inserting a 3½-inch and a 5¼-inch diskette into a disk drive

2. Format the diskette to the proper storage capacity using one of the following options. If you are using drive B instead of drive A, use B: instead of A: for the drive name in the commands.

   - If you are formatting a 3½-inch double-density diskette in a double-density drive, a 3½-inch high-density diskette in a high-density drive, or a 3½-inch extra-high-density diskette in an extra-high-density drive, type **FORMAT A:** and press **[Enter]**. You do not need to use the Format Capacity switch because DOS will automatically format the diskette to the maximum capacity of the drive.
   - If you are formatting a 3½-inch double-density diskette in a high-density or extra-high-density drive, type **FORMAT A: /F:720** and press **[Enter].**
   - If you are formatting a 3½-inch high-density diskette in an extra-high-density drive, type **FORMAT A: /F:1.44** and press **[Enter].**

   DOS then prompts you to insert a new diskette into drive A or B, which you did in Step 1.

3. Press **[Enter]**. You will know DOS is formatting the diskette when you see the first message, "Checking existing disk format." See Figure 1-16. If the diskette is already formatted, you will see the message "Saving UNFORMAT information" as DOS saves information that allows you to unformat the diskette later. Then DOS informs you that it is formatting the diskette to a specific storage capacity. DOS then displays a percentage to show you how much of the formatting process is complete. When this percentage reaches 100%, DOS informs you that the formatting is complete. If DOS displays an error message at any time, try another diskette or ask your instructor or technical support person for assistance. If you experience difficulty formatting two diskettes in a row and if you are using the proper value for the Format Capacity switch, the disk drive might be malfunctioning.

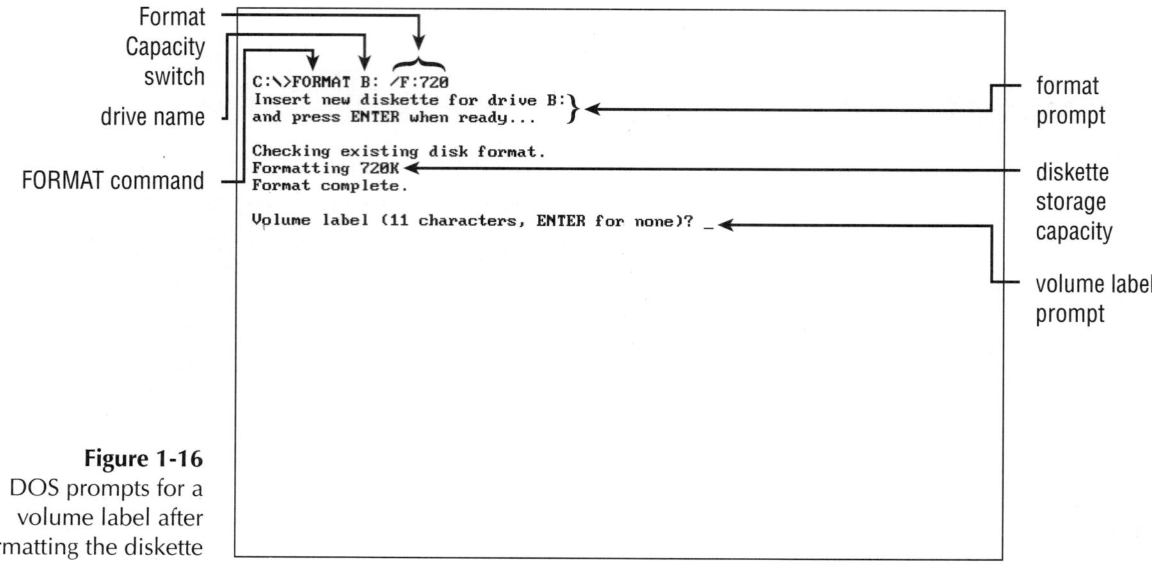

Figure 1-16
DOS prompts for a volume label after formatting the diskette

During the formatting operation, the diskette spins in the disk drive unit at approximately 300 to 360 rpm (revolutions per minute) and the drive light is on. You should *not* remove a diskette from, or insert a diskette into, a disk drive when the drive light is on. When the drive light is off, you can safely remove a diskette and insert another diskette.

Assigning a Volume Label

After DOS completes the formatting, it prompts for a volume label (Figure 1-16). A **volume label** is a name for the diskette, that usually identifies the type of information you will store on the diskette. For example, if you intend to store copies of your résumés and cover letters on a diskette, you could use the volume label JOB SEARCH. The volume label, or name, is one to 11 characters in length and can include spaces. Certain types of symbols, such as a period, are not allowed. If you attempt to use an invalid or unacceptable character, DOS will inform you of this problem and will prompt you again for the volume label.

You will need to choose a volume label that will be appropriate for both diskettes you will use as you work through this book. Because both diskettes will be duplicate copies of the data disk provided to your instructor and will contain files used in a business environment, you decide to use BUSINESS as the volume label.

To enter a volume label for your diskette during formatting:

1. Type **BUSINESS** and press **[Enter]**. DOS assigns the volume label to the diskette, displays information on how it formatted the diskette, assigns a volume name and serial number, and asks if you want to format another diskette (Figure 1-17).

```
C:\>FORMAT B: /F:720
Insert new diskette for drive B:
and press ENTER when ready...

Checking existing disk format.
Formatting 720K
Format complete.

Volume label (11 characters, ENTER for none)? BUSINESS

    730112 bytes total disk space
    730112 bytes available on disk

      1024 bytes in each allocation unit.
       713 allocation units available on disk.

Volume Serial Number is 2D44-1602

Format another (Y/N)?_
```

volume label

diskette storage specifications (yours might be different)

unique serial number

format prompt

Figure 1-17
DOS assigns a volume label to the diskette and asks if you want to format another diskette

Now format your second data diskette.

2. Type **Y** for "Yes" and press **[Enter]**. DOS prompts you to insert a new diskette into the drive. *If you already have two blank, formatted diskettes with the volume label BUSINESS, type* **N** *for No, then press* **[Enter]**. *You have finished formatting your diskettes and do not need to perform Steps 3 through 5.*
3. Insert another unformatted, 3½-inch double-density diskette, and press **[Enter]**. DOS repeats the formatting process.
4. When DOS prompts you for the volume label for this diskette, type **BUSINESS** and press **[Enter].**
5. When DOS asks if you want to format another diskette, type **N** for "No" and press **[Enter]**. DOS returns you to the DOS prompt.

Evaluating the Disk Storage Space Report

After formatting a diskette, DOS displays information on the storage capacity of the newly formatted diskette (Figure 1-17). Your storage capacities might be different. The first number shows the total amount of storage space on the diskette in bytes. The second number shows how much of this storage space is available for use, again in bytes. Usually, these two numbers are identical and indicate that you can use all of the formatted storage space available on the diskette. If these numbers are different, you will also see a message that indicates the diskette contains a certain number of bytes in bad sectors. When DOS formats a diskette, it checks the surface of the disk for defects. **Bad sectors** are defective areas on the diskette that DOS marks as unusable. You can still use the rest of the diskette. When DOS records information onto the diskette, it does not use sectors marked as defective or bad.

If DOS reports more than a few thousand bytes of bad sectors, the diskette itself could be defective. If you format another diskette and DOS does not report any bad sectors for that diskette, the first disk that you formatted was probably defective and should be thrown out. If you use a diskette with a large number of bad sectors, the condition might become worse and you could lose important information stored on the diskette.

On the next line, DOS reports on the size of each **allocation unit** and the total number of allocation units on the diskette. Although sectors represent the basic storage unit on a diskette, DOS uses an allocation unit, or **cluster**, as the minimum storage space when it records the contents of a file on a diskette. On high-density and extra-high-density diskettes, an allocation unit is the same size as a sector. This means that DOS stores information on these diskettes one sector at a time. On double-density diskettes, an allocation unit consists of two sectors, which means that DOS uses a minimum of two sectors to store information even if it needs less space than that for the file or for the end of the file. The remaining space in the allocation unit is unused and therefore wasted. The size of each allocation unit on your diskette might be different from that shown in Figure 1-17.

After DOS reports on how the storage space on the diskette is allocated, it identifies the serial number assigned to the diskette. The **serial number** is a unique ID number produced by DOS from the date and time on the computer system. The serial number represents another way to identify a diskette. Your serial number will be different from the one shown in Figure 1-17. Finally, DOS asks you if you want to format another diskette.

Caring for Diskettes

It is also important to protect your work by taking good care of your diskettes. Figure 1-18 summarizes guidelines you should follow.

- Store your diskettes in a safe, dry place—away from dust and other contaminants.
- Keep diskettes away from magnets and equipment that contains magnets, such as a telephone, stereo speaker, and color TV tube, as well as walk-through X-ray machines at airports, department stores, and libraries.
- Do not expose diskettes to extreme heat or extreme cold; for example, do not leave diskettes exposed to the hot sun in a car.
- Keep diskettes away from water, coffee, tea, and other liquids.
- Keep diskettes away from solvents.
- Place 5¼-inch diskettes in their sleeves when you are not using them.
- Hold 5¼-inch diskettes so that you do not touch any of the exposed surfaces of the diskette with your fingers.
- Do not bend 5¼-inch diskettes.
- Do not place paper clips on 5¼-inch diskettes.
- Use a felt-tip pen to record information on a 5¼-inch diskette's label; do not use a sharp pen or pencil.

Figure 1-18
Guidelines for the proper care of diskettes

CHANGING THE DEFAULT DRIVE

Now that you have formatted your diskettes, you are ready to make a duplicate copy of the data diskette provided to your instructor. You can perform this operation from drive C or from a diskette drive. You will find that many DOS operations are simpler if you change drives, because you do not need to specify the drive name in each DOS command that requires the drive name. If you omit the drive name, DOS assumes you want to use the drive from which you are currently working.

To change from one drive to another at the DOS prompt, you type the name of the drive followed by a colon (:) and press the Enter key. You *must* include the colon after the letter of the alphabet that identifies the drive. Otherwise, DOS will assume that you have entered a command. It will then look for the program instructions and inform you that you entered a "Bad command or file name" when it cannot find the program instructions. Also, do not confuse the semicolon (;) with the colon (:).

To change to the drive that contains your data diskette:

1. Be sure drive A or B contains one of the two diskettes you just formatted.
2. If your diskette is in drive A, type **A:** and press **[Enter]**. If your diskette is in drive B, type **B:** and press **[Enter]**. DOS updates the DOS prompt to show the new default drive. See Figure 1-19.

Figure 1-19
Changing the default drive from C to A

USING THE HELP SWITCH

Now you are ready to make copies of the diskette provided to your instructor. You can use the DISKCOPY command to duplicate a diskette. First, you decide to use the DOS Help switch to provide you with help information on how to properly use the DISKCOPY command. The **Help switch**, /?, displays a help screen with information on a specific DOS command. The syntax for this switch is as follows:

[***command***] **/?**

To access help information, you type a DOS command followed by /?. For example, to obtain help information on the DISKCOPY command, you type DISKCOPY /? and press the Enter key. The Help switch works with any DOS command.

To obtain help information on the DISKCOPY command:

1. Type **DISKCOPY /?** and press **[Enter]**. DOS displays a help screen that summarizes the features of the DISKCOPY command (Figure 1-20). *Be sure you type a Slash rather than a Backslash.* A Slash (/) leans to the right; a Backslash (\) leans to the left. If you type a Backslash, DOS displays the error message "Too many parameters," and then displays the DOS prompt again.

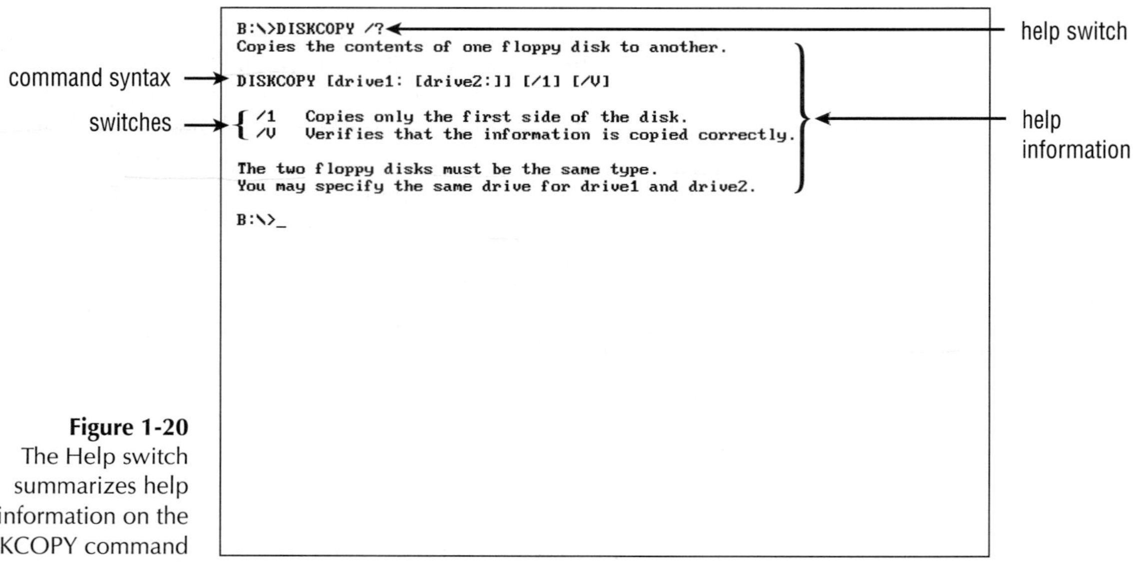

Figure 1-20
The Help switch summarizes help information on the DISKCOPY command

6.2

If you are using DOS 6.2, one additional switch—the /M switch—will appear on your screen.

Printing the Help Screen

You want to print a copy of this Help screen to use later for reference. Before you follow the next set of steps, ask your instructor or technical support person if the type of computer system you are using will permit you to print a screen. If not, skip these steps.

To print the Help screen:

1. Be sure the printer is operational. If necessary, ask your instructor or technical support person to show you how to use the printer.

2. Press **[Print Screen].** This key is located in the upper-right corner of the keyboard. If your keyboard has a key labeled PrtSc or [PrtScrn] rather than Print Screen, press **[Shift][PrtSc]** or **[Shift][PrtScrn]** (Print Screen).
3. If the printer does not automatically eject a sheet of paper, press the **Form Feed (FF) button** on the printer to advance the paper in the printer (Figure 1-21). If nothing happens when you press Form Feed, press the **On Line button**, press **Form Feed** again, and then press **On Line** a final time.

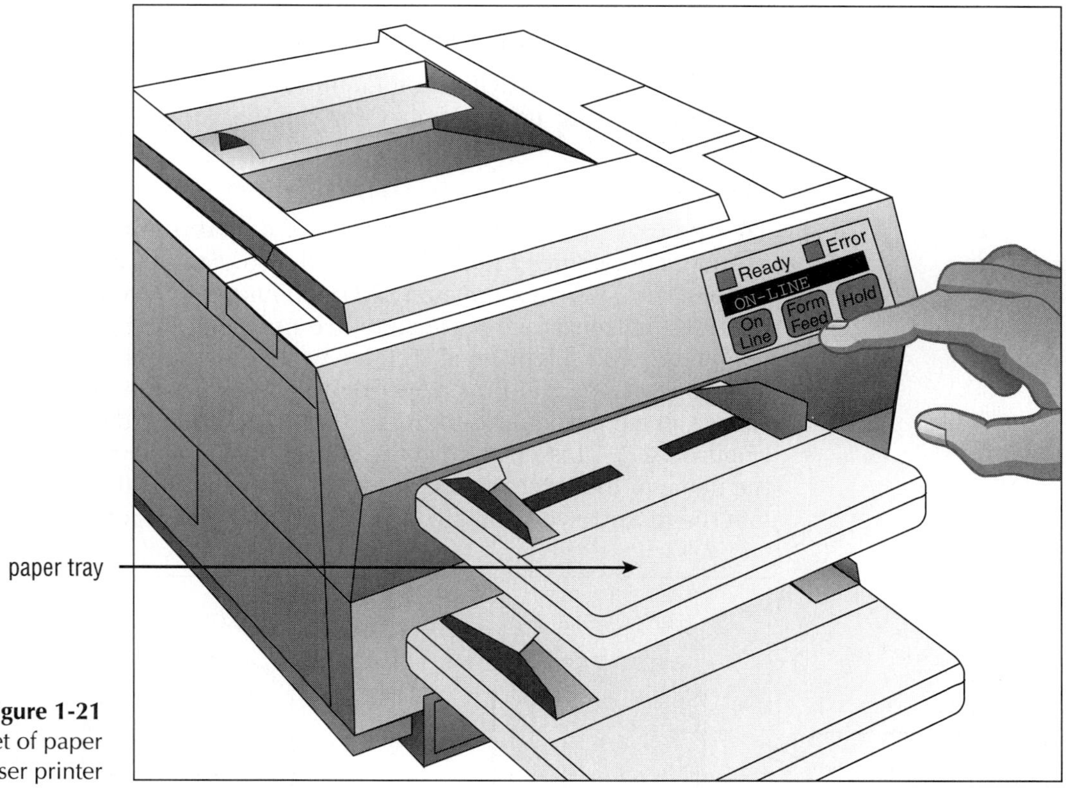

Figure 1-21
Ejecting a sheet of paper from a laser printer

4. Remove your printed copy of the Help screen from the printer.

MAKING A COPY OF A DISKETTE

It is important to copy the contents of diskettes that contain critical information, such as documents you create and software you use, onto other diskettes. You can keep the extra copies of your data diskettes and the original copies of software in reserve as **backup** copies. That way, if your working copy of a diskette fails, you can immediately make a duplicate of your backup copy. Then, you use the new copy as your working diskette.

If you examine your printed copy of the Help screen for the DISKCOPY command, you will note that this command copies the contents of one diskette to another. The notes for this command inform you that the two diskettes must be of the same type. That means the diskettes *must* be the same size *and* have the same storage capacity. For example, if you want to make a copy of a 3½-inch double-density diskette, you must use another 3½-inch double-density diskette for the new copy. You cannot perform a disk copy from a double-density diskette to a high-density diskette or vice versa. You cannot perform a disk copy from a 5¼-inch diskette to a 3½-inch diskette or vice versa.

You cannot use this command to make a copy of the contents of your hard disk drive. This command works only with diskettes.

Understanding the Syntax of the DISKCOPY Command

The help information tells you that the syntax for this external command is as follows:

DISKCOPY [*drive1:* [*drive2:*]] [/1] [/V]

6.2 In DOS 6.2, the DISKCOPY command has an additional switch, the **Multipass switch** (/M), that uses memory for the disk copy and requires you to swap diskettes.

DISKCOPY [*drive 1*:[*drive 2*:]] [/1] [/V] [/M]

This type of notation is an example of a **syntax diagram** that describes the proper way to enter the command and also displays required or optional parameters and switches for many DOS commands. Any parameters or switches included within square brackets are optional. In the case of the DISKCOPY command, you might need to specify one or two diskette drives for the disk copy operation. The first drive, **drive1**, is the name of the source drive. The **source drive** is the diskette drive that contains the diskette you want to copy (Figure 1-22). This diskette is the **source diskette**. The second drive, **drive2**, is the name of the target drive. The **target drive** is the diskette drive that will contain the diskette you copy to. This diskette is the **target diskette** (Figure 1-22).

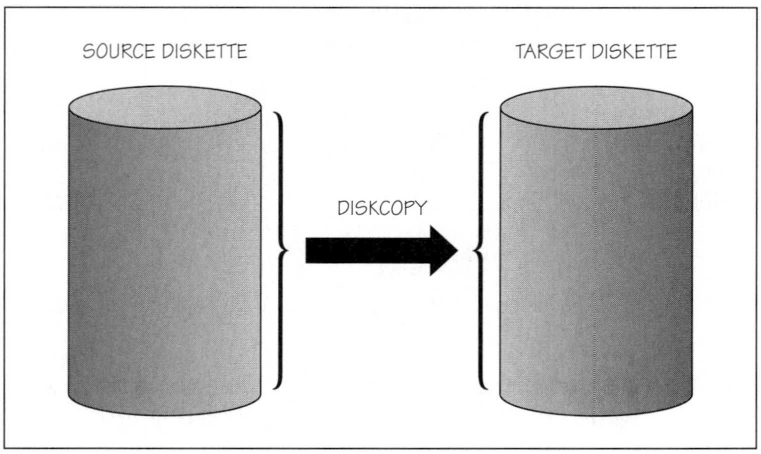

Figure 1-22
Copying an entire diskette to another diskette

If you specify only drive1, the DISKCOPY command assumes you want to use the same drive for the source and target disks. Because the DISKCOPY command requires that both diskettes be the same size and the same storage capacity, you often use the same drive for both the source and target disks. If you use the same drive for the source and target disks, you *must* switch diskettes during the disk copy operation. If you have two drives that are the same size *and* the same storage capacity, you can perform the disk copy using both drives. You insert your source diskette in one drive and your target diskette in the other drive.

5.0 *6.0*

In DOS 5.0 and 6.0, the DISKCOPY command has two optional switches. The /1 switch copies only the one side of a diskette. This switch is included for use with single-sided drives that were used on earlier computer systems. The Verify switch, /V, verifies that the information on the diskette is copied correctly. This switch is rarely used because the disk copy process is quite reliable and verification slows it down. In DOS 6.2, the DISKCOPY command has an additional switch, /M, which forces a multipass copy using memory only.

6.2

DOS 5.0 and 6.0 copy part of the contents of the source diskette into RAM, then copy that data from RAM to the destination diskette. As a result, you usually need to insert the source and destination diskettes more than once to complete the disk copy. DOS 6.2 can copy the contents of the source diskette to the hard disk and then to the destination diskette so that you do not need to swap diskettes repeatedly.

Using the DISKCOPY Command

You want to make two copies of the data diskette. Because this data diskette is a double-density diskette, you must use another double-density diskette for the target diskette. However, you can perform the disk copy in either a double-density or high-density disk drive.

Before you make copies of the data diskette, you should **write-protect** the diskette so that you do not inadvertently record over its contents. That way, the files are protected from accidental deletion. To write-protect a 3½-inch diskette, hold the diskette so that the label on the diskette faces away from you with the metal shutter at the bottom. On the upper-left side of the diskette, you will see a rectangular notch in the diskette. The rectangular notch contains a square plastic tab. With your fingernail, press on the square tab until it slides up and exposes an open, square hole in the diskette (Figure 1-23). The diskette is now write-protected.

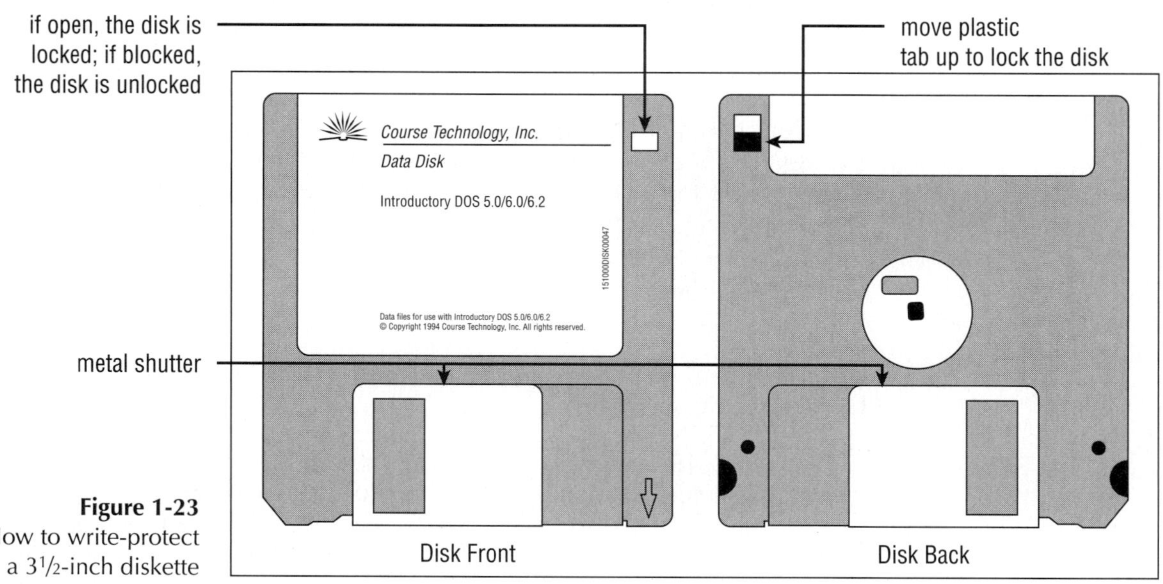

Figure 1-23
How to write-protect a $3^1/_2$-inch diskette

Now you are ready to make two copies of the data diskette.

To copy the data diskette:

1. Insert the data diskette provided by your instructor or technical support person.
2. Type **DISKCOPY** and press **[Enter]**. DOS prompts you to insert the **source diskette**, the diskette that you want to copy, and prompts you to press any key to continue. See Figure 1-24. The source diskette is the data diskette that you just inserted in the disk drive. *Because you did not specify a source drive and a target drive, DOS assumes that this disk drive will be used for both the source diskette and the target diskette.* You could also use the command DISKCOPY A: or DISKCOPY A: A: to copy the data diskette. If DOS displays the message "Bad command or file name," DOS cannot locate the program file for the DISKCOPY command on drive C. Ask your instructor or technical support person for assistance.

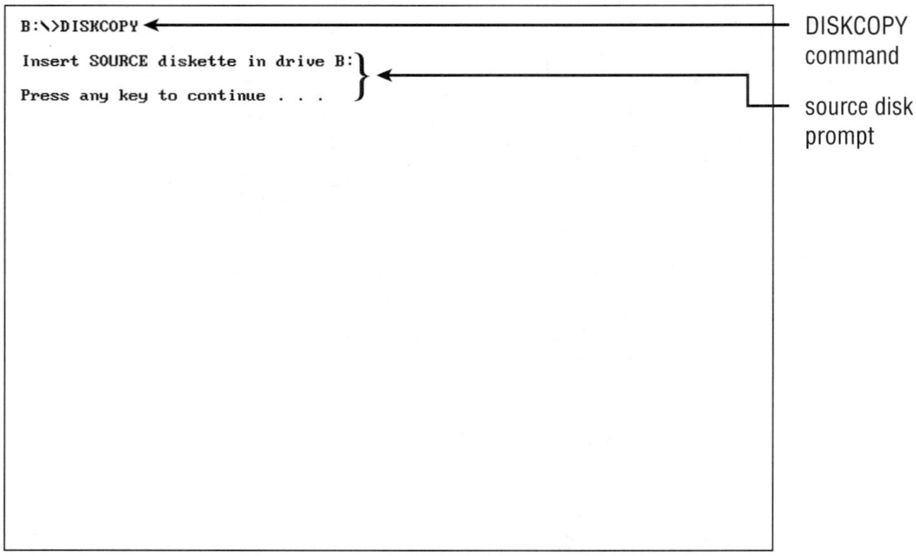

Figure 1-24 The DISKCOPY command prompts for the source diskette

Even though you were prompted to press "any key," you cannot press just any key. Certain keys, such as [Alt], [Ctrl], [Shift], [Caps Lock], [Scroll Lock], [Pause], and [Num Lock], do not work in this situation. Keys that do work include [Spacebar], [Enter], [Tab], [Esc], [Backspace], function keys, and cursor movement keys, as well as the keys with the letters of the alphabet, numbers, and symbols.

To continue the disk copy:

1. Press **[Spacebar]** or any other key to continue. DISKCOPY identifies the diskette specifications, including the number of tracks, the number of sectors per track, and the number of sides formatted on this diskette. It then stops and prompts you to insert the target diskette. See Figure 1-25.

```
B:\>DISKCOPY

Insert SOURCE diskette in drive B:

Press any key to continue . . .

Copying 80 tracks
9 sectors per track, 2 side(s)

Insert TARGET diskette in drive B:

Press any key to continue . . .
```

source diskette specifications

target diskette specifications

Figure 1-25
The DISKCOPY command prompts for the target diskette

2. When you are prompted for the target diskette, wait for the drive light to go off. Then remove the data diskette from the drive, insert your formatted diskette labeled "Tutorial Disk," and press **[Spacebar]** or any other key to continue. DISKCOPY copies data onto this new diskette. When the copying process is complete, DOS might prompt you to reinsert the source diskette. See Figure 1-26. If this occurs, the DISKCOPY program is ready to copy another part of the original data diskette. If you are using DOS 6.2, DISKCOPY might perform the copy in one pass, then ask if you want to create another copy of the same diskette. If this occurs in DOS 6.2, type **Y** for Yes, press **[Enter]**, skip Steps 4 and 5, and continue with Step 6.

```
B:\>DISKCOPY

Insert SOURCE diskette in drive B:

Press any key to continue . . .

Copying 80 tracks
9 sectors per track, 2 side(s)

Insert TARGET diskette in drive B:

Press any key to continue . . .

Insert SOURCE diskette in drive B:

Press any key to continue . . .
```

prompt for same source diskette

Figure 1-26
The DISKCOPY command prompts for the source diskette again

3. If prompted to insert the source diskette, wait for the drive light to go off. Then remove the target diskette from the diskette drive, reinsert the data diskette, and press **[Spacebar]** or any other key to continue. DISKCOPY continues the copy process. When it stops, you will be prompted to insert the target diskette again. See Figure 1-27.

```
B:\>DISKCOPY

Insert SOURCE diskette in drive B:

Press any key to continue . . .

Copying 80 tracks
9 sectors per track, 2 side(s)

Insert TARGET diskette in drive B:

Press any key to continue . . .

Insert SOURCE diskette in drive B:

Press any key to continue . . .

Insert TARGET diskette in drive B:

Press any key to continue . . .
```

Figure 1-27
The DISKCOPY command prompts for the target diskette again

4. When prompted to insert the target diskette, wait for the drive light to go off. Then remove the data diskette from the drive, reinsert the Tutorial Disk, and press **[Spacebar]** or any other key to continue. The DISKCOPY program copies the remainder of the data diskette from memory onto the target diskette. Then it asks if you want to copy another diskette.
5. Remove the newly prepared disk copy.
6. Insert the original source diskette (the data diskette), type **Y** for "Yes" and press **[Spacebar]** or any other key to continue. The DISKCOPY command will repeat the same process. However, this time the target diskette is your other diskette, the one labeled "Exercise Disk." After you make both copies of the data diskette, type **N** for "No" when asked whether you want to make another copy. DOS then returns you to the DOS prompt.

The DISKCOPY command performs a sector-by-sector copy of a diskette, so the new diskette that results from the disk copy operation is an identical copy of the original diskette, except for one feature. The new diskette has a different serial number.

FINISHING YOUR WORK SESSION

After you finish using a computer, you should remove any diskettes from the diskette drives. You might also need to shut off the power to the computer system.

To end your work session:

1. Be sure the DOS prompt is displayed on the screen.
2. Be sure the drive lights are off. Then remove any diskettes from the diskette drives. If you experience any difficulty, ask your instructor or technical support person to show you how to remove the diskettes.
3. If you are working in a computer lab, ask your instructor or technical support person if it is necessary to turn off the computer. If so, locate the power switch and turn it to the "off" position. Also locate the power switch for the monitor and turn it off.

◆

SUMMARY

In this tutorial, you learned that operating system software plays an important role in the management and use of a computer system. DOS is the predominant operating system software used on IBM microcomputers and IBM compatibles.

The primary storage media used on microcomputer systems are the hard disk and the diskette. Diskettes differ in their storage capacities and sizes and must be used in disk drive units that support them. Documents and programs are stored in files on a diskette or on a hard disk. Each file has a filename that you provide. The filename identifies the file's location on the disk and its contents. When you save a file to disk, you might also need to provide a drive name so that a document is stored on the correct drive.

After you boot a computer system, DOS displays the DOS prompt unless your computer system is customized. You can enter internal or external commands at the DOS prompt. In this tutorial, you used the VER command to display the version of DOS installed on your computer system. You also used the DATE and TIME commands to set, or verify, the date and time used by your computer system. You cleared the screen with the CLS command. You used the DOSKEY command to load a Terminate-and-Stay Resident program to keep track of commands that you entered at the DOS prompt. You recalled those commands with the Up and Down Arrow keys.

You formatted a diskette with the FORMAT command so that you can use the diskette in the computer system. The Format Capacity switch allows you to format double-density diskettes in high-density or extra-high-density disk drives and high-density diskettes in extra-high-density drives.

You changed the default drive by specifying the name of the drive you wanted to use as the new default drive. You used the Help switch to obtain help information on the DISKCOPY command, and you used the DISKCOPY command to make duplicate copies of a diskette.

Command Reference	
Syntax	**Use**
[*drive name*:]	Changes the current, or default, drive; for example, A: changes from the current drive to drive A, and drive A becomes the current drive
CLS	An internal command that clears the screen and displays the DOS prompt and cursor in the upper-left corner of the screen
DATE	An internal command that displays the date used on the computer system, prompts for a new date, and keeps or changes the date
DATE [*mm-dd-yy*]	An internal command that sets the date on the computer; for example, DATE 5-21-94 sets the date to May 21, 1994
DISKCOPY [*source*] [*target*]	An external command that makes a copy of a diskette
[DOS command] /?	Displays a screen with help information on the specified DOS command; for example, DATE /? displays help information on the DATE command
DOSKEY	An external command that keeps track of commands entered at the DOS prompt and that allows you to recall the commands with [↑] and [↓]
FORMAT *drive name*:	An external command that prepares a diskette for use on a computer system by formatting the diskette to the highest storage capacity of the disk drive; for example, FORMAT A: formats the diskette in drive A
FORMAT *drive name*: /F:*size*	An external command that prepares a diskette for use on a computer system by formatting the diskette to the specified storage capacity; for example, FORMAT A: /F:720 formats a 3½-inch double-density diskette to 720K

TIME	An internal command that displays the time used on a computer system, prompts for a new time, and keeps or changes the time
TIME [*hh:mm:ss*]	An internal command that sets the time on a computer system to a specific time; for example, TIME 10:30a sets the time to 10:30 a.m.
VER	An internal command that displays the version of DOS used on a computer system

QUESTIONS

1. Identify two important types of operations performed by operating system software.
2. On what types of systems do you use MS-DOS and PC-DOS?
3. What is a filename, and why is it important?
4. What is a drive name, and why is it important?
5. What is the current, or default, drive?
6. What is the difference between a cold and a warm boot?
7. What is the difference between an internal and an external command? Give an example of each type of command.
8. What information does the DOS prompt provide?
9. Name one reason it is useful to know the version of DOS installed on your computer system. How do you find out what that version is?
10. After you type a command at the DOS prompt, what must you do for DOS to execute the command?
11. If DOS displays the message "Bad command or file name" when you enter a command, what is the likely cause of the error?
12. How would you change the date on a computer system from March 20, 1994, to March 21, 1994?
13. What function key can you use at the DOS prompt to repeat the last DOS command that you entered?
14. What does DOSKEY do, and how do you use it?
15. When you check the time on your computer system, you find that the time is set at 7:15 a.m., but the time is actually 7:25 p.m. What command can you enter to correct this setting, and how would you enter it?
16. What does DOS do when it formats a diskette? What is a track? What is a sector?
17. What are the two common storage capacities for double-density and high-density diskettes?

18. What is an allocation unit?
19. What features account for the different storage capacities of double-density, high-density and extra-high-density diskettes?
20. What must you specify when you use the FORMAT command?
21. What command would you use to format a double-density diskette with a storage capacity of 720K in a high-density disk drive with a storage capacity of 1.44M?
22. What command would you use to format a high-density diskette with a storage capacity of 1.4M in an extra-high-density disk drive with a storage capacity of 2.88M?
23. What happens if you format a double-density diskette in a high-density drive and do not specify the storage capacity of the double-density diskette?
24. What is a volume label?
25. What is a switch? How are switches used? Give one example of a switch.
26. How do you change the default drive?
27. What is the Help switch and how do you use it?
28. What command can you use to make a copy of a diskette? How does it work?
29. What command would you enter to perform a disk copy if the DOS prompt is C:\ but the source and target diskettes are in drive A?
30. When you perform a disk copy, what two features must the diskettes have in common?

TUTORIAL ASSIGNMENTS

1. **Issuing DOS Commands**: After you boot your computer system and access the DOS prompt, use DOS commands to answer the following questions. List the full command that you use for each step, and answer the questions.
   a. What version of DOS is installed on your computer system?
   b. Clear the screen.
   c. Insert a formatted diskette into drive A or B and change to that drive.
   d. Clear the screen.
   e. After DOS executes a command, does DOS always return to the same drive? How can you tell?
2. **Setting the Time**: Assume that the time on your computer system is incorrect. Adjust the time in each of the following steps, list the full command or commands that you use, and answer the questions.
   a. What is the current setting for the time on your computer system?
   b. If the time is an a.m. time, change it to a p.m. time. If the time is a p.m. time, change it to an a.m. time. How did you verify this change?
   c. Change the time to 7:30 without specifying an a.m. or p.m. time. Then, check the time. Is DOS using an a.m. or a p.m. time? What does this feature tell you about DOS?
   d. Change the time to 7:30 p.m.
   e. Set the time back to the correct time.

3. **Using the Help Switch**: As you perform the following steps, list the command that you use, and answer any questions.
   a. Use the Help switch to display help information on the FORMAT command.
   b. What parameter does DOS require for the FORMAT command?
   c. What format capacities can you specify for the Format Capacity switch?
   d. Print a copy of this Help screen.
4. **Formatting Diskettes**: Format a new diskette using drive A or drive B. As you format the diskette, answer the following questions. *Be sure you use a new diskette for this exercise. If you format your Tutorial Disk or Exercise Disk, you will erase all the information on the diskette.*
   a. When DOS starts to format the diskette, what storage capacity does it use for the diskette?
   b. After the diskette is formatted, how many total bytes are available? Are there any bad, or defective, sectors? What is the size of an allocation unit on the diskette?
   c. You should be able to tell from the size of the allocation unit whether you are using a double-density or a high-density diskette. Which type of diskette are you using?
   d. Did you assign a volume label to the diskette? If so, what volume label did you use?
   e. Print a copy of the information DOS displays on the screen about the formatting process.
5. **Copying a Diskette**: Use the DISKCOPY command to make a copy of your Tutorial Disk from drive C. Since you have not made any changes to your Tutorial Disk or Exercise Disk, you can use the Exercise Disk as the target diskette. If you completed Tutorial Assignment 4 and formatted a new diskette, you can use that new diskette as your target disk. As you copy the Tutorial Disk, answer the following questions:
   a. The Tutorial Disk is a double-density diskette. What type of diskette must you use to perform the disk copy?
   b. What is the density of the diskette drive you are using?
   c. What command did you enter to perform a disk copy from drive C?
   d. Does the DISKCOPY command warn you that it is replacing the contents of the target diskette?

TUTORIAL 2

Displaying Directories

OBJECTIVES

In this tutorial you will learn to:

- Display a directory of filenames
- Use switches with the DIR command
- Display filenames one screen at a time
- Produce a wide directory
- Display files by name, extension, size, and date and time
- Use wildcards to select groups of files
- Combine wildcards and switches
- Specify default settings for the DIR command
- View the contents of the DOS environment
- Use a graphical user interface
- Start the DOS Shell
- Use a mouse
- Customize the DOS Shell for graphics mode
- Change the directory display in the DOS Shell
- Use wildcards in the DOS Shell
- Exit the DOS Shell

Imagine you are starting a small company with a business acquaintance. This company will prepare high-quality business documents for clients, such as résumés, cover letters, flyers, brochures, and newsletters. Your business partner has already created computer files for anticipating start-up costs, projecting income, and preparing checklists for equipment and insurance as well as templates for preparing client business documents. **Templates** are files that contain the general format or layout of a document but little or no data.

Your business partner provides you with a copy of this diskette. Before you meet with your partner to discuss the next phase in opening this business, you want to check the contents of the diskette to verify that it contains all the templates and start-up files that your new business needs.

◆

DISPLAYING A DIRECTORY

Your first step is to view the names assigned to the files on this diskette. You can use the DIR command to display a list, or **directory**, of the files stored on a diskette or a hard disk. When you use the DIR command, you must specify the name of the disk drive if it is different from the current drive. The format of the DIR command is

DIR [*drive name*]:

The DIR command is an internal command.

Before you start working with DOS, it is a good idea to install DOSKEY so that you can recall commands you previously entered at the DOS prompt. After you install this utility, DOSKEY stores a list of the commands that you enter at the DOS prompt in an area of memory called the **command stack**. You can then press [↑] (Up Arrow) or [↓] (Down Arrow) to step backward or forward through the list of commands in the command stack. Instead of repeatedly typing a command, you can use these arrow keys to find a copy of the command you need.

To activate DOSKEY:

1. Power on your computer system, and be sure you see the C:\> prompt displayed on the screen. If you see a prompt for some other drive, type **C:** and press **[Enter]** to change to drive C.
2. Type **DOSKEY** and press **[Enter]**. If you are using DOS 5.0 or 6.0, DOS will display the message "DOSKey installed" if DOSKEY is not already installed on your computer. If you do not see this message with DOS 5.0 or 6.0, DOSKEY is already installed. DOS 6.2 will not display a message.

Now you are ready to view a directory of the filenames stored on the diskette provided by your business partner.

To display a directory of filenames:

1. Insert the Tutorial Disk into drive A or B.
2. Type **DIR**, press **[Spacebar]**, type the name of the drive (**A:** or **B:**), and press **[Enter]**. Be sure you leave a space between the DIR command and

the drive name. Also, remember to type the colon (:) after the drive letter. DOS displays a directory of your diskette (Figure 2-1).

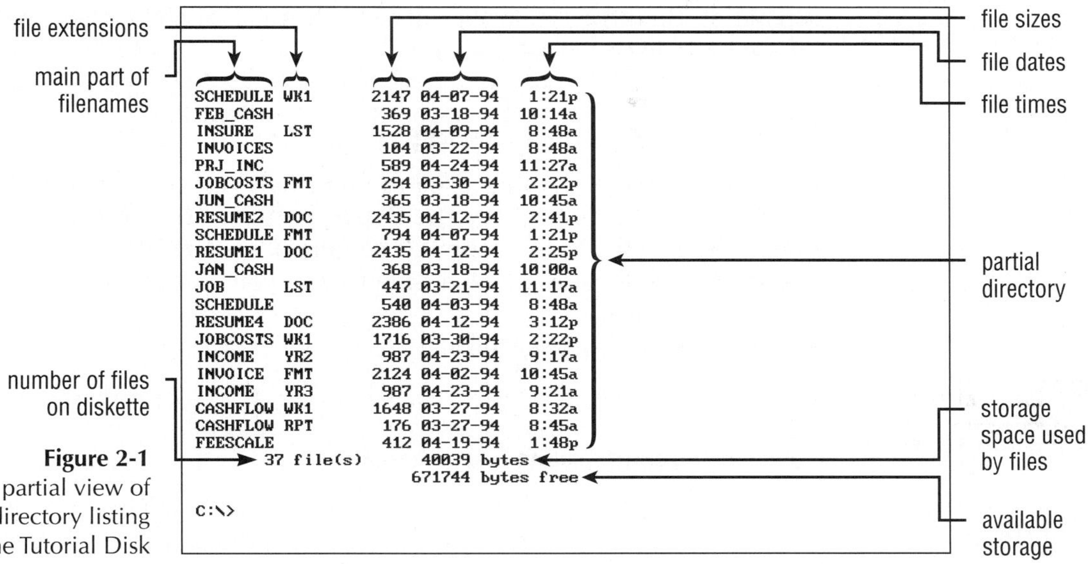

Figure 2-1
A partial view of the directory listing of the Tutorial Disk

Through a process called **scrolling**, DOS adjusts the screen view because the monitor can display only 25 lines at one time. Once DOS scrolls through the first part of the directory list, a partial directory remains on the screen. DOS lists the files in **disk order**—the order in which DOS keeps track of the files on the diskette. If your directory is listed in a different order from the one shown in Figure 2-1, ask your instructor or technical support person to restore the DOS default settings so that DOS displays the filenames in disk order.

The directory contains five columns of information:

- The first column shows the main part of the filename. As you learned in Tutorial 1, a filename can have two parts—the main part of the filename and an optional file extension. The main part of the filename is one to eight characters in length. For example, the last file on the list in Figure 2-1 is named FEESCALE.
- The second column shows the file extension for those files that have one. The file extension is one to three additional characters in length. The last file, FEESCALE, does not have a file extension. The file listed before it, CASHFLOW.RPT, has the file extension RPT, an abbreviation for "report." Because the main part of the filename and the file extension are listed in two separate columns on the directory listing for ease of use, you do not see a period separating the two parts of the filename, although you would always use one as a separator.
- The third column lists the size of each file in bytes (or characters). For example, FEESCALE is 412 bytes in size. When it displays file sizes, DOS 6.2 uses commas to offset every three places to the left of the decimal point.
- The fourth column shows the date that each file was either created or last modified. For example, FEESCALE was created or last saved on April 19, 1994. Each time you save a file to disk, DOS records the current date with the filename.
- The fifth column shows the time that each file was created or last modified. For example, FEESCALE was created or last saved at 1:48 p.m. DOS also records the time with the filename when you save a file to disk.

Below the directory listing, DOS shows the total number of files and the total disk storage space used by those files. The Tutorial Disk has a total of 37 files, which use 40,039 bytes of space. A total of 671,744 free bytes of space remain on the diskette. If your diskette has bad sectors, then the total space left on your diskette will be different.

Pausing a Directory Listing

Because you were unable to see the first part of this directory listing due to scrolling, you decide to try the Pause switch with the DIR command. The **Pause switch**, /P, modifies the DIR command so that DOS displays a directory listing one screen at a time, pausing to give you a chance to read the information on the screen.

Let's try the Pause switch.

To view a directory listing one screen at a time:

1. Press **[↑]** (Up Arrow) once to recall the command DIR A: or DIR B:. Press **[Spacebar]** and type **/P**. The command should now read "DIR A: /P." Press **[Enter]**. DOS displays the first screen, which contains part of the directory. See Figure 2-2. At the top of the screen, the DIR command displays the volume label. If you did not assign a volume name to the diskette when you formatted it, DOS will tell you that the volume in the drive has no label. In this figure, DOS also shows the diskette's serial number. On the third line, DOS informs you that you are seeing a directory for a specific disk drive. In Figure 2-2, the listing is for drive A. If your current drive is drive B, this line will read "Directory of B:\." At the bottom of this screen, DOS displays a prompt to press any key to continue. As noted in the previous tutorial, certain keys do not work.

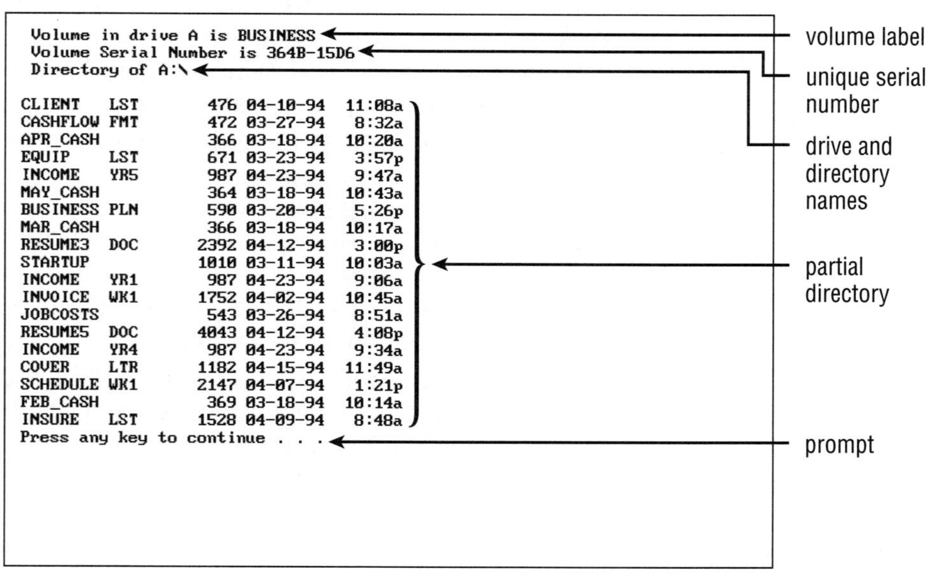

Figure 2-2
DOS pauses after displaying the first screen of the directory

2. Press **[Spacebar]** or any other key to continue. DOS displays the second, and last, screen with the remainder of the directory. See Figure 2-3. At the top of the directory listing on this screen, DOS displays the message "(continuing A:\)" to remind you that you are viewing a directory listing of the files stored in the root directory of drive A (or drive B).

```
Press any key to continue . . .

(continuing A:\)
INVOICES            104 03-22-94   8:48a
PRJ_INC             589 04-24-94  11:27a
JOBCOSTS FMT        294 03-30-94   2:22p
JUN_CASH            365 03-18-94  10:45a
RESUME2  DOC       2435 04-12-94   2:41p
SCHEDULE FMT        794 04-07-94   1:21p
RESUME1  DOC       2435 04-12-94   2:25p
JAN_CASH            368 03-18-94  10:00a
JOB      LST        447 03-21-94  11:17a
SCHEDULE            540 04-03-94   8:48a
RESUME4  DOC       2386 04-12-94   3:12p
JOBCOSTS WK1       1716 03-30-94   2:22p
INCOME   YR2        987 04-23-94   9:17a
INVOICE  FMT       2124 04-02-94  10:45a
INCOME   YR3        987 04-23-94   9:21a
CASHFLOW WK1       1648 03-27-94   8:32a
CASHFLOW RPT        176 03-27-94   8:45a
FEESCALE            412 04-19-94   1:48p
       37 file(s)        40039 bytes
                        671744 bytes free

C:\>_
```

drive and directory names

partial directory

Figure 2-3
DOS displays the next, and last, screen of the directory

Viewing a Wide Directory Listing

Another approach for viewing directory listings with many files is to use the Wide switch. The **Wide switch**, /W, displays filenames in five columns across the width of the screen and thus enables you to view more filenames at once. Although this switch displays the full filename, with a period separating the main part of the filename from the file extension, it does not show the file size, date, and time.

Let's view a directory listing using the Wide switch. Remember that you can use DOSKEY to recall the last command that you entered. Then you can modify, or **edit**, the command so it uses a different switch.

To view a wide directory listing:

1. Type **CLS** and press **[Enter]**. DOS clears the screen of the last directory listing.
2. Press **[↑]** (Up Arrow) twice to recall the last DOS command. Press **[Backspace]** until you delete the "P." Then type **W**. The command should read "DIR A: /W." Now press **[Enter]**. DOS produces a directory listing that includes all the files on the Tutorial Disk on one screen. See Figure 2-4 on the following page.

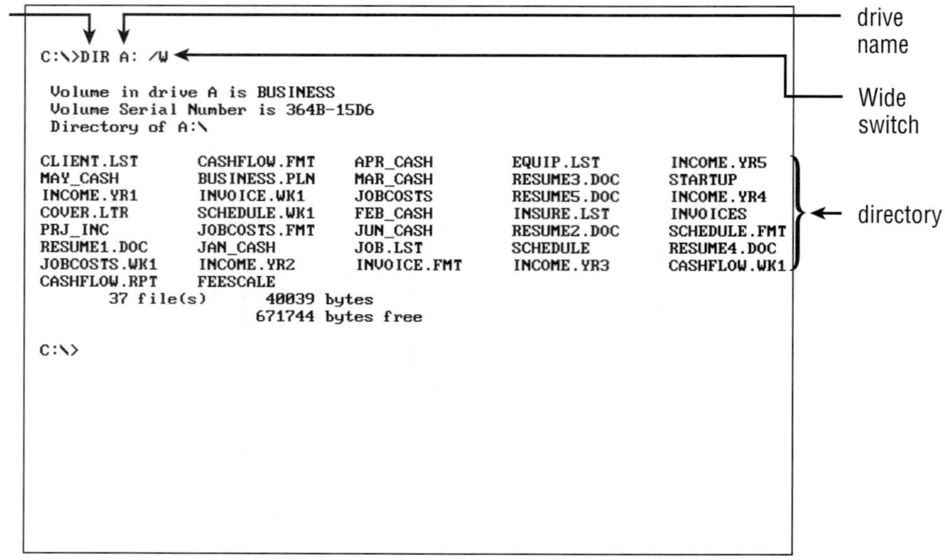

Figure 2-4
DOS displays a wide directory in five columns

Viewing a Directory of the Default Drive

The DIR command shows you a directory of the drive you specify. In the previous examples, you specified the name of the disk drive that contains your diskette. However, if you do not specify a drive name, DOS will look to the DOS prompt and display the directory for that drive. Many DOS commands operate in the same way.

To view a directory of a diskette drive without specifying the drive name:

1. Type **A:** or the drive name that contains your Tutorial Disk and press **[Enter]**. DOS updates the DOS prompt to show you the current drive.
2. Type **DIR /P** and press **[Enter]**. The DIR command displays a directory of your diskette one screen at a time, but you did not specify the drive name this time. Instead, DOS uses the current drive specified in the DOS prompt.
3. Press **[Spacebar]** or any other key to view the next screen and return to the DOS prompt.

Specifying a Sort Order for Directory Listings

Next, you want to verify that your business partner included the file that contains the business plan. Because DOS does not display the directory in an order that makes it easy to find a file, you decide to use the **Order switch**, /O, which displays filenames in alphabetical order. You can also combine this switch with the Pause switch to view one screen at a time. Let's try it.

To display the directory one screen at a time in alphabetical order by filename:

1. Press **[↑]** once to recall the last DOS command, DIR /P. Press **[Spacebar]** and type **/O**. *Be sure you type the letter "O" and not a zero for the Order switch.* The command should read "DIR /P /O." Now press **[Enter]**. DOS displays the first screen of filenames in alphabetical order. See Figure 2-5. The second file, BUSINESS.PLN, is the one that you want to locate.

file containing business plan

```
 Volume in drive A is BUSINESS
 Volume Serial Number is 364B-15D6
 Directory of A:\

APR_CASH           366 03-18-94  10:20a
BUSINESS PLN       590 03-20-94   5:26p
CASHFLOW FMT       472 03-27-94   8:32a
CASHFLOW RPT       176 03-27-94   8:45a
CASHFLOW WK1      1648 03-27-94   8:32a
CLIENT   LST       476 04-10-94  11:08a
COVER    LTR      1182 04-15-94  11:49a
EQUIP    LST       671 03-23-94   3:57p
FEB_CASH           369 03-18-94  10:14a
FEESCALE           412 04-19-94   1:48p
INCOME   YR1       987 04-23-94   9:06a
INCOME   YR2       987 04-23-94   9:17a
INCOME   YR3       987 04-23-94   9:21a
INCOME   YR4       987 04-23-94   9:34a
INCOME   YR5       987 04-23-94   9:47a
INSURE   LST      1528 04-09-94   8:48a
INVOICE  FMT      2124 04-02-94  10:45a
INVOICE  WK1      1752 04-02-94  10:45a
INVOICES           104 03-22-94   8:48a
Press any key to continue . . .
```

alphabetical directory

Figure 2-5
DOS displays the directory in alphabetical order by filename

2. Press **[Spacebar]** or any other key. DOS displays the filenames in the next, and last, screen in alphabetical order. DOS also returns to the DOS prompt.

Using Sort Order Parameters

The ability to display an alphabetical list of filenames is important for the daily operation of your business. However, you and your business partner want to quickly locate files with similar types of information by their file extensions, as well as recently created files by using the file date. Furthermore, you want to check file dates and file sizes periodically to determine how efficiently you are using disk space. When your disk begins to fill, you might need to store, or **archive**, large and less frequently used client files on other diskettes.

Your business partner informs you that you can use **sort order parameters** with the Order switch to view a directory in order by file extension, size, and date and time. These sort order parameters are codes added to the Order switch (Figure 2-6 on the following page).

Sort Order Parameters	Displays Filenames in Order By
/OE or /O:E	File extension only
/OEN or /O:EN	File extension, then by main part of filename
/OD or /O:D	File date and time
/OS or /O:S	File size
/ON or /O:N	Main part of filename only
/O or /ONE or /O:NE	By main part of filename and then by file extension

Figure 2-6
Sort order parameters for the Order switch

Your business partner also notes that you can reverse the sorting order by placing a minus sign in front of the optional parameter. For example, you use /O-S or /O:-S to display filenames in reverse order by file size.

You decide to try several of these sort order parameters. First, you want to locate your business files that contain the templates for producing résumés. These files have the file extension DOC (for "document"), so you would use the **Extension** (E) **sort order parameter** with the Order switch.

To view a directory one screen at a time in alphabetical order by file extension:

1. Press [↑] once to recall the last DOS command, DIR /P /O. Type **E**. *Be sure you do not include a space between the /O and E.* The command should read "DIR /P /OE." Then press **[Enter]**. DOS displays a directory and stops after the first screen of filenames. DOS first lists files without extensions, and then lists the files in alphabetical order by file extension. See Figure 2-7. The résumé template files are listed together by file extension. However, the main part of the filename is not listed in order.

filenames without file extensions

filenames with file extensions in alphabetical order by file extension

```
 Volume in drive A is BUSINESS
 Volume Serial Number is 364B-15D6
 Directory of A:\

APR_CASH            366 03-18-94  10:20a
MAY_CASH            364 03-18-94  10:43a
MAR_CASH            366 03-18-94  10:17a
STARTUP            1010 03-11-94  10:03a
JOBCOSTS            543 03-26-94   8:51a
FEB_CASH            369 03-18-94  10:14a
INVOICES            104 03-22-94   8:48a
PRJ_INC             589 04-24-94  11:27a
JUN_CASH            365 03-18-94  10:45a
JAN_CASH            368 03-18-94  10:00a
SCHEDULE            540 04-03-94   8:48a
FEESCALE            412 04-19-94   1:48p
RESUME3  DOC       2392 04-12-94   3:00p
RESUME5  DOC       4043 04-12-94   4:08p
RESUME2  DOC       2435 04-12-94   2:41p
RESUME1  DOC       2435 04-12-94   2:25p
RESUME4  DOC       2386 04-12-94   3:12p
CASHFLOW FMT        472 03-27-94   8:32a
JOBCOSTS FMT        294 03-30-94   2:22p
Press any key to continue . . .
```

Figure 2-7
DOS displays the directory in alphabetical order by file extension

2. Press **[Spacebar]** or any other key to continue. DOS displays the remainder of the sorted directory and the DOS prompt.

In a rush on a busy day, you might need to quickly locate important client files that you created or modified that day. You can display a directory in order by date by using the **Date** (D) **sort order parameter** with the Order switch. When you use this switch, DOS lists the files in order by date, from the file with the oldest date to the most recently created file. However, because you need to locate newly created files quickly, you can reverse this order by placing a minus sign in front of the Date sort order parameter. DOS lists the files in reverse order by date, with the most recently created files listed first.

To view a directory by file date from the most recent date:

1. Press [↑] once to recall the last DOS command, DIR /P /OE. Press **[Backspace]** until you delete the "E." Then type **-D**. *Be sure you do not include a blank space between the /O and -D.* The command should read "DIR /P /O-D." Then press **[Enter]**. DOS displays filenames in order from the most recent file dates to the oldest file date. See Figure 2-8.

```
 Volume in drive A is BUSINESS
 Volume Serial Number is 364B-15D6
 Directory of A:\

PRJ_INC              589 04-24-94  11:27a
INCOME   YR5         987 04-23-94   9:47a
INCOME   YR4         987 04-23-94   9:34a
INCOME   YR3         987 04-23-94   9:21a
INCOME   YR2         987 04-23-94   9:17a
INCOME   YR1         987 04-23-94   9:06a
FEESCALE             412 04-19-94   1:48p
COVER    LTR        1182 04-15-94  11:49a
RESUME5  DOC        4043 04-12-94   4:08p
RESUME4  DOC        2386 04-12-94   3:12p
RESUME3  DOC        2392 04-12-94   3:00p
RESUME2  DOC        2435 04-12-94   2:41p
RESUME1  DOC        2435 04-12-94   2:25p
CLIENT   LST         476 04-10-94  11:08a
INSURE   LST        1528 04-09-94   8:48a
SCHEDULE WK1        2147 04-07-94   1:21p
SCHEDULE FMT         794 04-07-94   1:21p
SCHEDULE             540 04-03-94   8:48a
INVOICE  WK1        1752 04-02-94  10:45a
Press any key to continue . . .
```

decreasing date order

decreasing time order

Figure 2-8
DOS displays the directory in reverse order by file date and time

2. Press **[Spacebar]** or any other key to continue. DOS displays the remainder of the directory. Files with the oldest file dates are listed last in the directory.

Finally, you want to check file sizes periodically to determine how efficiently you are using storage space on your diskette. You can use the **Size** (S) **sort order parameter** of the Order switch to list files from the smallest to the largest, or in reverse order from the largest to the smallest. Because large files have the greatest impact on the availability of disk space, let's list file sizes in reverse order.

To view a directory in reverse order by file size:

1. Press [↑] to recall the last DOS command, DIR /P /O-D. Press **[Backspace]** until you delete the "D." Then type **S**. The command should read "DIR /P /O-S." Then press **[Enter]**. DOS displays the first screen of directory information. The files are listed in reverse order by file size, starting with the largest file on the diskette. See Figure 2-9.

```
 Volume in drive A is BUSINESS
 Volume Serial Number is 364B-15D6
 Directory of A:\

RESUME5  DOC       4043 04-12-94   4:08p
RESUME2  DOC       2435 04-12-94   2:41p
RESUME1  DOC       2435 04-12-94   2:25p
RESUME3  DOC       2392 04-12-94   3:00p
RESUME4  DOC       2386 04-12-94   3:12p
SCHEDULE WK1       2147 04-07-94   1:21p
INVOICE  FMT       2124 04-02-94  10:45a
INVOICE  WK1       1752 04-02-94  10:45a
JOBCOSTS WK1       1716 03-30-94   2:22p
CASHFLOW WK1       1648 03-27-94   8:32a
INSURE   LST       1528 04-09-94   8:48a
COVER    LTR       1182 04-15-94  11:49a
STARTUP            1010 03-11-94  10:03a
INCOME   YR5        987 04-23-94   9:47a
INCOME   YR1        987 04-23-94   9:06a
INCOME   YR4        987 04-23-94   9:34a
INCOME   YR2        987 04-23-94   9:17a
INCOME   YR3        987 04-23-94   9:21a
SCHEDULE FMT        794 04-07-94   1:21p
Press any key to continue . . .
```

decreasing order by file size

Figure 2-9
DOS displays the directory in reverse order by file size

2. Press **[Spacebar]** or any other key to continue. DOS displays the remainder of the directory. The last files in the directory are the smallest files on the diskette.

By using this last option, you can quickly locate the largest files on the first screen and decide whether to archive these files.

Displaying Directory Listings in Lowercase

By default, DOS displays filenames in uppercase, and many people find the filenames difficult to read. If you use the **Lowercase switch**, /L, DOS displays the filenames in lowercase so that the filenames are easier to read. Let's try it.

To display an alphabetical directory in lowercase:

1. Press [↑] until you recall the command, DIR /P /O-S. Press **[Backspace]** until you delete the "-S." Next, press **[Spacebar]** and type **/L**. The command should read "DIR /P /O /L." Then press **[Enter]**. DOS displays the first screen of directory information. The filenames are listed in alphabetical order and in lowercase. See Figure 2-10.

```
 Volume in drive A is BUSINESS
 Volume Serial Number is 364B-15D6
 Directory of A:\

apr_cash            366 03-18-94  10:20a
business pln        590 03-20-94   5:26p
cashflow fmt        472 03-27-94   8:32a
cashflow rpt        176 03-27-94   8:45a
cashflow wk1       1648 03-27-94   8:32a
client   lst        476 04-10-94  11:08a
cover    ltr       1182 04-15-94  11:49a
equip    lst        671 03-23-94   3:57p
feb_cash            369 03-18-94  10:14a
feescale            412 04-19-94   1:48p
income   yr1        987 04-23-94   9:06a
income   yr2        987 04-23-94   9:17a
income   yr3        987 04-23-94   9:21a
income   yr4        987 04-23-94   9:34a
income   yr5        987 04-23-94   9:47a
insure   lst       1528 04-09-94   8:48a
invoice  fmt       2124 04-02-94  10:45a
invoice  wk1       1752 04-02-94  10:45a
invoices            104 03-22-94   8:48a
Press any key to continue . . .
```

lowercase filenames

Figure 2-10
DOS displays the directory in alphabetical order by filename and in lowercase

2. Press **[Spacebar]** or any other key to continue. DOS displays the remainder of the directory in lowercase and the DOS prompt.

The DIR command and its wide assortment of switches are invaluable for identifying which files are stored on a diskette or for locating information on files. If you forget which diskette contains a client file that you need, you can quickly check a diskette's contents with this command. The DIR command is also useful when you are looking for a specific copy of a file. You can check the dates and times of each version of that file to find the one you need.

USING WILDCARDS

The diskette provided by your business partner contains 37 files. You expect the number to increase as your business gets under way. When you need to use a group of files, such as the résumé templates, you want to select them without having to view the names of all the other files on the diskette. To simplify the process of selecting files with similar filenames, you can use **wildcards** to substitute for part or all of a filename when executing the DIR command and other DOS commands that operate on files.

There are two wildcard characters—the question mark and the asterisk. The **question mark** (?) substitutes for a single character in a filename, whereas the **asterisk** (*) substitutes for one or more characters. You can also combine wildcards with switches to improve the results of your selections.

Using the Question Mark Wildcard

One common use of the question mark wildcard is to select a group of files that have filenames that are identical except for one character. For example, the résumé template files on your diskette are named RESUME1.DOC, RESUME2.DOC, RESUME3.DOC, RESUME4.DOC, and RESUME5.DOC. The only difference in the names of these files is the character in the seventh position of the main part of the filename. To view a directory of just these files, you can substitute the question mark wildcard for the seventh character. Let's select these files.

To select the résumé template files using the question mark wildcard:

1. Type **CLS** and press **[Enter]**. DOS clears the screen of the last directory.
2. Type **DIR RESUME?.DOC /O** and press **[Enter]**. DOS displays an alphabetical directory with the five résumé template files. See Figure 2-11. You can also omit the file extension by typing DIR RESUME? /O, and DOS will produce the same selection. If you do not specify a file extension, DOS automatically selects filenames with or without a file extension.

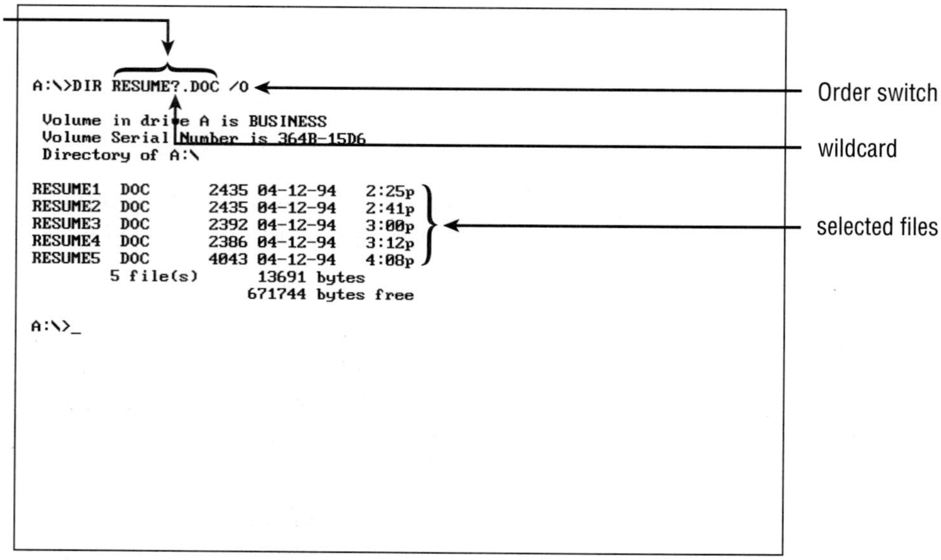

Figure 2-11
DOS displays a directory after using the question mark wildcard to select a group of files with similar filenames

The filename included with a DIR command, with or without wildcards, is called a **file specification**. DOS uses the file specification to select a single file with a specific filename or a group of files with similar filenames.

Next, you want to display a directory of your business files that track cash flow on a monthly basis. The files are named JAN_CASH, FEB_CASH, MAR_CASH, APR_CASH, MAY_CASH, and JUN_CASH. The first three characters in these filenames are different. To select these files as a group, you decide to use a question mark wildcard for each of the first three characters.

To view a directory of your monthly cashflow files in date order:

1. Press [↑] until you recall the CLS command and press **[Enter]**.

2. Type **DIR ???_CASH /OD** and press **[Enter]**. To type the underscore (_), press [Shift] and the key with the underscore and dash symbols. DOS displays your six monthly cashflow files. The Date (D) sort order parameter lists the files in month order by using the file date *and* time. See Figure 2-12.

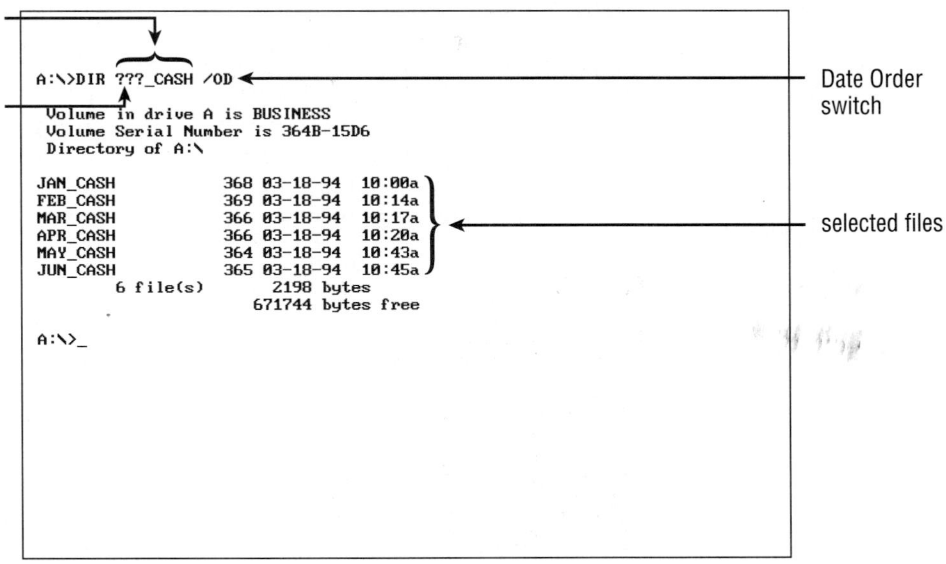

Figure 2-12
DOS displays a directory after using question mark wildcards to select a group of files with similar filenames

It is important to note that you cannot use an asterisk in place of the three question mark wildcards. If you do, DOS ignores anything after the asterisk and selects all the files.

Using the Asterisk Wildcard

You next want to display a directory of the files that contain your business checklists for insurance, equipment, jobs, and clients. Each of these files has the file extension LST. Because the filename represents more than one character, you use the asterisk wildcard to substitute for the main part of the filename.

To select your business checklist files with the asterisk wildcard:

1. Press [↑] until you recall the CLS command and press **[Enter]**. DOS clears the screen.
2. Type **DIR *.LST /O** and press **[Enter]**. DOS displays the names of all files with the LST file extension. See Figure 2-13 on the following page. The asterisk substitutes for any combination of characters in the main part of the filename.

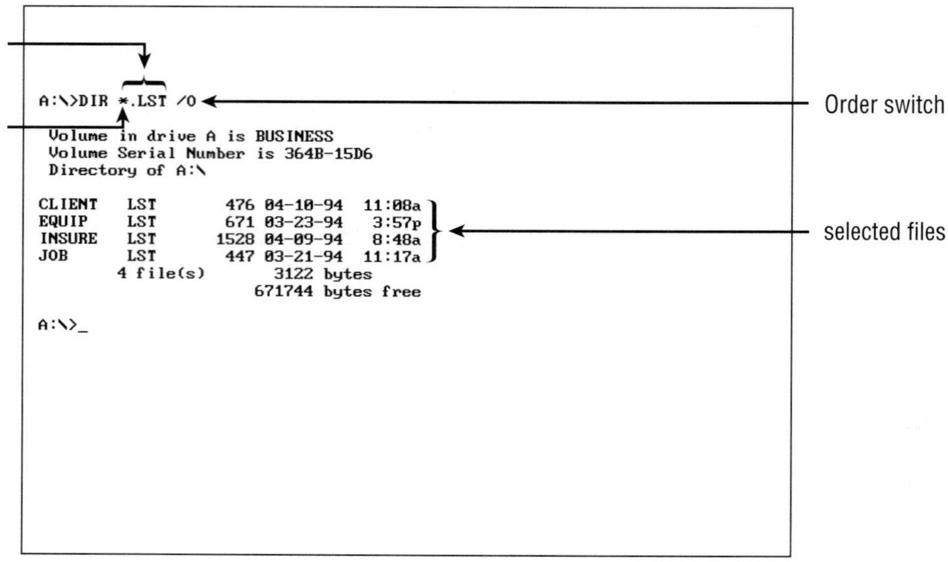

Figure 2-13
DOS displays a directory after using the asterisk wildcard to select a group of files with the same file extension

Another common use of the asterisk wildcard is to select all filenames that begin with a certain character or combination of characters. For example, suppose you want to locate the business file that contains your projected income for the first six months of your business, but you do not remember its exact name or even whether it has a file extension. All you remember is that "P" is the first character of the filename.

To locate this file:

1. Press [↑] until you recall the CLS command and press **[Enter]**. DOS clears the screen.
2. Type **DIR P*.*** and press **[Enter]**. DOS locates one file that meets this condition, and its filename is PRJ_INC. See Figure 2-14. You can obtain the same result by just typing "DIR P*" and pressing the Enter key. If you do not use an asterisk for the file extension, DOS assumes you want filenames with or without a file extension.

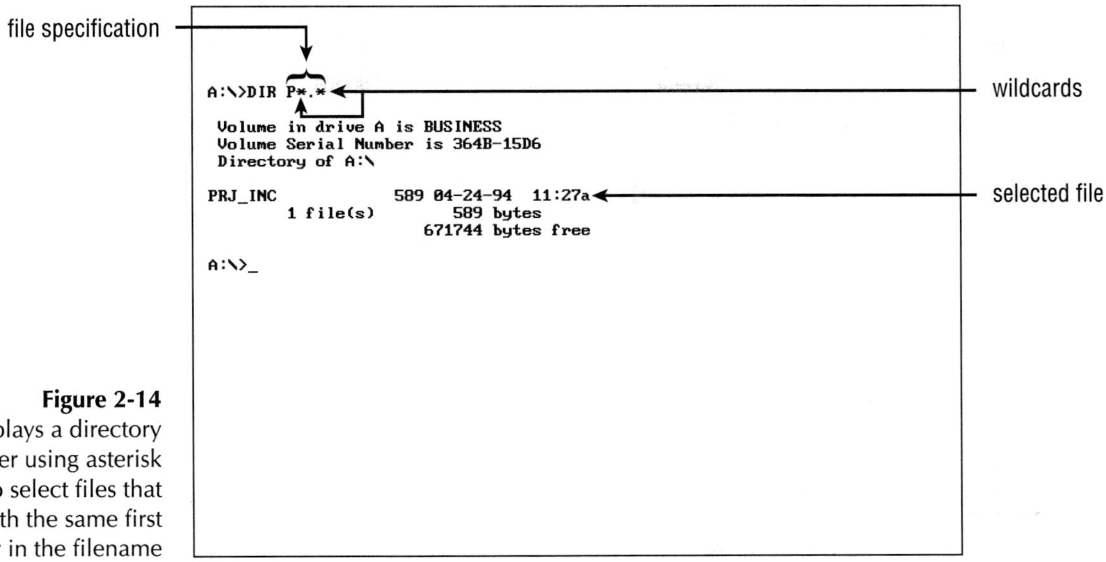

Figure 2-14
DOS displays a directory after using asterisk wildcards to select files that start with the same first character in the filename

In your business, you can use wildcards with switches as one more tool for quickly locating and selecting files.

SPECIFYING DEFAULT SWITCHES

After examining the use of various switches for the DIR command, you realize that you and your business partner will commonly use the Order and Pause switches for directory listings. Rather than enter these switches manually each time you need them and rather than recall them with DOSKEY, you can specify default switches for the DIR command. DOS will automatically use these switches each time you enter the DIR command.

DOS stores important settings in a small area of memory called the **DOS environment**. As you work on your computer, DOS checks the DOS environment if it needs a specific setting. DOS assigns each setting in the DOS environment to an **environment variable**. For example, DOS uses the DIRCMD environment variable for default switches for the DIR command.

The SET command is an internal command that assigns a setting to an environment variable. Its syntax is as follows:

SET *environment variable = string*

The **string** is the setting that you want to assign to the environment variable. For example, if you want to store the Pause and Order switches in the DOS environment for use with the DIR command, you enter the following command at the DOS prompt:

SET DIRCMD=/P /O

Now, whenever you enter "DIR" at the DOS prompt, DOS will execute your command as though you had entered "DIR /P /O." Later, if you prefer to use another setting, you can repeat this command and specify new switches.

When you assign a setting to the DIRCMD environment variable, you must *not* leave a blank space between DIRCMD and the equal sign. If you include a space, DOS does not use the new setting when you enter the DIR command.

If you want to view the contents of the DOS environment, you type the SET command and press the Enter key.

This DOS feature will save you and your business partner valuable time as you search diskettes and hard disks for files. You decide to use this feature for the remainder of your work session on the computer.

To specify default switches for the DIR command:

1. Type **SET DIRCMD=/P /O** and press **[Enter]**. DOS displays the DOS prompt. If DOS displays an error message indicating that you are out of environment space, the DOS environment does not contain any additional room to store new settings. Ask your instructor or technical support person to adjust the size of the DOS environment, and then try again.

Now verify that this setting is stored in the DOS environment.

2. Type **SET** and press **[Enter]**. DOS displays settings in the DOS environment. See Figure 2-15. Your settings will be different. The variable DIRCMD and the Pause and Order switches are listed as the last setting in the DOS environment. Later, you will examine the use of some of these other settings.

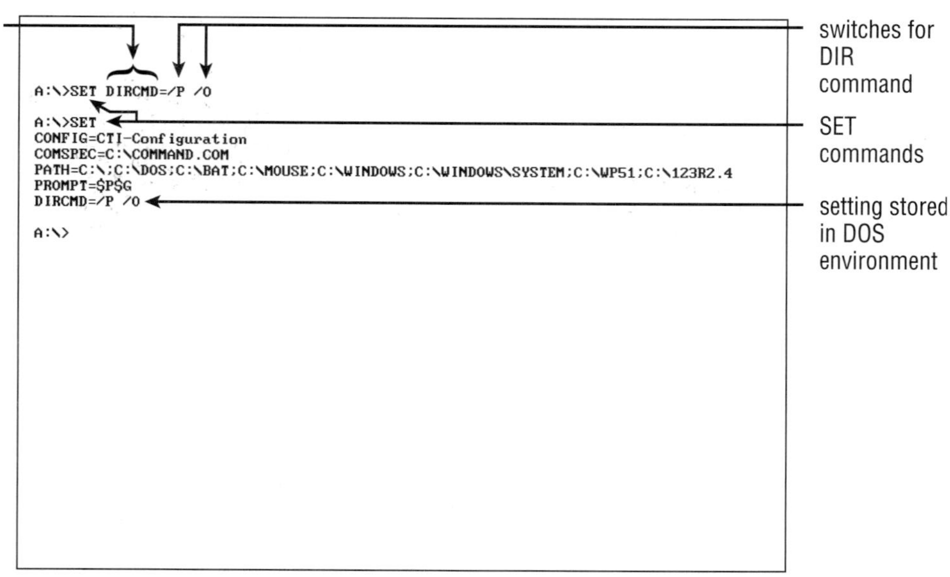

Figure 2-15
Settings stored in the DOS environment (your settings will be different)

Now display a directory of your business files.

3. Type **DIR** and press **[Enter]**. *Do not type any switches.* Because you have set the /P and /O switches as defaults, DOS automatically pauses after each screen and displays an alphabetical directory. See Figure 2-16.

```
 Volume in drive A is BUSINESS
 Volume Serial Number is 364B-15D6
 Directory of A:\

APR_CASH            366 03-18-94  10:20a
BUSINESS PLN        590 03-20-94   5:26p
CASHFLOW FMT        472 03-27-94   8:32a
CASHFLOW RPT        176 03-27-94   8:45a
CASHFLOW WK1       1648 03-27-94   8:32a
CLIENT   LST        476 04-10-94  11:08a
COVER    LTR       1182 04-15-94  11:49a
EQUIP    LST        671 03-23-94   3:57p
FEB_CASH            369 03-18-94  10:14a
FEESCALE            412 04-19-94   1:48p
INCOME   YR1        987 04-23-94   9:06a
INCOME   YR2        987 04-23-94   9:17a
INCOME   YR3        987 04-23-94   9:21a
INCOME   YR4        987 04-23-94   9:34a
INCOME   YR5        987 04-23-94   9:47a
INSURE   LST       1528 04-09-94   8:48a
INVOICE  FMT       2124 04-02-94  10:45a
INVOICE  WK1       1752 04-02-94  10:45a
INVOICES            104 03-22-94   8:48a
Press any key to continue . . .
```

Figure 2-16
The DIR command uses switches stored in the DOS environment to display a directory in alphabetical order and to pause after each screen

4. Press **[Spacebar]** or any other key to continue. DOS redisplays the DOS prompt.

This setting stays in the DOS environment and remains in effect until you specify a new setting, remove this setting, or turn off your computer. To specify a new setting, you enter "SET DIRCMD=" with a list of the new switches you now want to use. To remove this setting from the DOS environment, you type "SET DIRCMD=" without any settings and press the Enter key. Each time you start your computer, you can use this command to specify default switches for the DIR command.

You also can temporarily override these settings by entering the DIR command with the new switch that you want to use. For example, you might want to locate the file that your business partner most recently worked on today. Let's try this feature.

To display filenames in order by date:

1. Press [↑] once to recall the last command, DIR. Press **[Spacebar]** and type **/O-D**. The command should read "DIR /O-D." Then, press **[Enter]**. DOS displays the filenames in reverse order by date and time. See Figure 2-17 on the following page. Because you changed the parameter associated with the /O switch, DOS overrides the default setting for the Order switch in the DOS environment. However, DOS still uses the Pause switch.

```
 Volume in drive A is BUSINESS
 Volume Serial Number is 364B-15D6
 Directory of A:\

PRJ_INC              589 04-24-94  11:27a
INCOME   YR5         987 04-23-94   9:47a
INCOME   YR4         987 04-23-94   9:34a
INCOME   YR3         987 04-23-94   9:21a
INCOME   YR2         987 04-23-94   9:17a
INCOME   YR1         987 04-23-94   9:06a
FEESCALE             412 04-19-94   1:48p
COVER    LTR        1182 04-15-94  11:49a
RESUME5  DOC        4043 04-12-94   4:08p
RESUME4  DOC        2386 04-12-94   3:12p
RESUME3  DOC        2392 04-12-94   3:00p
RESUME2  DOC        2435 04-12-94   2:41p
RESUME1  DOC        2435 04-12-94   2:25p
CLIENT   LST         476 04-10-94  11:08a
INSURE   LST        1528 04-09-94   8:48a
SCHEDULE WK1        2147 04-07-94   1:21p
SCHEDULE FMT         794 04-07-94   1:21p
SCHEDULE             540 04-03-94   8:48a
INVOICE  WK1        1752 04-02-94  10:45a
Press any key to continue . . .
```

decreasing order by date

Figure 2-17
DOS displays a directory in reverse date order, overriding one of the switches in the DOS environment

2. Press **[Spacebar]** or any other key to continue. DOS redisplays the DOS prompt.

This time-saving tool not only simplifies directory operations, but can also streamline your daily business operations and improve efficiency and productivity.

This is a good opportunity to stop for a few minutes and take a break.

USING COMMAND LINE AND GRAPHICAL USER INTERFACES

Now that you are familiar with entering DOS commands at the DOS prompt, you are ready to learn a more visual approach for interacting with DOS. Your business partner tells you about the DOS Shell and explains that it simplifies command operations and saves time and effort.

When you enter a DOS command at the DOS prompt, you are using a **command line interface,** also called a **text user interface** (abbreviated **TUI**, pronounced "tooey"). An **interface** refers to the way in which you interact with the computer system. When you use DOS, your interface is the DOS prompt. When you use a command line interface, you enter commands on a line-by-line basis and wait for the results of each command operation. The only information displayed on the screen is the DOS prompt with the name of the drive and directory. This is the type of interface you have been using so far in these tutorials.

All versions of DOS allow you to interact with DOS using the command line interface. However, starting with DOS 4.0, you can also use a **graphical user interface** (abbreviated **GUI**, pronounced "gooey"), which provides a more visual frame of reference and additional on-screen information for interacting with the operating system. The DOS GUI is the DOS Shell. In the DOS Shell, you work with menus, windows, and **icons** (graphical images or pictures) that represent objects in a computer system, such as a disk drive, directory, program, or file. The DOS Shell contains all the tools you need to work with DOS and your computer system.

The DOS Shells in DOS 4.0 and 4.01 are different from the ones in DOS 5.0, 6.0, and 6.2. However, the DOS Shells in DOS 5.0, 6.0, and 6.2 are almost identical to each other.

Because a picture is worth a thousand words, let's view the DOS Shell so that you have a better idea of what constitutes a graphical user interface.

USING THE DOS SHELL

You decide to compare the use of the DOS Shell with the use of commands at the DOS prompt so that you and your business partner can choose the most effective and efficient way to work on your computer systems to complete business contracts. As an afterthought, you realize that you might complete some of your contract work in client offices. You must know how to work from the DOS Shell *and* from the DOS prompt in the event that the DOS Shell is not available on your clients' computers.

In order to view the DOS Shell, DOS must be able to locate the program that displays this graphical user interface. If you are using a computer system with a hard disk or if you are working on a network, this program must be installed on the hard disk or network in order to be available for your use. Check with your instructor or technical support person to be sure the DOS Shell program is installed on your computer or network.

To access the DOS Shell:

1. If necessary, insert your Tutorial Disk in a diskette drive and change to that drive.
2. Type **DOSSHELL** (as one word with no spaces) and press **[Enter]**. After DOS loads the DOS Shell program into the computer's memory from drive C or the network drive, you will see the DOS Shell screen. See Figure 2-18 on the following page. Because there are different ways to customize the screen view of the DOS Shell, your view might be different from the one in the figure. If you are unable to access the DOS Shell, or if your screen looks different from the screen in Figure 2-18, check with your instructor or technical support person.

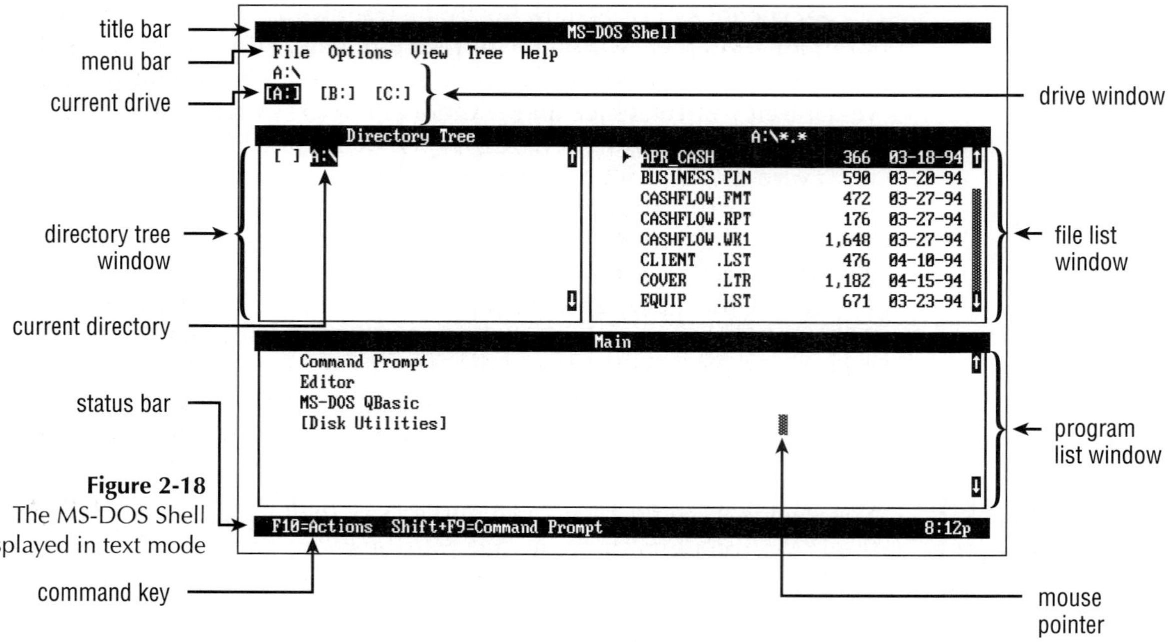

Figure 2-18
The MS-DOS Shell displayed in text mode

The view of the DOS Shell as shown in Figure 2-18 is referred to as text mode. In **text mode**, DOS uses standard keyboard characters and symbols to represent drives, directories, programs, and files. When you install DOS, the DOS Shell is automatically installed in text mode. On your system, the DOS Shell might be configured for graphics mode. See Figure 2-19. In **graphics mode**, the DOS Shell uses icons to represent drives, directories, programs, and files. These icons provide a more user-friendly and informative interface. If your screen view looks different from Figure 2-18 or Figure 2-19, see your instructor or technical support person for help in returning it to the default setting or to the setting initially installed with DOS.

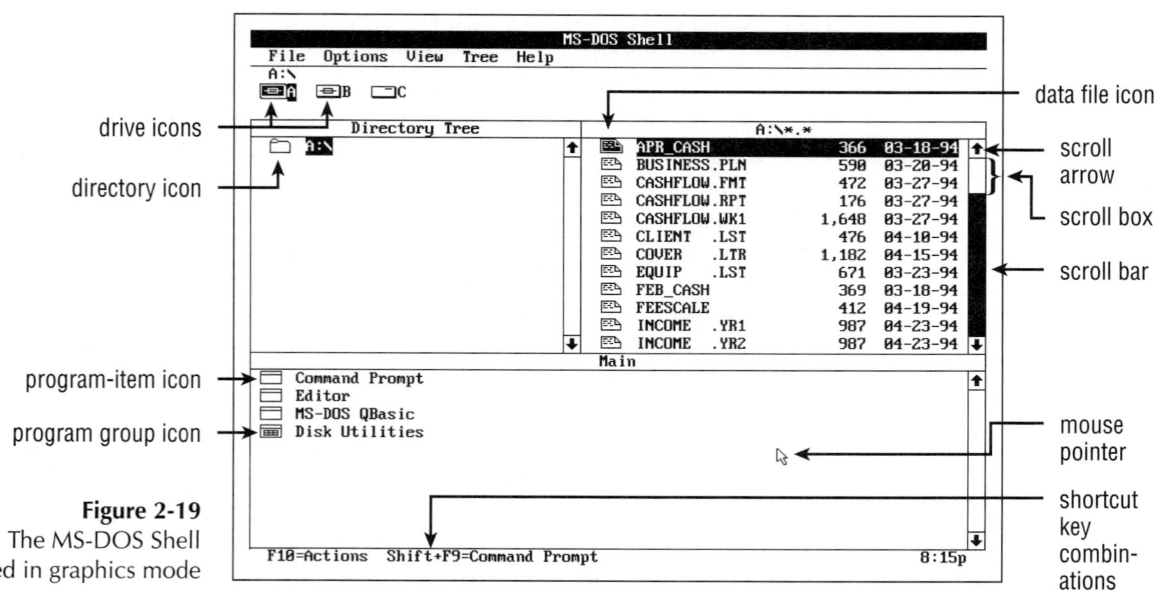

Figure 2-19
The MS-DOS Shell displayed in graphics mode

The DOS Shell screen is divided into areas, or **windows**, which you can customize. At the top of the screen is a **title bar** with the title "MS-DOS Shell." The **menu bar** on the next line contains the following menu names: File, Options, View, Tree, and Help. When you select one of these menu names, a list of options appears. You can select and execute commands from these menus.

The **drive window**, located immediately below the menu bar, shows the current directory and the drives available on your computer system. If your computer system contains a hard drive and two diskette drives, the DOS Shell will list drives A, B, and C. If you are using a network, the DOS Shell will also list network drives, such as drive F, G, or H. The DOS Shell highlights the icon for the current drive. One of the advantages of using the DOS Shell is that you know immediately which drives are included on your computer system.

The DOS Shell uses the **directory tree window** to represent the organization of files on a hard disk or diskette. Currently, all the files on your Tutorial Disk are stored in the root directory of the diskette. The **root directory** is the first and most important directory on a hard disk or diskette. The FORMAT command creates the root directory when it formats a hard disk or diskette. To the right of the directory tree window, the **file list window** shows the files contained in the root directory of your diskette.

The window at the bottom of the screen, with the title "Main," is called the **program list window**, which displays the list of program groups or programs that you can access from the DOS Shell. The **Command Prompt** option allows you to temporarily exit to the DOS prompt. The **Editor** option allows you to use the MS-DOS Editor, a simple text editing utility, from the DOS Shell. The **MS-DOS QBasic** option allows you to use the Quick BASIC programming language included with DOS. The **Disk Utilities** option contains a group of options for using DOS utilities, such as the one for formatting diskettes. You can add software applications, such as WordPerfect or Lotus 1-2-3, to this list so that you can use them directly from the DOS Shell. This feature allows you to organize and access all of the programs you commonly use on your computer system.

Below the Main window is the status bar. The **status bar** displays the shortcut key "F10=Actions" for accessing the menu bar and "Shift+F9=Command Prompt" for temporarily exiting the DOS Shell to display the DOS prompt. Although it is not shown on the status bar, you can also use the Alt (Alternate) key to access the menu bar. The status bar also displays the current time on the far right.

As you work in a window, your reference point is a **selection cursor**, a special type of cursor used in the DOS Shell to highlight a drive, directory name, filename, or program name. When you load the DOS Shell, the selection cursor highlights the current drive in the drive window. You move the selection cursor from window to window by pressing the Tab key or by using a mouse. A **mouse** is a hand-held device that moves a mouse pointer around the screen in the direction that you move the mouse. Once you load the DOS Shell, the **mouse pointer** becomes active and appears as a rectangle in text mode or as an arrow in outline in graphics mode. You use the mouse pointer to select an option displayed on the screen.

You can use the mouse in the DOS Shell, but you cannot use the mouse at the DOS prompt. If you have a mouse connected to your computer system and want to learn how to use it, read the next section. If you are not using a mouse, skip the next section.

USING THE MOUSE

You can perform the following types of operations with the mouse:

- When you **point** with the mouse, you move the mouse pointer to a specific area of the screen so that it highlights a menu, command, drive name, filename, icon, or another object displayed on the screen.
- To **click** the left mouse button, you quickly press and release it. Clicking permits you to select a command, drive name, filename, icon, or object on the screen or a specific area of the screen. Note that your mouse might include a right mouse button. When working in the DOS Shell, you use only the *left* mouse button.
- When you **double-click** the left mouse button, you quickly press it twice. You double-click to execute a command.
- When you **drag** the mouse, you hold down the left mouse button, move the mouse to highlight the area you want to select, and then release the mouse button. You would use this feature, for example, to select a group of filenames or to select and move an object on the screen.

In some cases, you can perform operations more easily with the mouse than with the keyboard; in other instances, the keyboard is easier to use. In these tutorials, you will be given instructions for using both the keyboard and the mouse to complete particular steps. The mouse instructions are indicated by a small mouse icon to the left of the steps.

CUSTOMIZING THE DOS SHELL

You prefer to switch the DOS Shell from text mode to graphics mode on the computer system in your business office so that you and your business partner can work with, and benefit from, a graphical user interface. Before you can use graphics mode, however, you must have a graphics adapter (or card) and a monitor that supports graphics mode.

If you are working in a computer lab, you must have permission to change the display mode of the DOS Shell. If you are using the DOS Shell on a network, your network might not permit changes to the configuration of programs such as the DOS Shell. Ask your instructor or technical support person if you can change from the default text mode to graphics mode. If you do not have permission to change the display mode of the DOS Shell, read but do not execute the following steps so that you understand the general process for making this change. You might need to customize the DOS Shell on another computer system in the future.

To customize the DOS Shell so that it uses graphics mode:

1. Press **[F10]** (Actions) to access the menu bar, press **[→]** (Right Arrow) to highlight the Options menu, and press **[Enter]**.

   If you are using the mouse, click on the menu name **Options**.

The DOS Shell displays the Options drop-down menu. See Figure 2-20. Notice that the commands on the Options drop-down menu are listed in two ways: with or without an ellipsis. Those commands that are followed by an *ellipsis* (...) are commands that display dialog boxes. Many *dialog boxes* display options from which you can select so that the DOS Shell can complete a command. Some dialog boxes display information, such as warnings. Commands without an ellipsis are those that the DOS Shell executes immediately. To select a command using the keyboard, you move the selection cursor with [↓] (Down Arrow) and press the Enter key, or you can type the underlined, boldface, or otherwise highlighted character in the menu or command name. For example, to choose the Colors option, you could type "o." If you are using the mouse, you can click the menu name or command.

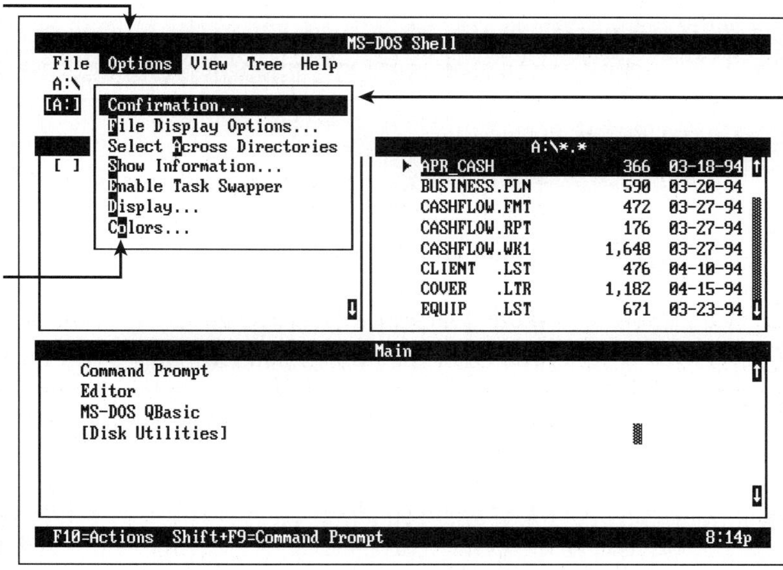

Figure 2-20
The drop-down Options menu in the DOS shell

2. Press [↓] (Down Arrow) until you highlight the Display command. Press **[Enter]**.

   If you are using the mouse, click **Display**.

   The DOS Shell displays the Screen Display Mode dialog box. See Figure 2-21 on the following page. The Screen Display Mode dialog box is a *list box*, which lists options for using text and graphics mode, depending on the capabilities of your video display adapter and monitor. As shown in Figure 2-21, you can customize the DOS Shell to work in text mode with 25, 43, or 50 lines per screen, or in graphics mode with 25 lines per screen. To view the remaining options for graphics mode—30, 34, 43, and 60 lines per screen—you first have to adjust the view of the list box with the selection cursor or the *scroll arrows* on the *scroll bars* at the right side of the dialog box. When you use the mouse to click a scroll arrow, the DOS Shell adjusts your view in the dialog box's window. The more lines you display per screen, the smaller the characters appear on the screen and the higher the resolution. A setting of 30 or 34 lines per screen works well in graphics mode.

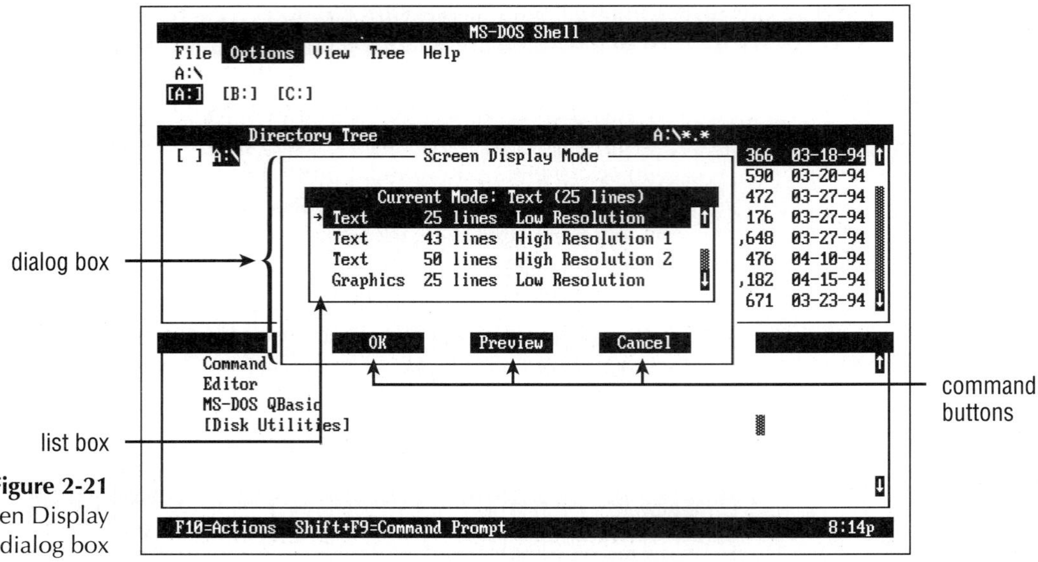

Figure 2-21
The Screen Display Mode dialog box

3. Press [↓] (Down Arrow) to highlight the graphics mode that you want to use and press **[Enter]**.

   If you are using the mouse, adjust the display in this dialog box by clicking **one of the scroll arrows** in the scroll bar. Next, click the **graphics mode** that you want to use and then click **OK**.

   The DOS Shell updates the display mode from text to graphics and sets the number of lines displayed on the screen. The remaining figures in this text use graphics mode with 30 lines per screen.

In graphics mode, diskette drives are represented by an icon that looks similar to the outward appearance of a diskette drive. Hard drives are represented by an icon in the shape of a system unit with a small dash in the upper-right corner of the icon. A directory, such as the one for A:\ in the directory tree window, is represented by a file folder icon. Data files in the file list window are represented by an icon of a sheet of paper with writing on it and with its upper-right corner folded down. Programs and program files are represented by a rectangular icon with a bar across the top; program groups have similar icons with a rectangular grid in the icon.

Because graphical user interfaces are common on most computer systems in use today, the figures of the DOS Shell in this textbook will use graphics mode to illustrate the advantages and features of working with a full graphical user interface.

DISPLAYING DIRECTORIES IN THE DOS SHELL

One advantage of using the DOS Shell is that it automatically displays filenames in alphabetical order. However, you can change the sort order, and you can select groups of files with the Options menu. In your business, an alphabetical list or a list in order by date are the best options for locating important business files quickly. To compare how you control the directory display within the DOS Shell to that at the DOS prompt, you decide to list files in order by date using the DOS Shell.

To view your business files in order by date using the DOS Shell:

1. Press **[F10]** (Actions) to access the menu bar, press [→] to highlight the Options menu, and press **[Enter]**.

   If you are using the mouse, click **Options**.

   The DOS Shell displays the drop-down Options menu.

2. Press [↓] to highlight File Display Options and press **[Enter]**.

   If you are using the mouse, click **File Display Options**.

   The DOS Shell displays the File Display Options dialog box. See Figure 2-22.

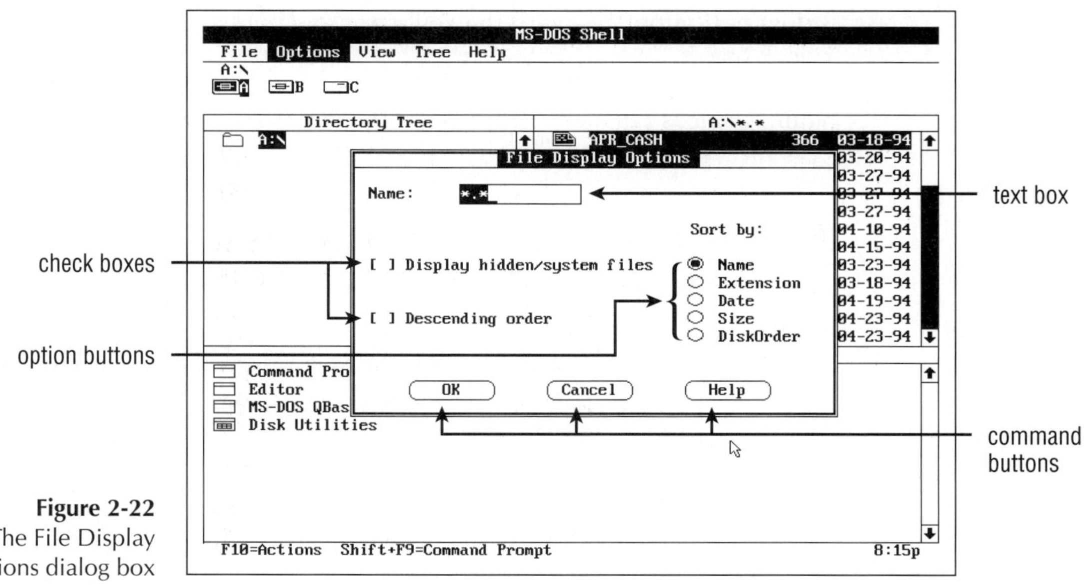

Figure 2-22
The File Display Options dialog box

In a dialog box, you may see one or more **text boxes**, in which you can change the entry. For example, in Figure 2-22, the Name text box shows the current type of file selection—***.*** (pronounced "star-dot-star"). This notation indicates that the DOS Shell is selecting all files. It uses the first asterisk wildcard to select any combination of characters in the main part of the filename and the second asterisk wildcard to select any combination of characters in the file extension.

This dialog box provides options for displaying hidden files and system files. **Hidden files** are files that are not displayed in a directory in order to protect them from inadvertently being deleted. **System files** are the program files that constitute DOS. System files are also hidden to protect them. If you select the **check box** next to "Display hidden/system files" by placing a check mark (an "X") in this box, the DOS Shell will display any hidden or system files included in a directory. If you are using the keyboard, you can use the Tab key to move the cursor to the check box and press the Spacebar to change the setting. If you are using the mouse, you can change the setting by clicking the check box.

The **option buttons** listed under "Sort by" allow you to display a directory in order by name, extension, date and time, size, and disk order. You can select only one of these options, and the files are automatically displayed in ascending order (from A to Z or 0 to 9). If you want to reverse the order (from Z to A or 9 to 0), you can select the check box next to "Descending order." You select option buttons with the keyboard and mouse in the same way you select check boxes.

You want to display a directory so that you can view the files that you and your business partner worked on in the last two days.

To arrange the directory in reverse order by date:

1. Press **[Tab]** twice to highlight the check box for descending order, and then press **[Spacebar]** to check this box.

   If you are using the mouse, click the **Descending order check box**.

   The DOS Shell displays a check mark in the check box for descending order. If you do not see a check mark, repeat this step.

2. Press **[Tab]** to select the Name option button under "Sort by." You cannot see the cursor. Press [↓] until you highlight the Date option button. As you press [↓], DOS Shell moves the dot to the next option.

   If you are using the mouse, click the **Date option button box**.

   The DOS Shell displays a dot in the option button for the Name. If you do not see a dot next to this option, repeat this step.

3. Press **[Enter]** to select OK.

   If you are using the mouse, click **OK**.

   DOS Shell saves the new settings, closes the dialog box, and updates the directory display. See Figure 2-23. You can now see the business files that you and your partner worked on in the last two days. These settings remain in effect until you change them.

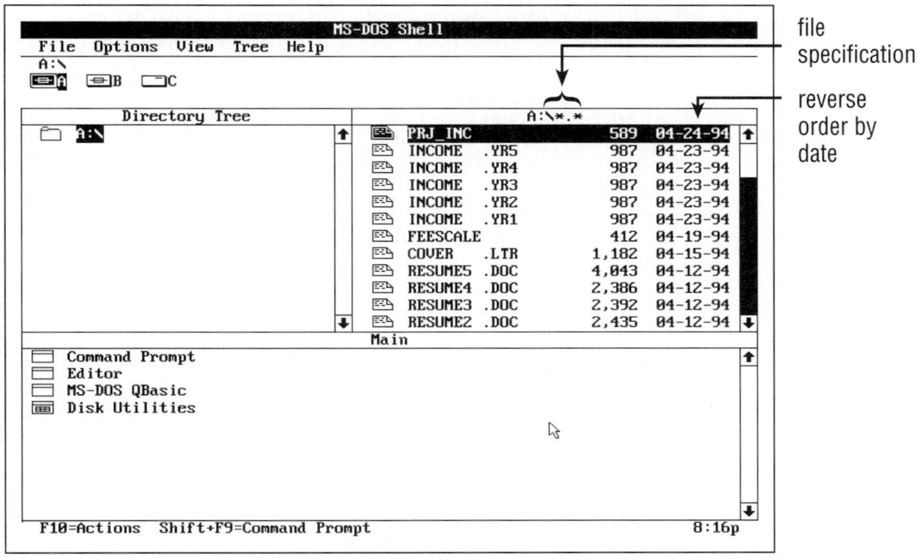

Figure 2-23
The DOS Shell displays a directory of files in descending order by date and time in the file list window

Using Wildcards in the DOS Shell

Next, you want to check the diskette for your yearly income projection template files. You and your partner agreed to name these files INCOME and use a file extension with YR and a single digit representing the year. You can select these files by specifying wildcards on the File Display Options dialog box.

To view a directory of the yearly income projections in order by file extension:

1. Press **[F10]** (Actions) to access the menu bar, press [→] (Right Arrow) to highlight the Options menu, and press **[Enter]**.

   If you are using the mouse, click **Options**.

   The DOS Shell displays the drop-down Options menu.

2. Press [↓] to highlight File Display Options and press **[Enter]**.

   If you are using the mouse, click **File Display Options**.

   The DOS Shell displays the File Display Options dialog box, and the Name text box is highlighted. To replace the default file selection criteria, you must type a new condition over it.

3. Type ***.YR?** to replace *.* in the Name text box. Press **[Tab]** twice to select the Descending Order check box. Then press **[Spacebar]** to remove the check mark.

   If you are using the mouse, type ***.YR?** and click the **Descending order check box**.

   In this operation, you are combining the use of the asterisk and question mark wildcards to select a group of files with similar file extensions.

4. Press **[Tab]** to select the Date option button under Sort by. Press [↑] to select Extension.

   If you are using the mouse, click the **Extension option button**.

5. Press **[Enter]**.

   If you are using the mouse, click **OK**.

   The DOS Shell closes this dialog box with the new settings. DOS updates the file list window and shows that there are five template files for income projections for the first five years of your new business. See Figure 2-24. When you and your business partner meet, you can work on the first year's projection.

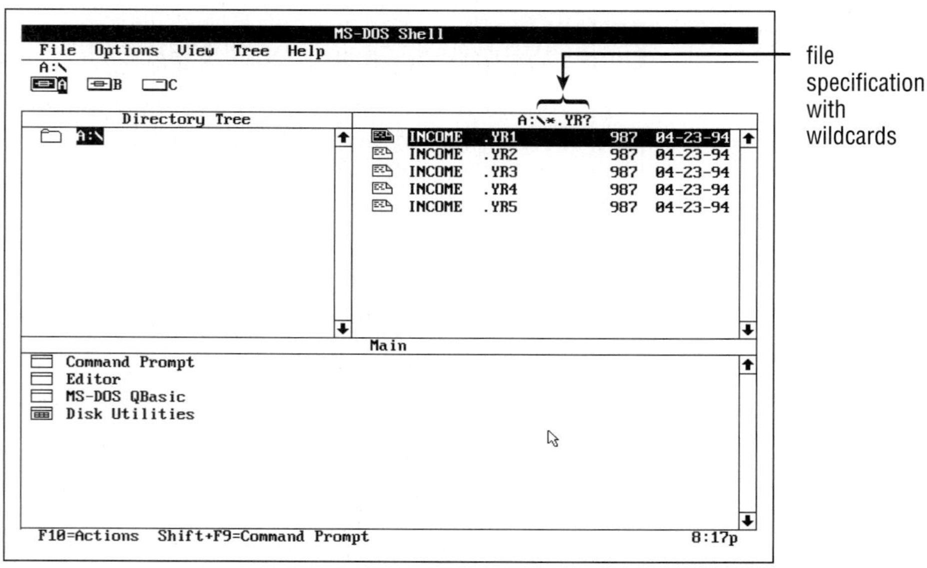

Figure 2-24
The DOS Shell uses wildcards to select a group of files with similar filenames and displays the filenames in ascending order by file extension

As you work with the DOS Shell, you and your business partner will usually want files displayed alphabetically by filename, so you decide to change the file display options back to the DOS Shell's default settings.

To specify the default settings for the filename display:

1. Press **[F10]** (Actions) to access the Menu Bar, press [→] to highlight Options, and press **[Enter]**.

   If you are using the mouse, click **Options**.

   The DOS Shell displays the drop-down Options menu.
2. Press [↓] to highlight File Display Options and then press **[Enter]**.

   If you are using the mouse, click **File Display Options**.

   The DOS Shell displays the File Display Options dialog box.
3. Type ***.*** in the Name text box, press **[Tab]** three times to select the Extension option button, and press [↑] to select the Name option button.

   If you are using the mouse, type ***.*** in the Name text box and click the **Name** option button.
4. Press **[Enter]**.

   If you are using the mouse, click **OK**.

   The DOS Shell stores the new settings and updates the Files window.

EXITING THE DOS SHELL

Your workday is almost over. Now that you know how to select sort orders and groups of files with the DOS Shell, you are ready to exit the DOS Shell. You can exit the DOS Shell with the Exit command on the File menu, or you can bypass the menu and use the shortcut key for this command, "Alt+F4." You can also use the shortcut key [F3] (Exit), even though the DOS Shell does not show this shortcut key on the status bar.

To exit the DOS Shell:

1. Press **[F10]** (Actions) to access the menu bar and press **[Enter]** to select the File menu.

   If you are using the mouse, click **File**.

   The DOS Shell displays the drop-down File menu. See Figure 2-25 on the following page. You can use some, but not all, of the commands on this menu. In this figure, the DOS Shell underlines and highlights those commands that you can use. For example, you can use the Open, Run, and Exit commands. You cannot use other commands, such as Move, Copy, Delete, and Rename, because you cannot use these commands on drives. However, if you move the selection cursor to the file list window, then the DOS Shell will highlight these commands when you next access the File menu because you can use these commands on files. Note that the DOS Shell displays shortcut key combinations for certain commands. You can bypass this menu by using those shortcut keys.

Because the appearance of commands on this menu depends on the capabilities of your graphics adapter and the screen colors you choose to use, your view of the File menu might be different from that in Figure 2-25. The DOS Shell might display those commands that you cannot use in gray, it might dim them, or it might not show those commands at all.

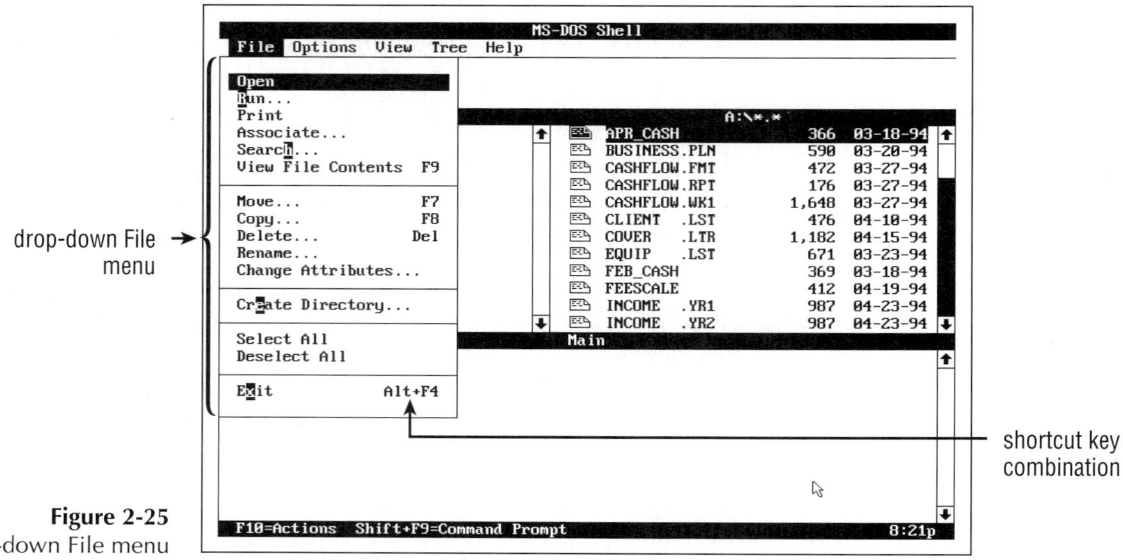

Figure 2-25
The drop-down File menu

2. Type **X** to select the Exit command. You can type the highlighted or underlined character shown in a menu option to select that command.

   If you are using the mouse, click **Exit**.

   DOS displays the DOS prompt for the current drive.

◆

SUMMARY

In this tutorial, you learned how to use the Directory (DIR) command to display a list of the names of files stored on a diskette. You used the Pause switch to display filenames one screen at a time and the Wide switch to display filenames in five columns across the screen. You used the Order switch and its optional sort order parameters to display filenames in order by name, extension, size, date, and time. You also reversed this order by placing a minus sign in front of the sort order parameter. You used the Lowercase switch to display filenames in lowercase rather than uppercase. As you worked with various switches for the DIR command, you used DOSKEY to recall and edit previously entered commands.

You substituted the question mark and asterisk wildcards for part or all of a filename to select groups of files with similar filenames. You also combined these two wildcards with each other and with switches to control the directory display.

You used the SET command to specify default switches for the DIR command and to view the contents of the DOS environment. You displayed a directory with these default switches, and you overrode a switch in the DOS environment.

You worked with the DOS command line interface at the DOS prompt and with the DOS Shell graphical user interface. After loading the DOS Shell, you explored its screen features and its windows. You switched the DOS Shell screen display from text to graphics mode to take full advantage of the graphical user interface.

You used the File Display Options command on the Options menu to change the sort order for displaying files and to select groups of files with wildcards. You returned these settings to the default settings used by the DOS Shell and then you exited the DOS Shell with the Exit command on the File menu.

Command Reference

DOS Commands	
DIR [*drive name:*]	An internal command that displays a directory listing of the diskette in the current drive, another drive, or a hard drive
DIR [*file specification*]	An internal command that displays a directory listing of a file or group of files on the diskette in the current drive, another drive, or a hard drive
DIR /L	An internal command that displays a directory listing in lowercase
DIR /O	An internal command that displays a directory listing in alphabetical order by filename and file extension
DIR /O<*sort order*> or DIR /O:<*sort order*>	An internal command that displays a directory listing in order by using a sort order parameter. The sort order parameters include: D File date and time E File extension N Main part of filename S File size
DIR /O-<*sort order*> or DIR /O:-<*sort order*>	An internal command that displays a directory listing in reverse order by using a sort order parameter. The sort order parameters include: D File date and time E File extension N Main part of filename S File size

DIR /P	An internal command that displays a directory listing and pauses after each screen
DIR /W	An internal command that displays a directory listing in five columns across the width of the screen, without specifying file sizes, dates, or times
DOSSHELL	An external command that loads the DOS Shell graphical user interface
SET	An internal command that displays settings stored in the DOS environment
SET DIRCMD=	An internal command that removes the default settings assigned to the DIRCMD environment variable from the DOS environment
SET DIRCMD=[*switches*]	An internal command that assigns default switches to the DIRCMD environment variable in the DOS environment for use with the Directory (DIR) command
DOS Shell Commands	
File Exit	Exits the DOS Shell
Options Display	Changes the screen display mode for the DOS Shell from text to graphics mode, or vice versa
Options File Display Options	Displays a file selection in the file list window

QUESTIONS

Use your DOS Exercise diskette to assist you with these questions.

1. What types of information does the DIR command provide on files stored on a diskette or hard disk?
2. What does DOS do if you enter the DIR command and do not specify a disk drive?
3. What does the Pause switch do? Give an example of how you would enter a DIR command with this switch.
4. What does the Wide switch do? Give an example of how you would enter a DIR command with this switch.

5. What does the Order switch do? Give an example of how you would enter a DIR command with this switch.
6. List four sort order parameters that you can use with the Order switch.
7. How can you reverse a sort order parameter when you use the Order switch?
8. What command would you enter at the DOS prompt to display filenames in alphabetical order by file extension only?
9. What command would you enter at the DOS prompt to display filenames in order by file size, from the smallest to the largest file?
10. What command would you enter at the DOS prompt to display filenames in order by file size, from the largest to the smallest file?
11. What command would you enter at the DOS prompt to display filenames in order by date and time, starting with the oldest date and time?
12. What command would you enter at the DOS prompt to display filenames in order by date and time, starting with the most recent date and time?
13. What command would you enter at the DOS prompt to display filenames first in order by file extension, then by the main part of the filename?
14. What does the Lowercase switch do? Give an example of how you would enter a DIR command with this switch.
15. What is a wildcard? What wildcards can you use with DOS? Give an example of how you can use each wildcard.
16. What is the DOS environment, and what does DOS store in the DOS environment?
17. How can you view the contents of the DOS environment?
18. What command would you enter to store in the DOS environment switches for displaying filenames in order by date, one screen at a time, and using lowercase?
19. What command would you enter to remove default switches or settings stored in the DOS environment for the Directory command (DIR)?
20. What command would you enter to display an alphabetical list of all files that have WP for a file extension?
21. What is a command line interface?
22. What is a graphical user interface?
23. What is the DOS Shell? How does it differ from the DOS prompt?
24. What two operating modes can you specify in the DOS Shell?
25. What is the default order used by the DOS Shell to display filenames in the file list window?
26. What DOS Shell command controls the display of filenames in the file list window?

27. How do you use wildcards in the DOS Shell to select groups of filenames to display in the file list window?
28. Name three ways to exit the DOS Shell.
29. What is an icon, and how does the DOS Shell use icons?
30. What is the difference between text mode and graphics mode in the DOS Shell?

TUTORIAL ASSIGNMENTS

Use your Exercise Disk for the following Tutorial Assignments.

1. **Displaying a Directory:** Insert your Exercise Disk into drive A or drive B. Then, perform the following operations from the DOS prompt on drive C. List the command that you use to accomplish each step.
   a. Display a directory of all files on the diskette in drive A or drive B from drive C.
   b. Change to drive A or drive B.
   c. Display a directory of drive A without specifying the drive name.
   d. Display a directory of drive C.
2. **Using Switches**: Perform the following operations from the DOS prompt on drive C. List the command that you use to accomplish each step.
   a. Display a directory of all files on the diskette in drive A in alphabetical order by filename and file extension.
   b. Display a directory of all files on the diskette in drive A in reverse order by file size.
   c. Display a directory of all files on the diskette in drive A in reverse order by date and in lowercase.
   d. Print the directory, or partial directory, displayed on the screen.
3. **Using Wildcards**: Perform the following operations from the DOS prompt on drive A. List the command that you use to accomplish each step.
   a. Display an alphabetical directory of all files with "I" as the first character in the filename.
   b. Display an alphabetical directory of all files with "DOC" for the file extension.
   c. Display an alphabetical directory of all files with "WK" as the first two characters of the file extension and any character after "WK".
   d. Print the directory displayed on the screen.
   e. Display an alphabetical directory of all files with "JOB" as the first three characters of the filename.
   f. Display a directory of all files with "LST" as the file extension, in date order.
4. **Specifying Default Settings for the Directory Command in the DOS Environment**: Perform the following operations from the DOS prompt. List the command that you use to accomplish each step.
   a. Display the settings in the DOS environment.
   b. Print the DOS environment settings displayed on the screen.

c. Assign switches to an environment variable so that DOS automatically displays filenames one screen at a time in alphabetical order by filename and in wide mode.
d. Check the newly entered setting in the DOS environment.
e. Display a directory using the switches in the DOS environment.
f. Override the Order switch in the DOS environment and display a directory in file size order.
g. Restore the original settings for the DIRCMD variable in the DOS environment. If the DOS environment did not contain a setting for this variable, remove the switches that you assigned to this variable.

5. **Using the DOS Shell**: Perform the following operations from the DOS Shell. Assume that you are currently using drive A and that DOS Shell is configured to operate in text mode. List the commands and steps for each of these operations.
   a. Load the DOS Shell.
   b. Change the operating mode from text mode to graphics mode.
   c. Specify that DOS Shell display filenames in disk order.
   d. Select all filenames that start with "S" and display them in date order.
   e. Select all filenames with the "WK1" file extension and display them in descending date order.
   f. Return the file specification to the default setting of all files (*.*) and the default sort order to name so that the DOS Shell shows all the filenames in the File List window in alphabetical order by name.

TUTORIAL 3

Working with Files

OBJECTIVES

In this tutorial you will learn to:

- Understand the importance and features of ASCII files
- View the contents of a text file
- Redirect the output of a DOS command
- Use the MORE filter
- Print text files
- Copy files
- Rename files
- Delete files
- Compare file operations from the DOS prompt and the DOS Shell

After carefully evaluating two job offers, you accept a position with a small business that produces business documents for clients. On your first day at your new job, your supervisor takes you on a short tour of the office and its facilities and introduces you to the other staff members. Your supervisor also provides you with an overview of how the company meets the business needs of its clients.

You are assigned a job for a specific client for whom you will produce the appropriate business documents from existing template files, each of which contains a general format for a specific type of document. As you recall, **templates** are files that contain the general format or layout of a document but little or no data. When you start a client job, you first check the contents of files that you intend to use to verify that you are starting with the correct files. Then you copy the template files to produce new files as your working copies. After you modify the new files for your client, you print either drafts or final copies of the documents. When you complete a client job, you make duplicate, or backup, copies of the files you produced in the event you encounter a problem with the original copies of those files. You also may be required to move files from one disk to another. Once a week, you reserve some time to check the files on your diskette and you archive or delete files that you no longer need.

Your supervisor emphasizes that many client jobs require you to meet tight deadlines, so you must know how to perform these operations quickly and efficiently. Although the office staff uses the DOS Shell to simplify and automate routine file operations like the ones described, you must also know how to work from the DOS prompt. Some clients request that you complete these jobs in their offices, and because they might not have the DOS Shell on their systems, you must be prepared to work under conditions different from those at your office. Your supervisor asks that you compare and contrast file operations from the DOS prompt and the DOS Shell as you work so that you are familiar with both approaches.

◆

GETTING STARTED

Your first client needs a résumé prepared in two different formats. Before you start, you decide to specify default settings for displaying directories, activate DOSKEY, and check the files on the template diskette provided you by your supervisor. The tutorial assumes you will use the CLS command to clear the screen before issuing a command, except in certain cases where it is necessary to show two or more steps in one figure.

To activate DOSKEY:

1. Power on your computer system, and be sure you see the C:\> prompt displayed on the screen. If you see a prompt for some other drive, type **C:** and press **[Enter]** to change to drive C.

5.0 *6.0* *6.2*

2. Type **DOSKEY** and press **[Enter]**. If you are using DOS 5.0 or 6.0, DOS will display the message "DOSKey installed" if DOSKEY is not already installed on your computer. If you do not see this message with DOS 5.0 or 6.0, DOSKEY is already installed. DOS 6.2 will not display a message.

Now specify default switches for the Directory command.

3. Type **SET DIRCMD=/P /O** and press **[Enter]**. DOS displays the DOS prompt. If DOS displays an error message indicating that you are out of environment space, ask your instructor or technical support person to adjust the size of the DOS environment, and then try again.

Next, verify that this setting is stored in the DOS environment.

4. Type **SET** and press **[Enter]**. DOS displays all the settings currently stored in the DOS environment. See Figure 3-1. The variable DIRCMD and the Pause and Order switches are listed as the last setting entered in the DOS environment.

settings in the DOS environment (yours might be different)

```
C:\>DOSKEY
DOSKey installed.

C:\>SET DIRCMD=/P /O

C:\>SET
CONFIG=CTI-Configuration
COMSPEC=C:\COMMAND.COM
PATH=C:\;C:\DOS;C:\BAT;C:\MOUSE;C:\WINDOWS;C:\WINDOWS\SYSTEM;C:\WP51;C:\123R2.4
PROMPT=$P$G
DIRCMD=/P /O

C:\>
```

default switches for the DIR command

Figure 3-1
The DOS environment contains settings for the DIRCMD variable as well as other settings

Now you are ready to view a directory of the template files on the diskette provided by your supervisor.

To display a directory of your working diskette:

1. Insert your Tutorial Disk into drive A (or drive B).
2. Type **A:** (or **B:**) to change to drive A (or drive B).
3. Type **DIR** and press **[Enter]**. *Do not type any switches.* DOS displays an alphabetical directory and pauses after each screen. See Figure 3-2.

```
 Volume in drive A is BUSINESS
 Volume Serial Number is 364B-15D6
 Directory of A:\

APR_CASH             366 03-18-94  10:20a
BUSINESS PLN         590 03-20-94   5:26p
CASHFLOW FMT         472 03-27-94   8:32a
CASHFLOW RPT         176 03-27-94   8:45a
CASHFLOW WK1        1648 03-27-94   8:32a
CLIENT   LST         476 04-10-94  11:08a
COVER    LTR        1182 04-15-94  11:49a
EQUIP    LST         671 03-23-94   3:57p
FEB_CASH             369 03-18-94  10:14a
FEESCALE             412 04-19-94   1:48p
INCOME   YR1         987 04-23-94   9:06a
INCOME   YR2         987 04-23-94   9:17a
INCOME   YR3         987 04-23-94   9:21a
INCOME   YR4         987 04-23-94   9:34a
INCOME   YR5         987 04-23-94   9:47a
INSURE   LST        1528 04-09-94   8:48a
INVOICE  FMT        2124 04-02-94  10:45a
INVOICE  WK1        1752 04-02-94  10:45a
INVOICES             104 03-22-94   8:48a
Press any key to continue . . .
```

Figure 3-2
The first screen of a directory with filenames in alphabetical order

4. Press **[Spacebar]** or any other key to continue. DOS displays the remainder of the directory and the DOS prompt.

You notice that this diskette contains general business files as well as client template files. Your supervisor suggested that you examine the general business files so that you become familiar with the business and can contribute ideas toward its growth.

THE IMPORTANCE OF ASCII FILES

Before you start on the client job at hand, you want to examine some of the business template files. These files, and many of the other files on your diskette, are ASCII (pronounced "ask key") files. An **ASCII file** is a simple file format in which data is stored as text. The name ASCII stands for **A**merican **S**tandard **C**ode for **I**nformation **I**nterchange. Computer companies recognize this standard coding format for storing information in a file and adapt their software packages to use, or **support**, this file format. The primary feature of an ASCII file is that users can read and decipher the contents of the file if it is displayed on the screen. In other words, the information is stored in a readable format.

In contrast, files produced by word processing software store formatting codes for special features, such as boldface and underlining, and you must use that software when you work on the file. However, most types of word processing software work with ASCII files. Furthermore, many of these word processing packages can automatically convert ASCII files into the file format typically used by that software. One advantage of storing general-use business template files as ASCII text files is that you can use them with whatever word processing application is available. In your business, this provides you with flexibility when working off-site at client offices.

The terms **DOS files**, **DOS text files**, **text files**, and **print files** also refer to ASCII files. Although you can store documents as ASCII files, many of the important configuration and initialization files on your computer system are

ASCII files. Therefore, it is important to become familiar with this file format and the DOS commands that operate on ASCII files.

The original ASCII character set contains codes for 128 characters, such as letters of the alphabet, numbers, and symbols as well as control codes. **Control codes** are codes for the use of the Ctrl (Control) key with another key. For example, when you press the Tab key to indent a line while creating an ASCII file, you insert a tab code, [Ctrl][I]. At the end of each line in an ASCII file, there is an ASCII code for a carriage return, [Ctrl][M]; a line feed, [Ctrl][J]; or both. Some ASCII files contain a form feed code, [Ctrl][L], to indicate a page break and the start of a new page. The last character in an ASCII file is a special type of code—an **end-of-file (EOF) code**, [Ctrl][Z].

Each ASCII character is assigned a numerical code, called the **ASCII code** or **ASCII value**. In the original ASCII character set, these values range from 0 (zero) to 127, for a total of 128 codes. The extended ASCII code has values that range from 0 (zero) to 255. The 128 additional codes include values for European characters, graphics characters, and scientific characters. You can produce an ASCII control code or character by pressing and holding [Alt] while you type the ASCII value *on the numeric keypad*. In some cases, applications programs redefine these codes. Figure 3-3 contains examples of ASCII characters and codes for both the original and extended ASCII character sets.

ASCII Character	Type of Character	ASCII Value
^I	Control code for a tab	009
Esc	Escape key	027
9	Number	057
A	Uppercase letter	065
a	Lowercase letter	097
£	British pound	156
╔	Graphics line	201
σ	Sigma symbol	229
÷	Division symbol	246

Figure 3-3
Examples of ASCII characters and codes

Viewing the Contents of an ASCII File

Because an ASCII file contains information stored as text, you can use the TYPE command, an internal DOS command, to display the contents of an ASCII file on the screen. The syntax of the TYPE command is as follows:

TYPE [*drive:*][*path*]*filename*

If you use the TYPE command, you do not need to start a program and then retrieve a file to view its contents. However, you cannot use the TYPE command to view the contents of a program file or a file produced by an application such as Lotus 1-2-3. If you do, DOS attempts to interpret the file's contents as ASCII characters and displays unintelligible symbols on the screen or no symbols at all. Also, you can use the TYPE command to view the contents of only one file at a time.

In your job, you want to become familiar with the client fee scale and with the two résumé template files that you need to use for your first client. You decide to use the TYPE command to examine the file with the fee scale and the first résumé template file.

To view the contents of the file with your company's fee scale:

1. Type **TYPE FEESCALE** and press **[Enter]**. The file named FEESCALE does not have a file extension. DOS displays the contents of this ASCII file on the screen, and then displays the DOS prompt. See Figure 3-4. The fee scale reflects the current rates for work in your region.

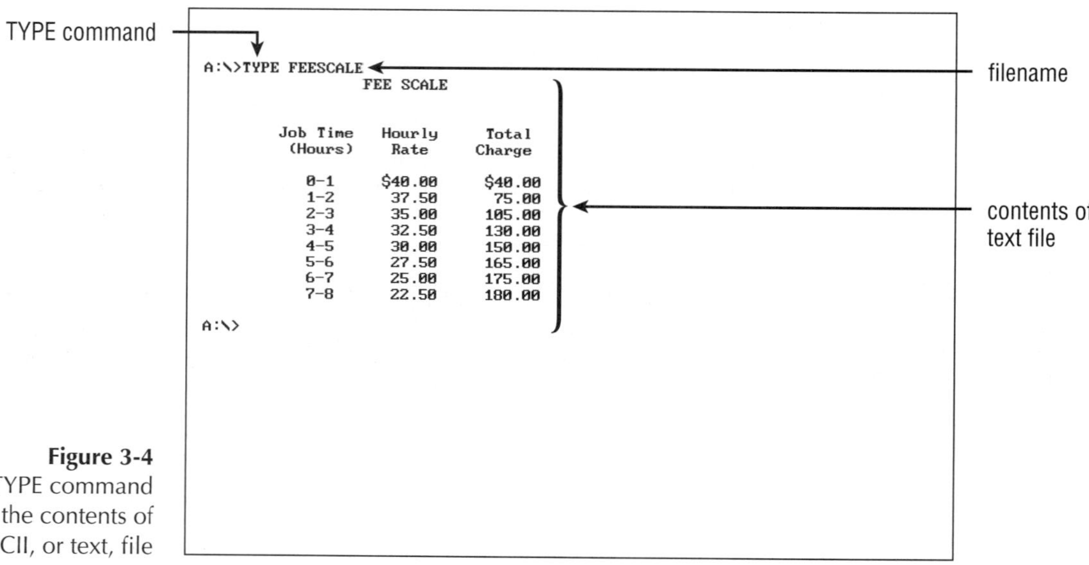

Figure 3-4
The TYPE command displays the contents of an ASCII, or text, file

Now view the contents of the file with the first résumé template.

2. Type **TYPE RESUME1.DOC** and press **[Enter]**. Unlike FEESCALE, the file named RESUME1.DOC does have a file extension. DOS displays the contents of this ASCII file on the screen, followed by the DOS prompt. Because the file contains more than 25 lines, DOS scrolls to adjust the screen view. The last half-page of the file remains displayed on the monitor. See Figure 3-5. This template identifies the type of information required to complete this résumé for a client.

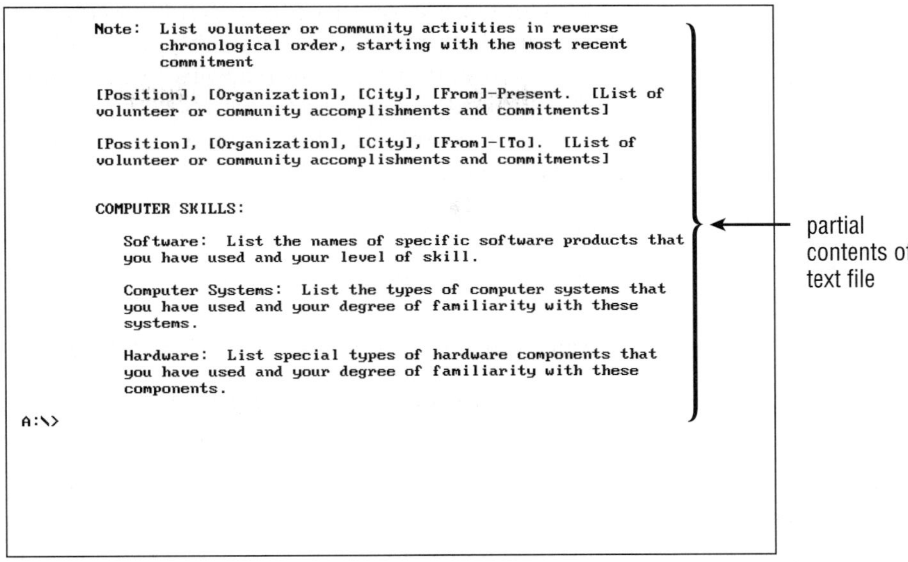

Figure 3-5
A partial view of the contents of an ASCII file

The scrolling was so quick that you were unable to view the entire contents of the file. To control the scrolling, you must use two other DOS features with the TYPE command: the MORE filter and the pipe operator.

PIPING OUTPUT TO THE MORE FILTER

The TYPE command does not have a Pause switch, and it is not uncommon for ASCII files to contain more than 25 lines of text. To display only one screen at a time and avoid automatic scrolling, you must send the output of the TYPE command to the MORE filter. A **filter** is a DOS command that can modify the output of another DOS command. The MORE filter, or command, displays a screen of output, pauses, and displays a More prompt, which permits you to continue when you are ready.

To combine the MORE filter with another DOS command, you use the pipe redirection operator. The **pipe operator** (¦) redirects the output of one DOS command operation so that it then becomes the input for another DOS command. For example, the following command will display the output of an ASCII file one screen at a time:

TYPE RESUME1.DOC ¦ MORE

The first command, TYPE, produces the output, and DOS stores this output in a temporary file on disk. After the TYPE command completes its operation, DOS uses the contents of the temporary file on disk as the input for the MORE filter. The MORE command displays the contents of the temporary file one screen at a time. After MORE displays the entire contents of the temporary file, DOS deletes the temporary file from disk. This transfer of data from one DOS command to another is called **piping**.

In order to complete this operation without error, DOS must be able to create a temporary, or **intermediate**, file. If the default disk drive is write-protected or if it does not contain enough space for the temporary file, DOS displays the error message "Intermediate file error during pipe."

If the computer's power fails during a piping operation, the temporary file remains on disk. You can recognize the temporary file because it is assigned a filename that you or a software application is not likely to use—names such as ACAPCPGB, AKCEDKAO, or APBNCMGA. These files might contain information or, if you interrupt a DOS command operation, these files might be empty (i.e., have a file size of zero bytes).

Let's try a piping operation so that we can view the entire contents of the résumé template file.

To display the contents of the résumé template file one screen at a time:

1. Type **TYPE RESUME1.DOC ¦ MORE** and press **[Enter]**. *Be sure you press the key with a vertical bar (the one that contains a space in the middle of the character) for the pipe operator.* DOS displays the first part of this ASCII file. See Figure 3-6. Your monitor might show a different number of lines. In this part of the résumé template file, you enter the client's name, address, telephone number, professional goals, and areas of expertise.

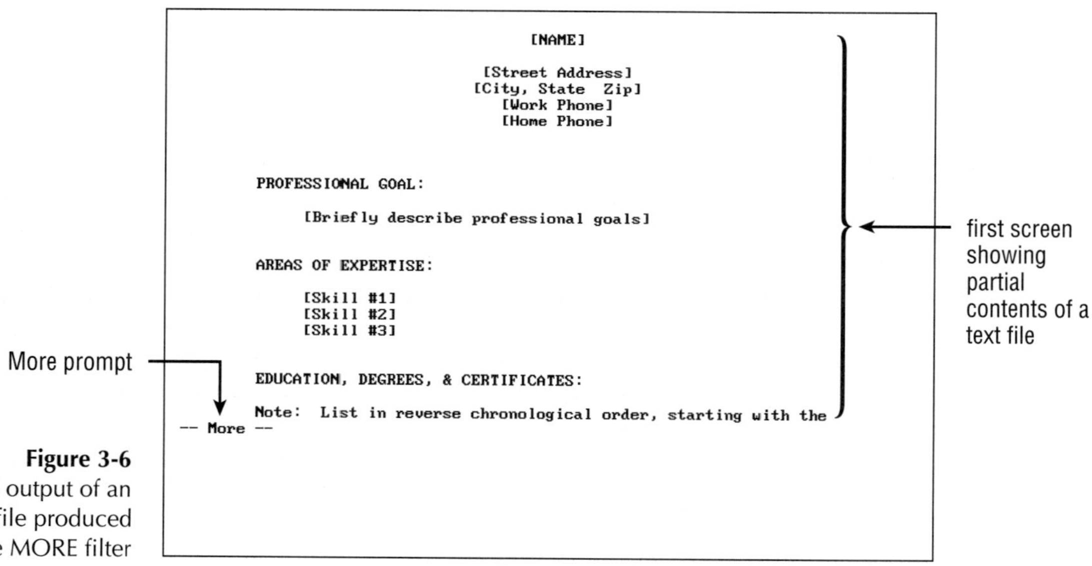

Figure 3-6
Paged output of an ASCII file produced by the MORE filter

2. Press **[Spacebar]** or any other key to continue. DOS displays the next part of this ASCII file, where you enter the client's educational background and degrees as well as professional experience.
3. Press **[Spacebar]** or any other key to continue. DOS displays the next part of this ASCII file, where you enter the client's volunteer experience and computer skills.
4. Press **[Spacebar]** or any other key to continue. DOS displays the remainder of this ASCII file, and then displays the DOS prompt.

You can use the TYPE command, the pipe operator, and the MORE filter to view the contents of "read me" files included with software packages. When software manufacturers release a software package, they include files with the latest information on the use of the product. These files are ASCII files with names such as README, READ.ME, or README.DOC, and they are copied to your hard disk when you install the software. You can then examine these files for important information that you might need to configure the software application so that it works well with the hardware components of your computer system.

You can also use the pipe operator and the MORE filter with any other DOS command that produces more than a full screen of output so that you can view all the information.

VIEWING ASCII FILES IN THE DOS SHELL

Next you want to use the DOS Shell to examine the other résumé template file. As you have discovered, the DOS Shell allows you to work with DOS in a menu-driven and more visually pleasing way than is possible when you work at the DOS prompt. In the file list window, the DOS Shell displays the names of files in the current drive and directory. From this window, you can select commands on the File menu that operate on one or more files. Let's use the DOS Shell to view the contents of an ASCII file.

To access the DOS Shell:

1. Be sure the current drive contains your Tutorial Disk. If necessary, change your current drive.
2. Type **DOSSHELL** and press **[Enter]**. The DOS Shell shows the names of the files in the root directory of drive A (or drive B). The files are listed in alphabetical order—the default order used by the DOS Shell. See Figure 3-7. If the DOS Shell does not list files in alphabetical order on your system, the DOS Shell is using some other order, such as disk order. Also, you might notice other differences if the DOS Shell is customized on your computer.

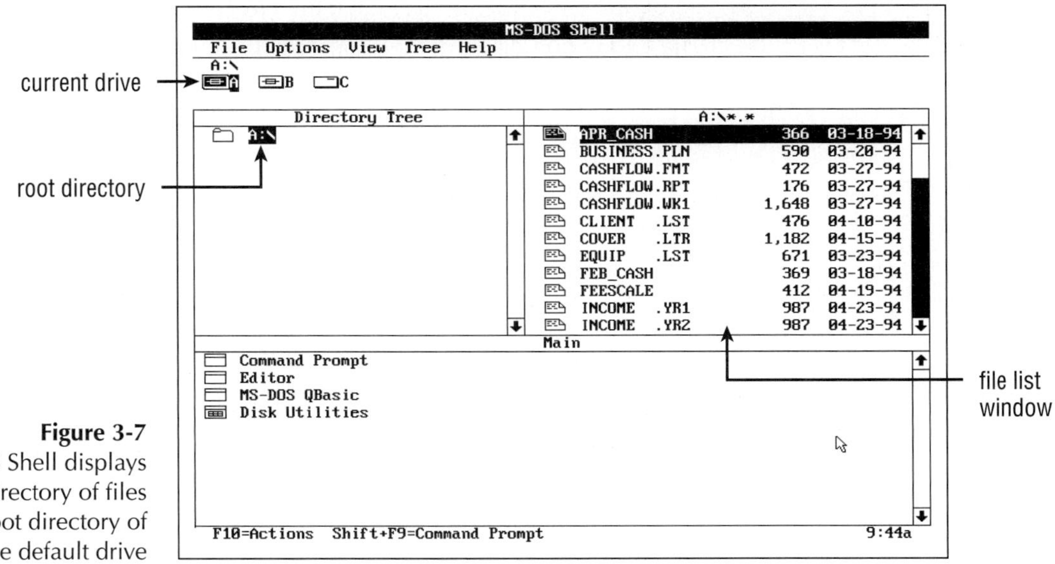

Figure 3-7
The DOS Shell displays a partial directory of files in the root directory of the default drive

3. If the filenames in the file list window are not in alphabetical order, press **[F10]** (Actions), type **O** for the Options menu, and type **F** for File Display Options. The DOS Shell displays the File Display Options dialog box. If necessary, type ***.*** in the Name text box to select all files. If the Descending Order check box has an X, press **[Tab]** until you select this check box, then press **[Spacebar]** to remove the X so that you can use Ascending Order. Press **[Tab]** until you select the Sort By option buttons, point to the Name sort option, and press **[Enter].**

   If the filenames in the file list window are not in alphabetical order and if you are using the mouse, click **Options**, and then click **File Display Options**. The DOS Shell displays the File Display Options dialog box. If necessary, type ***.*** in the Name text box to select all files. If the Descending Order check box has an X, click this **check box** to remove the X so that you can use Ascending Order. Click the **Name option**, then click **OK**.

   The DOS Shell now displays the filenames in the file list window in alphabetical order.

Now let's select the file list window.

4. Press **[Tab]** twice to move the selection cursor to the file list window.

   If you are using the mouse, click the **file list window title bar**.

   The DOS Shell then highlights the title bar for the file list window.

Next, let's select the résumé template file.

5. Type **R** to quickly move the selection cursor to the first file that starts with the letter "R." Then press [↓] (Down Arrow) until you highlight the file named RESUME5.DOC.

   If you are using the mouse, click [↓] (Down Scroll Arrow) on the vertical scroll bar to the right of the filenames until you see the filename RESUME5.DOC. Then click the filename **RESUME5.DOC**.

6. Press **[F10]** (Actions) to access the menu bar. Press **[Enter]** to select the File menu.

   If you are using the mouse, click the **File menu**.

   The DOS Shell displays the drop-down File menu. See Figure 3-8.

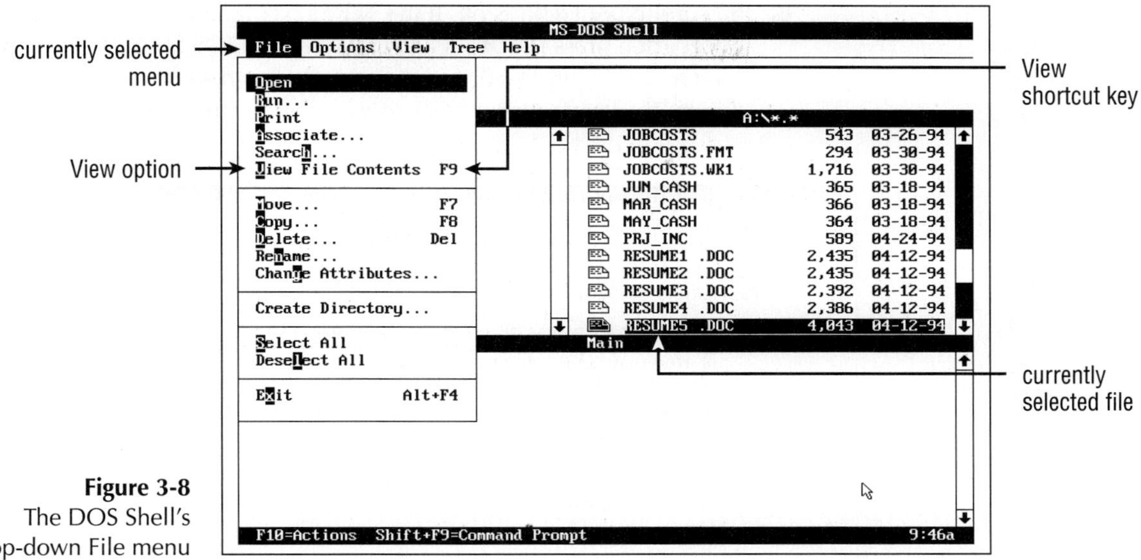

Figure 3-8
The DOS Shell's drop-down File menu

7. Press [↓] (Down Arrow) until you highlight the View File Contents command. Then press **[Enter]**. (Note that you can also use the shortcut View key [F9] to issue the command and bypass the menu.)

   If you are using the mouse, click the **View File Contents** command.

   The DOS Shell displays part of the file. See Figure 3-9. Your screen view might be different. Note that this screen has its own title bar, menu bar, and status bar. Below the menu bar, the DOS Shell provides information on how to use scrolling keys to view the rest of the file. By using [PgDn] (Page Down) and [PgUp] (Page Up), you can scroll forward and backward one screen at a time. You can also use [↓] (Down Arrow) and [↑] (Up Arrow) to adjust your screen view onto the file.

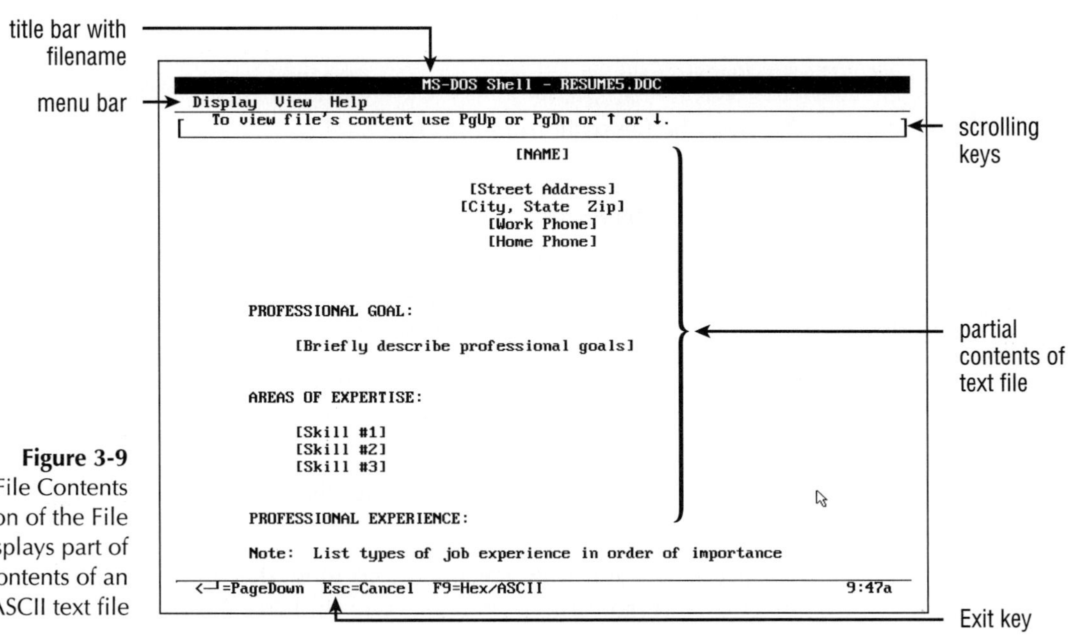

Figure 3-9
The View File Contents option of the File menu displays part of the contents of an ASCII text file

8. Be sure [Num Lock] is off. If the Num Lock light is on, press **[Num Lock]** once. Then press **[PgDn]** (Page Down). The DOS Shell displays the next screen. See Figure 3-10. As you can see, this résumé template is organized differently. It focuses on types of experience rather than on types of jobs.

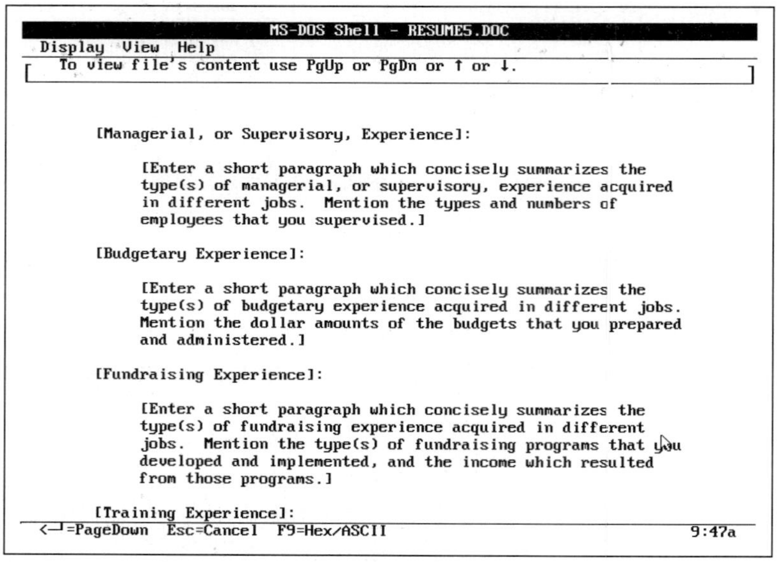

Figure 3-10
Scrolling to the next view of the résumé template file

9. Press **[PgDn]** repeatedly until you view the entire file. The DOS Shell will beep when there are no more screens to view.

Now let's exit this screen view of the file.

10. Press **[Esc]**. You return to the file list window.

While you are in the file list window, you decide to refresh your memory about the company's fee scale.

To view the fee scale from the DOS Shell:

1. Type **F** to move the selection cursor to the first filename that starts with the letter "F"—in this case, FEB_CASH.
2. Press [↓] (Down Arrow) to highlight the filename FEESCALE.

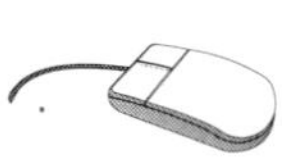

   If you are using a mouse, click the **scroll bar** until the filename FEESCALE appears. Then click **FEESCALE**.
3. Press **[F9]** (View) to examine the fee scale.
4. Press **[Esc]** to exit this screen view.

You are now ready to exit the DOS Shell.

5. Press **[F3]** (Exit). DOS displays the DOS prompt for the current drive.

Although you now know how to view the contents of a file from the DOS prompt and from the DOS Shell, you find the DOS Shell is faster and easier to use for your business needs. The DOS Shell automatically organizes filenames so that you can locate a file more quickly. When you view the contents of a file, it automatically pauses and displays the first screen. You can then adjust the view one screen at a time, or you can adjust that screen view in smaller increments than is possible at the DOS prompt. Furthermore, you can scroll backward through the document, which is not possible at the DOS prompt.

PRINTING AN ASCII FILE FROM THE DOS PROMPT

Next, you want to print copies of the two résumé template files that you will modify for your first client. Then, you can work with those printed copies until you become more familiar with all the files that you will use as an employee.

You can use the PRINT command to print a copy of an ASCII file. The PRINT command has a more complex syntax, with a variety of switches. However, if you want to print a file using the default settings for the PRINT command, you use the following syntax:

PRINT [[*drive:*][*path*]*filename*[...]]

The ellipsis option ([...]) after the filename indicates that you can specify more than one file. If you want to print a series of files, you list each filename separately and include a space between each filename. You might also need to specify the drive and path for each file. If you type "PRINT" without specifying a filename, PRINT displays a list of the files in the print queue. A **print queue** is a list of files that are waiting to be printed.

When you issue this command for the first time from the DOS prompt using the above syntax, DOS prompts you for the name of your printer port. As you may remember, a **port** is a connection between your computer system and another hardware component, such as a printer. Just as DOS assigns names to each of the disk drives, DOS assigns names to each of the ports in your computer system. Because it is possible to connect more than one printer to a computer system, DOS assigns the name PRN to the first printer port on your computer system. The other port names are LPT1, LPT2, and LPT3 for the first through third line printer, or parallel, ports; and COM1, COM2, COM3, and COM4 for the first through fourth communications, or serial, ports. In most cases, you can specify PRN or LPT1 as the printer port, and DOS will know which port to use.

To print a copy of the résumé template file:

1. Be sure the printer is on. If the printer is off, turn on the power switch.
2. Be sure the printer has paper and that the paper is properly aligned.
3. Be sure the printer is on-line and capable of receiving output from the computer. If the printer is off-line, press the **On Line button** once.
4. At the DOS prompt, type **PRINT RESUME1.DOC** and press **[Enter]**. DOS might prompt you for the name of the list device. A *list device* is a printer port—the name of the port DOS uses to list the contents of the file. If DOS does not prompt for the list device, the PRINT program is already loaded into memory.
5. If necessary, press **[Enter]** to accept the default list device, PRN, or if your printer port is different, type in the name of your printer port. DOS loads

the PRINT program into memory and informs you that the file is currently being printed. See Figure 3-11. If the printer does not print the file or if DOS displays an error message, check with your instructor or technical support person. You may need to specify the name of another printer port or check the status of the printer.

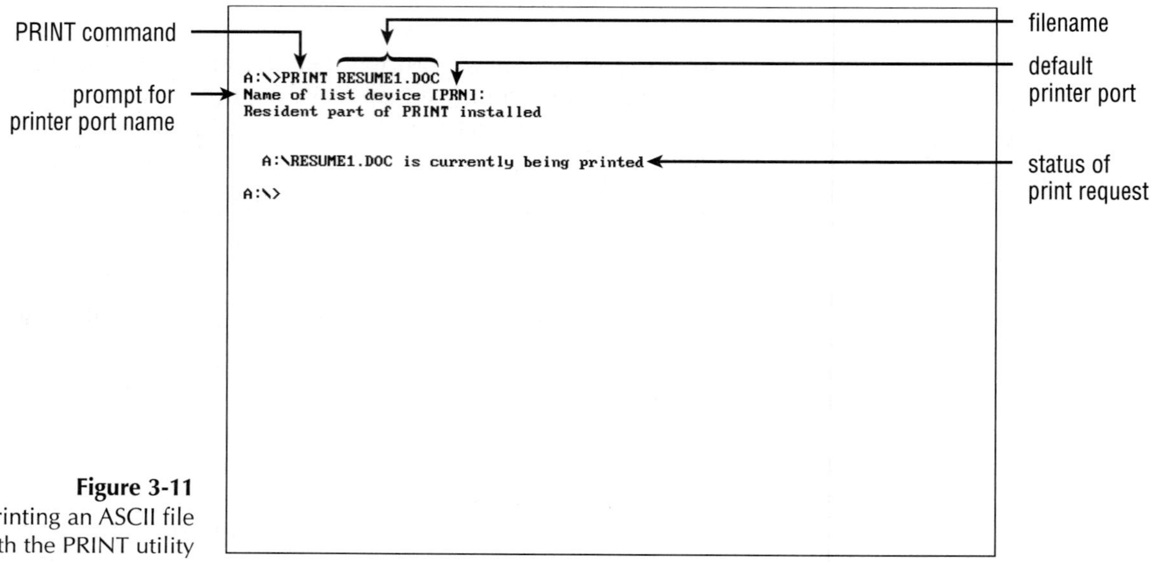

Figure 3-11
Printing an ASCII file with the PRINT utility

6. Remove your printed copy of the résumé template file from the printer.

The PRINT utility is another example of a Terminate-and-Stay-Resident (TSR) program. After DOS loads a TSR into memory, the TSR stays in memory as you work with other utilities or with software applications so that you can continue to use the TSR. The memory allocated to a TSR is not available for use by other programs. In contrast, if you load a software application or a utility that is not a TSR, the memory occupied by that program becomes available when you exit the software application or when the utility completes its intended function. You can access and remove, or unload, some TSRs from memory with the use of a **hot key**—a combination of keys that the TSR recognizes. To remove other TSRs, such as the PRINT utility, from memory, you must reboot your computer system; however, *do not* reboot your computer now.

PRINTING AN ASCII FILE FROM THE DOS SHELL

Next, you want to use the DOS Shell to print a copy of the other résumé template file. Before you can print from the DOS Shell, the PRINT program must be loaded into memory. You can load the PRINT utility before you load the DOS Shell, or you can use the Run option on the File menu in the DOS Shell to load the PRINT utility. Since you have already performed this step, the PRINT program is stored in RAM and ready for use with the DOS Shell.

To print the file with the other résumé template from the DOS Shell:

1. Type **DOSSHELL** and press **[Enter]**.
2. Press **[Tab]** twice to move the selection cursor to the file list window.

   If you are using the mouse, click the **file list window title bar**.

Now let's select the résumé template file.

3. Type **R** to quickly move the selection cursor to the first file that starts with the letter "R." Then, press [↓] (Down Arrow) until you highlight the file named RESUME5.DOC.

   If you are using the mouse, click the **down scroll arrow** on the vertical scroll bar to the right of the filenames until you see the filename RESUME5.DOC. Then, click the filename **RESUME5.DOC**.
4. Press **[F10]** (Actions), and then press **[Enter]** to select the File menu. Press [↓] (Down Arrow) twice to highlight the Print option, then press **[Enter]**.

   If you are using the mouse, click the **File menu** and then the **Print command**.

   The DOS Shell relays a request to the PRINT program to print a copy of the selected file.
5. Remove your printed copy of the résumé template file from the printer.
6. Press **[F3]** (Exit) to exit the DOS Shell.

You have completed the job for your first client, so you decide to take a short break before you start on your next task.

COPYING FILES

Your supervisor asks you to make a copy of one of the résumé template files and to revise it so that you have a new version of that résumé format. These résumé templates are invaluable in your job because they enable you to provide fast turnaround times for clients and to produce a variety of résumés in popular formats.

You can use the COPY command to copy the contents of an existing file into a new file on the same diskette (Figure 3-12). The COPY command is an internal command that you can use in a variety of ways. If you want to copy a file to another location, without specifying any switches, the syntax is as follows:

COPY [*source*] [*destination*]

The file that you copy is the **source file**—in this case, RESUME5.DOC. The new file that you produce from the copy operation is the **destination file**, or **target file**—in this case, RESUME6.DOC. You might need to specify all or part of the path for each file so that DOS can locate the source file and create a destination file where you need it. Recall that the full path includes the disk drive name, the directory name, and the filename. Because your current drive is the drive that contains your Tutorial Disk, all you need to specify are the source and target filenames.

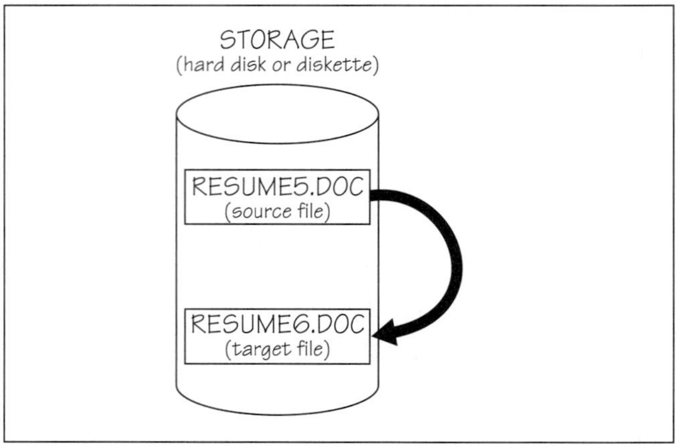

Figure 3-12
Copying a file to the same diskette with a new filename

5.0 ***6.0*** ***6.2***

Before you make a copy of a file, you should use the DIR command to verify that the destination disk or directory does not already contain a file with the same name as the one you intend to use for the new file if you are using DOS 5.0 or 6.0. If you inadvertently use an existing filename, DOS 5.0 and 6.0 will copy over that file without warning you, and you will lose that file's contents. By default, DOS 6.2 automatically asks for verification before it overwrites a file. After you make a copy of a file, you should verify that the copy operation worked.

To copy the file containing the format for preparing a résumé:

1. If necessary, power on your computer system, install DOSKEY, and specify default switches for the DIR command using the instructions on pages 55 through 58.
2. Be sure the current drive is the one with your Tutorial Disk. If this is not the case, you *must* specify the drive name for the source and target files in the next three steps.
3. Type **DIR RESUME**? and press **[Enter]** to check that the Tutorial Disk does not already contain a file named RESUME6.DOC. DOS assumes you want to use the current drive and that you want to include any file extensions. Also, filenames are displayed in alphabetical order because earlier you specified default switches in the DOS environment. You do not need to repeat those switches with the DIR command. Because your diskette does not contain a file named RESUME6.DOC, you are ready to perform the copy operation.
4. Type **COPY RESUME5.DOC RESUME6.DOC** and press **[Enter]**. DOS displays the message "1 file(s) copied" and then displays the DOS prompt again.

Now verify that the new file exists.

5. Press [↑] (Up Arrow) until you recall the command DIR RESUME? and then press **[Enter]**. The file RESUME6.DOC is shown in the directory. See Figure 3-13. Note that the new file contains the same number of bytes and date and time of creation as RESUME5.DOC. Because you have not yet made any changes to RESUME6.DOC, it is identical to RESUME5.DOC.

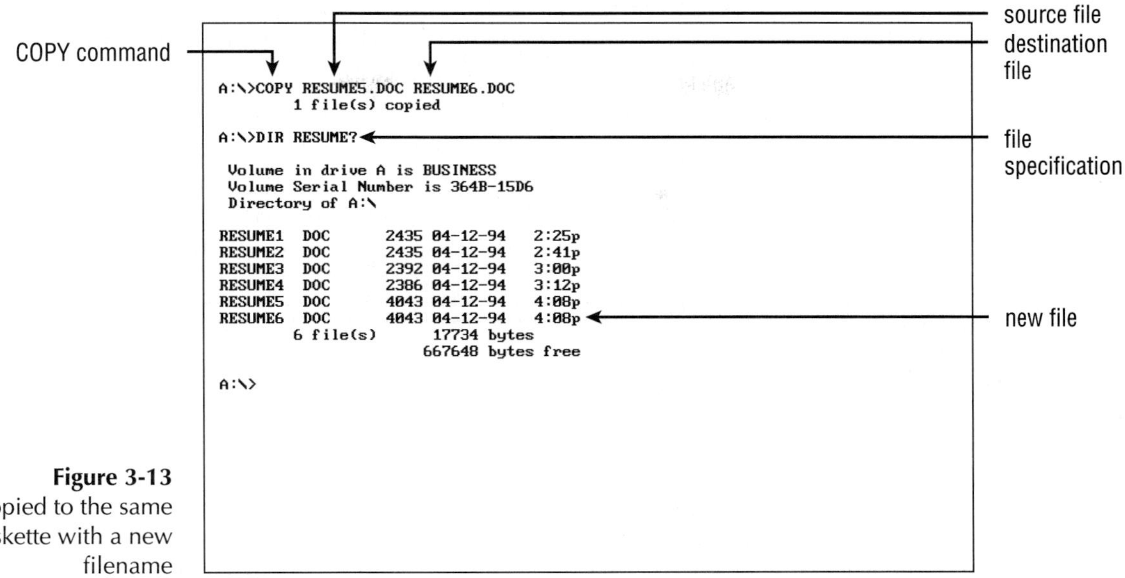

Figure 3-13
File copied to the same diskette with a new filename

The computer systems in your office have different types of disk drives to accommodate different types of diskettes. For example, your computer has a 3½-inch and a 5¼-inch high-density drive. Other computers have only one high-density drive for either a 3½-inch or a 5¼-inch diskette. Because you might work on one of the other computers, you will need to know how to copy from one disk drive to another as well as to and from a hard disk drive.

The next three sections describe how to copy files from one drive to another from the DOS prompt. Complete the section or sections that apply to the number of disk drives of the computer you are using.

Copying a File Using One Disk Drive

You want to copy the file RESUME6.DOC from your Tutorial Disk to your Exercises Disk so that you have a backup copy of this new file.

If you have a single disk drive, you can copy from one diskette to another diskette using the same drive. DOS treats this disk drive as drive A *and* drive B. If your computer has two diskette drives, skip this section because you *cannot* perform this operation.

To copy a file to another diskette using a computer *with only one diskette drive*:

1. Be sure drive A is the current drive.
2. Remove your Tutorial Disk, and insert your Exercise Disk into the diskette drive.
3. Type **DIR RESUME?** and press **[Enter]** to verify that you do not have a file named RESUME6.DOC on your Exercise Disk.
4. Remove your Exercise Disk, and insert your Tutorial Disk into the diskette drive.

5. Type **COPY RESUME6.DOC B:** and press **[Enter]**. After DOS copies the file, it prompts you to insert the diskette for drive B (the target diskette) and to press any key when you are ready.
6. Remove the Tutorial Disk, and insert your Exercise Disk. After the drive light goes off, press **[Spacebar]** or any other key. DOS displays the message "1 file(s) copied." See Figure 3-14. DOS copies the file to the target diskette and prompts you to insert the diskette for drive A (the source diskette) and to press any key when you are ready.

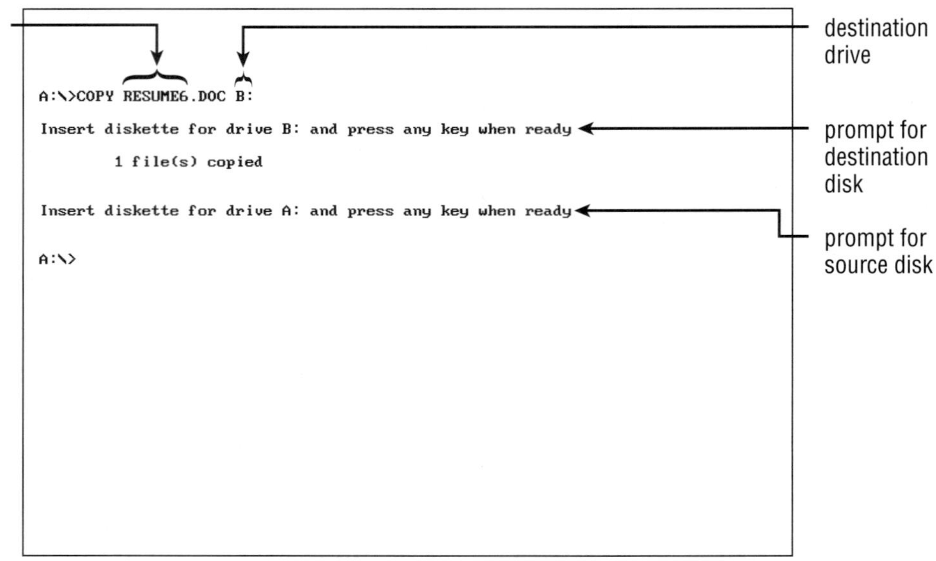

Figure 3-14
Copying a file to another diskette using a system with one diskette drive

7. Remove the Exercise Disk, and insert your Tutorial Disk. After the drive light goes out, press **[Spacebar]** or any other key. DOS displays the DOS prompt for drive A.
8. Remove your Tutorial Disk, and insert your Exercise Disk.

Now verify that the copy operation worked.

9. Press [↑] (Up Arrow) to recall the command DIR RESUME? and press **[Enter]**. You should see the filename RESUME6.DOC in the directory listing.
10. Remove the Exercise Disk, and insert your Tutorial Disk into the diskette drive.

Copying a File Using Two Disk Drives

A coworker has asked you to copy RESUME6.DOC from your diskette to his diskette, so that he can use it to prepare a résumé for one of his clients.

If your computer has two disk drives, you can copy a file from a diskette in one drive to a diskette in another drive, even if the diskettes are different sizes and have different storage capacities (Figure 3-15). You can copy a file from a 5¼-inch disk drive to another 5¼-inch disk drive, from a 3½-inch disk drive to another 3½-inch disk drive, from a 5¼-inch disk drive to a 3½-inch disk drive, and from a 3½-inch disk drive to a 5¼-inch disk drive.

To complete this section, you will copy a file from your Tutorial Disk to the diskette in the other disk drive. Therefore, you will need an additional formatted diskette that matches the size of your other disk drive. *See pages 19 through 27 for instructions on how to format a diskette.*

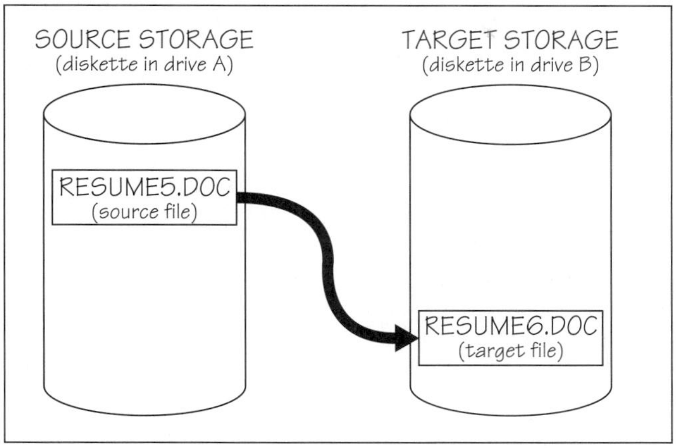

Figure 3-15
Copying a file from a diskette in drive A to a diskette in drive B

To copy a file from drive A to B, or from drive B to A:

1. If necessary, format an additional diskette for use in your other diskette drive as a destination diskette. *Do not format your Tutorial Disk or your Exercise Disk.*
2. Insert your Tutorial Disk (the source diskette) into one of the diskette drives.
3. Be sure you insert the newly formatted diskette (the destination diskette) that matches the size of the other diskette drive in the computer.
4. If you are copying from drive A to B, type **COPY A:\RESUME6.DOC B:** and press **[Enter]**. If you are copying from drive B to A, type **COPY B:\RESUME6.DOC A:** and press **[Enter]**. DOS copies this file from one diskette drive to another. If you specify the location of the source drive, you can copy from either drive. If you perform the copy operation from drive C, as shown in Figure 3-16, you must specify the drive name of both the source and target files. If you do not specify the name of the target file, DOS assumes you want to use the same name.

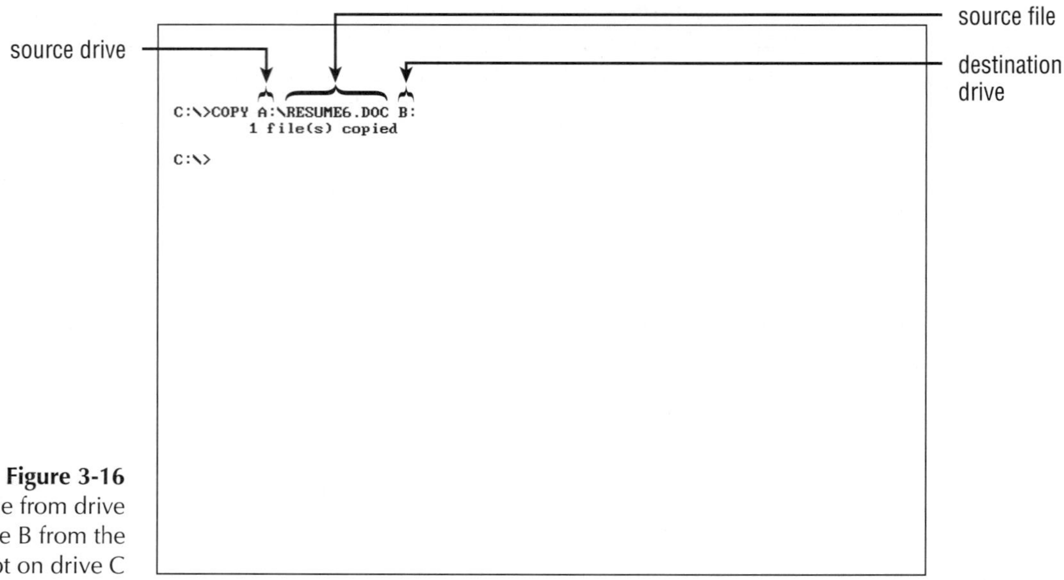

Figure 3-16
Copying a file from drive A to drive B from the DOS prompt on drive C

Next, you want to verify the copy operation.

5. If drive B contains your target diskette, type **DIR B:** and press **[Enter]**. If drive A contains your target diskette, type **DIR A:** and press **[Enter]**. You should see the filename RESUME6.DOC in the directory listing.

Copying a File or Files from a Diskette to a Hard Disk, and from a Hard Disk to a Diskette

You want to copy your résumé template file, RESUME6.DOC, from your diskette onto your hard disk drive so that you can prepare a résumé for one of your clients. You can copy files from a diskette to a hard drive, or vice versa (Figure 3-17). If you are completing the copy procedure in a computer lab, ask your instructor or technical support person for permission to copy to the root directory of the hard disk.

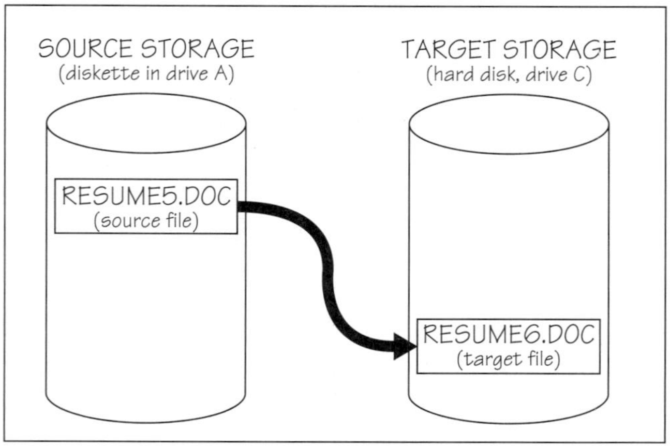

Figure 3-17
Copying a file from a diskette in drive A to a hard disk

To copy a file on your Tutorial Disk to the hard disk:

1. Be sure the current drive contains your Tutorial Disk.
2. Type **DIR C:\RESUME6.DOC** and press **[Enter]** to verify that the hard disk does not contain a file with the name RESUME6.DOC in the root directory. If you see the message "File not found," as shown near the top of Figure 3-18, you can complete the next two steps. If DOS informs you there is a file named RESUME6.DOC, ask your instructor or technical support person if you can copy over that file. Another student might have already copied that file to the hard disk drive. The volume label, serial number, and number of bytes free on your drive C will be different.

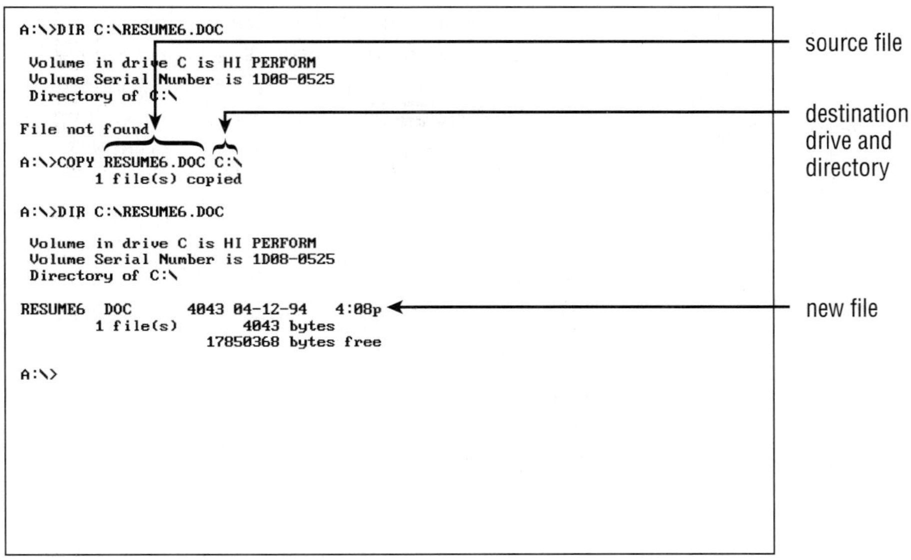

Figure 3-18
Copying a file from a diskette to the hard drive

3. Type **COPY RESUME6.DOC C:** and press **[Enter]**. The Backslash (\) in C:\ instructs DOS to copy the file to the root directory of drive C. If you do not specify a filename for the target file, DOS uses the same name as that of the source file.
4. Press **[↑]** (Up Arrow) until you recall the command DIR C:\RESUME6.DOC. Press **[Enter]** to verify the copy operation. DOS displays the name of the copied file. See Figure 3-18.

Later, after you prepare the client résumé, you will want to copy your client file from the hard drive to a diskette so that you have a backup, or duplicate copy, of that file. To copy from the hard disk to a diskette, you just reverse the process described above: You specify the source drive as drive C and the target drive as either drive A or drive B.

After copying RESUME6.DOC to the hard disk, you decide it might be a good idea to copy all the résumé template files to the hard disk so that you can quickly find the one you need for a client.

To copy the résumé template files on your Tutorial Disk to the hard disk:

1. Type **CLS** and press **[Enter]** to clear the screen.
2. Type **DIR C:\RESUME*.*** and press **[Enter]** to verify that the hard disk does not contain files in the root directory that start with the name RESUME, other than RESUME6.DOC, which you just copied to the hard disk. If DOS informs you there are other files that start with the name "RESUME," ask your instructor or technical support person if you can copy over those files. Another student may have already copied those files to the hard disk.
3. Type **COPY RESUME*.* C:** and press **[Enter]**. DOS copies the files to the root directory of the hard disk. See Figure 3-19. If you do not specify filenames for the target files, DOS uses the source filenames. If you are using DOS 5.0 or 6.0, DOS copies RESUME6.DOC to the hard disk again and overwrites the copy already stored there. If you are using DOS 6.2, DOS might ask if you want to overwrite the existing file on drive C. If this occurs, type **Y** for Yes and press **[Enter]**.

5.0

6.0

6.2

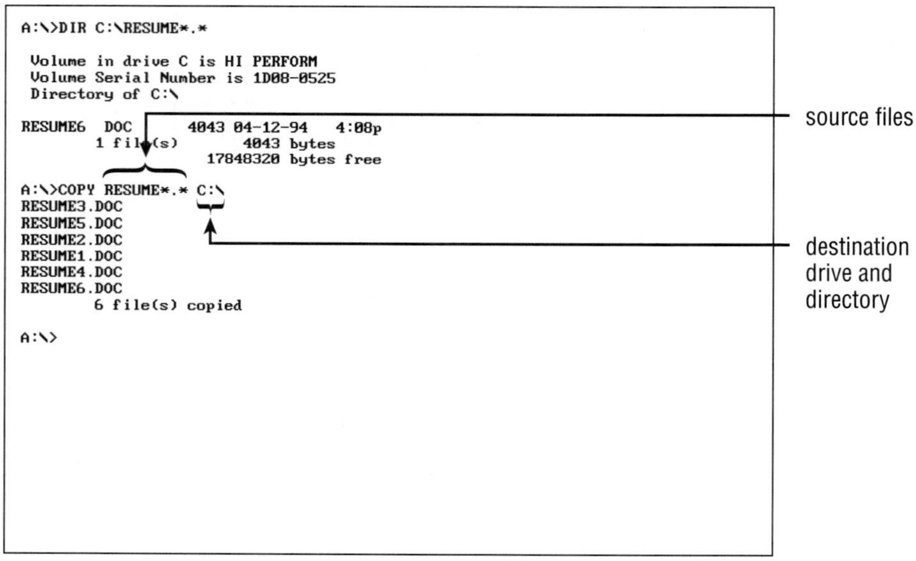

Figure 3-19
Copying files from a diskette in drive A to the hard disk

4. Press [↑] (Up Arrow) until you recall the command DIR C:\RESUME*.* and then press **[Enter]**. DOS displays the copied files and uses the default switches in the DOS environment to control the file display. See Figure 3-20.

```
A:\>DIR C:\RESUME*.*

 Volume in drive C is HI PERFORM
 Volume Serial Number is 1A81-8E17
 Directory of C:\

RESUME1  DOC       2435 04-12-94   2:25p
RESUME2  DOC       2435 04-12-94   2:41p
RESUME3  DOC       2392 04-12-94   3:00p
RESUME4  DOC       2386 04-12-94   3:12p
RESUME5  DOC       4043 04-12-94   4:08p
RESUME6  DOC       4043 04-12-94   4:08p
        6 file(s)       17734 bytes
                     24100864 bytes free

A:\>
```

new files on drive C

Figure 3-20
Verifying a copy operation to the hard disk

COPYING A FILE IN THE DOS SHELL

Next, you want to copy the template for projecting business income on a yearly basis so that you can produce a new template for projecting income on a quarterly basis. For each job, staff members will develop new files from this template and other templates. To work more efficiently, you want to learn how to use the DOS Shell to copy files.

To copy this template file using the DOS Shell:

1. Be sure the current drive contains your Tutorial Disk.
2. Type **DOSSHELL** and press **[Enter]**.
3. Press **[Tab]** twice to move the selection cursor to the file list window.

   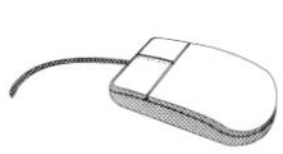

   If you are using the mouse, click the **file list window's title bar**.
4. Type **P** to select the first, and only, file that has the letter "P" at the beginning of its filename.

   If you are using a mouse, click in the **scroll bar** to the right of the filenames until the filename PRJ_INC comes into view; then, click **PRJ_INC**.
5. Press **[F10]** (Actions), press **[Enter]** to select the File menu, and type **C** to select the Copy command.

   If you are using the mouse, click **File**, then click **Copy**.

   Note that you can also use the shortcut Copy key, [F8]. The DOS Shell displays the Copy File dialog box. See Figure 3-21. Next to the From prompt is the name of the currently highlighted file, which is the source file. The DOS Shell will copy this file. Next to the To prompt, the DOS Shell displays the current drive and directory, which is also the target drive and directory. If you want to use another drive, you can type a new drive name. You can also specify a different filename for the copied file. Because this is the correct source file and target drive and directory, you do not need to make any changes.

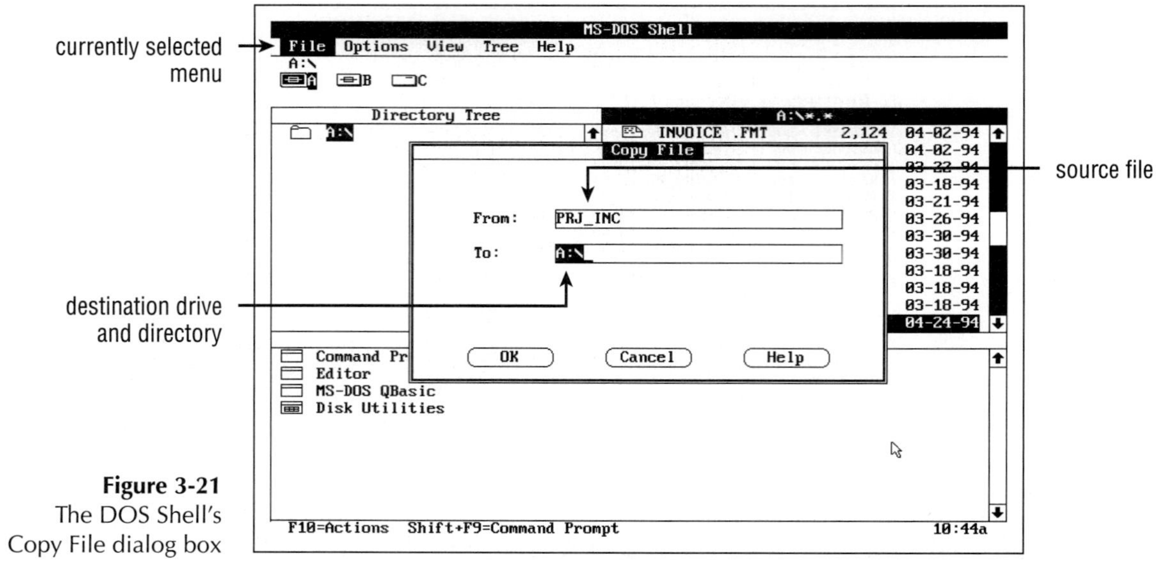

Figure 3-21
The DOS Shell's Copy File dialog box

6. Be sure [Num Lock] is off. Then press **[End]** to position the cursor so that you can enter a filename after the drive name.

   If you are using the mouse, click **after the drive name**.

   If you do not press [End] or click after the drive name, the filename that you type will write over the drive name. If this happens, you might need to retype the drive name before typing the filename.

7. Type **QTR_INC**. Then press **[Enter]**. *Remember to include the underline character in the filename.*

   If you are using the mouse, type **QTR_INC**, then click **OK**.

   The DOS Shell copies the file. If a file exists with this same filename, the DOS Shell will ask you to verify that you want to copy over that file.

8. Press [↓] (Down Arrow) to view the next filename. The next filename is RESUME1.DOC.

If your version of DOS does not display QTR_INC as the next filename, you must instruct the DOS Shell to reread your diskette and update the list of filenames in the file list window.

To reread your Tutorial Disk and update the file listing:

1. Press **[F10]** (Actions), press [→] (Right Arrow) twice to highlight View, and press **[Enter]** to select View. The DOS Shell displays the View menu. See Figure 3-22.

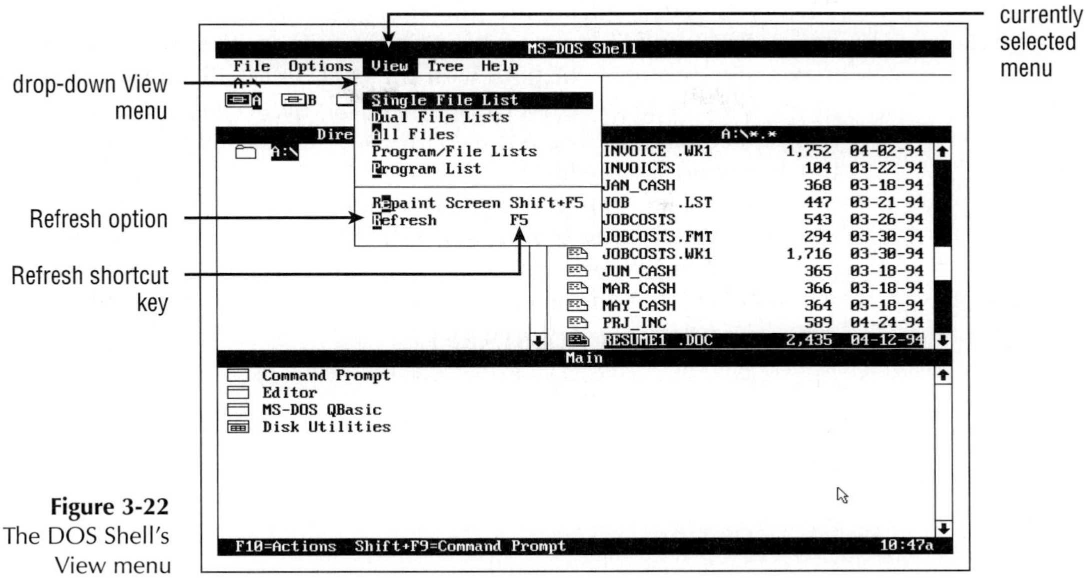

Figure 3-22
The DOS Shell's View menu

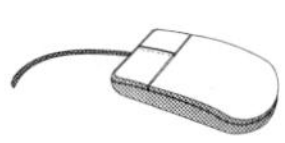

2. Press [↓] (Down Arrow) until you highlight Refresh and press **[Enter]**.

   If you are using the mouse, click the **View** menu, then click the **Refresh command**.

   You can also use [F5] (Refresh) to update the screen. The selection cursor returns to the drive window.
3. Press **[Tab]** twice to return to the file list window.

   If you are using the mouse, click the **file list window title bar**.
4. Type **Q** to highlight the new file QTR_INC. Note that this file currently has the same size and date as PRJ_INC. Because you have not yet made any changes to QTR_INC, it is identical to PRJ_INC.
5. Press **[F3]** (Exit) to exit the DOS Shell.

In your business, you can quickly make copies of your template files with the DOS Shell, as you have seen. You can then modify them to produce final copies of documents for clients.

RENAMING FILES

You want to rename some of the files on your diskette so that the filenames more clearly identify the contents of the files. Later, when you are facing deadlines, you will not need to spend valuable time checking to make sure you have the correct file. Again, you want to compare this type of file operation at the DOS prompt with the use of the DOS Shell.

You can use the RENAME command, or its abbreviated version, REN, to change the name of a file. If you use wildcards with these commands, you can change the names of a group of files. The general syntax for these internal commands is as follows:

RENAME [*drive:*][*path*]*filename1 filename2*

REN [*drive:*][*path*]*filename1 filename2*

When you specify *filename1* (the source filename), you must include the drive and path if the file is on another drive or in another directory. However, you *never* specify a drive or path with the destination filename. If you do, DOS displays an error message because it thinks you are attempting to move the file, and this command does not move files. The destination filename, *filename2*, is the new name for the file.

The first file that you want to rename is JOBCOSTS. You have two other files on your diskette that have JOBCOSTS as the main filename but that have descriptive file extensions. Because this file is a report, you want to rename it JOBCOSTS.RPT. You can enter the RENAME command in two ways:

REN JOBCOSTS JOBCOSTS.RPT

REN JOBCOSTS *.RPT

If you substitute an asterisk wildcard for the main part of the filename in the destination file, DOS assumes you want to use the same name as the source file. This feature saves keystroking.

To rename the JOBCOSTS file from the DOS prompt:

1. Be sure the current drive contains your Tutorial Disk.
2. Type **DIR JOBCOSTS** and press **[Enter]** to verify the file exists. DOS lists files with and without file extensions. See Figure 3-23.

file specification

```
A:\>DIR JOBCOSTS

 Volume in drive A is BUSINESS
 Volume Serial Number is 364B-15D6
 Directory of A:\

JOBCOSTS            543 03-26-94   8:51a
JOBCOSTS FMT        294 03-30-94   2:22p
JOBCOSTS WK1       1716 03-30-94   2:22p
        3 file(s)        2553 bytes
                       666624 bytes free

A:\>
```

selected files

Figure 3-23
Checking a directory before renaming a file

3. Type **REN JOBCOSTS *.RPT** and press **[Enter]**. DOS assumes that you want to rename the file on the current drive and that the main part of the new filename is the same. DOS will not let you rename a file if there is already a file by the name that you want to use. *You can also use RENAME instead of REN.*

4. Press **[↑]** (Up Arrow) until you recall the command DIR JOBCOSTS, and press **[Enter]** to verify the change. DOS added a file extension when it renamed the file. See Figure 3-24.

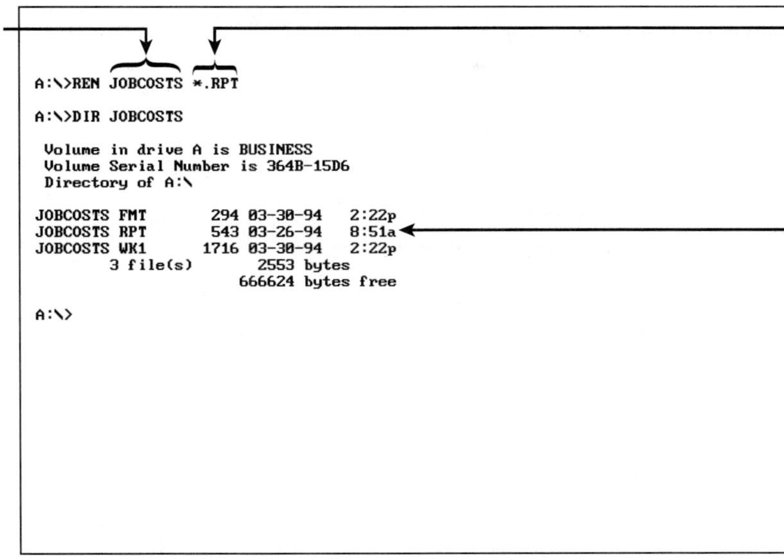

Figure 3-24
The REN command changes the name of a file

RENAMING FILES IN THE DOS SHELL

The next file that you want to rename is COVER.LTR. Because it is the letter sent with a client's résumé, you want to rename it RESUME.LTR. This time you want to use the DOS Shell to rename the file.

To rename the COVER.LTR file from the DOS Shell:

1. Be sure the current drive contains your Tutorial Disk. Then type **DOSSHELL** and press **[Enter]**.
2. Press **[Tab]** until the selection cursor moves to the file list window.

   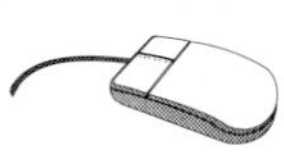

   If you are using the mouse, click the **file list window title bar**.
3. Press **[↓]** (Down Arrow) to highlight the filename COVER.LTR.

   If you are using the mouse, click the filename **COVER.LTR**.
4. Press **[F10]** (Actions), press **[Enter]** to select the File menu, and type **N** to select the Rename option.

   If you are using the mouse, click **File**, then click **Rename**.

   The DOS Shell displays the Rename File dialog box. See Figure 3-25. The Current name field shows the file's current name. Next to the New name prompt, you type the name you want to use.

selected file

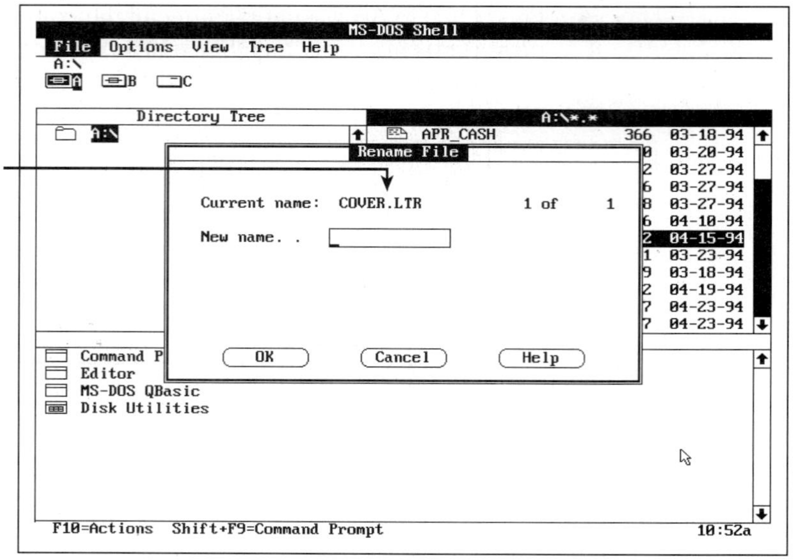

Figure 3-25
The DOS Shell's Rename File dialog box

5. Type **RESUME.LTR** and press **[Enter]**.

   If you are using the mouse, type **RESUME.LTR** and then click **OK**.

   After the DOS Shell renames the file, it places the new filename in the file list in alphabetical order. The original filename, COVER.LTR, is no longer displayed because you changed the filename.

6. Type **R** to display the filenames that start with the letter "R." The selection cursor moves to the filename RESUME.LTR. You successfully renamed the file with the cover letter for résumés.

7. Press **[F3]** (Exit) to exit the DOS Shell.

When you name a file, the name you select may be logical at the time, but later, you may realize that there is a better name for that file. You can rename it from the DOS prompt or the DOS Shell. The DOS Shell has the added advantage of updating the list of filenames quickly.

DELETING FILES

You realize that there are a couple of files you do not need and you want to remove them from your diskette so that they do not take up valuable space. You can delete files from the DOS prompt with the DEL or ERASE commands. The general syntax is as follows:

DEL [*drive:*][*path*]*filename*

ERASE [*drive:*][*path*]*filename*

Both commands are internal commands, and both produce the same results.

Deleting files from the DOS prompt is risky. If you use wildcards, you can inadvertently delete important files. DOS does not ask you if you are sure you want to delete a file or a group of files, except in one case. If you enter DEL *.* at the DOS prompt, DOS will automatically ask you if you want to delete all the files in the directory. As a precautionary measure, you should first test your file specification with the DIR command. If the DIR command selects the files you expect, then you can use the DEL or ERASE command with the same file specification.

You can also use the **Prompt for Verification switch**, /P. When you use this switch, DOS displays a prompt and asks you to verify whether or not you want to delete the file.

You no longer need the JOB.LST file, so you decide to delete it.

To delete the file named JOB.LST at the DOS prompt:

1. Be sure the current drive contains your Tutorial Disk.
2. Type **DIR JOB.LST** and press **[Enter]** to verify that the file exists. If you specify the exact name of a file, the directory listing will include only that file.
3. Type **DEL JOB.LST /P** and press **[Enter]**. DOS prompts for verification, displaying the message, "Delete (Y/N)?". *You can also use the ERASE command to achieve the same result.*
4. Type **Y**. You do not need to press the Enter key. DOS displays the DOS prompt after deleting the file.

Now you want to verify the deletion.

5. Press **[↑]** (Up Arrow) until you recall the command DIR JOB.LST, and then press **[Enter]**. The file JOB.LST is no longer on your diskette. See Figure 3-26.

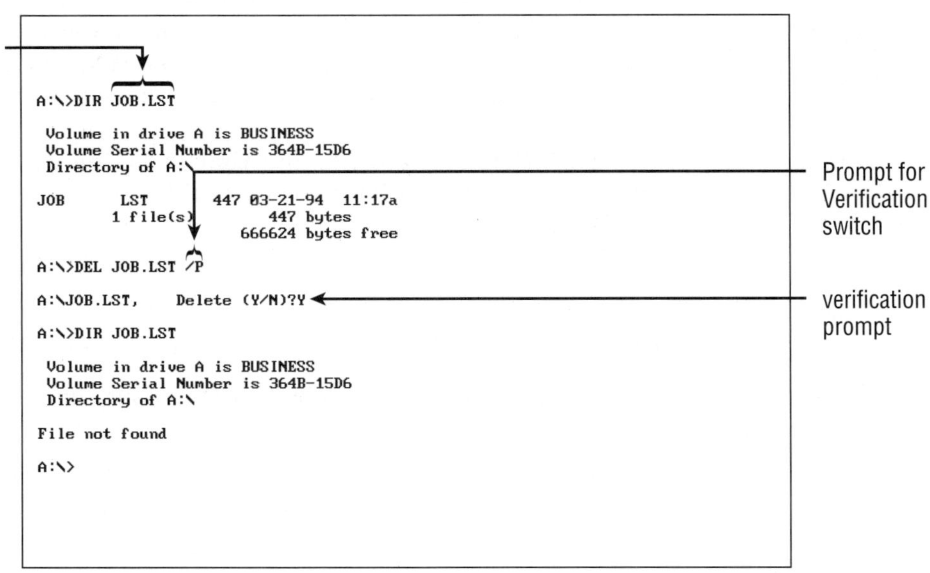

Figure 3-26
The DEL command deletes a file after prompting for verification

Deleting a File from Another Drive

While you are thinking of it, you decide to delete this same file from the duplicate copy of your Tutorial Disk. You decide to perform this operation from drive C so that you know how to delete a file from another drive. When you delete a file on another drive, you must specify the drive name and in some cases, the filename's path.

To delete a file from another drive:

1. Type **C:** and press **[Enter]**. DOS displays the prompt for drive C.
2. Remove the Tutorial Disk from the diskette drive and insert your Exercise Disk.
3. Type **DIR A:\JOB.LST** (or **DIR B:\JOB.LST**) and press **[Enter]** to verify that the file exists on the diskette in the diskette drive. The Backslash (\) tells DOS to check the root directory of the drive you specify for the filename.
4. Type **DEL A:\JOB.LST /P** (or **DEL B:\JOB.LST /P**) and press **[Enter]**. DOS prompts for verification. Again, you are specifying the file's exact location using the drive name and path (the Backslash).
5. Type **Y**. You do not need to press the Enter key. DOS displays the DOS prompt after deleting the file.

Now you want to verify the deletion.

6. Press **[↑]** (Up Arrow) until you recall the command DIR A:\JOB.LST or DIR B:\JOB.LST. Then press **[Enter]**. The file JOB.LST is no longer on your diskette.
7. Remove the Exercise Disk, and insert your Tutorial Disk into the diskette drive.
8. Type **A:** (or **B:**) to change to the disk drive that contains your Tutorial Disk.

DELETING FILES IN THE DOS SHELL

In the DOS Shell, you have more control over deleting files than you do at the DOS prompt. By default, the DOS Shell automatically displays a prompt asking you if you are sure you want to delete the selected file. Unlike working at the DOS prompt, in the DOS Shell you do not have to remember to use the Prompt for Verification switch.

SCHEDULE is another file that is taking up valuable space on your diskette. Because you have a copy of this file, you decide to use the DOS Shell to delete it.

To delete the file named SCHEDULE using the DOS Shell:

1. Be sure the current drive contains your Tutorial Disk. Then type **DOSSHELL** and press **[Enter]**.
2. Press **[Tab]** until the selection cursor moves to the file list window.

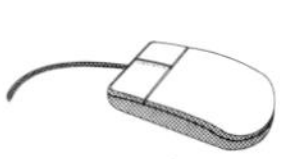

   If you are using the mouse, click the **file list window title bar**.
3. Type **S** and note that the DOS Shell moves the cursor to the first file that starts with the letter "S"—the file you want, SCHEDULE.

   If you are using the mouse, click in the **scroll bar** to the right of the filenames until the DOS Shell displays the filename SCHEDULE. Then click the filename **SCHEDULE**.

4. Press the shortcut key **[Del]** or **[Delete]**. The DOS Shell displays the Delete File Confirmation dialog box. See Figure 3-27. The cursor is positioned on the Yes button. (*You can also use the Delete command on the File menu to delete files.*)

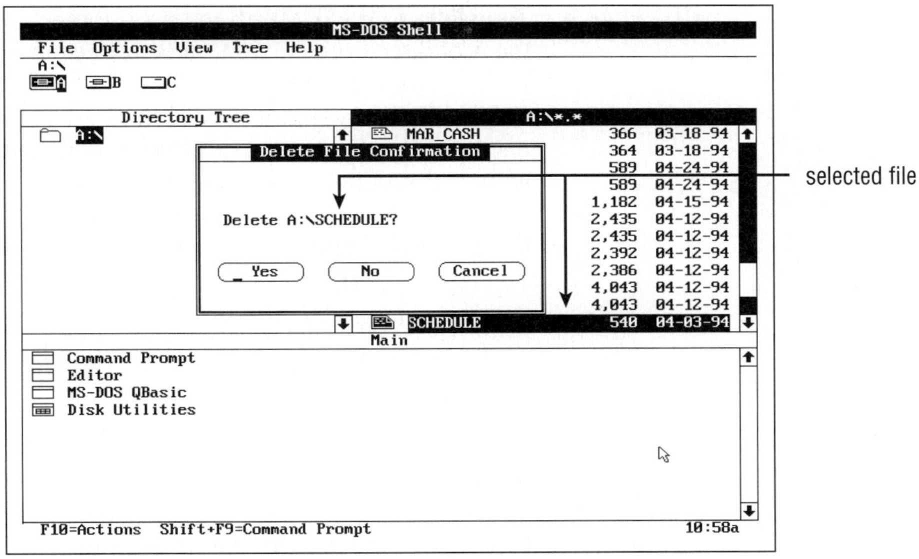

Figure 3-27
The DOS Shell's Delete File Confirmation dialog box

5. Press **[Enter]** to delete the file.

   If you are using the mouse, click the **Yes button**.

   The DOS Shell displays a dialog box that verifies it is deleting the filename you specified. Then the DOS Shell updates the file list.
6. Press [↓] (Down Arrow) twice. The filename SCHEDULE is no longer in the file list.
7. Press **[F3]** (Exit) to exit the DOS Shell.

When combined with the DIR command, the COPY, RENAME, and DEL commands assist you in one of the most important tasks you face when you use a computer system—managing your files. You can more easily and efficiently perform file operations from the DOS Shell, with less chance of inadvertently losing files.

FINISHING UP

If you completed the section of this tutorial where you copied the résumé template files from your Tutorial Disk to drive C, you will need to remove those files from your computer system's hard disk.

To remove the résumé template files from drive C:

1. Type **C:** and press **[Enter]** to change to drive C.
2. Remove your Tutorial Disk from drive A so that you do not inadvertently delete the résumé template files from that diskette.
3. Type **DIR C:\RESUME*.*** and press **[Enter]** to verify that these files are in the root directory of drive C. If the directory listing contains the filenames RESUME1.DOC, RESUME2.DOC, RESUME3.DOC, RESUME4.DOC, RESUME5.DOC, and RESUME6.DOC, complete the next step. If DOS displays other files in the directory listing, check with your instructor or technical support person before you attempt to delete files in the next step. If you do not see any files that start with the name "RESUME," you do not need to perform the next step.
4. Type **DEL C:\RESUME*.*** and press **[Enter]**. DOS deletes these files from the root directory of drive C.

◆

SUMMARY

In this tutorial, you learned the importance of ASCII files and studied many of their features. You viewed the contents of an ASCII file with the TYPE command at the DOS prompt and with the View File Contents option on the File menu in the DOS Shell. You used the pipe redirection operator and the MORE filter with the TYPE command at the DOS prompt to display the contents of an ASCII file one screen at a time. You printed an ASCII file with the PRINT command at the DOS prompt and with the Print option on the File menu in the DOS Shell.

You copied files with the COPY command at the DOS prompt and the Copy option on the File menu in the DOS Shell. You copied files to the same diskette, a different diskette, and a hard drive using a different or the same filename. You renamed files with the REN command at the DOS prompt and the Rename option on the File menu in the DOS Shell. You deleted files with the DEL command at the DOS prompt and with the Delete key in the DOS Shell.

You worked with filenames in the file list window in the DOS Shell, and you updated the directory with the Refresh option on the View menu.

Command Reference

DOS Commands	
COPY [*source*] [*destination*]	An internal command that copies the contents of a file (called the source file) and produces a new file (called the destination, or target, file)
DEL [*drive*:][*path*]*filename* [/P]	An internal command that deletes a file or a group of files; the Prompt for Verification switch (/P) asks you if you want to delete the file(s)
ERASE [*drive*:][*path*]*filename* [/P]	An internal command that deletes a file or a group of files; the Prompt for Verification switch (/P) asks you if you want to delete the file(s)
[*command-name*] ¦ MORE	A DOS filter, or external command, that modifies output of a DOS command and displays it one screen at a time
PRINT [[*drive*:][*path*]*filename*[...]]	An external command that prints a text file
RENAME [*drive*:][*path*]*filename1* *filename2* REN [*drive*:][*path*]*filename1* *filename2*	An internal command that renames a file or a group of files
*TYPE [*drive*:][*path*]filename*	An internal command that displays the contents of a text file on the screen
DOS Shell Commands	
File/Copy or [F8]	Copies one or more files
File/Delete, [Del], or [Delete]	Deletes a file
File/Print	Prints a text file from the DOS Shell after the PRINT program is loaded from the DOS prompt or from the DOS Shell
File/Rename	Renames one or more files
File/Run	Executes a DOS command from the DOS Shell
File/View File Contents or [F9]	Displays the contents of a text file
View/Refresh or [F5]	Updates the directory listing in the file list window after the DOS Shell rereads a diskette or hard disk

QUESTIONS

1. What is an ASCII file?
2. What control codes can an ASCII file contain?
3. What DOS command displays the contents of an ASCII file from the DOS prompt? Give an example of how to use this command.
4. How can you view the contents of a long ASCII file one screen at a time?
5. What is a DOS filter and how do you use it?
6. What is the pipe operator and how do you use it?
7. What does the MORE command do?
8. What are "read me" files, and why are they important?
9. How do you view an ASCII file from the DOS Shell?
10. What DOS command prints an ASCII file from the DOS prompt? What information does this command require?
11. What is a TSR?
12. How do you print an ASCII file from the DOS Shell?
13. Before you use the Print option on the File menu in the DOS Shell to print an ASCII file, what program must you first load into memory?
14. What does the COPY command do? What is the difference between a source file and a destination, or target, file?
15. What does DOS do when you copy a file but do not specify a drive name for the source file?
16. What does DOS do when you copy a file but do not specify a drive name for the target file?
17. What does DOS do when you copy a file to another disk but do not specify a filename for the new file?
18. What precaution should you take before you copy a file?
19. How do you copy a file in the DOS Shell?
20. What must you do in the DOS Shell to update the file list window?
21. What two commands can you use at the DOS prompt to change a filename?
22. What does DOS do if you rename a file and specify a drive for the destination file?
23. How do you rename a file in the DOS Shell?
24. What two commands can you use at the DOS prompt to delete a file?
25. Before you delete a file, what check should you perform?
26. What switch can you use when deleting a file from the DOS prompt to ensure you are deleting the correct file?
27. How do you delete a file from the DOS Shell?
28. How would you use the question mark wildcard to rename PROJBID1, PROJBID2, and PROJBID3 to PROJBID1.WP, PROJBID2.WP, and PROJBID3.WP in one step?
29. Assume drive A is the current drive. What command would you enter to copy the file named 94SALES from drive A to drive C?
30. Assume drive C is the current drive. What command would you enter to delete the file named MTGNOTES on drive B?

TUTORIAL ASSIGNMENTS

1. **Viewing and Printing the Contents of a Text File**: *Use your Tutorial Disk to perform the following operations from the DOS prompt.* List the command that you use to accomplish each step.
   a. Display the contents of the file named EQUIP.LST.
   b. Display the contents of the file named STARTUP.
   c. Print a copy of the file named RESUME2.DOC.

2. **Using the MORE Filter**: *Use your Tutorial Disk to perform the following operations from the DOS prompt.* List the command that you use to accomplish each step.
   a. Display the contents of the file named BUSINESS.PLN one screen at a time.
   b. Display the contents of the file named RESUME4.DOC one screen at a time.

3. **Copying Files**: *Use your Exercise Disk to perform the following operations from the DOS prompt.* List the command that you use to accomplish each step.
   a. Copy the file named SCHEDULE to produce a new file with the name WORKLOG.
   b. Copy the file named CASHFLOW.RPT to produce a new file with the name SUMMARY.
   c. Use question mark wildcards to copy JAN_CASH, FEB_CASH, MAR_CASH, APR_CASH, MAY_CASH, and JUN_CASH to produce files named JAN_CASH.RPT, FEB_CASH.RPT, MAR_CASH.RPT, APR_CASH.RPT, MAY_CASH.RPT, and JUN_CASH.RPT in one copy operation.

4. **Renaming Files**: *Use your Exercise Disk to perform the following operations from the DOS prompt.* List the command that you use to accomplish each step.
   a. Rename the file FEESCALE to FEES.
   b. Rename the file PRJ_INC to PRJ_INC.RPT.
   c. Use question mark wildcards to rename the files JAN_CASH, FEB_CASH, MAR_CASH, APR_CASH, MAY_CASH, and JUN_CASH to JAN-CASH, FEB-CASH, MAR-CASH, APR-CASH, MAY-CASH, and JUN-CASH in one operation.

5. **Managing Files in the DOS Shell**: *Use your Exercise Disk to perform the following operations from the DOS Shell.* List the steps for each of these operations, including the steps required to select a file.
   a. Copy the file CLIENT.LST to produce a new file named CUSTOMER.LST.
   b. Rename the file INVOICE.WK1 to INVOICES.WK1.
   c. Change the filename STARTUP to STARTUP.EST.
   d. View the contents of the file RESUME3.DOC.
   e. Print a copy of the file RESUME3.DOC.

TUTORIAL **4**

Using Subdirectories

OBJECTIVES

In this tutorial you will learn to:

- Create and change subdirectories
- Move files to subdirectories
- List and copy files in subdirectories
- Delete files in subdirectories
- Expand a directory structure
- View and print a directory tree

Your new business venture is growing rapidly! Your client files are increasing daily, and you want to more efficiently organize your client and business files on your hard disk and diskettes so that you can quickly locate important documents.

Most of the hard disks in your office have 120MB to 240MB of storage space and a variety of installed software packages and utilities, including Windows, WordPerfect, Lotus 1-2-3, and dBASE. Each software application includes hundreds of files and requires from 5MB to 15MB of hard disk storage space. Already, the majority of each hard disk's storage capacity is dedicated to these software applications and utilities that you use on a daily basis. Not only must you manage the use of the data files that you create with these software packages, but you must also manage the program files included with the software.

◆

MANAGING FILES

File management is one of the major tasks faced by any user of a computer system. This task is more complicated on a hard disk because of the enormous storage capacity of the drives and the number of files stored on them. To assist you in this task, DOS allows you to group related files together on a hard disk or diskette. You can then work with those grouped files as a separate unit, independent of all other files.

When you format a diskette or hard disk, DOS creates a special file, called a **directory file**, to keep track of information on files. When you use the DIR command, DOS shows you some of the information stored in this special directory file—the name, extension, size, date, and time of each file. The first directory created by the FORMAT command is called the **root directory**, or **main directory**.

After you format a diskette or hard disk, you can create other directories called subdirectories. A **subdirectory** is a directory that is *subordinate* to the root directory or to another subdirectory. Because each subdirectory is nothing other than a special file that tracks information about a group of files, a subdirectory is also a directory. (The term *directory* also describes the output produced by the DIR command.)

You can compare the use of drives, directories, subdirectories, and files to a filing cabinet's drawers, dividers, folders, and printed documents, respectively (Figures 4-1 and 4-2). Each drawer in a file cabinet is comparable to a disk drive. Within each drawer, each hanging folder corresponds to a DOS subdirectory. For example, you might have a file drawer labeled REPORTS, which contains different types of organizational reports, such as sales and budget reports. Within each hanging folder in the drawer, you might have folders that organize the reports by category, such as SALES and BUDGET. These folders correspond to subdirectories below the directory named REPORTS on your disk drive. Within each folder, the individual reports, such as SALES93.RPT and 95BUDGET, correspond to single files on your disk.

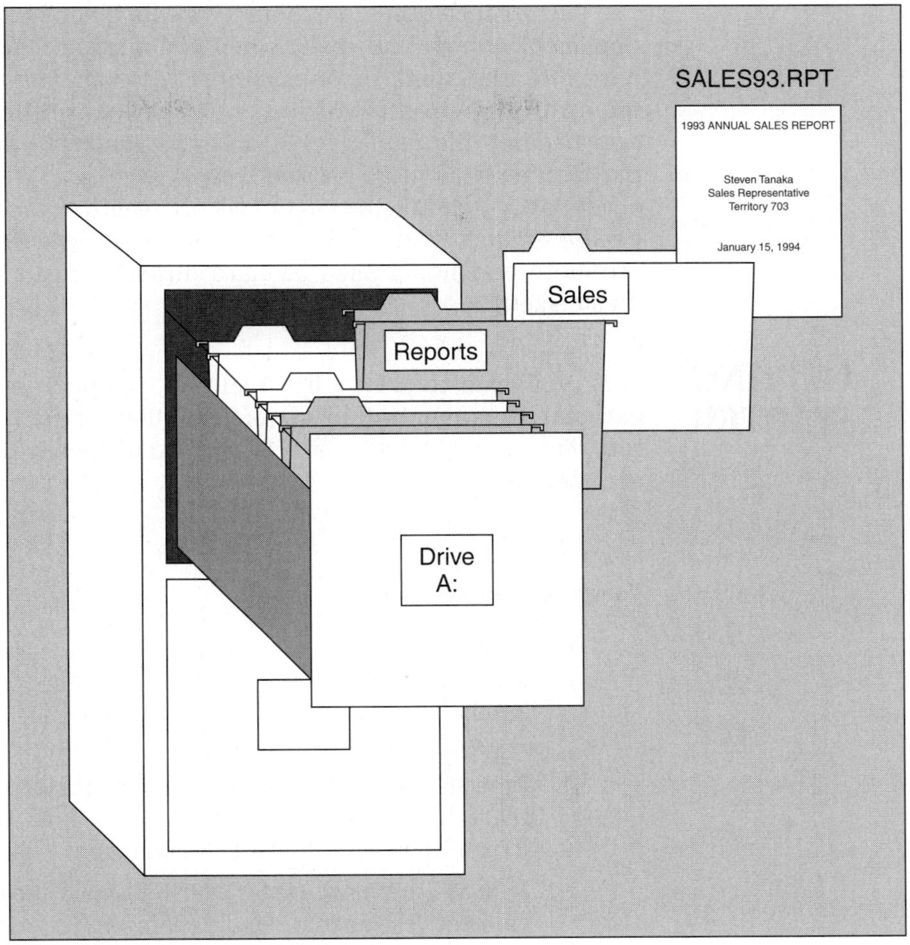

Figure 4-1
Organization of files in a filing cabinet

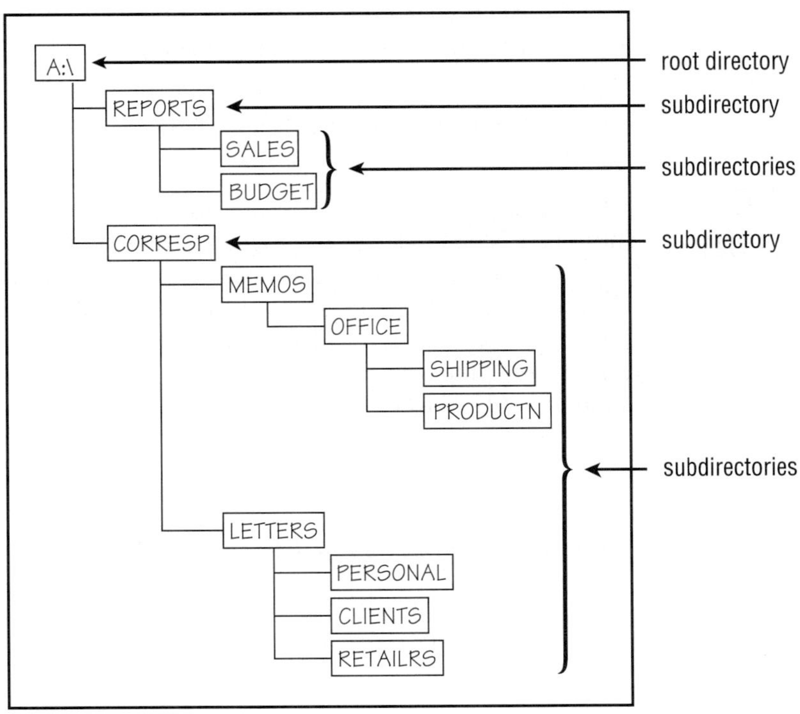

Figure 4-2
Organization of directories and subdirectories on a diskette or hard disk

The organization of documents within a filing cabinet enables you to find a document quickly and easily when you need it. Similarly, if you organize your hard disk into subdirectories, store files in the appropriate subdirectory, and maintain the subdirectories, you can locate files easily and quickly. By approaching file management in an organized way, you and your business partner can work more productively.

Before you tackle the larger task of organizing the files on your hard disk, you decide to start with the files on your client diskette. Although subdirectories are more commonly used on hard disks, you can also create subdirectories on a diskette.

GETTING STARTED

First, you want to print a list of all the files on your Tutorial Disk so that you can plan the organization of your subdirectories. Before you print this directory listing, you should install DOSKEY and specify default switches for the DIR command.

To set up your system:

5.0 *6.0* *6.2*

1. Type **DOSKEY** and press **[Enter]**. If you are using DOS 5.0 or 6.0, DOS will display the message "DOSKey installed" if DOSKEY is not already installed on your computer. If you do not see this message, DOSKEY is already installed. DOS 6.2 will not display a message.
2. Type **SET DIRCMD=/P /O** and press **[Enter]**. DOS will now display your client files and subdirectories in alphabetical order and pause after each screen when you use the DIR command.
3. Type **SET** and press **[Enter]**. DOS displays the contents of the DOS environment. You should see the setting you specified for the DIRCMD variable. If you do not, repeat Steps 2 and 3.
4. Insert your Tutorial Disk into a diskette drive. Then, type **A:** or **B:** to change to the drive that contains your Tutorial Disk.

You are now ready to print a directory listing of the filenames on your diskette.

PRINTING A DIRECTORY

DOS expects input from the keyboard and directs output to the monitor. Therefore, DOS uses the keyboard as the **standard input device** and the monitor as the **standard output device**. To send the output of a DOS command to the printer rather than the monitor, you must tell DOS to **redirect**, or change the destination of, that output with the **output redirection operator**, which is the greater-than symbol (>). After the redirection operator, you specify the name of your printer port.

Let's now produce the directory listing of your Tutorial Disk.

To redirect the output of the DIR command:

1. Be sure the printer is on, the paper is properly aligned in the printer, and the printer is on-line.

2. Type **DIR /-P > PRN** and press **[Enter]**. *Be sure you type a minus sign before the "P" in the /P switch.* /-P overrides the Pause switch setting in the DOS environment so that DOS does not pause after each screen. DOS still uses the Order switch in the DOS environment to print an alphabetical directory. Figure 4-3 shows a sample printout of the directory of the Tutorial Disk. Your volume serial number will be different. If you are using DOS 6.2, you will see commas every three places to the left of the decimal.

6.2

```
 Volume in drive A is BUSINESS
 Volume Serial Number is 142E-14F9
 Directory of A:\

APR_CASH              366 03-18-94  10:20a
BUSINESS PLN          590 03-20-94   5:26p
CASHFLOW FMT          472 03-27-94   8:32a
CASHFLOW RPT          176 03-27-94   8:45a
CASHFLOW WK1         1648 03-27-94   8:32a
CLIENT   LST          476 04-10-94  11:08a
EQUIP    LST          671 03-23-94   3:57p
FEB_CASH              369 03-18-94  10:14a
FEESCALE              412 04-19-94   1:48p
INCOME   YR1          987 04-23-94   9:06a
INCOME   YR2          987 04-23-94   9:17a
INCOME   YR3          987 04-23-94   9:21a
INCOME   YR4          987 04-23-94   9:34a
INCOME   YR5          987 04-23-94   9:47a
INSURE   LST         1528 04-09-94   8:48a
INVOICE  FMT         2124 04-02-94  10:45a
INVOICE  WK1         1752 04-02-94  10:45a
INVOICES              104 03-22-94   8:48a
JAN_CASH              368 03-18-94  10:00a
JOBCOSTS FMT          294 03-30-94   2:22p
JOBCOSTS RPT          543 03-26-94   8:51a
JOBCOSTS WK1         1716 03-30-94   2:22p
JUN_CASH              365 03-18-94  10:45a
MAR_CASH              366 03-18-94  10:17a
MAY_CASH              364 03-18-94  10:43a
PRJ_INC               589 04-24-94  11:27a
QTR_INC               589 04-24-94  11:27a
RESUME   LTR         1182 04-15-94  11:49a
RESUME1  DOC         2435 04-12-94   2:25p
RESUME2  DOC         2435 04-12-94   2:41p
RESUME3  DOC         2392 04-12-94   3:00p
RESUME4  DOC         2386 04-12-94   3:12p
RESUME5  DOC         4043 04-12-94   4:08p
RESUME6  DOC         4043 04-12-94   4:08p
SCHEDULE FMT          794 04-07-94   1:21p
SCHEDULE WK1         2147 04-07-94   1:21p
STARTUP              1010 03-11-94  10:03a
       37 file(s)         43684 bytes
                         668672 bytes free
```

Figure 4-3
A printed copy of the directory listing for your Tutorial Disk

3. If you need to eject the paper from the printer, press the **Form Feed button** on the printer. If the printer does not respond, press the **On Line button** to place the printer off-line. Then press the **Form Feed button**. After the printer ejects the page, press the **On Line button** to place the printer back on-line.

4. Remove your hardcopy from the printer.

CREATING SUBDIRECTORIES

After examining the types of files on your Tutorial Disk, you prepare a sketch of the subdirectory structure that you want to use to organize your files (Figure 4-4).

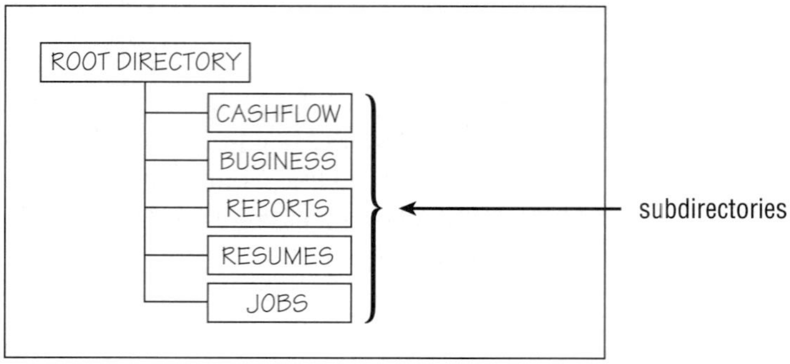

Figure 4-4
The planned directory structure for your Tutorial Disk

The DOS commands for creating a subdirectory are MD and MKDIR (both abbreviations for Make Directory). These internal commands have the following syntax:

MD [*drive:*] *path*
MKDIR [*drive:*] *path*

You must specify the drive name if you want to create the subdirectory on another drive. You also must specify the directory's path. In other words, you must identify its name and location relative to another directory, such as the root directory.

The rules for naming a subdirectory are the same as those for naming a file. Just as a filename identifies the type of document stored in the file, a subdirectory's name describes the types of files that you will store in the subdirectory.

Before you create a subdirectory, you should check the DOS prompt to be sure you create the subdirectory in the right place—just as you would read the label on a file cabinet drawer before placing a folder in it. You have learned that the prompt shows the current drive. It also tells you the current directory. For example, if you see A:\ or B:\ in the DOS prompt, the letters A and B indicate the drive name and the \ (Backslash) indicates that you are in the root directory. The \ (Backslash) is the notation DOS assigns to the root directory. If your DOS prompt looks like one of these examples, you are ready to create a subdirectory.

If DOS displays your prompt as A> or B>, you must use the PROMPT command to change the appearance of the DOS prompt. The syntax for this internal command is

PROMPT [*text*]

The text can consist of characters that you want to display as part of the prompt. You can also include special codes that customize the appearance of the DOS prompt. For example, if you enter PROMPT PG, the $P code instructs DOS to construct the prompt so that it shows the full path—the drive name and path for the current directory. The $G tells DOS to include the greater-than symbol (>) after the full path. This separates the path in the DOS prompt from commands that you enter at the DOS prompt.

Check your prompt to make sure it shows the path.

To change the prompt to display the current directory:

1. If your DOS prompt does not appear as A:\> or B:\>, type **PROMPT PG** and press **[Enter]**. DOS updates the DOS prompt to show the full path.

You are now ready to create a subdirectory. The first subdirectory that you create below the root directory will store files for tracking the cashflow in your business. You decide to name it CASHFLOW.

To create the CASHFLOW subdirectory:

1. Type **MD CASHFLOW** and press **[Enter]**. DOS creates the subdirectory below the root directory of the disk drive containing your diskette and displays the DOS prompt. If you perform this operation from another drive, such as drive C, you would include the drive name before the subdirectory name. Also, if the disk contains a file with the same name as the one you want to use as the subdirectory name, DOS will display an error message that tells you it is unable to create the directory.

Now verify that this new subdirectory exists.

2. Type **DIR C*** and press **[Enter]**. DOS displays a screen with an alphabetical list of the files in the root directory that begin with the letter "C," regardless of whether they have a file extension. See Figure 4-5. The first file in the directory listing is the name of your newly created subdirectory. DOS displays <DIR> next to each subdirectory name in a directory listing.

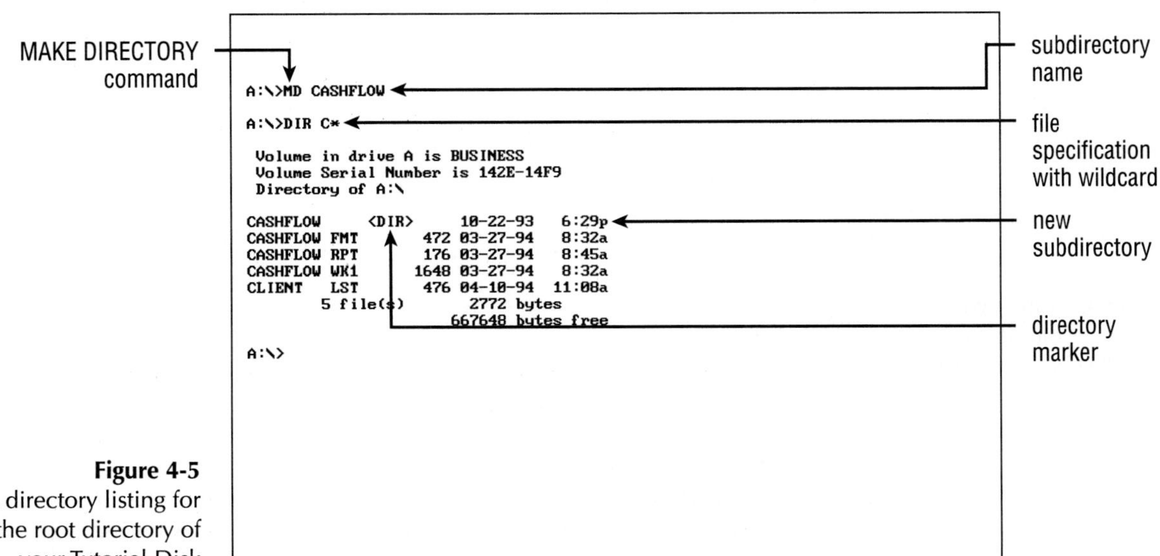

Figure 4-5
A directory listing for the root directory of your Tutorial Disk

CHANGING DIRECTORIES

Once you create a subdirectory, you can switch to that subdirectory by typing CD or CHDIR (both abbreviations for Change Directory) at the DOS prompt. These internal commands have the following syntax:

CD [*drive:*]*path*
CHDIR [*drive:*]*path*

If you specify a drive name, you change from one directory to another on that disk drive, even if you are working on another disk drive. When you specify the path, you are telling DOS the name of the directory that you want to change to and its location relative to another directory, such as the root directory.

After you change to a subdirectory, you can work more easily with the files stored in the subdirectory. Let's change to the CASHFLOW directory and examine its contents.

To change to the CASHFLOW subdirectory:

1. Type **CD CASHFLOW** and press **[Enter]**. DOS updates the DOS prompt to show the full path of the subdirectory. See Figure 4-6. The DOS prompt A:\CASHFLOW (or B:\CASHFLOW) tells you that CASHFLOW is a subdirectory below the root directory of the diskette in the current drive.

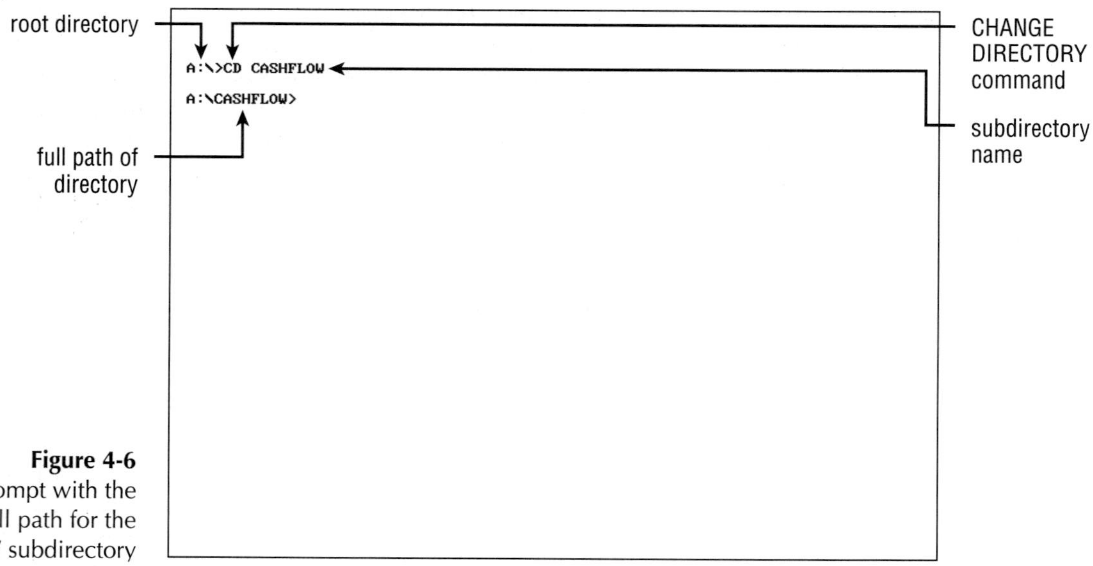

Figure 4-6
The DOS prompt with the full path for the CASHFLOW subdirectory

Now view the contents of this new subdirectory.

2. Type **DIR** and press **[Enter]**. DOS displays a directory listing for the current directory, CASHFLOW, on the current drive, and reports that there are two files in this subdirectory. See Figure 4-7. You do not see the names of files in the root directory.

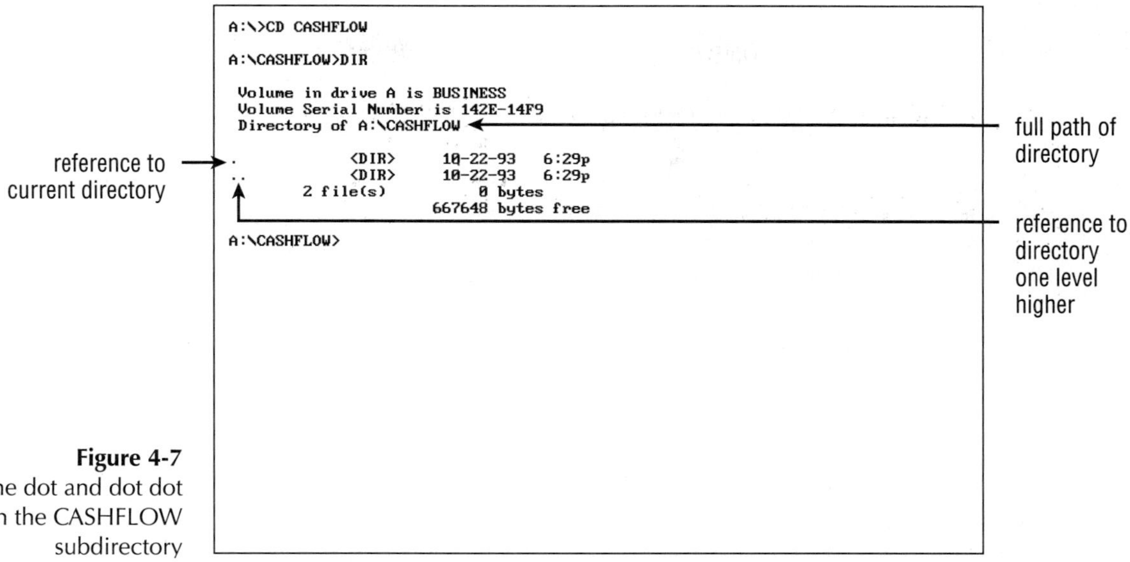

Figure 4-7
The dot and dot dot files in the CASHFLOW subdirectory

Whenever DOS creates a subdirectory, it always creates these two files. The first file, named . (pronounced "dot"), is a notation that refers to the current directory. The second file, named .. (pronounced "dot dot"), is a notation that refers to the directory one level higher than the current directory. The directory one level higher is also called the **parent directory**. In this case, the parent directory of CASHFLOW is the root directory. Every subdirectory has a parent directory. DOS uses the . and .. files to keep track of the current directory and the parent directory as you move from one directory to another.

Now that you have created one of the subdirectories planned for this diskette, you want to move the appropriate files to this subdirectory. To simplify this operation, you decide to return to the root directory where these files are currently stored. Again, you use the CD or CHDIR commands. For the root directory's name, you use the Backslash (\) symbol—the notation that identifies the root directory.

To return to the root directory from any subdirectory:

1. Type **CD ** and press **[Enter]**. DOS updates the DOS prompt and shows the root directory as the current directory. See Figure 4-8. If you type a Slash (/) instead of a Backslash (\), DOS will tell you that you have entered an invalid switch, because switches start with a Slash symbol. If you type CD and do not specify a directory name, DOS will display the name of the current directory.

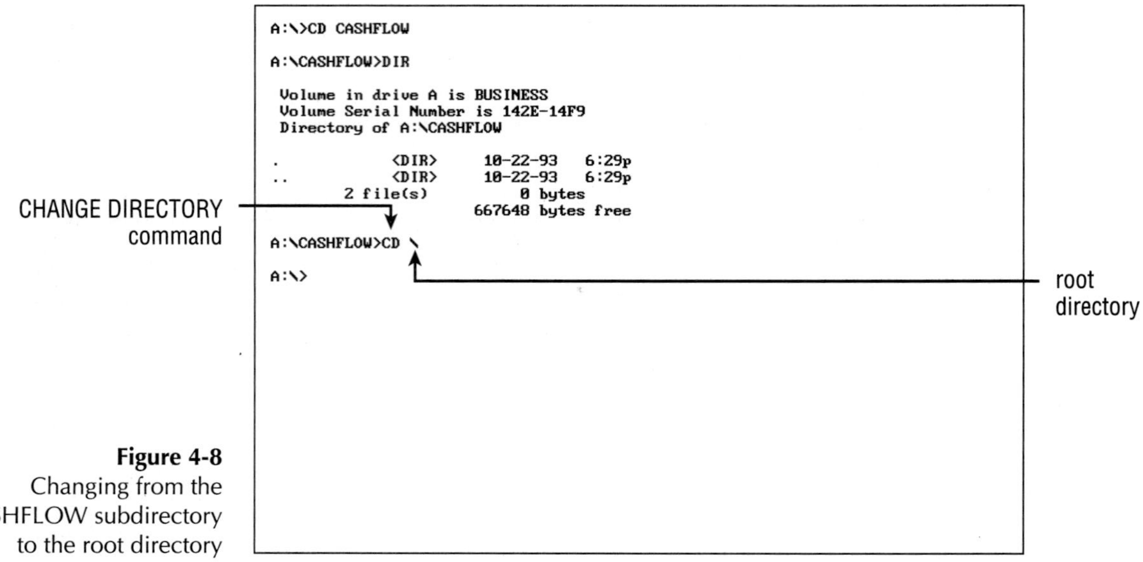

Figure 4-8
Changing from the CASHFLOW subdirectory to the root directory

MOVING FILES TO A SUBDIRECTORY

Next you check the printed copy of files on your diskette and highlight the files that you want to move to the CASHFLOW subdirectory (Figure 4-9).

```
 Volume in drive A is BUSINESS
 Volume Serial Number is 364B-15D6
 Directory of A:\

APR_CASH            366 03-18-94  10:20a
BUSINESS PLN        590 03-20-94   5:26p
CASHFLOW FMT        472 03-27-94   8:32a
CASHFLOW RPT        176 03-27-94   8:45a
CASHFLOW WK1       1648 03-27-94   8:32a
CLIENT   LST        476 04-10-94  11:08a
EQUIP    LST        671 03-23-94   3:57p
FEB_CASH            369 03-18-94  10:14a
FEESCALE            412 04-19-94   1:48p
INCOME   YR1        987 04-23-94   9:06a
INCOME   YR2        987 04-23-94   9:17a
INCOME   YR3        987 04-23-94   9:21a
INCOME   YR4        987 04-23-94   9:34a
INCOME   YR5        987 04-23-94   9:47a
INSURE   LST       1528 04-09-94   8:48a
INVOICE  FMT       2124 04-02-94  10:45a
INVOICE  WK1       1752 04-02-94  10:45a
INVOICES            104 03-22-94   8:48a
JAN_CASH            368 03-18-94  10:00a
JOBCOSTS FMT        294 03-30-94   2:22p
JOBCOSTS RPT        543 03-26-94   8:51a
JOBCOSTS WK1       1716 03-30-94   2:22p
JUN_CASH            365 03-18-94  10:45a
MAR_CASH            366 03-18-94  10:17a
MAY_CASH            364 03-18-94  10:43a
PRJ_INC             589 04-24-94  11:27a
QTR_INC             589 04-24-94  11:27a
RESUME   LTR       1182 04-15-94  11:49a
RESUME1  DOC       2435 04-12-94   2:25p
RESUME2  DOC       2435 04-12-94   2:41p
RESUME3  DOC       2392 04-12-94   3:00p
RESUME4  DOC       2386 04-12-94   3:12p
RESUME5  DOC       4043 04-12-94   4:08p
RESUME6  DOC       4043 04-12-94   4:08p
SCHEDULE FMT        792 04-07-94   1:21p
SCHEDULE WK1       2147 04-07-94   1:21P
STARTUP            1010 03-11094  10:03a
       37 file(s)      43684 bytes
                      668672 bytes free
```

Figure 4-9
Shading indicates the files you want to move to the CASHFLOW subdirectory

6.0 ***6.2***

If you are using DOS 6.0 or 6.2, you can use the MOVE command, an external command, to move these files in one step. If you want to move one or more files from one directory to another with the MOVE command, you use the following syntax:

MOVE [*drive:*][*path*]*filename destination*

The drive name, path, and filename are those of the source file or files you want to move to another location. You must specify the drive name for the source file or files if they are located on another drive. You must also specify the path if it is different from that of the current directory. The destination includes the path and name of the directory in which you want DOS to store the moved files. The destination might also include a drive name. If you are moving one file, you can also specify a new filename for that file. If you are moving a group of files, the destination must be a directory name.

For example, to move the file CLIENT.LST from the root directory of drive A to the BUSINESS subdirectory on drive A, you would enter this command:

MOVE CLIENT.LST BUSINESS

To move all the files with the file extension LST from the root directory of drive A to the BUSINESS subdirectory on drive A, you would enter this command:

MOVE *.LST BUSINESS

To move a file named BUSINESS.PLN from the current directory on drive C to drive A, you would enter this command:

MOVE BUSINESS.PLN A:

Be careful when moving files in DOS 6.0. If there is a file in the destination directory with the same filename as a source file you are moving, DOS 6.0 will overwrite the file in the destination directory. DOS 6.2 will automatically prompt you first.

5.0

If you are using DOS 5.0, you must move the files in two steps, because DOS 5.0 does not have a MOVE command. First, you use the COPY command to copy the files to the new subdirectory from the directory in which they are currently stored. You then use the DEL or ERASE command to delete the files from the original directory. It is always a good idea to verify these operations by using the DIR command.

Now you are ready to move your cashflow files to the CASHFLOW directory. Because these files have similar names, you can use wildcards to move the files as a group rather than moving one file at a time. Even though you work with DOS 6.0 and 6.2, you decide to use the COPY and DEL commands before you try the MOVE command. A number of your clients use DOS 5.0, so you should know how to move files in DOS 5.0.

To copy the cashflow files to the CASHFLOW subdirectory:

1. Type **DIR CASH*** and press **[Enter]**. DOS displays the names of the cashflow files you want to move. See Figure 4-10. You also see the CASHFLOW directory name with a directory marker, <DIR>, next to its name.

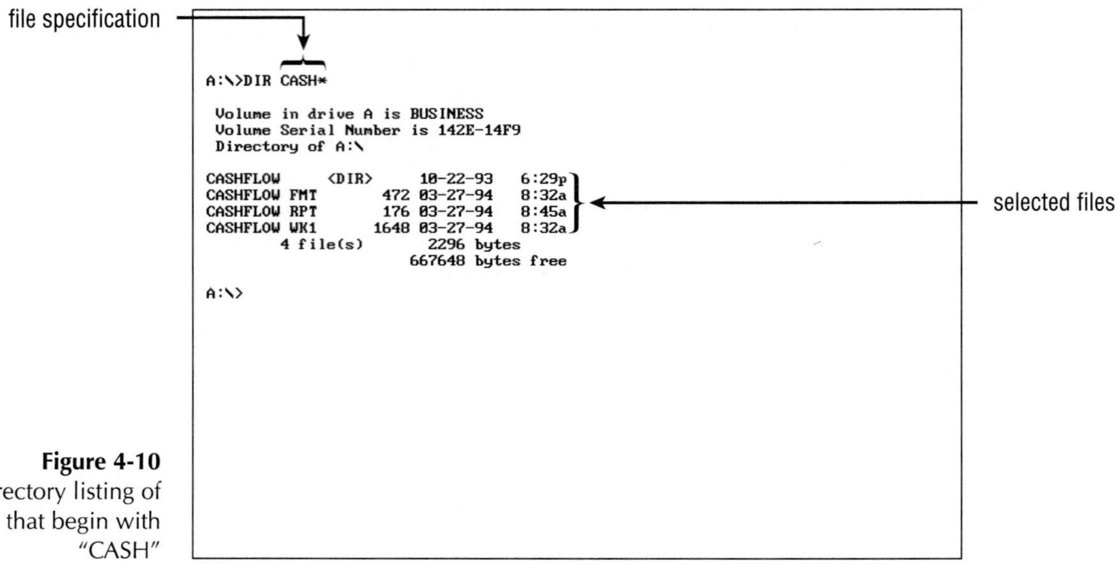

Figure 4-10
A directory listing of filenames that begin with "CASH"

2. Type **COPY CASH*.* CASHFLOW** and press **[Enter]**. As DOS copies these three files, it displays their filenames on the screen and tells you it copied three files. See Figure 4-11.

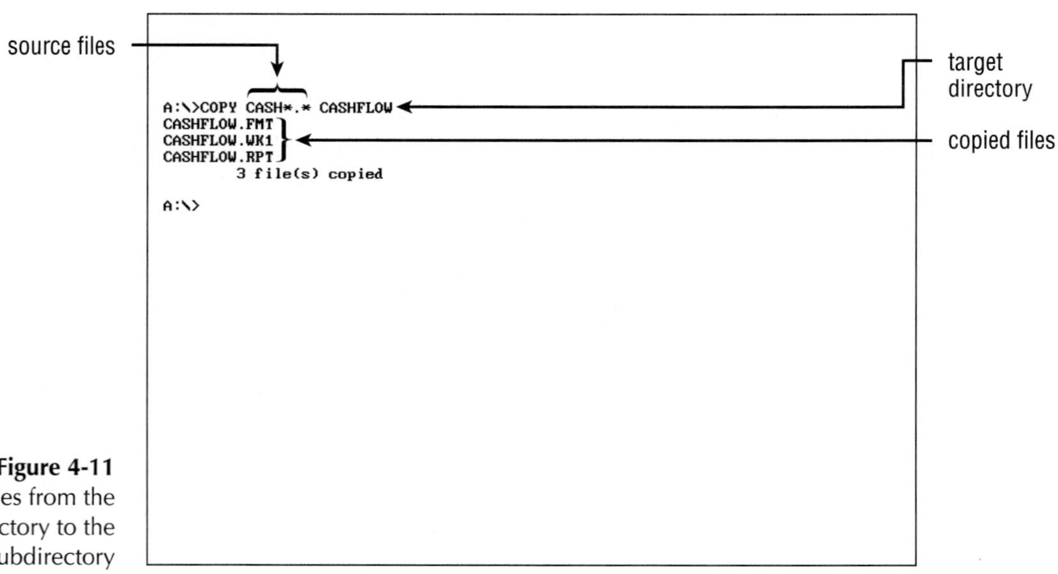

Figure 4-11
Copying files from the root directory to the CASHFLOW subdirectory

How does DOS know in this last command that CASHFLOW refers to the name of a subdirectory? The directory file for the root directory contains a list of all the files in the root directory of your diskette as well as all the names of subdirectories located below the root directory. During this copy operation, DOS examines this directory file and locates a subdirectory named CASHFLOW. It then copies the files you specified to that subdirectory. If the root directory did not contain a subdirectory named CASHFLOW, DOS would copy *and combine* all the files you specified into one larger file named CASHFLOW and store this new file in the root directory.

When you enter the COPY command, you can also use \CASHFLOW for the directory name, to indicate it is a subdirectory below the root directory. If you do not specify the Backslash (\) for the root directory and if the current directory is the root directory (as is the case here), DOS assumes the CASHFLOW subdirectory is located in the root directory.

Now you are ready to verify the copy operation.

To check the contents of the CASHFLOW directory:

1. Type **DIR CASHFLOW** and press **[Enter]**. The three copied files are now stored in the CASHFLOW subdirectory. See Figure 4-12.

```
A:\>DIR CASHFLOW

 Volume in drive A is BUSINESS
 Volume Serial Number is 142E-14F9
 Directory of A:\CASHFLOW

.            <DIR>        10-22-93   6:29p
..           <DIR>        10-22-93   6:29p
CASHFLOW FMT        472 03-27-94   8:32a
CASHFLOW RPT        176 03-27-94   8:45a
CASHFLOW WK1       1648 03-27-94   8:32a
        5 file(s)         2296 bytes
                        663552 bytes free

A:\>
```

directory

new files

Figure 4-12
The files copied to the CASHFLOW subdirectory

2. Press [↑] (Up Arrow) until you recall the command DIR CASH* and press **[Enter]**. The original versions of the three files copied to the CASHFLOW directory are still in the root directory.

You now have two copies of these files. One copy is in the CASHFLOW subdirectory and one copy is in the root directory. You do not need or want two copies of these files in two different directories, because you would not be using available disk space efficiently. You want to delete the original versions of the files in the root directory.

To delete the original files in the root directory:

1. Type **DEL CASH*.*** and press **[Enter]**. DOS deletes all files that match this file specification.

2. Press [↑] (Up Arrow) until you recall the command DIR CASH* and then press **[Enter]**. DOS displays an updated list of file and directory names in the root directory. See Figure 4-13. The DEL command deleted the original set of files that you copied to the CASHFLOW subdirectory, but it did not delete the CASHFLOW subdirectory.

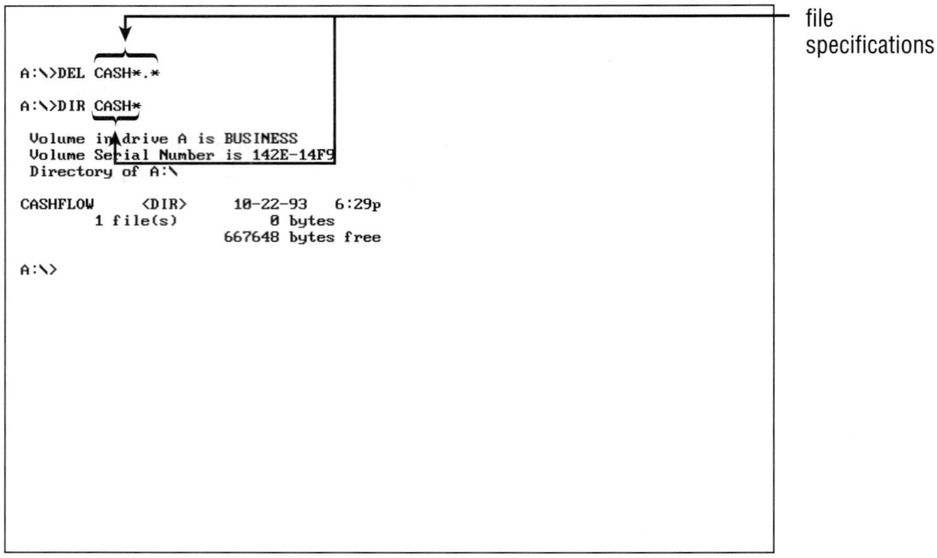

Figure 4-13
Verifying the deletion of files from the root directory

3. Press [↑] (Up Arrow) until you recall the command DIR CASHFLOW and press **[Enter]**. DOS displays the names of the files currently stored in the CASHFLOW subdirectory. The DEL command did not delete these files.

This use of the DEL command illustrates that DOS can treat a subdirectory as if it were a separate disk drive. The DEL command deleted files in the root directory without affecting the files in the CASHFLOW subdirectory. Furthermore, the DEL command did not delete, or remove, this subdirectory. The DEL command deletes only files; it cannot delete, or remove, a reference to a disk drive, and it cannot remove a subdirectory.

Moving Files with the Yearly Income Projections

Now, you are ready to move the files with the yearly income projections.

If you are using DOS 6.0 or 6.2, you will use the MOVE command. If you are using DOS 5.0, you will use the COPY and DEL commands.

Follow the steps in the section that describes how to perform these operations using the version of DOS on your system.

6.0 **6.2** **To move the files with the yearly income projections *using DOS 6.0 or 6.2*:**

1. Be sure the current drive contains your Tutorial Disk and that you are at the root directory of that diskette drive.
2. Type **MOVE INCOME.* CASHFLOW** and press **[Enter]**. As DOS moves each file, it verifies the operation. See Figure 4-14. The files are moved in disk order—the order in which the files were placed on the diskette.

```
A:\>MOVE INCOME.* CASHFLOW
a:\income.yr5 => a:\cashflow\income.yr5 [ok]
a:\income.yr1 => a:\cashflow\income.yr1 [ok]
a:\income.yr4 => a:\cashflow\income.yr4 [ok]
a:\income.yr2 => a:\cashflow\income.yr2 [ok]
a:\income.yr3 => a:\cashflow\income.yr3 [ok]

A:\>
```

Figure 4-14
DOS verifies a move operation of a selected group of files

3. Type **DIR CASHFLOW** and press **[Enter]**. DOS displays an updated listing of the CASHFLOW subdirectory. See Figure 4-15. This list includes the five moved files.

```
A:\>DIR CASHFLOW

 Volume in drive A is BUSINESS
 Volume Serial Number is 142E-14F9
 Directory of A:\CASHFLOW

.            <DIR>      10-22-93   6:29p
..           <DIR>      10-22-93   6:29p
CASHFLOW FMT        472 03-27-94   8:32a
CASHFLOW RPT        176 03-27-94   8:45a
CASHFLOW WK1       1648 03-27-94   8:32a
INCOME   YR1        987 04-23-94   9:06a
INCOME   YR2        987 04-23-94   9:17a
INCOME   YR3        987 04-23-94   9:21a
INCOME   YR4        987 04-23-94   9:34a
INCOME   YR5        987 04-23-94   9:47a
       10 file(s)        7231 bytes
                       667648 bytes free

A:\>
```

Figure 4-15
The current contents of the CASHFLOW subdirectory

4. Type **DIR INCOME.*** and press **[Enter]**. DOS finds no files with this file specification in the root directory, verifying that they have been moved.

If you are using DOS 6.0 or 6.2, skip to the section entitled "Moving the Monthly Income Report Files."

5.0

To move the files with the yearly income projections *using DOS 5.0*:

1. Type **COPY INCOME.* CASHFLOW** and press **[Enter]**. As DOS copies these files, it displays their filenames and tells you it copied five files. See Figure 4-16.

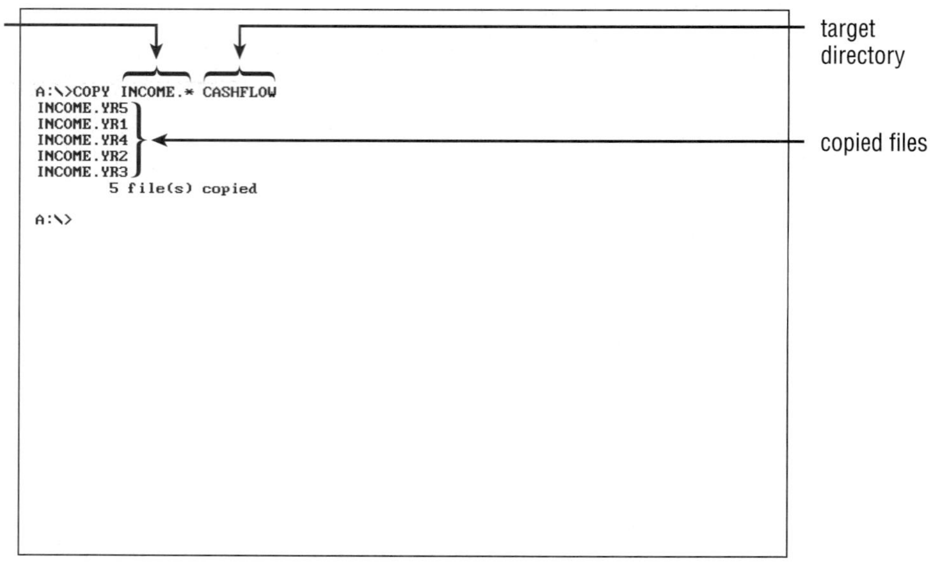

Figure 4-16
Copying files to the CASHFLOW subdirectory

2. Type **DIR CASHFLOW** and press **[Enter]**. The CASHFLOW directory contains the five files with names that begin with INCOME.

Now remove these files from the root directory.

3. Type **DEL INCOME.*** and press **[Enter]**. DOS deletes files that match this file specification.

Moving the Monthly Income Report Files

Now you are ready to move the monthly income report files to the CASHFLOW subdirectory. Again, follow the steps in the section below that describe how to perform these operations using the version of DOS on your system.

6.0 ***6.2***

To move the files with the monthly income reports *using DOS 6.0 or 6.2*:

1. Type **MOVE ???_INC CASHFLOW** and press **[Enter]**. As DOS moves each file that meets the file specification ???_INC, it verifies the operation.
2. Type **DIR CASHFLOW** and press **[Enter]**. The CASHFLOW directory contains two copied files, PRJ_INC and QTR_INC, that meet the file specification.

Now change to the CASHFLOW directory.

3. Type **CD CASHFLOW** and press **[Enter]**. DOS updates the DOS prompt to show that the current directory is CASHFLOW.

If you are using DOS 6.0 or 6.2, skip to the section entitled "Moving the Invoice Files."

5.0

To move the files with the monthly income reports *using DOS 5.0*:

1. Type **COPY ???_INC CASHFLOW** and press **[Enter]**. As DOS copies the two files that match this file specification, it displays their filenames.
2. Type **DIR CASHFLOW** and press **[Enter]**. The CASHFLOW directory contains the two copied files, PRJ_INC and QTR_INC.
3. Type **DEL ???_INC** and press **[Enter]**. DOS deletes files in the root directory that match this file specification.

Now change to the CASHFLOW directory.

4. Type **CD CASHFLOW** and press **[Enter]**. DOS updates the DOS prompt to show that the current directory is CASHFLOW.

Moving the Invoice Files

After examining the CASHFLOW directory, you realize that three other files belong in this subdirectory. You decide to move them from the root directory to the current directory. The source files are the files in the root directory that you want to copy, and the target file is the current subdirectory, CASHFLOW. Follow the steps in the section below that describe how to perform these operations using the version of DOS on your system.

6.0 *6.2*

To move the invoice files from the root directory to the current subdirectory *using DOS 6.0 or 6.2*:

1. Type **MOVE \INVOICE*.*** and press **[Spacebar]**. Type **.** (a period) and press **[Enter]**. As DOS moves each file that meets the specification INVOICE*.*, it verifies the operation. The Backslash (\) in the source specification tells DOS to look to the root directory for these files. Because you did not specify the source drive, DOS uses the current drive. The . (a period) after \INVOICE*.* is the target specification. It tells DOS that the target is the current directory. Remember, DOS uses a single dot to represent the current directory.
2. Type **DIR** and press **[Enter]** to verify the move operation. The CASHFLOW directory contains three filenames that begin with INVOICE. See Figure 4-17.

```
A:\CASHFLOW>DIR

 Volume in drive A is BUSINESS
 Volume Serial Number is 142E-14F9
 Directory of A:\CASHFLOW

.            <DIR>      10-22-93   6:29p
..           <DIR>      10-22-93   6:29p
CASHFLOW FMT        472 03-27-94   8:32a
CASHFLOW RPT        176 03-27-94   8:45a
CASHFLOW WK1       1648 03-27-94   8:32a
INCOME   YR1        987 04-23-94   9:06a
INCOME   YR2        987 04-23-94   9:17a
INCOME   YR3        987 04-23-94   9:21a
INCOME   YR4        987 04-23-94   9:34a
INCOME   YR5        987 04-23-94   9:47a
INVOICE  FMT       2124 04-02-94  10:45a
INVOICE  WK1       1752 04-02-94  10:45a
INVOICES            104 03-22-94   8:48a
PRJ_INC             589 04-24-94  11:27a
QTR_INC             589 04-24-94  11:27a
       15 file(s)      12389 bytes
                      667648 bytes free

A:\CASHFLOW>
```

Figure 4-17
A directory of the CASHFLOW subdirectory after a move operation

If you are using DOS 6.0 or 6.2, skip to the section entitled "Copying Files Within a Subdirectory."

5.0

To move the invoice files from the root directory to the current directory *using DOS 5.0*:

1. Type **COPY \INVOICE*.*** and press **[Spacebar]**. Type **.** (a period) and press **[Enter]**. DOS copies three files. See Figure 4-18. The Backslash (\) in the source specification tells DOS to look to the root directory for these files. Because you did not specify the source drive, DOS uses the current drive. The . (period) after \INVOICE*.* is the target specification. It tells DOS that the target is the current directory. Remember, DOS uses a single dot to represent the current directory.

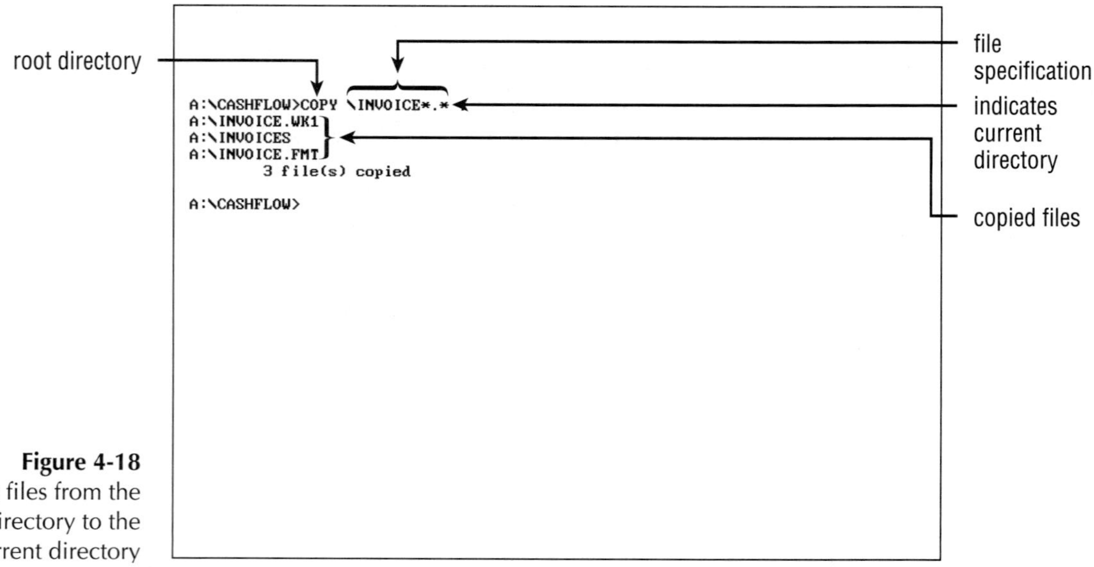

Figure 4-18
Copying files from the root directory to the current directory

2. Type **DIR** and press **[Enter]** to verify the move operation. The CASHFLOW directory contains the three files you copied to this subdirectory.

You can now remove these files from the root directory.

3. Type **DEL \INVOICE*.*** and press **[Enter]**. *Be sure you type the Backslash (\) before INVOICE*.*. If you forget the Backslash, you will delete the files that you just copied to the current directory.* DOS deletes files that match this file specification in the root directory.

4. Type **DIR** and press **[Enter]**. You should still see three filenames that begin with INVOICE. If you do not, you will need to repeat these steps.

COPYING FILES WITHIN A SUBDIRECTORY

To anticipate cash needs for your business venture, you want to project expected income and expenses. You also want to keep a record of your actual income and expenses so that you can later compare this information with your initial projections and improve your future projections.

Your new directory already contains files that you will use to project income and expenses. To save time and effort, you decide to copy these files so that you can modify them later to track actual income and expenses. Because you will use these two groups of files in conjunction with each other, you want to keep them in the same subdirectory.

To copy the cashflow files within the CASHFLOW subdirectory:

1. Be sure you are in the CASHFLOW subdirectory. The DOS prompt should contain the name of this directory.

2. Type **COPY CASHFLOW.* CASH.*** and press **[Enter]**. DOS copies three files and produces three new files with new filenames.

3. Type **DIR CASH*** and press **[Enter]** to view the new files. See Figure 4-19. Now there are six files that begin with CASH in the CASHFLOW subdirectory. At the end of the month, you can modify the three new files to track actual income and expense.

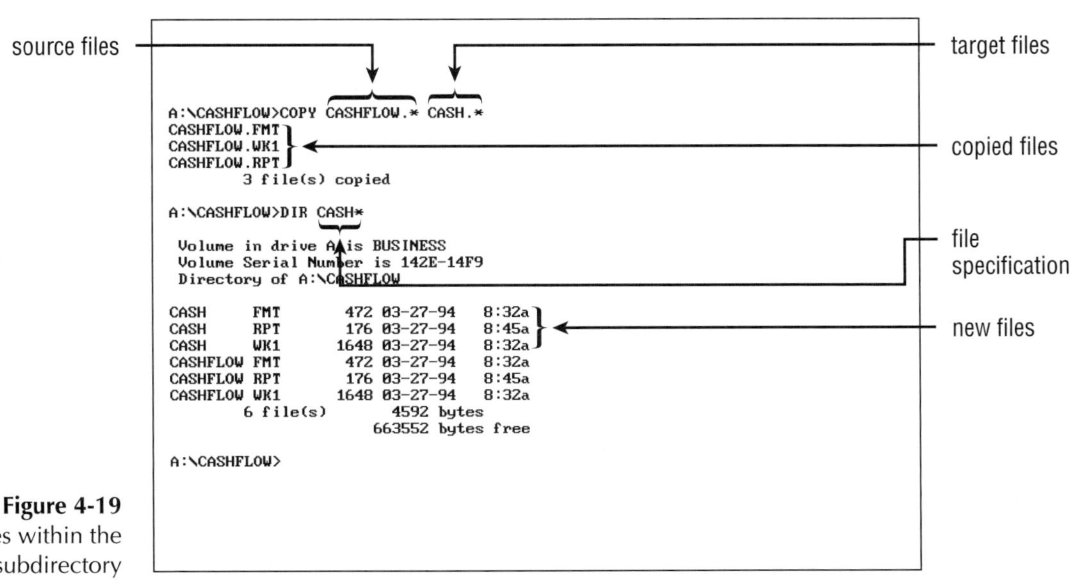

Figure 4-19
Copying files within the CASHFLOW subdirectory

Now you want to return to the root directory before you create other subdirectories.

4. Type **CD ** and press **[Enter]**.

EXPANDING A DIRECTORY STRUCTURE

Next you want to create a subdirectory named BUSINESS for your general business files. These files include the ones with your business plan, estimated start-up costs, and checklists for starting and maintaining this business.

To create the BUSINESS subdirectory:

1. Type **MD BUSINESS** and press **[Enter]**. DOS creates the subdirectory and displays the DOS prompt.
2. Type **DIR** and press **[Enter]**. From the directory listing, you can verify that you have created a new subdirectory. DOS first lists subdirectories in alphabetical order, then lists filenames in alphabetical order. Press **[Spacebar]** or any other key until you return to the DOS prompt.

You are now ready to move files to this new subdirectory. Follow the steps in the section below that describes how to perform these operations using the version of DOS on your system.

6.0 6.2

To move the general business files to this new subdirectory *using DOS 6.0 or 6.2*:

1. Type **MOVE BUSINESS.PLN BUSINESS** and press **[Enter]**. DOS moves one file to this subdirectory.
2. Type **MOVE STARTUP BUSINESS** and press **[Enter]**. DOS moves another file to the same subdirectory.
3. Type **MOVE *.LST BUSINESS** and press **[Enter]**. DOS moves three files with the LST file extension to this subdirectory.
4. Type **CD BUSINESS** and press **[Enter]**. DOS changes to the BUSINESS subdirectory.
5. Type **DIR** and press **[Enter]**. DOS displays a directory listing with the names of the five moved files. See Figure 4-20.

```
A:\>CD BUSINESS

A:\BUSINESS>DIR

 Volume in drive A is BUSINESS
 Volume Serial Number is 142E-14F9
 Directory of A:\BUSINESS

.            <DIR>       10-23-93  10:20a
..           <DIR>       10-23-93  10:20a
BUSINESS PLN        590 03-20-94   5:26p
CLIENT   LST        476 04-10-94  11:08a
EQUIP    LST        671 03-23-94   3:57p
INSURE   LST       1528 04-09-94   8:48a
STARTUP            1010 03-11-94  10:03a
        7 file(s)        4275 bytes
                       662528 bytes free

A:\BUSINESS>
```

Figure 4-20
The files moved to the BUSINESS subdirectory

If you are using DOS 6.0 or 6.2, skip to the section entitled "Creating a Directory for Reports."

5.0

To move the general business files to this new subdirectory *using DOS 5.0*:

1. Type **COPY BUSINESS.PLN BUSINESS** and press **[Enter]**. DOS copies one file to this subdirectory.
2. Type **COPY STARTUP BUSINESS** and press **[Enter]**. DOS copies another file to the same subdirectory.
3. Type **COPY *.LST BUSINESS** and press **[Enter]**. DOS copies three files that have the LST file extension to this subdirectory. See Figure 4-21.

```
A:\>MD BUSINESS

A:\>COPY BUSINESS.PLN BUSINESS
        1 file(s) copied

A:\>COPY STARTUP BUSINESS
        1 file(s) copied

A:\>COPY *.LST BUSINESS
CLIENT.LST
EQUIP.LST
INSURE.LST
        3 file(s) copied

A:\>
```

copy operations

Figure 4-21
The files copied to the BUSINESS subdirectory

4. Type **DIR BUSINESS** and press **[Enter]** to verify the move operation. This subdirectory contains the five files that you copied to it.

You can now delete these files from the root directory.

5. Type **DEL BUSINESS.PLN** and press **[Enter]**. Next, type **DEL STARTUP** and press **[Enter]**. DOS deletes these two files.
6. Type **DEL *.LST** and press **[Enter]**. DOS deletes the three files with the LST file extension.

Next, change to the BUSINESS directory.

7. Type **CD BUSINESS** and press **[Enter]**. DOS changes to the BUSINESS subdirectory.
8. Type **DIR** and press **[Enter]**. DOS displays the contents of the BUSINESS directory. The DEL command did not affect the files in this directory.

Creating a Directory for Reports

You also want to create a subdirectory for your monthly business cashflow reports. You want to name this directory REPORTS and create it below the root directory. Although you are still working in the BUSINESS subdirectory, you can create this new subdirectory if you provide DOS with enough of its path. You must specify the name of the root directory before the directory name—as \REPORTS—so that DOS creates this new subdirectory below the root directory (Figure 4-22). If you specify only the directory name REPORTS, DOS will create the new subdirectory below the current directory—the BUSINESS subdirectory (Figure 4-22). It is important to specify enough of the path so that DOS places the subdirectory in the correct location in the directory structure.

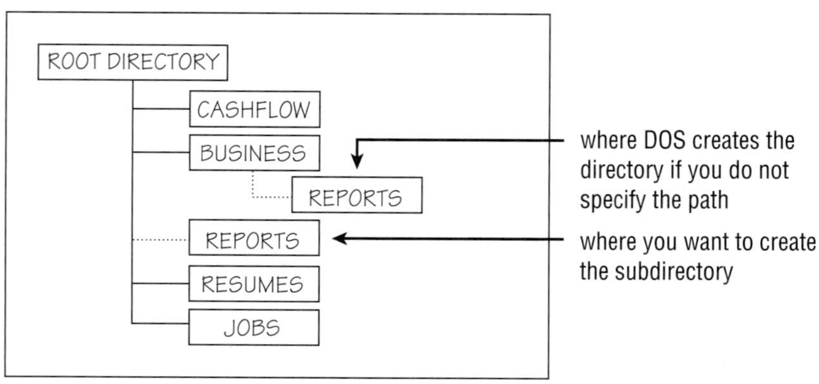

Figure 4-22
The importance of the path in specifying the location of a directory

To create the REPORTS subdirectory:

1. Type **MD \REPORTS** and press **[Enter]**. DOS creates this subdirectory and displays the DOS prompt.
2. Type **DIR ** and press **[Enter]**. From the directory listing, you can verify that you created this new subdirectory in the root directory. Press **[Spacebar]** or any other key until you return to the DOS prompt.

Now you can move files from the root directory to this new subdirectory. Follow the steps in the section below that describe how to perform these operations using the version of DOS on your system.

6.0 *6.2*

To move the monthly cashflow reports to the REPORTS subdirectory *using DOS 6.0 or 6.2*:

1. Type **MOVE \???_CASH** and press **[Spacebar]**. Type **\REPORTS** and press **[Enter]**. DOS moves six files that meet the file specification ???_CASH from the root directory to the REPORTS directory. You must specify the name of the root directory for the source files so that DOS knows where the files are located. You must also inform DOS that the target subdirectory is below the root directory; otherwise, DOS will assume it is below the current subdirectory. If there is a subdirectory by this same name below the current directory, DOS will move the files to a directory other than the one you want. If there is no subdirectory by this name, DOS will move and combine all the files into one larger file named REPORTS in the current directory.
2. Type **DIR \REPORTS** and press **[Enter]**. This operation verifies that the files are stored in the correct directory. See Figure 4-23.

current directory

path of new directory

```
A:\BUSINESS>DIR \REPORTS

 Volume in drive A is BUSINESS
 Volume Serial Number is 142E-14F9
 Directory of A:\REPORTS

.            <DIR>       10-23-93  10:25a
..           <DIR>       10-23-93  10:25a
APR_CASH           366 03-18-94  10:20a
FEB_CASH           369 03-18-94  10:14a
JAN_CASH           368 03-18-94  10:00a
JUN_CASH           365 03-18-94  10:45a
MAR_CASH           366 03-18-94  10:17a
MAY_CASH           364 03-18-94  10:43a
        8 file(s)         2198 bytes
                        661504 bytes free

A:\BUSINESS>
```

Figure 4-23
Viewing the contents of another subdirectory

3. Type **CD ** and press **[Enter]**. DOS returns to the root directory.
4. Type **DIR** and press **[Enter]**. DOS displays the names of the subdirectories and of the remaining files in the root directory of your Tutorial Disk. See Figure 4-24.

```
 Volume in drive A is BUSINESS
 Volume Serial Number is 142E-14F9
 Directory of A:\

BUSINESS     <DIR>        10-23-93  10:22a
CASHFLOW     <DIR>        10-22-93   6:29p
REPORTS      <DIR>        10-23-93  10:25a
FEESCALE             412 04-19-94   1:48p
JOBCOSTS FMT         294 03-30-94   2:22p
JOBCOSTS RPT         543 03-26-94   8:51a
JOBCOSTS WK1        1716 03-30-94   2:22p
RESUME   LTR        1182 04-15-94  11:49a
RESUME1  DOC        2435 04-12-94   2:25p
RESUME2  DOC        2435 04-12-94   2:41p
RESUME3  DOC        2392 04-12-94   3:00p
RESUME4  DOC        2386 04-12-94   3:12p
RESUME5  DOC        4043 04-12-94   4:08p
RESUME6  DOC        4043 04-12-94   4:08p
SCHEDULE FMT         794 04-07-94   1:21p
SCHEDULE WK1        2147 04-07-94   1:21p
       16 file(s)      24822 bytes
                      661504 bytes free

A:\>
```

alphabetical list of subdirectories below root directory

alphabetical list of filenames

Figure 4-24
The subdirectories and remaining files in the root directory

DOS 6.0 and 6.2 users: This is a good opportunity to take a break. Afterward, continue with the next section, entitled "Viewing the Directory Structure."

5.0

To move the monthly cashflow reports to the REPORTS subdirectory *using DOS 5.0*:

1. Type **COPY \???_CASH** and press **[Spacebar]**. Then type **\REPORTS** and press **[Enter]**. DOS copies six files from the root directory to the REPORTS directory. You must specify the name of the root directory for the source files so that DOS knows where the files are located. You must also inform DOS that the target subdirectory is below the root directory; otherwise, DOS will assume it is below the current subdirectory. If there is a subdirectory by the same name below the current directory, DOS will copy the files to a directory other than the one you want. If there is no subdirectory by this name, DOS will copy and combine all the files into one larger file named REPORTS in the current directory.
2. Type **DIR \REPORTS** and press **[Enter]**. This operation verifies that the files are stored in the correct directory. See Figure 4-23.
3. Type **DEL \???_CASH** and press **[Enter]**. *Be sure you type a Slash (\) before the file specification.* DOS deletes these files from the root directory.
4. Type **CD ** and press **[Enter]**. DOS returns to the root directory.
5. Type **DIR** and press **[Enter]**. DOS displays the names of your subdirectories and the names of the remaining files in the root directory of your Tutorial Disk. See Figure 4-24.

DOS 5.0 users: This is a good opportunity to take a break.

VIEWING THE DIRECTORY STRUCTURE

You want to view a graphical representation of the partially completed directory structure of your diskette. You can use the TREE command to display a directory tree from the DOS prompt. A **directory tree** is a diagrammatic representation of the directory structure of a hard disk or diskette. It shows the current directory and all subdirectories below the current directory. The TREE command is an external command with the following syntax:

TREE [*drive:*][*path*]

If you want to view a directory of another drive, you must specify its drive name. If you want to start with a specific subdirectory in the directory structure of a hard disk or diskette, you specify that directory's path. If you do not specify a drive or path, DOS assumes you want to view the directory structure of the current drive, starting with the current directory. If you want this directory tree to include the root directory and all subdirectories, you must start at the root directory or specify the root directory as the path.

To view a directory tree of your Tutorial Disk:

1. If necessary, power on your computer system, install DOSKEY, and specify default switches for the DIR command using the instructions on pages 56 through 58.
2. Be sure the current drive contains your Tutorial Disk. Also be sure the current directory is the root directory.
3. Type **CLS** and press **[Enter]** to clear the screen.
4. Type **TREE** and press **[Enter]**. DOS displays a diagrammatic representation of the directory structure of your diskette. See Figure 4-25. Next to the name of the drive, DOS displays a dot (.) to indicate that the directory tree starts at the current directory. The directory tree shows the three subdirectories you created earlier at the DOS prompt.

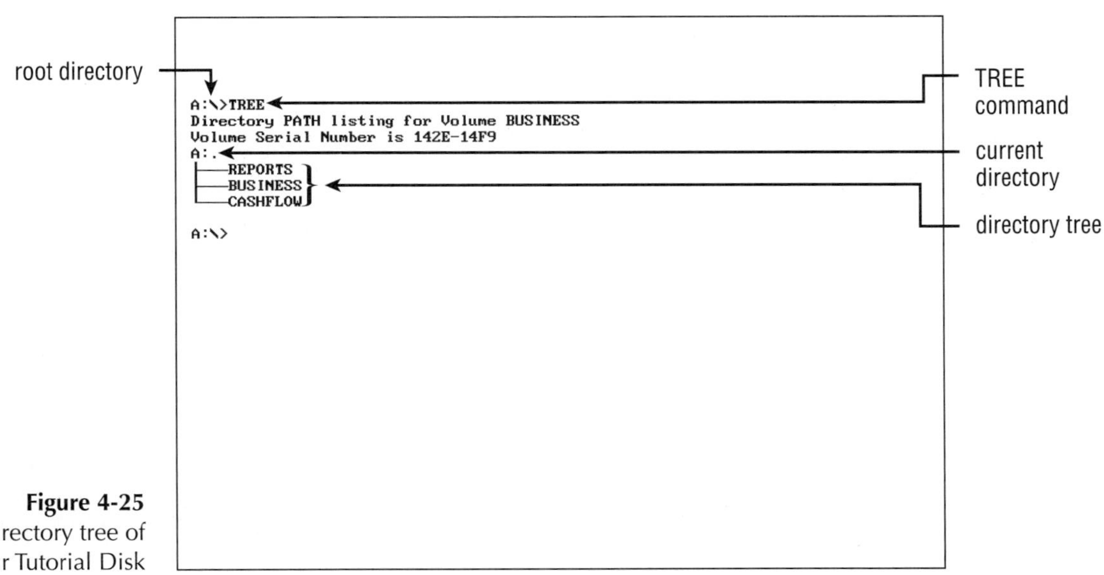

Figure 4-25
A directory tree of your Tutorial Disk

In this directory tree, you see the relationship of the subdirectories to the root directory. As you construct or revise the directory structure of your hard disk or diskettes from the DOS prompt to meet the changing needs of your business, you can quickly view the directory structure to verify directory operations and to refresh your memory of the disk's directory structure.

CREATING A SUBDIRECTORY IN THE DOS SHELL

You decide to create the additional subdirectories from the DOS Shell. As you have discovered, the DOS Shell provides a visual interface with menus and icons, automatically displays filenames, and simplifies DOS command operations. You will find that you can use the DOS Shell to move files from one subdirectory to another and to quickly verify these operations.

To load the DOS Shell:

1. Type **DOSSHELL** and press **[Enter]**. After DOS loads the DOS Shell, note that the directory tree window contains a diagrammatic representation of the directory structure of the diskette. See Figure 4-26.

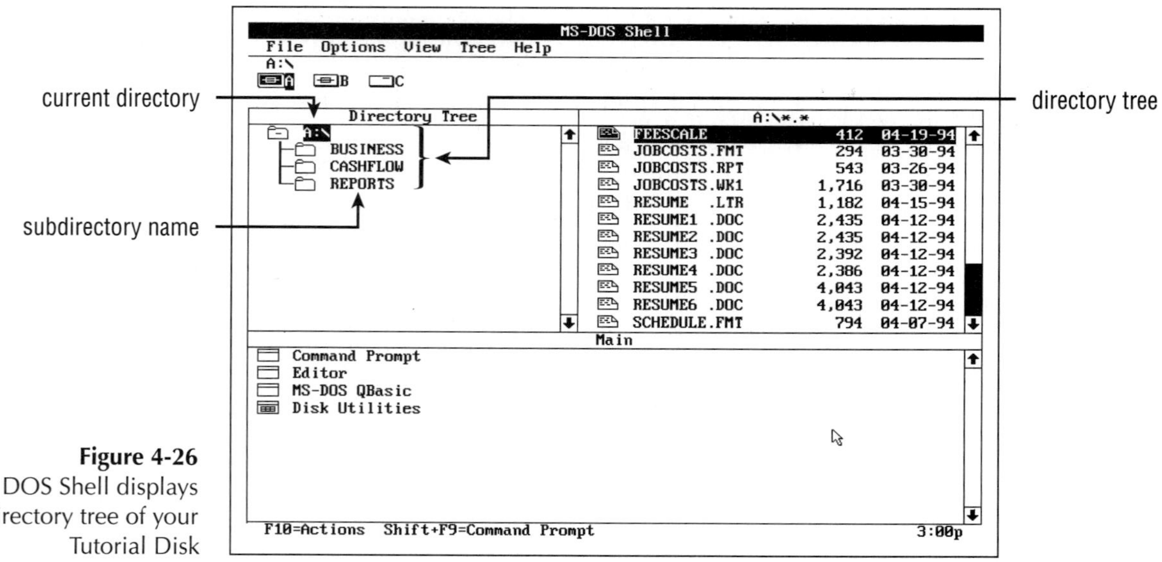

Figure 4-26
The DOS Shell displays a directory tree of your Tutorial Disk

This directory tree is similar to the one that the TREE command produces at the DOS prompt. The A:\ in the directory tree window is highlighted, indicating that it is the current directory. If your Tutorial Disk is in drive B, you will see B:\ in this window.

In the file list window, the DOS Shell shows the files stored in the root directory because that directory is the current directory. In the title bar for the file list window, the DOS Shell displays the file specification A:*.* (or B:*.*) to indicate that the list of files includes all files in the root directory of drive A (or drive B).

You need to create two more directories according to your original plan—RESUMES and JOBS.

To create the RESUMES subdirectory with the DOS Shell:

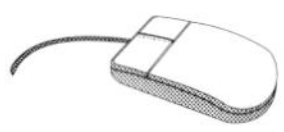

1. Press **[Tab]** to move the selection cursor to the directory tree window.

   If you are using the mouse, click the **directory tree window title bar**.

2. Press **[F10]** (Actions) to access the menu bar, press **[Enter]** to select the File menu, and then type **E** to select the Create Directory option.

   If you are using the mouse, click **File**, then click **Create Directory**.

   The DOS Shell displays the Create Directory dialog box. See Figure 4-27. The dialog box shows the parent directory name, which in this case is A:\, and prompts for the new directory name.

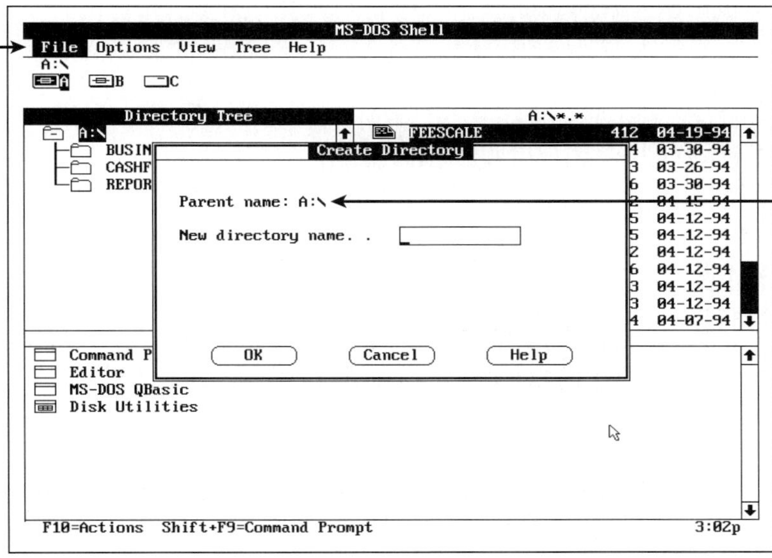

Figure 4-27 The DOS Shell's Create Directory dialog box prompts for a directory name

3. Type **RESUMES** and press **[Enter]**.

   If you are using a mouse, type **RESUMES** and click **OK**.

   The DOS Shell creates the RESUMES subdirectory on the current drive and updates the directory tree. See Figure 4-28.

new subdirectory

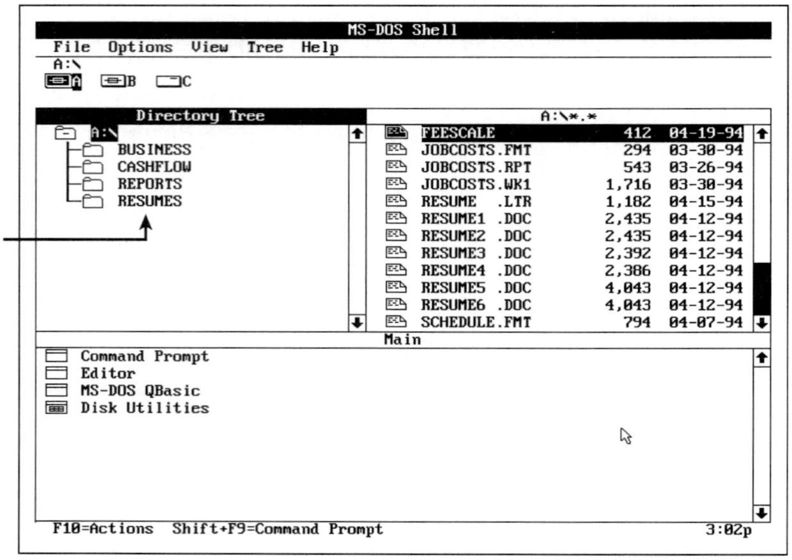

Figure 4-28
The DOS Shell adds a new subdirectory, RESUMES, to the directory tree

MOVING FILES IN THE DOS SHELL

You must now select the files to move to the RESUMES directory. Instead of moving the files one at a time, you can move them as a group in one step. Even if you use DOS 5.0, you do not need to copy the files to a new directory and then delete them from the original directory.

To move the résumé template files from the root directory to the RESUMES subdirectory:

1. Press **[Tab]** to move the selection cursor to the file list window.

   If you are using the mouse, click in the **file list window's title bar**.

2. Type **R** to move the selection cursor to the first file that starts with the letter "R"—RESUME.LTR.

   If you are using the mouse, click the filename **RESUME.LTR**.

   The DOS Shell highlights the filename RESUME.LTR.

3. Press and hold down **[Shift]** while you press **[↓]** (Down Arrow) to highlight all the files that have RESUME as the first six characters of the filename. The last filename in this group is RESUME6.DOC. Then release [Shift].

   If you are using the mouse, press and hold down **[Shift]** while you click **RESUME6.DOC**, the last filename you want to include in this selection. Then release [Shift].

   Figure 4-29 shows the selected files.

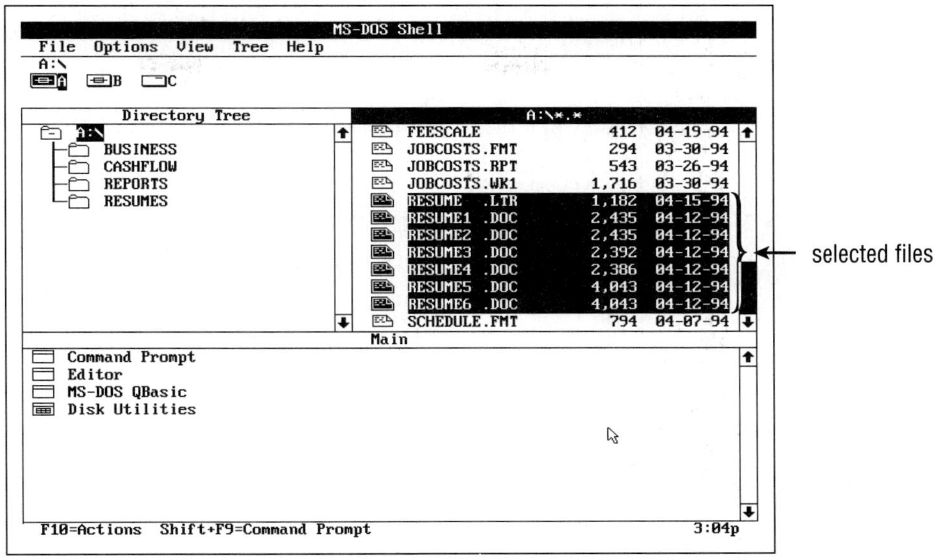

Figure 4-29
A group of selected files in the file list window

4. Press **[F10]** (Actions) and press **[Enter]** to select the File menu. Type **M** to select the Move option. (You can also use the shortcut Move key, **[F7]**.) The DOS Shell displays the Move File dialog box. See Figure 4-30. The selected files are listed in the first text box, next to the From prompt. The DOS Shell shows only a partial list of files in this text box. Your view might be different from that shown in Figure 4-30. The cursor is in the next text box, to the right of the To prompt. The DOS Shell assumes you want to move the files to the current directory. Press **[End]** to move the cursor past the path of the current directory. Then type **RESUMES** to specify the remainder of the path for the new subdirectory, and press **[Enter]**. *Be sure the target directory is A:\RESUMES (or B:\RESUMES).* The DOS Shell displays a "Moving file" dialog box as it moves the seven files to the RESUMES subdirectory. See Figure 4-31.

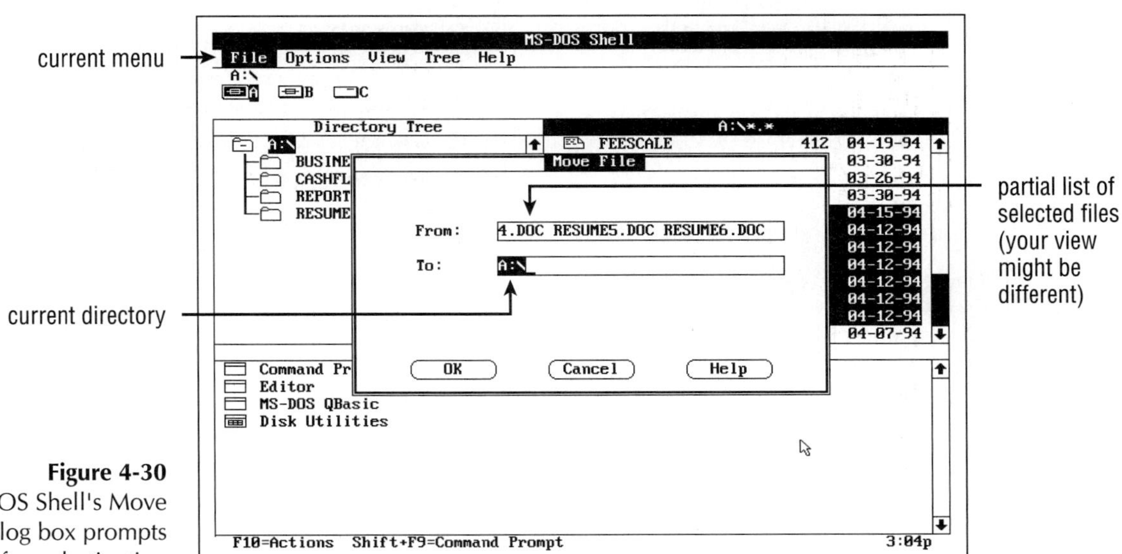

Figure 4-30
The DOS Shell's Move File dialog box prompts for a destination

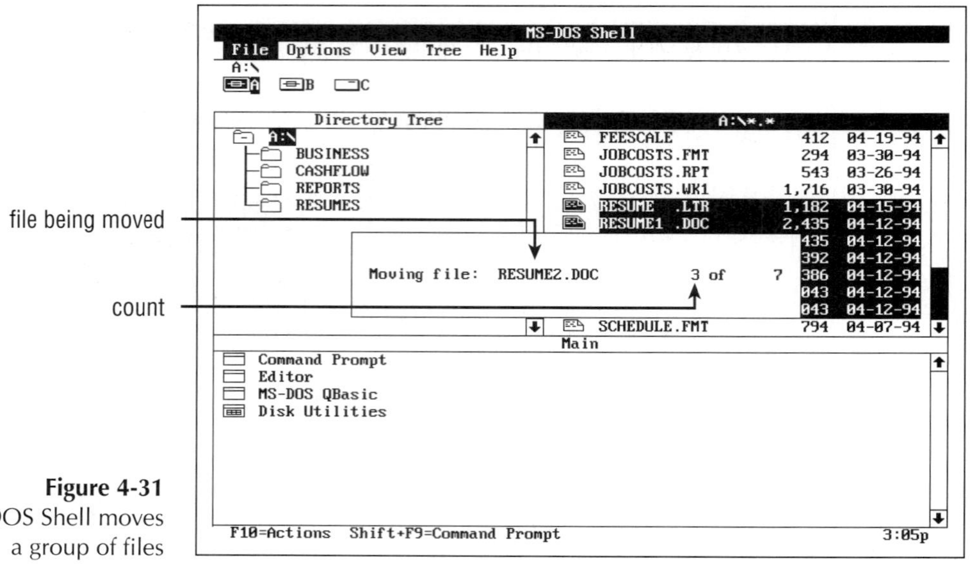

Figure 4-31
The DOS Shell moves a group of files

If you are using the mouse, click **one of the selected files**, hold down the left mouse button, and drag the pointer to the folder icon adjacent to the subdirectory name RESUMES in the directory tree window. As you point to this subdirectory, the pointer changes to an arrow if you are in text mode or a stack of documents or files if you are in graphics mode. See Figure 4-32. Release the mouse button. The DOS Shell displays the Confirm Mouse Operation dialog box and asks if you want to move the selected files to A:\RESUMES (or B:\RESUMES). See Figure 4-33. Click **Yes**. The DOS Shell moves the files to the RESUMES subdirectory.

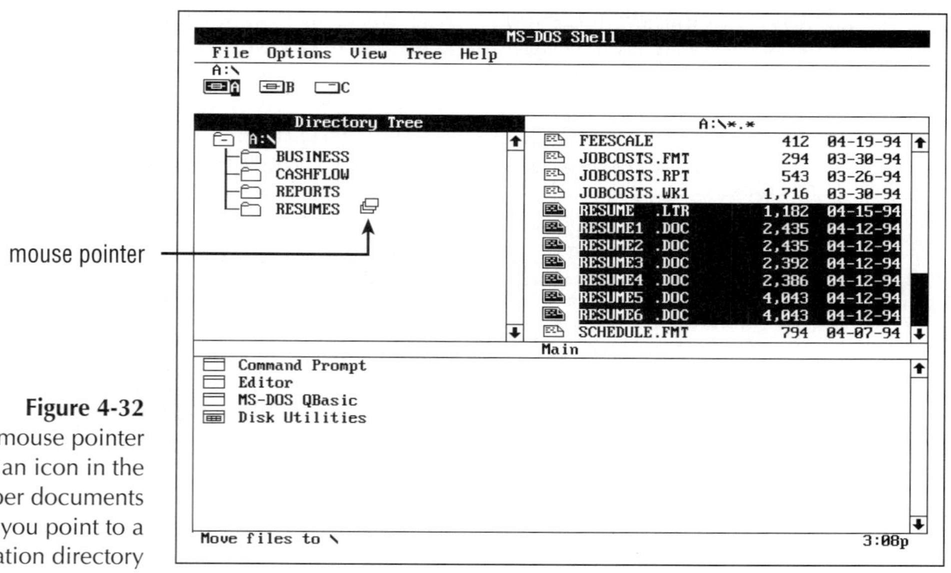

Figure 4-32
The mouse pointer changes to an icon in the shape of paper documents as you point to a destination directory

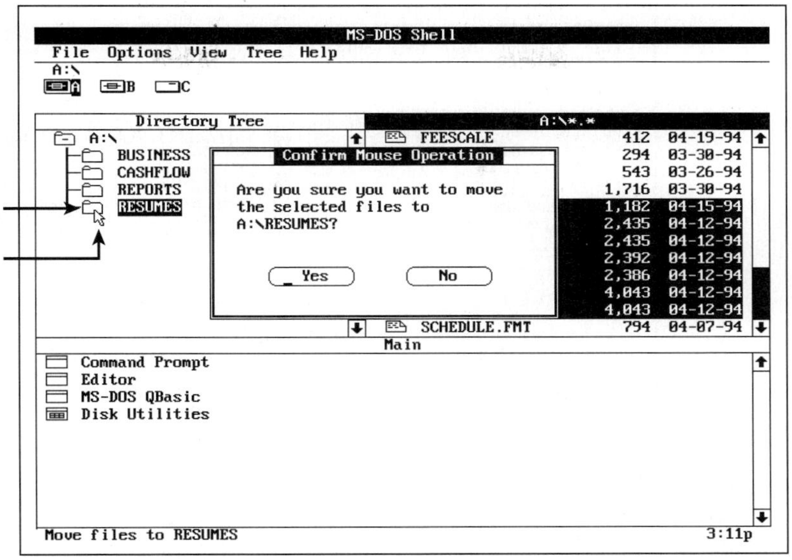

Figure 4-33
The Confirm Mouse Operations dialog box prompts you to verify a Move operation

REFRESHING THE DOS SHELL

You next want to verify these operations and be sure your business files are stored in the correct directory. If you now select the RESUMES subdirectory, you will not see any filenames listed in the file list window if you are using DOS 5.0 or 6.0. You must first use [F5] (Refresh) in DOS 5.0 and 6.0 so that the DOS Shell rereads your Tutorial Disk. DOS 6.2 automatically updates the file list.

To refresh the display of the files on your Tutorial Disk:

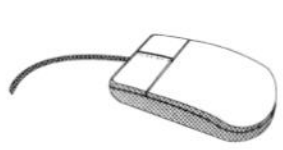

1. Press **[F5]** (Refresh).

   If you are using the mouse, click **View**, then click **Refresh**.

   The DOS Shell rereads your Tutorial Disk.

2. Press **[Tab]** to move the selection cursor to the directory tree window. Then press **[↓]** (Down Arrow) until you highlight the name of the RESUMES subdirectory.

   If you are using the mouse, click **RESUMES** in the directory tree window.

   The DOS Shell updates the file list window to show the files in the selected subdirectory. RESUMES contains the seven files that you just moved. See Figure 4-34.

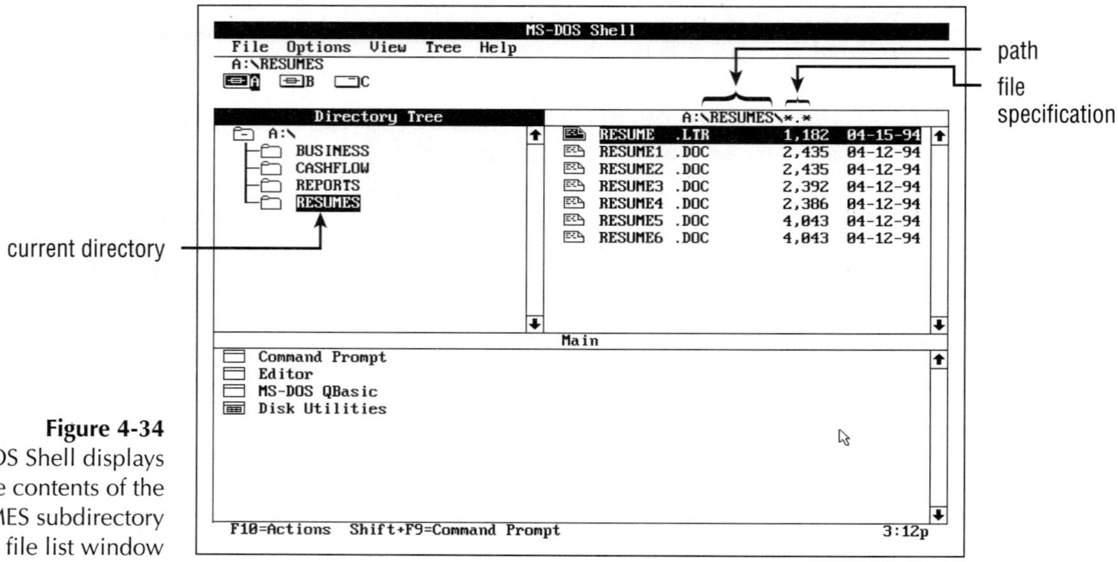

Figure 4-34
The DOS Shell displays the contents of the RESUMES subdirectory in the file list window

3. Press **[Home]** to move the selection cursor to the root directory.

   If you are using the mouse, click the **root directory icon**.

COMPLETING A DIRECTORY STRUCTURE WITH THE DOS SHELL

According to your organizational plan, you have one more subdirectory to create. This subdirectory, named JOBS, will contain the files that store information on each job that you do for a client.

To complete the directory structure:

1. Create the JOBS subdirectory according to your original plan for organizing subdirectories and files on your Tutorial Disk.
2. After you create the JOBS subdirectory, move the remaining files in the root directory to this subdirectory. You can select the file list window, and then use the Select All option on the File menu to select all the files at once.
3. Reread your Tutorial Disk.
4. Select the JOBS subdirectory. The DOS Shell updates the file list window to show the files in the JOBS subdirectory. See Figure 4-35.

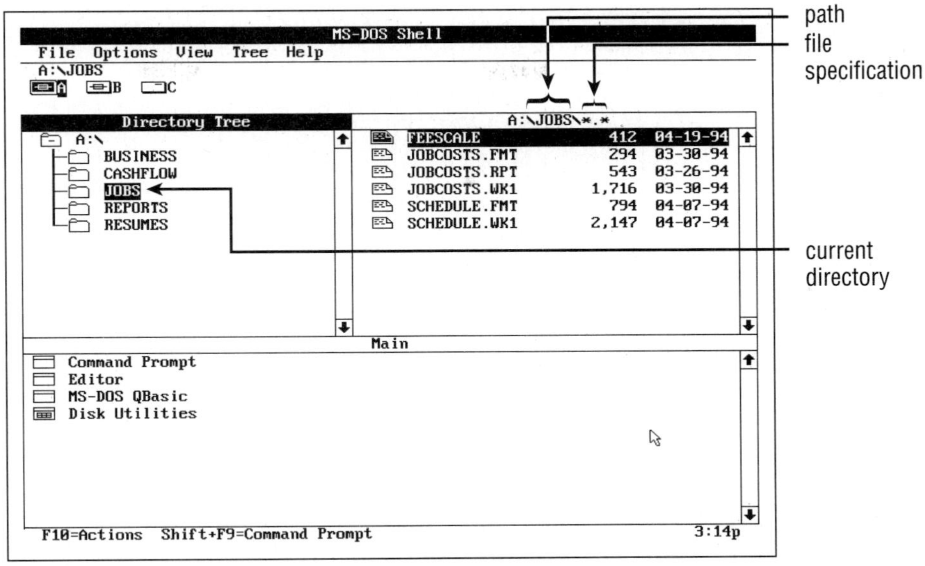

Figure 4-35
The DOS Shell displays the contents of the JOBS subdirectory in the file list window

5. Return to the root directory.

You have created five subdirectories and moved groups of files to those subdirectories using commands at the DOS prompt and in the DOS Shell. Because your Tutorial Disk has changed significantly, you might want to make a backup copy of it now. If you would like to make a backup copy, use the DISKCOPY command and refer to page 29 for help.

EXPANDING THE SUBDIRECTORY STRUCTURE

After reorganizing the files on your diskette into subdirectories, you realize that you could create several subdirectories below the CASHFLOW subdirectory and organize the files into smaller groups, which would allow you to work more easily with these files. You can also add more files to each subdirectory as the need arises. Figure 4-36 shows your updated plan for organizing the CASHFLOW subdirectory into three subdirectories—one called PRJCASH for storing cashflow projections for your business, one called INVOICES for storing files used to track the status of outstanding invoices, and one called SUMMARY for files with summary reports on your business.

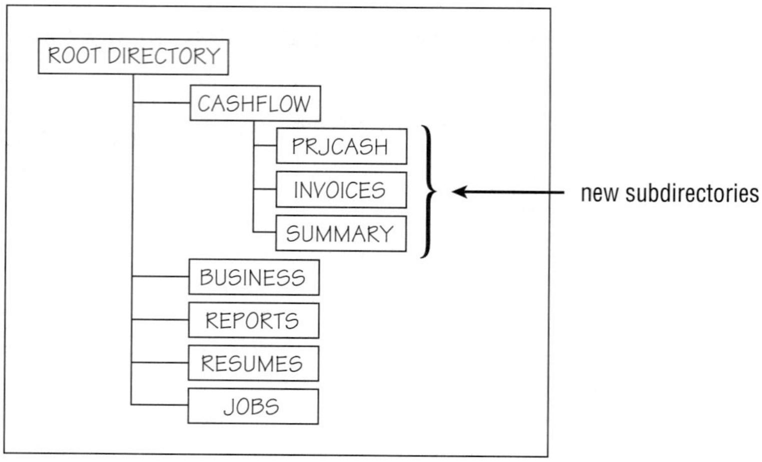

Figure 4-36
The revised directory structure of your Tutorial Disk

The first subdirectory you will create is PRJCASH. This subdirectory will contain the five files that begin with the word INCOME (but which have different file extensions), as well as the files PRJ_INC and QTR_INC. You decide to use the DOS Shell to create the subdirectory.

To create the PRJCASH subdirectory below the CASHFLOW subdirectory:

1. Be sure the current drive contains your Tutorial Disk.
2. Be sure the selection cursor is on the root directory in the directory tree window.
3. Press [↓] (Down Arrow) twice to highlight the subdirectory named CASHFLOW.

   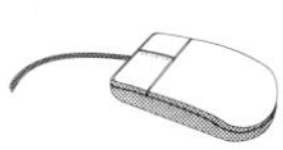

   If you are using the mouse, click the subdirectory name **CASHFLOW** in the directory tree window.

   The DOS Shell selects this subdirectory and updates the file list window.
4. Press **[F10]** (Actions) to access the menu bar, press **[Enter]** to select the File menu, and then type **E** to select the Create Directory option.

   If you are using the mouse, click **File**, then click **Create Directory**.

   The DOS Shell displays the Create Directory dialog box. The parent directory's name is A:\CASHFLOW (or B:\CASHFLOW).
5. Type **PRJCASH** and press **[Enter]**.

   If you are using the mouse, type **PRJCASH** and click **OK**.

   The DOS Shell creates the PRJCASH subdirectory below the current directory. See Figure 4-37.

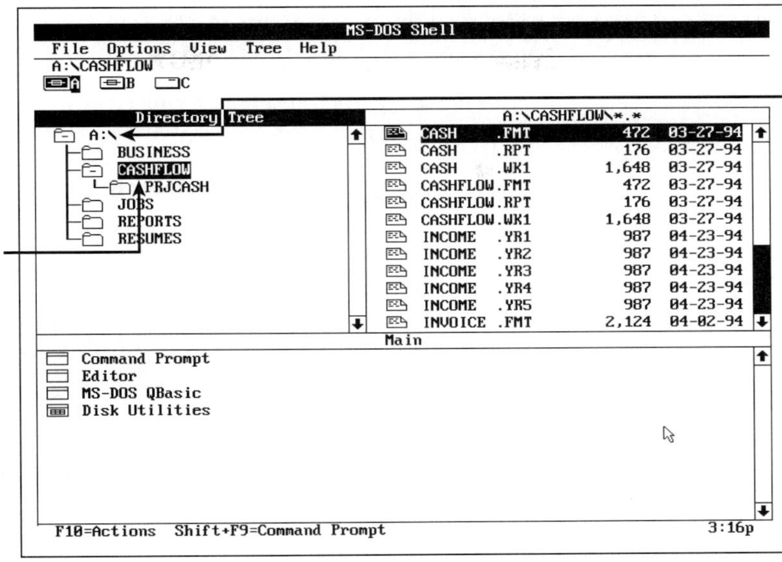

current directory

new subdirectory

Figure 4-37
The directory tree shows the newly added PRJCASH subdirectory below the CASHFLOW subdirectory

6. Press **[Tab]** to move to the file list window.

   If you are using the mouse, click the **file list window title bar**.

Now you are ready to select the files to move.

7. Type **I** to move the selection cursor to the filename INCOME.YR1.

   If you are using the mouse, click the filename **INCOME.YR1**.

8. Press and hold down **[Shift]** while you press [↓] (Down Arrow) and select INCOME.YR1, INCOME.YR2, INCOME.YR3, INCOME.YR4, and INCOME.YR5.

   If you are using the mouse, press and hold down **[Shift]**, click the filename **INCOME.YR5**, and release [Shift].

Extending a File Selection

You need to add two more files to your selection, but they do not follow the files you just highlighted on the file list. If you are using the keyboard, you can use [Shift][F8] (Add) to add more files to the selection. You point to each additional file and press [Spacebar]. If you are using a mouse, you can hold [Ctrl] while you click on each file you want to add to the selection.

To add the files PRJ_INC and QTR_INC:

1. Press and hold down **[Shift]** while you press **[F8]** (Add). Then release both [F8] and [Shift]. The ADD indicator appears in the lower-right corner of the status bar. Type **P** to move the selection cursor to the file PRJ_INC. Press **[Spacebar]** to add this file to the selection. Press [↓] (Down Arrow) to highlight QTR_INC. Finally, press **[Spacebar]** to add this file to the selection.

If you are using the mouse, click the **scroll bar** until you see the filename QTR_INC. Press and hold **[Ctrl]** while you click **PRJ_INC** and then **QTR_INC**. Release [Ctrl].

Figure 4-38 shows the selected files.

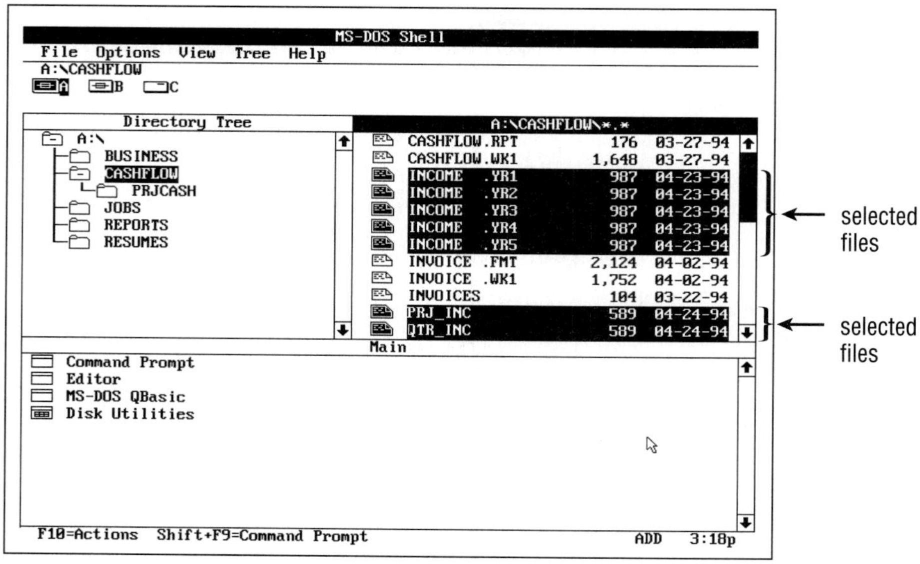

Figure 4-38
Extending a selection in the file list window to include two groups of files

Now move the selected files.

2. Press **[F7]** (Move). The DOS Shell displays the Move File dialog box with the directory name A:\CASHFLOW (or B:\CASHFLOW). Press **[End]** and type **\PRJCASH**. You *must* type the Backslash (\) before PRJCASH to separate the name of this subdirectory from its parent directory name. See Figure 4-39 to be sure you enter the path correctly. Then press **[Enter]**.

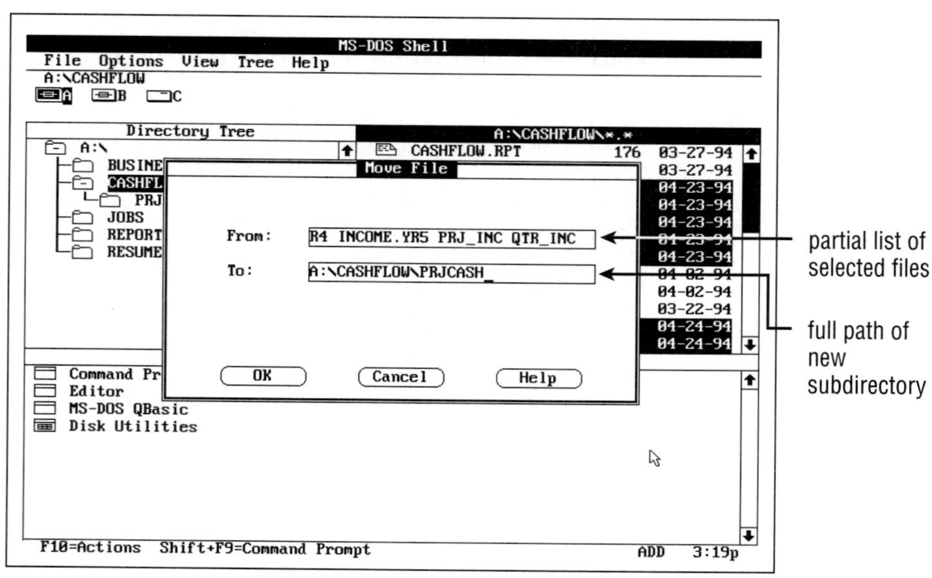

Figure 4-39
Specifying the full path of the target subdirectory

If you are using the mouse, click **one of the selected files**, hold down the mouse button, and drag the pointer to the folder icon next to the subdirectory name PRJCASH in the directory tree window. Then release the left mouse button. The DOS Shell displays the Confirm Mouse Operation dialog box and asks you if you want to move the files to A:\CASHFLOW\PRJCASH (or B:\CASHFLOW\PRJCASH). Click **Yes**.

The DOS Shell moves the files to the PRJCASH subdirectory.

You want to verify these operations before your make any more subdirectories.

3. Press **[F5]** (Refresh) to refresh the display of files on your diskette.

   If you are using the mouse, click **View**, then click **Refresh**.

EXPANDING THE DIRECTORY TREE

After you tell the DOS Shell to refresh the display of files on a diskette, it automatically collapses the directory tree so that you see only the subdirectories below the root directory. However, the DOS Shell places a plus sign (+) next to the subdirectory name CASHFLOW to indicate that there are subdirectories below it. You can use the Expand All option on the Tree menu to display the entire directory tree.

To expand the directory tree and include these subdirectories as part of the directory tree:

1. Press **[F10]** (Actions), press **[→]** (Right Arrow) three times to highlight the Tree menu, and press **[Enter]** to select Tree.

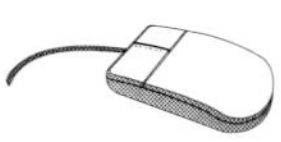

   If you are using the mouse, click **Tree**.

   The drop-down Tree menu appears with options for controlling the display of the directory tree.

2. Press [↓] (Down Arrow) *twice* to highlight Expand All and press **[Enter]** to select this option.

   If you are using the mouse, click **Expand All**.

   The DOS Shell expands the directory tree, so you can view the files in each of the subdirectories below the CASHFLOW subdirectory.

3. Press **[Tab]** to move the selection cursor to the directory tree window. Press [↓] (Down Arrow) until you highlight the subdirectory name PRJCASH.

   If you are using the mouse, click the subdirectory name **PRJCASH**.

   The file list window displays the files that you moved to the PRJCASH subdirectory. See Figure 4-40. Note the full path in the title bar of the file list window.

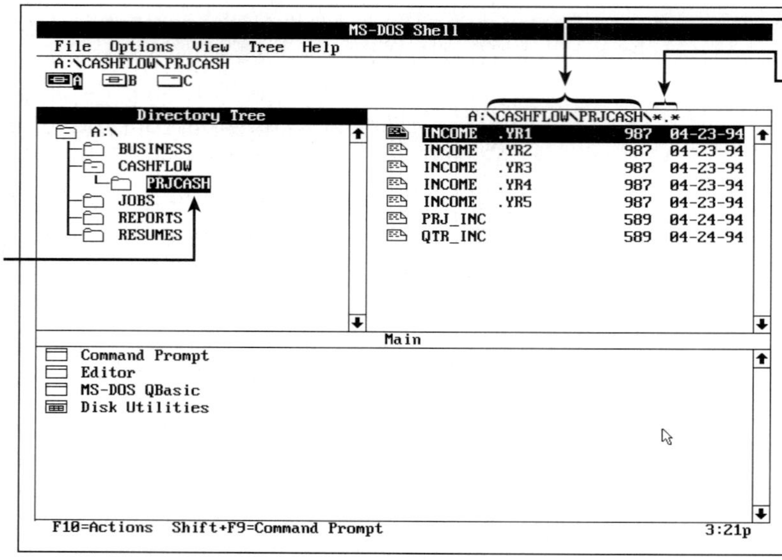

Figure 4-40
The DOS Shell displays the contents of the PRJCASH subdirectory in the file list window

Creating a Directory for Invoice Files

Because a new business must stay on top of its cash flow, you want to be able to quickly examine the status of outstanding invoices. You decide to create another new subdirectory below the CASHFLOW directory and move the invoice-tracking files to that subdirectory.

To create the INVOICES subdirectory:

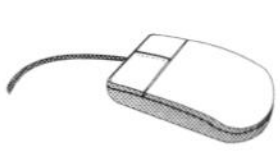

1. Press [↑] (Up Arrow) to select the CASHFLOW subdirectory.

   If you are using the mouse, click the subdirectory name **CASHFLOW**.

2. Press **[F10]** (Actions) to access the menu bar, press **[Enter]** to select the File menu, and type **E** to select the Create Directory option.

   If you are using the mouse, click **File**, then click **Create Directory**.

3. Type **INVOICES** and then press **[Enter]**.

   If you are using the mouse, type **INVOICES** and click **OK**.

   The DOS Shell displays the Create Directory dialog box and displays the message "Access denied." See Figure 4-41. An error has occurred. The subdirectory name that you specified is also the name of an existing file. The dialog box asks you to verify whether you want to continue or not. You have two options—rename the file or select another name for the new subdirectory. You decide to rename the file.

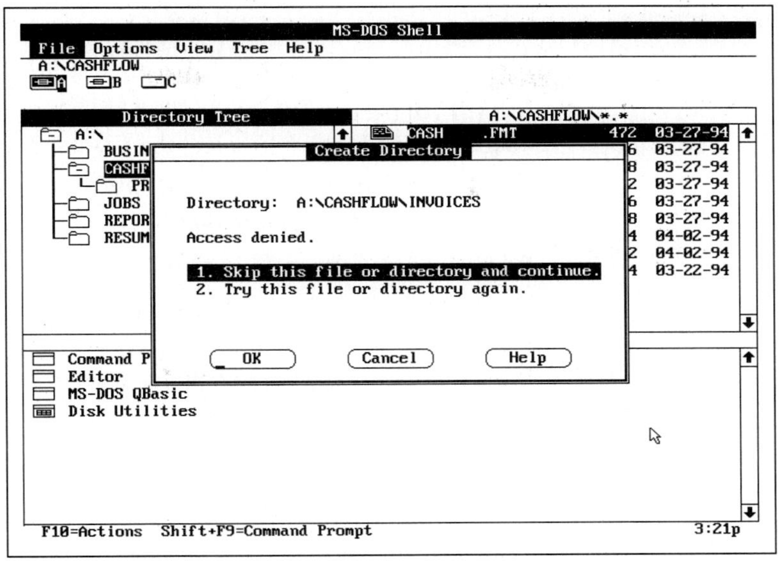

Figure 4-41
The DOS Shell's Create Directory dialog box warns of an error

4. Press **[Enter]**.

   If you are using the mouse, click **OK**.

   The DOS Shell skips this directory and lets you continue.

5. Press **[Tab]** to move the selection cursor to the file list window.

   If you are using the mouse, click the **file list window title bar**.

6. Type **I** to select the first filename that starts with the letter "I." Then press [↓] (Down Arrow) twice to highlight the filename INVOICES.

   If you are using the mouse, click the **scroll arrow** until you see the filename INVOICES. Then click **INVOICES**.

7. Press **[F10]** (Actions), press **[Enter]** to select File, and type **N** for the Rename command.

   If you are using the mouse, click **File**, then click **Rename**.

   The DOS Shell displays the Rename File dialog box.

8. Type **INVOICE.RPT** and press **[Enter]**.

   If you are using the mouse, type **INVOICE.RPT** and click **OK**.

   The DOS Shell renames the file and updates the file list window.

Now that you have renamed the INVOICES file, you can create a subdirectory with the name INVOICES.

To create the INVOICES subdirectory:

1. Press **[Shift][Tab]** (Backtab). This returns you to the directory tree window. This key combination is called the **Backtab key** because it allows you to move back to the previous window.

If you are using the mouse, click the **CASHFLOW** subdirectory in the directory tree window.

2. Be sure the DOS Shell highlights the subdirectory name CASHFLOW.
3. Press **[F10]** (Actions) to access the menu bar, press **[Enter]** to select the File menu, and type **E** to select the Create Directory option.

   If you are using the mouse, click **File**, then click **Create Directory**.
4. Type **INVOICES** and press **[Enter]**.

   If you are using the mouse, type **INVOICES** and click **OK**.

   The DOS Shell positions the INVOICES subdirectory below CASHFLOW in the directory tree.
5. Press **[Tab]** to move the selection cursor to the file list window.

   If you are using the mouse, click the **file list window title bar**.
6. Type **I** to select the first filename that starts with the letter "I."

   If you are using the mouse, click the **first filename that starts with the letter "I."**
7. Press and hold **[Shift]** while you press [↓] (Down Arrow) twice to select the three invoice files. Then release [Shift].

   If you are using the mouse, press **[Shift]** and then click the filename **INVOICE.WK1** to select the three invoice files.
8. Press **[F7]** (Move). The DOS Shell displays the Move File dialog box. Press **[End]**, type **\INVOICES** and press **[Enter]**.

   If you are using the mouse, click **File**, then click **Move**. When the DOS Shell displays the Move File dialog box, click **after the path**. Then type **\INVOICES** and click **OK**.

   The DOS Shell moves the files to the INVOICES subdirectory.

You are now ready to reread the Tutorial Disk.

To update the file list window:

1. Press **[F5]** (Refresh).

   If you are using the mouse, click **View**, then click **Refresh**.

   The DOS Shell rereads your Tutorial Disk.
2. Press **[F10]** (Actions) and type **T** to select the Tree menu.

   If you are using the mouse, click **Tree** to select the Tree menu.
3. Type **A** to select Expand All.

   If you are using the mouse, click **Expand All**.

   The DOS Shell expands the directory tree.

Now verify the move operation.

4. Press **[Tab]** to move the selection cursor to the directory tree window.

   If you are using a mouse, click the **directory tree window title bar**.
5. Press [↓] (Down Arrow) until you highlight the directory name INVOICES.

If you are using a mouse, click the directory name **INVOICES**.

DOS displays the newly moved files in the file list window.

6. Press [↑] (Up Arrow) to select the CASHFLOW subdirectory.

Creating a Directory for Summary Files

You have one more subdirectory to create according to your revised plan. This subdirectory, which you want to call SUMMARY, will store the files that contain the cashflow summaries.

To create the SUMMARY subdirectory:

1. Create the SUMMARY subdirectory under the CASHFLOW directory, according to your revised plan for organizing subdirectories and files on your Tutorial Disk.
2. After you create the SUMMARY subdirectory, move the remaining files in the CASHFLOW directory to this subdirectory.
3. Reread your Tutorial Disk, then expand the directory tree.
4. Move to the directory tree window and select the SUMMARY subdirectory. The DOS Shell shows the files that you moved to the SUMMARY subdirectory. See Figure 4-42.

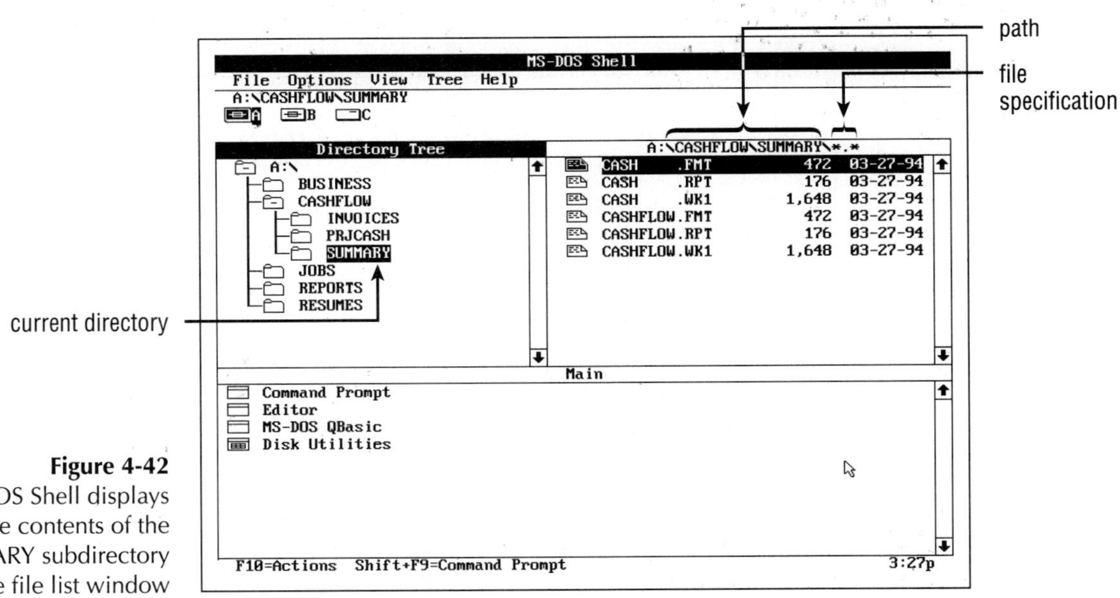

Figure 4-42
The DOS Shell displays the contents of the SUMMARY subdirectory in the file list window

5. Select the root directory before you exit the DOS Shell.
6. Exit the DOS Shell.

Navigating the Directory Tree at the DOS Prompt

In the DOS Shell, you selected and viewed the contents of directories below the CASHFLOW subdirectory by moving the selection cursor in the directory tree window. Now you want to learn how to navigate within the directory tree at the DOS prompt so that you can use both approaches in the daily operations of your business and when you work in client offices.

There are two techniques you can use: You can change to a subdirectory in one step by specifying its full path or you can traverse the directory tree one subdirectory at a time by specifying the directory's name. However, in some cases you might also need to specify part of the path.

You want to examine each of the subdirectories of CASHFLOW and return to the root directory. First, let's change to the INVOICES directory by specifying its full path.

To change to the INVOICES subdirectory in one step:

1. Be sure you are at the root directory of the drive that contains your Tutorial Disk.
2. Type **CD CASHFLOW\INVOICES** and press **[Enter]**. The DOS prompt shows that the current directory is the INVOICES subdirectory.
3. Type **DIR** and press **[Enter]** to view the files in this subdirectory. See Figure 4-43.

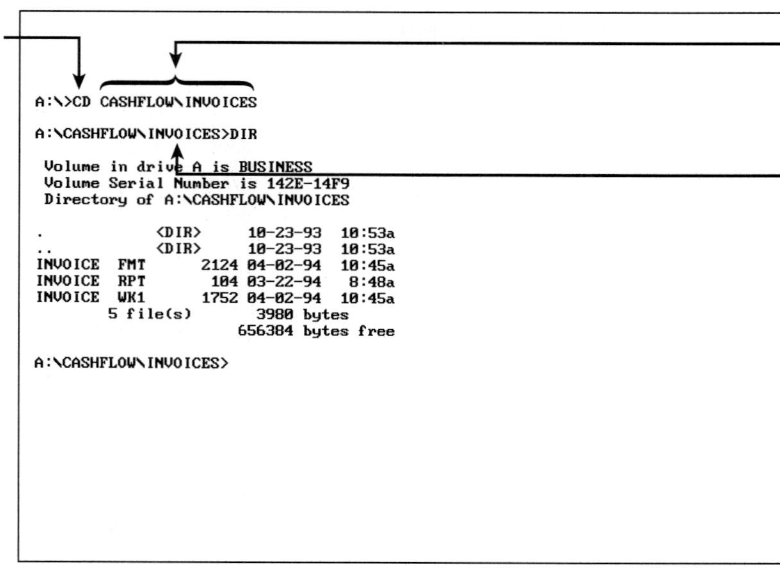

Figure 4-43
Displaying the contents of the INVOICES subdirectory, positioned two directories below the root directory

4. Type **CD ** and press **[Enter]**. As you can tell from the DOS prompt, DOS moved up two directories to the root directory.

Stepping Down the Directory Tree

You next want to examine the CASHFLOW and the PRJCASH subdirectories. You can step down the directory tree one directory at a time.

To change to the CASHFLOW subdirectory and then the PRJCASH subdirectory:

1. Type **CD CASHFLOW** and press **[Enter]**. The DOS prompt shows that the current directory is the CASHFLOW subdirectory.
2. Type **DIR** and press **[Enter]**. DOS displays a list of the subdirectories below CASHFLOW. See Figure 4-44.

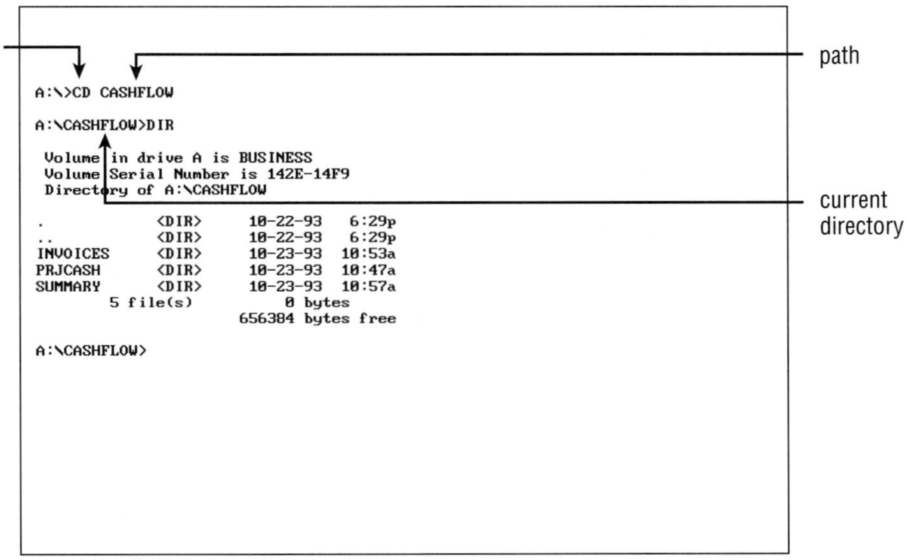

Figure 4-44
The subdirectories below the CASHFLOW directory

3. Type **CD PRJCASH** and press **[Enter]**. The DOS prompt shows that the current directory is the PRJCASH subdirectory, which is positioned below the CASHFLOW subdirectory.
4. Type **DIR** and press **[Enter]** to view the files in this subdirectory.

Stepping Up the Directory

You first want to return to the CASHFLOW directory and then to the root directory. If you change to a subdirectory and then want to move one level higher in the directory tree to its parent directory, you can use one of these variations of the Change Directory commands:

CD ..

CHDIR ..

Because .. (dot dot) refers to the parent directory of the current directory, you can change to a parent directory without specifying its full path.

Let's return to the root directory, one directory level at a time.

To change to the parent directory of PRJCASH:

1. Type **CD ..** and press **[Enter]**. Remember, the DOS prompt shows that the current directory is the CASHFLOW subdirectory. You can now use this same command to move to the parent directory of CASHFLOW.
2. Type **CD ..** and press **[Enter]**. The DOS prompt shows that you are at the root directory. See Figure 4-45.

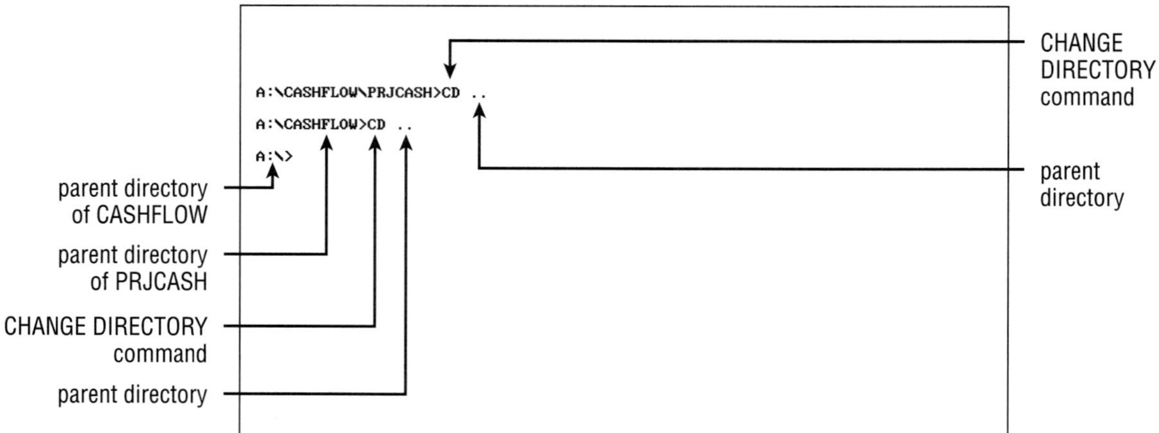

Figure 4-45
Stepping up one directory level at a time to return to the root directory

Next you want to change to the SUMMARY subdirectory, examine its files, and switch to the INVOICES subdirectory before returning to the root directory.

To traverse the subdirectories of CASHFLOW:

1. Type **CD CASHFLOW\SUMMARY** and press **[Enter]**. The DOS prompt shows that the current directory is SUMMARY.
2. Type **DIR** and press **[Enter]** to view the files in this subdirectory.
3. Type **CD ..\INVOICES** and press **[Enter]**. This command tells DOS to change to the INVOICES subdirectory, which is below the parent directory of SUMMARY. The DOS prompt shows that the current directory is INVOICES. See Figure 4-46. You could also enter CD \CASHFLOW\INVOICES to achieve the same result.

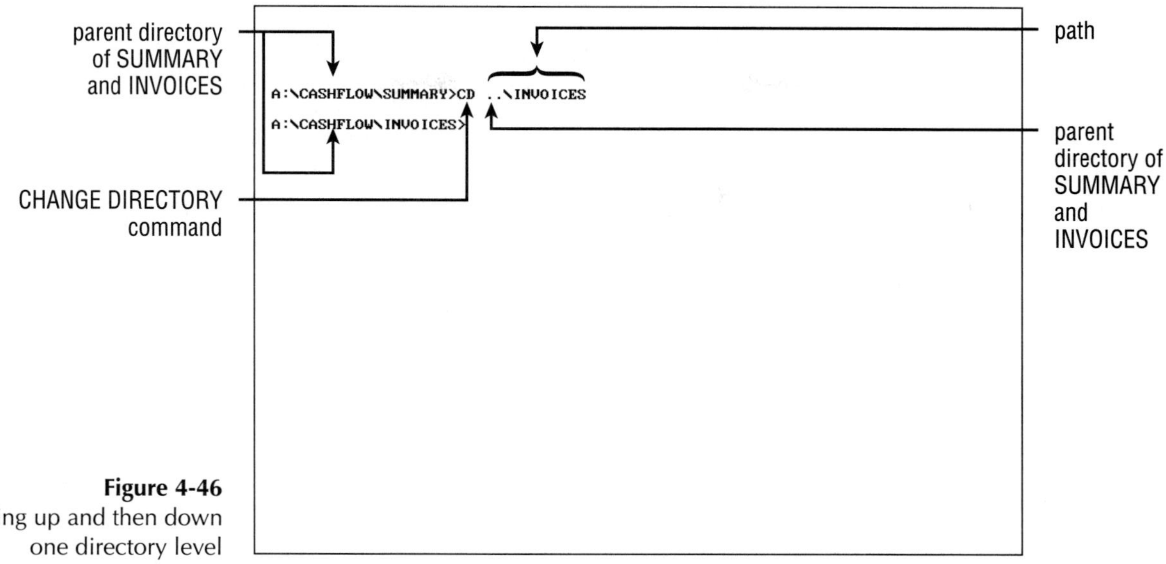

Figure 4-46
Moving up and then down one directory level

4. Type **CD ** and press **[Enter]** to return to the root directory.

You can use the same techniques to navigate the more complex directory structure of your hard disk in order to locate client or business files.

PRINTING A DIRECTORY TREE FROM THE DOS PROMPT

You want to print a copy of your directory tree and the files contained in each of the subdirectories. If the diskette fails or becomes damaged, you can quickly reconstruct the subdirectory structure and restore your business files to the proper subdirectories.

Earlier you used the TREE command to view a directory tree at the DOS prompt. You can use a variation of the same command to view filenames by directory. You can then redirect that output to print a copy of the directory tree. The **Filename switch** (/F) displays the directory tree and lists the filenames in each directory. When you print this information, you can also include the **ASCII switch** (/A) if your printer cannot print the graphics lines in the directory tree. If you use the ASCII switch, DOS substitutes other symbols for the graphics lines. Let's try it.

To display a directory tree of your Tutorial Disk:

1. Be sure the current disk drive contains your Tutorial Disk.
2. Be sure you are at the root directory. If not, type **CD ** and press **[Enter]**.
3. Type **TREE /F** and press **[Enter]**. The TREE command displays the directory tree and lists the filenames in each subdirectory. The first part of this directory tree scrolls off the screen.

4. Be sure the printer is on and on-line, and that the paper is properly aligned in the printer.
5. Type **TREE /F /A > PRN** and press **[Enter]**. You can redirect the output of any DOS command to the printer by using the output redirection operator (>) and the name of your printer port. If your printer can print graphics characters, you can perform this operation without the /A switch.
6. If necessary, press the **Form Feed button** on the printer. If the printer does not respond, press the **On Line button** to place the printer off-line. Then press **Form Feed** again. After the printer ejects the page, press the **On Line button** to place the printer back on-line. Figure 4-47 shows the printed copy of the directory tree with filenames.

```
Directory PATH listing for Volume BUSINESS
Volume Serial Number is 142E-14F9
A:.
+---REPORTS
|       APR_CASH
|       MAY_CASH
|       MAR_CASH
|       FEB_CASH
|       JUN_CASH
|       JAN_CASH
|
+---BUSINESS
|       BUSINESS.PLN
|       STARTUP
|       CLIENT.LST
|       EQUIP.LST
|       INSURE.LST
|
+---RESUMES
|       RESUME.LTR
|       RESUME1.DOC
|       RESUME2.DOC
|       RESUME3.DOC
|       RESUME4.DOC
|       RESUME5.DOC
|       RESUME6.DOC
|
+---JOBS
|       FEESCALE
|       JOBCOSTS.FMT
|       JOBCOSTS.RPT
|       JOBCOSTS.WK1
|       SCHEDULE.FMT
|       SCHEDULE.WK1
|
\---CASHFLOW
    +---INVOICES
    |       INVOICE.FMT
    |       INVOICE.RPT
    |       INVOICE.WK1
    |
    +---SUMMARY
    |       CASH.FMT
    |       CASH.RPT
    |       CASH.WK1
    |       CASHFLOW.FMT
    |       CASHFLOW.RPT
    |       CASHFLOW.WK1
    |
    \---PRJCASH
            INCOME.YR1
            INCOME.YR2
            INCOME.YR3
            INCOME.YR4
            INCOME.YR5
            PRJ_INC
            QTR_INC
```

subdirectory

files in subdirectory

lines in directory tree

Figure 4-47
A printed copy of the directory tree with filenames listed by directory

For a quick overview of the subdirectory structure of a hard disk or diskette, use the TREE command at the DOS prompt or view the directory tree from the DOS Shell. You can then locate specific subdirectories and periodically evaluate the organization of subdirectories on diskettes or hard disks.

◆

SUMMARY

In this tutorial, you learned how to work with subdirectories from the DOS prompt and from the DOS Shell. You created subdirectories with the MD, or Make Subdirectory, command at the DOS prompt and with the Create Directory option on the File menu in the DOS Shell. You learned how to navigate from one subdirectory to another with the use of the CD, or Change Subdirectory, command at the DOS prompt and by selecting subdirectories from the DOS Shell. You also learned how to change to a parent directory and to return to the root directory.

You used the DIR command and the DOS Shell to display the contents of subdirectories. You used the COPY command at the DOS prompt and the Copy option on the File menu in the DOS Shell to copy files from one subdirectory to another. In DOS 6.0 and 6.2, you moved files from one directory to another with the MOVE command at the DOS prompt. In DOS 5.0, you moved files with the COPY and DEL commands. You also used the Move option on the File menu in the DOS Shell to move files. You deleted files from a directory with the DEL command.

You viewed the directory tree of your Tutorial Disk with the TREE command at the DOS prompt and in the directory tree window in the DOS Shell. You also printed a directory tree from the DOS prompt with the TREE command and included filenames by directory.

Command Reference	
DOS Commands	
CD [*drive:*]*path* CHDIR [*drive:*]*path*	Internal commands that change from one directory to another
CD .. CHDIR ..	Internal commands that change to the directory above the current directory
CD \ CHDIR \	Internal commands that change from the current directory to the root directory
MD [*drive:*]*path* MKDIR [*drive:*]*path*	Internal commands that create, or make, a subdirectory
MOVE [*drive:*][*path*]*filename destination*	*DOS 6.0 and 6.2*: An external command that moves one or more files to another drive, directory, or drive and directory
PROMPT [*text*]	An internal command that customizes the appearance of the DOS command; for example, PROMPT PG displays the full path in the DOS prompt
TREE [*drive:*][*path*] [/F] [/A]	An external command that displays a diagram of the directory tree; the /F switch includes filenames with the directory tree, and the /A switch displays the lines in the directory tree with ASCII characters
DOS Shell Commands	
File Create Directory	Creates a subdirectory
File Move	Moves one or more files to another directory
Tree/Expand All	Expands the directory tree to show all subdirectories

QUESTIONS

1. What command would you enter to create a subdirectory named TOOLS below the root directory of the current drive? Assume the current directory is the root directory.
2. What command would you enter to create a subdirectory named WP51 (for WordPerfect 5.1) below a directory named \TOOLS? Assume the current directory is \TOOLS, and assume \TOOLS is a subdirectory below the root directory.
3. What command would you enter to change from the root directory to a subdirectory named TOOLS on the current drive?
4. What command would you enter to change to a subdirectory named WP51 below a directory named TOOLS? Assume the current directory is TOOLS.
5. What command would you enter to change from a subdirectory named \TOOLS\WP51 to the root directory?
6. List two commands that you could use to change from a subdirectory named \TOOLS\WP51 to the subdirectory named \TOOLS.
7. How do you move files from one subdirectory to another at the DOS prompt in DOS 5.0?
8. How do you move files from one subdirectory to another at the DOS prompt in DOS 6.0 and 6.2?
9. What command would you enter to display a directory tree from the root directory? Assume the current directory is the root directory.
10. What command would you enter to display a directory tree from the root directory? Assume the current directory is the TOOLS directory (below the root directory).
11. How would you create a subdirectory named CREDIT below the root directory in the DOS Shell?
12. How would you change from the root directory to another subdirectory named \CREDIT\CARDS in the DOS Shell?
13. How would you move files from a subdirectory named CARDLIST to another named CREDIT\CARDS in the DOS Shell?
14. How can you control the display of the directory tree in the DOS Shell?
15. After you move files in the DOS Shell, how can you update the file lists for each directory?
16. Suppose you have a subdirectory named \MARKETS on drive C. If this subdirectory is below the root directory of drive C, what command would you enter at the DOS prompt to change to this subdirectory? Assume the current directory is the root directory of drive C.
17. If there is a subdirectory named FUTURE below \MARKETS on drive C, what command would you enter to change to that subdirectory from the root directory? Assume the current directory is the root directory of drive C. What command would you enter to return to the root directory of drive C in one step?

18. Suppose you have a subdirectory named BENEFITS on drive C. This subdirectory is below the root directory of drive C. What command would you enter at the DOS prompt to display a list of the files in this subdirectory from the root directory of drive C?
19. Suppose you have a subdirectory named BIDS below the root directory and another subdirectory named 1994 below the one named BIDS. Assume these subdirectories are located on drive C. What is the full path of the subdirectory BIDS? Of the subdirectory 1994? Assume the current directory is the root directory of drive C. What command would you enter at the DOS prompt to change from the root directory to the 1994 subdirectory in one step? What command would you enter to change to its parent directory?
20. Suppose you have just created a new subdirectory named C:\WPFILES. You want to move all the files from the root directory with the file extension DOC to this new subdirectory. What command or commands would you enter at the DOS prompt to perform this operation? Assume the current directory is the root directory of drive C.
21. You keep all your work files in a subdirectory named C:\WORK. The number of files in this subdirectory now exceeds 50. You want to create a new subdirectory named C:\MEMOS and copy all the files with the file extension MEM from the subdirectory C:\WORK to C:\MEMOS. Then you want to delete those files from C:\WORK. List the steps and commands that you would use to accomplish this operation. Assume you are working at the DOS prompt and assume the current directory is the root directory of drive C.
22. You are working in the file list window of the DOS Shell. The DOS Shell is displaying the files in the root directory of drive C. You want to move all of the files with a file extension LTR to a subdirectory named LETTERS positioned immediately below the root directory of drive C. List the steps that you would follow to perform this operation.
23. You are working in the file list window of the DOS Shell. You want to select another subdirectory named \PAYROLL so that you can view the files in that subdirectory. List the steps that you would follow to change to this subdirectory.
24. After you power on your computer system, the DOS prompt appears as **C>**. You want to change the prompt so that you can see the full path of each subdirectory as you change from one subdirectory to another. What command can you enter at the DOS prompt so that the DOS prompt shows the full path? Assume you are working at the root directory of drive C. After you enter this command, what does the DOS prompt look like?
25. When you view a directory listing of a subdirectory, you see two files—one named . (dot) and the other named .. (dot dot). What do these two files represent?
26. What is a parent directory?
27. How can you display a directory tree from the DOS prompt so that it includes filenames for all directories? Assume you are working at the root directory of drive C.

28. How can you redirect a copy of a directory tree, with filenames by subdirectory, to the printer?
29. How does DOS designate a subdirectory in a directory listing produced with the DIR command so that you can distinguish the subdirectory from files?
30. How do you expand the directory tree in the DOS Shell?

TUTORIAL ASSIGNMENTS

1. **Displaying a Directory Listing**: *Use your Tutorial Disk to perform the following operations from the DOS prompt.* List the command that you use to accomplish each step.
   a. Display an alphabetical list of all files in the subdirectory named BUSINESS one screen at a time from the root directory.
   b. Display an alphabetical list of all files in the root directory from the subdirectory named BUSINESS.
   c. Display an alphabetical list of all files in the JOBS subdirectory while working in the CASHFLOW subdirectory.
   d. Display an alphabetical list of all files in the CASHFLOW\INVOICES subdirectory from the root directory.
   e. Change to the CASHFLOW subdirectory, and display a directory tree with filenames for the CASHFLOW directory and its subdirectories.

2. **Creating Subdirectories at the DOS Prompt**: *Use your Exercise Disk to perform the following operations from the DOS prompt.* Start at the root directory, and list the command that you use to accomplish each step.
   a. Create a subdirectory named CLIENTS below the root directory.
   b. Change to the CLIENTS subdirectory.
   c. Create a subdirectory named REPORTS below the CLIENTS directory.
   d. Create a subdirectory named PROJECTS below the CLIENTS directory.
   e. Create a subdirectory named BIDS below the root directory.
   f. Change to the root directory.
   g. Display a directory tree.
   h. Print a directory tree.
3. **Creating Subdirectories and Moving Files at the DOS Prompt**: *Use your Exercise Disk to perform the following operations from the DOS prompt.* List the command that you use to accomplish each step.
   a. From the root directory, create a subdirectory named DOCUMENT below the root directory.
   b. Change to the DOCUMENT subdirectory.
   c. Create a subdirectory named RESUMES below the DOCUMENT directory.
   d. Move all files in the root directory with a file extension of DOC to the RESUMES subdirectory.
   e. Change to the root directory.
   f. First display, then print, a directory tree with filenames.

4. **Creating Subdirectories from the DOS Shell**: *Use the Exercise Disk to perform the following operations from the DOS Shell.* List the step or steps for each of these operations.
   a. Create a subdirectory named 123FILES below the root directory.
   b. Move all the files in the root directory with the file extension WK1 and FMT to the subdirectory named 123FILES.
   c. Create another subdirectory named FINANCES below the root directory.
   d. Change to the subdirectory FINANCES and create a subdirectory named CASHFLOW below FINANCES.
   e. Move all the files in the root directory that have CASH as the last four characters of an eight-character filename and any file extension to the subdirectory named CASHFLOW.
   f. Exit the DOS Shell.
   g. First display, then print, a directory tree with filenames.
5. **Navigating Directories at the DOS prompt and in the DOS Shell**: *Use your Tutorial Disk to perform the following operations.* Be sure you start at the root directory of drive A or drive B. List the step or steps for each of these operations.
   a. Change to the REPORTS subdirectory.
   b. Change to the SUMMARY subdirectory below the CASHFLOW directory.
   c. Change to the JOBS subdirectory.
   d. Change to the root directory.
   e. Load the DOS Shell.
   f. Expand the directory tree.
   g. Change to the BUSINESS subdirectory.
   h. Change to the PRJCASH subdirectory below the CASHFLOW directory.
   i. Change to the root directory.
   j. Exit the DOS Shell.

TUTORIAL 5

Managing a Hard Disk

OBJECTIVES

In this tutorial you will learn to:

- Evaluate a hard disk's directory structure
- Reorganize a directory structure
- Rename a subdirectory
- Remove a subdirectory
- Locate files within a directory structure
- Eliminate file fragmentation and optimize a disk
- Check for computer viruses

Imagine that your supervisor asks you to evaluate the organization of subdirectories and files on the hard disks of your office computer systems and to recommend more efficient approaches for storing and accessing business and client records. Once you complete your evaluation, he wants to hold a general staff meeting to discuss your recommendations and develop a consensus for improving the performance of the computer systems. Ultimately, your goal is to standardize the computer systems so that staff members can work efficiently and easily on any of the computers.

◆

GETTING STARTED

To simplify the task of examining the organization of files in subdirectories, you decide to install DOSKEY and specify default switches for the DIR command.

To set up your system:

5.0 *6.0* *6.2*

1. After you power on your computer system, access drive C.
2. Type **DOSKEY** and press **[Enter]**. If you are using DOS 5.0 or 6.0, DOS will display the message "DOSKey installed" if DOSKEY is not already installed on your computer. If you do not see this message with DOS 5.0 or 6.0, DOSKEY is already loaded. DOS 6.2 will not display a message.
3. Type **SET DIRCMD=/P /O** and press **[Enter]**. DOS will now display your client files and subdirectories in alphabetical order and will pause after each screen.
4. Type **SET** and press **[Enter]** to verify that you correctly entered the switches for the DIRCMD environment variable. If not, repeat Step 3.

VIEWING THE DIRECTORY STRUCTURE OF A HARD DISK DRIVE

You want to display and then print the directory structure of the hard drive on one of the office computer systems. Because most hard disk drives have a complex, multi-tiered directory tree, you can pipe the output of the TREE command to the MORE filter so that you can view the directory tree one screen at a time.

To display a directory tree of a hard disk drive:

1. Type **TREE | MORE** and press **[Enter]**. DOS displays the first part of the directory tree, displays the More prompt, and pauses. Figure 5-1 shows the first page of a directory tree of a hard disk drive. Your directory will be different.

```
Directory PATH listing for Volume BUSINESS
Volume Serial Number is 07BD-0D01
C:.
├───DOS
├───UTIL
├───COLLAGE
├───WP51
│   ├───LEARN
│   ├───MACROS
│   ├───GRAPHICS
│   │   └───STYLES
│   └───PROJECTS
│       ├───BIDS
│       ├───REPORTS
│       ├───CONTRACT
│       ├───CASHFLOW
│       │   ├───INVOICES
│       │   └───REPORTS
│       ├───MEMOS
│       └───LETTERS
├───DATABASE
│   ├───REPORTS
│   └───TUTORIAL
├───GRAPHICS
-- More --
```

Figure 5-1
A paged view of a directory tree for a hard disk drive

2. Press **[Spacebar]** or any other key to continue. Repeat this process until you view the entire directory tree.

PRINTING THE DIRECTORY STRUCTURE OF A HARD DISK

Now you want to print a copy of the directory tree so that you can evaluate the directory structure of this hard disk. You will redirect the output of the TREE command to the printer port.

To print the directory tree:

1. Be sure the printer is on and on-line, and that the paper is properly aligned in the printer.
2. Type **TREE > PRN** and press **[Enter]**. DOS redirects the output and prints the directory tree. See Figure 5-2. If you experience difficulty, ask your instructor or technical support person for assistance. DOS must be able to locate the printer port.

```
Directory PATH listing for Volume BUSINESS
Volume Serial Number is 07BD-0D01
C:.
├───DOS
├───UTIL
├───COLLAGE
├───WP51
│   ├───LEARN
│   ├───MACROS
│   ├───GRAPHICS
│   │   └───STYLES
│   └───PROJECTS
│       ├───BIDS
│       ├───REPORTS
│       ├───CONTRACT
│       ├───CASHFLOW
│       │   ├───INVOICES
│       │   └───REPORTS
│       ├───MEMOS
│       └───LETTERS
├───DATABASE
│   ├───REPORTS
│   └───TUTORIAL
├───GRAPHICS
├───INVOICES
├───123R2.4
│   ├───WYSIWYG
│   ├───REPORTS
│   ├───CASHFLOW
│   │   ├───REPORTS
│   │   ├───PROJECTS
│   │   └───PRJINC
│   ├───TAXES
│   ├───INVOICES
│   └───TUTORIAL
├───MOUSE
├───WINDOWS
│   ├───SYSTEM
│   └───TEMP
├───RESUMES
└───RECORDS
    ├───91INCOME
    ├───92INCOME
    ├───93INCOME
    ├───CASHFLOW
    ├───INVOICES
    ├───PRJCASH
    └───REPORTS
```

Figure 5-2
A printed copy of a directory tree for a hard disk

3. If necessary, press the **Form Feed button** on the printer. If the printer does not respond, press the **On Line button** to place the printer off-line. Then press **Form Feed** again. After the printer ejects the page, press the **On Line button** to place the printer back on-line.

EVALUATING THE ORGANIZATION OF DIRECTORIES ON A HARD DISK

As you examine the printed copy of the directory structure shown in Figure 5-2, you notice that the hard disk contains subdirectories, positioned below the root directory, for software applications, utilities, DOS, and Windows. The DOS subdirectory contains the DOS system utilities. The DOS 5.0, 6.0, and 6.2 installation programs automatically create this subdirectory. The MOUSE subdirectory contains the software for operating the mouse. The UTIL subdirectory contains other utility software. The WINDOWS subdirectory contains program files for the Windows operating environment.

The WP51 and 123R2.4 subdirectories contain the software for the WordPerfect 5.1 and Lotus 1-2-3 Release 2.4 applications, respectively. The 123R2.4 subdirectory illustrates that subdirectories, like filenames, can have file extensions. Positioned below these two subdirectories are other subdirectories, such as a tutorial subdirectory, that contain additional files provided with the software application. You assume the DATABASE and GRAPHICS subdirectories contain software for these types of applications, document files, or perhaps both program and data files. Other subdirectories contain specialized software.

Some client and business files are stored in the INVOICES, RESUMES, and RECORDS subdirectories, which are located below the root directory. Other client and business files are stored in subdirectories that already contain applications software or in subdirectories subordinate to the applications software directory. For example, the WP51 and 123R2.4 directories contain subdirectories for client files.

After examining this directory tree, you realize that you can improve the directory structure of this hard disk. First, you can consolidate subdirectories and files into one directory. For example, you can consolidate the four INVOICE subdirectories into one so that invoice files are easier to locate. This consolidation will also reduce the chances of saving different versions of the same file in different subdirectories.

Second, you can separate files produced by software applications from the program files for those applications. For example, you can separate the WordPerfect software in the WP51 directory from the subdirectories that contain client files produced by WordPerfect, and staff members would no longer need to look for a client file among hundreds of program files.

Third, you can move files currently stored in the root directory to the appropriate subdirectory so that only important system files would remain in the root directory.

Finally, you can reduce the complexity of the directory structure by limiting the number of subdirectory levels. For example, rather than having a MEMOS subdirectory three levels below the root directory, you can place it directly beneath the root directory. When you use the DIR command to display the contents of the root directory, the directory listing will look like a table of contents. Then you and other staff members can quickly distinguish software directories from client directories. Furthermore, DOS works faster and more efficiently with a directory structure that contains fewer directory levels.

RECOMMENDING A NEW DIRECTORY STRUCTURE

You prepare and submit to your supervisor a summary of your findings and a diagram that illustrates the proposed directory structure for the office computers (see Figure 5-3). In this report, you emphasize the importance of organizing information by project, client, business records, and software use, and the importance of using a consistent approach when adding new directories. You also recommend that software and client subdirectories be positioned directly below the root directory, and that the directory structure contain no more than two or three levels of subdirectories.

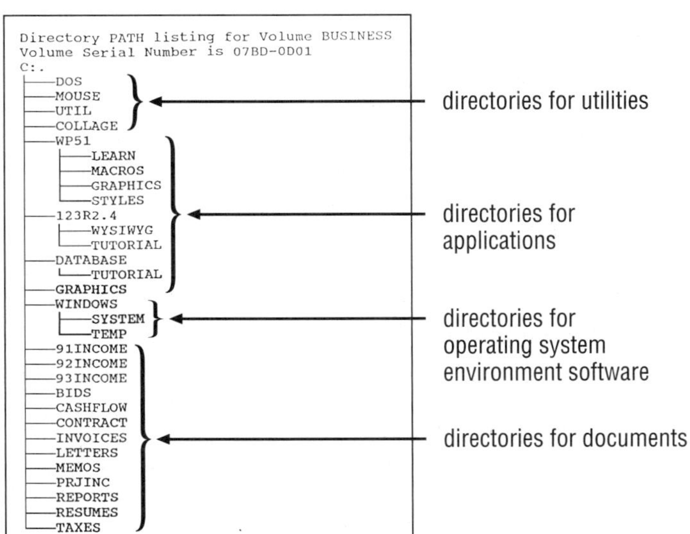

Figure 5-3
A proposed directory structure for a hard disk

After your supervisor reviews this report, he calls a general staff meeting to discuss the recommendations and to adopt a course of action. The general staff consensus is to proceed with your recommendations. Your supervisor asks that you first test your proposal on a copy of your client diskette before you actually revamp the directory structure of the hard drives in the office.

Before you can start the test, you need a printed copy of the directory tree on your client diskette. You can then prepare a sketch of a new directory structure for this disk.

To print the directory tree:

1. Insert your Tutorial Disk into drive A or drive B, and change to that drive.
2. Be sure the printer is on and on-line, and that the paper is properly aligned in the printer.
3. Type **TREE > PRN** and press **[Enter]**. DOS redirects the output and prints the directory tree. See Figure 5-4. The order of subdirectories in your tree might be different.

```
Directory PATH listing for Volume BUSINESS
Volume Serial Number is 17D9-3710
B:.
├───REPORTS
├───BUSINESS
├───RESUMES
├───JOBS
└───CASHFLOW
    ├───INVOICES
    ├───SUMMARY
    └───PRJCASH
```

Figure 5-4
A directory tree of the Tutorial Disk

4. If necessary, press the **Form Feed button** on the printer. If the printer does not respond, press the **On Line button** to place the printer off-line. Then press **Form Feed** again. After the printer ejects the page, press the **On Line button** to place the printer back on-line.

DEVELOPING A STRATEGY FOR REORGANIZING A DIRECTORY STRUCTURE

The CASHFLOW directory has three subdirectories: INVOICES, PRJCASH, and SUMMARY. You decide to position these subdirectories below the root directory. To make these changes from the DOS prompt, you must create a new subdirectory, move all the files from the original subdirectory to the new subdirectory, and remove the original subdirectory.

To create a new subdirectory, you use the MD (Make Directory) command as follows:

MD [*drive*:]*path*

You specify the path and name of the subdirectory. You must also specify the drive if you are creating the subdirectory on another disk drive. The directory name cannot be the same as a filename.

6.0 *6.2*

If you are using DOS 6.0 or 6.2, you can use the MOVE command to move files from one directory to another:

MOVE [*drive*:][*path*]*filename destination*

You specify the name of the file or files you want to move and the destination. If the file or files you want to move are located in another directory, you also must specify the name of that directory. If the file or files you want to move are located on another drive, you must specify the drive name for the file(s). The destination is the name of the directory where you want to move the file or files.

5.0

If you are using DOS 5.0, you must use the COPY command to copy all the files in the original subdirectory to the new subdirectory. After you verify the copy operation, you can use the DEL command to erase the files from the original subdirectory.

To remove a subdirectory, you use the RD or RMDIR (Remove Directory) command. The subdirectory that you remove *must* be empty. The subdirectory *cannot* contain any files *or* subdirectories. Also, you *cannot* remove the root directory with this command. The syntax for this internal command is as follows:

RD [*drive*:]*path*

You specify the path and name of the subdirectory. If the subdirectory is located on another drive, you also must specify the drive name.

MODIFYING THE DIRECTORY STRUCTURE

Now you are ready to reorganize the directory structure of your diskette. You decide to position the INVOICES subdirectory below the root directory. First, you need to create a new INVOICES subdirectory.

To create a new INVOICES subdirectory:

1. Be sure you are at the root directory of drive A or drive B.
2. Type **MD \INVOICES** and press **[Enter]**. DOS creates this subdirectory below the root directory of the disk drive containing your diskette and displays the DOS prompt.

Now verify that this new subdirectory exists:

3. Type **TREE** and press **[Enter]**. DOS displays an updated directory tree. See Figure 5-5. The order of subdirectories in your tree might be different.

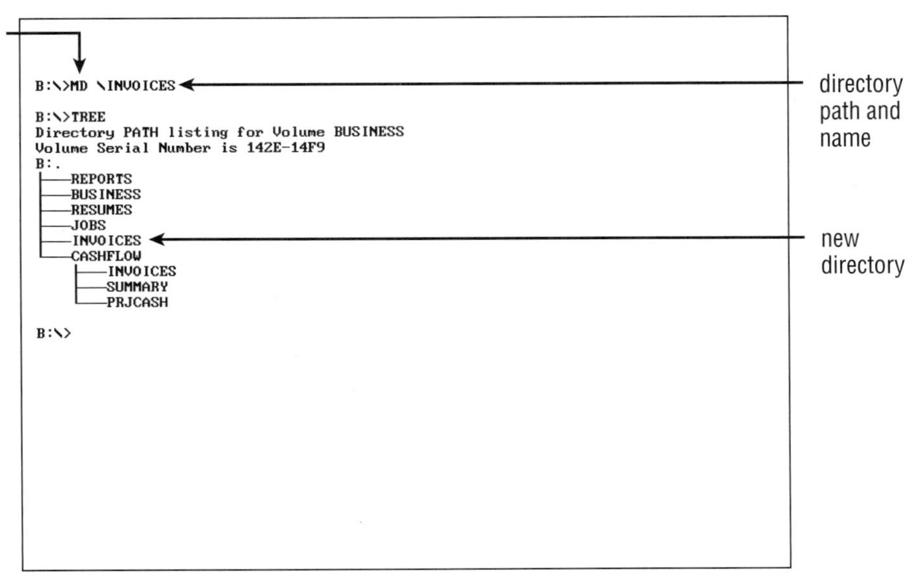

Figure 5-5
Expanding the directory structure by adding a new subdirectory

Moving Files from Directory to Directory

Now you are ready to move the files from the original INVOICES directory to the new INVOICES directory. Follow the steps in the section below for the version of DOS that you are using on your computer.

6.0 *6.2*

To move these files *using DOS 6.0 or 6.2*:

1. Type **MOVE \CASHFLOW\INVOICES*.* \INVOICES** and press **[Enter]**. The source files are the files in the INVOICES subdirectory located below the CASHFLOW directory. The destination directory is the INVOICES subdirectory located below the root directory. The backslash before \CASHFLOW\INVOICES and \INVOICES completes the path for these subdirectories and emphasizes that CASHFLOW and INVOICES are located below the root directory of the current drive. DOS displays a list of the files that it moves.

DOS 6.0 and 6.2 users should skip the next step list and proceed directly to the section entitled "Verifying a Move or Copy Operation."

5.0

To move these files *using DOS 5.0*:

1. Type **COPY \CASHFLOW\INVOICES \INVOICES** and press **[Enter]**. The source files are the files in the INVOICES subdirectory located below the CASHFLOW directory. The destination, or target, directory is the INVOICES subdirectory located below the root directory. The backslash before \CASHFLOW\INVOICES and \INVOICES completes the path for these subdirectories and emphasizes that CASHFLOW and INVOICES are located below the root directory of the current drive. DOS displays a list of the files that it copies.

Verifying a Move or Copy Operation

You now want to verify the move or copy operation to ensure the files are stored in the correct subdirectory.

To verify a move or copy:

1. Type **DIR \INVOICES** and press **[Enter]**. DOS displays the names of the three files that it moved into this new directory.
2. Type **DIR \CASHFLOW\INVOICES** and press **[Enter]**.

   6.0 *6.2* If you are using DOS 6.0 or 6.2, DOS displays a directory listing of this subdirectory, showing that it is empty.

   5.0 If you are using DOS 5.0, DOS displays a directory with the names of the files you copied. You must delete these files before you can remove the directory.

5.0

3. *If you are using DOS 5.0,* type **DEL \CASHFLOW\INVOICES** and press **[Enter]**. DOS asks you to verify this operation. Type **Y** and press **[Enter]**.

Removing an Empty Directory

Now you are ready to remove the \CASHFLOW\INVOICES directory, which is empty.

To remove a directory:

1. Type **RD \CASHFLOW\INVOICES** and press **[Enter]**. DOS displays the DOS prompt.
2. Type **DIR \CASHFLOW** and press **[Enter]**. The CASHFLOW directory no longer has a subdirectory named INVOICES. See Figure 5-6.

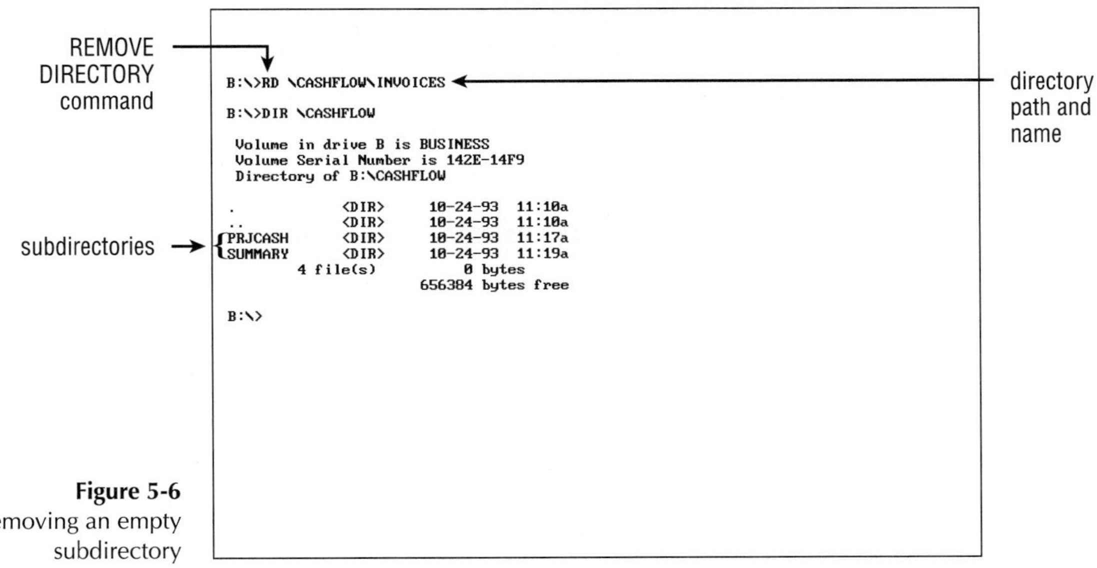

Figure 5-6
Removing an empty subdirectory

REORGANIZING A DIRECTORY STRUCTURE WITH THE DOS SHELL

You decide to move the other two subdirectories in the DOS Shell. Like working at the DOS prompt, you create a new subdirectory, move all the files from the original subdirectory to the new subdirectory, and delete the original subdirectory. Based on your previous experience, you anticipate that it will be easier working in the DOS Shell than it is working at the DOS prompt.

To start the DOS Shell:

1. Type **DOSSHELL** and press **[Enter]**. DOS loads the DOS Shell and displays the directory structure of the Tutorial Disk in the directory tree window.

Next, expand the directory tree.

2. Press **[F10]** (Actions) to access the menu bar, type **T** for the Tree menu, and type **A** for the Expand All option.

If you are using the mouse, click **Tree**, then click **Expand All.**

The DOS Shell expands the directory tree to show all subdirectories. See Figure 5-7. Your view of the directory tree and file list windows will be different if you are using text mode. You can switch to graphics mode by using the Display option on the Options menu.

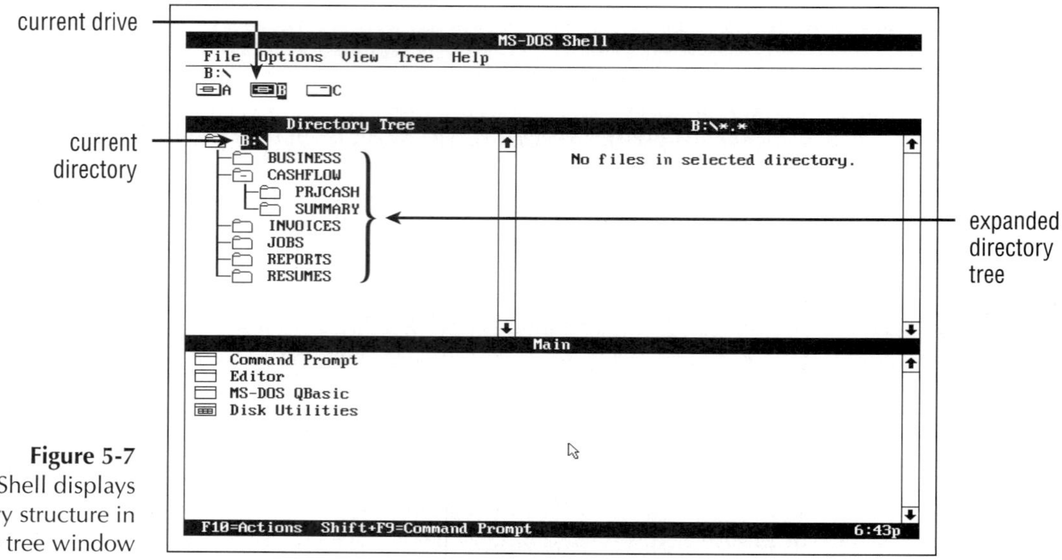

Figure 5-7
The DOS Shell displays the directory structure in the directory tree window

Now you can create your new SUMMARY subdirectory.

3. Press **[Tab]** to move the selection cursor to the directory tree window.

   If you are using the mouse, click the **root directory** in the directory tree window.

4. Press **[F10]** (Actions) to access the menu bar, press **[Enter]** to select the File menu, and type **E** to select the Create Directory option.

   If you are using the mouse, click **File**, then click **Create Directory**.

   The DOS Shell displays the Create Directory dialog box. The dialog box shows the parent name, in this case B:\, and prompts for the new directory name.

5. Type **SUMMARY** and press **[Enter]**.

   If you are using the mouse, type **SUMMARY** and click **OK**.

   The DOS Shell creates the SUMMARY subdirectory on the current drive below the root directory, and then updates the directory tree. See Figure 5-8.

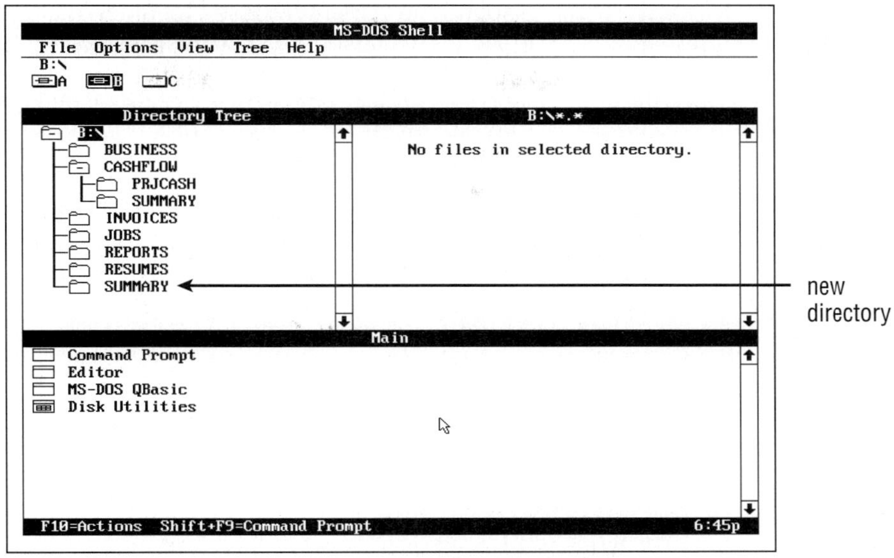

Figure 5-8
The newly created SUMMARY directory added to the directory tree below the root directory

Moving Files from Directory to Directory

You are now ready to move the files from the \CASHFLOW\SUMMARY directory to the \SUMMARY directory. Because both directories have the same name, SUMMARY, you must distinguish between the directories by specifying their paths.

To move the files to the new directory:

1. Press [↓] (Down Arrow) until you highlight the SUMMARY subdirectory *located below the \CASHFLOW directory. Do not select the \SUMMARY subdirectory.*

   If you are using the mouse, click the **folder icon** next to the \CASHFLOW\ SUMMARY directory.
2. Press **[Tab]**. The DOS Shell moves the selection cursor to the file list window.

   If you are using the mouse, click the **file list window title bar**.
3. Press **[F10]** (Actions) and press **[Enter]** to select the File menu. Type **S** for the Select All option.

   If you are using the mouse, click **File**, then click **Select All**.

   DOS selects all the files in the file list window.
4. Press **[F7]** (Move). The DOS Shell displays the Move File dialog box with a partial view of the selected files in the From text box. Type **\SUMMARY** to specify the name for the target directory, and press **[Enter]**. *You must type the Backslash before the directory name so that the DOS Shell knows exactly where you want to move the files.* The DOS Shell moves the files to the \SUMMARY subdirectory.

   If you are using the mouse, move the mouse pointer next to the selected files. Hold down the left mouse button and drag the pointer to the folder icon adjacent to the subdirectory name SUMMARY in the directory tree window. Be sure you select the SUMMARY directory that is located below the root directory. Then release the mouse button. The DOS Shell displays the Confirm Mouse Operation dialog box and asks if you want to move the selected files to A:\SUMMARY or B:\SUMMARY. Click **Yes**. The DOS Shell moves the files to this subdirectory.

Removing an Empty Directory

You can now remove the \CASHFLOW\SUMMARY directory, which is empty. To remove a directory in the DOS Shell, you select the directory and press the Delete key.

To remove this empty subdirectory:

1. Press **[Del]** or **[Delete]**. The DOS Shell displays the Delete Directory Confirmation dialog box. See Figure 5-9.

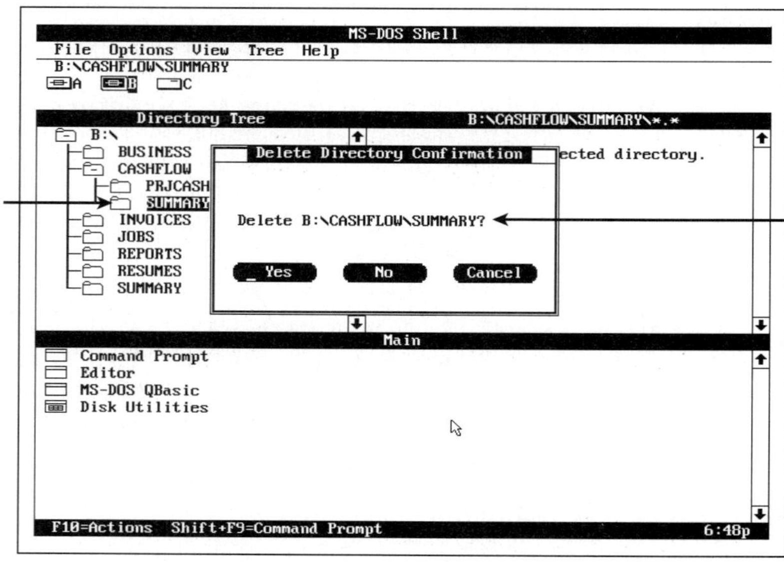

Figure 5-9
The DOS Shell's Delete Directory Confirmation dialog box

2. Press **[Enter]** to select the Yes button.

   If you are using the mouse, click **Yes**.

   The DOS Shell removes the SUMMARY subdirectory that is located below the CASHFLOW directory.

You next want to verify these operations to be sure your business files are stored in the correct subdirectory. But first you might need to reread your Tutorial Disk and refresh the display of files in the file list window.

To refresh the display of the files on your Tutorial Disk:

1. Press **[F5]** (Refresh). The DOS Shell rereads your Tutorial Disk.

Next, expand the directory tree.

2. Press **[F10]** (Actions) to access the menu bar, type **T** for the Tree menu, and type **A** for the Expand All option.

   If you are using the mouse, click **Tree**, then click **Expand All**.

   The DOS Shell expands the directory tree to show all subdirectories.

3. Press **[Tab]** to move the selection cursor to the directory tree window. Type **S** to move the selection cursor to the \SUMMARY subdirectory.

   If you are using the mouse, click the **\SUMMARY** subdirectory that is located below the root directory in the directory tree window.

   The DOS Shell shows that the files are now in this subdirectory.

4. Press **[Home]** to select the root directory.

   If you are using a mouse, click the **root directory** in the directory tree window.

Completing the Reorganization of the Directory Structure

According to your plan, you also want to create a subdirectory named \PRJCASH, which will be located below the root directory, to move the files from \CASHFLOW\PRJCASH to \PRJCASH, and to remove \CASHFLOW\PRJCASH.

To complete the reorganization of the directory structure of your Tutorial Disk:

1. Create the \PRJCASH subdirectory according to your plan for reorganizing subdirectories on your Tutorial Disk.
2. After you create this subdirectory, move the files in the \CASHFLOW\PRJCASH subdirectory to \PRJCASH.
3. If necessary, reread your Tutorial Disk and expand the directory tree.
4. Select the \PRJCASH subdirectory and verify that this subdirectory contains the moved files.
5. Remove the \CASHFLOW\PRJCASH subdirectory, and then remove the \CASHFLOW subdirectory.
6. Select the root directory. Your directory tree should look like the one shown in Figure 5-10.

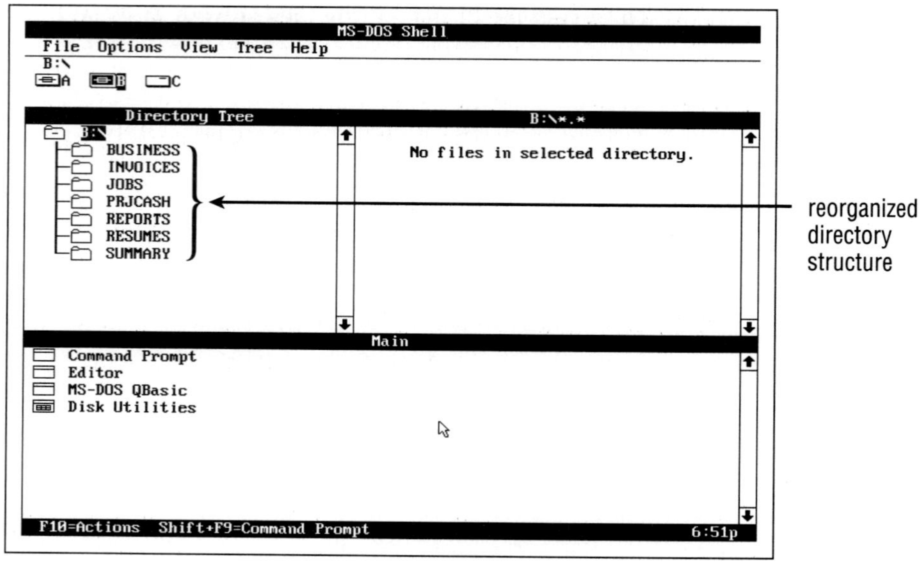

Figure 5-10
The reorganized directory structure for the Tutorial Disk

Because you have successfully restructured the directories on your client diskette, you have the necessary skills and correct plan to actually reorganize the directory structure of the hard disk drives in your office.

RENAMING DIRECTORIES

You decide to change the name of the SUMMARY subdirectory to CASHFLOW because this directory contains files with the company's cashflow reports. If you work at the DOS prompt, you must create a directory, move files, and then delete the original directory. In contrast, if you work in the DOS Shell, you can use the Rename option on the File menu to rename files and subdirectories in one step. In a business workplace, features such as this one save you and your business time and money.

To rename the SUMMARY subdirectory:

1. Type **S** to move the selection cursor to the SUMMARY subdirectory.

   If you are using the mouse, click the **SUMMARY** subdirectory below the root directory in the directory tree window.

2. Press **[F10]** (Actions) and press **[Enter]** to select the File menu. Type **N** to select the Rename option.

   If you are using the mouse, click **File**, then click **Rename**.

   The DOS Shell displays the Rename Directory dialog box. See Figure 5-11.

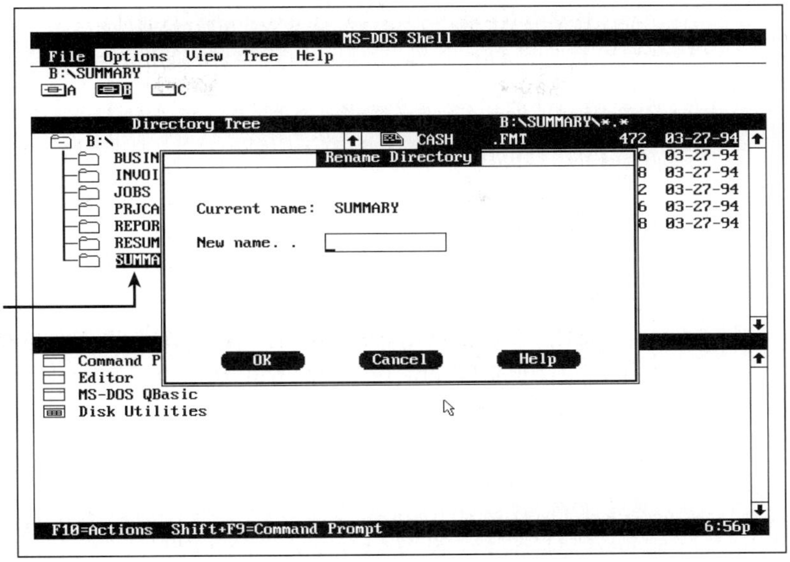

currently selected directory

Figure 5-11
The DOS Shell's Rename Directory dialog box

3. Type **CASHFLOW** and press **[Enter]**.

   If you are using the mouse, type **CASHFLOW**, then click **OK**.

   The DOS Shell renames this subdirectory and updates the directory tree. You can now exit the DOS Shell.

4. Press **[F3]** (Exit) to exit the DOS Shell and return to the DOS prompt.
5. Be sure you are at the root directory. If not, type **CD ** and press **[Enter]**.
6. Type **DIR** and press **[Enter]**. DOS displays a directory listing of the contents of the root directory of the Tutorial Disk. The directory structure reads like a table of contents in alphabetical order. See Figure 5-12.

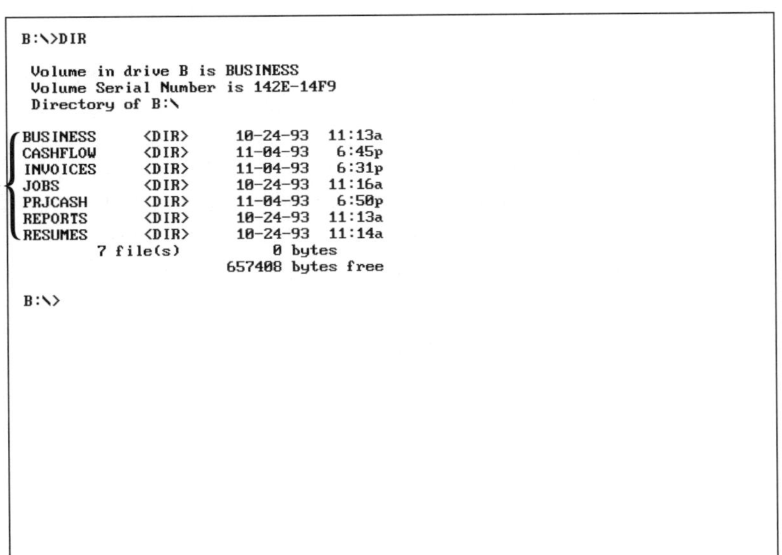

subdirectories in alphabetical order

Figure 5-12
A "table of contents" for the Tutorial Disk

Documenting the Directory Structure

To complete this process, you want to document the new directory structure of your client diskette.

To print the directory tree:

1. Be sure the printer is on and on-line, and that the paper is properly aligned in the printer.
2. Type **TREE > PRN** and press **[Enter]**. DOS redirects the output and prints the directory tree. See Figure 5-13. The order of subdirectories in your directory tree might be different.

```
Directory PATH listing for Volume BUSINESS
Volume Serial Number is 142E-14F9
B:.
├───REPORTS
├───BUSINESS
├───RESUMES
├───JOBS
├───INVOICES
├───CASHFLOW
└───PRJCASH
```

Figure 5-13
A printed copy of the reorganized directory tree

3. If necessary, press the **Form Feed button** on the printer. If the printer does not respond, press the **On Line button** to place the printer off-line. Then press **Form Feed** again. After the printer ejects the page, press the **On Line button** to place the printer back on-line.

LOCATING FILES IN DIRECTORIES

Your supervisor asks you to update some important business files on your client diskette before you leave for a two-week vacation. He gives you a list of the changes for your quarterly job costs report and the company's insurance and client check lists.

If you are working at the DOS prompt, you can expedite this task by using the Subdirectory Search switch (/S) to search through directories for one or more files. You can look for a single file by name, or you can use wildcards to expand the scope of a search and look for a group of files.

Before you use this switch, you must decide where in the directory tree you want to start the search. In most cases, you will return to the root directory and start the search from the top of the directory tree. DOS will then search through all the directories, starting with the root directory. If it locates a file or files using the file specification that you provide, it shows the full path of the directory and the filename, size, date, and time. If DOS locates files with the same name but in different directories, it lists each occurrence of the file.

The first file you need to locate contains the job costs report.

To locate the file named JOBCOSTS.RPT at the DOS prompt:

1. Type **DIR JOBCOSTS.RPT** (without the /S switch) and press **[Enter]**. DOS reports that it found no file by that name. Because you did not include the /S switch, DOS limited its search to the root directory. It did not search the directories below the root directory.

2. Press [↑] (Up Arrow) to recall the DIR JOBCOSTS.RPT command. Then press **[Spacebar]**. Type **/S** and press **[Enter]**. DOS locates the file in the directory JOBS. See Figure 5-14.

```
B:\>DIR JOBCOSTS.RPT

 Volume in drive B is BUSINESS
 Volume Serial Number is 142E-14F9
 Directory of B:\

File not found

B:\>DIR JOBCOSTS.RPT /S

 Volume in drive B is BUSINESS
 Volume Serial Number is 142E-14F9

Directory of B:\JOBS

JOBCOSTS RPT        543 03-26-94   8:51a
        1 file(s)         543 bytes

Total files listed:
        1 file(s)         543 bytes
                       657408 bytes free

B:\>
```

file specification

path of file

Subdirectory Search switch

located file

Figure 5-14
Locating a file with the DIR command's Subdirectory Search switch

Searching for Files in the DOS Shell

To locate the files with the insurance and client lists, you decide to use the DOS Shell. The Search option on the File menu will search an entire disk for one or more files, based on a file specification that you provide.

Let's start the DOS Shell and locate these files.

To locate a group of files in the DOS Shell:

1. Type **DOSSHELL** and press **[Enter]**. DOS loads the DOS Shell.
2. Press **[F10]** (Actions), press **[Enter]** to select the File menu, and type **H** for the Search option.

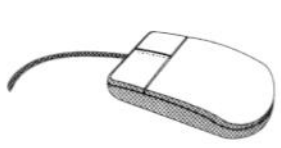

   If you are using the mouse, click **File**, then click **Search**.

   The DOS Shell displays a Search File dialog box. See Figure 5-15. The DOS Shell shows the default file specification for searches. The check in the check box shows that the DOS Shell will search the entire disk.

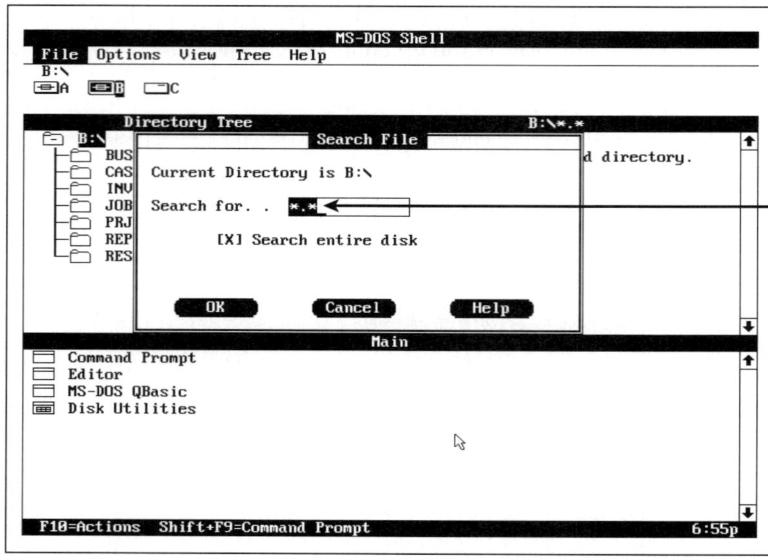

Figure 5-15
The DOS Shell's Search File dialog box

3. Type ***.LST** and press **[Enter]**.

   If you are using a mouse, type ***.LST** and click **OK**.

   DOSSHELL displays a screen labeled "Search Results for: *.LST" that alphabetically lists the files that meet this specification. See Figure 5-16. The two files that you want to locate, INSURE.LST and CLIENT.LST, are included in this selection. The DOS Shell also shows the full path of each file so that you know exactly where the files are stored. In the DOS Shell, you do not need to specify an Order switch or a Subdirectory Search switch.

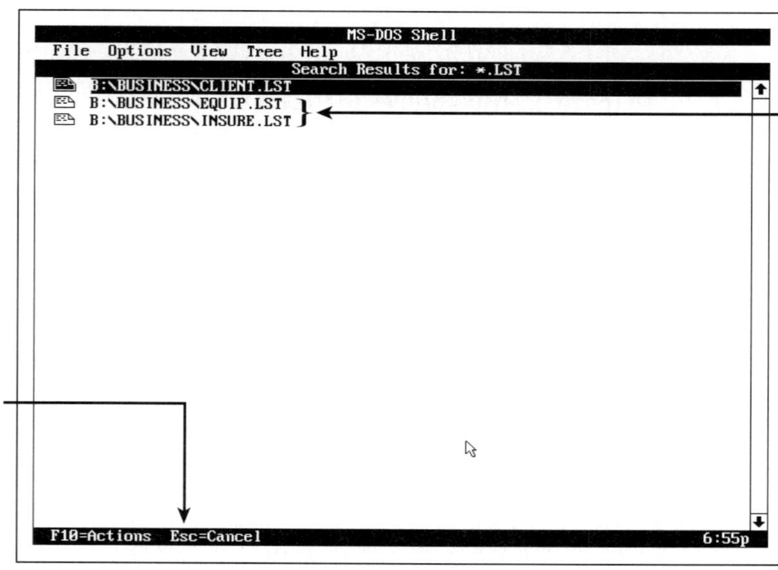

Figure 5-16
Locating files with the LST file extension in the DOS Shell

4. Press **[Esc]** to exit this screen view.
5. Press **[F3]** to exit the DOS Shell.

Now you have two useful tools for locating files quickly, either from the DOS prompt or from the DOS Shell. You also can use this feature to quickly locate duplicate copies of files stored in various directories or to locate different versions of the same file stored in different directories.

This is a good opportunity to stop for a few minutes and take a break.

DEFRAGMENTING HARD DISKS AND DISKETTES

Your company purchased your computer system approximately a year ago. Over the last several months, you have noticed that its performance is not optimal. DOS takes longer to display directories, load software applications, and load document files from the hard disk drive than it used to. Your supervisor suggests that you run the Microsoft defragmenting utility that was introduced with DOS 6.0. A **defragmenting utility** is a program that rearranges files on a hard disk or a diskette so that all sectors of each file are stored in consecutive sectors. If you are using DOS 5.0, you do not have the Microsoft defragmenting utility and cannot complete the steps in this section of the tutorial. However, you can read the introductory material so that you are familiar with the use of a defragmenting utility.

How Does File Fragmentation Occur?

As you create, modify, and save files to a hard disk or diskette, DOS attempts to store the different parts of a file in **contiguous**, or adjacent, sectors on the hard disk or diskette. However, over time, as you add, delete, and modify files, DOS may not be able to store all parts of a file in consecutive sectors. Instead, DOS must store different parts of a file in **noncontiguous**, or nonadjacent, sectors that are scattered across the surface of a diskette. The file is then called a **fragmented** file.

Each time you issue a command to retrieve a file from a hard disk or diskette, DOS must locate each of the file sectors and reassemble those sectors so that the program you are using can work with the entire file or with a portion of a large file. Likewise, when you issue a command to save a new or modified file to a hard disk or diskette, DOS must locate available sectors for that file. If a file is stored in noncontiguous sectors, it takes DOS longer to read the file from the hard disk or diskette and to write the file to the hard disk or diskette. The problem is compounded if all or a majority of the files on a hard disk or diskette are fragmented.

Let's examine a simple example of how file fragmentation occurs. (As you follow this example, remember that it applies to both hard disks and diskettes.) Assume you have used a client diskette heavily over the last year. You have added files to the diskette, and you have deleted and modified files on the diskette. As a result of these changes, DOS has used all of the clusters on the diskette at one time or another. Let's also assume that part of this diskette contains three files (Figure 5-17). You have a file with a client résumé that occupies three clusters, a file with a brief letter that occupies the next available cluster, a file with a client report that occupies the next four clusters, and two previously used clusters that are now available for use again. You decide you no longer need the letter, so you delete the file with the letter from the diskette. By removing this file, you have created an available cluster (Figure 5-18). Now you prepare a bid for a client and save it to the same diskette. DOS uses the cluster that was previously occupied by the letter and the next two available clusters—which happen to be located after the clusters containing the client report (Figure 5-19). Thus, the file with the client bid becomes a fragmented file because it is stored in noncontiguous sectors. From this example, you can see that if you reduce the size of files or delete files from a diskette, you free up clusters that DOS might use later for part of a file. If you increase the size of files or add new files to a diskette, DOS will store the files in noncontiguous clusters if the diskette does not contain enough consecutive clusters to hold the entire file.

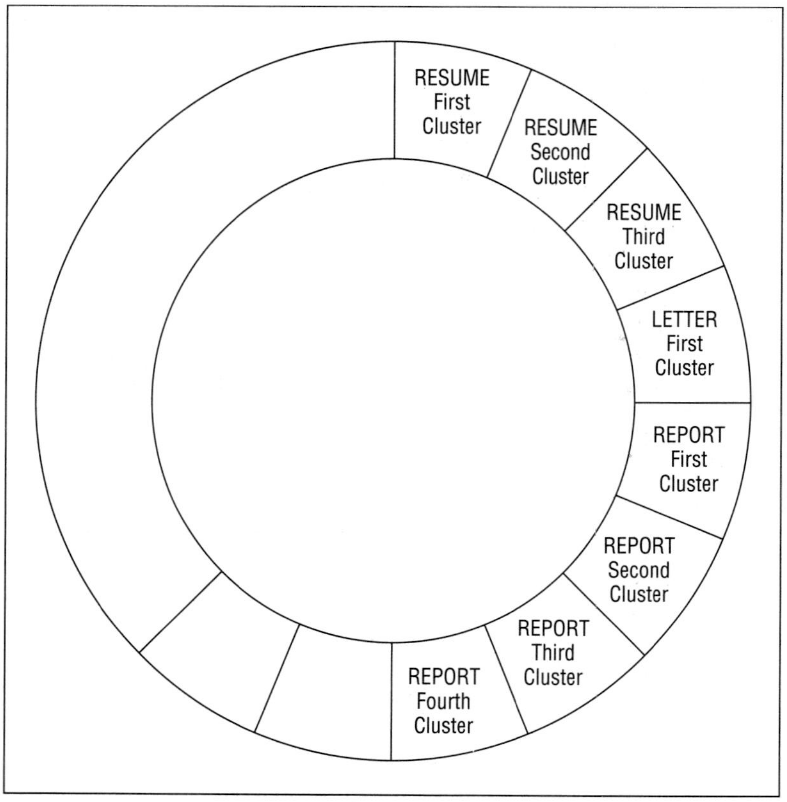

Figure 5-17
An example of the arrangement of files in contiguous clusters on a hard disk or diskette

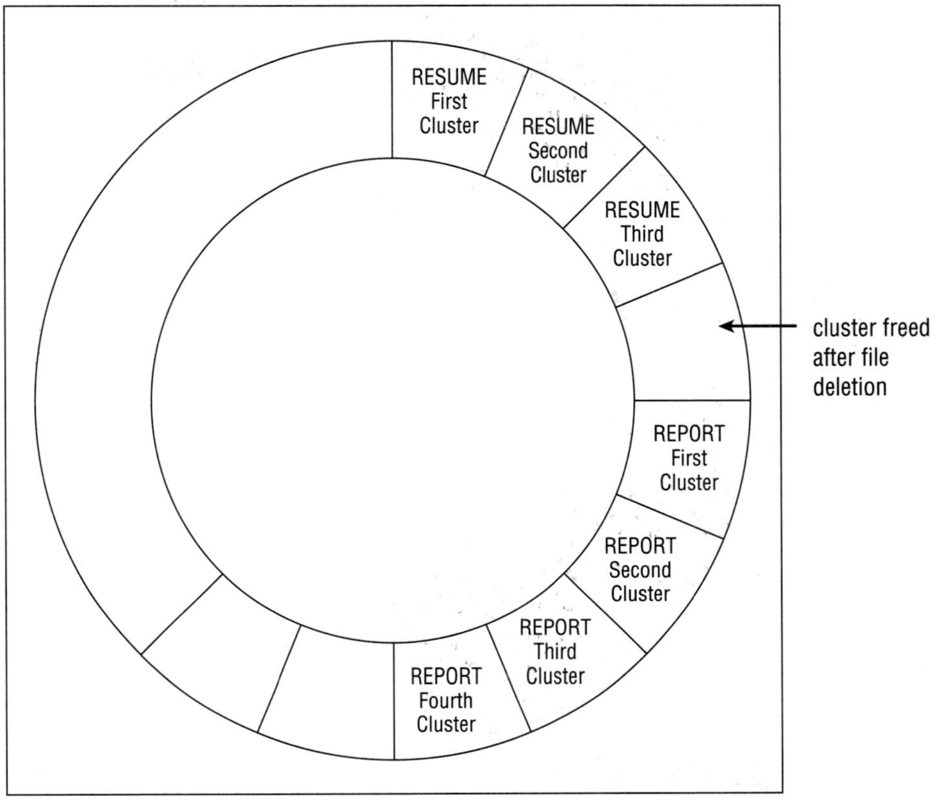

Figure 5-18
DOS frees a cluster after a file deletion

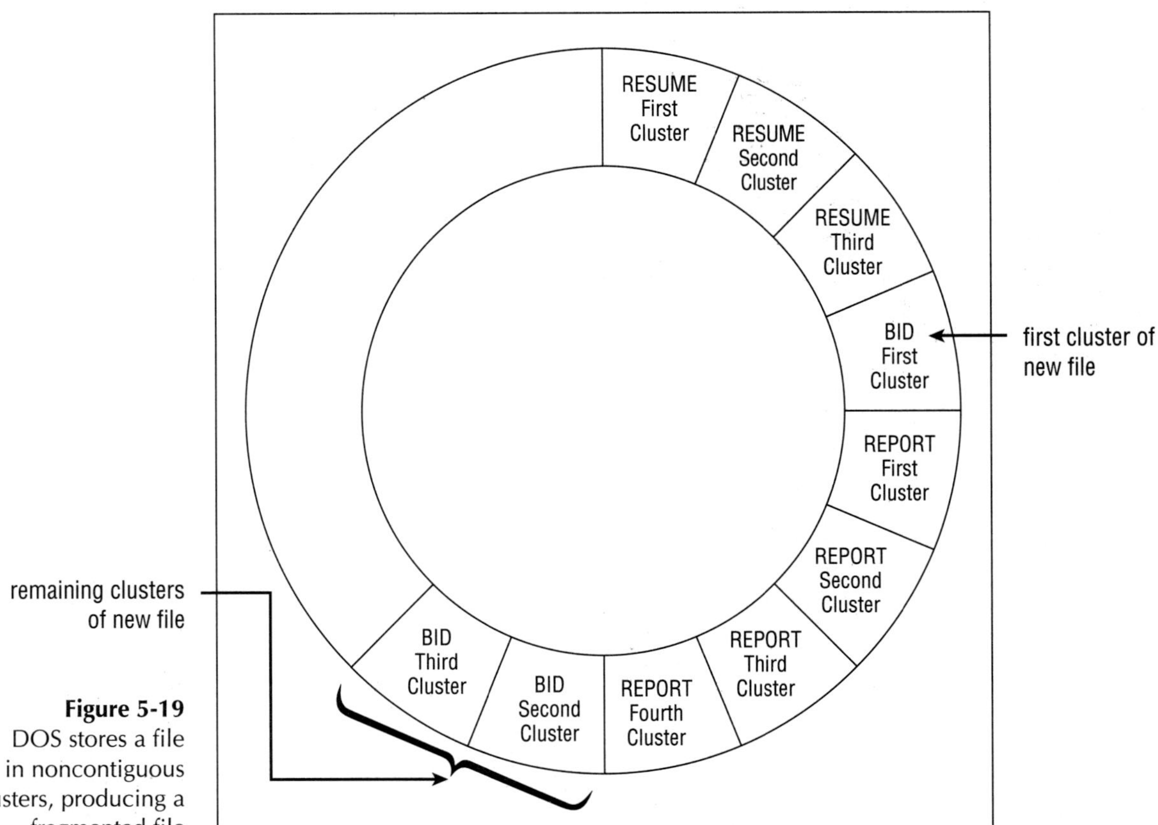

Figure 5-19
DOS stores a file in noncontiguous clusters, producing a fragmented file

Using the DOS Defragmenting Utility

To eliminate or reduce file fragmentation, you can use the Defragmenter utility introduced in DOS 6.0. This utility examines a hard disk or diskette and recommends one of three types of optimization: None, Unfragment Files Only, and Full Optimization. If the Defragmenter informs you that no optimization is necessary, the hard disk or diskette is not fragmented, or the amount of fragmentation is minimal and does not affect the performance of the computer system. If the utility recommends "Unfragment Files Only," it will eliminate file fragmentation by storing each part of a file in adjacent sectors. This option may result in unused storage space between files on the hard disk or diskette, a condition that can later contribute to file fragmentation. If the utility recommends Full Optimization, it will not only eliminate file fragmentation but also the unused storage space between files. If you select this option and fully optimize a hard disk or diskette that contains subdirectories, the Defragmenter moves the subdirectory files to the outer edge of the hard disk or diskette so that DOS can quickly access information stored in these files.

The Defragmenter also arranges files in order during the optimization process. You can specify a sort criterion: Unsorted, Name, Extension, Size, or Date and Time. You also can specify a sort order: Ascending or Descending. When you specify **ascending sort order**, files are arranged in alphabetical order by filename or file extension, in order by file size from the smallest to the largest file, or in order by date and time from the oldest file to the most recently used file. When you specify **descending sort order**, files are arranged in reverse alphabetical order by filename or file extension, in reverse order by file size from the largest to the smallest file, and in reverse order by date and time from the most recently used file to the oldest file.

DEFRAG is an external command, with the following general syntax:

DEFRAG [*drive:*]

The drive is optional. If you do not specify a drive, the utility assumes you want to defragment the current drive.

You cannot use the Defragmenter to optimize files on a network hard disk drive. Also, you cannot load Windows, temporarily exit to the DOS prompt, and then run this utility. If you do, you may lose data. You must run this utility from the DOS prompt. Windows has its own version of this Defragmenter, which you can use while working in Windows.

5.0

If DOS 5.0 is installed on your computer system, you do not have the Defragmenter. However, you can purchase other utility software, such as The Norton Utilities, and use its defragmenter to optimize your hard disk and diskettes.

Checking the Directory Structure

Before you use this utility on the computers in your office, you want to test it on your client diskette. Let's view the directory tree before you optimize your client diskette.

To display the directory tree:

1. Be sure the current drive is the one with your Tutorial Disk. If necessary, switch to drive A or drive B. If your monitor displays unusual graphics characters for borders, outlines, or symbols, press **[ESC]** to display the Optimize menu. Then type **X** for Exit to return to the DOS prompt. Type **DEFRAG /G0** (the letter "G" followed by the number "0") and press **[ENTER]**. The *No Graphics Characters* switch (/G0) disables the graphics mouse and graphic character set so you should be able to view the Defragmenter screens properly.
2. Type **TREE** and press **[Enter]**. DOS displays the directory tree. The subdirectories are not listed in alphabetical order in the directory tree. See Figure 5-20.

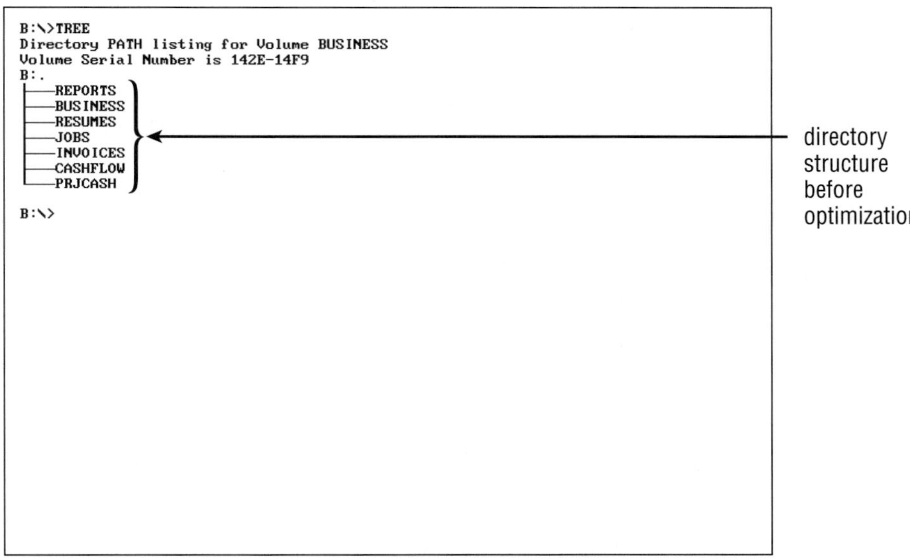

Figure 5-20
The directory tree before optimizing the Tutorial Disk's directories and files

Loading the Defragmenter

5.0

If you are using DOS 6.0 or 6.2, you can now load the Defragmenter.

If you are using DOS 5.0, skip the remainder of this section and start with the section entitled "Checking for Computer Viruses," or you can read this section and examine the figures so that you are familiar with the use of a defragmenter.

6.0 6.2

To load the Defragmenter *using DOS 6.0 or 6.2*:

1. Type **DEFRAG** and press **[Enter]**. DOS loads the utility, and the Defragmenter prompts you to select the drive to be optimized. See Figure 5-21. In this instance, the current drive is drive B and it is automatically highlighted. Your screen view will be different if you are using graphics mode.

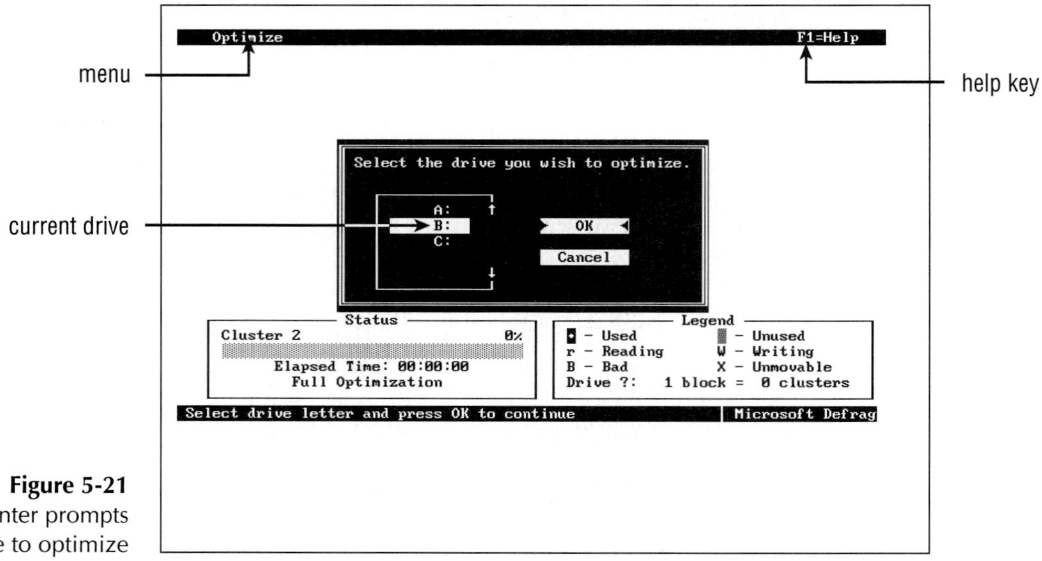

Figure 5-21
The Defragmenter prompts for a drive to optimize

2. Press **[Enter]** to select the current drive.

   If you are using the mouse, click **OK**.

   The Defragmenter reads and analyzes information from the diskette and recommends the type of optimization. See Figure 5-22. In this example, the Defragmenter states that the diskette in drive B is not fragmented and recommends no optimization. The Defragmenter might display a different recommendation for your diskette and the organization of clusters with data might differ from that shown in Figure 5-22.

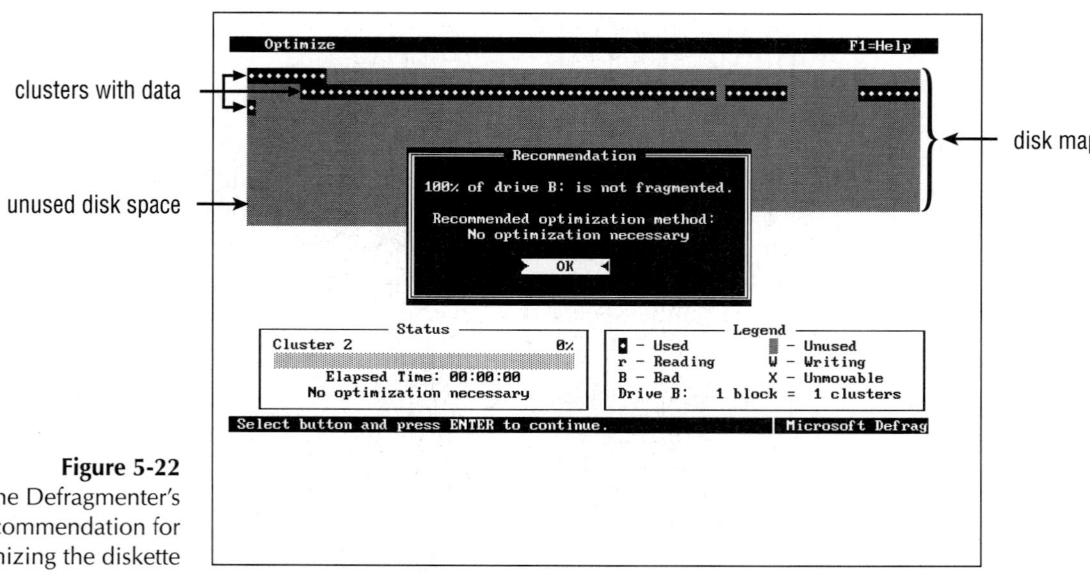

Figure 5-22
The Defragmenter's recommendation for optimizing the diskette

Understanding the Map of Disk Space Usage

In the background of the screen display, the Defragmenter maps the usage of storage space on the diskette: A rectangle with a dot represents a cluster with data; a rectangle without a dot is an empty cluster (Figure 5-22). A **cluster** is the minimum amount of storage space that DOS allocates to a file. If you use the Defragmenter on a hard disk drive, each rectangle represents a number of clusters.

The map also shows that there is empty space between files on this diskette. Although the Defragmenter recommends no optimization for this diskette, you can still optimize the diskette so that you are familiar with the use of this utility. Let's examine the Optimize menu and its options.

To display the Optimize menu:

1. If the Defragmenter recommends "No Optimization," press **[Enter]**. If the Defragmenter recommends "Full Optimization" or "Unfragment Files Only," press **[Esc]**.

   If you are using the mouse and if the Defragmenter recommends "No Optimization," click OK. If the Defragmenter recommends "Full Optimization" or "Unfragment Files Only," press **[Esc]**.

   The Defragmenter displays the Optimize menu. See Figure 5-23.

Optimize menu →

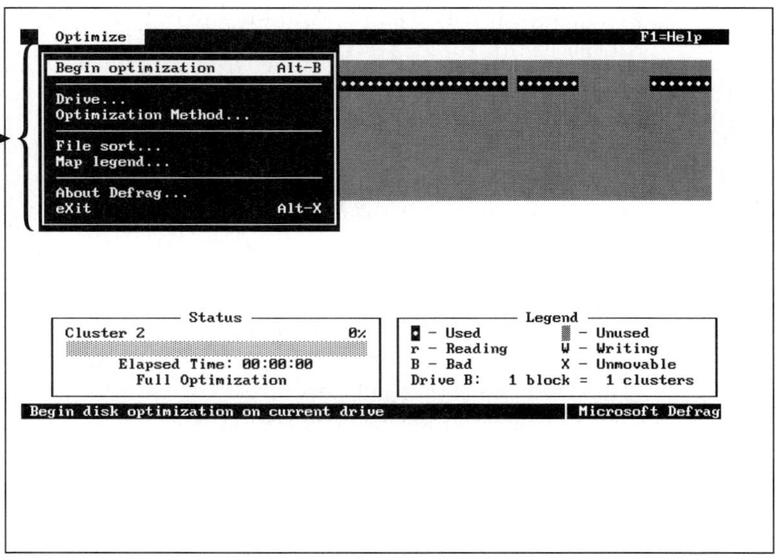

Figure 5-23
The Defragmenter's Optimize menu

Now view an explanation of disk space usage.

2. Press [↓] until you highlight the Map legend option. Then press **[Enter]**.

   If you are using the mouse, click **Map legend**.

   The Defragmenter displays a Disk Map Legend window with information on the notations used to describe disk space usage. See Figure 5-24.

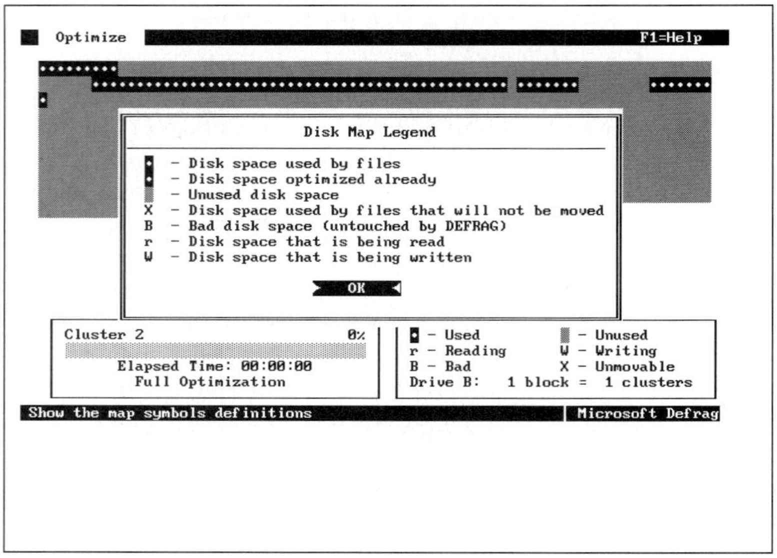

Figure 5-24
The Defragmenter's Disk Map Legend informational dialog box

On the map, a rectangle with a dot represents disk space currently in use by a file. If a rectangle is highlighted, that disk space is already optimized. A small rectangle with shading and no dot indicates unused disk space. If a rectangle contains an "X," the clusters contain an operating system file that cannot be moved. If a rectangle contains a "B," the cluster contains a defective, and therefore unusable, sector. These options are summarized in the Legend box.

Let's return to the Optimize menu.

To exit the Disk Map Legend window:

1. Press **[Enter]**.

   If you are using the mouse, click **OK**.

   The Optimize Menu reappears.

Selecting an Optimization Method

You can choose one of two types of optimization from the Optimize menu: Unfragment Files Only or Full Optimization. If you use Unfragment Files Only, the Defragmenter stores each part of a file in consecutive sectors on a diskette or a hard disk. However, it might leave unused space between files. If you use Full Optimization, the Defragmenter will arrange each part of a file in consecutive sectors and will eliminate any unused storage space between files. Also, it can sort the files and directories during the process.

You can select an optimization method that is different from the one recommended by the Defragmenter. If you do not want to optimize a diskette or hard disk, you can exit the Defragmenter without making any changes. If you want to optimize your diskette or hard disk, you select the Optimization Method menu option from the Optimize menu and choose either "Unfragment Files Only" or "Full Optimization."

Let's use full optimization so that you can see the full process for optimizing a disk.

To select full optimization:

1. Press [↑] (Up Arrow) until you highlight the Optimization Method option. Then press **[Enter]**.

   If you are using the mouse, click **Optimization Method**.

   The Select Optimization Method dialog box appears. See Figure 5-25. In this figure, the Defragmenter automatically highlights the first option, Full Optimization. (The Defragmenter might highlight the other option for your Tutorial Disk.) The Unfragment Files Only option eliminates file fragmentation but not unused space between files. If necessary, press [↑] (Up Arrow) to select Full Optimization, then press **[Spacebar]**.

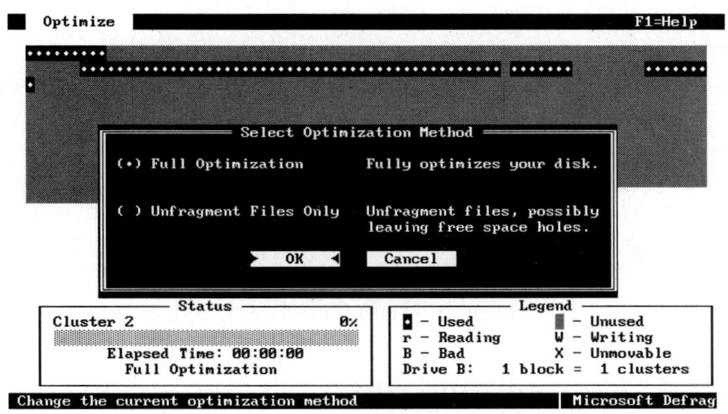

Figure 5-25
The Defragmenter's Select Optimization Method dialog box

2. Press **[Enter]** to select Full Optimization.

   If you are using the mouse, click **Full Optimization**.

   The Optimize Menu appears.

3. Press [↓] (Down Arrow) once to highlight the File sort option. Then press **[Enter]**.

   If you are using the mouse, click **File sort**.

   The File Sort dialog box appears. See Figure 5-26. You can specify the Sort Criterion and the Sort Order. The Sort Criterion options box shows that the default is Unsorted. If you use this option, files are stored on the diskette in the order in which you placed them on the diskette.

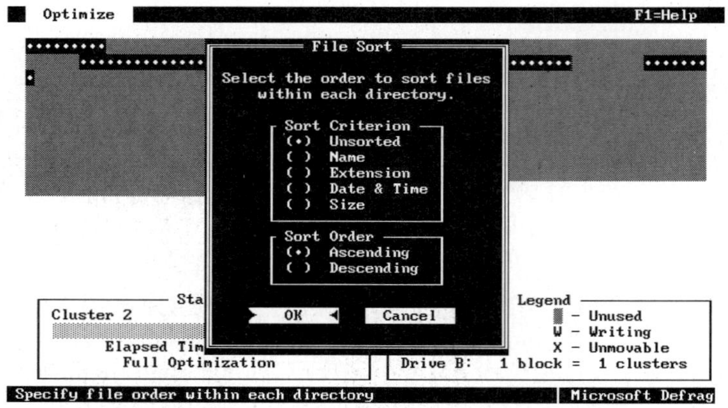

Figure 5-26
The Defragmenter's File Sort dialog box

4. Press [↓] to highlight the check box for the next option, Name, and press **[Spacebar]** to select this option.

   If you are using a mouse, click **Name**.

   A dot appears in the check box. The Defragmenter will now arrange files and directories in order by filename. The default Sort Order is Ascending.

5. Press **[Enter]**.

   If you are using the mouse, click **OK**.

   The Optimize menu reappears.

6. Press **[Home]** to highlight Begin Optimization and press **[Enter]**.

   If you are using a mouse, click **Begin Optimization**.

The Defragmenter first optimizes directories and places directory files in order at the outer edge of the diskette (Figure 5-27). It then optimizes files within each directory. As the Defragmenter reads data from the diskette and writes it back onto the diskette, you can see it rearrange the small rectangles that represent storage space used by files on the diskette. The Defragmenter will label clusters that it is reading from the diskette with an "r," and clusters that it is writing to the diskette with a "W." After the optimization, which may take only seconds, the Defragmenter displays a dialog box that tells you it has finished condensing (Figure 5-28). (In the Status box, the last processed cluster and the elapsed time on your computer might be different.) If you examine the disk storage map, you can see that the files are now arranged in order from the outer edge of the diskette and that there is no unused storage space between files.

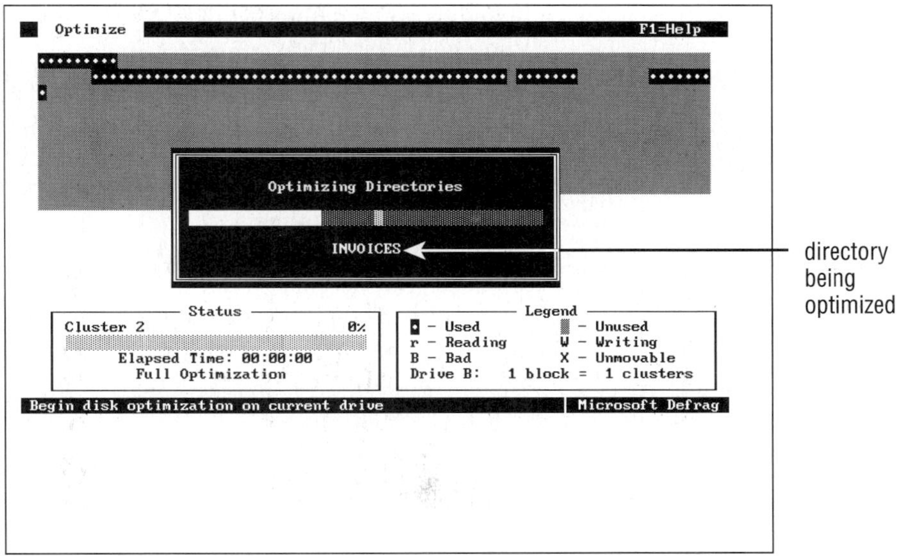

Figure 5-27
The Defragmenter optimizes directories on the diskette

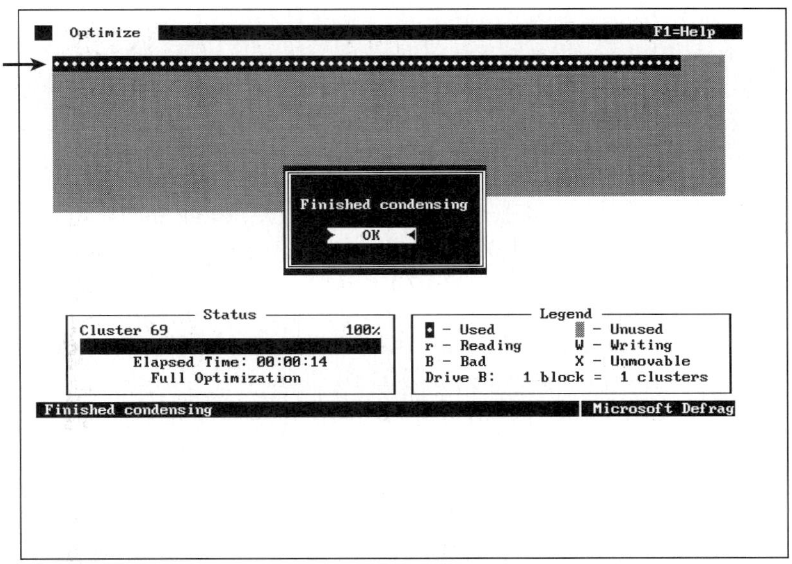

Figure 5-28
The Defragmenter optimizes and condenses the diskette

Now that the optimization is complete, let's exit the Defragmenter.

To exit the Defragmenter:

1. Press **[Enter]**.

   If you are using the mouse, click **OK**.

   A dialog box appears with three options: Another Drive, Configure, or Exit DEFRAG. The Configure option allows you to perform another optimization.

2. Press [→] until you highlight Exit DEFRAG, then press **[Enter]**.

If you are using a mouse, click **Exit DEFRAG**.

You return to the DOS prompt.

3. Type **TREE** and press **[Enter]**. DOS displays a directory tree. The subdirectories are now listed in alphabetical order. See Figure 5-29.

```
B:\>TREE
Directory PATH listing for Volume BUSINESS
Volume Serial Number is 142E-14F9
B:.
├───BUSINESS
├───CASHFLOW
├───INVOICES
├───JOBS
├───PRJCASH
├───REPORTS
└───RESUMES

B:\>
```

optimized and sorted directory structure

Figure 5-29
The optimized directory structure

Optimizing a hard disk drive takes more time than optimizing a diskette. The amount of storage space on a hard drive, the degree of fragmentation, and the type of optimization that you choose will affect the time required to optimize a hard disk. For example, in one instance, the Defragmenter fully optimized a 116M hard disk in 7 minutes 58 seconds. This hard disk was 1% fragmented and had 93MB of data, 362 directories, and 5,423 files. It optimized 47,921 clusters of data. Larger hard disks with greater file fragmentation will take longer. After a hard disk is optimized, you will see an immediate improvement in the speed and performance of your computer system.

CHECKING FOR COMPUTER VIRUSES

A coworker just informed you that she discovered a computer virus on one of her client diskettes. She recommends that you check your hard disk and your client diskettes immediately before you lose valuable client documents.

Computer viruses are programs that adversely affect the performance of a computer system. These programs might even damage the hard drive or some other hardware component. For example, the Michelangelo virus activates on the artist Michelangelo's birthday (March 6) each year, and can destroy all the information on a hard disk and render the hard disk unusable. The media coverage of the Michelangelo virus, first identified in 1992, increased the general public's awareness of the dangers of computer viruses.

Currently, more than 2,000 computer viruses have been identified, and two or three new ones are discovered every week. These viruses affect computer systems in many different ways. Like the Michelangelo virus, most computer viruses are transferred from one computer system to another by users sharing or trading diskettes. Because computer viruses can rapidly spread from one computer system to another via infected diskettes, you must frequently check your diskettes and hard disk for the appearance of computer viruses. Many computer systems and networks are set up so that a special program, called an **antiviral program**, automatically checks for the presence of viruses when the computer systems are turned on and when a diskette is inserted into a disk drive.

Sites of Infection

The majority of computer viruses infect one of three areas on a computer system: the boot sector of a hard disk or diskette, the hard disk partition table, and program files with certain types of file extensions. When you format a diskette, DOS creates a boot sector in the first sector on the first track of the first side of the diskette. The **boot sector**, or **boot record**, is a hidden file that contains information about the version of DOS used to format the diskette and the physical characteristics of the diskette, such as the number of bytes per sector, sectors per cluster, maximum number of files per disk, total number of sectors, and sectors per track. If the diskette is a boot, or system, disk, the boot sector also contains a **bootstrap loader program**, which locates and loads DOS from the diskette. If the diskette is not a boot disk, then the boot sector does not contain this program, but instead contains common error messages, such as the "Non-System disk or disk error" message that appears if you attempt to boot from a diskette that is not a boot disk. The hard drive from which DOS boots a computer system also contains a boot record. The boot sector, or record, is very important because DOS uses the information in this file to work with a hard disk or diskette.

The **hard disk partition table** is another important file. It contains information that identifies where each drive starts and which drive on the hard disk is the boot drive. If a computer virus affects the boot sector of a diskette or hard drive or the hard disk partition table, DOS is unable to work with the diskette or hard disk.

Computer viruses also commonly attach to program files with the file extensions COM or EXE and, in some cases, to **overlay files** (modules of program code) with the file extension OVL and **device drivers** (program code for managing hardware) with the file extension SYS. When the virus attaches itself, the program files increase in size and may not function properly. Some computer viruses even keep re-infecting and increasing the size of program files.

Computer Virus Activity

When certain types of computer viruses gain access to a computer system, they immediately affect the performance of that system. Other computer viruses can remain dormant until they are triggered by an event, such as a specific date or time. Once activated, that computer virus might destroy or overwrite the boot sector or hard disk partition table, destroy file linkages so that DOS cannot recognize what parts of a file belong to a given file, destroy data files, modify program files so that they do not operate properly or at all, disable ports such as LPT1 and COM1, disable diskette drives, and reformat the hard disk.

The two computer viruses most frequently found are the Stoned and Michelangelo viruses. They account for approximately one-half of all current infections on computer systems. The Stoned virus destroys or overwrites the boot sector and destroys file linkages. The Michelangelo virus infects diskettes inserted into a computer and, once it gains access to the hard disk, damages file linkages, damages or overwrites the boot sector, and reformats the hard drive. As is typical of many computer viruses, the Stoned and Michelangelo viruses are small—only 512 bytes in size.

Anti-Viral Software

Software manufacturers have developed a class of software, called **anti-viral software**, to protect computer systems from viruses. This software usually includes a program for scanning a diskette or hard drive for the presence of computer viruses, a program for cleaning or eliminating computer viruses from a diskette or hard drive, and a program that monitors for the presence of computer viruses on the computer system and on diskettes inserted into disk drives.

Anti-viral software locates computer viruses in three ways. First, it checks for computer virus signatures. A **signature** is a sequence of program code unique to a specific virus or a family of viruses that affect a computer system in similar ways. Second, it checks for suspicious activity, such as attempts to modify the operating system files. And, finally, this software checks locations where computer viruses hide, such as memory, the boot sector, the hard disk partition table, and program files.

Microsoft Corporation introduced the Microsoft Anti-Virus utility in DOS 6.0 to check for the presence of computer viruses. If Microsoft Anti-Virus locates a virus that it recognizes, it can eliminate the virus from a diskette or hard disk. If it does not recognize a virus, either the program is not able to detect it or it is a newly introduced virus. As with other types of software, you must periodically purchase updates of anti-viral software so that it can check for new computer viruses.

5.0

DOS 5.0 does not have the Microsoft Anti-Virus utility. However, you can purchase an anti-viral software product similar to Microsoft Anti-Virus and use it to check your computer for viruses.

Starting Microsoft Anti-Virus

To ensure the integrity of your client diskette, you want to check it for the presence of computer viruses and remove any viruses that are found. To start the Microsoft Anti-Virus from the DOS prompt, you use the following external command:

MSAV [*drive:*]

"MSAV" is an abbreviation for Microsoft Anti-Virus. If you do not specify a drive, MSAV assumes you want to check for computer viruses on the current drive.

5.0

If you are using DOS 5.0, you cannot complete the steps in this section because DOS 5.0 does not include the Microsoft Anti-Virus utility. Skip to the Summary section, or you can read the steps and examine the figures in this section to familiarize yourself with the process of checking for the presence of computer viruses with an anti-viral utility like Microsoft Anti-Virus.

6.0 6.2

To start the Microsoft Anti-Virus *using DOS 6.0 or 6.2*:

1. Be sure the current drive contains your Tutorial Disk.
2. At the DOS prompt, type **MSAV** and press **[Enter]**. The Microsoft Anti-Virus Main Menu appears. See Figure 5-30. The Main Menu contains five options. The status bar shows the options that are available through the function keys. For example, [F1] accesses Help. Your screen view will look different if you are using graphics mode.

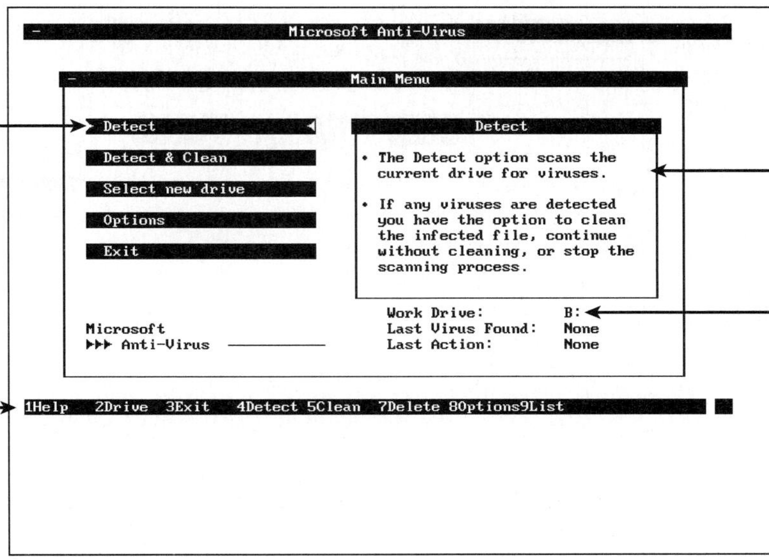

Figure 5-30
The Microsoft Anti-Virus Main Menu

If your monitor displays strange or unusual graphics characters for borders, outlines, or symbols, type **X** for Exit and then press **[Enter]** for OK to return to the DOS prompt. Then type **MSAV /BF** and press **[Enter]**. Microsoft recommends that you use the *BIOS Font switch* (/BF) to disable the graphics mouse and graphics character set if the graphics characters do not display properly. If this switch does not work, type **X** (for Exit), press **[Enter]** for OK to return to the DOS prompt again, then type **MSAV /NF** and press **[Enter]**. The *No Fonts switch* (/NF) does not use graphics characters.

Displaying Information on Computer Viruses

The Microsoft Anti-Virus utility contains information on over 1,000 computer viruses. You can display information on a specific virus with [F9] (List). Let's examine information on the two most common computer viruses.

To display information on the Michelangelo and Stoned viruses:

1. Press **[F9]** (List). Microsoft Anti-Virus displays the Virus List. See Figure 5-31. Your Virus List might be different because Microsoft provides an option for periodic upgrades to this utility. The computer viruses are listed in alphabetical order. The names of *variants,* or functionally similar computer viruses,

are listed beneath the name of the more common virus in the family. For example, Red State is a variant of AirCop.

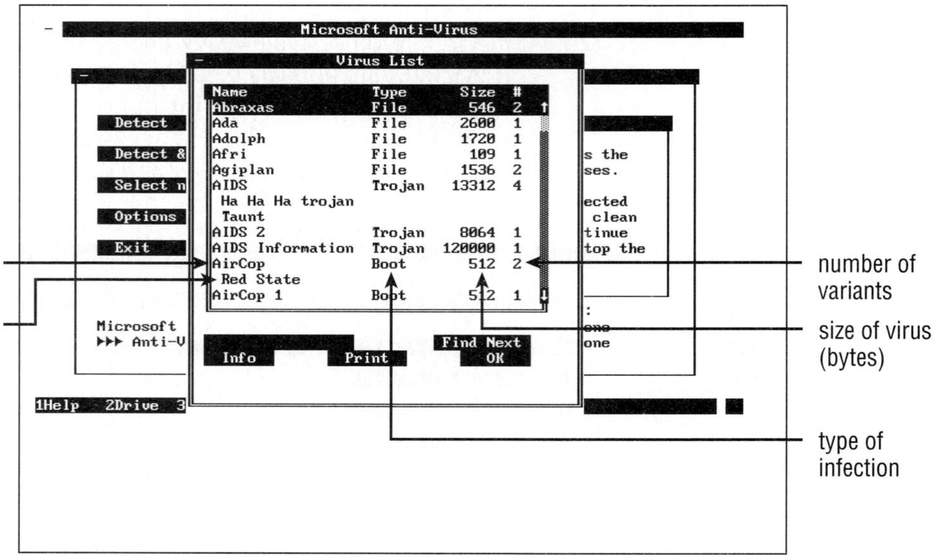

Figure 5-31
The Virus List dialog box

2. Type **Mic** (for Michelangelo). Microsoft Anti-Virus searches for the first computer virus name that starts with these three letters, and it locates the listing for the Michelangelo virus. See Figure 5-32. The Type column tells you that the Michelangelo virus is a *boot sector virus,* a type of virus that replaces the boot sector with its own program code to guarantee that it is automatically loaded into memory when the computer system boots. The last column shows that there are five variants of this computer virus.

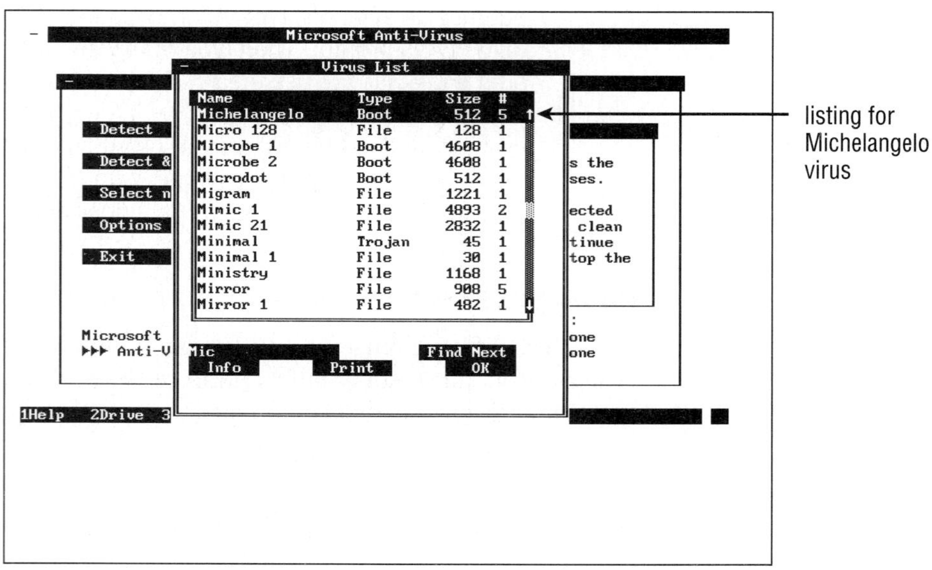

Figure 5-32
The listing for the Michelangelo computer virus

3. Press **[Enter]**. Microsoft Anti-Virus displays a Virus Characteristics window with information on the Michelangelo virus. See Figure 5-33. From this information, you can tell that it infects the boot sector of diskettes and the hard disk partition table. It stays, or remains *resident,* in memory after a computer system boots and continues to infect the computer system and any diskettes inserted into disk drives. Microsoft Anti-Virus also lists its side effects, i.e., how it affects the computer system.

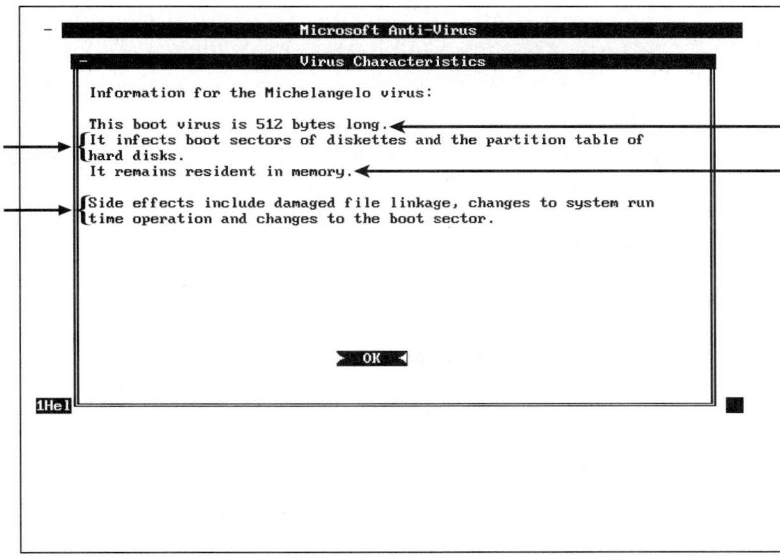

Figure 5-33
Information on the Michelangelo virus in the Virus Characteristics window

4. Press **[Enter]**.

   If you are using the mouse, click **OK**.

   Microsoft Anti-Virus displays the Virus List screen.

5. Press **[Backspace]** three times to delete the characters "Mic" (for Michelangelo).
6. Type **Sto** (for Stoned). Microsoft Anti-Virus locates the listing for the Stoned virus, another boot sector virus.
7. Press **[Enter]**. Microsoft Anti-Virus displays the Virus Characteristics window for this virus. Like the Michelangelo virus, it infects the boot sector of diskettes as well as the hard disk partition table, and it remains resident in memory.
8. Press **[Enter]**.

   If you are using the mouse, click **OK**.

   Microsoft Anti-Virus displays the Virus List.

9. Press **[Esc]** to exit the Virus List.

Scanning a Disk

You are now ready to scan your client diskette for computer viruses. The scanning process only checks for the presence of computer viruses; it does not remove them from the diskette or hard disk.

To scan the Tutorial Disk:

1. Be sure the first option, Detect, is highlighted or selected. Press **[Enter]**. Microsoft Anti-Virus scans the disk.

Microsoft Anti-Virus first checks the computer's memory (RAM) for viruses (Figure 5-34). Computer viruses load themselves into memory once they gain access to a computer system. After Microsoft Anti-Virus checks memory, it checks the files in each of the directories on the Tutorial Disk (Figure 5-35). The full path of each file is listed in the upper-left corner as each file is checked. When the system check is complete, an informational window, titled "Viruses Detected and Cleaned," shows the types of drives and files that the utility checked (Figure 5-36). Your scan time might be different.

If your diskette contained a computer virus, Microsoft Anti-Virus would sound an alarm and display a message window with information on the virus and a suggestion for removing the virus. To remove the virus, you would return to the Main Menu and use the menu option "Detect & Clean."

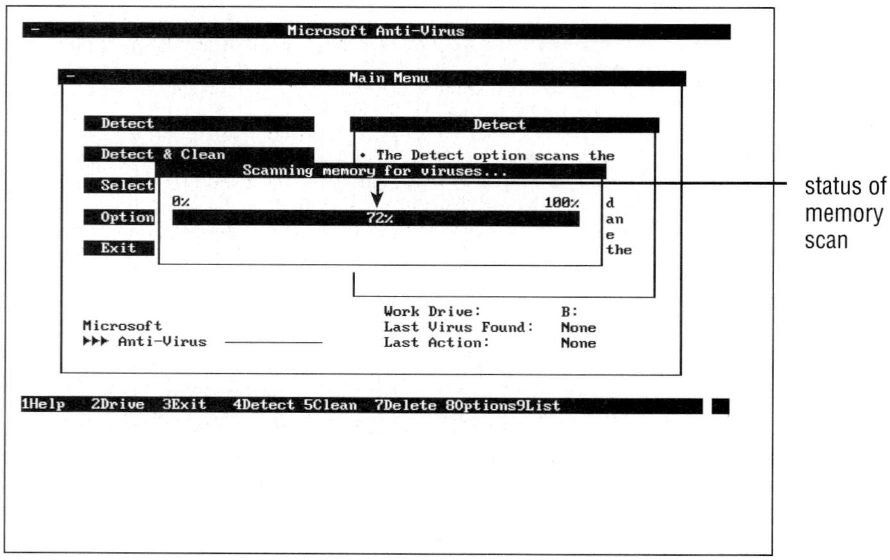

Figure 5-34
The memory scan for computer viruses

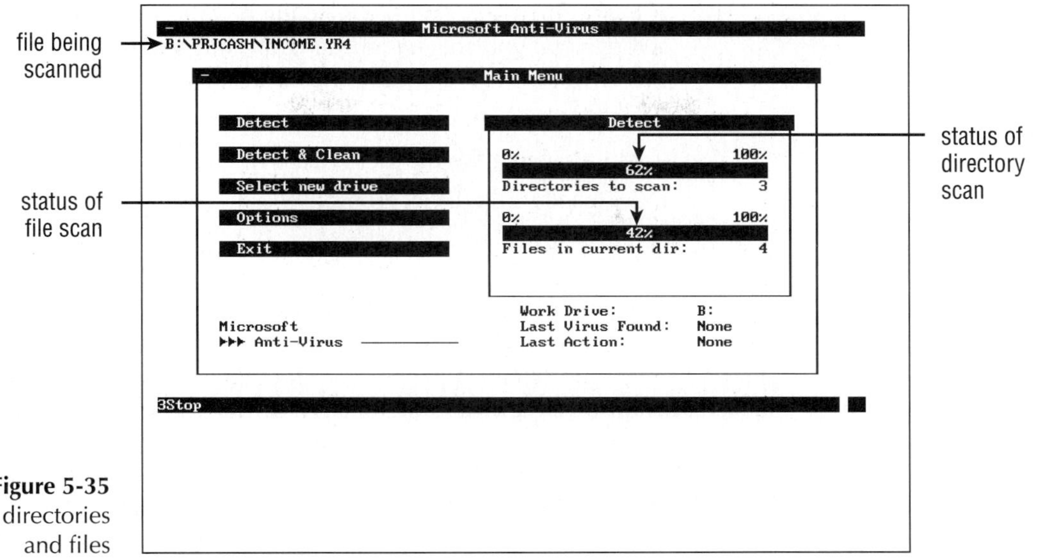

Figure 5-35
Scanning directories and files

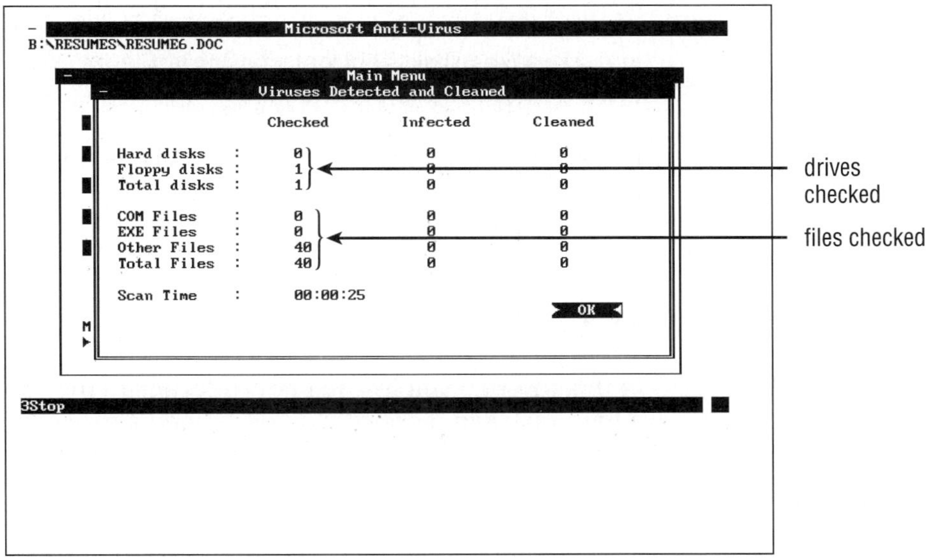

Figure 5-36
The Viruses Detected and Cleaned informational window

Let's return to the Main Menu and exit Microsoft Anti-Virus.

To return to the Main Menu:

1. Press **[Enter]**.

   If you are using the mouse, click **OK**.

   The Main Menu appears.
2. Press [↓] until you highlight Exit, and press **[Enter]**.

   If you are using a mouse, click **Exit**.

A Close Microsoft Anti-Virus dialog box appears. Note that you can save settings that you specify in Microsoft Anti-Virus. By using the Options menu option, you can customize Microsoft Anti-Virus.

3. Press **[Enter]**.

   If you are using the mouse, click **OK**.

   DOS displays the DOS prompt.

The Detect option only checks for computer viruses; it does not remove them. If a virus is found, you have an opportunity to copy important files from the hard disk drive or diskette before you remove the computer virus, because, in some cases, the "clean" process can damage a program or data file.

The first time that Microsoft Anti-Virus scans a hard disk or diskette, it creates small files named CHKLIST.MS in each directory that contains programs. These files contain checksums for each program file. A **checksum** is a calculated value based on characteristics of the program file, including its size, date, and time. The next time you use Microsoft Anti-Virus, it will compare the values in these checksum files with newly calculated values for the same program files to determine if the program files have changed. If the checksums do not match, a computer virus might have infected the program. Your Tutorial and Exercises Disks will not contain a file named CHKLIST.MS because these disks do not contain program files.

You now have another important tool for maintaining the integrity of your files and for preventing damage to the computer systems and disks in your office.

◆

SUMMARY

In this tutorial, you learned how to evaluate the organization of directories on a hard disk and diskette. You developed a plan for reorganizing directories on your Tutorial Disk. You modified the directory structure from the DOS prompt and with the DOS Shell so that you and DOS could more easily and quickly locate files and access information on a diskette. You used commands at the DOS prompt and the DOS Shell to move subdirectories and their files, as well as to rename and remove subdirectories. You used the Subdirectory Search switch with the DIR command at the DOS prompt and the Search option on the File menu in the DOS Shell to locate a single file or a group of files within the directory structure of your diskette.

You used the Defragmenter utility in DOS 6.0 and 6.2 to optimize the directory structure, the organization of files, and storage space usage on your diskette. You used the Microsoft Anti-Virus utility in DOS 6.0 and 6.2 to scan your Tutorial Disk for the presence of computer viruses. You also learned how to locate information about specific viruses.

Command Reference	
DOS Commands	
DEFRAG [*drive:*]	An external command for a DOS utility that optimizes directories and eliminates or reduces file fragmentation
DIR [*file specification*] /S	An internal command that searches through subdirectories for filenames that match the file specification and then displays the full path of matching filenames
MSAV [*drive:*]	An external command for a DOS utility that checks for the presence of computer viruses and, if necessary, cleans or removes computer viruses from a diskette or hard drive
RD [*drive:*]*path*	An internal command that removes an empty subdirectory from the directory structure of a diskette or hard drive
DOS Shell Commands	
File Search	Locates all filenames in all directories that match a file specification and then displays the full path of the filenames

QUESTIONS

1. What command would you use to view the directory structure of a hard disk drive one screen at a time from the DOS prompt?
2. What command would you use to print the directory structure of a hard disk drive from the DOS prompt?
3. List four factors that you can use to evaluate the organization of subdirectories on a hard disk?
4. What command removes a subdirectory at the DOS prompt? List three conditions under which this command will not work?
5. Describe the three basic steps required to move a subdirectory from one level to another level in the directory tree at the DOS prompt.
6. Describe the three basic steps required to move a subdirectory from one level to another in the directory tree in the DOS Shell.
7. How do you rename a subdirectory in the DOS Shell?

8. What switch can you use with the DIR command to locate files with similar file specifications stored in different directories on a hard disk drive? Give an example.
9. How do you locate a file, or set of files, in the DOS Shell?
10. What is file fragmentation, and why is it a problem?
11. List two ways that you can optimize a hard disk or diskette with the Defragmenter utility.
12. What sort criteria can the Defragmenter use to arrange files on a diskette or hard disk?
13. What sort orders can the Defragmenter use to arrange files on a diskette or hard disk?
14. When you view the usage of disk space with the Defragmenter, how does this utility identify disk space occupied by files versus unused disk space?
15. What is a computer virus?
16. Name one computer virus commonly found on computer systems and describe how it affects the computer system?
17. List the three sites on a computer system commonly infected by viruses.
18. What is a boot sector, or boot record? What information does it contain? Why is it important to DOS?
19. What is a hard disk partition table? What information does it contain?
20. List three types of program operations commonly performed by anti-viral software?
21. What is a computer virus signature?
22. How does a boot sector virus affect a computer system?
23. What is a checksum? How does Microsoft Anti-Virus use checksums to check for computer viruses?
24. What is the most common vehicle for the transmission of computer viruses?
25. You have a directory named OLDFORMS on drive C that is below the root directory, and you want to remove this directory. Assume this directory has files that you no longer need. What command(s) would you use to remove this directory?
26. You want to locate a file named 93TAXES.REC. What command would you enter from the root directory to check all subdirectories so that you could find this file?
27. You keep all your work files in a directory named C:\WORK. The number of files in this directory now exceeds 50. You want to create a new directory named C:\MEMOS so that you can copy all the files with the file extension MEM (for "Memo") from the directory C:\WORK to C:\MEMOS. Then you want to delete those files from C:\WORK. List the steps and commands you would use to accomplish these operations. Assume you are working at the DOS prompt.
28. What command would you enter at the DOS prompt to locate a file named 93BUDGET.DOC on drive C? Assume that you are working on drive D in a subdirectory named \BUDGET and that the file could be stored in any of the directories on drive C.

29. What command would you enter at the DOS prompt to locate all the budget document files on drive C for the last three years? Assume that the files begin with two digits for the year—91, 92, and 93—and that you are working in a subdirectory named \CASHFLOW on drive C. Also, the files might contain any combination of characters after the year and any file extension.
30. What command would you enter at the DOS prompt to locate all the tax records on drive C for the last three years? Assume that all the files have the file extension REC and that you are working in the directory named C:\EARNINGS.

TUTORIAL ASSIGNMENTS

1. **Evaluating the Directory Structure of a Hard Disk**: After examining the directory structure of a hard disk, you make the following observations:
   - DOS utilities, such as the programs for formatting and making copies of diskettes, are stored in the root directory along with programs for other software utilities.
   - The WordPerfect directory, WP51, contains several hundred program files included with this software application and several hundred document files produced over a several-year period.
   - The same version of Lotus 1-2-3 is installed twice in two separate directories at different levels in the directory tree.
   - The hard disk contains seven levels of subdirectories.

   Describe how you would reorganize and improve the directory structure of the hard disk and resolve the problems described above.
2. **Reorganizing the Directory Tree**: *Use your Exercise Disk for this Tutorial Assignment.* Complete the following steps from the DOS prompt.
   a. Print a copy of the directory tree for the Exercise Disk.
   b. Print a copy of the directory of all the files in all the directories on the Exercise Disk.

   Evaluate the organization of directories and files on the Exercise Disk. Then prepare a diagram of a new directory structure for the diskette.
   c. Create the new directory structure based on your diagram. After you create each new directory, move files from the root directory or from any existing directories to their new directories. Use your best judgment in determining where to place files. Be sure no files remain in the root directory.
   d. Print a copy of the new directory structure of the Exercise Disk.
3. **Locating Files**: *Use your Tutorial Disk to perform the following operations from both the DOS prompt and the DOS Shell.* List the command that you use to accomplish each step.

   Using the DOS Prompt:
   a. Display an alphabetical list, one screen at a time, of all files in all directories that have filenames with the file extension "RPT."
   b. Display an alphabetical list, one screen at a time, of all files in all directories that have "WK" as the first two characters of the file extension.

Using the DOS Shell:

c. Display an alphabetical list of all files in all directories that have a "DOC" file extension.

d. Display an alphabetical list of all files in all directories that have "CASH" as the last four characters of an eight-character filename.

6.0 *6.2*

4. **Optimizing a Diskette**: *Use your Exercise Disk to complete this Tutorial Assignment.* As you perform the following steps, answer the questions.
   a. Load the Defragmenter.
      (1) What drive does the Defragmenter select?
      (2) Is this drive your current drive?
   b. Select the current drive.
      (1) What percentage of the disk is not fragmented?
      (2) What is the recommended optimization method?
      (3) How many clusters are in a block?
   c. Select Full Optimization.
   d. Specify a Sort Criterion that arranges files in order of file size.
   e. Specify a Sort Order that arranges files from the largest size to the smallest size in each directory.
   f. Optimize the diskette. After optimization, describe the arrangement of used and unused storage space on the diskette.
   g. Exit the Defragmenter.

6.0 *6.2*

5. **Scanning for Computer Viruses**: *Use your Exercise Disk to complete this Tutorial Assignment.* As you perform the following steps, answer the questions.
   a. Load Microsoft Anti-Virus.
      (1) What drive does the Microsoft Anti-Virus select?
      (2) Is this drive your current drive?
   b. Scan the Exercises Disk for computer viruses.
      (1) How many viruses did Microsoft Anti-Virus find?
      (2) How many files did it check on the diskette?
   c. If necessary, remove any computer viruses from the diskette.
   d. Display information on the Dark Avenger computer virus, another common and destructive virus.
      (1) What type of virus is it?
      (2) How many variants are there?
      (3) What is the size of the Dark Avenger virus?
      (4) What site or sites does the Dark Avenger infect?
      (5) Does it remain resident in memory?
      (6) What side effects does the Dark Avenger produce?
   e. Exit Microsoft Anti-Virus.

TUTORIAL **6**

Backing Up a Hard Disk

OBJECTIVES

In this tutorial you will learn to:

- Distinguish between types of backups
- Back up a hard disk
- Perform a system compatibility test for backups
- Create setup files for backups
- Restore backed-up files
- Perform extended copies
- Develop a backup strategy

The end of the month is rapidly approaching and it is time for the monthly backup of computer files. When you perform this backup, you start a new **backup cycle** and back up all your client and business files for the last month onto diskettes. After you finish the backup, you will have a complete set of all the important files that you use on a daily basis in your business. If you should inadvertently delete a file during your daily work, you can restore a copy of that file from your **backup set**. If your hard disk fails, you can repair or replace the hard disk and restore all your client and business files from your backup diskettes.

If you do not back up a hard disk and if that disk fails, you will have to reconstruct all your client and business files. Microsoft Corporation estimates that it would take an average of 2,000 hours to replace lost files on a typical hard disk. If you are operating a business, you cannot afford to lose important files, nor can you afford the time and cost required to reconstruct them. A regular backup of your hard disk is like an insurance policy because it protects your investment in your business.

◆

BACKING UP FILES, DISKETTES, AND HARD DISKS

DOS provides several commands for backing up files and disks. You can use the COPY command to make a duplicate copy of a single file or, with the use of wildcards, duplicate copies of a group of files. For example, after you create an important business file and save it to your hard disk, you can take a few seconds and immediately copy that file to a diskette so that you have a **backup**, or duplicate copy, of the file. If you should inadvertently delete, overwrite, or damage that business file, you can immediately copy the duplicate copy of the file from the diskette to the hard disk and continue your work.

However, the COPY command has limitations. For example, although you can copy one or more files in a directory, you cannot copy more than one directory at a time. Therefore, you cannot use this command to back up an entire hard disk. Also, if you are copying files to a diskette and the space on that diskette fills up before you are able to copy all the files you want, the COPY command stops and tells you that the diskette is full. You can continue the copy operation on another diskette, but you must specify a new COPY command with a new file specification so that you do not copy the same set of files again. This command does not automatically start where it left off, and it cannot split a file between diskettes. The COPY command, therefore, is most useful for quick backups of a single file or a set of files.

You also can use the DISKCOPY command to make a backup copy of a diskette. For example, if you store important client files on a diskette and work from that diskette, you can take a few minutes and make a backup copy of the client diskette. If your original working diskette fails, you can make a duplicate copy of the backup diskette and use the duplicate copy as your new working diskette. If you inadvertently delete an important client file, you can copy that file from your backup diskette.

Like the COPY command, the DISKCOPY command has its limitations. You cannot use the DISKCOPY command to back up the contents of a hard disk. Use of DISKCOPY is limited to copying diskettes. However, if you store most of your work on a diskette, you will find the DISKCOPY command useful.

In all versions of DOS except DOS 6.2, you can use the BACKUP utility to back up all or part of a hard disk. The BACKUP utility can copy one directory after another to a series of diskettes. You can copy part of the directory tree or the entire directory tree and each directory's files. During the backup operation, the BACKUP utility uses all of the storage space available on a diskette and can split a file between two diskettes. When a diskette is full, the BACKUP utility stops and prompts you to insert another diskette.

To recover a file or group of files from backup copies produced with the BACKUP utility, you must use the RESTORE command because the backed-up files are stored in a special format on the backup diskettes. You should use the RESTORE command that comes with the version of DOS that you used to create the backup copies. Otherwise, you might not be able to restore files from your backup diskettes. A BACKUP utility in another version of DOS might store the backed-up files in a different format than does the version of DOS you used.

DOS 6.0 and DOS 6.2 contain a new backup utility called MSBACKUP. You can use MSBACKUP like the BACKUP utility to back up all or part of a hard disk onto diskettes. You can also use this utility to restore files to a hard disk from backup diskettes. MSBACKUP is intended as a replacement for the BACKUP and RESTORE utilities in DOS 6.0 and later versions of DOS. Not only does it improve the speed, efficiency, and reliability of backups, but it offers a variety of options for performing backups. If you are using DOS 5.0 or an earlier version of DOS, you must use the separate BACKUP and RESTORE utilities. If you are using DOS 6.2, you must use the MSBACKUP utility to back up your hard disk, because the DOS 6.2 installation program removes the BACKUP utility from your DOS subdirectory.

You want to back up the directory on your hard disk that contains your client and business records. This directory has the same name as your business, AceForms. Before you can back up this directory and its subdirectories, however, you must perform some preliminary operations.

GETTING STARTED

Your instructor or technical support person will have created a directory named AceForms on your hard disk drive for this tutorial. *Before you make changes to that hard drive, be sure you have permission from your instructor or the technical support person in your computer laboratory. If you are using a network without a hard disk drive C, ask your instructor for directions on how to complete this tutorial.*

You will begin by installing DOSKEY and specifying switches for the DIR command in the DOS environment. Then you will format your Tutorial Disk and Exercise Disk so that you can use them as backup diskettes for this tutorial. *Because the formatting will eliminate all files and directories on the Tutorial Disk and Exercise Disk, be sure you have completed all previous tutorials.*

To set up your system:

1. After you power on your computer system, access the DOS prompt for your hard drive.

5.0 6.0

2. Type **DOSKEY** and press **[Enter]**. If you are using DOS 5.0 or 6.0, DOS will display the message "DOSKey installed" if DOSKEY is not already installed on your computer. If you do not see this message with DOS 5.0 or 6.0, DOSKEY is already loaded. DOS 6.2 will not display a message.

6.2

3. Type **SET DIRCMD=/P /O** and press **[Enter]**. DOS will now display your client files and subdirectories in alphabetical order and pause after each screen.
4. Type **SET** and press **[Enter]** to verify that you correctly entered the switches for the DIRCMD environment variable. If not, repeat Step 3.

Formatting Diskettes for a Backup

Next you need to format the Tutorial Disk and Exercise Disk before you can perform the backup operation. As noted earlier, be sure you do not need any of the information on these diskettes. When you reformat a diskette, you can use the **Unconditional Switch** (/U) with the FORMAT command to erase all information from the diskette.

To format a diskette:

1. Insert your Tutorial Disk into drive A or drive B and, if necessary, close the drive door.
2. Format the diskette to the proper storage capacity using one of the following options:
   - If you are formatting a double-density diskette in a double-density drive, a high-density diskette in a high-density drive, or an extra-high-density diskette in an extra-high-density drive, type **FORMAT A: /U** (or **FORMAT B: /U**) and press **[Enter]**. You do not need to use the Format Capacity switch because DOS will automatically format the diskette to the maximum capacity of the drive.
   - If you are formatting a double-density diskette in a high-density or extra-high-density drive, type **FORMAT A: /F:720 /U** (or **FORMAT B: /F:720 /U**) and press **[Enter]**.
   - If you are formatting a high-density diskette in an extra-high-density drive, type **FORMAT A: /F:1.44 /U** (or **FORMAT B: /F:1.44 /U**) and press **[Enter]**.

DOS then prompts you to insert a diskette into drive A or drive B.

3. Press **[Enter]**. After DOS completes the formatting, it prompts for a volume label.
4. Press **[Enter]** to indicate that you do not want a volume label assigned to this diskette. DOS asks you whether you want to format another diskette.
5. Type **Y** and press **[Enter]**. DOS prompts you to insert a diskette into the diskette drive.
6. Remove your Tutorial Disk from the drive, and insert your Exercise Disk or an unformatted diskette *with the same storage capacity* as the one you just formatted. Press **[Enter]**. DOS formats this diskette to the same storage capacity and prompts for a volume label.
7. Press **[Enter]** to indicate that you do not want a volume label assigned to this diskette. DOS asks you whether you want to format another diskette.
8. Type **N** and press **[Enter]**. DOS displays the DOS prompt.

USING THE BACKUP UTILITY

You can use the BACKUP command in DOS 5.0 and 6.0 to back up all or part of a hard disk onto diskettes. Although the setup program for DOS 6.2 removes this utility from the DOS subdirectory when you install DOS 6.2, DOS 6.2 users should read this discussion to become familiar with the BACKUP utility's use and syntax. You might need to use this utility on a computer that has DOS 5.0 or 6.0 installed. The general syntax for this external command is:

BACKUP *source destination-drive*:

The source might be an entire hard drive, part of the directory structure of a hard drive, a group of files in a subdirectory, or even a single file. The destination drive is the name of the diskette drive to which BACKUP will copy files. The source and destination drives are required parameters.

If you back up an entire hard drive or part of the directory structure, you should use the **Subdirectory switch** (/S) so that DOS backs up all subdirectories and files below the directory or drive that you specify. For example, to back up an entire hard disk (drive C) to drive A, you use the following command:

BACKUP C:*.* A: /S

This command instructs DOS to start at the root directory of drive C and back up all files in the root directory and in all subdirectories below the root directory to drive A.

If you want to start at a specific directory, you specify the path and directory name. For example, to back up a directory named BIDS on drive C and all subdirectories and files below this directory to drive A, you would enter the following command:

BACKUP C:\BIDS A: /S

Another useful switch is the **Log File switch** (/L). When you use this switch, the BACKUP command creates a file that contains a list of the full path and filename of all the backed-up files. For example, to back up a BIDS directory on drive C and create a log file named 070994.LOG (for July 9, 1994) in a directory named LOGS on drive C, you would enter the following command:

BACKUP C:\BIDS A: /S /L:C:\LOGS\070994.LOG

After the /L in the Log File switch, you type a colon, followed by the drive name and path (C:), directory name (\LOGS), and filename of the log file (070994.LOG). During the backup operation, you will see a message that BACKUP is logging to this file.

Viewing the Contents of the AceForms Directory

Before you back up your data directory, you want to view its contents.

To view the contents of the AceForms directory:

1. Be sure you are at the root directory of the hard drive you are using. The remainder of these steps will assume drive C for the source drive and drive A for the destination drive. If you are using different drive names for the source and destination drives, substitute your drive names whenever you enter commands that require them.
2. Type **DIR \ACEFORMS /S** and press **[Enter]**. DOS displays the contents of the AceForms directory, directory by directory. It lists the directory names and filenames in alphabetical order and pauses after each screen. See Figure 6-1. *If DOS reports "File not found," ask your instructor or technical support person to create this directory and its files before you continue.*

```
 Volume in drive C is HI PERFORM
 Volume Serial Number is 1A81-8E17

Directory of C:\ACEFORMS

.            <DIR>      06-02-94   1:20a
..           <DIR>      06-02-94   1:20a
BUSINESS     <DIR>      06-02-94   1:20a
CASHFLOW     <DIR>      06-02-94   1:20a
INVOICES     <DIR>      06-02-94   1:20a
JOBS         <DIR>      06-02-94   1:20a
PRJCASH      <DIR>      06-02-94   1:20a
REPORTS      <DIR>      06-02-94   1:20a
RESUMES      <DIR>      06-02-94   1:20a
        9 file(s)          0 bytes

Directory of C:\ACEFORMS\BUSINESS

.            <DIR>      06-02-94   1:20a
..           <DIR>      06-02-94   1:20a
BUSINESS PLN        590 03-20-94   5:26p
CLIENT   LST        476 04-10-94  11:08a
EQUIP    LST        671 03-23-94   3:57p
Press any key to continue . . .
```

subdirectories

files

Figure 6-1
A partial directory listing of the AceForms subdirectory

3. Keep pressing **[Spacebar]** or any other key until you view the entire directory listing and return to the DOS prompt.

Next, because you are responsible for preparing, updating, and maintaining these documents for your company, you want to verify the contents of one of the AceForms subdirectories, the one named REPORTS.

To view the contents of a subdirectory below AceForms:

1. Type **DIR \ACEFORMS\REPORTS** and press **[Enter]**. DOS displays the contents of this subdirectory. See Figure 6-2. *If DOS reports "File not found" or if you do not see the same filenames as shown in Figure 6-2, ask your instructor or technical support person to create this directory and its files before you continue.*

6.2 *If you are using DOS 6.2, you cannot complete the sections of this tutorial that illustrate the use of the BACKUP and RESTORE utilities. Instead, skip these sections and continue with the section entitled "Using MSBACKUP."*

5.0 ***6.0*** *If you are using DOS 5.0 or 6.0, continue with the next section, entitled "Backing Up the AceForms Directory."*

```
C:\>DIR \ACEFORMS\REPORTS

 Volume in drive C is HI PERFORM
 Volume Serial Number is 1A81-8E17
 Directory of C:\ACEFORMS\REPORTS

.            <DIR>      06-02-94   1:20a
..           <DIR>      06-02-94   1:20a
APR_CASH            366 03-18-94  10:20a
FEB_CASH            369 03-18-94  10:14a
JAN_CASH            368 03-18-94  10:00a
JUN_CASH            365 03-18-94  10:45a
MAR_CASH            366 03-18-94  10:17a
MAY_CASH            364 03-18-94  10:43a
        8 file(s)        2198 bytes
                     27471872 bytes free

C:\>
```

directory path and name

Figure 6-2
A directory listing of the \ACEFORMS\REPORTS subdirectory

Backing Up the AceForms Directory

Now you are ready to back up the AceForms directory and all its subdirectories and files.

To back up the AceForms directory:

1. Be sure you are at the root directory of drive C.
2. Type **BACKUP C:\ACEFORMS A: /S /L:C:\DOS\LOGFILE1** (or **BACKUP C:\ACEFORMS B: /S /L:C:\DOS\LOGFILE1**) and press **[Enter]**. *If your DOS subdirectory has another name, use that name with the Log File switch.* BACKUP prompts you to insert backup diskette 01 into the diskette drive you specified, warns you that all files in the root directory will be erased, and prompts you to press any key when you are ready to continue. See Figure 6-3.

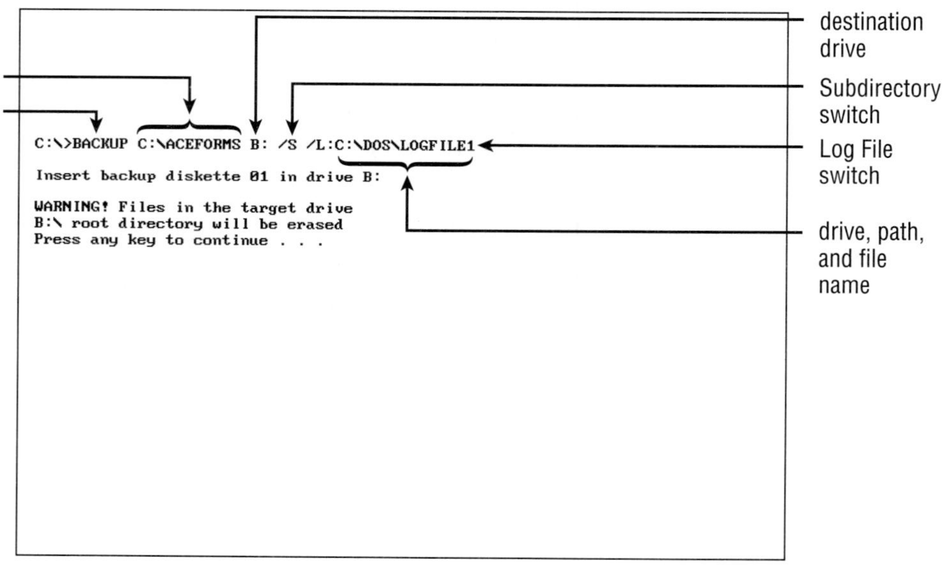

Figure 6-3
The BACKUP utility prompts for the first backup diskette

3. Insert your Tutorial Disk in the appropriate disk drive, then press **[Enter]**. BACKUP informs you that it is backing up to drive A and logging to a file named C:\DOS\LOGFILE.001. It displays the full path and filename of each file as it backs up each file to the diskette drive. See Figure 6-4. After the backup is complete, DOS displays the DOS prompt. If BACKUP fills the first diskette, it will prompt you for another diskette.

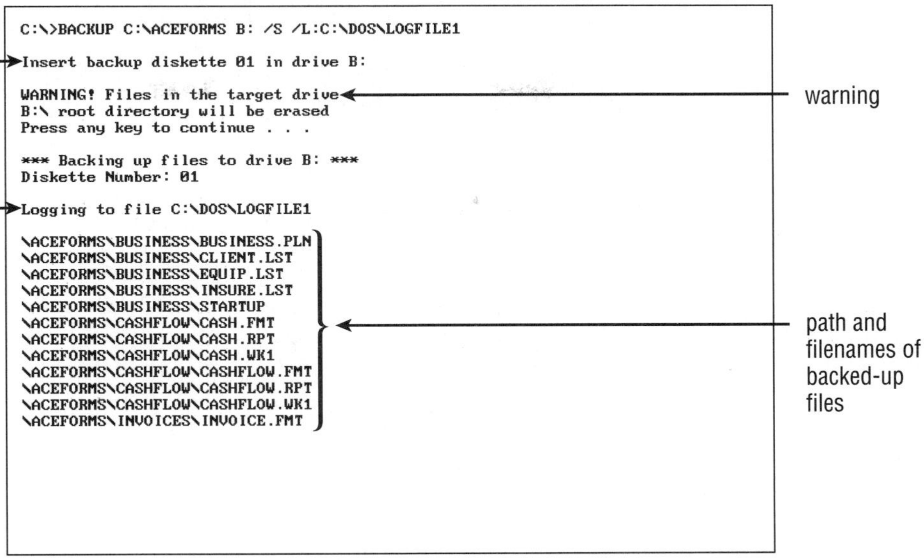

Figure 6-4
Backing up files and logging the backup

Checking the Backup Process

Now you want to view a directory of the backup diskette so that you can see which files the BACKUP utility stored on your Tutorial Disk. You also want to examine the log file.

You should not automatically assume a backup worked. You should always check the backup diskette to verify the backup. If there are no files on the backup diskette or if the files are zero bytes in size, the backup did not work. You should then repeat the backup.

To view the contents of the Tutorial Disk:

1. Type **DIR A:** (or **DIR B:**) and press **[Enter]**. DOS shows you that the BACKUP command assigned the volume name BACKUP.001 to the diskette and that it created two files. See Figure 6-5. The BACKUP.001 file contains all the files that the BACKUP command backed up to this diskette. These files are stored together to maximize the use of disk space on the backup diskette. The CONTROL.001 file contains information about the backed-up files, including the path names. In both cases, the file extension identifies the diskette number. In this example, these files use 47,969 bytes of storage space.

```
C:\>DIR B:

 Volume in drive B is BACKUP  001
 Volume Serial Number is 2F51-14E4
 Directory of B:\

BACKUP   001      45980 11-06-93   1:39p
CONTROL  001       1989 11-06-93   1:39p
        2 file(s)      47969 bytes
                      681984 bytes free

C:\>
```

backup volume label

backup file

control file

Figure 6-5
A directory listing of the backup diskette

Now view the contents of the log file.

2. Type **TYPE C:\DOS\LOGFILE1 | MORE** and press **[Enter]**. DOS pages the output and displays the first part of the information stored in the log file. See Figure 6-6. The log file contains the disk number, the full path, and filename of each file. In DOS 6.0, you see the date and time of the backup at the beginning of the log file.

6.0

```
11-06-1993  13:38:30
001   \ACEFORMS\BUSINESS\BUSINESS.PLN
001   \ACEFORMS\BUSINESS\CLIENT.LST
001   \ACEFORMS\BUSINESS\EQUIP.LST
001   \ACEFORMS\BUSINESS\INSURE.LST
001   \ACEFORMS\BUSINESS\STARTUP
001   \ACEFORMS\CASHFLOW\CASH.FMT
001   \ACEFORMS\CASHFLOW\CASH.RPT
001   \ACEFORMS\CASHFLOW\CASH.WK1
001   \ACEFORMS\CASHFLOW\CASHFLOW.FMT
001   \ACEFORMS\CASHFLOW\CASHFLOW.RPT
001   \ACEFORMS\CASHFLOW\CASHFLOW.WK1
001   \ACEFORMS\INVOICES\INVOICE.FMT
001   \ACEFORMS\INVOICES\INVOICE.RPT
001   \ACEFORMS\INVOICES\INVOICE.WK1
001   \ACEFORMS\JOBS\FEESCALE
001   \ACEFORMS\JOBS\JOBCOSTS.FMT
001   \ACEFORMS\JOBS\JOBCOSTS.RPT
001   \ACEFORMS\JOBS\JOBCOSTS.WK1
001   \ACEFORMS\JOBS\SCHEDULE.FMT
001   \ACEFORMS\JOBS\SCHEDULE.WK1
001   \ACEFORMS\PRJCASH\INCOME.YR1
001   \ACEFORMS\PRJCASH\INCOME.YR2
-- More --
```

backup diskette number

date and time of backup

path and filenames of backed-up files

Figure 6-6
Viewing the contents of the backup log file

3. Press **[Spacebar]** or any other key to continue. DOS displays the next screen with names of the backed-up files. If necessary, press **[Spacebar]** or any other key to view the next and last screen, then return to the DOS prompt.

REMOVING A DIRECTORY

Your supervisor informs you that a coworker will now be responsible for the monthly cashflow reports. He asks you to copy those files to the hard disk in your coworker's computer. Because you have already backed up your files, you can remove the directory that contains the monthly cashflow reports.

You will use the DEL command to remove the files from this directory and the RD (Remove Directory) command to remove the directory itself.

To remove the REPORTS directory:

1. Type **CD \ACEFORMS** and press **[Enter]**. DOS changes from the root directory to the ACEFORMS subdirectory.
2. Type **DEL REPORTS** and press **[Enter]**. DOS asks you to verify that you want to delete the entire directory.
3. Type **Y** for Yes and press **[Enter]**.
4. Type **RD REPORTS** and press **[Enter]**. DOS removes the directory.
5. Type **DIR** and press **[Enter]**. The directory listing does not contain the name of the REPORTS subdirectory, so you know DOS has removed the directory.

Soon after you remove this directory, the Finance Manager asks you for a copy of one of the monthly cashflow reports. You decide to quickly restore this directory to your hard disk from your backup set so that you can print a copy of the report for her.

RESTORING FILES FROM A BACKUP SET

The RESTORE command restores all or part of the files from a backup set to your hard disk. The general syntax of this external command is

RESTORE *source-drive: target-drive:*[*path*[*filename*]]

The source drive is the diskette drive that you will use for the backup diskettes. The target drive is the name of a drive, directory, group of files, or a single file that you want to restore to the hard disk. The source and target drives are required parameters. You can also use the Subdirectory switch (/S) to restore all subdirectories and their files below the drive or directory that you specify for the target drive.

If you want to view the contents of a backup set without restoring to the hard disk, you can use the **Display switch** (/D). This switch is useful if you want to verify that you have the right backup set or if you want to verify that the files you need to restore are on a particular backup set.

Before you restore the files to the REPORTS directory, you want to view the contents of the backup diskette using the Display switch.

To view the contents of the backup set:

1. Type **RESTORE A: C:\ACEFORMS\REPORTS*.* /D /S** (or **RESTORE B: C:\ACEFORMS\REPORTS*.* /D /S**) and press **[Enter]**. RESTORE prompts you to insert the first backup diskette into the specified drive.
2. Press **[Enter]**. DOS displays the full paths and filenames of the backed-up files for the \ACEFORMS\REPORTS directory on the backup diskette. See Figure 6-7.

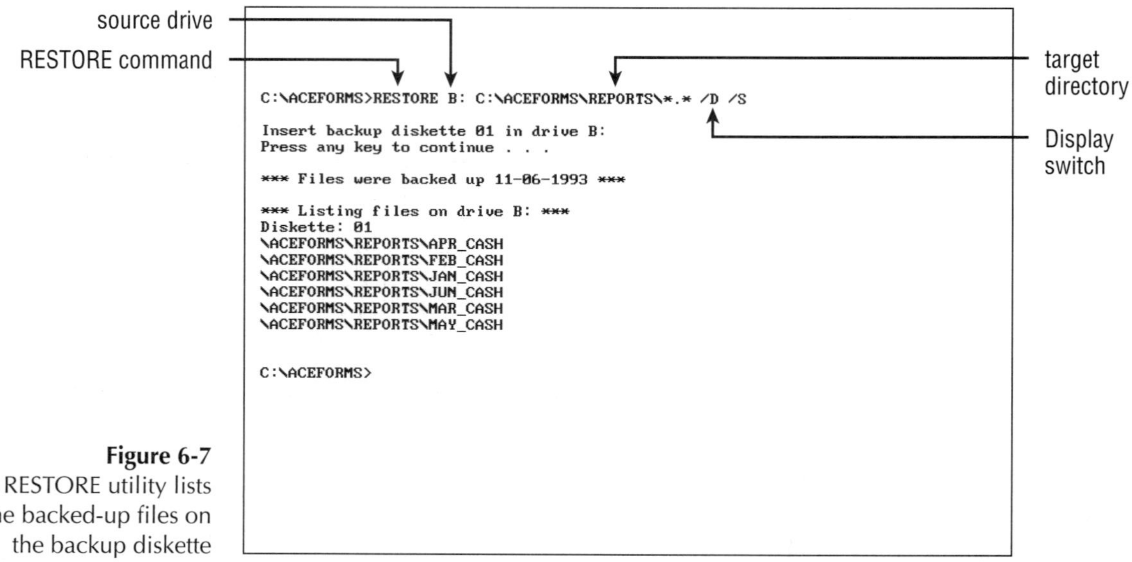

Figure 6-7
The RESTORE utility lists the backed-up files on the backup diskette

Now restore the REPORTS directory.

3. Type **RESTORE A: C:\ACEFORMS\REPORTS*.*** (or **RESTORE B: C:\ACEFORMS\REPORTS*.***) and press **[Enter]**. RESTORE prompts for diskette 01.
4. Press **[Enter]**. RESTORE displays the paths and names of the files it restores to the hard disk. See Figure 6-8. It restores only the REPORTS directory and its files.

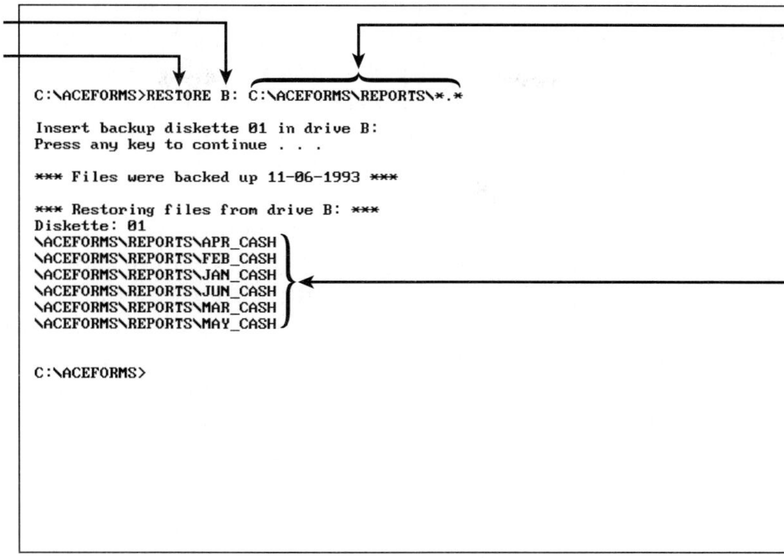

Figure 6-8
Restoring directories and files to the hard disk

Now verify the restore operation.

5. Type **DIR REPORTS** and press **[Enter]**. DOS displays the names of files in the REPORTS directory. DOS recreated the directory before it restored the files.
6. Type **CD ** to return to the root directory.

You have successfully backed up part of the directory tree of a hard disk, removed a directory, and restored a directory from a backup set.

Performing a Backup and Restore from the DOS Shell

You can execute the BACKUP and RESTORE utilities in one of three ways:

- You can use the Run option on the File menu to load and execute the BACKUP and RESTORE utilities. If you use this approach, you temporarily leave the DOS Shell and work with the BACKUP and RESTORE utilities. After the operation is complete, you return to the DOS Shell.
- You can temporarily exit the DOS Shell with the key combination [Shift][F9] (Command Prompt). Then, at the DOS prompt, you execute the BACKUP and RESTORE utilities. When you are ready to return to the DOS Shell, you type "EXIT" and press the Enter key.
- You can use the DOS Utilities program-group icon in the Main window in the DOS Shell. After you select this icon, the DOS Shell displays options for common DOS operations, including "Backup Fixed Disk" and "Restore Fixed Disk." The DOS Shell displays dialog boxes that prompt you for the parameters of each command.

In each case, you temporarily exit the DOS Shell and use the BACKUP and RESTORE utilities just as you would at the DOS prompt.

This is a good opportunity to stop for a few minutes and take a break.

USING MSBACKUP

The **MSBACKUP utility** in DOS 6.0 and 6.2 is a menu-driven utility that provides you with a variety of options for backing up and restoring files. You also can run compatibility tests and verify backups.

If you are using DOS 5.0, you will not be able to complete this section because DOS 5.0 does not contain the MSBACKUP utility. You may, however, want to read this information so that you are familiar with the capabilities of this backup utility.

When you use MSBACKUP, you specify a variety of settings for a backup. These settings are stored in a special type of file called a **setup file**. MSBACKUP provides you with an initial setup file, named DEFAULT.SET. You can specify any additional settings or modify any existing settings you need, then save all the settings in a new setup file with a different name. You can create and save up to 50 setup files with settings for different types of backups. Whenever you need to perform the same type of backup again, you recall the setup file that you need.

During a backup, MSBACKUP also creates a backup catalog. A **backup catalog** is a file that contains information about the files you backed up. MSBACKUP assigns a name to the file using the following guidelines: The first two characters of the filename are the letters of the drives you backed up. If you back up only one drive, the same drive letter is used twice. The third character is the last digit of the current year. The fourth and fifth characters are digits for the current month. The sixth and seventh characters are digits for the current day. The eighth, and last, character is a letter of the alphabet that distinguishes one backup from another performed the same day. One of three file extensions is assigned to identify the type of backup. For example, the backup catalog name CC40709A.FUL indicates that drive C was backed up on July 9, 1994. It was the first backup performed that day (indicated by the letter "A") and it was a full backup (the default). A **full backup** indicates the start of a new backup cycle.

Later, when you examine backup strategies, you will learn about the types of backups, the value of each type of backup, and how you can combine them into an effective backup strategy.

The syntax for the MSBACKUP external command is

MSBACKUP

6.0 ***6.2***

If you are using DOS 6.0 or 6.2, you are ready to configure and perform backup and restore operations with MSBACKUP.

If you are using DOS 6.0, you must format your Tutorial Disk again to remove the backup files produced with the BACKUP utility, following the steps below. If you are using DOS 6.2, you do not need to format your Tutorial Disk.

5.0

If you are using DOS 5.0, you will not be able to complete this section because DOS 5.0 does not contain the MSBACKUP utility. If you are using DOS 5.0, skip to the section entitled "Using XCOPY for Backups."

6.0 6.2

To prepare your Tutorial Disk *in DOS 6.0 and 6.2:*

1. Format your Tutorial Disk using the instructions on pages 56 through 58.
2. Be sure you are at the root directory of your hard disk drive.

Now start MSBACKUP.

3. Type **MSBACKUP** and press **[Enter]**.

   After you load the MSBACKUP utility, MSBACKUP will display one of two screens:

   - MSBACKUP will display an Alert dialog box that informs you that you must configure MSBACKUP for your computer system before you can perform any backups. See Figure 6-9. If the Alert dialog box is displayed, follow the instructions in the following section, "Running a Compatibility Test."

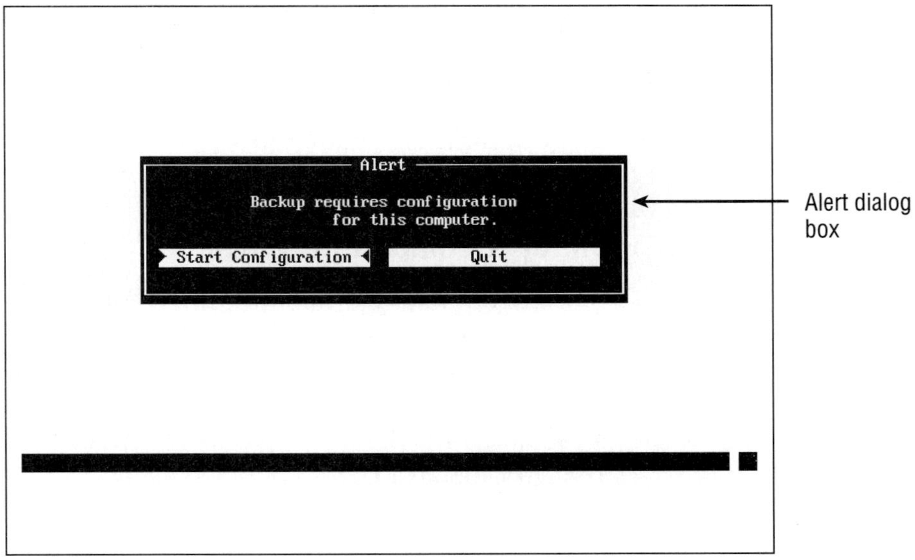

Figure 6-9
The MSBACKUP utility displays a configuration Alert dialog box

6.0 6.2

   - If you are using DOS 6.0, MSBACKUP will read information from your hard disk and then display the Microsoft Backup 6.0 menu. If you are using DOS 6.2, it will immediately display the Microsoft Backup 6.0 menu. See Figure 6-10. MSBACKUP is already configured for use on your computer system. *If your system is already configured, do not run the compatibility test to reconfigure the system.* Skip the next section, entitled "Running a Compatibility Test," and continue this tutorial at the section entitled "Backing Up a Directory."

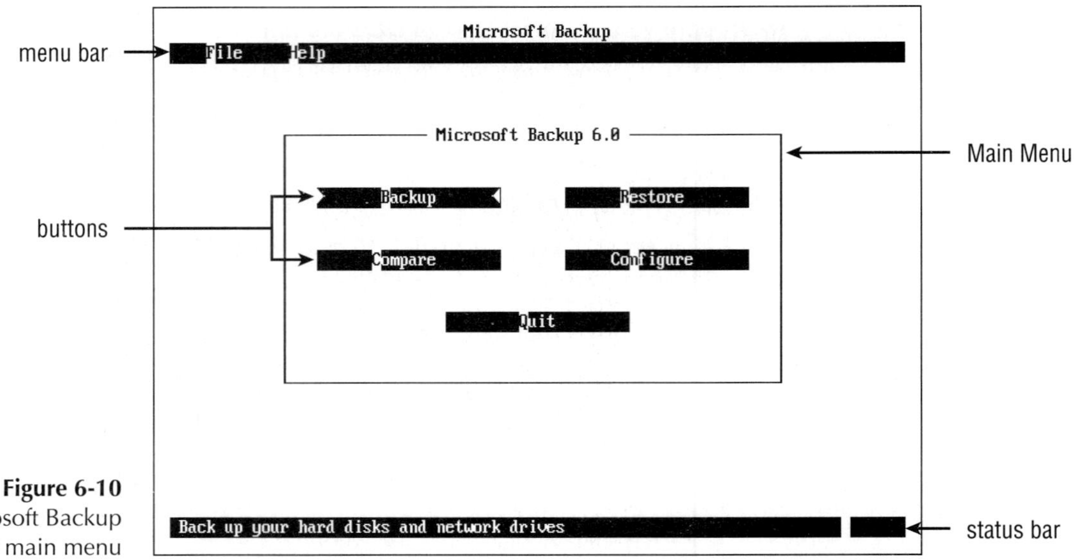

Figure 6-10
The Microsoft Backup 6.0 main menu

Your view of the MSBACKUP may differ from those in Figures 6-9 and 6-10 if you are using graphics mode.

Running a Compatibility Test

During the compatibility test, MSBACKUP automatically configures itself, performs a test backup, and checks for errors in the backup process. *Complete the steps in this section only if the MSBACKUP utility requires configuration.*

To configure MSBACKUP:

1. Press **[Enter]** to select the Start Configuration menu option.

   If you are using the mouse, click **Start Configuration**.

   MSBACKUP displays a Video and Mouse Configuration dialog box and instructs you to accept the configuration as shown. See Figure 6-11. MSBACKUP has already determined the characteristics of the video display and mouse.

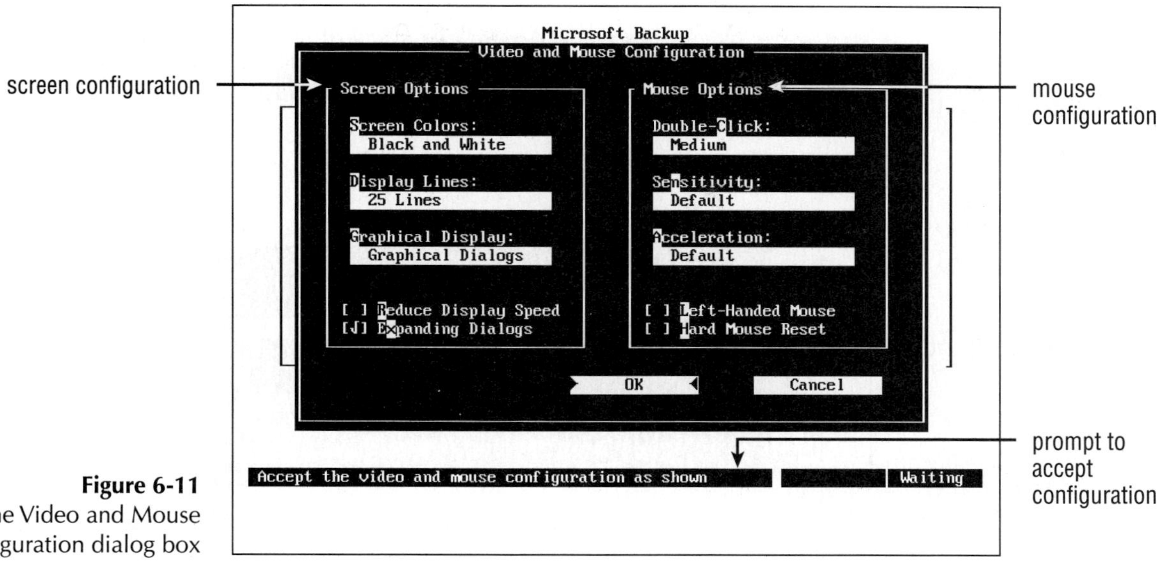

Figure 6-11
The Video and Mouse Configuration dialog box

2. Press **[Enter]** to accept the configuration.

   If you are using the mouse, click **OK** to accept the configuration.

   MSBACKUP displays a Floppy Drive Change Line Test dialog box. See Figure 6-12. MSBACKUP explains that this test will determine whether it can detect when a disk is changed in the diskette drive. It also asks you to remove any diskettes from the diskette drives.

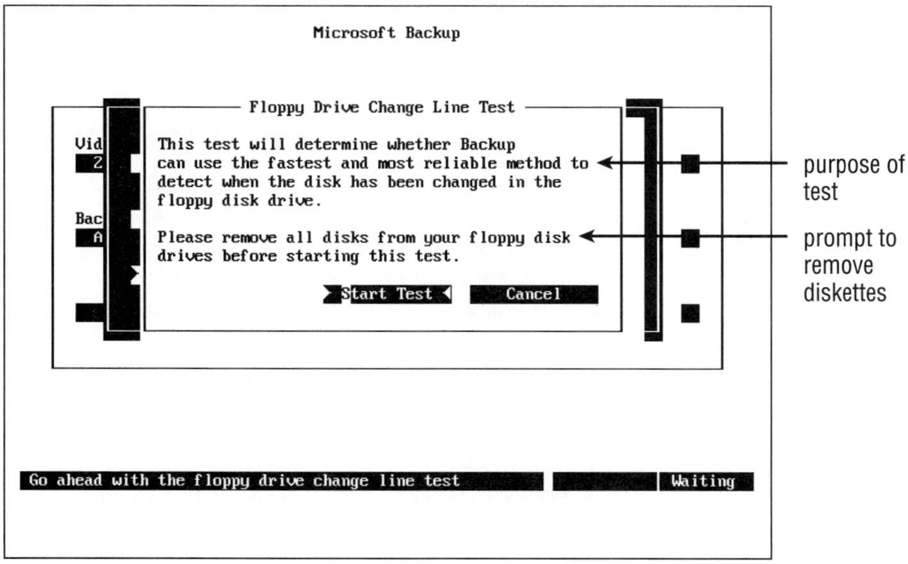

Figure 6-12
The Floppy Drive Change Line Test dialog box

3. If necessary, remove any diskettes from drive A and drive B.
4. Press **[Enter]** to select Start Test.

   If you are using the mouse, click **Start Test**.

MSBACKUP tests your system and displays a Backup Devices dialog box, which shows the size, storage capacities, and densities of the diskette drives in your computer system. MSBACKUP again prompts you to accept the configuration as shown. See Figure 6-13.

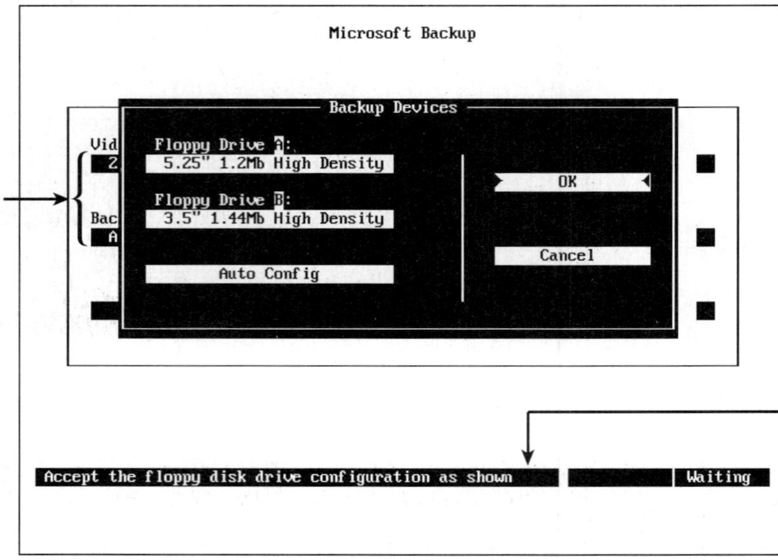

Figure 6-13
The Backup Devices dialog box

5. Press **[Enter]** to accept the configuration.

   If you are using the mouse, click **OK** to accept the configuration.

   MSBACKUP displays a Configure dialog box. It then tests the processor speed and performs a hard disk read test. Next, it displays a Floppy Disk Compatibility Test dialog box that explains that it intends to do a small backup and compare. See Figure 6-14. It informs you that it will automatically perform this test, for which you will need two diskettes.

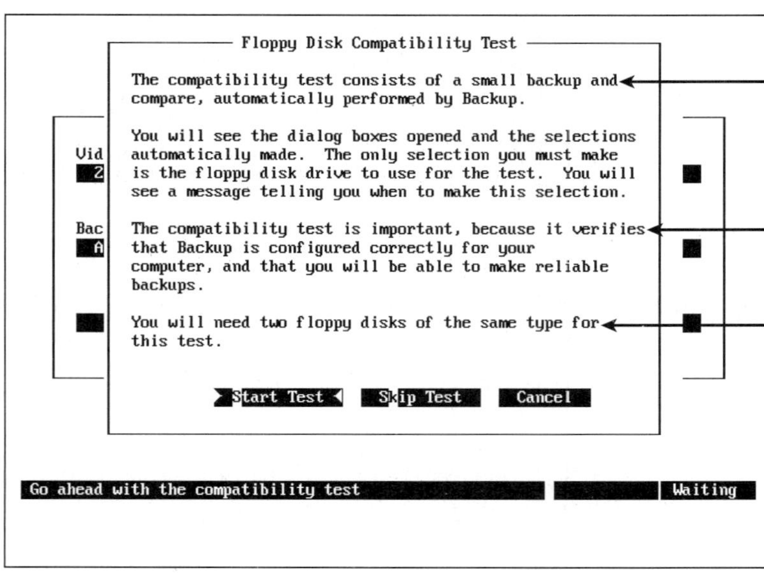

Figure 6-14
The Floppy Disk Compatibility Test dialog box

6. Press **[Enter]** to select Start Test.

   If you are using the mouse, click **Start Test**.

   MSBACKUP reads information and examines all files on the hard disk, and automatically selects files from the DOS subdirectory to back up. It displays an Alert dialog box, which tells you that it will pause to let you select a drive for the backup test.

7. Press **[Enter]** to select Continue.

   If you are using the mouse, click **Continue**.

   MSBACKUP displays a Backup To dialog box so that you can select a drive. See Figure 6-15. If your computer system has one or more high-density drives, you will see options for using those drives to perform a backup on either high-density or double-density diskettes. Your drive options might be different.

drive options

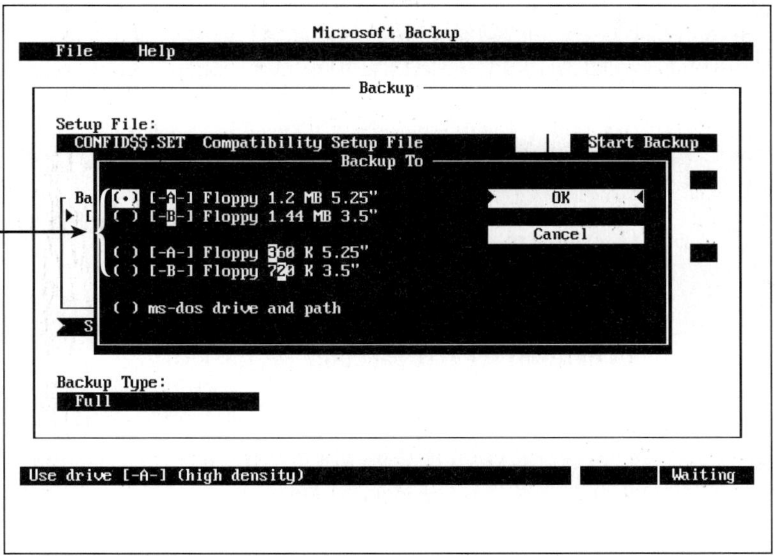

Figure 6-15
The Backup To dialog box for selecting a drive

8. Highlight the option for the drive you intend to use for a backup. You can use the [↓] (Down Arrow) and [↑] (Up Arrow) keys to select the drive. Then press **[Spacebar]** to select the backup drive. *Be sure you select the right capacity for the backup.*

   If you are using the mouse, click on the **option for the drive you intend to use** as the backup drive. *Be sure you select the correct capacity for the backup.*

9. Press **[Enter]** to save the drive setting.

   If you are using the mouse, click **OK** to save the drive setting.

   MSBACKUP displays an Alert dialog box and prompts you to insert diskette #1 in the drive you selected for the backup. See Figure 6-16.

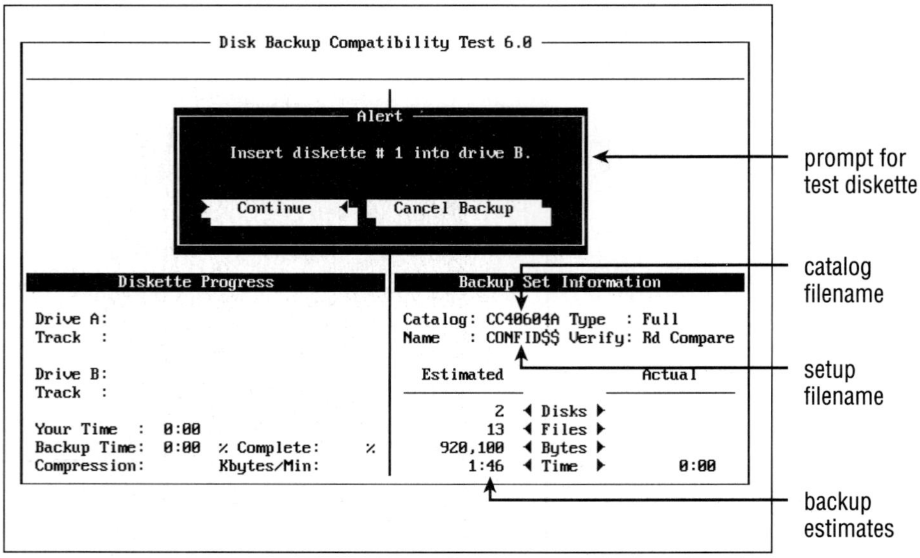

Figure 6-16
An Alert box prompts for a backup test diskette

Performing the Test Backup

Now you will perform a test backup with MSBACKUP as part of the Compatibility Test.

To perform the test backup:

1. Insert your Tutorial Disk and press **[Enter]**.

   If you are using the mouse, insert your Tutorial Disk and click **Continue**.

   If you insert a diskette with directories and files, MSBACKUP will display an Alert box and prompt you as to whether you want to overwrite the disk. If this occurs, press **[Enter]** or if you are using the mouse, click **Overwrite**. MSBACKUP displays a Disk Backup Compatibility Test 6.0 dialog box and records selected DOS files on the diskette. The Diskette Progress dialog box shows the drive, track number, and percentage of the backup that is complete. After this operation is done, MSBACKUP displays the message "Insert Diskette # 2." Wait until MSBACKUP displays an Alert dialog box that prompts you to insert the next diskette in the same drive.

2. Remove your Tutorial Disk, and insert your Exercise Disk. Then press **[Enter]**.

   If you are using the mouse, click **Continue**.

   MSBACKUP backs up files to the second diskette. After the backup is complete, MSBACKUP displays a Backup Complete dialog box, which includes information on how many files were backed up, how many backup diskettes were used, the total number of bytes required for the backup, the total time required for the backup, and the number of kilobytes backed up per minute. See Figure 6-17.

   6.2

   DOS 6.2 backs up more files then DOS 6.0. If you are using DOS 6.2, your summary information might be different, and you might not see part of the directory tree for the hard disk.

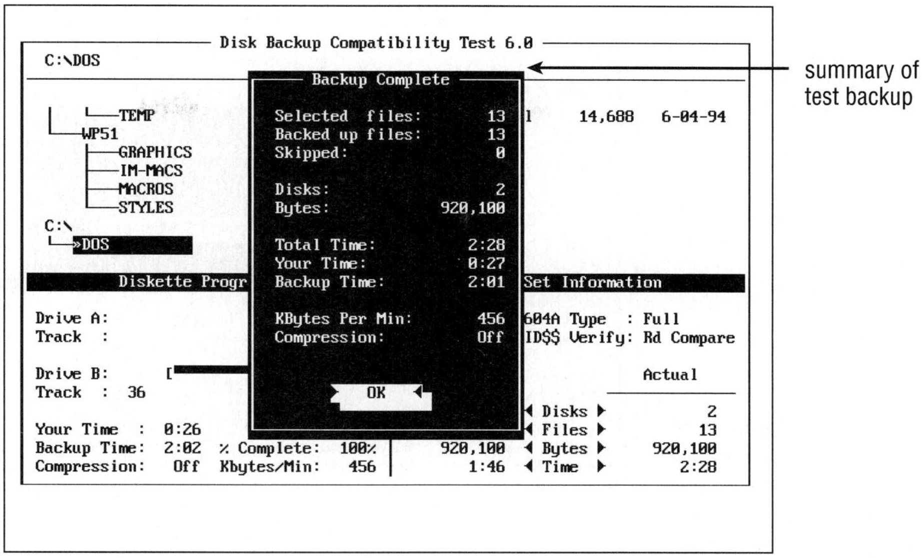

Figure 6-17
The Backup Complete dialog box

Verifying the Backup Process

Now you will check to be sure the backup process worked.

To verify the backup process:

1. Press **[Enter]** to continue.

   If you are using the mouse, click **OK** to continue.

   MSBACKUP then proceeds to the second part of the compatibility test, where it compares the backed up files on the diskette with the original files on the hard disk to check for errors in the backup process. After a series of operations, MSBACKUP prompts you to insert diskette #1 into the backup drive. See Figure 6-18. In this figure, note that the catalog file's name is CC40604A.FUL. The name of your catalog file will be different.

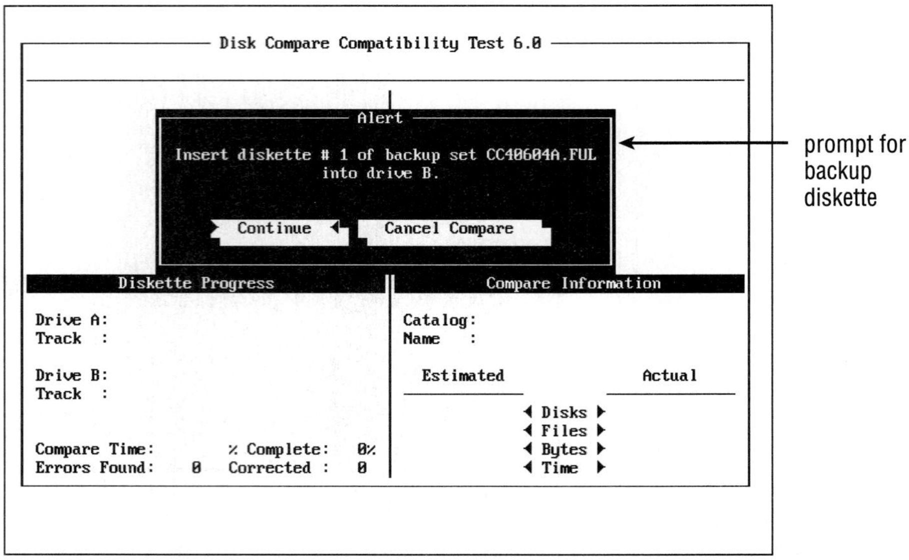

Figure 6-18
An Alert box prompts for the first diskette in a backup set (your catalog filename will be different)

2. Remove your Exercise Disk, and insert your Tutorial Disk in the diskette drive used for the backup.
3. Press **[Enter]** to continue.

   If you are using the mouse, click **Continue**.

   MSBACKUP checks the backup files for errors, then prompts for the next diskette.
4. Remove your Tutorial Disk, and insert your Exercise Disk in the same diskette drive.
5. Press **[Enter]** to continue.

   If you are using the mouse, click **Continue**.

   6.2

   MSBACKUP checks the backup files on the second diskette for errors. When the operation is complete, MSBACKUP displays a Compare Complete dialog box. See Figure 6-19. DOS 6.2 compares more files than DOS 6.0. This summary reports that MSBACKUP found no errors. If MSBACKUP reported errors, backups you make with this utility might be unreliable. You should perform another backup and compare the results. If MSBACKUP still reports problems, you might need to reconfigure MSBACKUP or service your diskette drive.

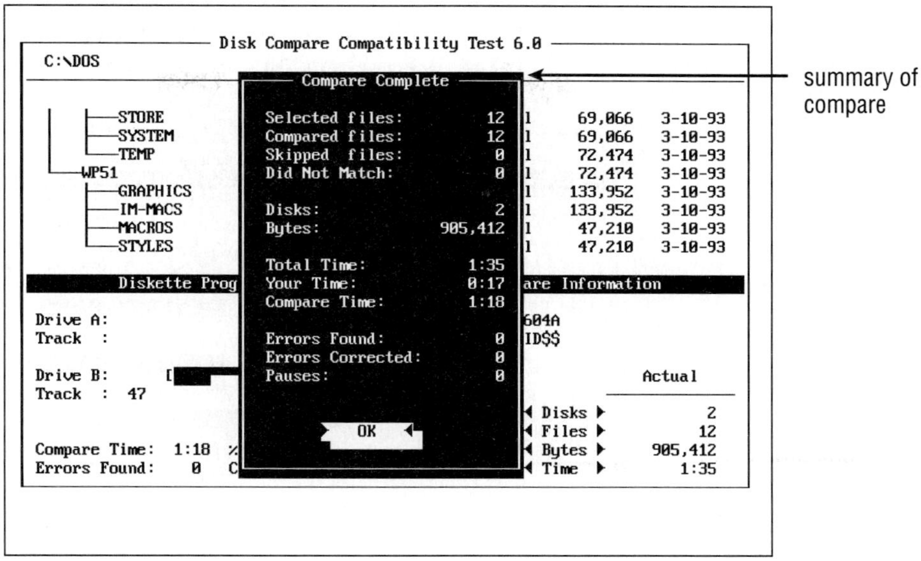

Figure 6-19
The Compare Complete dialog box

6. Press **[Enter]** to continue.

   If you are using the mouse, click **OK** to continue.

   MSBACKUP should display a Compatibility Test dialog box that tells you the compatibility test was successful and that you can perform backups reliably on your computer system. If MSBACKUP reports problems with the Compatibility Test, check with your instructor or technical support person.

7. Press **[Enter]** to continue.

   If you are using the mouse, click **OK** to continue.

   MSBACKUP displays the Configure Menu so that you can save configuration changes. See Figure 6-20.

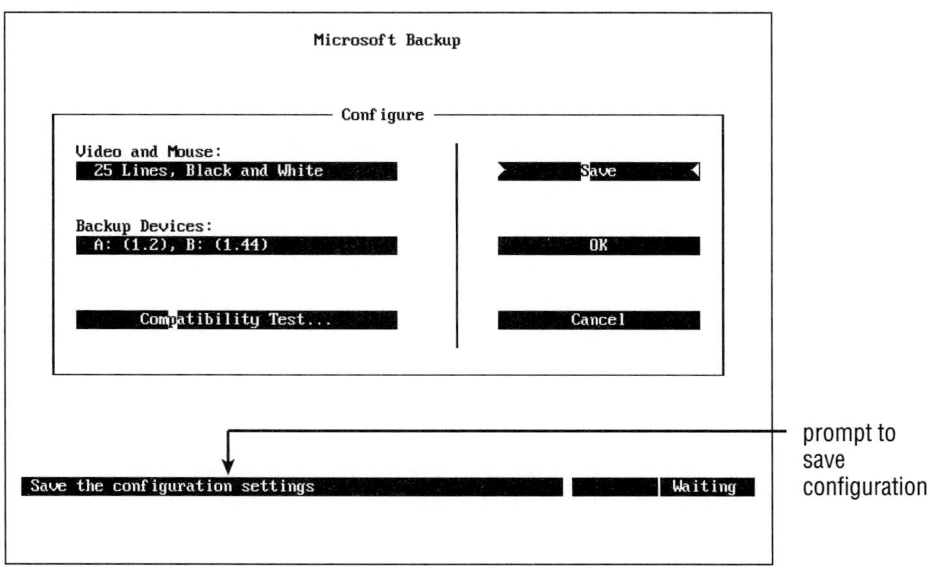

Figure 6-20
A Configure dialog box for saving configuration settings

8. Press **[Enter]** to save the configuration settings.

   If you are using the mouse, click **Save**.

   MSBACKUP displays the Microsoft Backup 6.0 menu. See Figure 6-21.

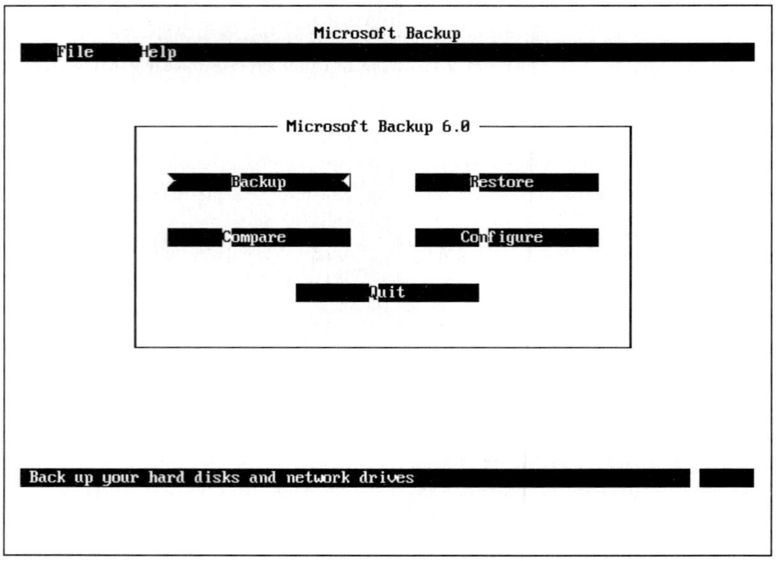

Figure 6-21
The Microsoft Backup 6.0 main menu

You must now temporarily exit MSBACKUP so that you can format the diskettes for the next part of the tutorial.

To exit MSBACKUP 6.0 or 6.2:

1. Type **Q** to select Quit.

   If you are using the mouse, click **Quit**.

   You exit MSBACKUP and return to the DOS prompt.

Now format the diskettes.

2. Format your Tutorial Disk and Exercise Disk using the instructions on pages 56 through 58.

Backing Up a Directory

You want to back up the AceForms directory on your hard disk. MSBACKUP will not only back up the files in each of the subdirectories, but it will also record the directory structure so that you can restore the entire directory later to the same hard disk or another hard disk.

To load MSBACKUP and select the Backup option:

1. Type **MSBACKUP** and press **[Enter]**. If you are using DOS 6.0, MSBACKUP will read the information from your hard disk, including the name and path of every file, then will display the MSBACKUP 6.0 menu. If you are using DOS 6.2, it will immediately display the Microsoft Backup 6.0 menu.
2. Type **B** (or press **[Enter]**) to select Backup.

   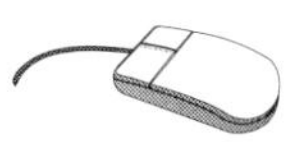

   If you are using the mouse, click **Backup**.

   MSBACKUP displays the Backup screen. See Figure 6-22. The Backup From box shows drive C as the default drive from which to back up files. The Backup To box might show drive A (or drive B) as the default drive for the backup. The Backup Type box shows the default type as Full. The Setup File box shows the name of the default setup file, DEFAULT.SET. MSBACKUP uses the last settings that were in effect.

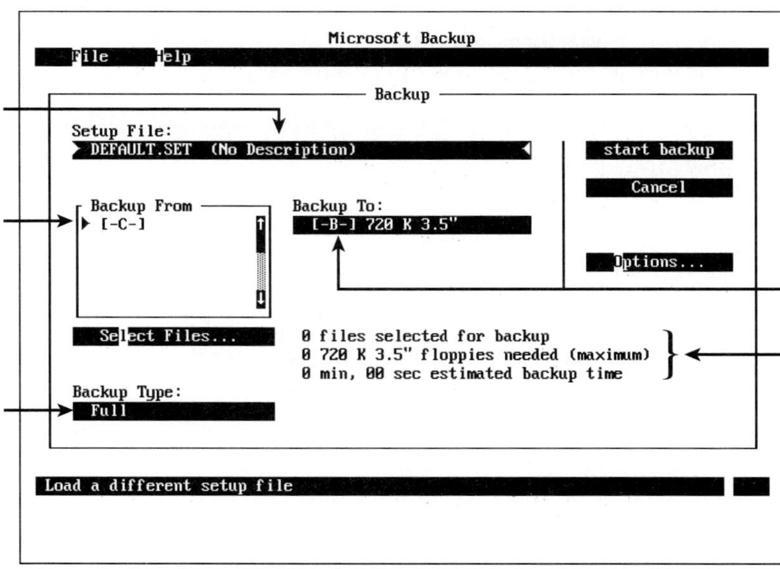

Figure 6-22
The Backup screen

Creating a Setup File

Now you want to save the default setup file under a new name so that it will store the settings you use to back up the AceForms directory, and then you'll select the files to back up.

To assign a new name to the default setup file:

1. Press and hold **[Alt]** while you press **F** to access the File menu.

If you are using the mouse, click **File**.

MSBACKUP displays its File menu. See Figure 6-23.

currently selected menu

File menu

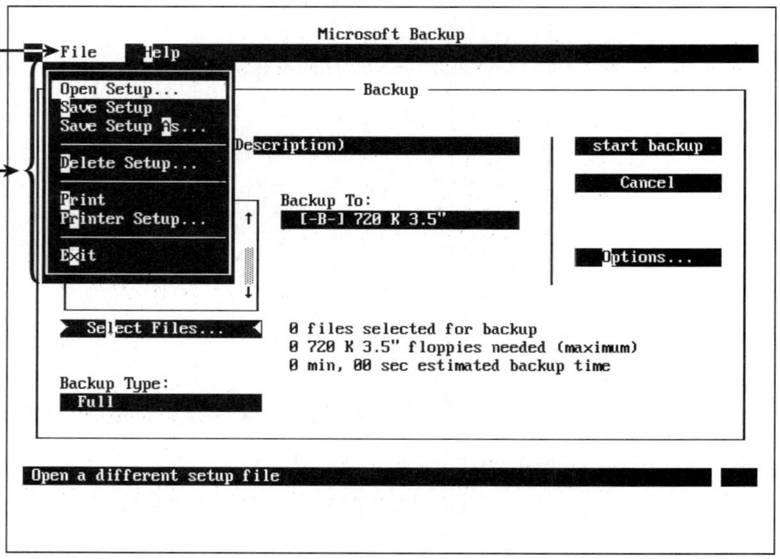

Figure 6-23
The Microsoft Backup File menu

2. Press [↓] (Down Arrow) until you highlight Save Setup As, then press **[Enter]**.

If you are using the mouse, click **Save Setup As**.

MSBACKUP displays a Save Setup File dialog box. See Figure 6-24.

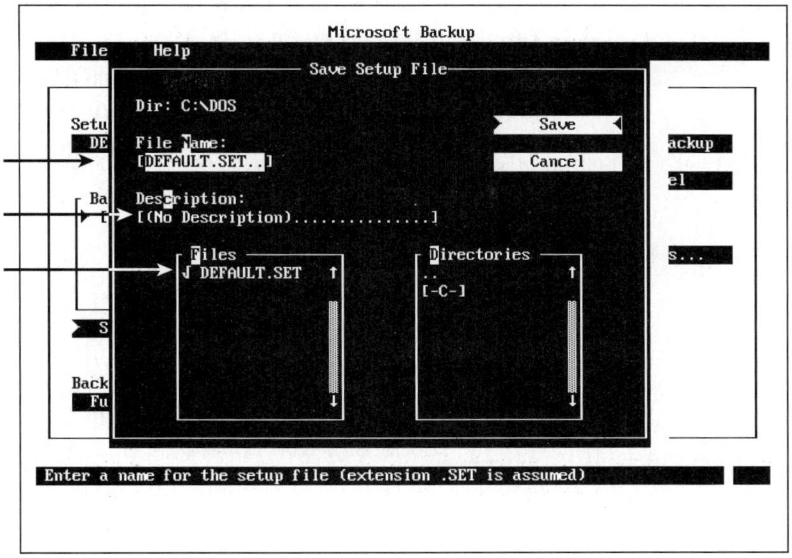

Figure 6-24
The Save Setup File dialog box

3. Type **ACEFORMS** in the File Name text box, then press **[Tab]** to select the Description text box.

   If you are using the mouse, type **ACEFORMS** and click the **Description** text box.

4. Type **(Client Files)** *including the parentheses* and press **[Enter]**.

   If you are using the mouse, type **(Client Files)** *including the parentheses* and click **OK**. MSBACKUP returns to the Backup screen. The new name of the setup file is ACEFORMS.SET. See Figure 6-25.

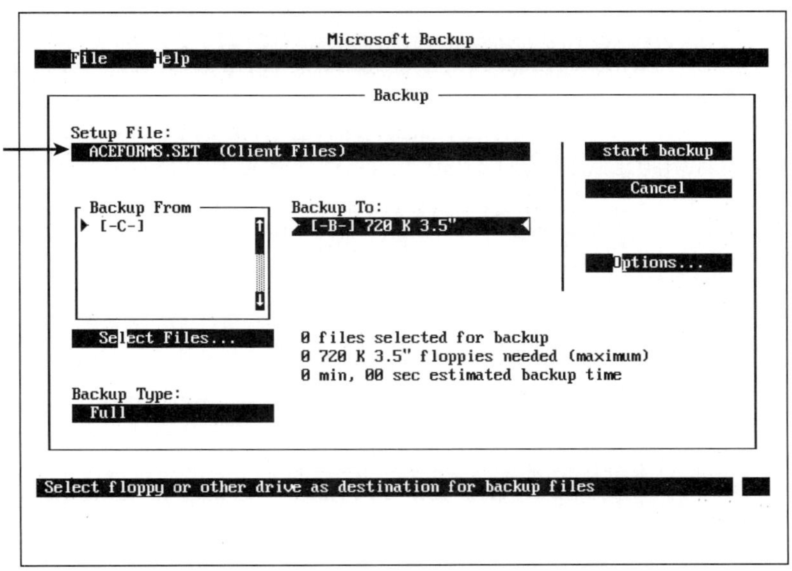

Figure 6-25
The Backup screen with the new setup filename

Changing the Settings in a Setup File

Next you will modify the default settings from the DEFAULT.SET setup file and save them under the new setup filename, ACEFORMS.SET.

If the drive setting in the Backup To list box is not the one you want to use, you can change the setting for the backup drive.

To specify the drive you want to use:

1. Type **A** for Backup To. Use [↓] (Down Arrow) to highlight the backup drive name with the proper storage capacity. Press **[Spacebar]** to select this drive. Press **[Enter]** to save this setting.

   If you are using the mouse, click **Backup To**, click the **backup drive name** with the proper storage capacity, and click **OK**.

   MSBACKUP returns to the Backup screen.

Now you're ready to select the directories and files for the backup.

To select the directories and files for the backup:

1. Type **L** for Select Files.

   If you are using the mouse, click **Select Files**.

   MSBACKUP reads disk information and displays the Select Backup Files screen. See Figure 6-26. On this screen, you see the current drive (in this case, C:), the specification for selecting files (in this case, C:*.*), a window with a partial view of the directory tree for the current drive, and a window with filenames and other file information.

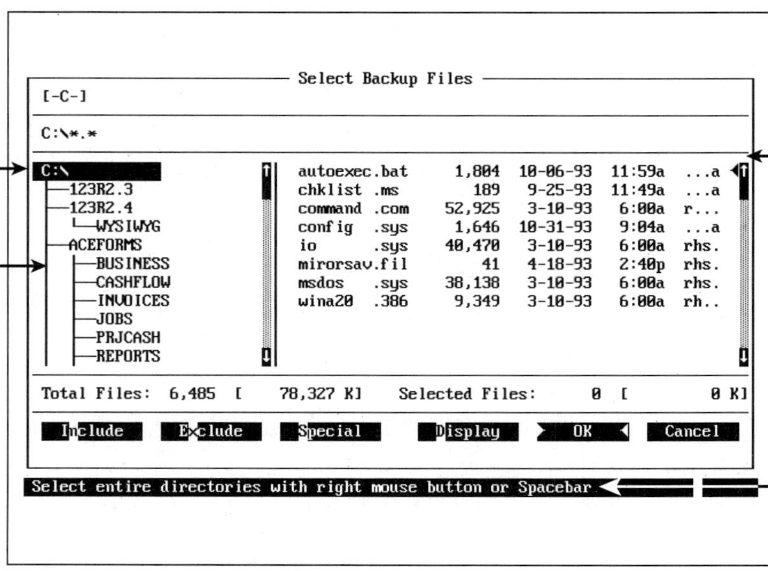

Figure 6-26
The Select Backup Files screen

2. Press [↓] (Down Arrow) until you highlight the ACEFORMS directory in the directory tree window. Press [↓] (Down Arrow) to highlight the BUSINESS subdirectory. Then press **[Spacebar]** to select this directory.

   If you are using the mouse, click **ACEFORMS** in the directory tree window with the right mouse button, then double-click the **BUSINESS** subdirectory.

   MSBACKUP selects this subdirectory for the backup; an arrow in the directory tree points to this subdirectory.

3. Select each of the remaining subdirectories under the ACEFORMS directory: CASHFLOW, INVOICES, JOBS, PRJCASH, REPORTS, and RESUMES.

4. Press [↑] (Up Arrow) to highlight the ACEFORMS directory name. Figure 6-27 shows the selected subdirectories.

directories selected for backup

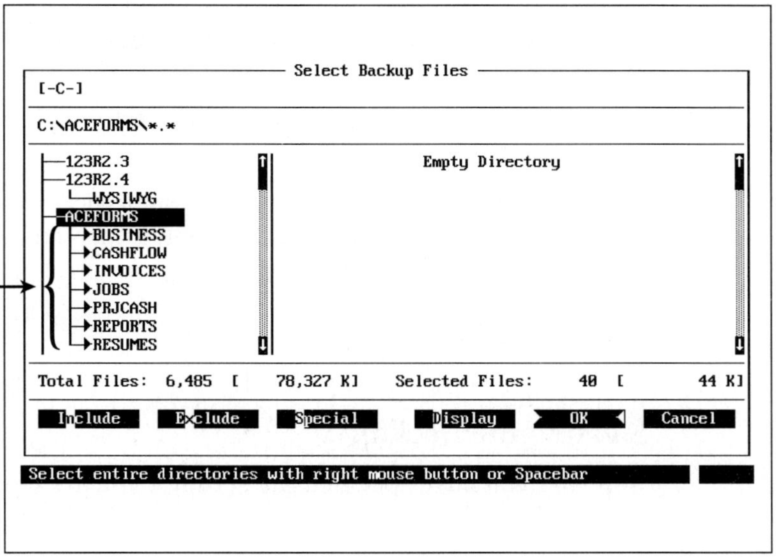

Figure 6-27
MSBACKUP points to the subdirectories selected for backup

5. Press **[Enter]** to save these settings.

   If you are using the mouse, click **OK** to save these settings.

   MSBACKUP displays the Backup screen and shows you that 41 files are selected for the backup, including the catalog file. See Figure 6-28. In this case, MSBACKUP indicates that one 720K 3.5-inch diskette is needed for the backup and indicates an estimated backup time of 15 seconds. (MSBACKUP's recommendation on your computer might be different.)

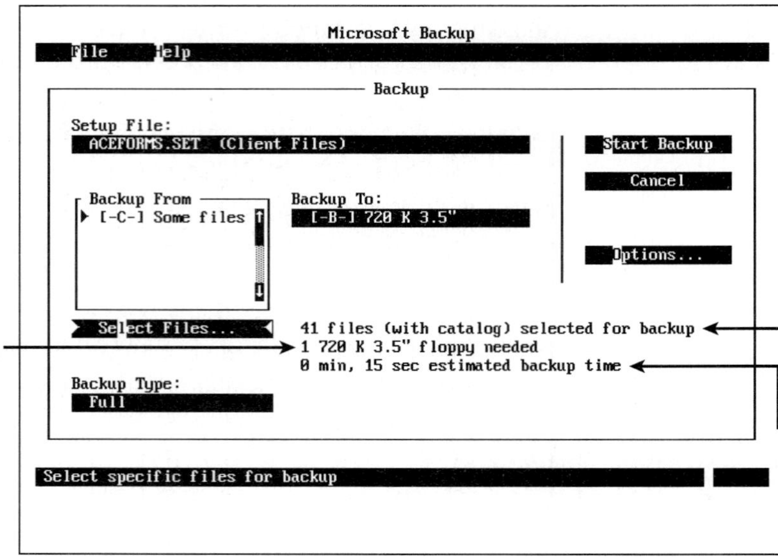

Figure 6-28
The Backup screen's recommendations for the backup (your screen might be different)

6. Press and hold **[Alt]** while you press **F** to access the File menu. Press [↓] (Down Arrow) to select Save Setup, then press **[Enter]**.

   If you are using the mouse, click **File,** then click **Save Setup**.

   MSBACKUP saves your new settings under the setup file named ACEFORMS.SET.

Starting the Backup

Now that you have specified the settings, you are ready to start the backup.

To back up the AceForms directory:

1. Type **S** to select Start Backup.

   If you are using the mouse, click **Start Backup**.

   MSBACKUP creates a catalog for the backup, loads the Backup program, and displays an Alert dialog box, which prompts you to insert the first diskette. See Figure 6-29.

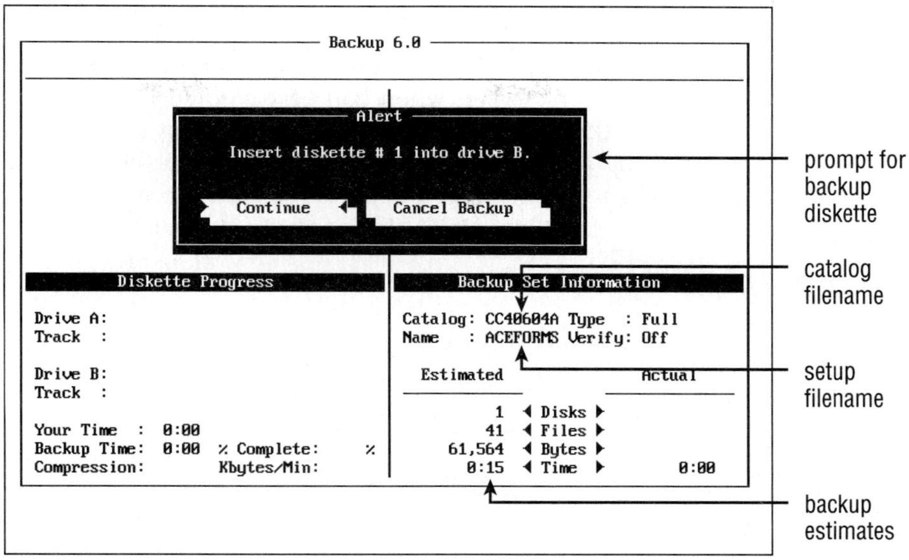

Figure 6-29
An Alert box prompts for the first backup diskette

2. Insert your Tutorial Disk in the diskette drive and press **[Enter]**.

   If you are using the mouse, insert your Tutorial Disk in the diskette drive and click **Continue**.

   MSBACKUP displays a Backup Complete dialog box. See Figure 6-30. In this example, MSBACKUP backed up 41 files occupying 61,564 bytes of storage space at a compression ratio of 1.9 to 1. It reduced the storage space required for these files by almost one-half. MSBACKUP might report different results on your computer.

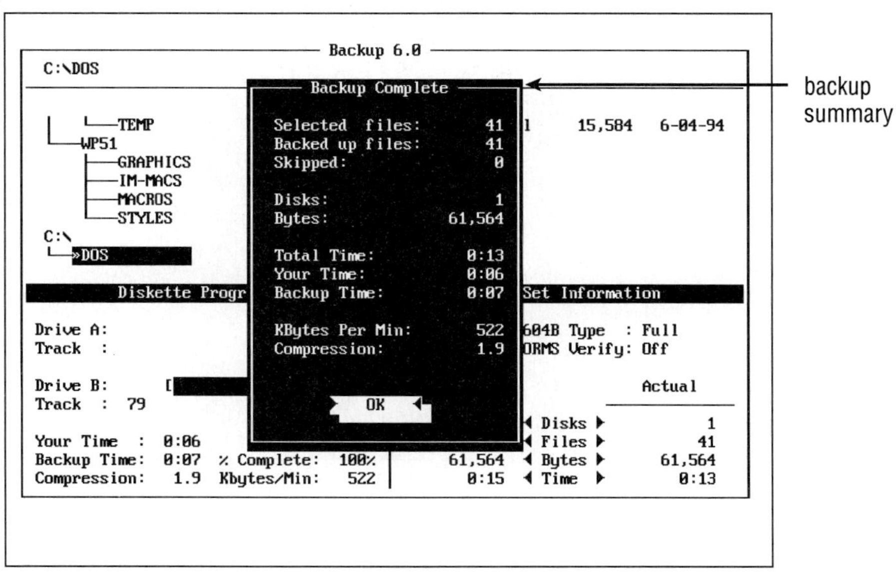

Figure 6-30
The Backup Complete dialog box

3. Press **[Enter]** to continue.

   If you are using the mouse, click **OK** to continue.

   The Microsoft Backup 6.0 menu appears.

Verifying the Backup

If you want to verify the backup operation, you could perform a Compare operation. However, when you first configure MSBACKUP, it verifies the reliability of the backup process by performing a compare on a test backup. If you change or reconfigure hardware in your computer system, you should reconfigure MSBACKUP to guarantee reliable backups.

Let's exit MSBACKUP and check the contents of the backup diskette.

To exit MSBACKUP:

1. Type **Q** for Quit.

   If you are using the mouse, click **Quit**.

   DOS displays the DOS prompt.

Now check the backup disk.

2. Type **DIR A:** (or **DIR B:**) and press **[Enter]**. DOS displays the contents of the backup diskette. See Figure 6-31. In this example, the volume name is ACEFORMSFUL, and the backup file is named CC40604A.001. This file contains all of the files backed up to this disk, and all the files are stored together in one file to maximize the use of disk space. This backup filename indicates that drive C was backed up on June 4, 1994, was the first backup (A) performed that day, and that the file was stored on the first diskette (001) in the backup set.

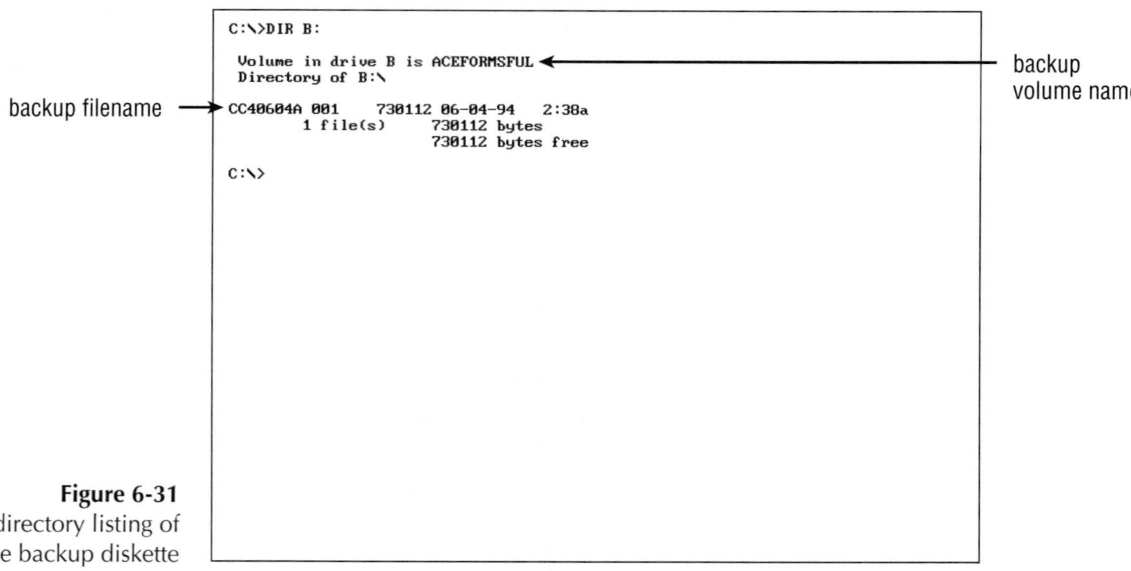


```
C:\>DIR B:

 Volume in drive B is ACEFORMSFUL
 Directory of B:\

CC40604A 001    730112 06-04-94   2:38a
        1 file(s)      730112 bytes
                       730112 bytes free

C:\>
```

Figure 6-31
A directory listing of the backup diskette

Removing Part of the Directory Tree

Your supervisor informs you that your new computer system has arrived. He asks you to remove your client and business files from your old computer because an employee in another department will use it. Fortunately, you have just backed up your hard disk's files onto diskettes, so you can remove your data directory.

In DOS 6.0 and 6.2, you can use the DELTREE command to delete part of the directory tree. The syntax is

DELTREE [*drive:*]*path*

You specify the path and directory name of the subdirectory you want to delete. The DELTREE command starts at the subdirectory you specify and removes all files and all subdirectories positioned below that directory. You specify the drive if the directory is on another disk drive. Be careful when you use this command, because you can quickly delete a large amount of information from a disk.

5.0 DOS 5.0 does not contain the DELTREE command. If you want to delete a subdirectory and all its subordinate directories in DOS 5.0, you must first delete all the files in the subdirectory and its subordinate directories with the DEL or ERASE command. Next, you use the RD or RMDIR (Remove Directory) command to remove each subdirectory, starting from the innermost directory and working your way to the parent directory.

6.0 6.2 **To remove the AceForms directory *using DOS 6.0 and 6.2*:**

1. Type **DELTREE ACEFORMS** and press **[Enter]**. DOS asks if you are sure you want to remove this directory and all its subdirectories.
2. Type **Y** for Yes, then press **[Enter]**. DELTREE informs you that it is "Deleting aceforms..."

Now verify this operation.

3. Type **DIR ACEFORMS** and press **[Enter]**. DOS tells you that it found no such file. See Figure 6-32. You have successfully deleted the directory, its subdirectories, and all the files in each of the subdirectories.

```
C:\>DELTREE ACEFORMS
Delete directory "aceforms" and all its subdirectories? [yn] y
Deleting aceforms...

C:\>DIR ACEFORMS

 Volume in drive C is HI PERFORM
 Volume Serial Number is 1A81-8E17
 Directory of C:\

File not found

C:\>
```

verification of directory deletion

Figure 6-32
Verifying removal of part of a directory tree

Restoring Directories and Files

After unpacking and setting up your new computer system, you install the software applications you need. You are now ready to restore the client and business files from your backup set so that you can return to work.

To restore files from a backup set:

6.0

6.2

1. Type **MSBACKUP** and press **[Enter]**. If you are using DOS 6.0, MSBACKUP will read information from your hard disk, including the full path and name of all files, then will display the Microsoft Backup 6.0 menu. If you are using DOS 6.2, it will immediately display the Microsoft Backup 6.0 menu.
2. Type **R** to select Restore.

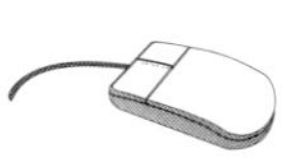

   If you are using a mouse, click **Restore**.

   MSBACKUP displays a Restore screen with the current settings for the last backup. See Figure 6-33. If you had actually switched to a new computer system, you would have had to copy the setup files from your old computer or create new setup files on your new computer system. By default, MSBACKUP saves setup files in your DOS subdirectory.

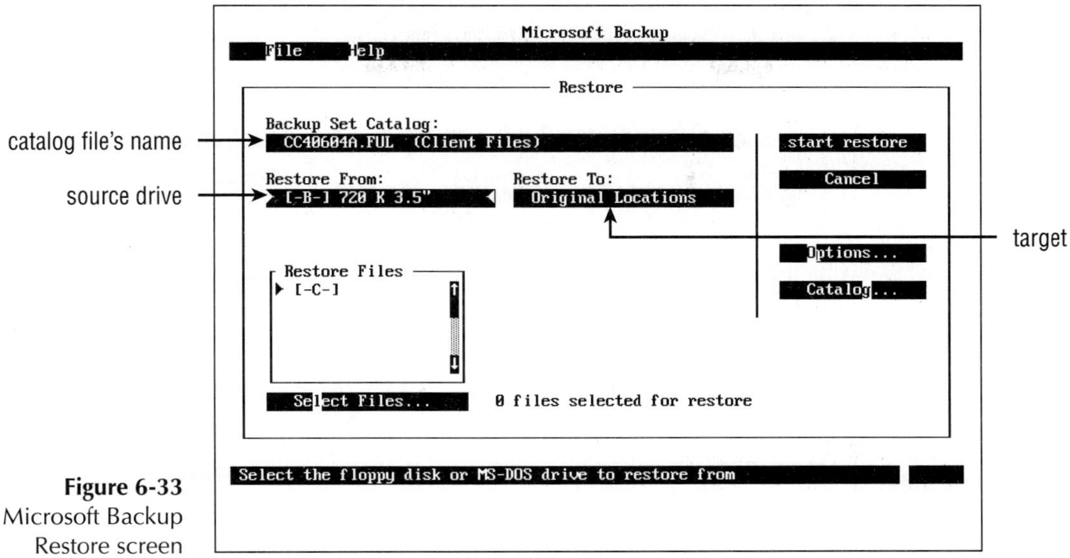

Figure 6-33
The Microsoft Backup Restore screen

3. If MSBACKUP does not display the name of your setup file, type **K** to select Backup Set Catalog. Select the catalog file's name in the Catalog Files box, then press **[Enter]** to select the Load button.

   If you are using the mouse, click the **list box** for Backup Set Catalog. Click the **catalog file's name** in the Catalog Files list box, then click **Load**.

4. If MSBACKUP does not display the name of your backup drive or if you need to specify a different storage capacity for that drive, type **E** to select Restore From. Highlight the backup drive option you want to use and press **[Spacebar]** to select that option. Press **[Enter]** to return to the Restore screen.

   If you are using the mouse, click **Restore From**, click the **backup drive option** you want to use, and click **OK** to return to the Restore screen.

5. Type **I** to select Restore Files. Highlight the drive name of the hard disk you want to use, then press **[Spacebar]**.

   If you are using the mouse, click the name of the hard drive.

   MSBACKUP displays "All Files" next to [-C-] (or your hard drive name) and automatically selects 40 files. See Figure 6-34.

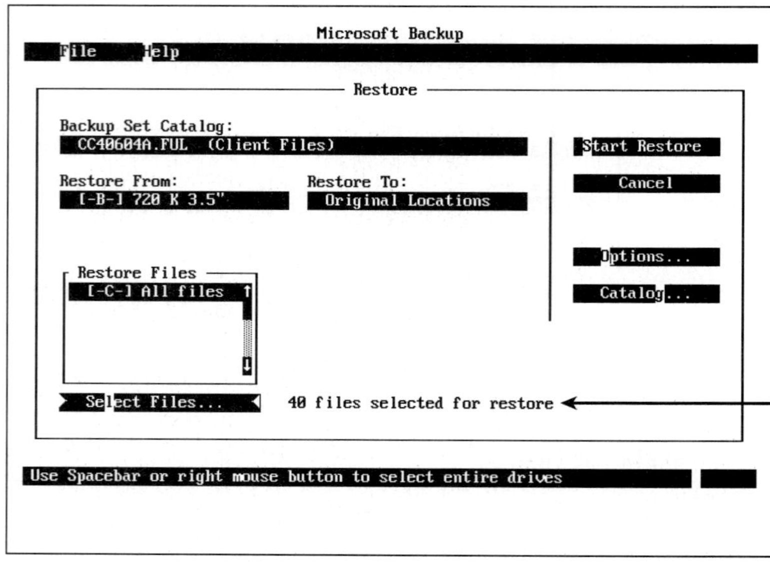

Figure 6-34
Microsoft Backup selects 40 files to restore

To start the restore:

1. Press and hold **[Alt]** while you press **S** to select Start Restore. If MSBACKUP does not respond, press and hold **[Alt]** while you press **S**.

   If you are using the mouse, click **Start Restore**.

   MSBACKUP displays an Alert dialog box prompting for diskette #1 for a specific backup set. See Figure 6-35.

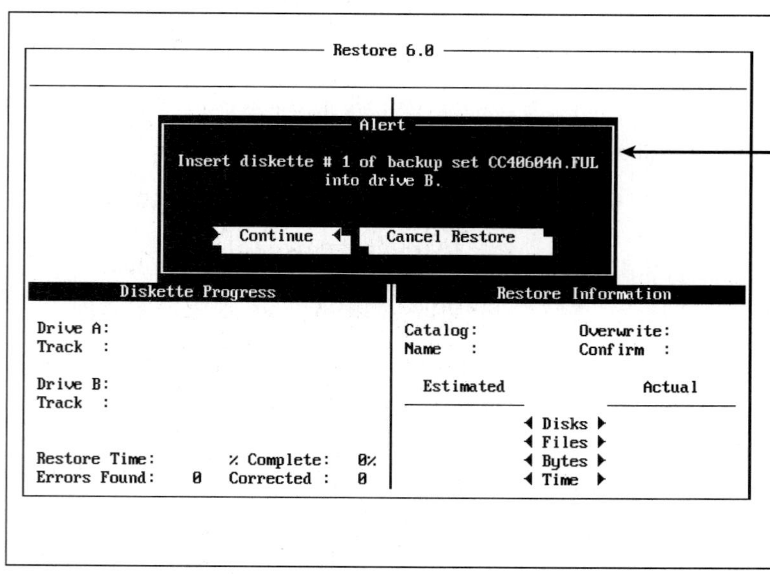

Figure 6-35
An Alert box prompts for the first diskette in a backup set

2. Press **[Enter]** to continue.

   If you are using the mouse, click **Continue**.

   MSBACKUP restores files directory by directory and displays a Restore Complete dialog box with information on the restore process. See Figure 6-36.

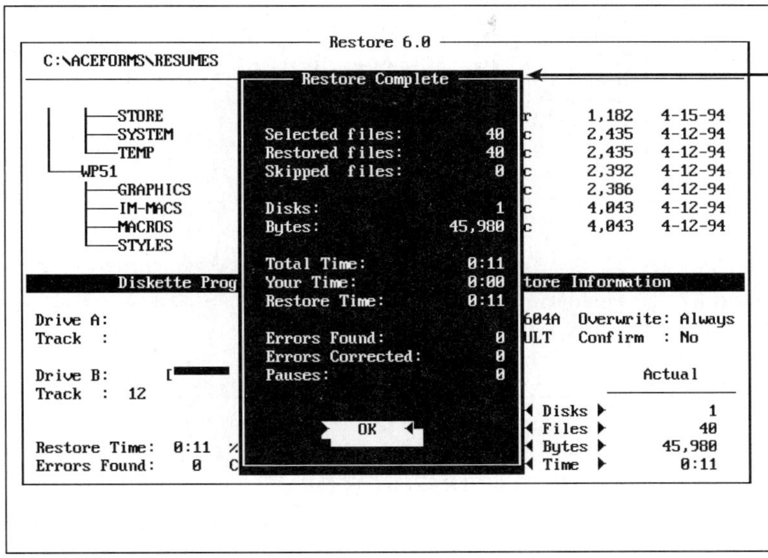

Figure 6-36
The Restore Complete dialog box

3. Press **[Enter]**.

   If you are using the mouse, click **OK**.

   If you are using DOS 6.0, MSBACKUP will read information from your hard disk and then display the Microsoft Backup 6.0 menu. If you are using DOS 6.2, it will immediately display the Microsoft Backup 6.0 menu.

Verifying the Restore

Now you want to exit MSBACKUP and verify the restore operation.

To exit MSBACKUP:

1. Type **Q** for Quit.

   If you are using the mouse, click **Quit**.

   You exit MSBACKUP and return to the DOS prompt.

Now verify the restore.

2. Type **DIR ACEFORMS** and press **[Enter]**. DOS displays the subdirectories in the AceForms directory. See Figure 6-37. MSBACKUP recreated the entire directory tree.

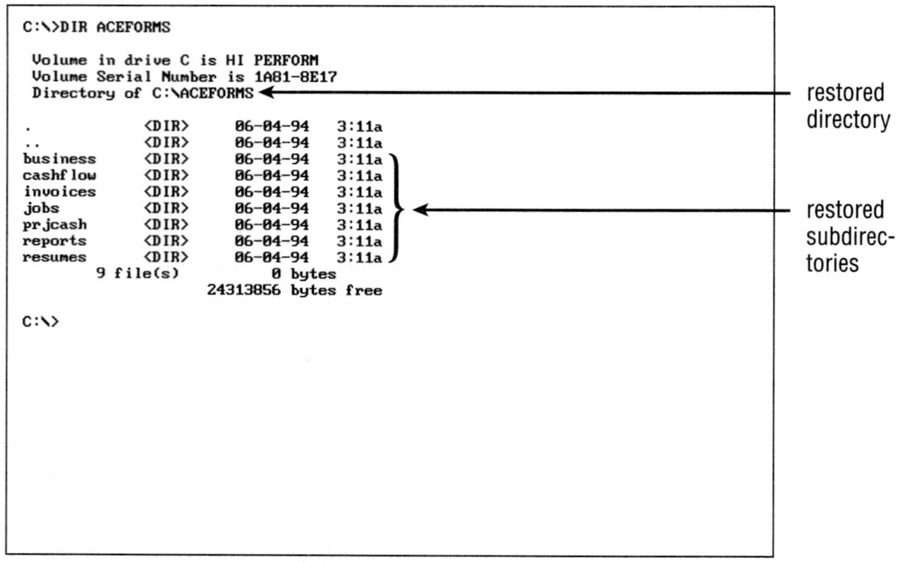

Figure 6-37
A directory listing of subdirectories restored by MSBACKUP

3. Type **TREE ACEFORMS /F ¦ MORE** and press **[Enter]**. DOS displays a directory tree, starting with the AceForms directory, lists the files in each subdirectory, and pauses after displaying the first screen of information. See Figure 6-38.

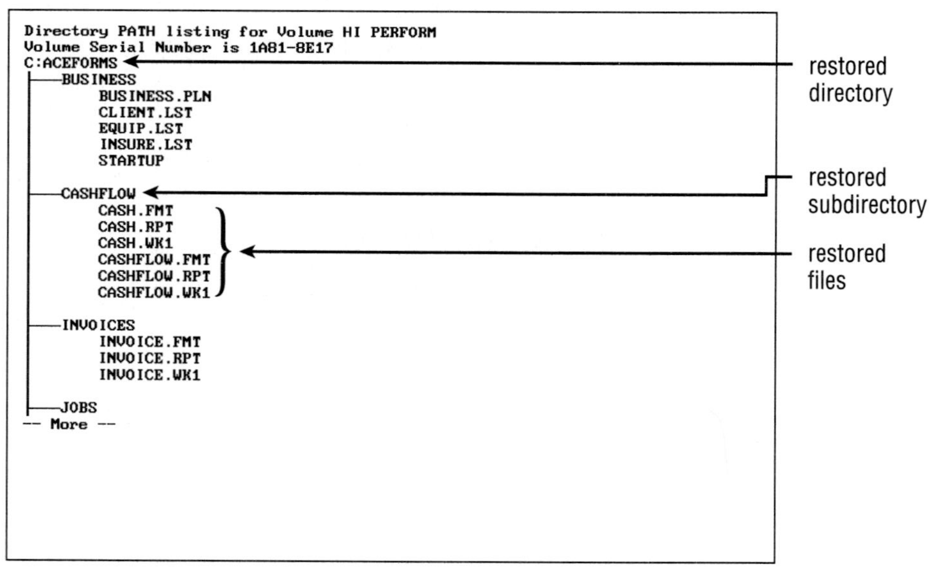

Figure 6-38
A partial directory tree with restored files listed by subdirectory

4. Press **[Spacebar]** or any other key to continue. Repeat this process until you view the entire directory tree and return to the DOS prompt.

You have successfully backed up part of the directory tree of a hard disk, removed part of the directory tree, and restored the same directory tree from a backup set.

USING XCOPY FOR BACKUPS

Occasionally, you need to work on client and business files on your home computer. You decide to copy your data directory from your hard drive in the office to a diskette you can use on your home computer system.

In DOS 5.0, 6.0, and 6.2, you can use the XCOPY command to make backups. The XCOPY is similar to the COPY command, except it can copy more than one directory. The "X" in XCOPY stands for "Extended" to indicate that the XCOPY command is a more extensive command than COPY. The general syntax of this external command is

XCOPY *source* [*destination*]

The *source* is a directory, a group of files, or a single file and is a required parameter. The *destination* is the name of the drive *or* directory to which you want to copy the files. You can omit the destination if you want to copy to the current drive or directory. If you want to include all the subdirectories located below a directory, you can include the Subdirectory switch (/S).

Like the COPY command, XCOPY has some limitations. You cannot use it to make a backup copy of the contents of an entire hard disk. Like COPY, XCOPY automatically stops when it fills a diskette. It does not automatically prompt for another diskette as the MSBACKUP and Backup utilities do. However, like COPY, you can use the files produced with XCOPY because the files are not combined into one larger file on the backup diskette.

Before you use XCOPY, you need to format your Tutorial Disk.

To prepare a diskette:

1. Format your Tutorial Disk using the instructions on pages 56 through 58.

Now copy a directory with XCOPY.

2. Type **XCOPY C:\ACEFORMS*.* A: /S**
   (or **XCOPY C:\ACEFORMS*.* B: /S**)
   and press **[Enter]**. XCOPY copies the directories
   and files to your data diskette. See Figure 6-39.

source directory
source drive
xcopy command
source files
destination drive
Subdirectory switch

```
C:\>XCOPY C:\ACEFORMS\*.* A: /S
Reading source file(s)...
C:\ACEFORMS\BUSINESS\BUSINESS.PLN
C:\ACEFORMS\BUSINESS\CLIENT.LST
C:\ACEFORMS\BUSINESS\EQUIP.LST
C:\ACEFORMS\BUSINESS\INSURE.LST
C:\ACEFORMS\BUSINESS\STARTUP
C:\ACEFORMS\CASHFLOW\CASH.FMT
C:\ACEFORMS\CASHFLOW\CASH.RPT
C:\ACEFORMS\CASHFLOW\CASH.WK1
C:\ACEFORMS\CASHFLOW\CASHFLOW.FMT
C:\ACEFORMS\CASHFLOW\CASHFLOW.RPT
C:\ACEFORMS\CASHFLOW\CASHFLOW.WK1
C:\ACEFORMS\INVOICES\INVOICE.FMT
C:\ACEFORMS\INVOICES\INVOICE.RPT
C:\ACEFORMS\INVOICES\INVOICE.WK1
C:\ACEFORMS\JOBS\FEESCALE
C:\ACEFORMS\JOBS\JOBCOSTS.FMT
C:\ACEFORMS\JOBS\JOBCOSTS.RPT
C:\ACEFORMS\JOBS\JOBCOSTS.WK1
C:\ACEFORMS\JOBS\SCHEDULE.FMT
C:\ACEFORMS\JOBS\SCHEDULE.WK1
```

Figure 6-39
Copying a directory, its subdirectories, and each subdirectory's files (your screen will show more files)

Now verify the copy operation.

3. Type **TREE A:** (or **TREE B:**) and press **[Enter]**. DOS shows you the directory tree of the diskette in drive A (or drive B). See Figure 6-40. XCOPY reproduced the directory structure exactly.

```
C:\>TREE B:
Directory PATH listing
Volume Serial Number is 0C3F-0AD9
B:.
├───BUSINESS
├───CASHFLOW
├───INVOICES
├───JOBS
├───PRJCASH
├───REPORTS
└───RESUMES

C:\>
```

copied subdirectories

Figure 6-40
A directory tree of the diskette

4. Type **TREE A: /F ¦ MORE** (or **TREE B: /F ¦ MORE**) and press **[Enter]**. Figure 6-41 shows a partial directory tree with filenames. XCOPY copied files to the correct directories on this disk.

```
Directory PATH listing
Volume Serial Number is 0C3F-0AD9
B:.
├──BUSINESS  <──────────── copied subdirectory
│       BUSINESS.PLN ┐
│       CLIENT.LST   │
│       EQUIP.LST    ├ <── copied files
│       INSURE.LST   │
│       STARTUP      ┘
│
├──CASHFLOW
│       CASH.FMT
│       CASH.RPT
│       CASH.WK1
│       CASHFLOW.FMT
│       CASHFLOW.RPT
│       CASHFLOW.WK1
│
├──INVOICES
│       INVOICE.FMT
│       INVOICE.RPT
│       INVOICE.WK1
│
├──JOBS
-- More --
```

Figure 6-41
A partial directory tree of the diskette, with files listed by subdirectory

You can reverse this operation and copy a directory structure to a hard disk with the versatile XCOPY command.

FINISHING UP

If you completed this tutorial in a computer lab, you should remove files produced by MSBACKUP from the computer system.

To remove backup files from the hard disk:

6.0 *6.2*

1. If you are using DOS 6.0 or 6.2, type **DEL \DOS\ACEFORMS.*** and press **[Enter]**. DOS deletes the catalog and setup files produced by MSBACKUP.
2. If you are using DOS 6.0 or 6.2, type **DEL \DOS*.BAK** and press **[Enter]**. DOS deletes files with the BAK (Backup) file extension produced by MSBACKUP.

5.0 *6.0*

3. If you are using DOS 5.0 or 6.0, type **DEL \DOS\LOGFILE1** and press **[Enter]**. DOS deletes the BACKUP log file.

DEVELOPING A BACKUP STRATEGY

To protect your time and investment in the files that you produce on your computer system, you should develop a backup strategy that will enable you to restore files to your computer system if you inadvertently delete those files or if your hard disk fails.

As part of a backup strategy, you should perform a full backup at regular intervals, such as every month or quarter. A **full backup** represents the start of a **backup cycle** and can include the entire contents of your hard disk. Or, in the interest of saving time and effort, you might want to limit your full backups just to the document or data files on your computer system. These files are obviously quite important because you are constantly changing and updating them.

You do not need to repeatedly back up directories that contain installed software, because software settings change infrequently or not at all. After you install and configure a software application on your computer system, you might want to back it up once so that you can install a new copy later if the need arises. It is quicker to restore software from a backup copy than it is to reinstall the original software application and respecify its default settings.

If you perform a full backup monthly, you can perform either an incremental or a differential backup on a weekly or daily basis. An **incremental backup** includes only those files that have *changed* since your last full or last incremental backup. You can combine full and incremental backups to guarantee that you can restore all the files you have worked on during a backup cycle. For example, after you perform a full backup, you can perform your first incremental backup at the end of the first week. This backup will include all files that changed during the first week. At the end of the second week, you perform your second incremental backup. This backup includes all files that changed during the second week. At the end of the third week, you perform your third and last incremental backup. This backup includes all files changed during the third week. At the end of the month, you perform a new full backup and start a new backup cycle. Although you could reuse the same diskettes, it is a good habit to keep two or three of the most recent backup sets and alternate them. When you are ready to perform another full backup, you use your oldest backup set. If you need to restore files to a hard disk, you can restore your last full backup and then each of the incremental backups in the order in which you produced them.

One advantage of incremental backups is that you have different versions of the same file stored in different backup sets, and you therefore can locate a specific version of a file. To perform an incremental backup with BACKUP in DOS 5.0 and 6.0, you use the **Modified switch** (/M) to select all files that were *created* or *modified* since the last backup, whether it was a full or an incremental backup. You can also include the **Add switch** (/A) to add the next set of backup files to the existing set of backup diskettes. To perform an incremental backup with MSBACKUP in DOS 6.0 and 6.2, you specify Incremental as the Backup Type on the Backup screen.

A **differential backup** includes all files altered since your last full backup. This type of backup takes longer than an incremental backup and keeps only the most recent version of files. For example, after you perform a full backup, you can perform your first differential backup at the end of the first week. This backup will include all files that were created or modified during the first week since the full backup. At the end of the second week, you perform your second differential backup. This backup will include all files that were created or modified during the first and second weeks, again since the full backup. At the end of the third week, you perform your third and last differential backup. This backup will include all files created and modified during the first, second and third weeks since the full backup. At the end of the month, you perform a new full backup and start a new backup cycle. Just as with an incremental backup, it is a good habit to keep two or three of the most recent backup sets and alternate them rather than reuse the same set of diskettes for each differential backup. When you are ready to perform another full backup, you use your oldest backup set. If you need to restore files to a hard disk, you can restore files from your last full backup and your last differential backup in that backup cycle.

To perform a differential backup with BACKUP in DOS 5.0 and 6.0, you use the **Date switch** (/D) to select all files since the date of the last full backup. If you performed a full backup on June 30, 1994, you would perform each differential backup (of the entire hard drive) in July with the following command:

BACKUP C:*.* A: /S /D:7-1-94

BACKUP would then backup all files created or modified on or after July 1, 1994. Again, you should rotate backup sets of both the full and the differential backups.

To perform a differential backup with MSBACKUP in DOS 6.0 and 6.2, you specify Differential for the Backup Type on the Backup screen.

When you use MSBACKUP in DOS 6.0 and 6.2, it creates a backup catalog file that tracks information for each backup. It uses the file extension FUL for full backups, INC for incremental backups, and DIF for differential backups. It also creates a **master catalog** file that keeps track of all backups performed during a backup cycle. You can use the master catalog to restore a complete backup cycle.

No matter what type of backup strategy you choose to implement, you should have at least two and maybe three backup sets of a full backup and an incremental or differential backup. If one of the backup sets fails, then you can use one of the other backup sets. It is also common practice to save full backups done at one-year intervals and to store one set of backups off-site.

Like insurance, these backups are invaluable when you need them. You may find yourself in a situation where you need to reconstruct all your company's business records after a major disaster, like an earthquake or fire, or some other incident, like a theft. A couple of years ago, the news media reported that thieves stole a computer system that belonged to a small business. The owner of the company claimed that the only thing that she wanted the thieves to return was her backups.

◆

SUMMARY

In this tutorial, DOS 5.0 and 6.0 users learned how to use BACKUP to backup files from a hard disk to diskettes and how to use RESTORE to restore files from diskettes to a hard disk. You learned how to use the Subdirectory and Log File switches with BACKUP and the Subdirectory and Display switches with RESTORE. You also learned of the importance of the Modified and Date switches when performing incremental and differential backups.

DOS 6.0 and 6.2 users learned how to use MSBACKUP to backup files from a hard disk to diskettes and to restore files from diskettes to a hard disk. You also learned how to perform a compatibility test and to configure MSBACKUP for the hardware in your computer system. DOS 6.0 and 6.2 users also deleted a part of the directory tree of a hard disk with the DELTREE command.

You learned how to use XCOPY and its Subdirectory switch to copy a directory, its subdirectories, and each subdirectory's files from a hard disk to a diskette.

You learned about the importance of developing a backup strategy. You learned about the use of full, incremental, and differential backups as well as their advantages and disadvantages. You learned how to integrate these backups in an overall backup strategy.

Command Reference	
DOS Commands	
BACKUP *source destination-drive:*	*DOS 5.0 and 6.0*: An external command that backs up an entire hard drive, a directory, a group of files, or a single file onto a set of backup diskettes. Common switches include: /S Subdirectory switch for backing up all subdirectories located below the specified drive or directory /L Log File switch for specifying the name of a file that stores information on backed-up files /M Modified switch for backing up only those files that changed since the last backup /A Add switch for adding another backup set to an existing set of backup diskettes /D Date switch for performing a backup of all files created or modified on or after a certain date

DELTREE [*drive:*]*path*	*DOS 6.0 and 6.2*: An external command that deletes a directory tree, all its subdirectories, and all files in the specified directories
MSBACKUP	*DOS 6.0 and 6.2*: An external command that backs up an entire hard drive, a directory or combination of directories, a group of files, or a single file from a hard disk to a set of backup diskettes; restores selected directories or files from a set of backup diskettes to a hard disk; and performs a compatibility test to verify the backup process
RESTORE *source-drive: target-drive:*[*path*[*filename*]]	*DOS 5.0, 6.0, and 6.2*: An external command that restores an entire hard disk, a directory, a group of files, or a single file from a set of backup diskettes. Common switches include: /S Subdirectory switch for restoring all subdirectories located below the specified drive or directory /D Display switch for displaying a list of path names and filenames of files stored on a set of backup diskettes
XCOPY *source* [*destination*]	*DOS 5.0, 6.0, and 6.2*: An external command that copies a directory and its subdirectories and files, a group of files, or a single file to another disk. Common switches include: /S Subdirectory switch for copying all subdirectories located below the specified directory

QUESTIONS

1. List the advantages and disadvantages of using the COPY command for backups.
2. List the advantages and disadvantages of using the DISKCOPY command for backups.
3. What happens when you use the Subdirectory switch with BACKUP?
4. What is the Log File switch, how do you use it with BACKUP, and what advantage does it provide?
5. After you back up a directory that contains several hundred files, you check your backup disk's directory and find that there are only two files—BACKUP.001 and CONTROL.001. Where did BACKUP store all the files? What is the difference between these two files? What is the significance, if any, of the file extension?
6. What types of information does BACKUP store in a log file?
7. What command can you use to restore files backed up with the BACKUP command?
8. How can you display the contents of a backup disk produced with BACKUP without actually restoring the files?
9. When using BACKUP, how can you select only those files that have changed since the last backup?
10. When using BACKUP, how can you add new backup files to an existing backup set?
11. When using BACKUP, how can you select only those files created or modified since the last backup?
12. What is a setup file, and how do you use it?
13. Explain the conventions used to name backup catalog files.
14. What is the purpose of MSBACKUP's compatibility test?
15. How do you save settings for a setup file in MSBACKUP?
16. Name one way in which you can select an entire directory from the MSBACKUP Select Backup Files screen.
17. Name two options that MSBACKUP automatically uses during a backup.
18. After you back up a directory that contains several hundred files, you check your backup diskette and find that there is one file named CC40709A.FUL. What drive did MSBACKUP back up? What type of backup did it perform? What is the date of the backup?

19. What command can you use in DOS 6.0 to remove an entire directory and all its subordinate directories and files?
20. One of your backup sets contains the backup file CC40922A.FUL. What drive did MSBACKUP back up? What type of backup did it perform? What is the date of the backup?
21. Name three advantages of using MSBACKUP over BACKUP?
22. How does XCOPY differ from COPY? What advantage, if any, does it have over the COPY command?
23. What is a full backup, and what phase does it represent in a backup cycle?
24. What is an incremental backup?
25. How can you use a full and an incremental backup in a backup cycle?
26. What is a differential backup?
27. How can you use a full and a differential backup in a backup cycle?
28. What is a master catalog file?
29. How many backup sets should you have of a hard disk drive, and where should you store those backup sets, if at all possible?
30. Assume you use MSBACKUP to perform a full backup of drives C and D on October 31, 1994. What name would MSBACKUP assign to the backup file?

TUTORIAL ASSIGNMENTS

1. **Developing a Backup Strategy**: Suppose you want to develop a backup strategy for your hard disk. What backup strategy would you choose based on the following factors, and how would you implement this backup strategy?

   Use the following factors in choosing a backup strategy:

   - You create and modify many different files each work day.
   - You want to keep different versions of the same file in the event you need to restore a specific version of a file.
   - You store all your work files in one branch of the directory tree on your hard disk.

   Explain how you would implement these backups with either MSBACKUP (in DOS 6.0 or 6.2) or BACKUP (in DOS 5.0 or 6.0).

2. **Backing Up Directories with BACKUP in DOS 5.0 and 6.0**: This Tutorial Assignment assumes that the AceForms directory you used in this tutorial is stored on the hard disk you are using. Perform the following operations, and describe the commands or selections you make for each step.
   a. Unconditionally format a diskette to use for the backup.
   b. Back up the BUSINESS directory, and create a log file in the DOS directory.
   c. Back up the RESUMES directory to the same backup diskette, and log the backup process to the same log file. Note: BACKUP automatically adds to the existing file.
   d. Display the contents of the log file.
   e. Display a list of the backed-up files on the backup diskette.
   f. Remove the RESUMES directory from the hard disk.
   g. Restore the RESUMES directory to the hard disk.
   h. Verify the restore operation.

3. **Backing Up Directories with MSBACKUP in DOS 6.0 and 6.2**: This Tutorial Assignment assumes that the AceForms directory you used in this tutorial is stored on the hard disk you are using. Perform the following operations, and describe the commands or selections you make for each step.
   a. Unconditionally format a diskette to use for the backup.
   b. Load the MSBACKUP utility.
   c. Create a setup file from DEFAULT.SET to store settings that you specify for a backup.
   d. Select the CASHFLOW and PRJCASH directories for the backup.
   e. Perform the backup.
   f. Exit MSBACKUP and remove the CASHFLOW directory.
   g. Load MSBACKUP and restore the CASHFLOW directory.
   h. Exit MSBACKUP and verify the restore operation.
4. **Using XCOPY to Back Up a Directory**: This Tutorial Assignment assumes that the AceForms directory you used in this tutorial is stored on the hard disk you are using. Perform the following operations, and describe the commands or selections you make for each step.
   a. Unconditionally format a diskette to use for the backup.
   b. Back up the INVOICES directory with the XCOPY command.
   c. Display a directory tree of the backup diskette to verify its directory structure.
   d. Back up the REPORTS directory with the XCOPY command.
   e. Display a directory tree of the backup diskette to verify its directory structure.
   f. Remove the INVOICES directory from the hard disk.
   g. Restore the INVOICES directory to the hard disk.
   h. Verify the restore operation.
5. **Comparison of BACKUP and MSBACKUP in DOS 6.0**: One of the important considerations people face when backing up their computer system is the amount of time required for the backup. In DOS 6.0, you can use either BACKUP or MSBACKUP to back up your hard disk. In this exercise, you will compare the differences between these two backup utilities by calculating the time required for each of these utilities to back up a directory and its subdirectories and files.

This Tutorial Assignment assumes that the AceForms directory that you used in this tutorial is stored on the hard disk that you are using. Perform the following operations.

Using BACKUP:

a. Unconditionally format a diskette to use for the first backup.
b. Record the time in minutes and seconds when you start the first backup.
c. Use BACKUP to back up the entire AceForms directory to the backup diskette, and create a log file in the DOS directory.
d. Record the time in minutes and seconds when the backup ends. Calculate the amount of time required for the backup.
e. Unconditionally format the diskette so that you can use it for the second backup.
f. Record the time in minutes and seconds when you start the second backup.

Using MSBACKUP:

g. Load MSBACKUP, create a new setup file, specify backup settings, select the AceForms directory and its subdirectories, save the settings in the setup file, and perform a full backup of the AceForms directory.
h. After the backup is complete, exit MSBACKUP and record the time in minutes and seconds when you end the backup process. Calculate the amount of time required for the backup.

Although this backup is on a smaller scale than one you would normally perform on a computer system, compare the differences in time required for the two types of backups. Based only on this time difference, which backup utility would you choose to use? What other factors might affect your decision to use one of the two backup utilities?

TUTORIAL 7

Exploring Windows 3.1

OBJECTIVES

In this tutorial you will learn to:

- Start Windows 3.1
- Use the Windows graphical interface
- Identify the elements of a window
- Adjust the Program Manager window
- Use the Control-menu box
- Select menus from the menu bar
- Obtain help information
- Open the Main Group
- Examine applications in the Main Group
- Set the date and time
- Use the MS-DOS Prompt icon
- Move a window and change its size
- Tile and cascade windows
- Exit Windows

At a meeting of your workgroup, your supervisor and coworkers discuss the possibility of using Windows on each of the computer systems in the office. Most of your coworkers agree that Windows provides a friendlier and more visual interface than the DOS prompt and the DOS Shell. Several coworkers also emphasize that Windows contains a variety of applications for customizing, managing, and using your computer system and its resources, including files, disks, and software applications. Your supervisor notes that you can switch between applications easily as you work. Everyone agrees that the next logical step is to install Windows on each computer system and to become familiar with the basics of using the program.

◆

THE WINDOWS 3.1 GRAPHICAL USER INTERFACE

When you work from the DOS prompt, you are using a command-line interface that requires you to know how to enter and execute commands. The only real information that this interface provides is the name of the current drive and directory.

In contrast, the DOS Shell, as you have learned, uses a **graphical user interface** (GUI) that provides a more visual and supportive working environment than DOS. For example, you can view the directory tree for a disk drive, and you can easily select a directory and view its files. You can select commands from menus that clearly identify your options, and you can use the mouse to point and select commands and objects on the screen. Many DOS operations, such as renaming, moving, copying, and deleting files, are easier to perform in the DOS Shell than at the DOS prompt.

In contrast to the DOS Shell, Windows 3.1 provides an even richer graphical user interface and many more options for working with drives, directories, applications, and files. You can open more than one application at a time and quickly switch from one application to another. Each application is displayed in its own window so that you can distinguish and work with different applications in different windows. Also, Windows 3.1 includes a variety of additional applications that you will find useful in your daily work.

STARTING WINDOWS

You are ready to examine the basic features of Windows 3.1. The instructions that follow describe how to start Windows 3.1 from the DOS prompt. If your computer setup is different, follow the instructions provided by your instructor or technical support person on how to start Windows.

To start Windows 3.1 from the DOS prompt:

1. Be sure you see the operating system prompt for drive C on your monitor.
2. Type **WIN** and press **[Enter]**. As Windows loads into memory, you see the Windows 3.1 logo. As you work in Windows, you may also see the image of an hourglass when Windows wants you to wait until it has finished performing an operation. If this is the first time you have used Windows, you will next see the Program Manager and Main Group windows. See Figure 7-1. Your initial view might be different from that shown in Figure 7-1; for example, you might see more than one window and different icons.

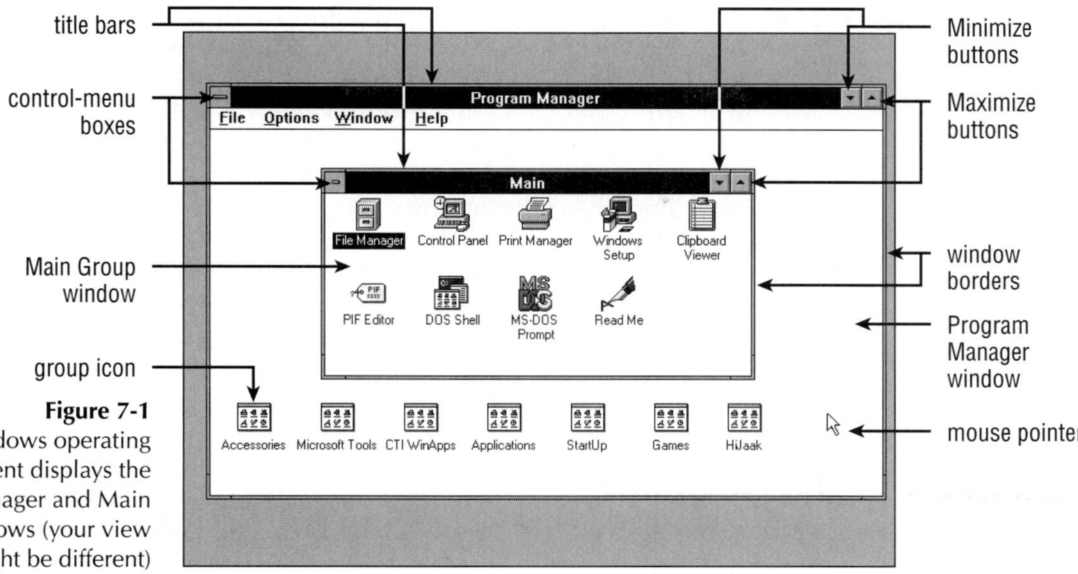

Figure 7-1 The Windows operating environment displays the Program Manager and Main Group windows (your view might be different)

THE WINDOWS DESKTOP

You can compare your view of Windows to your desktop on a busy workday. Your desktop contains a variety of tools as well as printed copies of documents. Windows organizes your screen into **windows**, or views, so that you can work with the tools available through Windows. In this sense, you can compare windows on your screen to "in" and "out" boxes as well as desk accessory organizers on your desktop. One of the advantages of using Windows is that you can customize your screen view to meet your needs.

The Program Manager window automatically appears when you load Windows. **Program Manager** is a software application that manages the use of other Windows components. You start other applications from the Program Manager, and use it to organize applications and files into logical groups within Windows for ease of access and use. The Main Group window contains applications specific to Windows. Before you examine these applications, let's look more closely at the organization of a window.

Identifying the Elements of a Window

Each window contains the same basic elements, so that you have a standardized operating environment. Each window contains a **window border**, which appears as a double outline, around the window's contents. Each window has a title that appears on its **title bar**. For example, as you can see in Figure 7-1, the Program Manager title appears on the title bar for the Program Manager window. Each window also contains a set of **icons**, or pictures, that represent software and hardware components that you can use.

The Program Manager window contains a set of icons known as group icons. A **group icon** represents a set of related applications that Windows displays when you select that icon. For example, if you select the Accessories Group icon, Windows displays another window that includes icons for Write, a word-processing program; Paintbrush, a drawing program; Calculator, an on-screen calculator program; Calendar, a calendar and daily appointment book program; Cardfile, a program for organizing addresses and other information, much like a Rolodex; and Clock, an on-screen clock program.

If the Main Group window is open, you will see a variety of icons in this window. Each of the icons in a group window is called a **program-item icon**, and each represents an application for a specific task. When you select one of these program-item icons, Windows opens a window that displays the application. For example, one of the icons in the Main Group window appears as a filing cabinet. This icon is the File Manager icon. **File Manager** is an application for managing the use of drives, directories, and files.

If your copy of DOS 6.0 or 6.2 is installed for use with Windows, you might also see a Microsoft Tools Group in the Program Manager window. If you open the Microsoft Tools Group, you will find an Undelete icon for undeleting files from Windows, a Backup icon for using Microsoft Backup from Windows, and an Anti-Virus icon to check for computer viruses from Windows.

Each window contains a **Control-menu box** in the upper-left corner next to the title bar. This Control-menu box contains a short horizontal bar in a square. If you click the Control-menu box, Windows displays a drop-down Control menu that you can use to adjust windows or to exit the application window. If you double-click the Control-menu box, Windows closes the current application and its window.

Each window also contains a Minimize and Maximize button in the upper-right corner next to the title bar. You can use these buttons to adjust the size of a window. The **Minimize button** appears as a triangle pointing downward, and the **Maximize button** appears as a triangle pointing upward. When you click the Minimize button, Windows reduces the window to an icon and displays the icon at the bottom of the screen. When you click the Maximize button, Windows enlarges the window to fill the entire screen and the Maximize button changes to a **Restore button**, which has one triangle pointing upward and another pointing downward. You use the Restore button to return the window to its original size.

As you work with Windows, you will discover that the mouse is indispensable. Although you can perform most operations in Windows with the keyboard, you will find that the mouse is easier to use than the corresponding key combinations. The **mouse pointer** appears as an arrow in outline; however, its shape may change as you perform specific tasks. *Because it is assumed you will use the mouse rather than the keyboard in these Windows tutorials, the mouse icon you became familiar with in the DOS tutorials does not appear in the text of the two Windows tutorials.*

Now you are ready to explore Windows 3.1. However, you do not want to change any settings until you know more about the use of Windows 3.1. In the steps that follow, you will use a mouse to point and select options.

To get started:

1. If the Main Group window appears in front of the Program Manager window, double-click the **Control-menu box** in the upper-left corner of the Main Group window. The Control-menu box is to the left of the title bar. Windows closes the Main Group window and reduces the window to an icon. See Figure 7-2. If multiple windows are open, you can double-click

each window's Control-menu box until you close all windows *except* the Program Manager window. Your Program Manager window might contain different icons. If you need assistance, ask your instructor or technical support person to adjust your view so that only the Program Manager window is open.

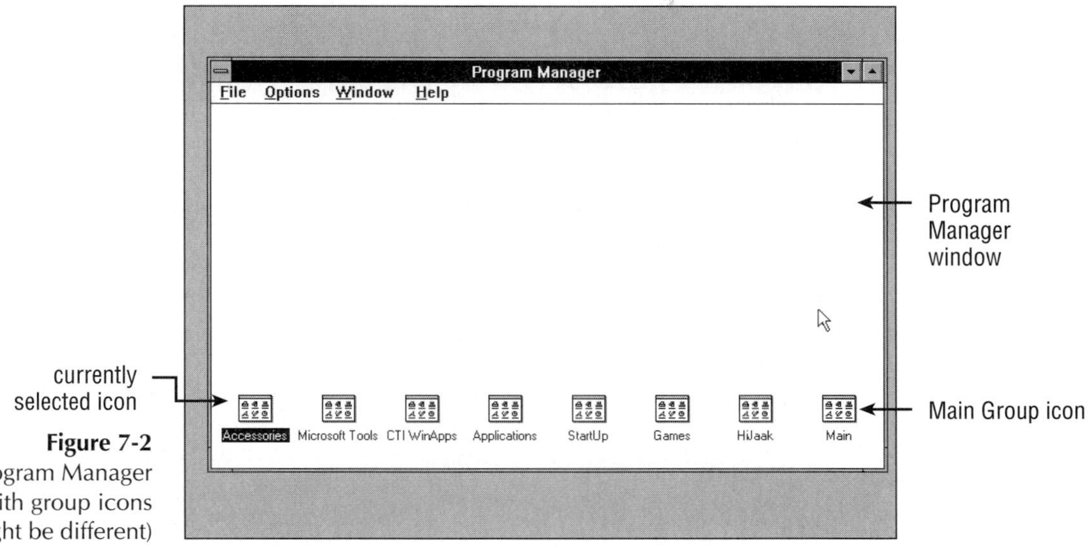

Figure 7-2
The Program Manager window with group icons (yours might be different)

Now adjust the size of the Program Manager window.

2. Click the **Minimize button**. The Minimize button is located to the immediate right of the title bar and contains a triangle that points downward. Windows converts the Program Manager window to an icon that appears at the bottom of the screen. See Figure 7-3.

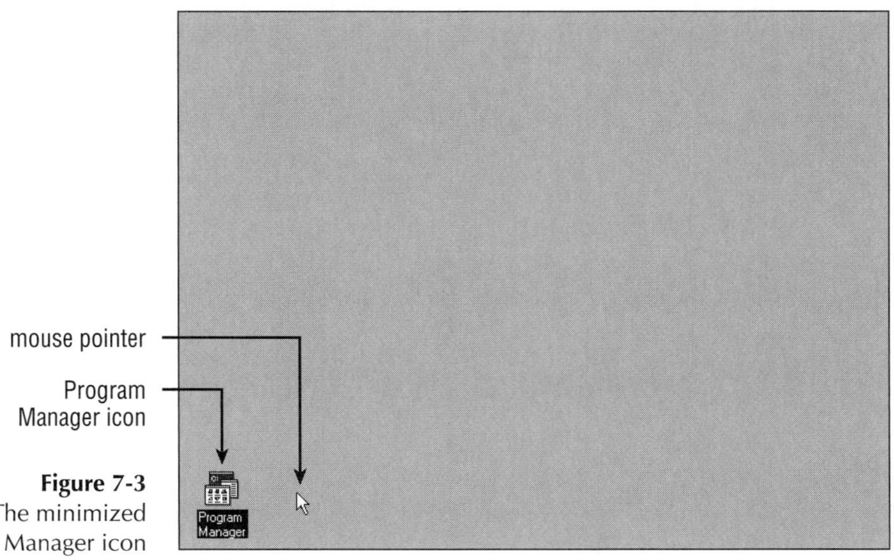

Figure 7-3
The minimized Program Manager icon

3. Double-click the **Program Manager icon**. Windows displays the Program Manager window at its original size. If you click the Program Manager icon once, Windows displays a Control menu. See Figure 7-4. You can click the Restore option on the menu to return the Program Manager window to its original size.

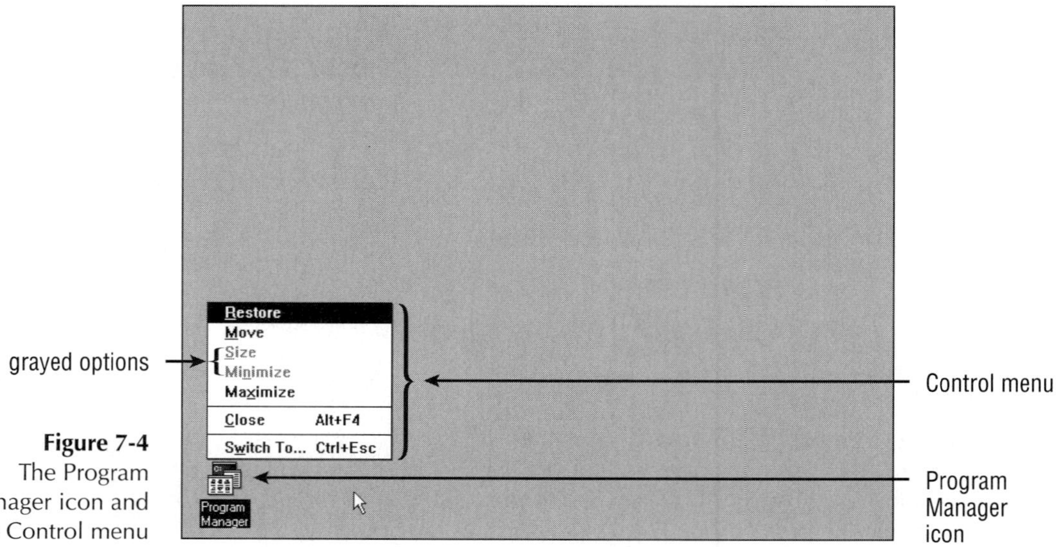

Figure 7-4
The Program Manager icon and the Control menu

4. Click the **Maximize button**. The Maximize button is located to the far right of the title bar and contains a triangle that points upward. Windows displays a full-screen view of the Program Manager window. See Figure 7-5. It also converts the Maximize button to a Restore button that contains two triangles, one pointing upward and the other pointing downward.

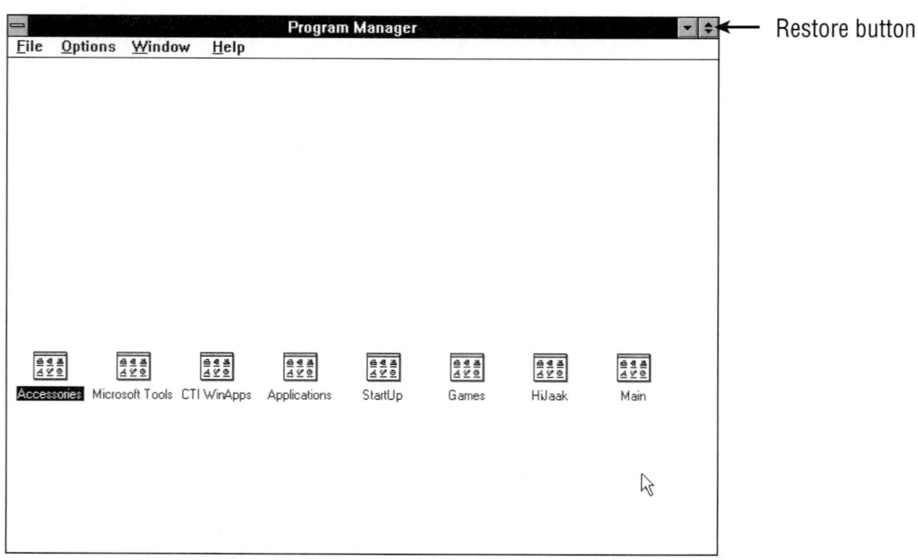

Figure 7-5
The maximized Program Manager window

5. Click the **Restore button**. Windows returns the Program Manager window to its original size. It also converts the Restore button to a Maximize button.

Using the Control Menu

You can also adjust the Program Manager Window with the Control-menu box. Let's view the Control menu and try these same operations.

To display the Control menu:

1. Click the **Control-menu box** in the Program Manager window. The Control-menu box is located in the upper-left corner of the window to the left of the title bar, and it contains a bar icon. Windows displays the Control menu. See Figure 7-6. This menu contains commands for minimizing, maximizing, and restoring the size of a window, as well as commands for moving, sizing, and closing a window. (If you inadvertently double-click the Control-menu box, Windows displays an Exit Windows dialog box and asks if you want to exit Windows. If this occurs, click the Cancel button to return to Program Manager and try again.)

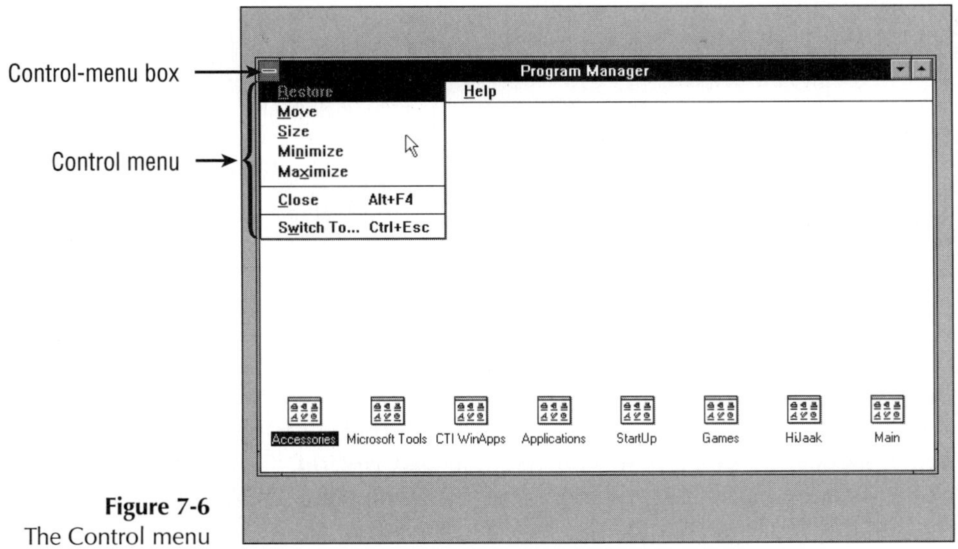

Figure 7-6
The Control menu

2. Click the **Minimize option**. Windows again converts the Program Manager window to an icon that appears at the bottom of the screen.
3. Click the **Program Manager icon**. Windows displays a Control menu instead. Click **Restore** to return the Program Manager window to its original size.
4. Click the **Control-menu box**. Then click **Maximize**. Windows again displays a full-screen view of the Program Manager window.
5. Click the **Control-menu box**. Then click **Restore**. Windows returns the Program Manager window to its original size.

EXAMINING THE PROGRAM MANAGER MENUS

Now that you are familiar with the Control menu and buttons for sizing a window, let's examine the menus on the menu bar.

To display the File menu:

1. Click **File**. Program Manager displays the File menu. See Figure 7-7. Like the DOS Shell menus, the Program Manager menus display a list of commands and, in some cases, shortcut keys for certain commands. Commands that are shown in gray are unavailable for use because they do not apply to the current window.

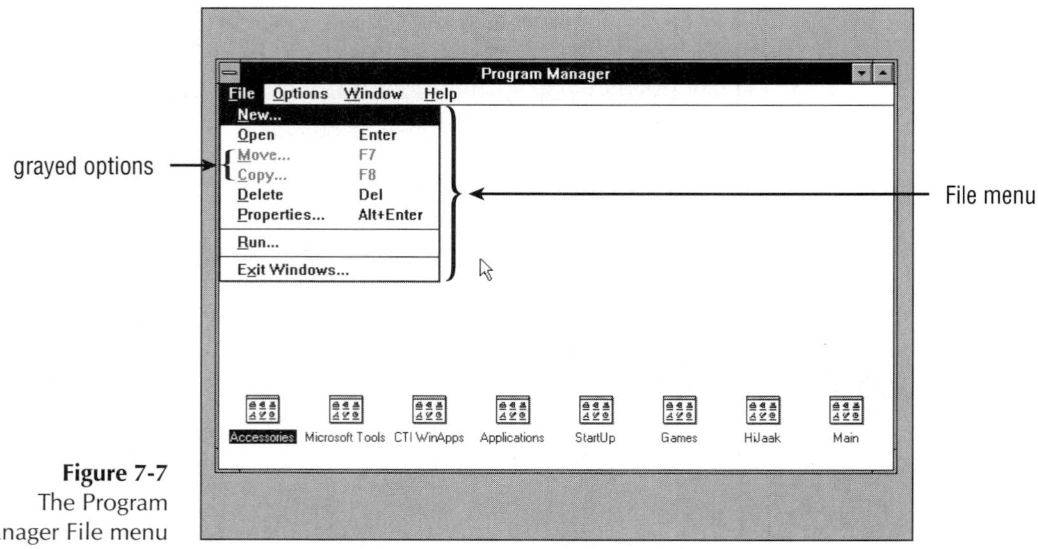

Figure 7-7
The Program Manager File menu

On the File menu, you use the New option to create a new group, Open to open a group, Delete to delete a group icon, and Properties to redefine settings for a group. The Run option executes a DOS command from within Windows. Menu options followed by an ellipsis indicate that a dialog box appears when that option is chosen. You can use the last option, Exit Windows, to exit Windows and return to the DOS prompt. You can also exit Windows by double-clicking the Program Manager's Control-menu box.

The Options Menu

Next let's look at the Options menu. This menu allows you to select some default settings for the operation of Windows.

To display the Options menu:

1. Click **Options**. Program Manager closes the File menu and displays the Options menu. See Figure 7-8.

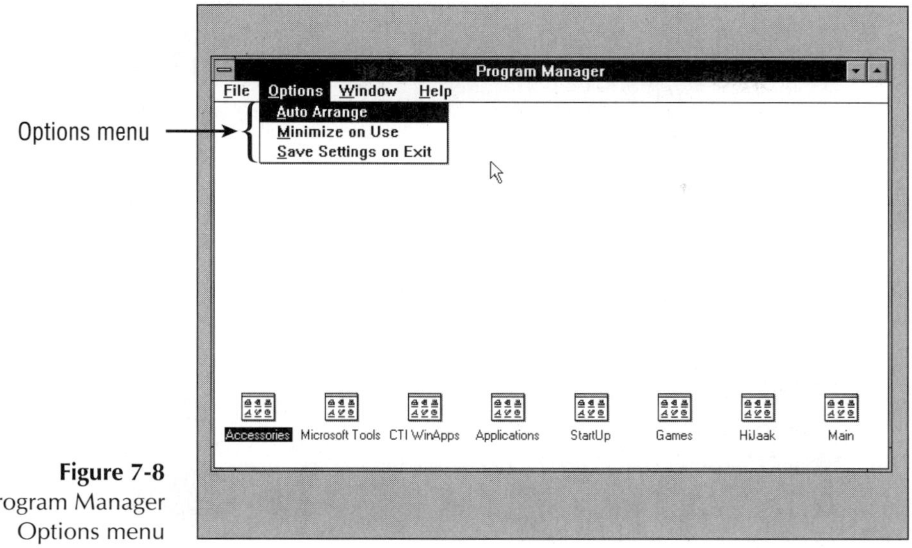

Figure 7-8
The Program Manager Options menu

The options on this menu can be toggled on or off. When an option is activated, a check mark appears next to it. When an option is deactivated, the check mark disappears. If you activate the Auto Arrange option, Windows will automatically adjust the position and arrangement of icons in a window as you change the size of the window. If you activate the Minimize on Use option, the Program Manager will appear as an icon, not an open window, when Windows loads. If you activate the Save Settings on Exit option, any changes you make to Windows are saved when you exit Windows.

The Window Menu

You can use the Window menu to control the arrangement of windows on the screen and to select groups. Let's examine the Window menu.

To display the Window menu and its options:

1. Click **Window**. Program Manager closes the Options menu and displays the Window menu. See Figure 7-9. Your list of group icons will be different.

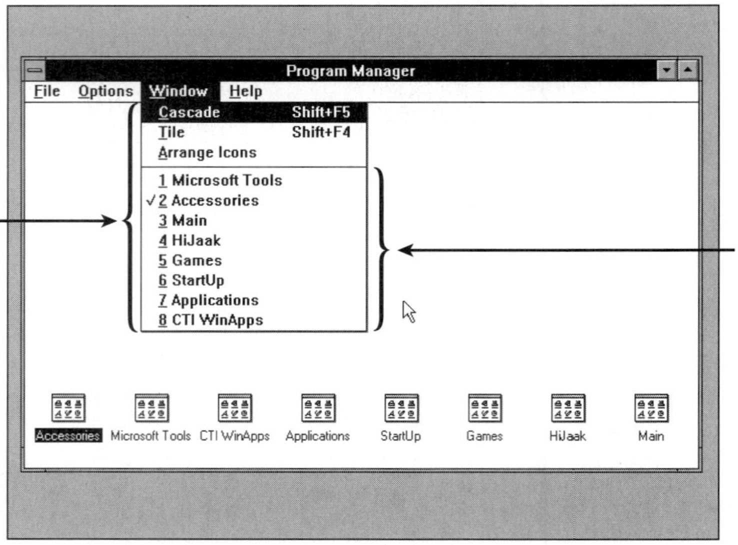

Figure 7-9
The Program Manager Window menu

The Cascade option overlaps windows so that you can see the title bars of each window. In contrast, the Tile option arranges windows side by side. Although the windows are smaller, you can see each window. You can use the Arrange Icons option to arrange icons in even rows in a window. The second part of the menu is a numbered list of options; each group icon is assigned a number so that you can quickly open a group from this menu by typing the number or clicking the option. Your list of group icons will be different from Figure 7-9.

USING HELP

The last menu, Help, takes you into the Windows Help system, which puts help information on procedures, commands, and terms at your fingertips to assist you in the use of Windows. You can also learn more about Windows through a built-in Windows tutorial. Let's look more closely at the Help menu.

To display the Help menu:

1. Click **Help**. Program Manager closes the Window menu and displays the Help menu. See Figure 7-10.

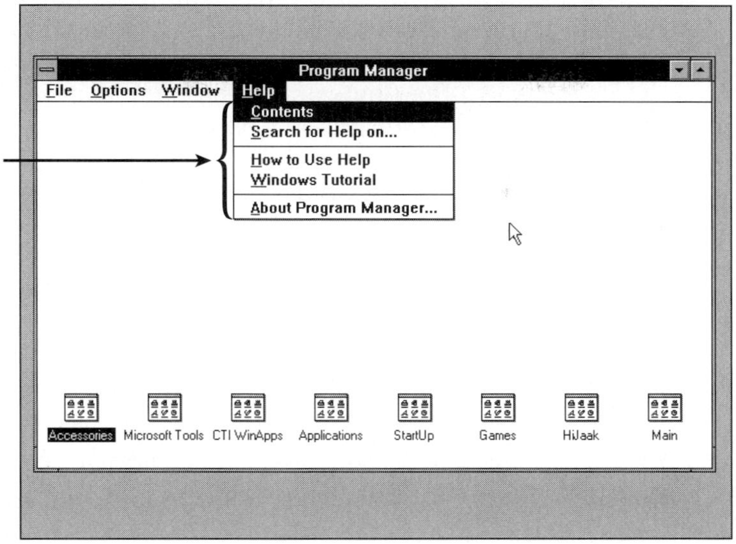

Figure 7-10
The Program Manager Help menu

2. Click **Contents**. After the Program Manager displays the Program Manager Help window, click the Program Manager Help **Maximize button**. See Figure 7-11. The text in the Help window explains the value of the Program Manager, and it lists procedures under "How To" and menu options under "Commands." If you click one of the underlined options, Windows Help displays help information on that option.

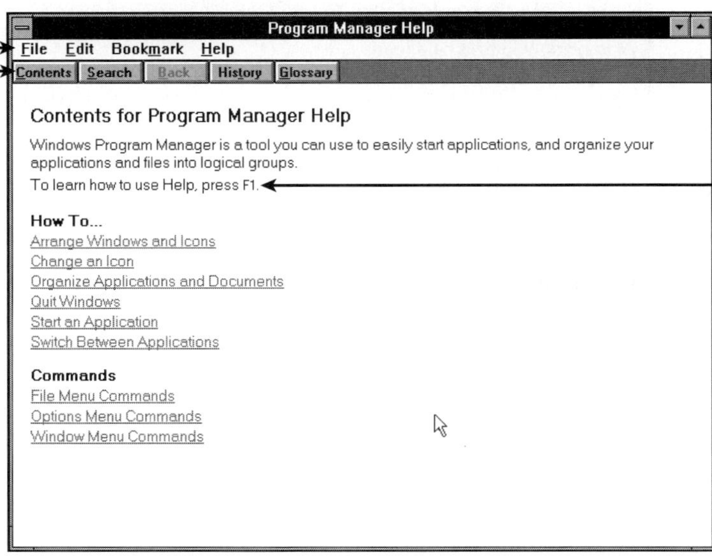

Figure 7-11
The Program Manager Help window

The Help window contains Help menus, Help buttons, and a list of topics for which help information is available. The Help File menu allows you to open a help file on a Windows application, print information displayed on a help topic, specify printer settings, or exit Help. The Edit menu command allows you to copy text from a help screen to another application via the Clipboard or to **annotate**, or add, comments to a help screen. (The **Clipboard** is an area of memory used to temporarily store data.) The Bookmark menu allows you to assign a name to a certain help screen. Later, you can quickly return to the same help screen by indicating the bookmark name. The Help menu allows you to return to the Contents for Program Manager Help screen, adjust help windows, and view the Windows version, mode, and copyright information.

The Contents button on the Help button bar provides help information on the application you are using. The Search button allows you to locate help information on a specific topic by entering a word or phrase. The Back button takes you back to the previous screen you viewed. (The Back button is grayed in Figure 7-11 because you are viewing the first screen; there is no previous screen.) The History button displays the last 40 topics you examined. The Glossary button provides definitions of Windows terms.

Let's examine help information on arranging windows and icons.

To obtain "How To..." help information:

1. Move the mouse pointer to the first underlined option, "Arrange Windows and Icons." The mouse pointer changes to a hand with a finger pointing to this option.
2. Click **Arrange Windows and Icons**. Windows Help displays help information on arranging windows and icons. See Figure 7-12. Windows Help explains how to use three commands to arrange windows and icons on the screen.

Help text

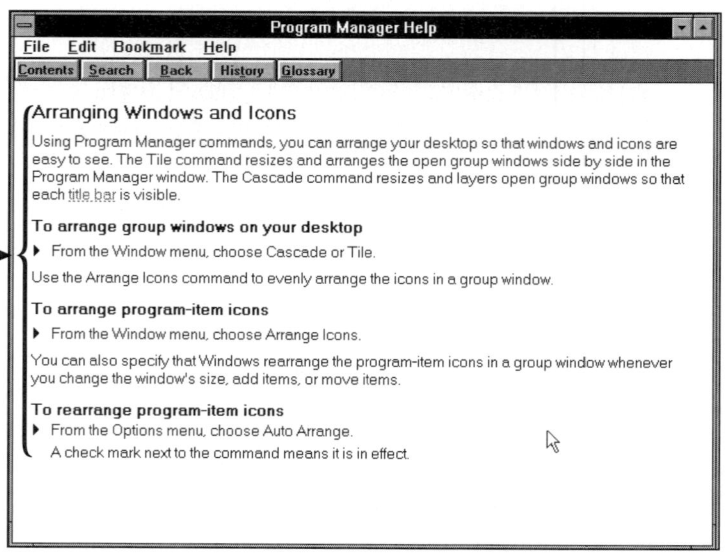

Figure 7-12
Help information on arranging windows and icons

Now view the glossary's definition of an icon.

3. Click the **Glossary button** on the Help button bar. Windows Help displays a glossary window. See Figure 7-13. Terms are listed in alphabetical order.

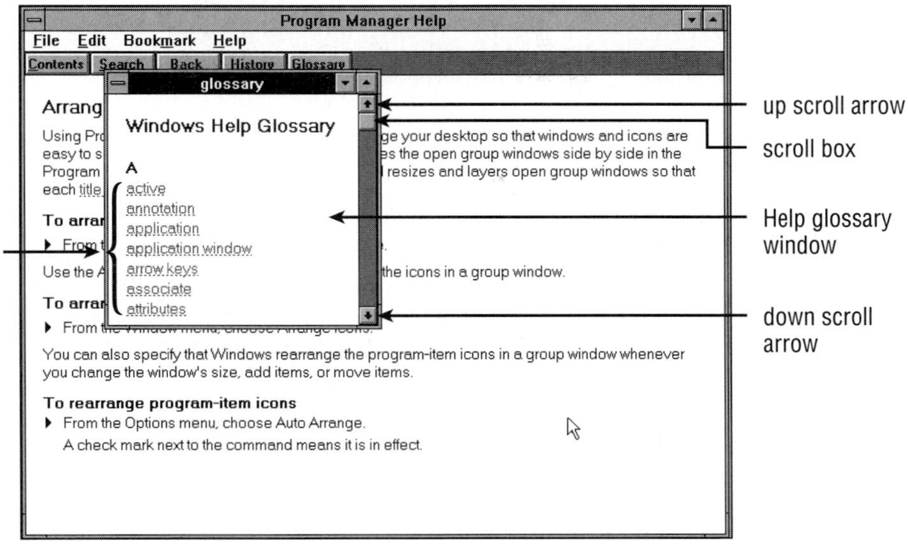

Figure 7-13
The Windows Help Glossary window

4. Drag the **scroll box** halfway down the scroll bar located on the right side of the glossary window, or click the **down scroll arrow**, until you see terms that start with the letter "I."
5. Click the term **icon**. Windows Help displays a Help window for this term. See Figure 7-14.

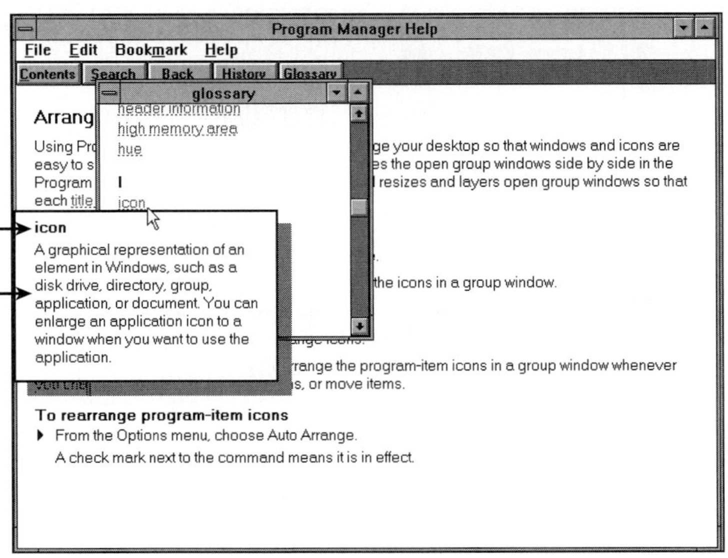

Figure 7-14
Help information for the term "icon"

6. Click the **right mouse button**. The Help window closes.
7. Double-click the **Control-menu box** for the glossary window. Windows Help closes the glossary window and returns you to the Help window on arranging windows and icons.

8. Double-click the **Control-menu box** for the Program Manager Help window. Windows closes the Program Manager Help window and displays the Program Manager window.

Now that you are familiar with the Program Manager's menus, let's examine an important group, the Main Group.

OPENING THE MAIN GROUP

The **Main Group** contains a set of Windows applications for managing the resources on your computer system and, therefore, is one of the more important tools within Windows. Program items in this group enable you to manage files and directories, configure your computer system, customize Windows, control printing, specify new applications, and exit to the DOS prompt.

Let's open this window and examine some of these uses.

To open the Main Group:

1. If you have opened windows other than Program Manager, close them by double-clicking the **Control-menu box** for each window. Leave the Program Manager window open; do not exit Windows.
2. Double-click the **Main icon**. Windows displays the Main Group window and its program items. See Figure 7-15.

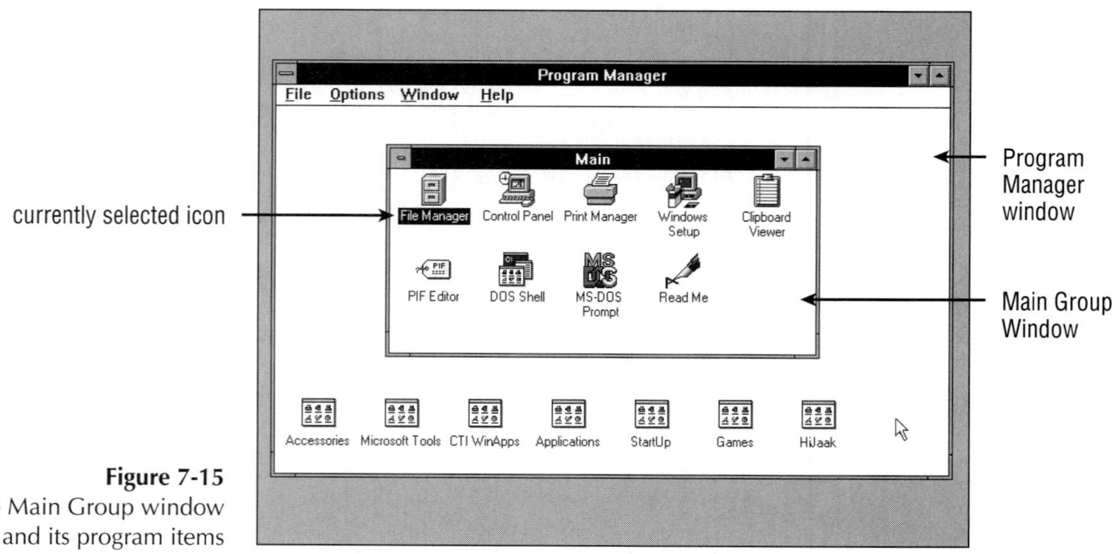

Figure 7-15
The Main Group window and its program items

3. Double-click the **File Manager icon**. Windows displays the File Manager window. The File Manager title bar displays a drive and file specification for the root directory of drive C. See Figure 7-16. If you do not see the specification C:*.* in the title bar, click the **up scroll arrow** until you see the icon for the root directory, then click the **root directory icon**. The File Manager contains drive icons, a directory tree window, and a contents list window, all of which look similar to the equivalent features in the DOS Shell. Using File Manager and its menus, you can perform disk, directory, and file operations from within Windows. (The next tutorial examines the File Manager in detail.)

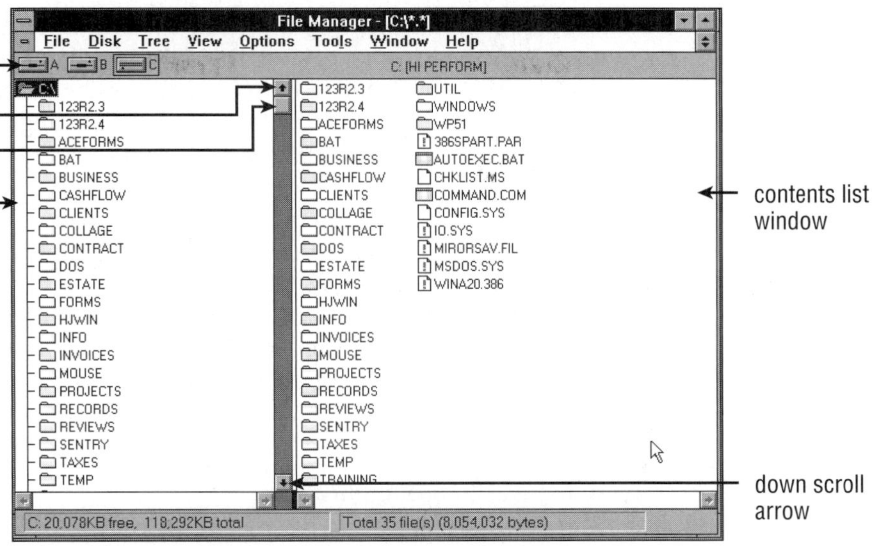

Figure 7-16
The File Manager window (your view will be different)

4. Double-click the **Control-menu box**. Windows closes the File Manager window and displays the Main Group window.
5. Double-click the **Control Panel icon**. Windows displays the Control Panel window. See Figure 7-17. The Main Group window is now behind the Control Panel window.

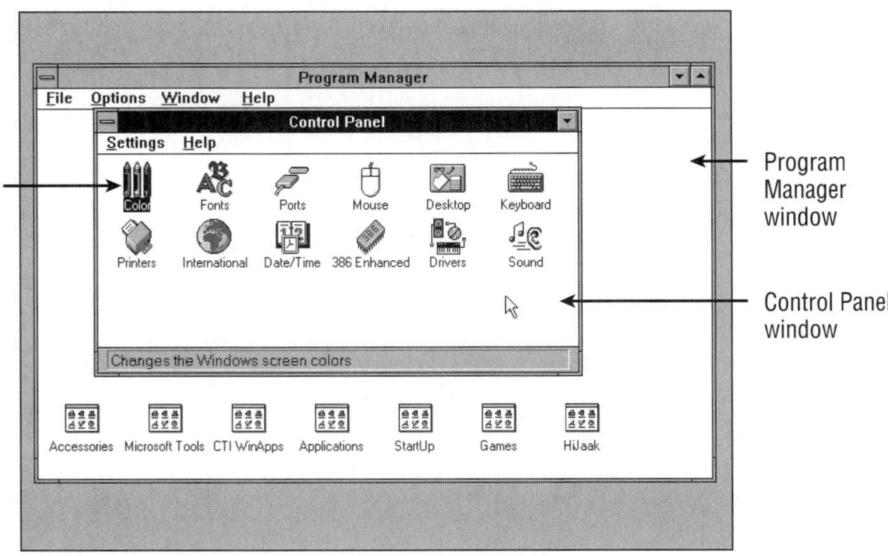

Figure 7-17
The Control Panel window

The Control Panel

The **Control Panel** contains program items for customizing and configuring Windows and your computer system. For example, you can use the Color application to select or design a color scheme for Windows, the Fonts application to specify a font for the Windows screen display, and the Desktop application to further customize the Windows desktop.

You can use the Ports application to configure your computer system's serial ports, the Mouse application to customize the use of the mouse, the Keyboard application to adjust the keyboard's operation, and the Printers application to install and configure printers. You can use the International application to specify and use international settings, such as for currency. If you have a 386 or 486, you will see international settings such as for currency as well as the 386 Enhanced icon. On a 386 or 486, you can use this application to specify the Windows operating mode, and you can install and configure device drivers for hardware components with the Drivers option. **Device drivers** are programs that allow Windows and DOS to work with specific types of hardware components that you add to your computer system.

The Date/Time application in the Control Panel group allows you to view or change the date and time on your computer system. Let's examine this option.

To use the Date/Time application:

1. Double-click the **Date/Time icon**. Windows displays the Date & Time dialog box. See Figure 7-18. If you want to change the date, you double-click the month, day, or year and then click the up or down triangle to the right of the date to adjust that component in one direction or the other.

Date/Time application window

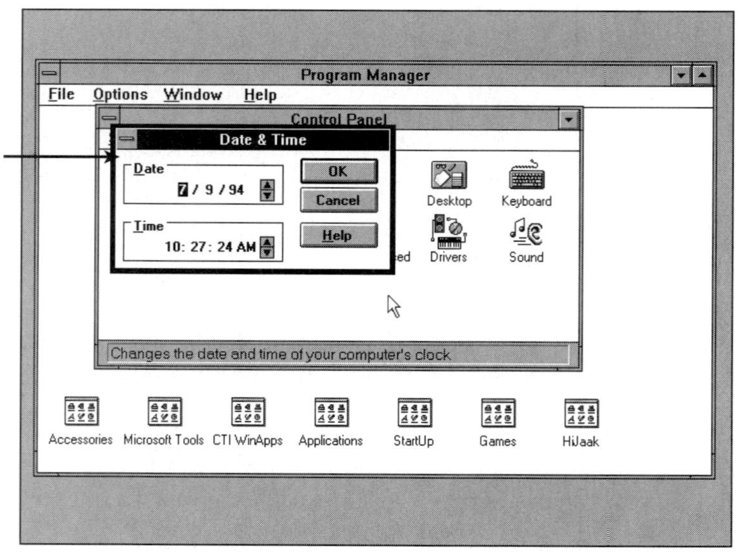

Figure 7-18 The Date & Time dialog box

2. Click **OK**. Windows closes the Date & Time dialog box.
3. Double-click the **Control-menu box** for the Control Panel. Windows closes the Control Panel window, and you see the Main Group window.

Using the MS-DOS Prompt

Occasionally you might want to work from the DOS prompt. If you select the MS-DOS Prompt icon in the Main Group, you temporarily exit to the DOS prompt so that you can issue a DOS command. Let's try it.

To use the MS-DOS Prompt:

1. Double-click the **MS-DOS Prompt icon**. Windows displays the DOS prompt, the DOS version, and information on how to return to Windows. When you exit Windows from the MS-DOS Prompt, Windows loads a second copy of the Command Interpreter so that you can work from the DOS prompt.
2. Type **TREE C:\ ¦ MORE** and press **[Enter]**. DOS displays the first part of the directory tree of drive C. Continue to press **[Spacebar]** or any other key until you view the entire directory tree.
3. Type **EXIT** and press **[Enter]**. You must return to Windows by entering the EXIT command. Now your screen returns to Windows.
4. Double-click the **Control-menu box** for the Main Group. Windows closes the Main Group window and displays the Program Manager window.

MOVING A WINDOW

If you need to adjust your view of a window or its position on the screen, you can easily move the window using the mouse. You click the window's title bar and drag the window to its new location. You can also move a window by using the Move command on the Control menu. You can use the same techniques to move dialog boxes.

Let's adjust the position of the Program Manager window.

To move a window using the mouse:

1. Click the **Program Manager title bar**, hold down the left mouse button, and drag the window to a new location on the screen. As you move the mouse pointer, you see an outline of the window that you are moving. See Figure 7-19.

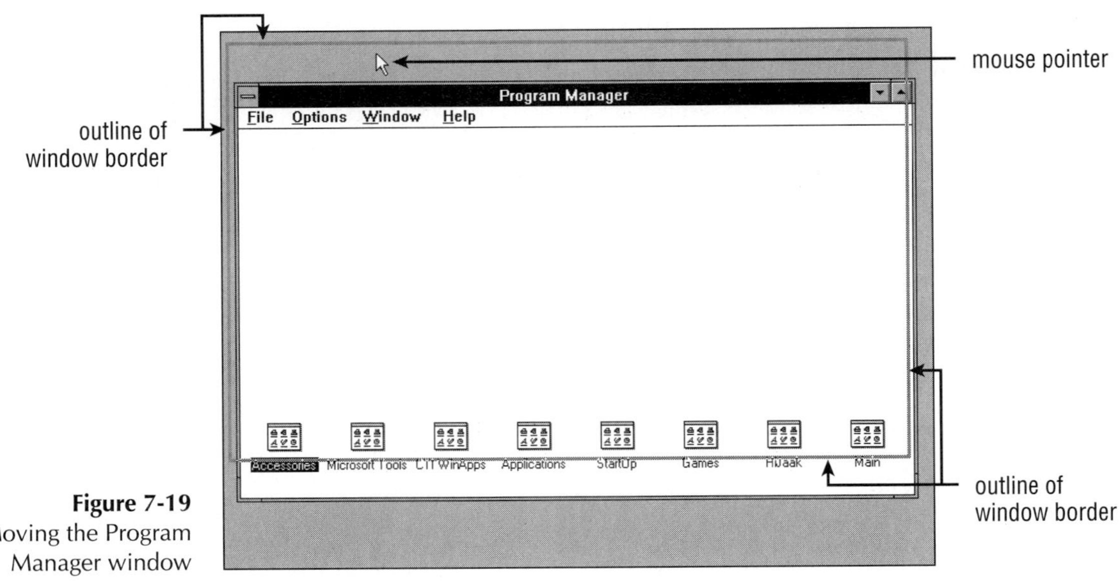

Figure 7-19
Moving the Program Manager window

2. Release the mouse button. The Program Manager window moves to its new location.

Now move the window using the Control menu.

3. Click the **Control-menu box**, then click **Move**. The mouse pointer changes to a four-headed arrow, and the window has an outline around it.
4. Use the keyboard arrow keys to move an outline of the window to a new location. Then press **[Enter]**.

CHANGING THE SIZE OF A WINDOW

You can also change the size of a window. You might need to enlarge a window to see all of the applications available in that window. Or you might want to reduce the size of a window so that you can open and view another window on the same screen.

Let's adjust the size of the Program Manager window.

To change the size of a window:

1. Position the mouse pointer on the right border of the Program Manager window. The mouse pointer changes to a double-headed arrow. See Figure 7-20.

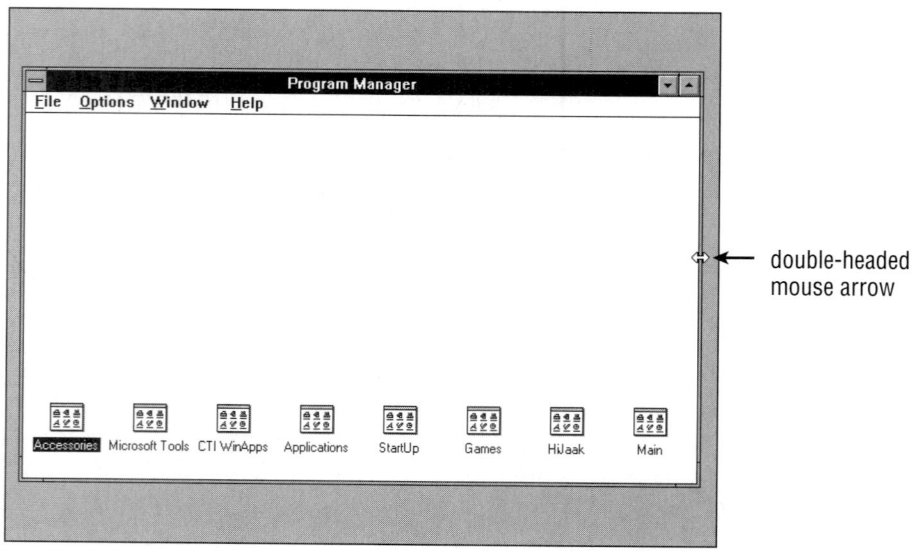

Figure 7-20
Positioning the mouse pointer on the right border of the Program Manager window

2. Click and hold the **left mouse button**. An outline of the window appears. Drag the double-headed arrow and window outline a short distance to the left. See Figure 7-21.

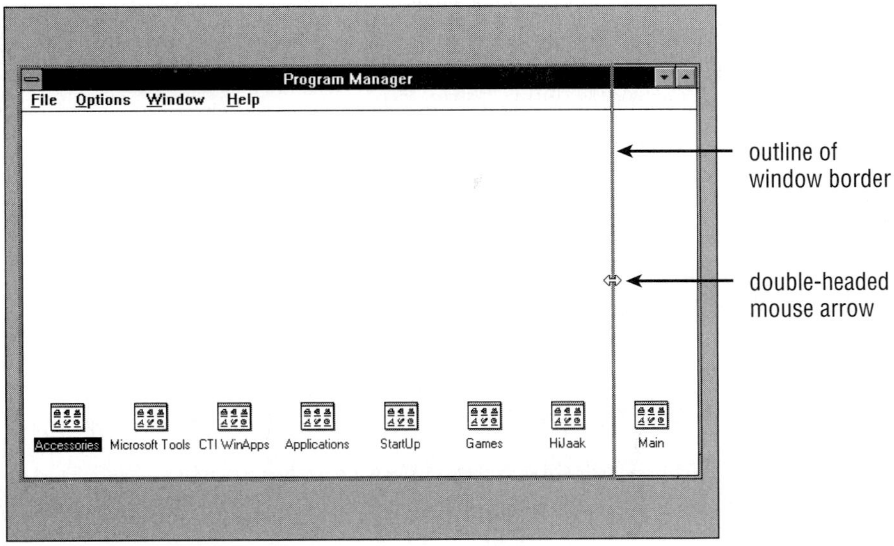

Figure 7-21
Dragging an outline of the Program Manager window

3. Release the mouse button. Windows adjusts the size of the window to match the outline that you specified. See Figure 7-22.

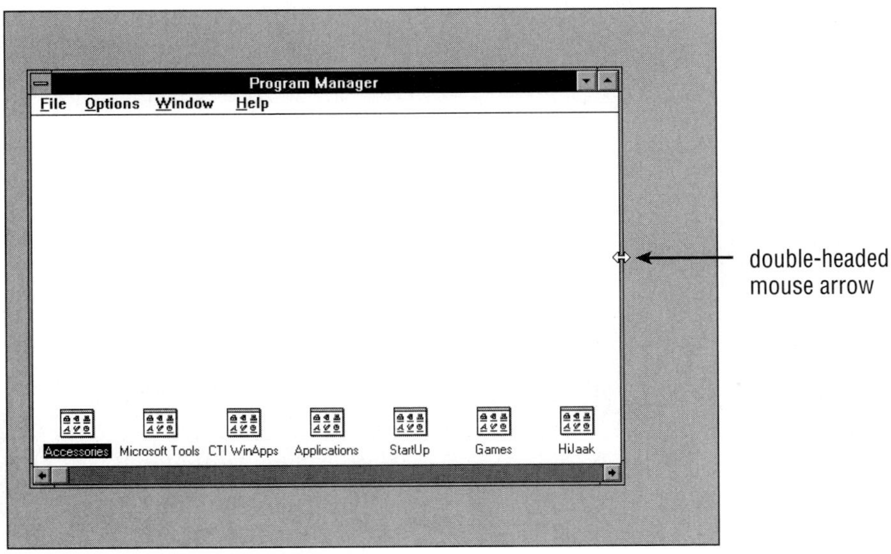

Figure 7-22
The Program Manager window adjusted for a new width

4. Position the mouse pointer on the bottom window border. The mouse pointer again changes to a double-headed arrow.
5. Click and hold the **left mouse button**. An outline of the window appears. Drag the double-headed arrow and window outline up a short distance, above the bottom row of icons.
6. Release the mouse button. Windows adjusts the size of the window to match the outline that you specified.
7. Click **Window**, then click **Arrange Icons**. Windows rearranges the icons within the window. See Figure 7-23.

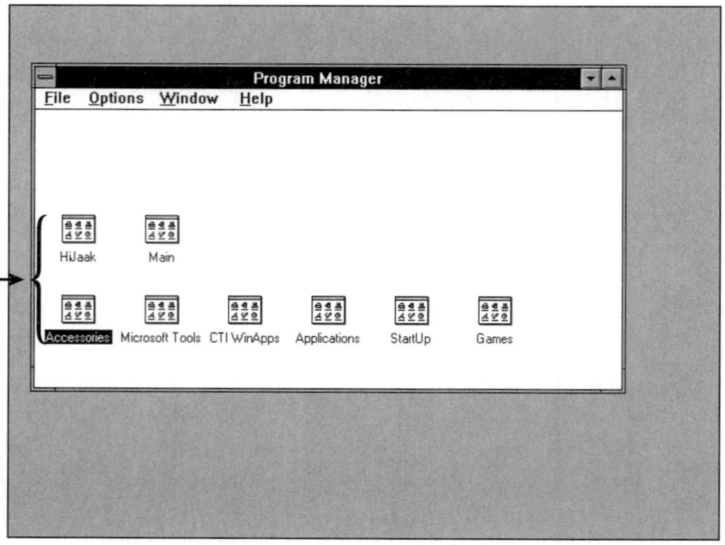

rearranged group icons

Figure 7-23
Rearranged icons in the Program Manager window

If you want to enlarge or decrease the width and height of a window at the same time, you position the mouse pointer on a window corner and drag the outline of the window until you redefine its size. Let's use this method to enlarge the Program Manager window.

To enlarge a window:

1. Position the mouse pointer on the bottom-right corner of the Program Manager window. See Figure 7-24. The mouse pointer changes to a double-headed arrow.

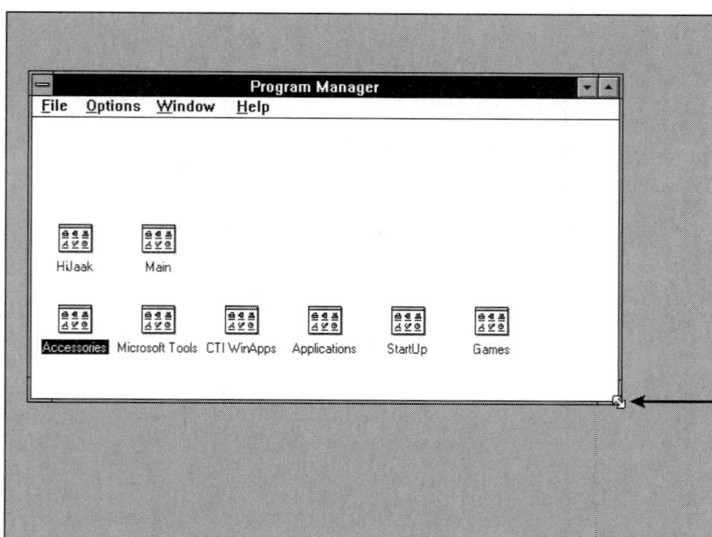

double-headed mouse arrow

Figure 7-24
Positioning the mouse pointer on the lower-right border

2. Click and hold the **left mouse button**. An outline of the window appears. Drag the double-headed arrow and window outline to the right and down. See Figure 7-25.

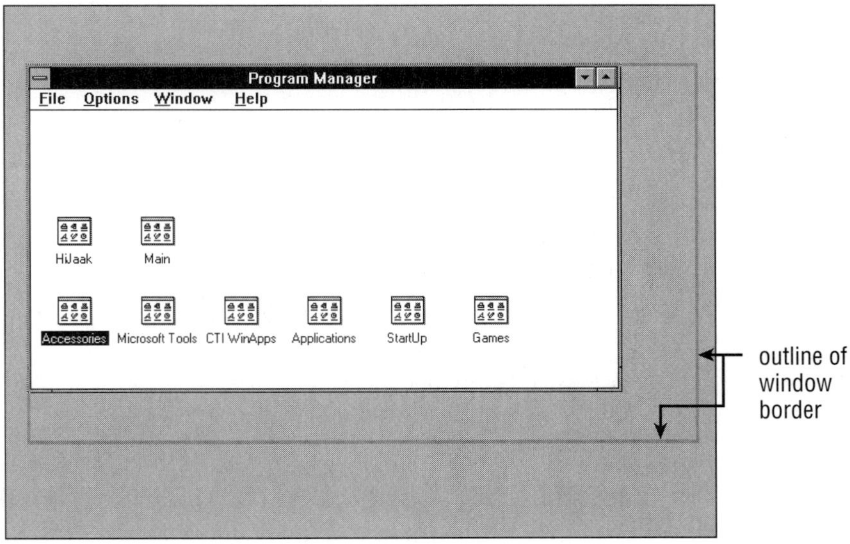

Figure 7-25
Enlarging the Program Manager window

3. Release the mouse button. Windows adjusts the size of the window to match the outline of the window that you specified and rearranges the icons.
4. Click **Window**, then click **Arrange Icons**. Windows rearranges the icons within the window.

CASCADING AND TILING WINDOWS

As you open one window after another, Windows overlaps the windows so that they appear similar to the arrangement of papers on a desktop. The **current window**, or **active window**, is the window with the highlighted title bar. By default, Windows displays only a part of each of the other windows that you previously opened. If you open multiple windows, one window may hide another window.

You can arrange the windows by cascading or tiling them. When you **cascade** windows, Windows places each window to the right and below the previous window. If you want to select a window, you click on that window. The contents of that window then appear above the other windows.

When you **tile** windows, Windows reduces the size of each window and arranges the windows side by side so that you can view each window at the same time. Although the windows are smaller and although you might not be able to view all the icons in a window, you can quickly switch from one window to another by clicking on the window you want to use. If you open new windows, Windows does not automatically cascade or tile the new windows.

You want to first tile and then cascade the Main and Accessories windows.

To open, tile, and then cascade the open windows:

1. If necessary, close all windows except Program Manager.
2. If necessary, click the **Maximize button** so that the Program Manager window occupies the full screen.
3. Click **Window**, then click **Arrange Icons**. Windows rearranges the icons within the window.
4. Double-click the **Main Group icon**. Windows displays the Main Group window and its program-item icons.
5. Double-click the **Accessories Group icon**. Windows opens and overlaps the Accessories Group window over the Main Group window. See Figure 7-26.

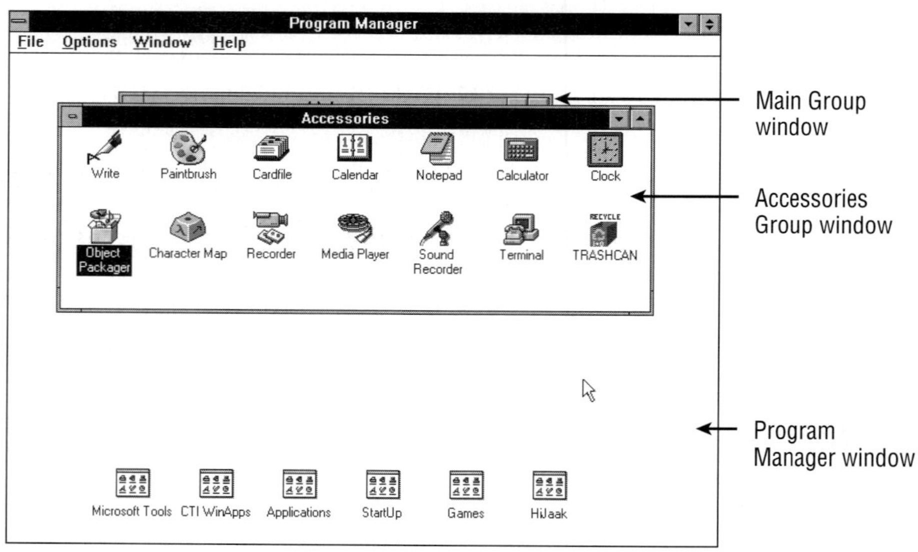

Figure 7-26
The Accessories Group window in front of the Main Group window

6. Click **Window**, then click **Tile**. Windows arranges the Main Group and Accessories Group windows side by side. See Figure 7-27. The Accessories Group window is the active, or current, window. Windows will add scroll bars at the bottom of a window or on the right side of a window if it cannot display all the icons in a window.

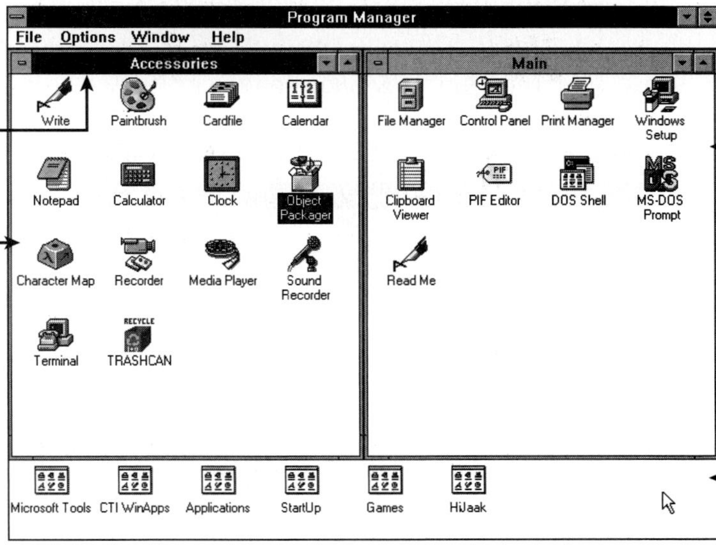

Figure 7-27
Tiling the Accessories Group and Main Group windows

7. Click **Window**, then click **Cascade**. Windows rearranges the windows so that they overlap one another. See Figure 7-28. Again, the Accessories Group window is the current window.

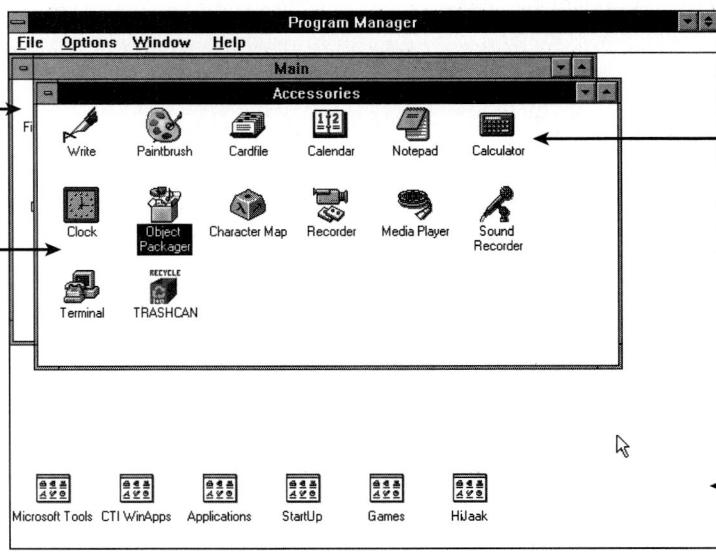

Figure 7-28
Cascading the Accessories Group and Main Group windows

Selecting a Window

You can change windows by clicking on the window you want to use or by using the Window menu to choose a window. Let's make the Main Group window the active window and then return to the Accessories Group window.

To select the Main Group window and make it active:

1. Click a **visible portion** of the Main Group window. Windows displays the Main Group window in front of the Accessories window. See Figure 7-29.

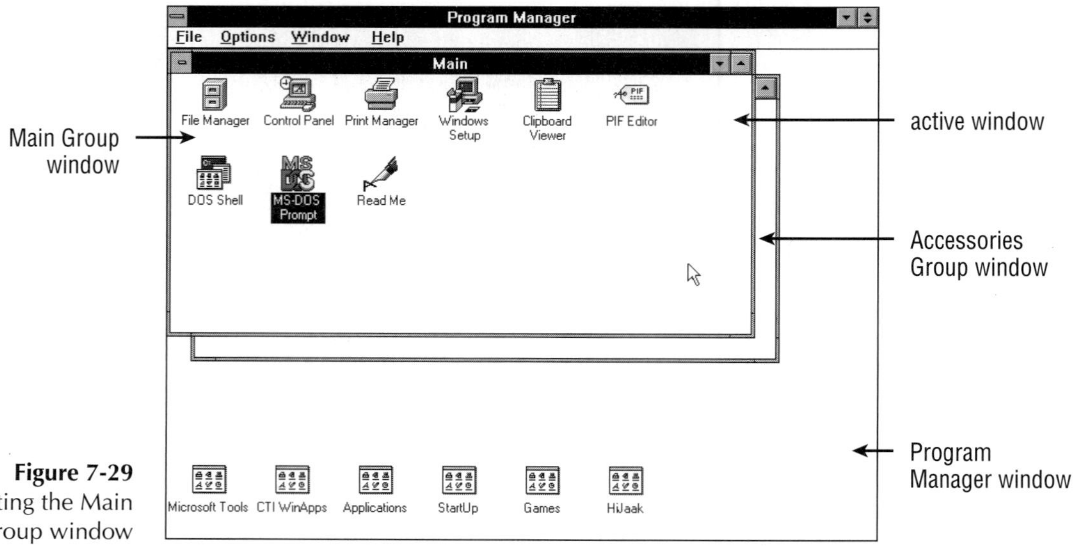

Figure 7-29
Selecting the Main Group window

Now select the Accessories Group window using the Window menu.

2. Click **Window**, then click **Accessories**. Windows displays the Accessories Group window in front of the Main Group window.

Next close both windows.

3. Double-click the **Control-menu box** for the Accessories Group window. Windows closes the Accessories Group window.
4. Double-click the **Control-menu box** for the Main Group window. Windows closes the Main Group window and you see the Program Manager window.

EXITING WINDOWS

You decide to exit Windows before you leave for lunch. You can exit Windows in one of three ways using the mouse. You can double-click the Program Manager Control-menu box. You can click the Program Manager Control-menu box and then select the Close command. Or you can select the Exit Windows command on the Program Manager's File menu.

To exit Windows:

1. If necessary, close all open windows by double-clicking each window's **Control-menu box**.
2. Double-click the Program Manager **Control-menu box**. Windows displays an Exit Windows dialog box and asks you to verify that you want to exit Windows.
3. Click **OK**. You exit Windows and return to the DOS prompt.

◆

SUMMARY

In this tutorial, you learned how to use and identify the components of the Windows 3.1 graphical user interface. You used the Control menu and the Minimize, Maximize, and Restore buttons to adjust the size of a window. You explored the command options available on the Program Manager File, Options, and Window menus. You examined how to use the Windows Help system.

You opened and examined applications in the Main Group, including the File Manager and the Control Panel. In the Control Panel, you examined the Date/Time application for viewing and changing the system date and time. You used the MS-DOS Prompt application to display the DOS prompt from within Windows, you executed a DOS command, and then returned to Windows.

You practiced the techniques for moving, sizing, tiling, cascading, and selecting windows.

Features Reference	
Windows Tools and Groups	
Accessories	A Program Manager group that contains a variety of Windows applications, such as a word processing application, a text editor, a drawing program, a calculator, a cardfile, a calendar, and a clock
Applications	A Program Manager group for installed software applications, such as word processing, electronic spreadsheets, and database applications
Control Panel	A group in the Main Group that contains applications for changing the configuration of your system
File Manager	An application in the Main Group for managing drives, directories, and files
Main Group	A Program Manager group that contains Windows system applications
MS-DOS Prompt	An application in the Main Group for temporarily exiting to the DOS prompt
Program Manager	A tool for starting applications and for organizing applications and files into groups
Windows Buttons	
Control-menu box	Displays the Control menu if you click; closes the open window if you double click
Maximize	Enlarges the window to fill the screen
Minimize	Reduces a window to an icon
Restore	Returns a window to its original size
Windows Commands	
File/Exit Windows	Exits Windows after all applications are closed
Help	Access the Windows Help system
Window/Arrange Icons	Arranges icons in even rows near the bottom of the Program Manager window
Window/Cascade	Arranges windows in an overlapping pattern
Window/Tile	Arranges windows side by side

QUESTIONS

1. What is Program Manager, and why is it important?
2. What is a group icon? Give an example.
3. What is File Manager, and why is it important?
4. What is a program-item icon? Give an example.
5. What is the Control-menu box, and how can you use it?
6. What does the Minimize button do?
7. What does the Maximize button do?
8. What does the Restore button do?
9. What does Auto Arrange on Program Manager's Options menu do?
10. How can you locate the definition for a Windows term?
11. How can you locate help information on a specific topic?
12. Name two important options available in the Main Group?
13. What is the Control Panel, and how can you use it? Give an example.
14. How can you set the date and time on your computer system from Windows?
15. What element of a window do you select when you want to move a window? To resize a window?
16. How can you enter commands from the DOS prompt without exiting Windows?
17. How do you move a window with the mouse?
18. How do you move a window with the Control menu?
19. How can you widen a window?
20. How can you adjust the width and height of a window at the same time?
21. What does Windows do when you tile windows?
22. What does Windows do when you cascade windows?
23. How do you reduce a window to an icon?
24. What other DOS graphical user interface is similar to Windows?
25. If you have not enabled Auto Arrange from the Program Manager's Options menu, how can you rearrange icons when you change the size of a window?
26. Name two ways to exit Windows.
27. How do you select a window behind the current window?
28. If you use the MS-DOS Prompt icon to exit Windows temporarily, how do you return to Windows from the MS-DOS Prompt?
29. How can you identify the current or active window?
30. What is the difference between a window and an icon?

TUTORIAL ASSIGNMENTS

1. **Using Windows Help**: Use Windows Help to answer the following questions.
   a. What two steps are required to start an application from a group?
   b. How can you arrange windows in an overlapping pattern?
   c. What is the function of the Control menu?
   d. What is a group?
   e. What is an icon?
   f. What is a program item?
   Close Windows Help and exit Windows.
2. **Sizing Windows**: Perform the following operations and list the steps or commands that you use.
   a. Load Windows.
   Use the mouse to:
   b. Minimize the Program Manager window.
   c. Restore the Program Manager window.
   d. Maximize the Program Manager window.
   e. Restore the Program Manager window to its original size.
   Use the Control menu to:
   f. Minimize the Program Manager window.
   g. Restore the Program Manager window.
   h. Maximize the Program Manager window.
   i. Restore the Program Manager window to its original size.
   Close all open windows and exit Windows.
3. **Adjusting Windows**: Perform the following operations and list the steps and commands that you use.
   a. Load Windows.
   b. Maximize the size of the Program Manager window.
   c. Rearrange the icons in the Program Manager window.
   d. Open the Main Group.
   e. Maximize the size of the Main Group window.
   f. Open the Applications window.
   Close all open windows and exit Windows.
4. **Moving Windows**: Perform the following operations and list the steps or commands that you use.
   a. Load Windows.
   b. Open the Main Group.
   c. Open the Accessories Group.
   d. Reduce the size of the Accessories Group window.
   e. Move the Accessories Group window so that you can see the Main Group window.
   f. Reduce the size of the Main Group window.
   g. Move the Main Group and Accessories Group windows so that they are side by side in the middle of the screen.
   Close all open windows and exit Windows.

5. **Arranging Windows**: Perform the following operations and list the steps and commands you use.
   a. Open the Main Group.
   b. Open the Accessories Group.
   c. Tile the windows.
   d. Maximize the Program Manager window.
   e. Open the Applications Group.
   f. Tile the windows.
   g. Cascade the windows.
   h. Select the Main Group.

   Close all open windows and exit Windows.

TUTORIAL **8**

Using File Manager

OBJECTIVES

In this tutorial you will learn to:

- Open and use File Manager
- Format a diskette
- Copy the contents of a diskette
- Change drives
- Expand the directory tree
- Select a directory
- Change the details displayed with filenames
- Modify the directory structure of a disk
- Rename a directory
- Create a directory
- Copy files from one directory to another
- Move directories

The director of your department informs you that one of your coworkers has resigned so that he can return to school. She asks you if you want to switch from part-time to full-time employment and assume the client responsibilities of the departing coworker. You tell her that you are definitely interested in a full-time position and in increasing your responsibilities and opportunities.

You ask your coworker for his client diskette so that you can make a copy of the diskette and familiarize yourself with his client files before he leaves. Because time is an important factor in completing client jobs, you want to ensure that the directories and files on his client diskette are organized in a manner that is similar to the way you currently organize your own client files.

◆

USING FILE MANAGER

Because you and other staff members have switched to the Windows operating environment, you decide to use File Manager to examine your coworker's client diskette.

File Manager is a Windows tool for viewing and organizing directories and files on a diskette or hard disk. You can use File Manager for the common types of operations that you perform at the DOS prompt and in the DOS Shell, such as creating, renaming, moving, and removing directories; copying and moving files from diskette to diskette or from directory to directory; renaming and deleting files; and viewing and printing documents.

Before you examine your coworker's client files, you want to format a diskette and make a copy of his client diskette using File Manager.

To get started:

1. If you are at the DOS prompt for drive C, type **WIN** and press **[Enter]**. If your computer setup is different, follow the instructions provided by your instructor or technical support person for starting Windows.
2. After you load Windows, close all open windows except Program Manager.
3. Double-click the **Main Group icon**. Windows displays the Main Group window. See Figure 8-1. The group icons in your Program Manager window and the application icons in your Main Group window will probably be different.

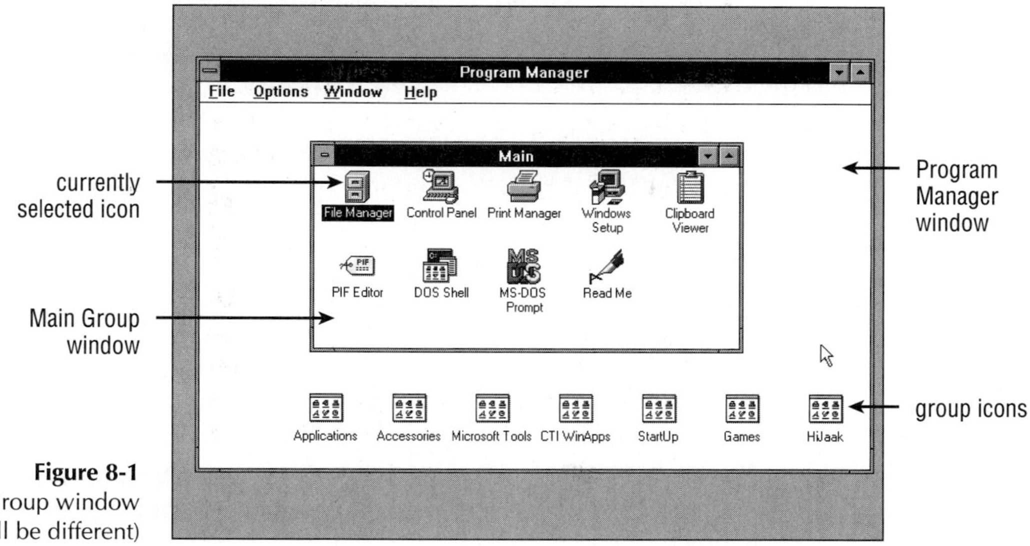

Figure 8-1
The Main Group window (yours will be different)

4. Double-click the **File Manager icon**. Windows displays the File Manager window and a directory window.
5. If File Manager does not occupy the full window, click the **Maximize button** for the File Manager window. See Figure 8-2.

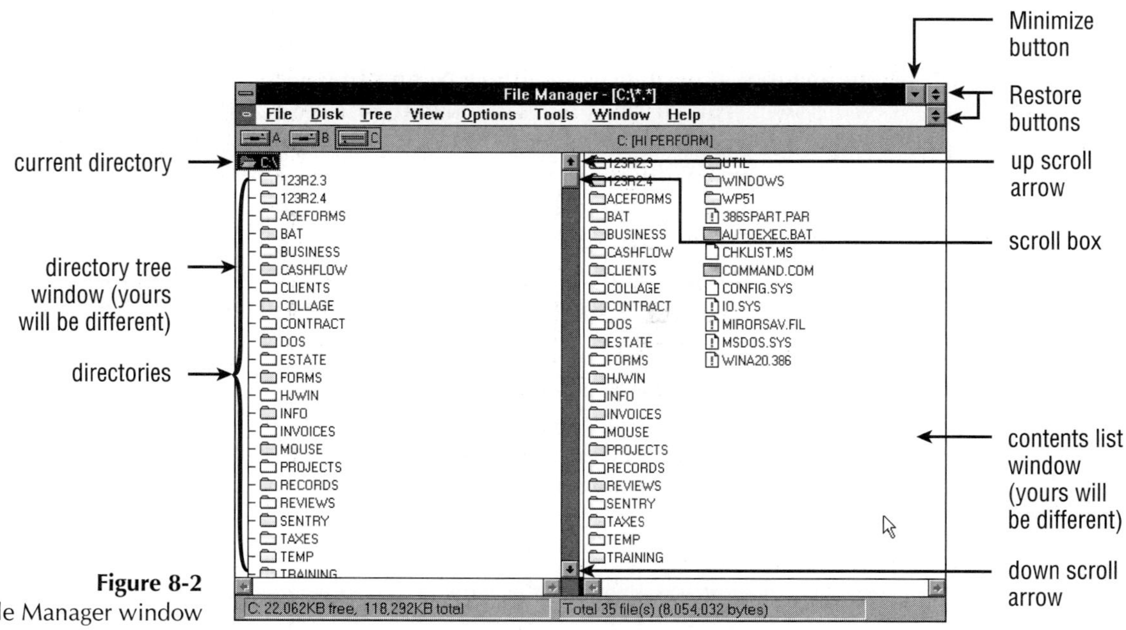

Figure 8-2
The File Manager window

6. If the window for drive C showing the directory structure and filenames does not occupy the full window, click the **Maximize button** for this window.

File Manager contains menus for managing drives, diskettes, directories, and files. The File Manager window contains a title bar with the path of the current directory, a Control-menu box, and Minimize and Maximize buttons. Like the DOS Shell, the File Manager window contains a drive icon for each disk drive (including network drives) on your computer, a directory tree window that shows the directory structure of your hard disk drive or a diskette, and a window that shows the contents of the current directory. Your directory tree will be different from that shown in Figure 8-2.

In the **directory tree window**, file folder icons represent directories. Also, only the first directory level below the root directory will be displayed. File Manager represents the current directory in the directory tree window as an open file folder. In Figure 8-2, the current directory is C:\.

The **contents list window** to the right of the directory tree window is equivalent to the DOS Shell's file list window. In this window, you see file folder icons for subdirectories positioned below the current directory; program file icons, such as the one for COMMAND.COM; and file icons, such as the one for IO.SYS, that appear as sheets of paper with the upper-right corner folded down. Your contents list window will be different from the one shown in Figure 8-2.

Each of these windows has a set of scroll bars for adjusting the screen view onto the window.

As you use File Manager in this tutorial, you will discover that drive, directory, and file operations are performed more easily from Windows than from DOS. However, it is important to understand how to perform these operations from DOS. Windows 3.1 is an operating *environment*, not an operating system. Even with Windows, DOS is required to boot your computer system and to manage its resources. After you load DOS, you can load Windows. Windows then works in conjunction with DOS, and DOS provides underlying support for Windows. The drive, file, and directory organization evident in Windows depends on the ability of DOS to manage drive, files, and directories. Furthermore, Windows does not have menus for all of the DOS commands. If you work on computers that do not have Windows, you must know how to perform drive, directory, and file operations from DOS.

The obvious value of Windows is that it simplifies the task of managing your computer and its resources through a friendly and easy-to-use interface.

FORMATTING A DISKETTE WITH FILE MANAGER

To begin, you must format two diskettes using the File Manager Disk menu. The Disk menu provides a more friendly user interface and lets you select the options that you need for formatting a diskette—including a disk drive, a formatting capacity, and a volume label.

To format a diskette:

1. Insert your Tutorial Disk into a diskette drive.
2. Click **Disk**. File Manager displays the Disk menu. See Figure 8-3. From this menu, in addition to formatting a diskette, you also can copy a diskette, assign a volume label to a diskette, make a system or boot diskette, and select a disk drive. You might even see other options, such as one for network connections.

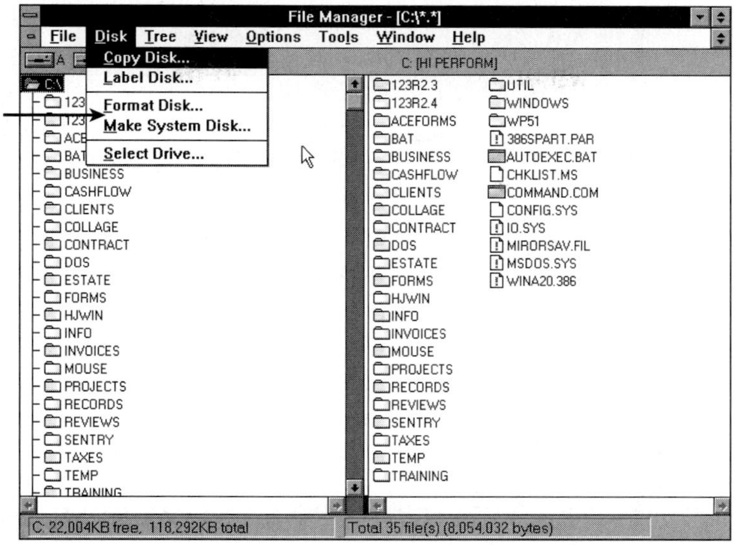

Figure 8-3
The File Manager Disk menu

3. Click **Format Disk**. File Manager displays the Format Disk dialog box. See Figure 8-4. The Disk In list box shows the default drive for formatting, and the Capacity list box shows the default formatting capacity (yours might be different) for the default drive.

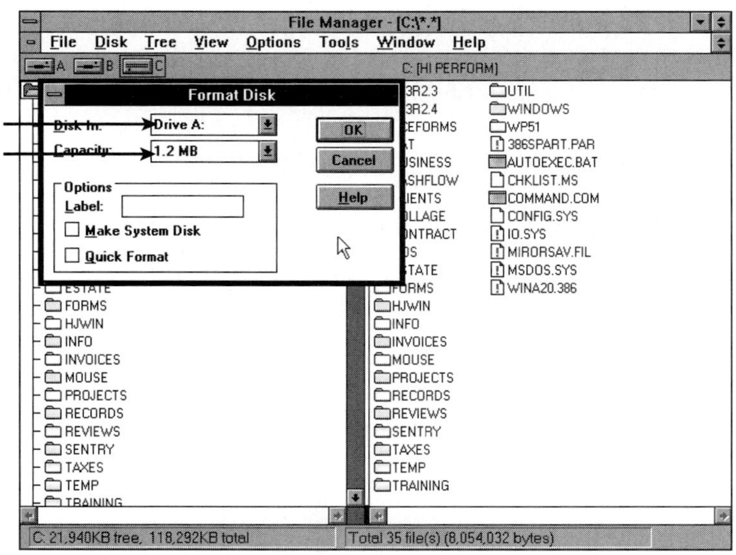

Figure 8-4
The Format Disk dialog box

4. If you need to specify another drive, click the **down arrow** to the right of the Disk In list box. File Manager displays a drop-down list box. See Figure 8-5. Click the **drive** that you want to use. File Manager displays the drive you selected in the Disk In list box.

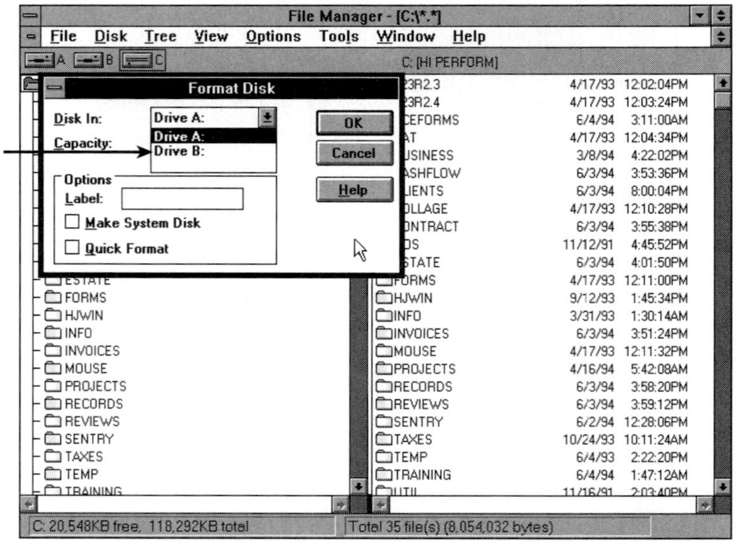

Figure 8-5
Selecting a disk drive from the Disk In drop-down list box

5. If you need to specify another format capacity, such as 720K for a double-density 3½-inch diskette, click the **down arrow** to the right of the Capacity list box. File Manager displays a drop-down list box. Click the **storage capacity** that you want to use. File Manager displays the new format capacity in the Capacity list box.

6. Click the **Label text box** to specify a volume label. The *insertion point cursor* appears as a flashing vertical bar, and the mouse pointer appears as an *I-bar*. See Figure 8-6.

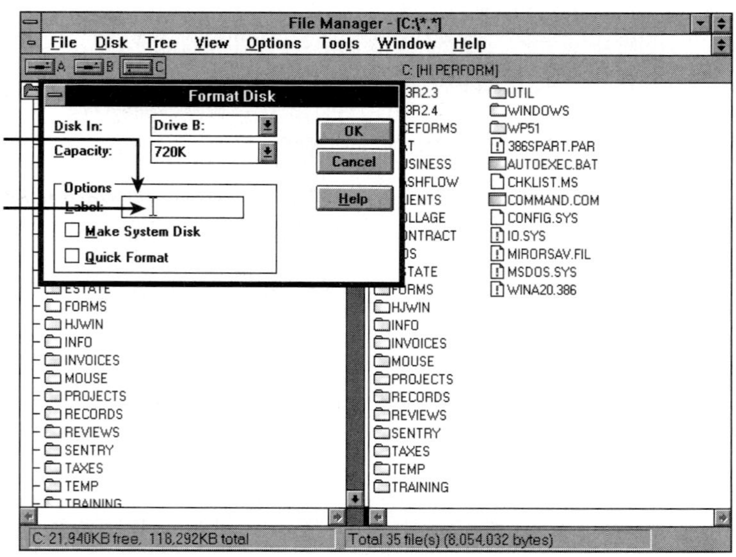

Figure 8-6
Selecting the Label text box

7. Type **BUSINESS** in the Label text box. Then click **OK**. File Manager displays a Confirm Format Disk dialog box and warns that it will erase all data on the disk.
8. Click **Yes**. File Manager displays a Formatting Disk dialog box. This dialog box shows the percentage of formatting completed. If you want to stop the formatting for any reason, click the **Cancel button**. When the formatting is complete, this dialog box informs you that File Manager is creating the root directory on the formatted diskette. It then displays a Format Complete dialog box with information on the total diskette space and available space, and asks if you want to format another diskette.

You need to format another diskette because you want to make a backup copy.

To format another diskette:

1. Remove the Tutorial Disk from the diskette drive, and insert your Exercise Disk.
2. Click **Yes**. File Manager displays the Format Disk dialog box. File Manager will use the same settings that you specified for the first diskette.
3. Click **OK**. File Manager displays the Confirm Format dialog box.
4. Click **Yes**. File Manager formats the diskette. When the formatting is complete, File Manager displays another Format Complete dialog box and asks if you want to format another diskette.
5. Click **No**. File Manager closes the dialog box and the Disk menu.

COPYING THE CONTENTS OF A DISKETTE WITH FILE MANAGER

Next you want to copy the contents of your coworker's diskette onto your newly formatted diskettes. To do so, you will use the Copy Disk option on the Disk menu. Making a duplicate copy of a diskette is easier with Windows than with DOS. If you use the DISKCOPY command at the DOS prompt in DOS 5.0 or 6.0, you must swap the source and target diskettes several times. In Windows, you insert the source and target diskettes only once. Not only is it easier and faster, but it is also less confusing and there is less chance for error.

Your instructor will prepare a Windows Data Disk (which contains the contents of your coworker's diskette) for you to copy. This Data Disk contains a directory structure similar to the one used in previous tutorials. You will need to borrow this diskette so that you can make duplicate copies of it.

To copy the Windows Data Disk onto your Tutorial Disk:

1. Insert the Windows Data Disk into the appropriate drive.
2. Click **Disk**, then click **Copy Disk**. File Manager displays the Copy Disk dialog box. See Figure 8-7. The default settings for the source and destination diskettes are shown in list boxes. If you need to change the drive for the source diskette, click the **down arrow** to the right of the Source In list box. Then click the **drive** you want to use from the drop-down list. If you need to change the drive for the destination diskette, click the **down arrow** to the right of the Destination In list box. Then click the **drive** you want to use from the drop-down list.

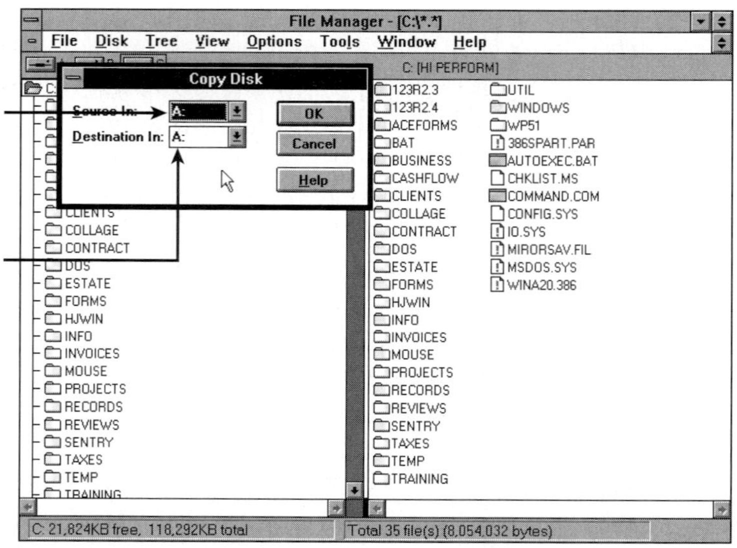

Figure 8-7
The Copy Disk dialog box

3. Click **OK**. If File Manager displays a Confirm Copy dialog box and warns that it will erase all data on the destination diskette, click **YES**. File Manager displays a Copy Disk dialog box that prompts you to insert the source diskette.
4. If necessary, insert your Windows Data Disk into the drive you specified.
5. Click **OK**. File Manager displays a Copying Disk dialog box that shows the percentage of formatting completed. When File Manager shows 49% completed, it has copied the source diskette. File Manager then displays a Copy Disk dialog box that prompts you to insert the destination diskette.

6. Remove the Windows Data Disk from the diskette drive, and insert your Tutorial Disk in the drive. Click **OK**. After the disk copy is complete, File Manager closes the dialog box and the Disk menu.
7. Remove your Tutorial Disk from the diskette drive, and insert the Windows Data Disk in the drive.
8. Repeat the same process to copy the contents of the Windows Data Disk to your Exercise Disk.
9. Remove your Exercise Disk, and insert your Tutorial Disk into the diskette drive.
10. Return the Windows Data Disk that you borrowed.

SELECTING A DRIVE WITH FILE MANAGER

Next you want to examine your copy of your coworker's client diskette. You can select a drive by clicking on the appropriate drive icon or by using the Disk menu and the Select Drive option. The current drive is shown in outline in the drive icon window.

To change drives:

1. Click the **drive icon** for the drive that contains your Tutorial Disk. File Manager updates the directory tree window and the contents list window. See Figure 8-8. The current directory is the root directory of the drive you selected, A:\ or B:\. The contents list window shows the directories in the root directory.

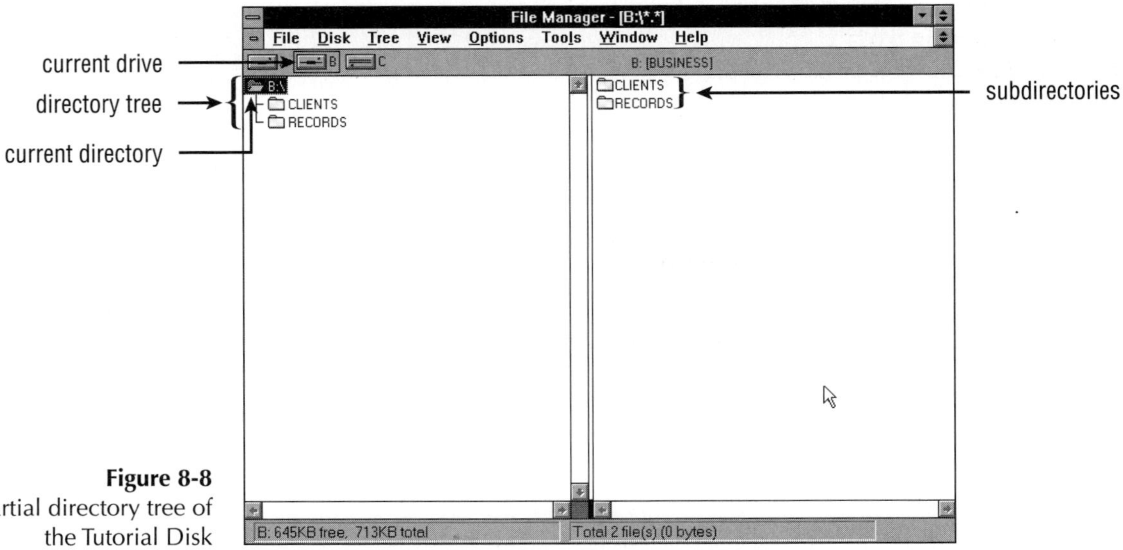

Figure 8-8
A partial directory tree of the Tutorial Disk

EXPANDING THE DIRECTORY TREE

Your coworker has organized his client diskette so that there are two directories positioned below the root directory—one named CLIENTS for client files and the other named RECORDS for business files. You want to expand the directory tree so that you can see the complete directory structure of this diskette. When you select a drive, File Manager shows you only the first level of subdirectories located below the root directory. You can use the Tree menu to expand the directory tree.

To view the entire directory structure:

1. Click **Tree**. File Manager displays the Tree menu. The Tree menu and its options are similar to those in the DOS Shell. You can expand one more level of the directory tree, expand one branch of the directory tree, expand the entire directory tree, or collapse a branch of the directory tree. You also can specify if you want File Manager to indicate branches of the directory tree that could be expanded.
2. Click **Expand All**. File Manager displays the entire directory tree of your Tutorial Disk. See Figure 8-9.

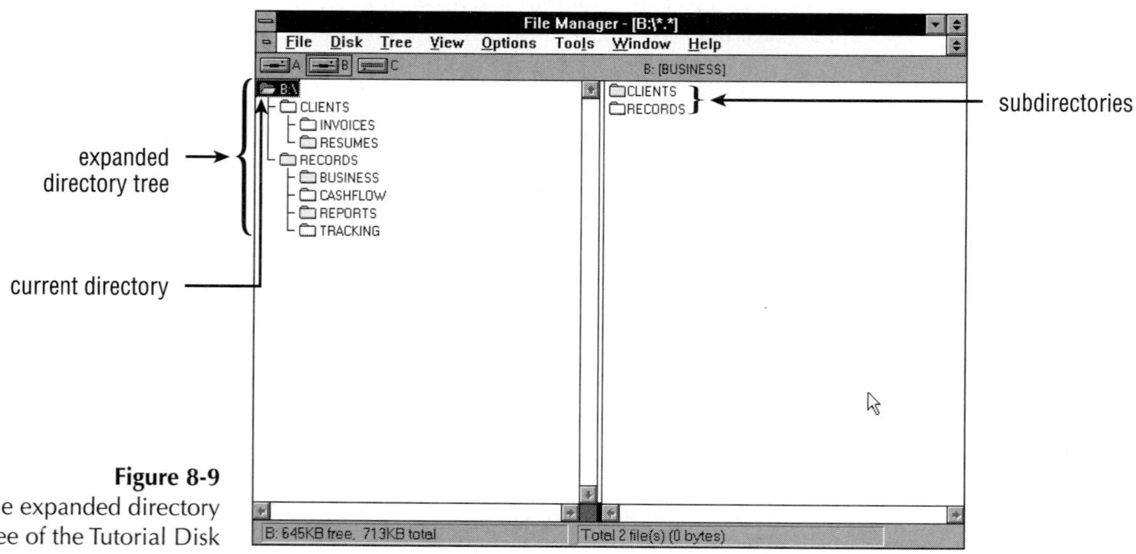

Figure 8-9
The expanded directory tree of the Tutorial Disk

SELECTING A DIRECTORY

You want to examine the files in the two client directories. The process is the same as in the DOS Shell. To select a directory, you click the directory folder icon or the directory name.

To select the INVOICES subdirectory:

1. Click the **INVOICES directory name** in the directory tree window. File Manager highlights the directory name and updates the contents list to show the files in this directory. See Figure 8-10.

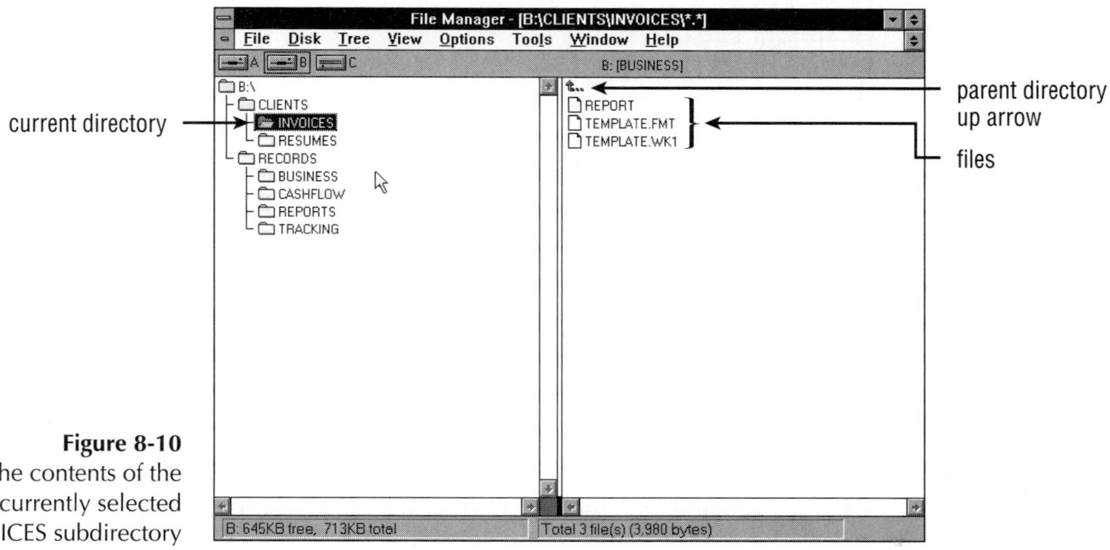

Figure 8-10
The contents of the currently selected INVOICES subdirectory

Now select the RESUMES directory.

2. Click **RESUMES** in the directory tree window. File Manager highlights this directory name and updates the contents list to show the files in this directory.

ORGANIZING THE DISPLAY OF FILENAMES

You want to see more detail on the client files than just the filename—you want to view the sizes, dates, and times of the files. By default, File Manager lists directories and files in alphabetical order in the contents list window. You can change the order of the listing and specify more detail with the View menu.

To change the view in the contents list window:

1. Click **View**. File Manager displays the View menu. See Figure 8-11. Check marks next to specific menu options indicate the current settings for displaying filenames in the contents list window.

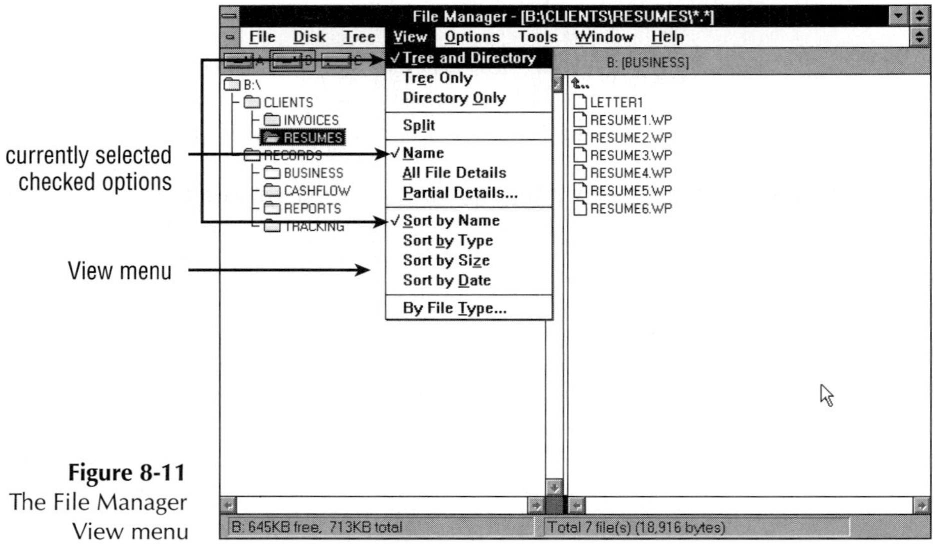

Figure 8-11
The File Manager View menu

2. If your View menu contains check marks next to options other than those shown in Figure 8-11, click **Tree and Directory**, click **View**, and click **Name**, and then click **View** and click **Sort by Name**.

The first three options on the View menu determine which window or windows you see. The check mark next to Tree and Directory instructs File Manager to display a directory tree window and a contents list window. You could adjust the display with the next two options to show only the directory tree window (Tree Only) or only the contents list window (Directory Only).

The Split option allows you to adjust the relative sizes of the two windows. The next three options allow you to determine how much information is displayed on files. The check mark next to Name instructs File Manager to display only the names of files. You can also choose to display all file details, or, by selecting Partial Details, choose only the file details you want.

The next four options determine the sort order of the files. The check mark next to Sort by Name instructs File Manager to list filenames in alphabetical order by name and extension. You can also quickly organize files by type (file extension), size (from the largest to the smallest), or date (from the most recent to the oldest).

The last option, By File Type, allows you to limit the display in the contents list window to specific groups of files—directories, programs, documents, and other types of files. You can also specify if you want to see system and hidden files. **System files** include the files that contain the DOS operating system. **Hidden files** are files that DOS does not display in a directory listing, such as the operating system files.

If you instruct File Manager to view all file details, it will display file sizes, dates, times, and attributes. **File attributes** are special characteristics assigned to a file by DOS. Each attribute is represented by a code—S for System file, H for Hidden file, R for Read-Only file, and A for Archive. You can retrieve Read-Only files, but you cannot modify or delete these files. DOS assigns the **Archive attribute** to files that you created or modified since your last backup.

Let's view all the details on these files.

To view all file details:

1. If necessary, click **View** to display the View menu. Click **All File Details**. File Manager displays details next to the filenames. See Figure 8-12. If your screen view does not show five columns of file information, including the filenames, you can adjust the width of this window. In Figure 8-12 only four columns of information are displayed.

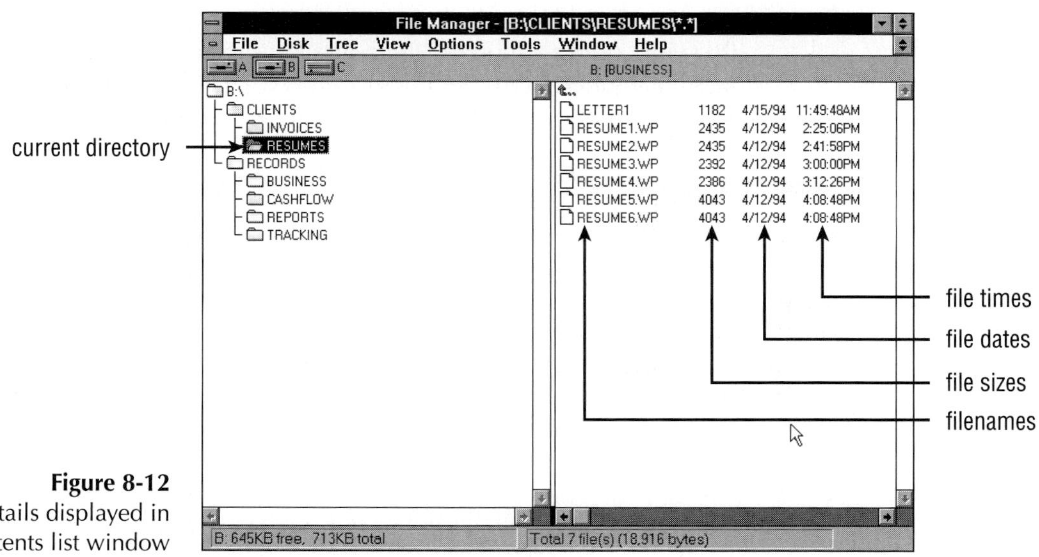

Figure 8-12
The file details displayed in the contents list window

2. If you need to expand the width of the contents list window, position the mouse pointer on the **split bar**—the thin vertical bar to the left of the filenames in the contents list window and to the right of the vertical scroll bar for the directory tree window. See Figure 8-13. The mouse pointer changes to a vertical bar with arrows pointing in both directions.

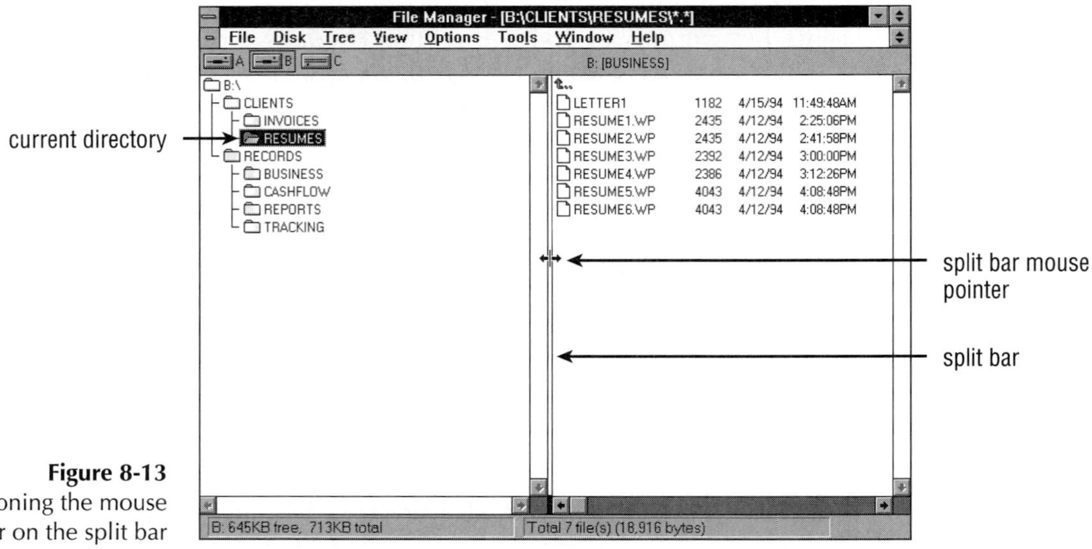

Figure 8-13
Positioning the mouse pointer on the split bar

3. Press and hold the **left mouse button** as you drag the split bar to the left a short distance. As you move the split bar, it appears as a dark vertical bar. Then release the left mouse button. File Manager adjusts the widths of the two windows, and you should be able to see all five columns of information. See Figure 8-14. If necessary, repeat Steps 2 and 3 to further adjust the width of this window. The last column in the contents list window lists file attributes. The Archive attribute indicates that these files are newly created or modified files that have not been backed up.

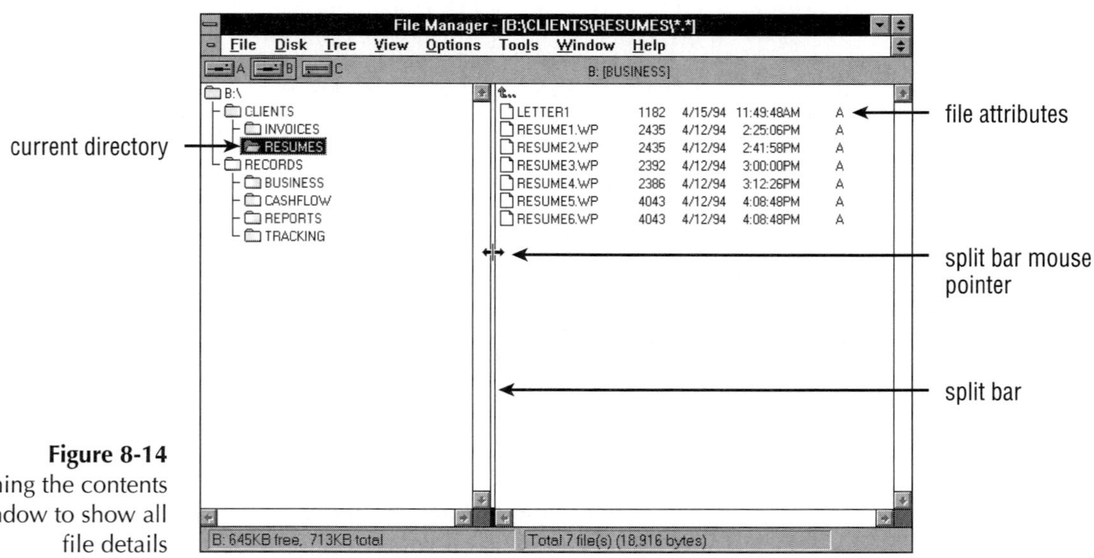

Figure 8-14
Widening the contents list window to show all file details

For your daily needs, you do not need to view file attributes. However, you may need to view more complex directory trees with more directory levels. You decide to adjust the display of file details. This time you also want to try the Split option on the View menu to adjust the width of the contents list window, as you did earlier using the split bar.

To view only the file sizes, dates, and times:

1. Click **View**, then click **Partial Details....** File Manager displays a Partial Details dialog box. Each of the four options—size, date, time, and file attributes—are checked.
2. Click the **check box** next to File Attributes. File Manager removes the "X" from this check box. See Figure 8-15.

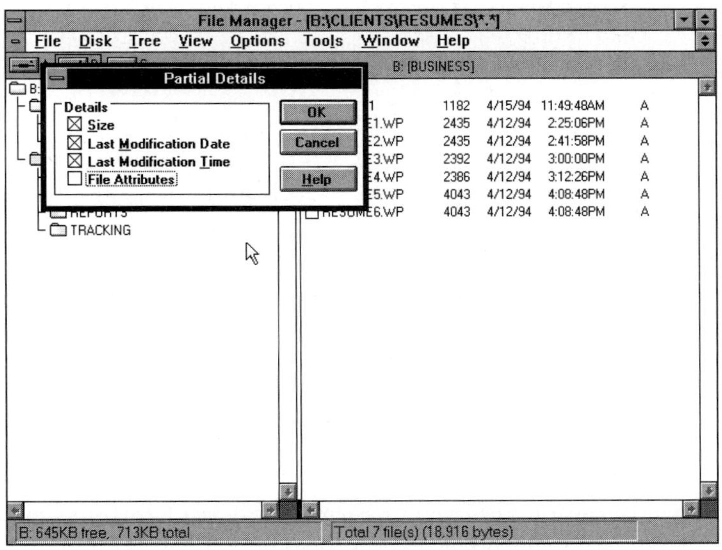

Figure 8-15
The Partial Details dialog box

3. Click **OK**. File Manager closes this dialog box and updates the display of the contents list window. You no longer see file attributes.

Now adjust the width of the contents list window again.

4. Click **View**, then click **Split**. File Manager displays a dark wide vertical bar with the mouse pointer next to it. See Figure 8-16. This split bar is easier to see and use. As you slide the mouse across the desktop, the split bar moves in the corresponding direction.

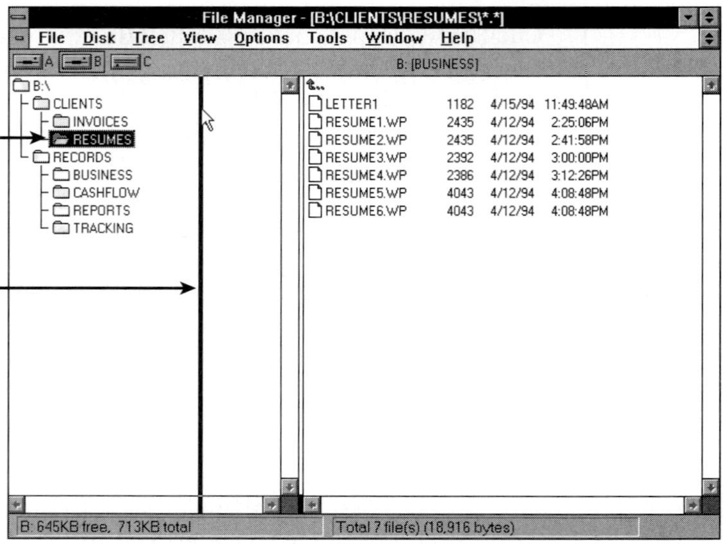

Figure 8-16
A split bar displayed by the Split option on the View menu

5. Drag the **split bar** to the right so that it is positioned where you want to separate the directory tree and contents list windows, then click the **left mouse button**. File Manager adjusts the width of this window.

6. If necessary, repeat Steps 4 and 5 to adjust the view so you see the file details that you specified.

RENAMING AND COPYING FILES

You need to copy the standard cover letter stored in the file named LETTER1 so that later you can produce a variation of this letter for résumés. You decide to rename it to COVER1.LTR with the Rename option on the File menu, and then copy it using the Copy option on the File menu. When you copy files, Windows automatically prompts you if you attempt to copy over an existing file.

To rename a file:

1. Click **LETTER1** in the contents list window. File Manager highlights this filename, and an outline appears around the current directory in the directory tree window. See Figure 8-17.

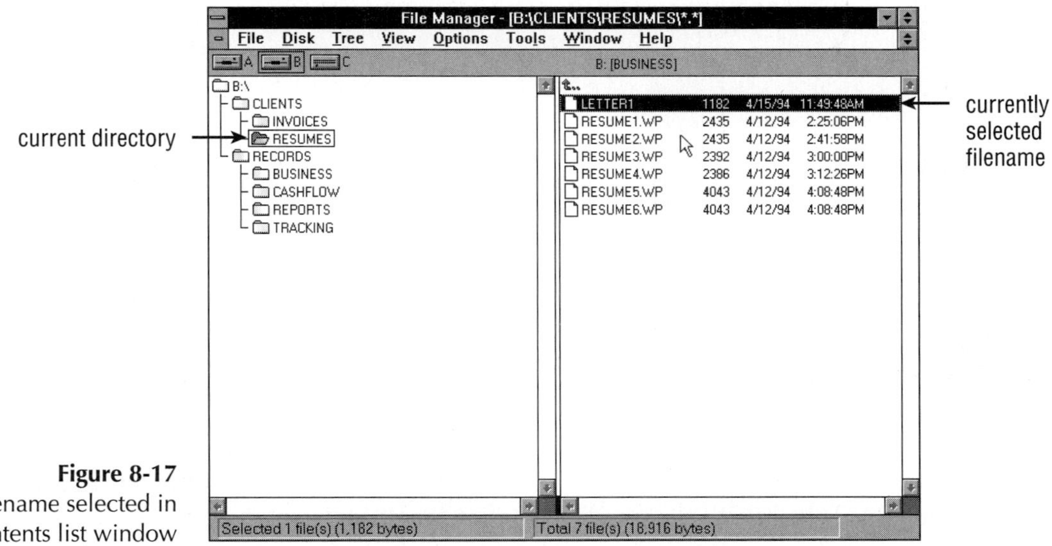

Figure 8-17
A filename selected in the contents list window

2. Click **File**, then click **Rename**. File Manager displays a Rename dialog box. See Figure 8-18.

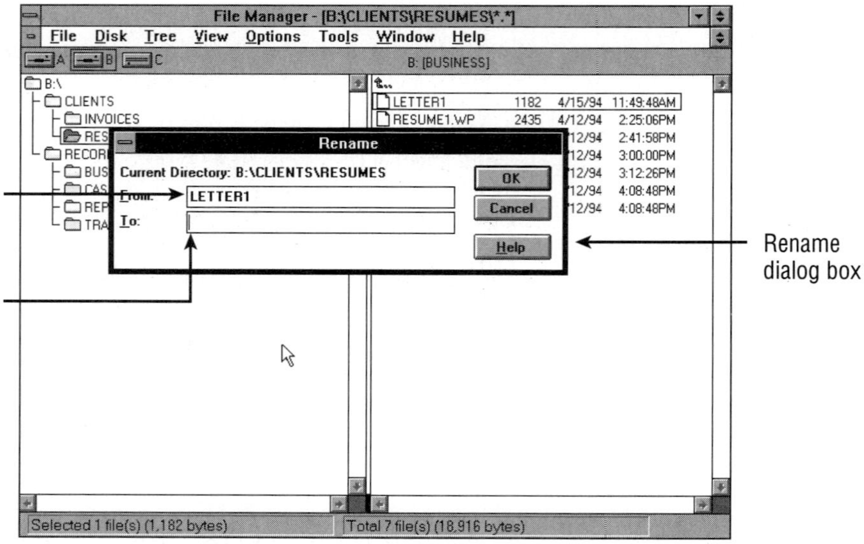

Figure 8-18
The Rename dialog box

3. In the To text box, type **COVER1.LTR** and click **OK**. File Manager renames the file and updates the contents list window. See Figure 8-19.

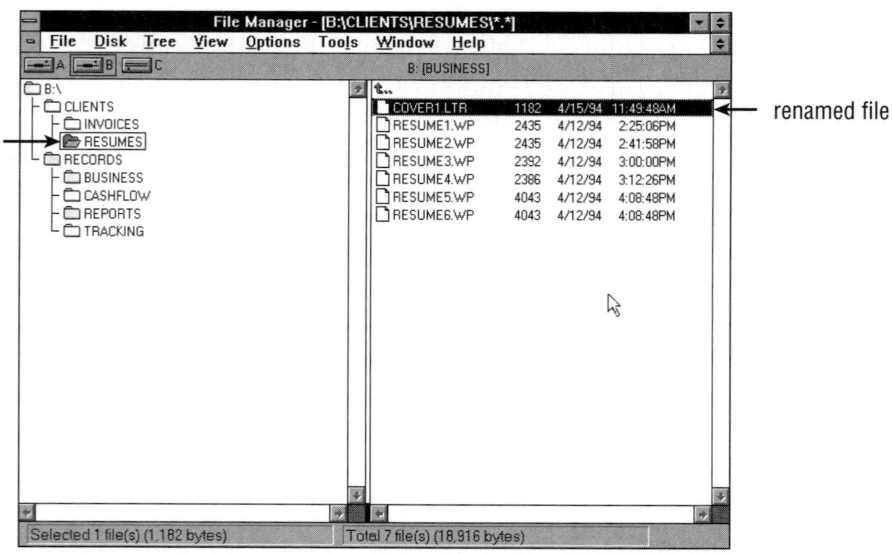

Figure 8-19
The renamed file in the contents list window

Now copy this file.

4. Be sure the file named COVER1.LTR is highlighted in the contents list window.

5. Click **File**, then click **Copy**. File Manager displays a Copy dialog box. See Figure 8-20. The dialog box shows the current directory and the file selected for the copy operation. You are automatically placed in the To text box.

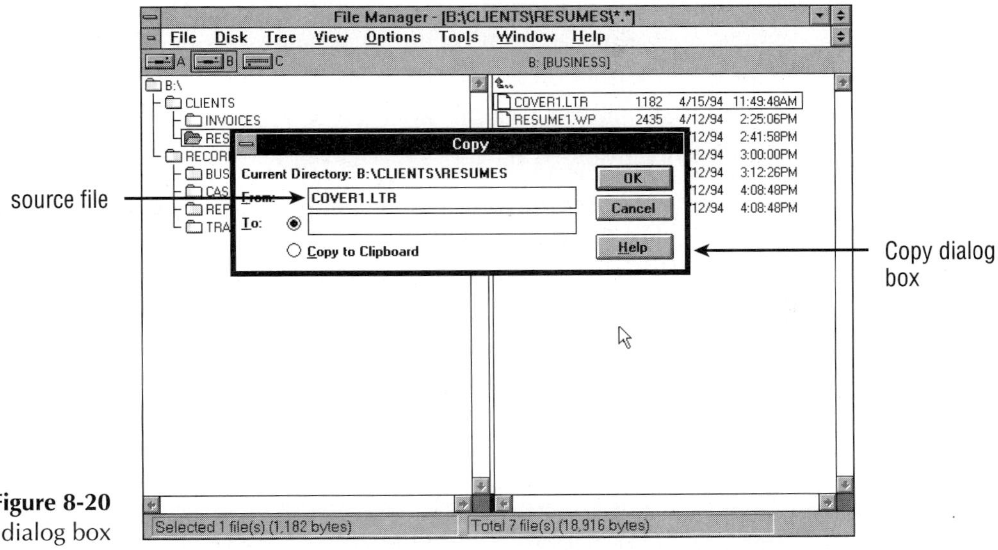

Figure 8-20
The Copy dialog box

6. In the To text box, type **COVER2.LTR** and click **OK**. File Manager copies COVER1.LTR, produces a new file named COVER2.LTR, and updates the contents list window. See Figure 8-21.

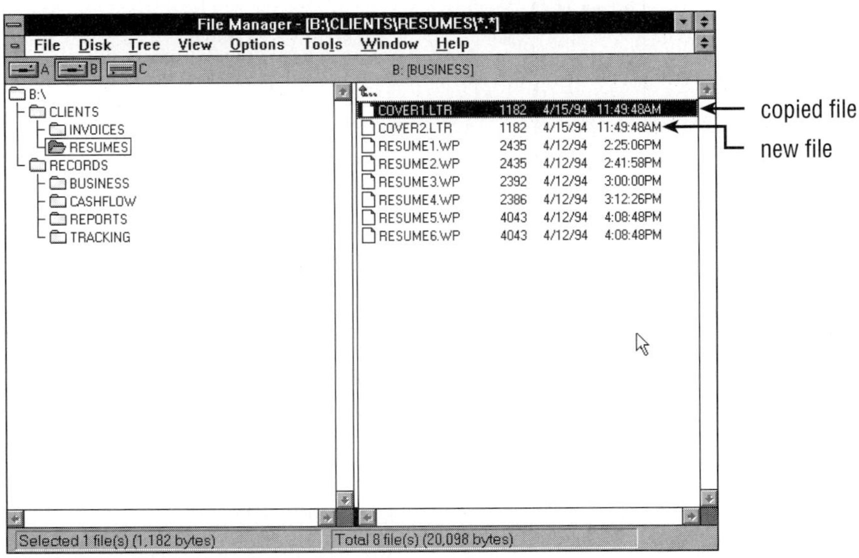

Figure 8-21
File Manager updates the contents list window to show the file produced by the copy operation

If you want to copy a file to another drive, you specify the drive name with the filename. If you want to copy a file to another subdirectory, you specify the path for that subdirectory with the filename. If you want to copy a file to a subdirectory on another drive, you specify both the drive name and path with the filename.

You also want to make a copy of the second résumé template file, so that you can produce a variation of this résumé for one of your clients.

To copy this file:

1. Click **RESUME2.WP** in the contents list window. File Manager highlights this filename.
2. Click **File**, then click **Copy**. File Manager displays a Copy dialog box.
3. Type **RESUME6.WP** and click **OK**. File Manager displays a Confirm File Replace dialog box. See Figure 8-22. In the dialog box, File Manager shows the drive, path, and filename for an existing file named RESUME6.WP and for the file you want to copy. It asks if you want to replace the existing file. You do *not* want to replace this file with a copy of RESUME2.WP.

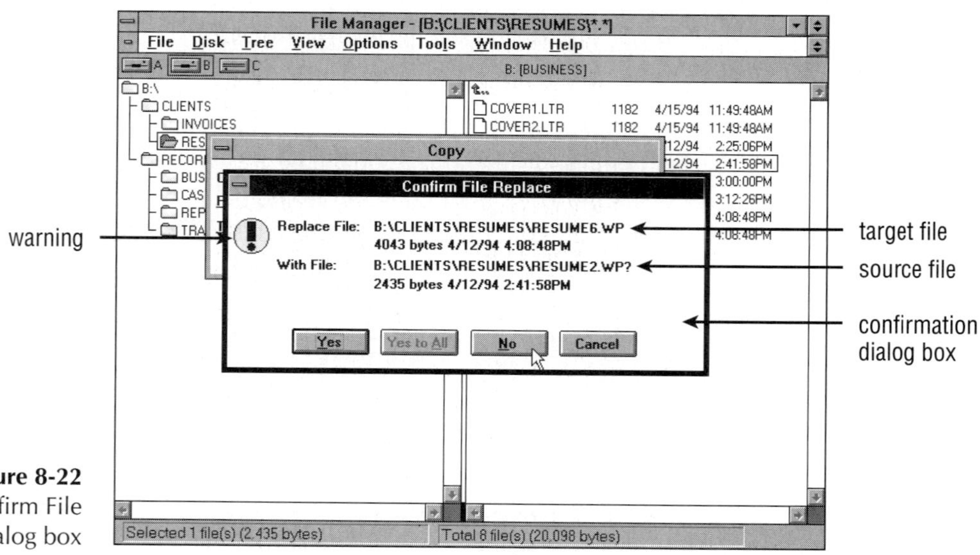

Figure 8-22
A Confirm File Replace dialog box

4. Click **No**. File Manager closes the dialog boxes and the File menu.

Now specify another filename for this copy operation.

5. Click **File**, then click **Copy**. File Manager displays a Copy dialog box.
6. Type **RESUME7.WP** and click **OK**. File Manager copies RESUME2.WP and produces a new file named RESUME7.WP. It then updates the contents list window.

MODIFYING THE DIRECTORY STRUCTURE

You decide to modify the directory structure so that it more closely resembles that of your own client diskette. You want to move those subdirectories currently positioned below the CLIENTS and RECORDS directories so that they are immediately below the root directory.

To move the INVOICES directory:

1. Click the **INVOICES directory name** in the directory tree window. File Manager updates the contents list window to show the files in this subdirectory.
2. Be sure the mouse pointer points to the INVOICES directory name or to the file folder icon. Then press and hold the **left mouse button** as you drag the mouse pointer, now represented as an arrow pointing to a sheet of paper, to the file folder for the root directory, A:\ or B:\. See Figure 8-23.

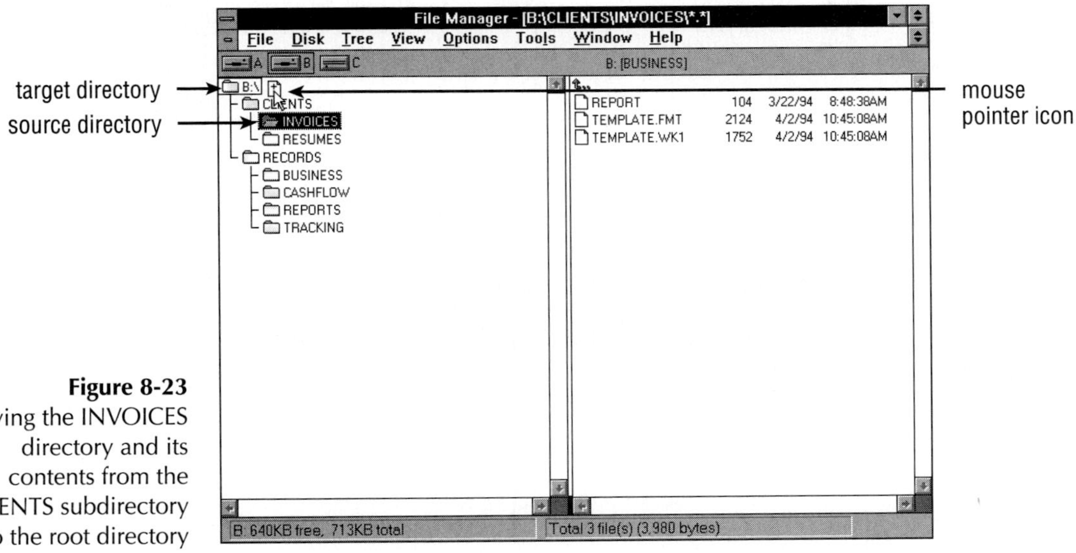

Figure 8-23
Moving the INVOICES directory and its contents from the CLIENTS subdirectory to the root directory

3. Release the left mouse button. File Manager displays a Confirm Mouse Operation dialog box and asks if you want to move the selected files or directories to A:\ or B:\. See Figure 8-24.

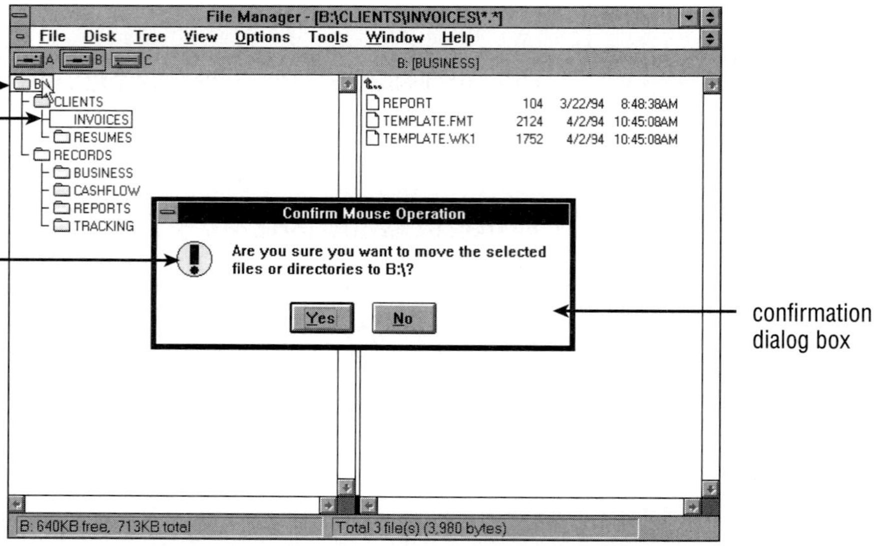

Figure 8-24
A Confirm Mouse Operation dialog box

4. Click **Yes**. File Manager displays a Moving dialog box and informs you that it is creating A:\INVOICES (or B:\INVOICES). It then moves the files in the original directory to the new directory. Finally, it removes the original directory. Figure 8-25 shows the modified directory tree.

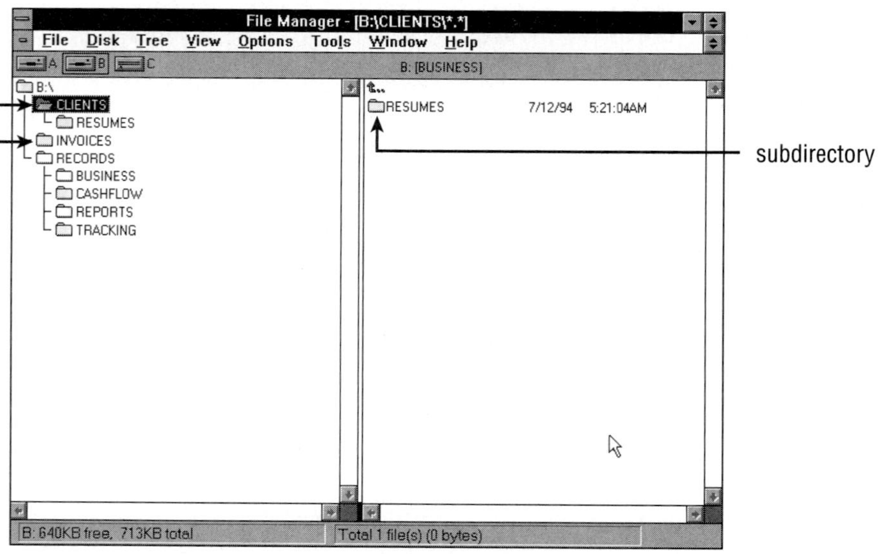

Figure 8-25
The modified directory tree after moving the INVOICES subdirectory

5. Click the **INVOICES file folder icon**. File Manager updates the contents list window to show the files in this directory.
6. Move the RESUMES directory using the same approach as you used for the INVOICES directory. Figure 8-26 shows the modified directory tree.

current directory

new directory

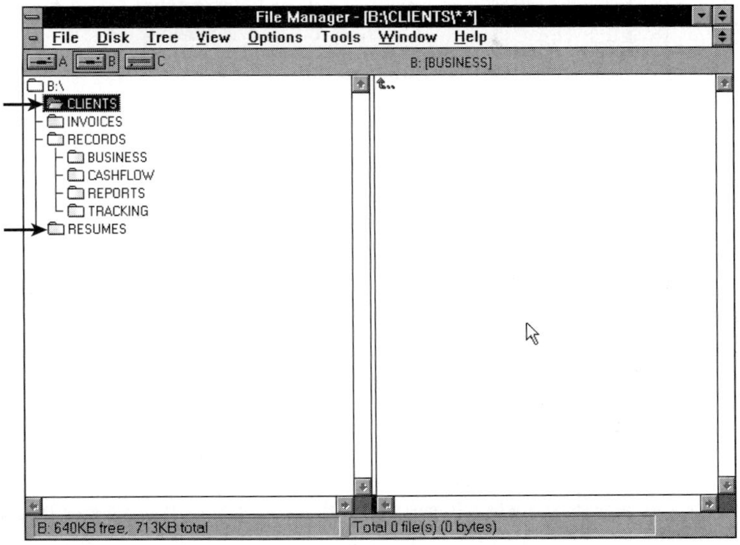

Figure 8-26
The modified directory tree after moving the RESUMES subdirectory

7. If necessary, click the **CLIENTS file folder icon**. The contents list window shows that this directory is now empty.

REMOVING A DIRECTORY

Now that you have moved the INVOICES and RESUMES subdirectories from the CLIENTS directory, you can remove the CLIENTS directory. As in the DOS Shell, you can remove the directory with one of the Delete keys.

To remove a directory:

1. Be sure the file folder icon for the CLIENTS directory is highlighted.
2. Press **[Delete]** or **[Del]**. (Instead of using this shortcut key, you could also use the Delete option on the File menu.) File Manager displays a Delete dialog box that shows the current directory. See Figure 8-27.

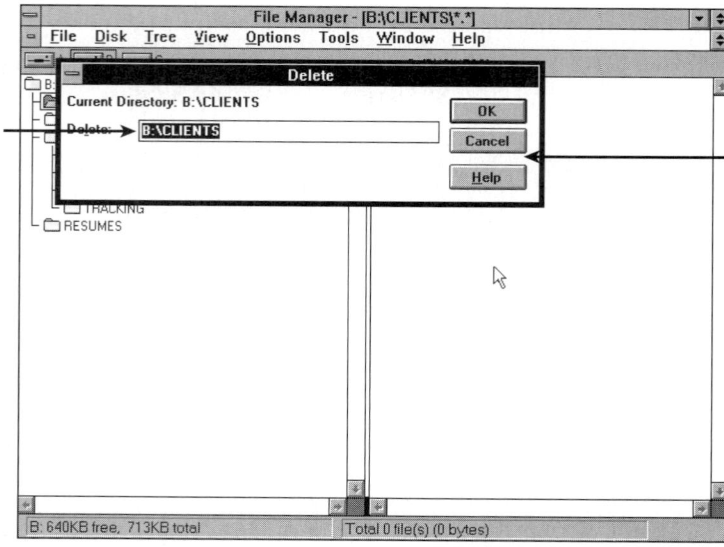

Figure 8-27
The Delete dialog box

3. Click **OK**. File Manager displays a Confirm Directory Delete dialog box.
4. Click **Yes**. File Manager removes the CLIENTS directory and updates the view of the directory tree. See Figure 8-28.

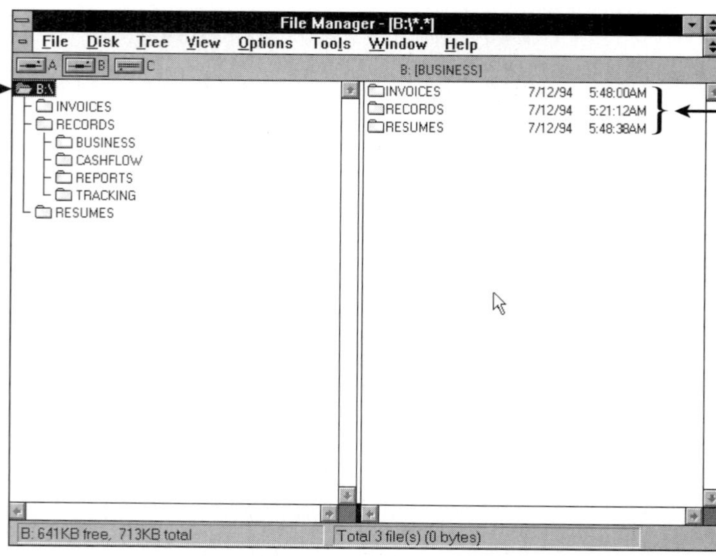

Figure 8-28
The updated directory tree after removing the CLIENTS directory

REORGANIZING THE DIRECTORY STRUCTURE

Next you want to move all the directories currently located below RECORDS so that they are immediately below the root directory. Follow the same process that you used to move the directories located below the original CLIENTS directory.

To make the final modifications to the directory structure:

1. Move all the directories below RECORDS and place them below the root directory.
2. Delete the empty directory RECORDS.
3. Click the **file folder icon** for the root directory. Your new directory tree should be identical to that shown in Figure 8-29.

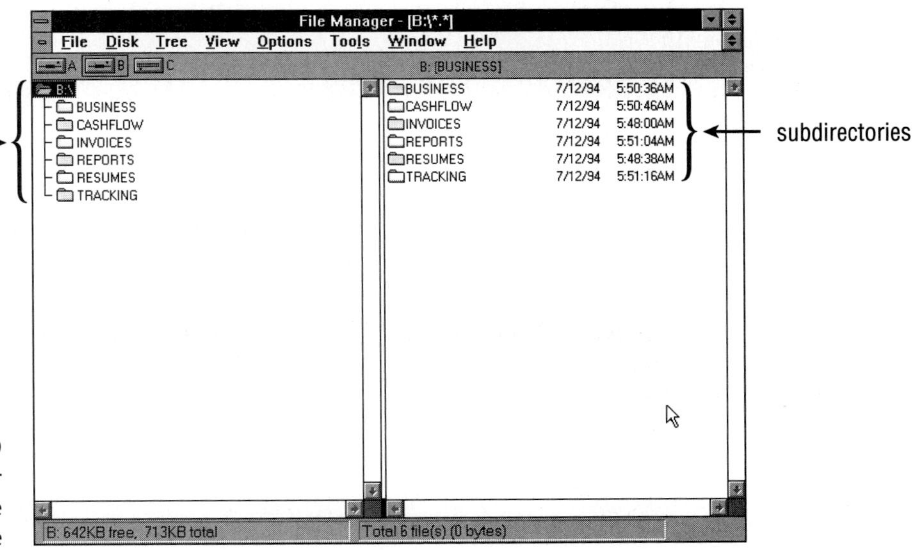

Figure 8-29
The directory tree after reorganizing the subdirectory structure

RENAMING A DIRECTORY

Now that you have reorganized the directory structure, you want to change the name of the TRACKING directory to JOBS so that it is similar to your own client diskette. The process for renaming directories is similar to that in the DOS Shell.

To rename the TRACKING directory:

1. Click the **TRACKING file folder icon**.
2. Click **File**, then click **Rename**. File Manager displays a Rename dialog box with the name of the current directory—the directory name that you want to change. See Figure 8-30.

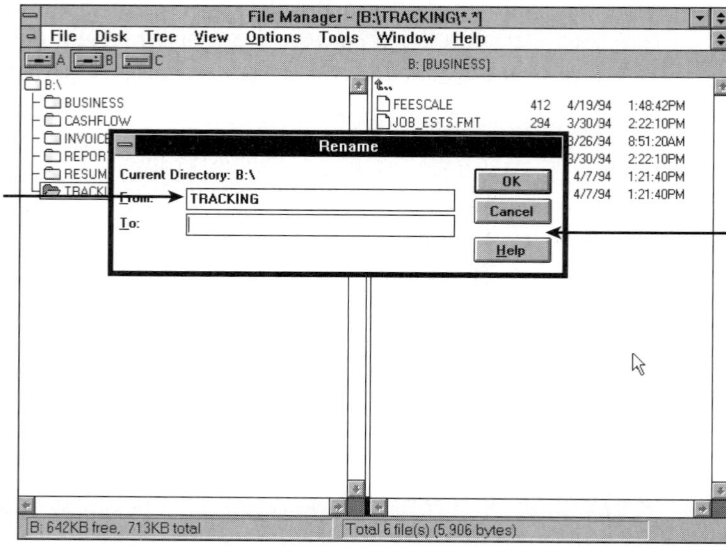

Figure 8-30
The Rename dialog box prompting for the directory to rename

3. In the To text box, type **JOBS** and click **OK**. File Manager updates the directory tree and displays the directory names in alphabetical order. See Figure 8-31.

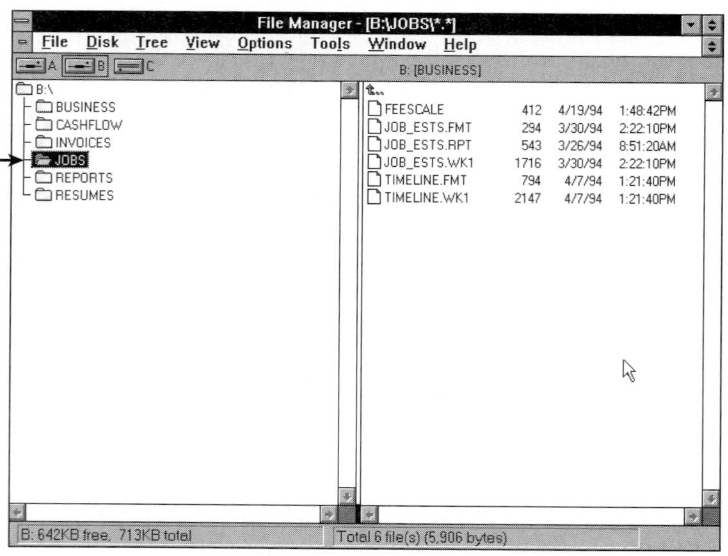

Figure 8-31
The updated directory tree after renaming a directory

CREATING A DIRECTORY

Your client diskette contains a directory named PRJCASH that contains income projection reports for the first five years as well as report formats for quarterly and yearly projected income. You want to modify this copy of your coworker's diskette so that it contains the same directory and the same set of files as the client diskette.

The process for creating a directory and moving files is similar to that used in the DOS Shell. Before you create a directory, you must select the directory that will be the parent directory of the new directory. In this case, you want the new directory to appear below the root directory.

To create a directory:

1. Click the **file folder icon** for the root directory, A:\ or B:\. File Manager highlights the directory name.
2. Click **File**, then click **Create Directory**. File Manager displays a Create Directory dialog box. See Figure 8-32. The current directory is A:\ or B:\. The insertion point cursor is positioned in the Name text box.

Create Directory dialog box

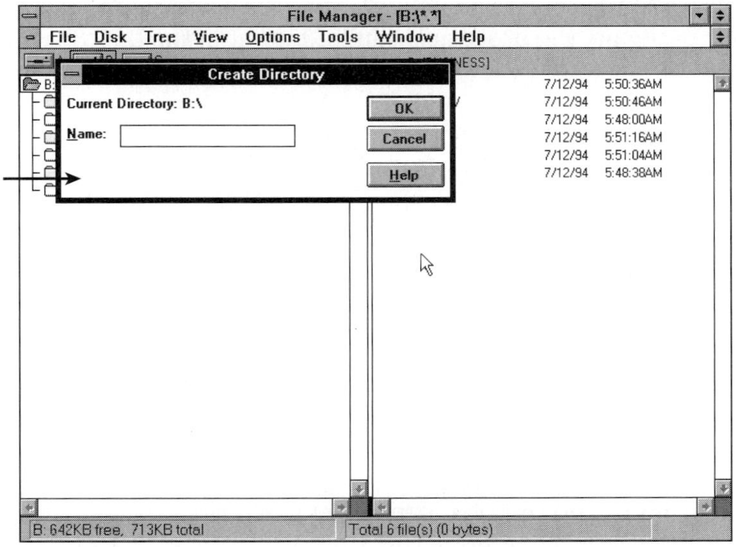

Figure 8-32
The Create Directory dialog box

3. In the Name text box, type **PRJCASH** and click **OK**. File Manager includes the new directory in the directory tree. See Figure 8-33.

new directory

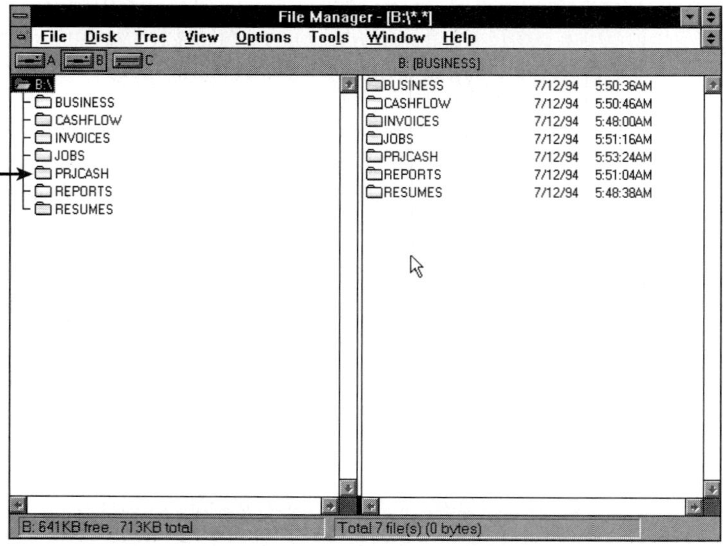

Figure 8-33
The directory tree after adding the PRJCASH subdirectory

MOVING FILES

Now you can move files from the CASHFLOW directory to the new directory. Again, the process is similar to that in the DOS Shell.

To move files:

1. Click the **CASHFLOW file folder icon**. File Manager updates the contents list window. The last seven files in this directory are the ones that you want to move.
2. Click **PRJ_SUM.RPT** in the contents list window. File Manager highlights this filename.
3. Press and hold **[Shift]** while you click the last filename, **YR5_INC.RPT**. File Manager highlights the names of the last seven files. See Figure 8-34.

current directory

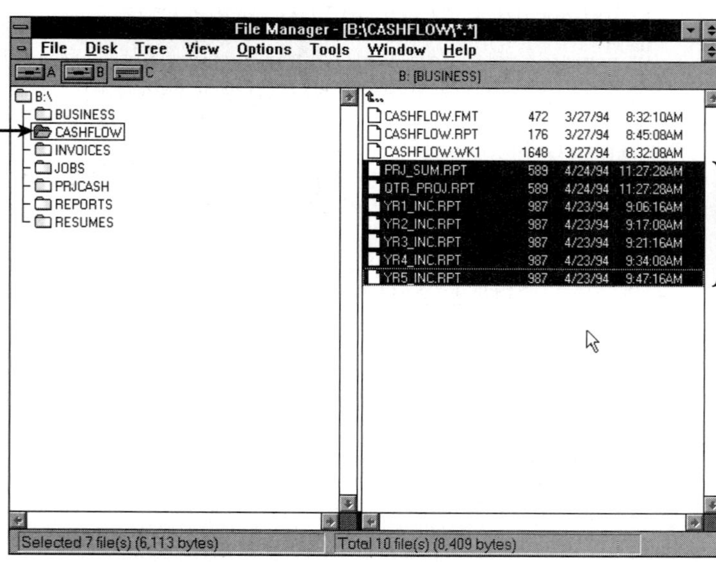

selected files

Figure 8-34
A selected group of files in the contents list window

4. Position the mouse pointer over the selected files. Press and hold the **left mouse button** as you drag the icon of a stack of papers to the PRJCASH directory name in the directory tree window. See Figure 8-35.

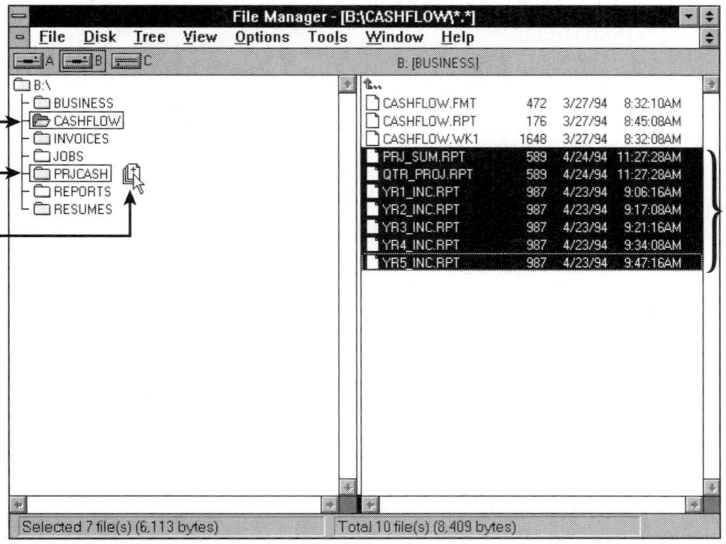

Figure 8-35
Moving a selected group of files to the PRJCASH subdirectory

5. After you position the icon representing a stack of papers on the PRJCASH directory name, release the left mouse button. File Manager displays a Confirm Mouse Operation dialog box and asks if you want to move the selected files to the PRJCASH directory.
6. Click **Yes**. File Manager displays a Moving dialog box. After it completes this operation, you see the remaining files in the CASHFLOW directory.
7. Click the **PRJCASH file folder icon**. File Manager updates the contents list window and shows you the files moved to this new directory. See Figure 8-36.

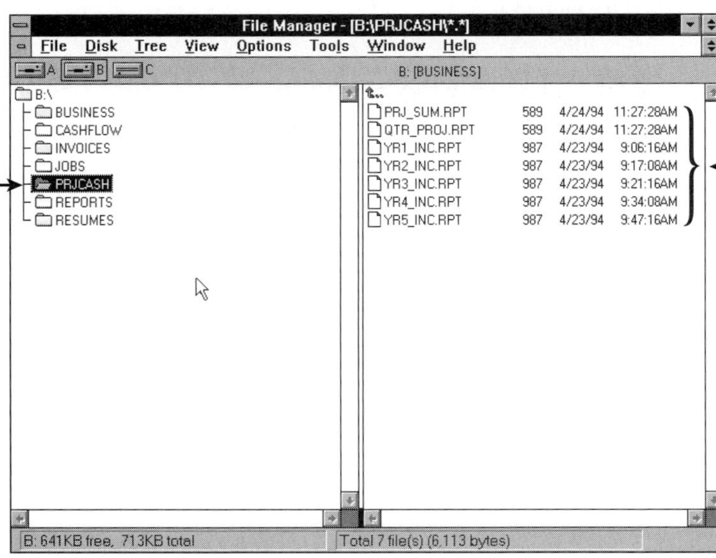

Figure 8-36
The files in the PRJCASH subdirectory

8. Click the **root directory icon** in the directory tree window.

EXITING WINDOWS

Now that you have completed your examination of a copy of your coworker's diskette and have reorganized the directories on this diskette, you are ready to exit Windows.

To exit Windows:

1. Double-click the **Control-menu box** for File Manager. Windows closes File Manager.
2. Double-click the **Control-menu box** for the Main Group. Windows closes the Main Group.
3. Double-click the **Control-menu box** for Program Manager. Windows prompts for verification.
4. Click **OK**. You return to the DOS prompt.

◆

SUMMARY

In this tutorial, you learned how to use File Manager and its directory window. You formatted and copied diskettes with File Manager. You changed drives and expanded the directory tree in the directory tree window. You selected a directory to examine the directory's files. You viewed full and partial details on files in the contents list window.

You used File Manager to modify the directory structure of a diskette. You moved directories, and their files, from one level in the directory tree to another level. You removed empty directories, renamed a directory, and created a directory with File Manager. You also moved files from one directory to another. When you completed these operations, you closed File Manager and its window.

Command Reference	
File Manager Commands	
Disk/Copy Disk	Copies the contents of a diskette from a source drive to another diskette in a destination drive
Disk/Format Disk	Formats a diskette in a specific drive to a specific storage capacity
File/Create Directory	Creates a directory below the current directory
File/Rename	Renames a directory or a file
Tree/Expand All	Expands the directory tree to include all subdirectories
View/All File Details	Displays the filename, extension, size, date, time, and attributes of files in the contents list window
View/Name	Displays filenames only in the contents list window
View/Partial Details	Specifies the details displayed on files in the contents list window
View/Sort by Name	Displays filenames in the contents list window in order by filename and file extension
View/Split	Displays a split bar so that you can visually adjust the relative widths of the directory tree window and the contents list window
View/Tree and Directory	Displays a directory tree window and a contents list window

QUESTIONS

1. What windows does File Manager display, and what information is displayed in each window?
2. What formatting options are available when you format a diskette in File Manager?
3. What advantage(s) does File Manager have over DOS when you need to format a diskette?

4. What advantage(s) does File Manager have over DOS 5.0 and 6.0 when you need to copy a diskette?
5. How do you select a drive with File Manager?
6. How can you expand the directory tree in the directory tree window in File Manager?
7. How do you select a directory in File Manager?
8. What three ways can you control the display of the File Manager window?
9. What three options are available for displaying information on files in the contents list window in File Manager?
10. What options are available for determining the sort order in the contents list window in File Manager?
11. If you indicate that you want to view all details on files in the contents list window, what information does File Manager display?
12. Name two ways to adjust the relative widths of the directory tree window and contents list window in File Manager.
13. What is a file attribute? Identify the four file attributes and the code that DOS and Windows use for each attribute.
14. How do you copy a file in File Manager?
15. How do you rename a file in File Manager?
16. How can you move a directory from one level of the directory tree to another with File Manager?
17. What three operations does File Manager perform when you move a directory?
18. How do you rename a directory in File Manager?
19. How do you create a directory in File Manager? What one consideration must you take into account before you create a directory?
20. Describe the steps you would use to move a group of files from one directory to another directory in File Manager?
21. What types of drives does File Manager display in its drive window?
22. Name three ways to identify the current directory in File Manager.
23. What types of icons does File Manager use for directories, program files, and document files?
24. How does the File Type option on the View menu affect the display in the contents list window?
25. What options are available in File Manager for controlling the display of the directory tree?
26. What is a split bar, and how do you use it in File Manager?
27. How do you remove a directory in File Manager?
28. What does File Manager do when you attempt to copy a file over an existing file?
29. What information must you specify if you want to copy a file to another drive in File Manager?
30. What information must you specify if you want to copy a file to another subdirectory in File Manager?

TUTORIAL ASSIGNMENTS

1. **Viewing File Details in File Manager**: *Use your Tutorial Disk for this Tutorial Assignment.* Start Windows, open File Manager, and switch to the drive that contains your Tutorial Disk. Perform the following operations in File Manager, list the commands or steps that you use for each operation, and answer any questions.
   a. Select the JOBS subdirectory.
   b. Display files in the contents list window with only the name and date. What file has the most recent date? The oldest file date?
   c. Display files in the contents list window with only the name and size. What file is the largest? What file is the smallest?
   d. Display files in the contents list window with all file details. Then remove file attributes from the display. If necessary, adjust the size of the contents list window. What information does File Manager display for the filename FEESCALE?
   e. Display files in the contents list window by name. What is the name of the first file? The last file?

   Close File Manager, then exit Windows.
2. **Changing the File Order in File Manager**: *Use your Tutorial Disk for this Tutorial Assignment.* Start Windows, open the Main Group, open File Manager, and switch to the drive that contains your Tutorial Disk. Perform the following operations in File Manager, list the commands or steps that you use for each operation, and answer any questions.
   a. Select the BUSINESS subdirectory.
   b. Display files in order by date. Does File Manager display the most recently created or the oldest file first? What is the name of the first file? The last file?
   c. Display files in order by size. Does File Manager display the largest or the smallest file first? What is the name of the first file? The last file?
   d. Display files in order by type. What part of the filename determines the sort order? What is the name of the first file? The last file?
   e. Display files in order by name. Does File Manager display filenames in alphabetical order by both the filename and file extension? What is the name of the first file? The last file?

   Close File Manager and exit Windows.
3. **Renaming and Copying Files**: *Use your Exercise Disk for this Tutorial Assignment.* Start Windows, open the Main Group, open File Manager, and switch to the drive that contains your Exercise Disk. If necessary, expand the directory tree. Then perform the following operations, list the commands and steps that you use for each operation, and answer any questions.
   a. Select the INVOICES subdirectory.
   b. Change the name of the file REPORT to REPORT.FRM.

c. Copy the file named REPORT.FRM to produce a new file named INTERIM.RPT.
d. Copy the file named REPORT.FRM to produce a new file named FINAL.RPT.
e. Select the REPORTS subdirectory.
f. Copy the file named JUN.RPT to produce a new file named SUMMARY.RPT.
g. Copy the file named JUN.RPT to produce a new file named JUL.RPT.

Exit Windows and, from the DOS prompt, use the TREE command to print the modified directory structure of your diskette with a list of filenames by directory.

4. **Moving Files**: *Use your Exercise Disk for this Tutorial Assignment.* Start Windows, open the Main Group, open File Manager, and switch to the drive that contains your Exercise Disk. If necessary, expand the directory tree. Then perform the following operations, list the commands and steps that you use for each operation, and answer any questions.

a. Select the RECORDS subdirectory.
b. Create a new subdirectory named LISTS positioned below the RECORDS directory.
c. Select the BUSINESS subdirectory.
d. Copy all the files with the file extension LST from this subdirectory to the LISTS subdirectory.
e. Select the RECORDS subdirectory.
f. Create a new subdirectory named SUMMARY positioned below the RECORDS directory.
g. Select the CASHFLOW subdirectory.
h. Copy the file named PRJ_SUM.RPT to the SUMMARY subdirectory. Then select and copy the files with the file specification YR?_INC.RPT to the SUMMARY directory.

Exit Windows and, from the DOS prompt, use the TREE command to print the modified directory structure of your diskette with a list of filenames by directory.

5. **Reorganizing the Directory Structure of a Diskette with File Manager**: *Use your Exercise Disk for this Tutorial Assignment.* Start Windows, open the Main Group, open File Manager, and switch to the drive that contains your Exercise Disk. If necessary, expand the directory tree. Then perform the following operations.

a. Move all the subdirectories currently located below CLIENTS to below the root directory.
b. Move all the subdirectories currently located below RECORDS to below the root directory.
c. Delete the empty subdirectory named RECORDS.
d. Change the name of the subdirectory called TRACKING to JOBCOSTS.

Exit Windows and, from the DOS prompt, print the modified directory structure of your diskette with a list of filenames by directory.

Glossary

Symbols

- . The notation used in a directory listing to refer to the current directory
- .. The notation used in a directory listing to refer to the directory one level higher than the current directory; the parent directory
- ? The question mark wildcard character that substitutes for a single character in the filename or file extension of a file specification
- * The asterisk wildcard character that substitutes for any and all characters in a filename or file extension of a file specification
- \ A notation that indicates the root directory; a notation that separates two directory names in a path or a directory name and filename in a file specification

8086 An obsolete microprocessor chip introduced in 1983-84, used in IBM XT compatibles, and capable of processing and transmitting 16 bits at a time, accessing 1MB of memory, and operating at a clock speed of 5-10MHz

8088 An obsolete microprocessor chip introduced in 1983, used in IBM PCs and PC/XTs, and capable of processing 16 bits at a time, transmitting 8 bits at a time, accessing 1MB of memory, and operating at a clock speed of 5-8MHz

80286 A microprocessor chip introduced in 1984, used in ATs (IBM PC/ATs and 286s), and capable of processing and transmitting 16 bits at a time, accessing 16MB of memory, and operating at a clock speed of 8-12 MHz

80386DX A microprocessor chip introduced in 1985, used in 386DXs, and capable of processing and transmitting 32 bits at a time, accessing 4GB of memory, and operating at a clock speed of 16-33MHz

80386SX A microprocessor chip introduced in 1988, used in 386SXs, and capable of processing 32 bits at a time, transmitting 16 bits at a time, accessing 16MB of memory, and operating at a clock speed of 16-20MHz

80486DX A microprocessor chip with a math coprocessor introduced in 1989, used in 486DXs, and capable of processing and transmitting 32 bits at a time, accessing 4GB of memory, and operating at a clock speed of 25-50MHz

80486SX A microprocessor chip with a disabled math coprocessor introduced in 1991, used in 486SXs, and capable of processing and transmitting 32 bits at a time, accessing 4GB of memory, and operating at a clock speed of 16-25MHz

80486DX2 A microprocessor chip with a math coprocessor introduced in 1992, used in 486DX2s, and capable of processing and transmitting 32 bits at a time, accessing 4GB of memory, and operating at a clock speed of 50-66MHz

A

A: The drive name assigned to the first diskette drive in a computer system

A prompt The DOS prompt for drive A

access hole The oval-shaped recording window on a 3½-inch diskette

access time The time required to read or write a byte of data to a disk

active window The currently selected window in Windows with a highlighted title bar

adapter card A circuit board that is inserted in the system unit and connected to the motherboard so that the computer system can work with a hardware component

add-in card A circuit board that is inserted in the system unit and connected to the motherboard so that the computer system can work with a hardware component

address bus The combination of address lines that access memory

address lines The electronic circuitry used to access specific storage locations in memory

allocation unit One or more sectors DOS uses as the minimum storage space when it allocates storage space on a disk to a file; a cluster

analog Varying continuously over a range, such as the amplitude of a sound wave signal

annotate To add comments to a Windows Help screen

anti-viral software A program that scans a disk for computer viruses and removes the viruses, or monitors a computer system for the presence of computer viruses

application software Software that allows a user to accomplish a specific task such as word processing, electronic spreadsheet, database, graphics, desktop publishing, or communications

archive attribute An attribute assigned to a file by DOS to indicate that the file was created or modified since the last backup

archive To store infrequently used files on diskettes

ascending order Arranged in alphabetical order from A to Z, in numerical order from the lowest to the highest value, or in date and time order from the most recent date to the oldest date

ASCII The abbreviation for *American Standard Code for Information Interchange*, a coding scheme for representing characters and symbols

ASCII code The numerical code for an ASCII control code or character

ASCII file A simple file format in which data is stored as text

ASCII value The numerical code for an ASCII control code or character

auto-park A safety feature that automatically moves or parks the read/write heads in a landing zone on the innermost surface of the hard disk when the computer's power is switched off

B

B: The drive name assigned to the second diskette drive in a computer system, or to the first disk drive if there is only one drive

B prompt The DOS prompt for drive B

backtab key A key combination, [Shift][Tab], that moves the selection cursor to the previous window in the DOS Shell

backup catalog A file that contains information about files backed up by MSBACKUP

backup copy An extra or duplicate of a diskette, file, or files kept in reserve in the event you need to restore the original diskette, file, or files

backup cycle A periodic cycle used to back up files on a hard disk

backup set A set of diskettes that contain duplicate copies of files stored on a hard disk

bad sector A defective area on a hard disk or diskette that DOS marks as unusable

binary digit A binary digit that consists of the number 1 or 0

bit An abbreviation for a binary digit that consists of the number 1 or 0

boot To start a computer system

boot disk A disk that contains the DOS system files and that is used to start a computer

boot record A hidden file that contains information about the version of DOS used to format a disk and the physical characteristics of the disk, such as the number of bytes per sector, sectors per cluster, maximum number of files per disk, total number of sectors, and sectors per track

boot sector virus A type of virus that replaces the boot sector with its own program code to guarantee that it is automatically loaded into memory when the computer system boots

boot sector A hidden file that contains information about the version of DOS used to format a disk and the physical characteristics of the disk, such as the number of bytes per sector, sectors per cluster, maximum number of files per disk, total number of sectors, and sectors per track

booting The process of powering on a computer system and loading DOS into memory

bootstrap loader program A program that is located in the boot record of a boot disk and that locates and loads DOS from the boot disk

byte A combination of eight bits used to encode a character, including letters of the alphabet, numbers, and symbols

C

C: The drive name assigned to the first hard-disk drive in a computer system

C prompt The DOS prompt for drive C

cascade To arrange each open window in Windows in an overlapping pattern to the right and below the previous window

central processing unit The microprocessor chip that processes data under the direction of instructions in a program

check box A box within a dialog box for selecting or removing an option

checksum A value calculated by Microsoft Anti-Virus for a program file, based on characteristics of the program file, including its size, date, and time

click To quickly press and release a mouse button

Clipboard An area of memory used by Windows to temporarily store data

clock rate The rate, in megahertz, at which the microprocessor executes program instructions

clock speed The rate, in megahertz, at which the microprocessor executes program instructions

cluster One or more sectors used by DOS as the minimum storage space when it allocates storage space on a disk to a file; an allocation unit

cold boot Starting a computer system by turning on the power switch

COM1: The device name DOS assigns to the first communications, or serial, port in a computer system

COM2: The device name DOS assigns to the second communications, or serial, port in a computer system

COM3: The device name DOS assigns to the third communications, or serial, port in a computer system

COM4: The device name DOS assigns to the fourth communications, or serial, port in a computer system

command An instruction to perform a task, issued by a user to a program

COMMAND.COM The MS-DOS and PC-DOS operating system file responsible for interpreting commands entered at the DOS prompt; locating and executing internal and external DOS commands; locating and loading an application, programming language, or utility; and executing commands stored in batch files

command interpreter The operating system file, usually COMMAND.COM, that interprets commands entered at the DOS prompt; locates and executes internal and external DOS commands; locates and loads an application, programming language, or utility; and executes commands stored in batch files

command line The line to the right of the DOS prompt where you enter commands

command line interface The use of the DOS prompt to interact with the operating system

command processor The operating system file, COMMAND.COM, that interprets commands entered at the DOS prompt; locates and executes internal and external DOS commands; locates and loads an application, programming language, or utility; and executes commands stored in batch files

command stack A small area of memory used by DOSKEY to keep track of commands entered at the DOS prompt

communications software Software that enables you to use your computer system to communicate with other computer systems in the same office or in other offices around the country or world with the use of a modem and a telephone line connection

compatibility test A backup test performed by MSBACKUP to configure a computer for a backup and to test the reliability of the backup process

computer virus A program that adversely affects the performance of a computer system

CON The device name DOS assigns to the console unit—the keyboard and monitor

contents list window The File Manager window that displays information on files in the current directory and on the current drive

contiguous sectors Adjacent sectors of a file on a hard disk or diskette

control code A code for the use of the Ctrl (Control) key with another key

control lines The electronic circuitry used to synchronize operations

Control Panel A group of Windows applications for customizing and configuring Windows and a computer system

Control-menu box A Windows button located to the left of the title bar and used to display a Control menu or to exit Windows

coprocessor An additional microprocessor that works in conjunction with the main microprocessor to dramatically increase the speed of mathematical calculations and processing of graphics

CPU The abbreviation for *central processing unit*, the microprocessor chip that processes data under the direction of instructions in a program

CRT The abbreviation for *cathode ray tube*, the main component of a monitor

current directory The directory or subdirectory that is currently in use and whose path is displayed as part of the DOS prompt

current drive The drive DOS uses to locate commands and files if no other drive is specified

current window The currently selected window in Windows with a highlighted title bar

cursor A blinking underscore character (_) or a small solid rectangle that identifies your current working position on the screen and that marks where the next character typed will appear on the screen

customize To configure a computer system to meet a specific set of needs

D

data Facts, figures, and images

data bus The electronic circuitry that connects the CPU with internal and external hardware

data file A file that contains a document or data

data lines The electronic circuitry used to transmit and receive data from other hardware components

database software Software for storing and managing large quantities of information in a table format

date stamp The date assigned by DOS to a file

default The setting or reference point DOS uses unless you specify another setting or reference point

default directory The directory or subdirectory that is currently in use and whose path is displayed as part of the DOS prompt

default drive The drive DOS uses to locate commands and files if no other drive is specified

defragmenting utility A program that rearranges files on a hard disk or a diskette so that all sectors of each file are stored in consecutive sectors

descending order Arranged in reverse alphabetical order from Z to A, in reverse numerical order from the highest to the lowest value, or in reverse date and time order from the oldest date to the most recent date

desktop publishing software Software used to produce high-quality, professional-looking documents for presentation or reproduction

destination file A file that DOS copies to

device A component within a computer system, such as a keyboard, mouse, system unit, monitor (or video display unit), disk drive, or printer

device driver A file with program code for managing hardware

device name A name DOS assigns to a device or hardware component

dialog box An outlined area of the screen where a program displays useful information, including messages and warnings, or options for you to select

differential backup A backup performed during a backup cycle that includes all files altered since the last full backup

digital Consisting of data stored in discrete units, such as 0s and 1s

directory A list of information on files stored on a diskette or a hard disk produced by the DIR command; the root directory or a subdirectory that tracks information on other files

directory file A special file created by DOS to keep track of information on files

directory tree A diagrammatic representation of the directory structure of a hard disk or diskette

directory tree window The area of the screen where the DOS Shell and the File Manager display a graphical representation of the directory structure of a hard disk or diskette

disk A device used to store program and data files

disk drive A hardware component that records data onto or retrieves data from storage media, such as a diskette or a hard drive

disk jacket A case that encloses and protects the flat, circular plastic disk that constitutes a diskette

disk map A visual representation of the organization of clusters on a hard disk or diskette

disk order The order in which DOS keeps track of files on a diskette or hard disk

diskette A commonly used storage medium that consists of a flat, circular plastic disk with a magnetic coating enclosed in a case for protection

DOS The abbreviation for *Disk Operating System*, the primary operating system software used on IBM and IBM-compatible microcomputers

DOS environment A small area of memory where DOS stores important settings that it and other programs use

DOS file A type of ASCII file

DOS prompt The command line interface for interacting with DOS

DOS text file A type of ASCII file

dot The notation used in a directory listing to refer to the current directory

dot dot The notation used in a directory listing to refer to the directory one level higher than the current directory; the parent directory

dot-matrix printer A type of impact printer that uses small pins in the print head to produce a character composed of an array, or matrix, of dots

double-click To quickly press twice and release a mouse button

double-density disk A 5¼-inch diskette with a storage capacity of 360K, or a 3½-inch diskette with a storage capacity of 720K

double-sided disk A type of diskette in which data is recorded on both sides of the disk

draft mode An operating mode in which a printer prints quickly but produces lower quality output

drag To hold down the left mouse button, move the mouse, and then release the mouse button, usually to select a group of filenames or to select and move an object or icon on the screen

drive icon An icon that represents a disk drive in a computer system

drive name A device name that consists of a letter of the alphabet and a colon, and that is assigned to a disk drive in a computer system

drive window An area of the screen where a program displays a list of the drives available in a computer system

drop-down menu A menu that drops down from the menu bar when you select a menu name

E

editing keys A set of keys that allow you to change or modify text

electronic spreadsheet A type of software application for performing calculations on numbers arranged in a table of columns and rows and for building models

ellipsis Three dots (...) next to a menu option that indicate a program will display a dialog box when you select the menu option

end-of-file code A control code, [Ctrl][Z], that marks the end of an ASCII file

environment variable A name that DOS associates with a setting stored in the DOS environment

EOF The abbreviation for *end of file*

executing Carrying out instructions in a program that is already loaded in memory

expansion slot A slot for inserting and attaching an adapter or add-in card to the motherboard

external command A command that is executed by DOS after DOS locates the program file containing the program instructions on disk and then loads the program instructions into memory

external modem A modem that consists of a separate hardware unit that connects to one of the serial ports on a computer system

extra-high-density diskette A 3½-inch diskette with a storage capacity of 2.88M

F

fax board An adapter inserted in the system unit and mounted on the motherboard for the purpose of sending and receiving facsimiles (faxes)

file A certain amount of storage space on a diskette or hard disk that is set aside for the contents of a program, document, or data file

file attribute A special characteristic assigned to a file by DOS

file extension An additional one to three characters included after the main part of a filename, usually to identify the type of data in the file

file folder icon A DOS Shell or Windows icon that represents a directory or subdirectory

file icon A DOS Shell or Windows icon that represents a file

file list window The area on the screen where the DOS Shell displays filenames for a specific directory and drive

File Manager A Windows application for managing the use of drives, directories, and files

file specification The use of a drive name, path, filename, and wildcards to select one or more files

filename A name assigned to a program, document, or data file to identify its contents

filter A DOS command that can modify the output of another DOS command

fixed disk An internal disk drive unit that consists of two or more unremovable metallic disks or platters with a magnetic coating on both surfaces of the disk

floppy disk A commonly used storage medium that consists of a flat, circular plastic disk with a magnetic coating and that is enclosed in a case for protection; also called a diskette

format To prepare a diskette for use in a computer

formatted diskette A diskette prepared by DOS so that DOS can store data on the diskette

fragmented file A file stored in non-contiguous, or non-adjacent, sectors on a hard disk or diskette

full backup A backup that marks the start of a backup cycle and that includes all or part of the contents of a hard disk

function keys A set of program-specific keys labeled [F1] through [F10] or [F12] used for specific tasks by a program, such as saving or printing

G

G A common abbreviation for *gigabyte*

GB A common abbreviation for *gigabyte*

gigabyte 1,024 megabytes, or approximately one billion bytes, of storage space

graphical user interface An interface that provides a more visual method for interacting with the operating system through the use of icons, menus, and multiple windows

graphics adapter A video display card mounted in an expansion slot on the motherboard to control the display of text and graphics on the monitor

graphics mode A video display mode for displaying graphic images as well as text

graphics software Software used to create illustrations, diagrams, graphics, charts, and freehand drawings

group icon An icon that represents a set of related applications in Windows

GUI The abbreviation for *graphical user interface*, an interface that provides a more visual method for interacting with the operating system through the use of icons, menus, and multiple windows

H

hardcopy The paper copy of computer output

hard disk An internal disk drive unit that consists of two or more unremovable metallic disks or platters with a magnetic coating on both surfaces of a disk, that stores substantially more data than a diskette, and that accesses data substantially faster than a drive unit for a diskette

hard disk partition table A file on a hard disk that contains information that identifies where each hard drive starts and which drive on the hard disk is the boot drive

hardware The physical components of a computer system

head crash A hard disk failure resulting from the read/write heads gouging the surface of a platter

head slot The oval-shaped recording window on a 5¼-inch diskette

help information information provided by a program to assist you with a program task

hidden file A file not displayed in a directory list

high-density disk A 5¼-inch diskette with a storage capacity of 1.2M, or a 3½-inch diskette with a storage capacity of 1.44M

hot key A combination of keys that activate a Terminate-and-Stay-Resident (TSR) utility

I

I-bar The mouse pointer used in Windows

IBMBIO.COM The PC-DOS operating system file responsible for assigning device names and handling input and output operations

IBMDOS.COM The PC-DOS operating system file that constitutes the core of DOS and that is responsible for drive, directory, and file management

icon An image or picture displayed on the screen to represent common objects—such as a drive, disk, program, or file—and tasks

impact printer A type of printer that produces a character on paper by striking a metallic element against an inked ribbon

incremental backup A backup performed during a backup cycle that includes only those files that have changed since the last full or last incremental backup

initialization file A file that contains initial settings used by a program

ink-jet printer A type of non-impact printer that sprays tiny dots of ink onto paper to form characters or graphics

input The process of providing program instructions, commands, and data to a computer system so that it can accomplish a useful task with the data

input device A hardware component, such as the keyboard or mouse, used to provide program instructions, data, and commands to a computer

insert mode A working mode in which the characters typed are inserted at the position of the cursor, and characters to the right of the cursor are shifted to the right

insertion point cursor A flashing vertical bar used as a cursor in Windows

integer A whole number

integrated software A software package that combines two or more applications into one product

interface The means or way in which you interact with a computer system

intermediate file A temporary file created by DOS during the processing of a command and that is deleted after the operation is complete

internal command A DOS command for which the program instructions are stored in the computer's memory as part of the operating system software

internal modem A modem that is mounted on a card and inserted into one of the expansion slots inside a computer

interrupt command The [Ctrl][Break] key combination, which interrupts a DOS command

I/O The abbreviation for *input/output*

IO.SYS The MS-DOS operating system file responsible for assigning device names and handling input and output operations

K

K A common abbreviation for *kilobyte*

KB A common abbreviation for *kilobyte*

kilobyte 1,024 bytes, or approximately 1,000 bytes, of storage space

L

LAN The abbreviation for *local area network*, a collection of computers and other peripherals joined by direct cable links and located relatively close to each other, usually in the same building, so that users can share hardware and software resources and files

landing zone The innermost surface of a hard disk where read/write heads rest when the computer's power is switched off

laptop computer A small, lap-size microcomputer

laser printer A type of non-impact printer that uses a laser beam to form an electrostatic, or electrically charged, image on a rotating photosensitive drum, which in turn attracts toner and uses heat to bond the toner to paper

LCD The abbreviation for *liquid crystal display*, a type of display medium used with laptops and notebooks

list box A box within a dialog box that lists options from which to choose

list device The name of a printer port DOS uses to list output

loading Copying programs or data into a computer's memory

local area network A collection of computers and other peripherals joined by direct cable links and located relatively close to each other, usually in the same building, so that users can share hardware and software resources and files

log file A file in which the BACKUP command stores a record of the path and filename of each file backed up on a hard disk

LPT1: The device name assigned by DOS to the first parallel port in a computer system

LPT2: The device name assigned by DOS to the second parallel port in a computer system

LPT3: The device name assigned by DOS to the third parallel port in a computer system

M

M A commonly used abbreviation for *megabyte*

macro A set of stored keystrokes or commands for an operation or set of operations that a program can automatically execute

main directory The first and most important directory created by the FORMAT command on a hard disk or diskette

Main Group A set of Windows applications for managing the resources on a computer system

mainframe computer A computer that has substantially greater capacities for storing and processing data than minicomputers and microcomputers, that operates 10 to 100 times faster than a microcomputer, and that requires a specially controlled environment

major upgrade A major change or major enhancement to a software package

map legend An explanation of the notations used by the Defragmenter to identify cluster usage on a hard disk or diskette

master catalog A file produced by MSBACKUP to keep track of all the backups performed during a backup cycle

Maximize button A Windows button for enlarging a window to fill the entire screen

MB A common abbreviation for *megabyte*

megabyte 1,024 kilobytes, or approximately one million bytes, of storage space

megahertz A unit of measurement representing millions of cycles per second

memory A set of storage locations where instructions and data are stored while you use a microcomputer

menu A list of command choices presented by a program

menu bar A bar near the top of the screen where programs, such as the MS-DOS Editor, the DOS Shell, Windows, and DOS utilities, display a list of menu names

MHz The abbreviation for *megahertz*

microcomputer A single-user, personal computer system

microprocessor A special computer chip that constitutes the central processing unit of a microcomputer and that processes data using program instructions

minicomputer A larger and more powerful computer that requires more office space than a microcomputer, operates 3 to 25 times faster, and stores and processes much larger quantities of data

Minimize button A Windows button for reducing a window to an icon

minor upgrade A minor change or minor enhancement to a software package

modem A hardware device that transmits and receives data between computers over telephone lines

modifier key A key that is pressed in conjunction with another key to change the keyboard output

monitor A TV-like video screen that displays input and output

motherboard The main system board with the microprocessor, supporting electronic circuitry and expansion slots

mouse A hand-held device used to position a pointer on the screen so that you can select options and perform specific operations

mouse pointer A type of cursor in the shape of an arrow or a rectangle that moves in the direction in which the mouse is moved over a desktop

MS-DOS Microsoft Disk Operating System; the brand of DOS used on IBM-compatibles

MS-DOS Prompt icon A Windows application for temporarily exiting to the DOS prompt

MSDOS.SYS The MS-DOS operating system file that constitutes the core of DOS and that is responsible for drive, directory, and file management

multitasking The ability to use several different programs at the same time

multiuser system A computer system that supports the use of several people, each with their own keyboard and monitor, at the same time

N

near-letter-quality mode An operating mode in which a printer produces typewriter-quality output but at a slower rate than when used in draft mode

network A collection of interconnected computers and peripherals that enables users to share software, hardware, and data

network board An adapter inserted into a computer on a network and joined by an electrical cable to the network server

network server A computer with a high-capacity drive that provides software and data to the other computers and peripherals on the network

NLQ The abbreviation for near-letter-quality

non-contiguous sectors Non-adjacent sectors of a file scattered across the surface of a hard disk or diskette

non-impact printer A type of printer that sprays ink or uses heat to fuse ink onto paper to produce an image of a character

notebook computer A small microcomputer that can easily fit into a briefcase

numeric keypad A set of keys on the right side of the keyboard used to enter numbers or to move the cursor

O

open file folder A Windows icon that indicates the current directory or subdirectory

operating environment An interface, such as Windows, between the operating system (DOS) and an application or utility

operating system software The software that manages and coordinates all the activities within a computer, including all the input and output operations to and from the peripherals

operating system The software that manages the operation of the computer system and the use of other software

operating system level Interacting with DOS through the DOS prompt after the operating system is loaded into memory

option button A small round button within a dialog box used for selecting an option

output The transmission of the results of computer processing to the user or to a storage site

output device A hardware component used to display, print, or store information that results from processing data

output redirection operator The greater-than symbol (>), used to redirect output

overlay file A file that contains a module of program code (such as a spelling checker) that is loaded into memory only when needed

overtype mode A working mode in which what you type replaces existing text on a character-by-character basis

P

parallel port A port or connection for transmitting data between the microprocessor and another component eight bits, or one byte, at a time

parameter An optional or required item of information

parent directory The directory one level higher than the current directory

park To position the read/write heads of a hard- disk drive in a landing zone on the innermost surface of the disk when the computer's power is switched off

path The sequence of directory and subdirectory names that identify the location of a subdirectory or a file

PC-DOS The abbreviation for Personal Computer Disk Operating System, the brand of DOS used on IBM microcomputers

Pentium A microprocessor chip with a math coprocessor introduced in 1993, used in Pentium PCs, and capable of processing 32 bites at a time, transmitting 64 bits at a time, accessing an unlimited amount of memory, and operating at a clock speed of 60-100MHz

peripheral An external hardware component, such as a printer or monitor, that is connected to the system unit

personal computer (PC) A single-user computer system

pipe operator A vertical-bar symbol (¦) that redirects the output of one DOS command operation so that it becomes the input for another DOS command

piping The process of redirecting the output of one DOS command operation so that it becomes the input for another DOS command

pixel An abbreviation for a picture element, the smallest element on a video monitor display that can be illuminated

platter A disk within a hard-disk drive unit

point To move the mouse pointer to a specific area of the screen, usually to highlight a menu, command, drive name, filename, icon, or another object displayed on the screen

port An electronic pathway or connection for passing data between the computer's microprocessor and its peripherals

POST The abbreviation for Power-On Self Test, a set of diagnostic programs for testing the system components at start-up

preformatted diskette A diskette formatted prior to sale

print file A type of ASCII file

print queue A list of files waiting to be printed

printer A hardware component that produces a paper copy of text or graphics processed by the computer

PRN The device name assigned by DOS to the first printer port in a computer system

processing The ways in which a computer uses input to produce meaningful information, including arithmetic computations, logical comparisons, rearrangement of data, and the production of images or pictures

program A detailed step-by-step set of instructions that tell the computer how to accomplish a task

program file icon A DOS Shell or Windows icon that represents a program

program file A file that contains program instructions for a software application, utility, or programming language

program list window The area on the screen where the DOS Shell displays a list of program groups or program items

Program Manager The primary Windows software application that acts as an interface between DOS and the user, that organizes applications as icons, and that manages other Windows components

program-item icon An icon in a Windows group window that represents an application for a specific task

programming language software Programs that enable you to design and write application software for use on a computer system

prompt A message or request for information displayed on the monitor by a program

R

RAM The abbreviation for Random-Access Memory

Random-Access Memory That part of a computer's memory used to store program instructions, input, processing, and output

read To retrieve instructions or data stored in memory or on disk

read/write head The magnetic mechanism on a read/write arm that reads data from or writes data to a disk

read/write arm The arm that moves across the surface of a hard disk or diskette to locate and read data or to record data onto the surface of the platter or diskette

Read-Only Memory The part of a computer's memory that includes instructions for starting the computer system, for testing the system components at startup (the POST, or Power-On Self-Test), for locating drives A and C, and for transferring the operating system software from the disk in drive A or C to Random-Access Memory

record A set of related information, for example, information about employees, clients, schedules, supplies, equipment, inventories, or catalog entries

redirect To change the destination of output or the source of input

resident Remaining in memory

resolution The sharpness and distinctness of an image

Restore button A Windows button for restoring a window to its original size

ROM The abbreviation for *Read-Only Memory*

root directory The first and most important directory created by the FORMAT command on a hard disk or diskette

S

scanner A device that you move over an image on paper to copy that image into the computer system and store it so that you can later enhance and print it

scroll arrows Up and down arrows on a scroll bar that indicate the direction in which you can move a window if you click with the mouse on the up or down arrow or scroll bar

scroll bar A bar with scroll arrows placed on the right side or bottom of a window so that you can adjust the view within the window with the mouse

scroll box A box in a scroll bar that is used to adjust the view of a window by large increments by moving the scroll box with the mouse

scrolling A process by which DOS adjusts the screen view

sector The basic unit of storage space on a diskette or hard drive that holds 512 bytes of data

selection cursor A special type of cursor used in the DOS Shell and in Windows to highlight a drive, directory name, filename, program name, or dialog box option

serial number A unique ID number produced by DOS from the date and time on a computer and assigned to a disk during formatting

serial port A port or connection for sending information between the microprocessor and another component one bit at a time

server A computer with a high-capacity drive that provides software and data to the other computers and peripherals on the network

setup file A file in which MSBACKUP stores settings for a specific type of backup

shutter The metal plate that covers the access hole of a 3½-inch diskette

signature A sequence of program code unique to a specific virus, or a family of viruses that affect a computer system in similar ways

software A collection of computer programs that enable a computer to perform a useful task

sort order parameter A parameter that determines the order in which information on files is listed with the DIR command

source drive The disk drive that contains a diskette you want to copy

source file The file that DOS copies

split bar The vertical bar used in File Manager to adjust the relative widths of the directory tree window and the contents list window

standard input device The keyboard, the device DOS uses for input

standard output device The monitor, the device DOS uses for output

status bar A bar near the bottom of the screen where programs, such as the MS-DOS Editor and the DOS Shell, display command keys, shortcut keys, uses for function keys, help information, cursor coordinates, and settings, such as the time

storage The process of recording data and information on some type of permanent storage medium, such as a disk or magnetic tape

string A sequence of characters or text used as a setting

subdirectory A directory that is subordinate to the root directory or to another subdirectory

supercomputer The largest and fastest computer that operates 50 to 10,000 times faster than a microcomputer and that handles complex problems such as weather forecasting, earthquake prediction, and petroleum surveying

SVGA The abbreviation for SuperVGA, a type of high-resolution video display adapter and monitor

switch An optional parameter that modifies the way in which a command operates

syntax diagram The notation that describes the proper way to enter a command with required or optional parameters and switches

syntax The keystrokes and order used to enter a command

system board The main board, or motherboard, of the microprocessor, supporting electronic circuitry and expansion slots

system bus The network of electronic circuitry (data, address, and control lines) responsible for transmitting data and signals between the microprocessor and various components as well as storing information on the location of instructions and data in memory

system date The current date on a computer system

system files The program files that constitute the operating system software

system prompt The DOS prompt that is displayed when you access the operating system level of the computer

system reset rebooting a computer system by pressing [Ctrl], [Alt], and [Del] simultaneously

system time The current time on a computer system

system unit The computer case that houses the microprocessor, memory, electronic circuitry, adapters, disk drives, and power supply

system utility software Special programs provided with operating system software to enhance the performance of your computer system, such as optimizing the use of memory, maximizing the use of storage space on a hard disk, correcting errors on a hard disk, obtaining technical or diagnostic information about your computer system, or preparing diskettes for use on a computer system

systems software The programs that manage the fundamental operations within a computer, such as starting the computer, loading or copying programs and data into memory, executing or carrying out the instructions in programs, saving data to a disk, displaying information on the monitor, and sending information through a port to a peripheral

T

target drive The disk drive used for the diskette to which DOS copies data

target file A file that results from a copy operation

template A file that contains the general format or layout of a document but little or no data

Terminate-and-Stay-Resident program A program that remains in memory and is active while you use other programs

text box A box within a dialog box for entering a response

text file A type of ASCII file

text mode A simple video display mode for displaying text, including letters, numbers, symbols, and special characters

text user interface The use of the DOS prompt to interact with the operating system

tile To arrange each open window in Windows side by side

time stamp The time assigned by DOS to a file

title bar A bar near the top of the screen where programs, such as the MS-DOS Editor, the DOS Shell, and Windows, display the name of a program, the name of the current screen, or a filename

toggle key An on/off key that alternates between two uses each time you press the key

toner A black, powdery substance used in laser printers to reproduce an image

track A concentric recording band on a diskette or hard disk for storing data

TSR An abbreviation for *Terminate-and-Stay-Resident*, a program that remains in memory and is active while you use other programs

TUI An abbreviation for *text user interface*, the use of the DOS prompt to interact with the operating system

typeover mode A working mode in which what you type replaces existing text on a character-by-character basis

U

unformatted diskette A blank diskette that has not been prepared for use in a computer

V

variant A computer virus that is functionally similar to a different virus

VGA An abbreviation for *video graphics array*, a type of video high-resolution display adapter and monitor

video card A video display card mounted in an expansion slot on the motherboard to control the display of text and graphics on the monitor

volatile Dependent on the availability of power, and therefore temporary

volume label A name assigned to a hard disk or diskette to identify the type of information contained on the disk

W

warm boot Starting a computer system by pressing [Ctrl], [Alt], and [Del] simultaneously

wildcard An asterisk or question mark that substitutes for all or part of a filename in a file specification

window border The double outline border around a window's contents in Windows

window An outlined area on the screen through which you use programs, view information, and display the contents of files

Windows A graphics-based operating environment designed to make your computer easier to use by acting as an interface between the operating system and an application or utility

word processing software Software for creating, editing, enhancing, and printing documents electronically

workstation A single-user microcomputer

write protect To protect a diskette so that a computer cannot record data onto the diskette

write To record instructions or data in memory or on disk

Index

A

Add switch (/A), 248
allocation units, 26
American Standard Code for Information Interchange. *See* ASCII
anti-viral programs, 195, 196–202
archive, 47
archive attributes, 299
ascending sort order, 186
ASCII code, 81
ASCII files, 80–91
  in DOS Shell, 85–89
  printing, 89–91
    from DOS prompt, 89–90
    from DOS Shell, 90–91
  viewing contents of, 81–85
ASCII switch (/A), 157–158
ASCII value, 81

B

Back button, 268
backslash (\), 9, 121
backup, 29
  differential, 249
  full, 220, 248–249
  hard disks, 208–252
  incremental, 248–249
  removing files, 247
  strategy for, 248–250
  using XCOPY, 245–247
backup catalog, 220
backup cycle, 208, 248
backup set, 208
  restoring from, 217–219, 240–245
  viewing contents of, 218–219
Backup utility, 209–217
  checking process, 215–217
  from DOS Shell, 219
  restoring files, 217–220
Bookmark menu, 268
booting, 10–11
  cold boot, 10
  warm boot, 11–12
boot record, 195
boot sector, 195
bootstrap loader program, 195

C

cascading windows, 277–279
CD command, 120–22, 155–156
CHDIR command, 120, 155
check box, 66
checksum, 202
clearing the screen, 18–19
click, 62
Clipboard, 267–268
clusters, 26, 189
CLS command, 18–19
cold boot, 10
colon (:), 9
COM, 6
COMMAND.COM, 12
command interpreter, 11–12
command line interface, 58–59, 258
command processor, 11
Command Prompt, 61
command stack, 17, 42
commands, 4
  editing, 45
  listed, 36–37, 71–72, 109, 160, 203, 250–251
  recalling last, 15–16
  syntax, 13
computers
  starting, 10–12
Contents button, 268
contents list window, 290
control codes, 81
Control menu, 263
  box, 260
Control Panel, 271–272
COPY command, 91, 123–125, 208
copying
  diskettes, 29–34
  files, 91–101
    from diskette to hard disk, 96–99
    in DOS Shell, 99–101
    with one disk drive, 93–94
    with two disk drives, 94–96
  Ctrl (Control) key, 81
current drive, 9
cursor, 12
  selection of, 61
customizing, computer systems, 11

D

data files, 7
  extensions, 8
date, changing, 14–16
date stamp, 14
Date switch (/D), 249
default drive, 9, 12
  changing, 27
  viewing directory, 46
default switches, 55–58
  overriding, 57
  setting, 78–79
DEFRAG command, 186
Defragmenter utility, 183, 186–194
  exiting, 193–194
  loading, 187–188
  map of space usage, 189–190
  optimization methods, 190–193
defragmenting disks, 183–194
DEL command, 104, 126
deleting files, 104–107, 125–126

DELTREE command, 239
descending sort order, 186
destination file, 91
device drivers, 195, 272
device names, 6
  list of, 6
dialog boxes, 63, 66
DIR command, 42, 114
directories, 9, 42
  changing, 120–122
  creating, 313–314
  displaying, 42–74
  information in, 43
  lowercase listing of, 50–51
  moving, 307–309
  pausing listing of, 44–45
  printing, 116–117
  removing, 217, 309–310
  renaming, 311–312
  saving to, 9
  sort orders, 46–50
    alphabetical, 46–47
    by date, 49
    in DOS Shell, 65–69
    by file extension, 48–49
    by file size, 50
    reversing, 48
    viewing contents of, 212–213
  wide listing of, 45–46
directory file, 114
directory tree, 137
  expanding, 132–136, 149–150, 296
  printing from DOS prompt, 157–158
  specifying path, 134–135
  viewing, 137–138
    at DOS prompt, 154–157
  window, 61, 290
disk, 4. *See also* diskettes, hard disk
DISKCOPY, 27–28, 31–34, 208–209
  switches, 30–31
  syntax, 30–31
diskettes, 4
  caring for, 26
  copying, 29–34
  formatting, 19–26, 210–211, 290–293
  removing, 24
  serial number, 26, 34
  storage capacities, 20–22
Disk Operating System (DOS). *See* DOS
disk order, 43
Disk Utilities, 61
Display switch (/D), 218
DOC file extension, 7
document files, 7–8
DOS (Disk Operating System)
  commands list, 71–72, 109, 160, 203, 250–251
  definition, 4
  environment, 55–57
  files, 80
  prompt, 12–13, 272–273
    changing, 118–119
  system files, 11
  system utilities, 168
  text files, 80
  version, 13–14
DOSKEY, 16–17, 42
  activating, 78–79
DOS Shell, 59–71
  ASCII files in, 85–89
  commands list, 72, 109, 160, 203
  customizing, 62–64
  default settings, 69
  deleting files in, 106–107
  exiting, 69–70
  and graphics mode, 62–64
  moving files in, 140–143
  refreshing, 143–144
  renaming files in , 103–104
  wildcards in, 67–69
dot dot file, 121, 155
dot file, 121
double-click, 62
drag, 62
drive names, 9
drive window, 61

E

Editor, 61
ellipsis (...), 63
end-of-file (EOF) code, 81
environment variable, 55–56
ERASE command, 104
EXE file extension, 6
execute, 11
external command, 13

F

F3 (Repeat key), 15–16
file attributes, 299
file list window, 61
  updating, 152–153
file management, 114–116
File Manager, 260, 288–316
  commands, 317
  copying diskettes in, 293–295
  copying files in, 303–306
  creating directories in, 313–314
  displays in, 297–302
  expanding directory tree in, 296
  formatting diskettes in, 290–293
  moving directories in, 307–309
  moving files in, 314–315
  removing directories in, 309–310
  renaming directories in, 311–312
  renaming files with, 303–305
  selecting directory with, 297
  selecting a drive with, 295
  starting, 288–290
Filename switch (/F), 157–158

filenames, 5–8
  choosing, 8
  invalid characters, 5–6
  root, 6
files, 5–7
  copying, 91–101
  directory of, 42–74
  displaying in order by date, 57–58, 65–67
  displaying in order by file extension, 67–68
  extensions, 6–8
  fragmentation of, 183–194
  moving groups of, 140–143, 147–149
  moving to subdirectory, 122–131, 140–143
  renaming, 101–104
    in DOS Shell, 103–104
  selecting groups of, 51–55
  viewing details of, 298–302
file specification, 52
filters, 83
Format Capacity switch, 20–21
FORMAT command, 20, 61, 210
full path, 9, 91

G

Glossary button, 268–270
graphical user interface (GUI), 59, 258
graphics mode, 60
  in DOS Shell, 62–64
GUI. *See* graphical user interface

H

hard disks, 4
  creating subdirectories on, 170–172
  defragmenting, 183–194
  locating files on, 180–183
  moving files on, 172–173, 175–176
  organization of, 168–170
  partitioning, 9
  printing directory tree, 167–168, 180
  removing subdirectories on, 171, 176
  renaming directories on, 178–180
  reorganizing with DOS Shell, 173–180
  viewing directory tree, 166–167
hard disk partition table, 195
Help, 27–29
  menu, 267–270
  printing screen, 28–29
Help switch (/?), 27–28
hidden files, 66, 299
History button, 268
hot keys, 90

I

icons, 59, 64, 259
INI file extension, 7
initialization files, 7
interface, 58
intermediate file, 83–84
internal command, 12

L

list box, 63
loading, 4
Log File switch (/L), 212
Lowercase switch (/L), 50–51

M

main directory. *See* root directory
Main Group, 270–273
master catalog, 249
Maximize button, 260, 262
MD command, 118–119, 170–172
menu bar, 61
menus, 59
Michelangelo virus, 194–196
Microsoft Anti-Virus utility, 196–202
  displaying information on viruses, 197–199
  exiting, 201–202
  scanning disks in, 199–201
Minimize button, 260–261
MKDIR command, 118
Modified switch (/M), 248
MORE filter, 83–85
mouse, 61–62, 260
mouse pointer, 61, 260
MOUSE subdirectory, 168
MOVE command, 123, 170–172
MSAV command, 196–197. *See also* Microsoft Anti-Virus utility
MSBACKUP utility, 209, 220–245
  backing up in, 231, 236–238
  and compatibility test, 222–226
    test backup, 226–230
  creating setup file in, 232–236
  exiting, 230, 238
  deleting part of Directory Tree in, 239–240
  restoring directories and files in, 240–245
MS-DOS, 4–5
  QBasic, 61
Multipass switch (/M), 30

O

operating system level, 12
operating system software, 4
  functions of, 4
  loading, 10–11
optimization, 189–193
option buttons, 66
Order switch (/O), 46–47
output redirection operator (>), 116
overlay files, 7, 195
OVL file extension, 7

P

parameter, 14
parent directory, 121
partitioning, 9
Pause switch (/P), 44–45

PC-DOS, 4–5
pipe operator, (¦), 83–85
piping, 83–85
point, 62
POST. *See* Power-On Self Test
Power-On Self Test (POST), 10–11
print files, 80
printing
  ASCII files, 89–91
  directories, 116–117
  directory tree, 157–158
PRINT utility, 90
program files, 6–7
program list window, 61
program-item icon, 260
Program Manager, 259, 264–270
  Help menu, 266–270
  Options menu, 264–265
  Window menu, 265–266

R

RD command, 171, 217
redirect, 116
Refresh command, 101
removing subdirectories, 171
RENAME command, 101–103
renaming files, 101–104
  in DOS Shell, 103–104
Repeat key (F3), 15–16
Restore button, 260, 263
RESTORE command, 217–219
RMDIR command, 171
root directory, 61, 114

S

Search button, 268
sectors, 19
  bad, 25–26
selection cursor, 61
SET command, 55–56
signature, 196
sort order parameters, 47–50
  Date (D), 49
  Extension (E), 48
  Size (S), 49–50
source diskette, 30
source drive, 30
source file, 91
split bar, 299–300
square brackets ([ ]), 14
standard input device, 116
standard output device, 116
star-dot-star (*.*), 66
status bar, 61
Stoned virus, 195–196
storage capacities, 20–22
storage space report, 25–26
string, 56
subdirectories, 9, 114–116
  changing, 120–122
  copying files within, 131–132
  creating, 117–119
    in DOS Shell, 138–140
  and extensions, 168
  moving files to, 122–131
    in DOS Shell, 140–143
Subdirectory Search switch (/S), 180–181, 211
support, 80
switches, 20–21
  and DISKCOPY, 30–31
  setting default, 55–58
symbols
  in filenames, 5
syntax, 13
syntax diagram, 30
system files, 11, 66, 299
system reset, 11
system utilities, 16

T

target diskette, 30
target drive, 30
target file, 91
templates, 42, 52, 78
Terminate-and-Stay Resident (TSR) utility, 17, 90
text boxes, 66
text files, 80
text mode, 60
  in DOS Shell, 63
text user interface (TUI), 58
tiling windows, 277–279
time
  setting, 17–18
  stamp, 14
title bar, 61, 259
tracks, 19
TREE command, 137
TSR. *See* Terminate-and-Stay Resident utility
TUI. *See* text user interface
tutorials
  conventions in, 10
  preparing diskettes for, 21
TYPE command, 81–83

U

Unconditional Switch (/U), 210

V

VER command, 13
viruses, computer, 194–202
volume label, 24–25

W

warm boot, 11–12
Wide switch (/W), 45–46
wildcards, 51–55
  asterisk (*), 51, 53–55, 102
  in DOS Shell, 67–69
  question mark (?), 51–53
window border, 259
windows, 59, 61, 259
  active, 277
  cascading, 277–279
  current, 277
  moving, 273–274
  resizing, 274–277
  selecting, 279–280
  tiling, 277–279
Windows 3.1, 258–282
  desktop, 259–263
  exiting, 281, 316
  features, 282
  File Manager, 288–316
write-protect, 31
XCOPY command, 245–247

DOS Quick Reference

All of the following commands and features apply to DOS 5.0, 6.0, and 6.2, unless otherwise noted

Status, Setup, & Help

[*DOS-command*] /?	Display help information for a command
drive-name:	Change to a specific drive
CLS	Clear screen
DATE [*mm-dd-yy*]	View or set system date
DOSKEY	Store commands entered at the DOS prompt for recall and editing
PROMPT [*text*]	Customize the appearance of the DOS prompt
PROMPT PG	Display the full path in the DOS prompt, followed by a greater-than symbol
SET	Display settings stored in the DOS environment
SET DIRCMD=	Remove settings assigned to the DIRCMD environment variable
SET DIRCMD=[*switches*]	Assign switches to the DIRCMD environment variable for use with the DIR command
TIME [*hh:mm:ss*][*a*¦*p*]	View or set system time
VER	Display DOS version

Disk Management

DISKCOPY [*drive1:* [*drive2:*]]	Copy contents of one diskette to another diskette using the named drive or drives
FORMAT *drive-name:*	Format diskette to maximum capacity of drive
FORMAT *drive-name:* /F:*size*	Format diskette to a specific storage capacity

Directories

DIR	Display a list of filenames for the current drive
DIR *drive-name:*	Display a list of filenames for a specific drive
DIR *directory-name*	Display a list of filenames for the specified directory
DIR *file-specification*	Select and display one or more filenames
DIR /L	Display a list of filenames in lowercase
DIR /O	Display a list of filenames in alphabetical order by filename and extension
DIR /O<*sort order*> DIR /O:<*sort order*>	Display a list of filenames using a sort order parameter, such as date and time (D), extension (E), main part of filename (N), or file size (S)
DIR /O-<*sort order*> DIR /O:-<*sort order*>	Display a list of filenames in reverse order using a sort order parameter, such as date and time (D), extension (E), main part of filename (N), or file size (S)
DIR /P	Display a list of filenames and pause after each screen
DIR *file-specification* /S	Search through subdirectories for filenames that match the file specification and then display the full path of the matching filenames
DIR /W	Display a list of filenames in five columns across the width of the screen, without file sizes, dates, or times

Subdirectory Management

CD [*drive:*]*path* CHDIR [*drive:*]*path*	Change from one directory to another
CD .. CHDIR ..	Change to the directory above the current directory
CD \ CHDIR \	Change from the current directory to the root directory
DELTREE [*drive:*]*path*	*DOS 6.0 and 6.2:* Delete a directory tree, all its subordinate subdirectories, and all files in the specified directories
MD [*drive:*]*path* MKDIR [*drive:*]*path*	Create a subdirectory
RD [*drive:*]*path* RMDIR [*drive:*]*path*	Remove an empty subdirectory from the directory structure of a diskette or hard disk
TREE [*drive:*][*path*] [/F] [/A]	Display a directory tree, with options to display filenames by directory (/F) and to use ASCII characters rather than graphics characters for the lines in the directory tree (/A)

File Management

DOS-command ¦ MORE	Display the output of a DOS command and pause after each screen
COPY *filename*	Copy the named file to the current drive and directory
COPY *filename1 filename2*	Copy the first named file to the current drive and directory, and assign a new name to the file
COPY *filename drive-name:*	Copy the named file to a specific drive and store the new copy of the file under the same name
COPY *filename directory-name*	Copy the named file to a specific subdirectory on the current drive
COPY *directory1 directory2*	Copy all the files in the first named directory to another directory on the current drive
DEL [*drive:*][*path*] *filename* [/P]	Delete a file or a group of files, with an option to prompt for verification (/P)
ERASE [*drive:*][*path*] *filename* [/P]	Delete a file or a group of files, with an option to prompt for verification (/P)

MOVE [*drive:*][*path*] *filename destination*	*DOS 6.0 and 6.2:* Move one or more files to another drive, directory, or drive and directory
PRINT [[*drive:*][*path*] *filename*[...]]	Print one or more text files
REN [*drive:*][*path*] *filename1 filename2* RENAME [*drive:*][*path*] *filename1 filename2*	Rename a file or a group of files
TYPE [*drive:*] [*path*]*filename*	Display the contents of a text file on the screen
XCOPY [*source*] [*destination*] [/S]	Copy all the files in a directory, a group of files, or a single file to another disk, with an option for copying all subdirectories located below the specified directory (/S)

Path & File Specifications

Use the conventions shown below when specifying drive, directory, and filenames. Wildcards can be used with the COPY, DEL, DIR, ERASE, MOVE, PRINT, REN, RENAME, and XCOPY commands to perform operations on groups of files.

CLIENT.LST	The file named CLIENT.LST is located on the current drive and in the current directory
\CLIENT.LST	The CLIENT.LST file is located in the root directory of the current drive
A:\CLIENT.LST	The CLIENT.LST file is located in the root directory of drive A
\BUSINESS\CLIENT.LST	The CLIENT.LST file is located in the BUSINESS directory, a subdirectory of the root directory on the current drive
C:\BUSINESS\CLIENT.LST	The CLIENT.LST file is located in the BUSINESS directory, a subdirectory of the root directory of drive C
\BUSINESS	The BUSINESS directory is a subdirectory of the root directory of the current drive
C:\BUSINESS	The BUSINESS directory is a subdirectory of the root directory of drive C
C:\BUSINESS\RECORDS	The RECORDS directory is a subdirectory of the BUSINESS directory, which is a subdirectory of the root directory of drive C
.	A wildcard specification for selecting all files
*.LST	A wildcard specification for selecting all files with the LST file extension
94BUDGET.*	A wildcard specification for selecting all files with the filename 94BUDGET and any or no file extension
RESUME?.DOC	A wildcard specification for selecting all files with RESUME as the first six characters of the filename, any character as the seventh character of the filename, and the file extension DOC

DOS Utilities

BACKUP [*source*] [*destination-drive:*] [/S] [/L] [/M] [/A] [/D]	Back up an entire hard drive, a directory, a group of files, or a single file onto diskettes, with options for backing up all subordinate subdirectories (/S), creating a log file (/L), backing up only those files that changed since the last backup (/M), adding another backup set to an existing set of backup diskettes (/A), and backing up all files created or modified on or after a certain date (/D)
DEFRAG [*drive:*]	*DOS 6.0 and 6.2:* Optimize directories and eliminate or reduce file fragmentation
MSAV [*drive:*]	*DOS 6.0 and 6.2:* Check for the presence of computer viruses and, if necessary, clean or remove computer viruses from a diskette or hard disk
MSBACKUP	*DOS 6.0 and 6.2:* Back up an entire hard drive, a directory or combination of directories, a group of files, or a single file from a hard disk to diskettes; restore directories or files from backup diskettes to a hard disk; or perform a compatibility test to verify a backup process
RESTORE [*source-drive:*] [*target-drive:* [*path*[*filename*]]] [/S] [/D]	Restore an entire hard disk, a directory, a group of files, or a single file from backup diskettes, with options for restoring all subordinate subdirectories (/S) and displaying a list of path names and filenames of files stored on the backup diskettes (/D)

DOS Keys

[Ctrl][Alt][Del]	Reboot computer
[Print Screen] or [Shift][PrtSc]	Print the information displayed on the screen
[F3]	Display last command entered at DOS prompt
[↑]	Recall last command entered at DOS prompt (if DOSKEY is loaded)

DOS Interfaces

DOSSHELL	Load the DOS Shell graphical user interface
WIN	Load the Windows graphical user interface

DOS Shell Quick Reference

DOS Shell Commands

[F10] (Actions) or [Alt] (Menu)	Access the menus on the menu bar
File/Copy or [F8] (Copy)	Copy one or more files
File/Create Directory	Create a subdirectory
File/Delete, [Del], or [Delete]	Delete a file or group of files
File/Exit or [F3] (Exit)	Exit the DOS Shell
File/Move	Move one or more files to another directory
File/Print	Print a text file
File/Rename	Rename one or more files or a directory
File/Run	Execute a DOS command from the DOS Shell
File/Search	Locate all filenames in all directories that match a file specification and then display the full path of the filenames
File/Select All	Select all files in the file list window
File/View File Contents or [F9] (View)	Display the contents of a text file
Options/Display	Change the screen display mode from text to graphics mode, or vice versa
Options/File Display Options	Display a file selection in the file list window
Tree/Expand All	Expand the directory tree to include all subdirectories
View/Refresh or [F5] (Refresh)	Update the list of filenames in the file list window

WINDOWS 3.1 QUICK REFERENCE

Windows Commands

File/Exit Windows	Exit Windows
Help	Access the Windows Help system
Options	Specify default options for Windows
Window/Arrange Icons	Rearrange all icons in the current window
Window/Cascade	Arrange windows in an overlapping pattern
Window/Tile	Arrange windows side-by-side

Windows Buttons

Control-menu	Display the Control menu if you click; close the open window if you double-click
Maximize	Enlarge a window to fill the screen
Minimize	Reduce a window to an icon
Restore	Return a window to its original size

File Manager Commands

Disk/Copy Disk	Copy the contents of a diskette from a source drive to a destination drive
Disk/Format Disk	Format a diskette in a specific drive to a specific storage capacity
File/Create Directory	Create a subdirectory below the current directory
File/Rename	Rename a directory or a file
Tree/Expand All	Expand the directory tree to include all subdirectories
View/All File Details	Display the filename, extension, size, date, time, and attributes of files in the contents list window
View/Name	Display filenames only in the contents list window
View/Partial Details	Specify the details displayed on files in the contents list window
View/Sort by Name	Display filenames in the contents list window in order by filename and file extension
View/Split	Display a split bar for visually adjusting the relative widths of the directory tree window and the contents list window
View/Tree and Directory	Display a directory tree window and a contents list window